World War II

Second Edition

World War II

A Short History

MICHAEL J. LYONS
North Dakota State University

Prentice Hall
Englewood Cliffs, New Jersey 07632

Library of Congress Cataloging-in-Publication Data

Lyons, Michael J.
World War II : a short history / Michael J. Lyons.—2nd ed.
p. cm.
Includes bibliographical references and index.
ISBN 0–13–501156–6
1. World War, 1939–1945. I. Title. II. Title: World War Two.
III. Title: World War 2.
D743.L96 1994
940.53—dc20 93–14685
CIP

The maps located on pp. 156, 168, 297, 305, 309, and 312 have been reprinted by permission of The Putnam Publishing Group from ATLAS OF THE SECOND WORLD WAR by Brigadier Peter Young and Richard Natkiel. Copyright © by Richard Natkiel.

Acquisitions editor: Stephen Dalphin
Editorial assistant: Caffie Risher
Editorial/production supervision and
interior design: Mary McDonald
Copy editor: Sherry Babbitt
Cover design: Patricia Kelly
Cover photo credit: AP/Wide World Photos
Prepress buyer: Kelly Behr
Manufacturing buyer: Mary Ann Gloriande

A Simon & Schuster Company
Englewood Cliffs, New Jersey 07632

Printed in the United States of America
10 9 8 7 6 5 4 3

ISBN 0-13-501156-6

Prentice-Hall International (UK) Limited, *London*
Prentice-Hall of Australia Pty. Limited, *Sydney*
Prentice-Hall Canada Inc., *Toronto*
Prentice-Hall Hispanoamericana, S.A., *Mexico*
Prentice-Hall of India Private Limited, *New Delhi*
Prentice-Hall of Japan, Inc., *Tokyo*
Simon & Schuster Asia Pte. Ltd., *Singapore*
Editora Prentice-Hall do Brasil, Ltda., *Rio de Janeiro*

To Joan

Contents

Preface

When the first edition of *World War II: A Short History* appeared in 1989, the conflict had already inspired over 70,000 volumes. The number has risen steadily since then. In this second edition, I have incorporated material from the vast array of new literature, along with suggestions from readers, most notably a completely new chapter on "Total War and the Home Fronts." I have also updated both the final chapter, "Aftermath," in an effort to link the war with the momentous transformation of Eastern Europe and the Soviet Union in the late 1980s and early 1990s, and the section on "Additional Reading." Finally, I have made numerous minor changes throughout the book.

My basic purpose in this edition is still the same as that which prompted me to write the first: to satisfy the needs of the college student in the classroom as well as those of the general reader. At the same time, I have sought to provide a relatively brief synthesis of the work of other scholars that the professional historian will find useful. With these aims in mind, I have endeavored neither to overestimate the average reader's knowledge of the subject nor to insult his or her intelligence by being too elementary. In pursuit of this elusive goal, I have attempted to fashion a book that is readable, informative, understandable, and interesting. Each reader will determine how well I have succeeded.

Though focusing primarily on the Second World War, I have examined the many factors that combined to cause that terrible calamity as well as the most significant effects of the conflict. Obviously, in a work of this scope, it has been necessary to deal selectively and summarily with the highly complex history of the decades preceding the outbreak of hostilities in 1939 and the period that followed the defeat of Germany and Japan in 1945. I have also striven to present a balanced account that does justice to both the European and Pacific theaters of operations and the connections between them. The global conflagration gave birth to innumerable controversies, and I have done my best to analyze the most important of these while presenting my own views as to the best interpretations to place on them.

Finally, the revelation in the early 1970s that the Western Allies had broken the German cipher and were intercepting enemy messages throughout much of the war has led to an ongoing reconsideration of the struggle. The process of obtaining and using this often vital information received the code name "Ultra." I have tried to demonstrate its role in achieving the eventual Allied victory.

Any author incurs numerous debts in writing and publishing a book. I certainly am no exception. Mine start with Professor Harold C.

Deutsch, whose masterful course at the University of Minnesota kindled my fascination with the Second World War. Thanks also go to the many students who enrolled in my own World War II course at North Dakota State University during a period of almost two decades. Their obvious interest helped stimulate my dedication to this project. Professor Archer Jones offered encouragement and advice during his years as dean of the College of Humanities and Social Sciences. I must also acknowledge my discussions, not to mention arguments, with Professor James D. Sadkovich, which helped to alter my view of Italy's performance in the war to some extent. My good friend and colleague Professor David B. Danbom provided me with inspiration by example as well as strong personal support. I also appreciate the encouragement and suggestions of Professor A. Harding Ganz. Janis Kirsch is the recipient of special appreciation for service above and beyond the call of duty. She typed my innumerable and often exasperating drafts for the first edition with speed, accuracy, and good humor, without so much as a murmur of discontent. Amy Ochoa performed admirably in preparing the revisions for this second edition.

I am indebted, too, for the many valuable suggestions offered by the readers who found my manuscript worthy of publication. These include James P. Shenton, Columbia University; Joseph W. Bendersky, Virginia Commonwealth University; David Detzer, Western Connecticut State University; John A. Maxwell, West Virginia University; Robin F. A. Fabel, Auburn University; Donald L. Layton, Indiana State University; and Robert Maddox, Pennsylvania State University. In addition, I would like to thank Steve Dalphin and his staff at Prentice Hall for their work in connection with the editorial process. Perhaps the reader will indulge a sentimental urge to recognize the assistance of my much abused vintage 1949 portable typewriter with the missing *x* key.

My gratitude for their encouragement also goes with much affection to my children—Mary, Mike, and Nancy. Finally, my wife, Joan, offered never-flagging but unobtrusive support. She also showed enormous patience with the appalling clutter of notes, books, and other paraphernalia that bore mute testimony to my labors.

I have done my utmost to eliminate mistakes from the following pages. Any errors that have eluded these efforts—whether in fact, interpretation, or otherwise—are solely my own.

Michael J. Lyons

World War II

1

World War I: The Great Turning Point

On June 28, 1914, a Serbian terrorist shot and mortally wounded Archduke Francis Ferdinand, the heir to the throne of the dual monarchy of Austria-Hungary, and his wife. The assassination triggered a crisis that within a month led to the outbreak of World War I. This conflict soon involved all the major European powers as well as Japan and eventually the United States. When the war ended, more than four years later, it had taken 8 million lives and had seriously weakened the predominant position in the world that Europe had long enjoyed. The effects of this great catastrophe lingered throughout the 1920s and 1930s and ultimately contributed to the start of World War II.

THE SOCIAL, POLITICAL, AND ECONOMIC CLIMATE IN EUROPE PRIOR TO WORLD WAR I

World War I has aroused more controversy regarding its origins than any other war. Although the crisis that followed the assassination led directly to the conflict, many factors helped create an atmosphere of tension in the decades before 1914. Some historians consider these factors as more important than the crisis itself and view the war as the inevitable result of their interaction.

Among the factors that contributed to World War I was the growth of nationalism throughout the nineteenth century. This process affected not only the Great Powers—Britain, France, Germany, Austria-Hungary, and Russia—but many smaller countries as well. Early twentieth-century nationalism tended to be of a narrow, selfish, and strident type. Rabid nationalists saw their own countries as superior and looked toward other countries with contempt and hostility. To be sure, most people were not so extreme in their outlook. But many took great pride in their nation and often exaggerated its accomplishments. Governments were willing to go to the brink of war or beyond to safeguard what they considered to be "national interests" or to avenge supposed insults to national honor. Their peoples were, if necessary, ready to die for these causes.

This burgeoning nationalism coincided with large-scale industrialization in much of Western and Central Europe and to a lesser extent in eastern portions of the continent. The nineteenth century also experienced a vast increase in population and the transformation of society in many countries from one that had traditionally been rural and agrarian to one that was largely urban and industrial. These changes occurred with relative speed and contributed to the erosion of traditional values, including religious beliefs, among many people. To some, nationalism became a sort of secular substitute for religion. The concentration of large portions of the population in cities and the development of more efficient communications and a popular press facilitated the dissemination of nationalistic propaganda.

The nineteenth and early twentieth centuries also witnessed the growth of representative political institutions in many countries and the extension of the right to vote in parliamentary elections to the poorer classes of society. The development of a system of mass education, at least at the primary level, played an important role in this democratizing trend. But at the same time, wealth and the actual exercise of political power remained concentrated in a small percentage of the population. Members of the wealthier classes continued to monopolize important governmental positions. The landowning aristocracy, which had dominated Europe for centuries, retained its importance and tended to merge with the wealthy capitalists, who controlled large industries, and directed powerful financial institutions. Industrial society held the promise of a better life, but to the poorer classes, expectations often proved greater than achievements. Although the standard of living rose, millions still remained victims of poverty. Many others who were not in such dire straits were nevertheless dissatisfied with their lives. And while countries such as Britain and France had become true democracies, the political systems of Germany and Austria had the appearance of democracy but lacked the substance. Their elected parliamentary institutions possessed only limited power, while the heads of state and their ministers controlled the formation and implementation of policy. In Russia, there was not even the appearance of democracy.

Many members of the industrial working class turned to labor unions and socialism as a way out of their dilemma. These movements opposed nationalism and appealed to the international solidarity of the workers. They also preached the need to preserve peace and opposed expenditures on armaments. Many Socialists subscribed in theory to the Marxist doctrine of revolution to overthrow the existing political and economic system. But in practice most of them were moderate and willing to work peacefully for reforms. Radical parties appealed to many from the lower middle class, especially small businessmen and independent craftsmen who felt threatened by Big Business and Big Labor. Others found solace in the emotional stimulus of nationalism, which cut across class lines.

Industrialization accelerated economic competition among European powers, which vied for markets and raw materials. But at the same time, they continued to enjoy a large volume of trade with one another. This tended to reduce the intensity of their competition. As patterns of trade became extensive within Europe and between the continent and other parts of the world, however, the economy grew more complex, international, and interdependent. Economic rivalry also provided an impetus to a new flowering of imperialism among the Great Powers in the late nineteenth century. They engaged in a scramble to acquire colonies and spheres of influence in Africa, Asia, and other parts of the "underdeveloped world." Although imperialistic rivalry led to some heated disputes, the powers had settled most of them well before 1914. But some of them had profound and ongoing effects.

THE GROWTH OF RIVALRY AMONG EUROPEAN NATIONS

The development of two rival alliance systems in the years prior to 1914 proved especially critical. The first of these, the Triple Alliance, was the creation of Otto von Bismarck. As minister-president of Prussia, Bismarck had been primarily responsible for combining the various German states in a united Germany and became the country's first chancellor in 1871. The new Germany represented the greatest triumph of nineteenth-century nationalism and became the leading military and industrial power in Europe. But Bismarck had made enemies during the unification process, most notably France, which Prussia had defeated in the Franco-Prussian War of 1870–71. This conflict eliminated French resistance to German unification and forced France to give up two provinces, Alsace and part of Lorraine, to

Germany. To provide his country with security against a possible French attempt to gain revenge and destroy his achievement, Bismarck set out to acquire allies.

His quest led to the formation of the Triple Alliance during the period 1879–82. This defensive alliance linked Germany, Austria-Hungary, and Italy. In the event that an outside power should attack one of the members of the alliance, the other two would be obligated to go to war. Bismarck also attempted to maintain a close relationship with Russia by negotiating a separate treaty with that country. But after his retirement in 1890, his successors allowed the agreement to lapse, fearing that it conflicted with Germany's other commitments. This action provided France with an opportunity to pursue friendlier relations with the Russians. These efforts culminated in a defensive alliance in 1894. Russia's need for capital to finance its industrialization program and France's willingness to provide the funds contributed to this agreement.

Britain later overcame its traditional dedication to what it called "splendid isolation" and made separate agreements with France in 1904 and Russia in 1907. Each of these agreements merely settled colonial issues that had caused problems in the past, but in the following years, Britain drew closer to both countries. This three-cornered relationship became the Triple Entente and served as a counterweight to the Triple Alliance.

The British tightened their connection with France largely because of their growing fear of Germany. The decision of the German emperor, William II, and Admiral Alfred von Tirpitz to increase greatly the size of Germany's navy, starting in 1898, contributed significantly to that concern. Britain had long possessed the world's largest navy. As an island nation dependent on massive imports of food and raw materials, it viewed any threat to its naval supremacy as a danger to its existence. But William and Tirpitz considered a large fleet necessary for a world power and questioned Britain's right to dictate naval strength.

The rather truculent nature of German foreign policy also alarmed the British, especially in connection with two crises over the North African territory of Morocco. In the first of these in 1905, Germany challenged France's efforts to transform Morocco into a protectorate, which Britain had sanctioned in their 1904 agreement. German leaders believed that if confronted by such a crisis, Britain would desert France, and this would wreck their newly formed friendship. But contrary to German expectations, the British supported the French and even initiated military staff talks with them. During the second crisis, in 1911, Germany again pressured France over its encroachment on Morocco, and again Britain sided with the French. This time, the two powers began naval staff talks. These ongoing discussions led to the development of plans to coordinate their armies and navies in case of war with Germany. In 1914, shortly before the outbreak of war, Britain and Russia inaugurated conversations between their naval staffs.

European powers also increased their military and naval strength and devised strategic plans that they intended to put into operation in case of war. New technology facilitated the creation of weapons of increasing sophistication and destructiveness, and industrialization enabled their mass production. As in the case of their alliances, the powers contended that these military and naval forces were necessary to defend them from aggression. But their staff officers drafted strategic plans that were offensive in character. In case of war, they intended to put them into operation as quickly as possible. They considered speed to be essential. In a crisis situation, demands for swift mobilization could create intolerable pressure on civilian officials to resort to war rather than wait for the other side to strike first.

THE SEEDS OF CONFLICT IN EUROPE

During the decade before 1914, the powers focused their attention to a large extent on the Balkan area of southeastern Europe, where a number of crises erupted. Austria-Hungary and

Russia had long been rivals for political and economic influence in the Balkans. The emergence of nationalism among the various Balkan peoples complicated this rivalry. These national groups had been subject to the rule of the Ottoman Turks for centuries. But during the late nineteenth and early twentieth centuries, the Ottoman Empire declined to such an extent that it earned the unenviable reputation as the "sick man of Europe." The Balkan nationalities took advantage of this weakness gradually to win their independence. By 1913, the Turks had lost all of their Balkan holdings except for the predominantly Turkish area bordering the straits that linked the Black Sea with the Mediterranean.

Among the states that emerged from this long process was an independent Serbia. Its existence posed a special problem for the dual monarchy of Austria-Hungary, which was a glaring exception in an age of nation-states. It was a multinational empire, consisting of minorities that differed from one another in language, customs, historical development, and religion. In fact, the two dominant nationalities—the Austrians, who were ethnically German, and the Hungarians—comprised less than half the population. The Austro-Hungarian government had long viewed nationalism as a force that, if successful, would lead to the country's disintegration into its component national parts. Among the dual monarchy's nationalities was a Serbian minority that lived in territories bordering Serbia. The Serbian government hoped eventually to absorb these kinsmen into a "greater Serbia." To complicate matters even more, Russia treated Serbia as a client state. Both the Russians and Serbs were Slavic peoples. In the early twentieth century, Austria-Hungary became obsessed by what it viewed as "the Serbian menace." This menace materialized with the creation of a secret Serbian nationalist society that took the name Union of Death or the Black Hand. It was this organization that carried out the assassination of Francis Ferdinand in 1914.

The Austro-Hungarian government responded to the assassination with outrage; however, it could not decide how it should deal with Serbia. At this critical point, Germany pledged to support whatever action the dual monarchy deemed necessary, even if it meant war with Serbia's protector, Russia. Armed with this "blank check," Austria-Hungary finally issued an ultimatum to Serbia that, if accepted, would have reduced the nation to a virtual satellite state. Although the Serbs agreed to comply with most of the ultimatum's demands, they balked at certain points that they felt were incompatible with their independence. Austria-Hungary responded by declaring war on July 28, hoping to deal with Serbia in isolation.

THE WAR SPREADS

But Russia rallied to Serbia's aid by mobilizing its reserves, an act preparatory to military action. Since the Russians assumed that war with Austria-Hungary would also mean war with Germany, they had only one plan, which provided for mobilization against both countries. Germany now became alarmed and, taking for granted that a conflict with Russia would also embroil it in hostilities with France, issued ultimatums to both. Germany asked Russia to cease mobilization and France to declare neutrality in case of war between Germany and Russia. Neither agreed to accept these demands, and by August 3 Germany was at war with both powers.

Despite a close relationship with France, Britain hesitated at first but entered the conflict when Germany sent forces into tiny Belgium. This violated an agreement that the Great Powers had made in 1839 to guarantee Belgium's permanent neutrality. The British had traditionally opposed any power that attempted to seize this area because of its location across the Channel from Britain. Germany justified its aggression on grounds of military necessity. Germany's strategic plan provided for an invasion of France by way of Belgium. The British responded to this action by declaring war on Germany.

Italy refused to support its partners in the Triple Alliance, contending that Austria-Hungary and Germany were the aggressors. Italy pointed to the fact that its only obligation was to take action in case of an attack on one of them. The Italians remained interested onlookers until April 1915, when they sided with the Allies—Britain, France, and Russia. They did so in return for Allied promises of compensation at Austria-Hungary's expense as well as in the Middle East and Africa. Japan also declared war on Germany but confined its efforts to the Far East and Pacific, where the Japanese quickly seized a number of German colonial outposts. The Central Powers—Germany and Austria-Hungary—managed to lure Turkey and Bulgaria into the conflict on their side.

The war that came in 1914 was not inevitable. To be sure, conflicting national interests and the existence of the alliances contributed to the outbreak of hostilities. But the war was nevertheless the result of the inability of the powers to solve the 1914 crisis. This failure was due to human error, especially Germany's blank check, Austria-Hungary's belief that it could localize the war, and Russia's decision to mobilize. It does not appear that any of the Great Powers desired a general conflict, but once the Austro-Hungarians issued their ultimatum to Serbia, the crisis took on a momentum of its own. The necessities of mobilization and strategic plans quickly swept Europe into war.

Civilians and soldiers alike greeted the outbreak of war with nationalist pride and enthusiasm. To them, it was a great adventure. Millions lined the streets to cheer and throw flowers to the brave warriors as they marched through Berlin, Vienna, and Paris. One young German recruit was so overjoyed when he received his uniform and weapons that he shouted, "War is like Christmas!" The mood soon changed.

MISCALCULATIONS AND ILLUSIONS

At first, none of the European powers realized the type of conflict they had unleashed. Most leaders, both civilian and military, seriously underestimated the length of the war, its costliness in lives and wealth, and its impact on the very foundations of European politics and society. They expected a short war, basing their assumption on the fact that since the defeat of Napoleon in 1815, most European wars had been brief, lasting only a few weeks or months. The Great Powers also anticipated that the development and mass production of powerful new weapons in the years leading up to 1914 would give the advantage to the offense rather than the defense. It seemed obvious that the side that possessed the greatest offensive strength would win.

The Central Powers especially counted on a short war because a long conflict was almost certain to go against them. The Allied countries possessed larger manpower reserves, greater industrial strength, and access to the resources of the rest of the world. They also used their superior naval strength to impose a blockade that cut off the Central Powers from the other continents. The Allies virtually encircled their enemies, with Britain and France on the west, Russia on the east, and Italy on the south. Despite the fact that German armies operated within the borders of both France and Russia from 1914 on, the Central Powers were in effect the besieged nations, at least until the collapse of Russia late in the war.

Germany, the most powerful of the Central Powers, had taken a two-front war for granted in its long-range military planning. But the Germans realized that they could not win such a conflict unless they defeated France and Russia one at a time in quick, decisive fashion. Their strategic plan, which aimed at accomplishing the first stage of this task, was not new. It was the work of General Alfred von Schlieffen, who had retired as chief of staff in 1906. Schlieffen called for the Germans to concentrate powerful forces in the west while remaining on the defensive against Russia. He envisioned a thrust through Belgium that would avoid the fortifications along France's northeastern border. German troops would then swing into France, led by an overwhelmingly powerful right wing that would advance to the southwest of Paris before wheeling to the east. If all went according to plan, the Germans would encircle the main enemy armies and force France to capitulate within six weeks. After this great victory, Germany would shift its strength eastward to deal with the Russians.

When the war began, General Helmuth von Moltke, who had taken over as chief of staff, put the Schlieffen plan into effect. At first, the Germans carried out their offensive with considerable skill and were nearing Paris by early September. But Moltke had reduced the striking power of the right wing to strengthen his forces along the German border where he anticipated a French attack. He also shifted additional troops to the eastern front to help resist an unexpected Russian offensive. As a result, the German spearhead did not have sufficient strength to execute its turn to the southwest of Paris. Instead, it had to shorten its front and wheel to the northeast of the capital, and as it did, the French counterattacked the German flank.

In the desperate struggle that followed, the Allies forced the Germans to halt their offensive. This First Battle of the Marne proved to be the decisive encounter of the war. It denied Germany a quick victory and condemned it to fight a prolonged two-front conflict. Although Moltke received the blame for the German failure, it appears that the Schlieffen plan had little chance of success under any circumstances. It was far too ambitious and would soon have encountered such extreme supply problems that it would have failed even if Moltke had attempted to carry out Schlieffen's instructions to the letter. In fact, a stronger right wing would have compounded these logistic difficulties.

A LONG AND BLOODY DEADLOCK

As the short-war illusion faded, hostilities on the western front degenerated into a bloody war of attrition. The two sides began to dig in and gradually created opposing systems of trenches, extending across southwestern Belgium and northern France from the English Channel to the Swiss border. The front had no flanks, and thus for the next four years both the Allies and Germany tried to break the deadlock by means of direct assaults using millions of men. Unfortunately, the new and terrible weapons, which the Great Powers had developed prior to the war, proved especially well suited for defensive warfare. They included vastly improved rifles, the machine gun, and artillery of tremendous range and velocity. This concentrated firepower prevented either side from gaining a breakthrough and inflicted hundreds of thousands of casualties in each major offensive.

Another deadlock developed on the eastern front, even though this vast area provided far greater room for maneuver. After halting Russia's offensive in the great Battle of Tannenberg in August 1914, the Germans carried out a major offensive in 1915 that drove the enemy out of much of its western territory. The Russians suffered appalling casualties, and the Germans captured over a million prisoners. But despite this demoralizing setback, Russia refused to make peace. This confronted the Germans with a dilemma. Should they continue to advance deeper into the vast expanse of Russia or halt their operations and concentrate on the western front during 1916? After considerable debate, they chose the latter solution.

The man most responsible for this decision was General Erich von Falkenhayn, who had succeeded Moltke as chief of staff. Falkenhayn had devised a master plan to win the war in the west during 1916. It involved a huge offensive against the French fortress city of Verdun with the purpose of inflicting such heavy losses that France would be forced to leave the war. This assault, designed to "bleed France white," began in February and continued for months. It did cost the French 375,000 casualties, but the Germans suffered 335,000 of their own, and France did not make peace.

Britain was active, too. It had started the war with a small volunteer military force but resorted to conscription early in 1916 and by the summer had created a mass army. General Sir Douglas Haig, commander of the British Expeditionary Force, opened an offensive along the Somme River in July 1916 with French assistance. But his hopes for a major breakthrough proved as illusory as Falkenhayn's dream of victory at Verdun. The British suffered almost 60,000 casu-

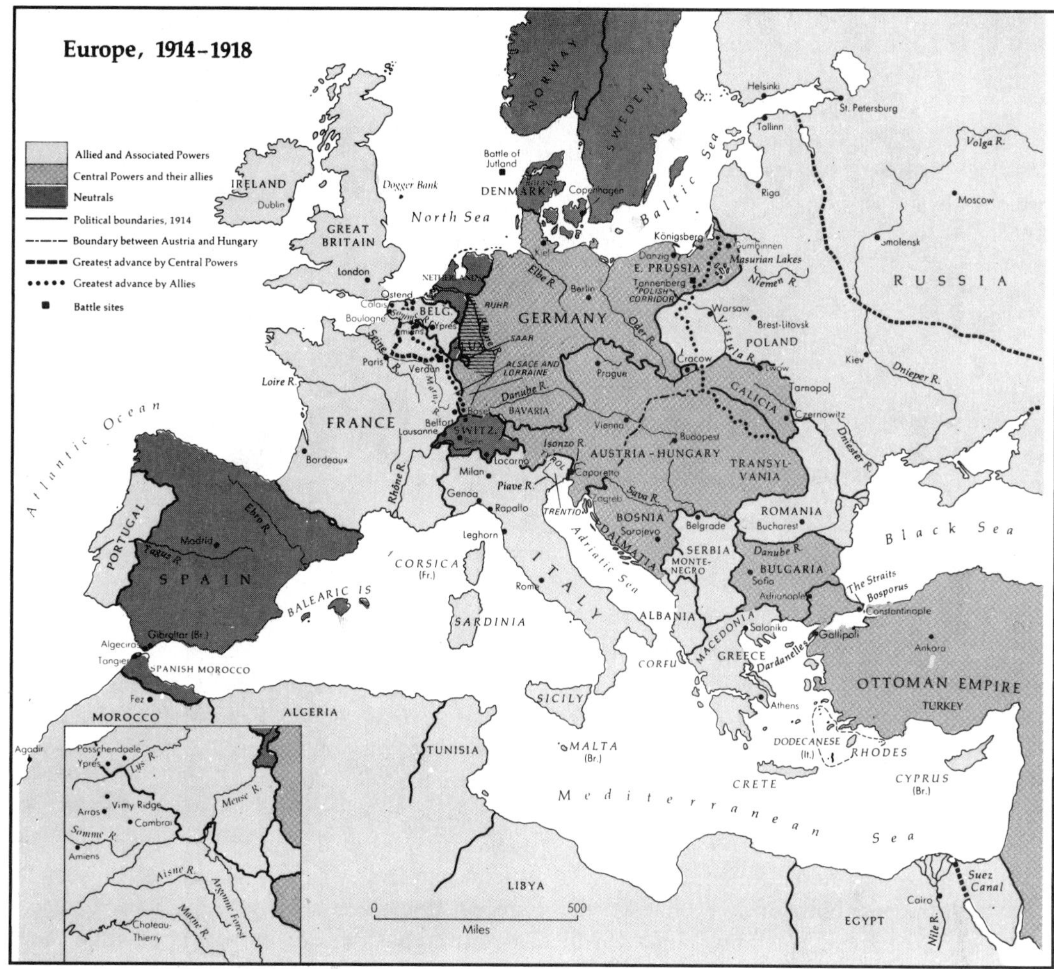

Europe, 1914–18

alties on the first day, and the Battle of the Somme continued until November. When it ended, the British had sustained 420,000 casualties, the French 200,000, and the Germans 450,000. This fearful carnage had resulted in no appreciable change in the battle line.

The Russians also returned to the offensive in the summer of 1916. Under the leadership of General Alexei Brusilov, they scored impressive early successes against the Austro-Hungarians, but, as usual, their drive eventually stalled. Again, casualties were high for both sides, the Russians suffering most with close to half a million dead, wounded, and missing and another 400,000 prisoners. Hundreds of thousands of others deserted.

The horrible events of 1916 struck the belligerent powers with stunning psychological impact. Verdun, although a French victory, left the army on the verge of rebellion. When France resorted to another suicidal offensive in the spring of 1917, large-scale mutinies actually took place. The British had to shoulder most of the burden during the remainder of the year, while the French restored order and morale among their forces. The Brusilov offensive had virtually fin-

FIGURE 1-1 Allied troops advance on the western front. (*National Archives*)

ished both the Russian and Austro-Hungarian armies as important factors in the war. Even the proud German army was never quite the same after Verdun and the Somme and found itself stretched too thin in too many places.

On the home front, war weariness increased, and support for peace grew among the civilian populations. The winter of 1916–17 was particularly harsh, adding to the suffering. Both sides toyed with the possibility of a negotiated settlement, while President Woodrow Wilson of the United States and Pope Benedict XV offered their help as mediators. But neither side was willing to settle for a peace without compensation.

THE RESORT TO TOTAL WAR

Instead of peace, the Western Powers and Germany resorted to a total-war approach and stronger leadership completely dedicated to victory. In Britain, David Lloyd George, a fiery Welshman, became prime minister in December 1916. The equally combative Georges Clemenceau, who had earned the nickname "the Tiger," took over as premier of France in 1917. The governments of both countries assumed virtual dictatorial power and subordinated everything to their war efforts, but at least civilian officials remained in charge.

In Germany, the military increasingly dominated the government. Field Marshal Paul von Hindenburg, a veteran of the Franco-Prussian War, succeeded Falkenhayn as chief of staff after the failure at Verdun. He and General Erich Ludendorff pressured Chancellor Theobold von Bethmann-Hollweg out of office in 1917 when he appeared too receptive to a negotiated peace. Bethmann's successor proved to be little more than a puppet for Hindenburg and Ludendorff.

The governments of all three countries concentrated their economies almost totally on the war effort. They allocated resources as well as labor and coordinated production to an unprecedented degree. Their achievements were remarkable. The task of large-scale economic mobilization proved far more difficult for Austria-Hungary, Italy, and Russia. Their less well developed economies and weaker governmental structures left them more dependent on aid from their allies. Russia's isolation from the Western Powers also sharply limited the amount of assistance it could receive. All the warring countries appealed to their peoples for support and continued sacrifice.

The European powers had blundered into the

conflict so unexpectedly in 1914 that they initially had few, if any, clear war aims. All of them believed they were fighting in defense of their national independence or at least national interests. None of them considered itself to be the aggressor. Of the major powers, only Italy entered the war with definite aims but had had over seven months to ponder them. Soon after hostilities began, however, other belligerents formulated specific war aims. With the realization that the struggle was going to be long and bloody, leaders and important segments of the public concluded that it must result in gains that would help justify the terrible slaughter and the strain on their economies.

THE TERRITORIAL IMPERATIVE

On the Allied side, France hoped from the start to regain Alsace-Lorraine. But as time passed, French leaders began to covet Germany's coal-rich Saar, a small area bordering France on the northeast. They also favored removing German control over the Rhineland, the region to the west of the Rhine River, and establishing an independent Rhenish state. This would create a buffer between France and Germany. The French also hoped to weaken Germany to such an extent that it would be unable to make war on France in the future. And they hoped to acquire German colonies in Africa as well as Turkish possessions in the Middle East. Britain had no territorial ambitions in Europe but, like France, desired colonial compensation at the expense of Germany and Turkey.

Russia expected to oust Turkey from control of the straits. This cherished dream had long been contrary to the interests of both Britain and France, which had desired to keep Russian naval power out of the Mediterranean. But in 1915, fearing that Russia might make a separate peace, the Western Powers conceded Russia control over the straits after the war. Italy had entered the conflict to obtain territory along the Austrian border—the Trentino on the north as well as the port city of Trieste and the peninsula of Istria to the east. Italy also desired a sizable strip of Austria's coastline along the Adriatic Sea.

As for the Central Powers, Austria-Hungary had been confused from the start about what it expected to gain from the conflict. In fact, Hungarian leaders had agreed to war only on condition that Austria-Hungary would not acquire any Serbian territory. They believed that the absorption of additional Serbs would only create greater internal problems. And the Austro-Hungarians immediately suffered defeats at the hands of not only the Russians but the Serbs as well. This ominous beginning seemed to indicate the wisdom of seeking a quick end to the war. Instead, they continued to persevere, and Germany came to their rescue with the 1915 offensive, which drove the Russians deep into their own territory. The Germans also directed a campaign in which their troops joined with those of Austria-Hungary and Bulgaria to crush Serbia. But this salvation ultimately proved fatal to the dual monarchy because the war became more and more unpopular with the subject nationalities, kindling desires for independence. Austria-Hungary's increasing reliance on its ally also transformed the empire into a German satellite. As the war continued, its primary aim came to be one of self-preservation.

By far the most extensive aims were those of Germany, although these fluctuated according to the fortunes of war. They provided for absorption of an additional iron-rich slice of French Lorraine as well as Luxembourg and either annexation of Belgium or its conversion into a satellite state. The Germans harbored far greater ambitions in Eastern Europe. These included acquisition of almost all of Russia's western territory—the provinces bordering the Baltic Sea, Poland, and the vast area of the Ukraine. Germany's intentions in these areas are not clear, but it certainly planned some annexations and the establishment of satellite states. The Germans also anticipated keeping Austria-Hungary in the role of a satellite as well as establishing a sphere of influence in the Balkans. They visualized creating a German-dominated European customs union that would make them economically supreme. In addition to this vast increase of German power in Europe, they also proposed to take over a number of French, British, and Belgian colonies in Africa.

REVOLUTION IN RUSSIA

As the war continued, the pressures on each of the powers increased steadily. Russia was the first to crack under the strain. Although the Russian economy had experienced some industrialization in the years prior to 1914, it still remained primitive compared to those of Germany and Britain. It proved quite inadequate to supply the needs of both the armed forces and the civilian population. Shortages of all kinds developed early and became more pronounced as the conflict continued. The Russian transportation system also broke down under the unprecedented demands of modern warfare. To make matters worse, the government of Czar Nicholas II was inefficient, corrupt, and unpopular. War weariness became greater in Russia than in any other country as the army suffered its series of staggering defeats.

During the winter of 1916–17, shortages of many goods, including food, became even more acute. Early in March 1917, a revolt broke out in Petrograd, the capital. It started as demonstrations against the food shortage that soon became riots. Workers showed their sympathy by going on strike. The government ordered the city's army garrison to put down the unrest, but the soldiers deserted to the rebels. Revolution spread rapidly to other cities, and it soon became apparent that virtually no one was willing to defend the discredited regime. Within a week, Czar Nicholas II had bowed to increasing demands for his abdication, ending the 300-year rule of the Romanov dynasty.

The revolutionaries established a provisional government to lead the country until a constituent assembly could draft a constitution for a permanent political system. But the provisional government was reluctant to hold elections for the assembly in the unsettled atmosphere and also refused to seek a negotiated peace. Instead, it tried to provide more efficient and inspiring leadership that would lead the army to victory. With the utter failure of a final offensive in July, however, it became clear that this was an impossible task. But still the provisional government continued the war. This obstinate policy and the refusal to call elections for the constituent assembly eroded the government's support. Its failure to enact a land reform program also alienated the peasants. Workers and soldiers increasingly rallied to the Bolsheviks, a revolutionary Marxist Socialist party.

Under the leadership of Vladimir Lenin, the Bolsheviks sought to win control of the soviets, councils which workers and soldiers had organized early in the revolution. The soviets had remained in existence despite the formation of the provisional government and represented a potential source of opposition to its rule. By October, the Bolsheviks had gained a majority in the soviets of Petrograd, Moscow, and several other industrial cities. In early November, they moved against the provisional government, which found itself almost as bereft of support as the czarist regime had been in March. The Bolsheviks quickly gained control of much of European Russia.

Lenin had promised to secure peace if the Bolsheviks came to power and now set out to fulfill that pledge. It proved difficult because the Germans insisted on exceedingly harsh terms. It was not until March 1918 that the Bolsheviks finally agreed to the Treaty of Brest-Litovsk. This settlement, along with later supplementary arrangements, required Russia to give up most of its Baltic provinces, much of Russian Poland, and the Ukraine, as provided in the German war aims. Germany also extracted such far-reaching trade concessions that Russia became a virtual economic dependency.

THE U.S. ROLE

Meanwhile, the United States had entered the war on the side of the Allies in April 1917. Many Americans had been sympathetic to the Allied cause from the start of the war. They had much more in common with democratic Britain and France than with the more authoritarian regimes of the Central Powers. They also were appalled by the German shooting of Belgian hostages in reprisal for civilian attacks on soldiers, the shelling of the beautiful Gothic cathedral at Reims, France, and the sinking of the British ocean liner *Lusitania* with the loss of over 1,000 lives, including 128 Americans. Allied propaganda proved especially effective at portraying the Germans as barbaric "Huns." And American loans to Allied powers created an economic stake in their victory.

But the primary factor that brought the United States into the war was Germany's policy of unrestricted submarine warfare, which resulted in the sinking of several American ships in early 1917. This policy was a calculated risk designed to force Britain out of the war. The Germans realized that the British were dependent on large-scale imports of food and other supplies. They hoped that with the help of a greatly increased submarine force, they would be able to starve Britain into submission by sinking large numbers of both Allied and neutral ships in the waters around the British Isles. The gamble failed. Not only did it bring the United States into the war, but the British were able to combat the submarine menace and continue the struggle.

Despite a large population and great economic resources, America was a negligible military power in early 1917, with only 110,000 men under arms. Before the United States could help in the actual fighting, it had to raise a mass army through conscription, train it and transport it to France. This new and powerful force was not ready for action until the summer of 1918. In the months that followed Russia's departure from the war, Germany attempted to defeat the British and French before America became a factor. The Germans unleased a series of offensives between March and July 1918, but the French and British managed to hold out, and during the last German offensive, fresh American divisions began to make a major contribution. After stopping the final German drive, the Allies took over the offensive and, under the leadership of Marshal Ferdinand Foch, applied unrelenting pressure. On August 8, "the black day of the German army,"

FIGURE 1-2 Emperor William II of Germany.

the whole enemy front began to fall back. German military leaders realized that they had lost the war.

AN END TO THE NIGHTMARE

Soon afterward, dramatic events unfolded far to the southeast. An Allied army had been encamped in northern Greece since 1915, when it had arrived too late to prevent neighboring Serbia from being overrun by the Central Powers. But in September 1918, it went over to the offensive, led by French Marshal Louis Franchet d'Esperey. By the end of the month, it had forced Bulgaria out of the war. Turkey, now isolated to the southeast, capitulated a month later as Allied troops pushed into Serbia.

In late October, Italian forces, which had suffered a near catastrophic defeat in the Battle of Caporetto a year earlier, also won a major victory over the Austro-Hungarians in the Battle of Vittorio Veneto. Confronted by these two critical developments, Austria-Hungary's army disintegrated, and the various subject nationalities began to declare their independence. The dual monarchy signed an armistice on November 4. Soon afterward, Charles, the last emperor of the Hapsburg dynasty, which had ruled Austria since 1276, abdicated.

Germany's position was now hopeless. With its army in full retreat and its allies gone, morale began to crack. Naval mutinies and sporadic civilian revolts broke out. Demand for an end to the war and even to the monarchy, which had been the form of government since the unification of Germany in 1871, grew ever more insistent. The Emperor William II, realizing the weakness of his position, abdicated and fled into exile in neutral Holland. On November 11, a new republican government accepted an armistice.

The long nightmare was over. But although the Allies had defeated the Central Powers, in a larger sense none of the European belligerents had really won. The war had cost the lives of at least 8 million soldiers and had left another 20 million wounded. There were few families that did not mourn the loss of loved ones. An atmosphere of gloom and uncertainty persisted long after the fighting stopped. The war had also seriously disrupted the European economies, which had concentrated on production of war materiel for over four years at the expense of normal peacetime manufacturing. Overseas markets were gone, and all the belligerents were deeply in debt. Devastation abounded in many parts of the continent. And although peace had returned, wartime hatreds lingered. So did the questions. How could it have happened? How could the leaders have allowed it to continue for so long? What did it accomplish? Could anything be worth the price? Among the casualties was the old confident Europe, long the focal point of the world. It was gone, perhaps forever.

2

The Legacy of World War I

Although the war had ended, turmoil still afflicted much of Europe. The Austro-Hungarian Empire had vanished from the map. The relative unity and stability it had given to Central Europe was no more. A jumble of small, weak states had taken its place, creating a vacuum of power. In Russia, the Bolsheviks had not been able to savor their victory over the provisional government for long. Various anti-Bolshevik forces had challenged their right to rule, and civil war had erupted during the summer of 1918. It continued to rage in the aftermath of World War I. Defeat had reduced Germany to a state of shock, bitterness, and disillusionment. And while Britain, France, and Italy engaged in victory celebrations, mourning for millions of dead, who had paid the price for this triumph, tended to restrain their joy. Now that they were free from the grim reality that had haunted them for four long years, Europeans looked to the future with both hope and uncertainty. But hatred of recent enemies persisted.

THE PEACE OF PARIS

It was in this atmosphere that the victorious Allies met in January 1919 to draft the settlement that liquidated the war—the Peace of Paris. They refused to invite either Germany or Russia to attend the conference. After four years of bitter warfare, the European Allies, especially the French, had little inclination to sit across the bargaining table from the despised Germans. Resentment over the Bolshevik government's separate peace with Germany and fear of its doctrine of world revolution prompted the decision to bar Russia from participation. The outcome of the Russian civil war was also uncertain, and the Allies hoped that the anti-Bolshevik forces would win. The Allies had refused to grant diplomatic recognition to the new regime and had even intervened in the civil war during 1918. British and French forces had landed at Russian ports on the Arctic and Black seas, ostensibly to prevent war materiel, which the Western Allies had sent to the provisional government, from falling into the hands of the Germans. But they also provided aid to the anti-Bolshevik forces. American and Japanese units had gone ashore at Vladivostok in East Asia to help the escape of Czech prisoners of war who intended to join the Allies. With the end of World War I, the original justification for intervention was no longer valid, and the Western Allies withdrew during 1919. The Japanese remained for three more years.

Delegations representing 27 nations convened in Paris, but the leaders of the Great Powers actually made the major decisions. They started as the Big Four, consisting of President Wilson of the United States, France's Premier Clemenceau, British Prime Minister Lloyd George, and Italian Premier Vittorio Orlando. But Orlando walked out of the conference in protest when the Western Powers refused to grant Italy the extensive compensation it had expected along the Adriatic Coast. The others were not impressed with Italy's performance in the war, and Wilson was opposed to giving the Italians territory that contained predominantly South Slav populations. As a result, they agreed to grant only the Trentino, Trieste, and Istria. Although Orlando did return later, the Big Three—Wilson, Clemenceau, and Lloyd George—essentially molded the settlement.

The most important portion of the Peace of Paris was the Treaty of Versailles, which provided the settlement for Germany. It represented a compromise, essentially between the views of Wilson and those of Clemenceau. Wilson desired a peace of reconciliation that would be lenient with the Germans and, he hoped, they would accept as final. He had issued a statement of war aims—the Fourteen Points—in January 1918. His position was highly idealistic and included such unselfish aims as the creation of an international peacekeeping organization, disarmament, the securing of the right of all peoples to govern themselves, an end to secret diplomatic agreements, and the establishment of freedom of trade between nations. He could afford to be unselfish. The United States had suffered far less from the war than had the European Allies. In fact, in terms of economic and political power, America had gained a great deal from the conflict. It had taken over markets that the European powers were not able to supply due to their concentration on the war and had achieved a highly favorable balance of trade in the process. The European Allies had also turned to the United States for loans to help them finance their war efforts. In 1919, they were all deeply in debt, whereas America had become a creditor nation on a massive scale.

FIGURE 2-1 Victorious Allied troops march through London. (*National Archives*)

Wilson firmly believed that the United States had a special calling to lead the world into a new age of peace and democracy. He looked with disapproval at the traditionally cynical attitude of European countries in the realm of power politics. The president looked upon himself as an alternative to Lenin, the architect of the Bolshevik victory in Russia and the chief advocate of a new Marxist world order. Wilson wanted to build an international system based on liberal capitalism, free trade, and democracy, with a League of Nations dedicated to preserving peace as its cornerstone.

At least some of Wilson's Fourteen Points differed rather dramatically from the war aims of the European Allies. Britain and France agreed to the Fourteen Points as the basis for negotiation but not as a hard-and-fast blueprint for settlement. But the German government accepted the armistice in the belief that Wilson's proposal would be the framework for a lenient peace. Actually, the Germans were unduly optimistic about the Fourteen Points, which contained a provision for an independent Poland with access to the sea.

This meant that Germany would lose territory to the new Polish state, including a corridor to the Baltic Sea that would divide Germany into two parts, something extremely unpalatable to most Germans.

Clemenceau desired a harsh peace that would keep Germany permanently crippled or at least postpone its ability to make war for as long as possible. The French leader hated the Germans and was contemptuous of Wilson. Clemenceau had experienced two German invasions of France during his lifetime—in 1870 and, of course, in 1914. He was determined that it should never happen again. In pursuit of that goal, he sought to deprive Germany of some territory, reduce the German armed forces to impotence, and require heavy payments for war damages. He also hoped to bind France, Britain, and the United States in a peacetime alliance that would safeguard France against the possibility of a German revival.

Lloyd George started out as another proponent of a harsh peace, but by the time the conference opened, he had modified his approach. He became something of a mediator between the more extreme views of Wilson and Clemenceau and performed capably in this role. As he later commented, "I think I did as well as might be expected, seated as I was between Jesus Christ and Napoleon Bonaparte."

The Treaty of Versailles, which was the fruit of the Big Three's efforts, was neither as lenient as Wilson had preferred nor as harsh as Clemenceau had desired. Both men had yielded on many points to obtain what they considered essential. Wilson won approval for his League of Nations, which he hoped would mediate future international disputes peacefully. Clemenceau gained restrictions on Germany that he considered necessary to safeguard France's security.

Certainly the treaty was not nearly as severe as the peace that the Germans would have imposed had they won the war. The Treaty of Brest-Litovsk had been the first installment of that projected peace of iron. But many Germans, who had been most insistent on extensive gains for their own country, considered the Versailles settlement outrageously unfair. They also found it difficult to believe that Germany had really suffered defeat. Allied troops had not reached the German border before the war ended. There were few signs of destruction in Germany. The armistice had provided for occupation of the Rhineland and several bridgeheads on the Rhine's east bank, but most of Germany remained free of an Allied presence.

Indeed, the story was already circulating that the German army had not actually been beaten. According to this account, the new republic had betrayed the army by hastily accepting the armistice. This "stab in the back" legend plagued the republic throughout its existence and also contributed significantly to the German refusal to accept the new treaty as final. Indeed, the republic's first chancellor, Friedrich Ebert, unwittingly provided impetus to the legend when he greeted German troops arriving back in Berlin in 1918 with the words, "As you return unconquered from the field of battle, I salute you."

By comparison to Brest-Litovsk, the territorial provisions of the Versailles treaty were, for the most part, fair. As everyone expected, France regained the provinces of Alsace and Lorraine. Belgium also received minor border changes in its favor, and a plebiscite resulted in Denmark gaining a slice of Danish-populated territory along Germany's northern border. In the case of the coal-rich Saar, the peacemakers provided a temporary compromise settlement. Clemenceau wanted to annex the area to France as compensation for the destruction of French coal mines during the war. But Wilson and Lloyd George withheld their approval. Instead, the three men agreed to place the area under the administration of the newly established League of Nations for 15 years. They also provided for French operation of the coal mines during this period. But the agreement stipulated that the population, which was solidly German, would have the right to determine the permanent fate of the Saar by plebiscite in 1935.

A much more important provision concerned the Rhineland. In keeping with French war aims,

Territorial Settlements in Europe, 1919–26

Clemenceau favored its separation from Germany and the establishment of an independent Rhenish state. Again, Wilson and Lloyd George refused and secured another compromise. Under this agreement, the Rhineland remained part of Germany, but the Allies were to maintain troops there for 15 years. When this period expired, they were to withdraw their forces, and the entire area was to remain permanently demilitarized, along with a 50-kilometer-wide strip on the Rhine's east bank. The Big Three hoped that this solution would provide a buffer area that would shield France and Belgium from a possible German invasion, or at least give them advance warning of such an attack. To reconcile Clemenceau to this compromise, Wilson and Lloyd George made a remarkable commitment to safeguard French security. If Germany attacked France, this "guarantee treaty" bound the United States and Britain to support the French militarily. It represented a sig-

FIGURE 2-2 The Big Four at the Paris Peace Conference. From the left: Vittorio Orlando (Italy), David Lloyd George (Britain), Georges Clemenceau (France), Woodrow Wilson (U.S.). (*AP/Wide World Photos*)

nificant departure from the traditional peacetime policies of both countries.

But by far the most far-reaching and controversial territorial changes took place in the east. In keeping with Polish national aspirations and Wilson's Fourteen Points, the Big Three agreed that Germany must surrender a substantial amount of territory to the revived state of Poland. This included the province and city of Posen (Poznan in Polish) and, most important, a strip of land that linked the major portion of the new country with the Baltic Sea to the north. Without this "Polish corridor," Poland would be a landlocked state, and its only access to the sea would be through Germany.

Unfortunately, the corridor also divided the bulk of Germany from the province of East Prussia, which was certain to anger the Germans. Transfer of these territories also righted a historic wrong. They had belonged to Poland until its neighbors—Prussia, Austria, and Russia—removed the country from the map by a series of three partitions in the late eighteenth century. They also contained a majority of Poles, although large German minorities were present as well. The population pattern was so mixed that unless the peacemakers insisted on the transfer of many Germans to the west or Poles to the east, this was unavoidable. Farther south, the industrial area of Upper Silesia also proved troublesome. Again, the population was mixed, and the Big Three ordered a plebiscite, which resulted in less than half the disputed area going to Poland.

Wilson, Clemenceau, and Lloyd George found it far less easy to justify the detachment of the large city of Danzig from Germany. Danzig's population was German, but since it was the only major port in the vicinity of the Polish corridor, the Poles coveted its harbor facilities. Another compromise provided a solution of sorts. Danzig and the surrounding area became a free state under League of Nations supervision, but Poland received the right to unrestricted use of the port.

Separation of the smaller port of Memel in extreme northeastern East Prussia also proved difficult to justify. Memel, like Danzig, was a German city, but the border strip extending to the south contained a predominantly Lithuanian population. Again, the treaty placed the entire area under League administration. But the new state of Lithuania, small though it was, took advantage of Germany's weakness to seize Memel in 1921.

The treaty also provided for the total dismantling of Germany's overseas empire and the distribution of its colonies to various Allied powers as "mandated territories" under League of Nations supervision. In theory, the occupying powers were to prepare their mandates for eventual independence. But in practice, they governed most of them as colonies. Britain and France were the principal beneficiaries in Africa, while Japan gained Germany's enclaves along the coast of China as well as the Marshall, Caroline, and Mariana island chains in the Pacific.

France, of course, was determined to weaken Germany's ability to make war. The Allies agreed to limit the German army to a volunteer force of only 100,000 men and prohibited the existence of any kind of reserve. To facilitate this, soldiers were to serve 12-year enlistments, which would prevent short-term training for a large number of men. Tanks, heavy artillery, and other "offensive" weapons were banned. The Big Three also ordered the dissolution of the general staff, the war academy, and the cadet schools, which they considered breeding grounds for Prussian militarism. The German navy received bad news, too. It was to consist of only six warships, none of which was to be over 10,000 tons, and there were to be no submarines. Finally, the treaty prohibited Germany from maintaining a military air force.

To compensate Allied powers for damages inflicted by German forces during the war, the treaty provided that Germany pay reparations. This was not unusual. The Germans fully expected to make such payments and had accepted the principle during the armistice negotiations. Germany had imposed a heavy war indemnity on France after the Franco-Prussian War and on Russia in the Treaty of Brest-Litovsk. Clemenceau and Lloyd George originally asked that, in addition to paying for civilian damages, reparations cover all Allied costs in fighting the war. Wilson blocked this proposal as much too extreme but did allow inclusion of the cost of war pensions for Allied soldiers. At the same time, he renounced any American claim to reparations. The peace conference did not establish the final amount.

Instead, the Big Three appointed a commission to study the problem and set the total. Germany was to pay $5 billion in cash and commodities during the interim period. The Reparations Commission announced the final bill in May 1921 as $33 billion in gold. It set annual payments of about $500 million for 66 years. American experts considered the burden to be considerably beyond Germany's ability to pay. The great British economist John Maynard Keynes agreed and attacked it in the most scathing terms, predicting that it would unhinge the postwar economy. The Germans were even more critical. Although, in proportion to values at the time, the amount was equivalent to the indemnity imposed on France in 1871, they greeted the announcement with a wave of protest.

In an effort to justify reparations, the Allied leaders inserted a clause in the treaty that required Germany to admit that the Central Powers had been responsible for the war. It became known as the "war guilt" clause, and it was, to say the least, politically unwise. The Germans found it highly offensive and unfair. It did not actually contain the term *guilt* or specifically blame the Central Powers for starting the war. But it did charge them with responsibility for the "loss and damage" suffered by the Allies and referred to "the aggression" of Germany and its partners. The Germans interpreted this to mean guilt.

In addition to the German settlement, the treaty contained the agreement or covenant that established the League of Nations. Wilson visualized the League as a collective security organization that would deter aggression and would work to provide peaceful solutions to disputes between nations. The covenant created a League assembly to which every member nation would belong. The assembly had the right to consider all issues, but the actual decision-making power, in most cases, lay with the League council. The council would include five permanent members—Britain, France, Italy, the United States, and Japan—as well as four nonpermanent members that the assembly would select for limited terms.

The covenant declared that any war involving member states or any crisis that might lead to war fell within the League's jurisdiction. It stated that members must submit all disputes for investigation, arbitration, and settlement. If a member ignored this obligation and went to war, the League could take action against the aggressor power. But the question of what these measures would entail proved difficult. Clemenceau insisted that the only way to secure meaningful collective security was the creation of an international army that could enforce League decisions. But Wilson and Lloyd George refused to agree to such a far-reaching commitment. Ultimately, the only coercive power that the League possessed was the authority to impose economic sanctions. This involved cutting off trade between League members and the aggressor power. The Big Three refused to allow either Germany or Russia to join the organization, a decision which undermined the validity of the League from the start.

Despite Wilson's dream, the United States also did not become a member of the League. This was due to a quarrel between the president and Republican leaders in the Senate who refused to accept the League without modifications that they considered necessary to safeguard American sovereignty. But Wilson refused to compromise, and the Treaty of Versailles failed to obtain the two-thirds majority necessary for ratification. The Senate finally passed a resolution in 1921 accepting all provisions of the treaty except those establishing the League.

Britain and France reacted to the Senate's action with mixed emotions. The British to some extent were relieved that they had escaped from American influence, which had been strong during the latter part of the war and the peace conference. But they had never shared Wilson's enthusiasm about the League and now saw considerably less reason for optimism. The French had been even more skeptical of the League and viewed America's withdrawal from Wilson's commitment with alarm. Of far greater concern to them, however, was the failure of the Senate to act on the guarantee treaty, which would have provided for Anglo-American support for France if attacked by Germany. This agreement became a casualty of the quarrel over the League. Britain subsequently used the American failure to act as grounds for abandoning its own commitment.

OTHER TREATIES AND TERRITORIAL CHANGES

Two other treaties recognized that Austria-Hungary had ceased to exist and that a number of new countries had come into being in Central Europe. Even the Austrians and Hungarians had severed the connection between themselves and created separate states. This necessitated individual agreements—the Treaty of St. Germain with Austria and the Treaty of Trianon with Hungary.

The disintegration of Austria-Hungary led to the formation of two other new countries—Czechoslovakia and the Kingdom of Serbs, Croats, and Slovenes, which later became Yugoslavia. All of Czechoslovakia's territory had formerly been part of Austria-Hungary. Yugoslavia consisted of a merger of prewar Serbia and Montenegro with the portions of Austria-Hungary that had contained Serbs, Croats, and Slovenes.

Czechoslovakia based its independence on a union of the Czechs, who lived in the western provinces of Bohemia and Moravia, and the Slovaks, who inhabited the eastern area of Slovakia. Although the two groups were related Slavic peoples, the Czechs were considerably more numerous and more advanced politically and economically. They played the predominant role in the new state. The country also included substantial German, Hungarian, and Ukrainian minorities. The Germans were the largest and most important of these. Three million of them resided in the frontier areas of Bohemia and Moravia. This border region came to be known as the Sudetenland.

The Serbs, Croats, and Slovenes of Yugoslavia also were related Slavic peoples. But the Serbs outnumbered the others, and had previous experience governing Serbia. They dominated the new state from the start, much to the chagrin of the Croats, the second largest group, who considered themselves culturally superior to the Serbs. A religious difference also increased antagonism between the two peoples. The Serbs were predominantly Orthodox, while the Croats were Catholic. If this were not enough, Yugoslavia contained other national minorities as well.

Another national group, the Poles in Galicia, the extreme northeastern portion of Austria-Hungary, joined their kinsmen in territories formerly under German and Russian domination to create the independent state of Poland. Unfortunately, eastern Galicia contained a majority of Ukrainians, who now found themselves under Polish rule. To the southeast, the Rumanians in the provinces of Transylvania and the Banat joined the prewar state of Rumania. But these areas also contained Hungarian and Yugoslav minorities. Finally, the Italians in the Trentino, Trieste, and Istria merged with Italy. Here, too, other nationalities were present—Germans in the southern Trentino, Slovenes in Trieste and Istria.

The creation or enlargement of all of these states posed major problems. Most of them were small multinational states and were not remotely strong enough to be great powers. As a result, they had internal problems and much of central Europe became a "power vacuum." This posed the danger that some time in the future, stronger outside nations would attempt to move into the area and fill the vacuum. Finally, the small countries engaged in a myriad of border disputes with their neighbors. The peacemakers attempted to settle these quarrels and established commissions to help adjust borders as much as possible in keeping with national aspirations. But this proved a formidable task due to the mixed population patterns of the region, and in some cases, countries would not be economically or strategically viable if they did not include territories inhabited by minorities.

The Sudetenland, with its predominantly German population, provided the most notable example of this. It was vital to Czechoslovakia because it contained important industries and natural resources as well as hilly, heavily wooded terrain that served as an easily defensible border. In view of these factors, Wilson, Clemenceau, and Lloyd George agreed that the Sudetenland must go to Czechoslovakia rather than to Austria or Germany. The Big Three also violated the principle of national self-determination in regard to Austria. The Austrians doubted that their severely truncated state would prove economically viable and asked that they be allowed to merge with their fellow Germans across the border. Allied leaders rejected this request because they opposed any increase in Germany's size. Both decisions held the potential for trouble. The Sudeten Germans remained unreconciled to their position as citizens of Czechoslovakia, and many Austrians continued to favor union with Germany. The republican government of Germany also cherished the dream of eventually absorbing Austria.

The Paris Peace Conference played only a minor role in the settlement for Eastern Europe. With its defeat at the hands of the Allies, Germany had to relinquish control over the territories it had wrested from Russia at Brest-Litovsk. Since the Russian civil war prevented the Bolshevik government from retaking these areas, various national groups established independent states. These included Finland in the far north and three small countries along the shore of the Baltic—Estonia, Latvia, and Lithuania. The region inhabited by Poles became a part of the new Poland, and the people of the Ukraine also established their separate national identity. Finally, Rumania annexed Bessarabia, an area of mixed Rumanian and Ukrainian population.

In most cases, the peacemakers took no action in regard to these territories other than to recognize their independence. But the British foreign secretary, Lord Curzon, did propose an eastern border for Poland that roughly followed the linguistic division between Poles to the west and Belorussians and Ukrainians to the east. The Poles were not at all interested in the "Curzon line" and demanded restoration of their eighteenth-century boundary. This would have included most of the Ukraine as well as Belorussia just to the north. They went to war to enforce this claim in 1920 but ultimately had to settle for a line about 150 miles east of the Curzon line.

The Big Three were pleased by the changes in Eastern Europe, because the new nations were all anti-Russian and anti-Communist. It became customary to refer to this entire tier of countries as the *cordon sanitaire,* a barrier that helped sanitize the West from the spread of communism. But it was a weak barrier. None of the new states was strong, and all of them feared the revival of Germany and Russia, both of which dreamed of revising the Eastern European settlement. One of the fledgling countries, the Ukraine, failed to maintain its independence for long. By 1920, the Russian government had reasserted its control over Ukrainian territory.

Two additional treaties dealt with the minor members of the Central Powers—the Treaty of Neuilly with Bulgaria and the Treaty of Sèvres with Turkey. The Bulgars lost a strip of territory along the coast of the Aegean Sea to Greece and two small border areas to Yugoslavia. The Allies forced Turkey to relinquish all of its remaining Balkan territory to Greece with the exception of the great city of Constantinople (soon to be renamed Istanbul). Greece also gained a number of Turkish islands in the Aegean and the right to administer a substantial amount of territory on Turkey's Asian coastline. Although there were Greeks in this area, the majority of the population was Turkish. The treaty also took away all of Turkey's Arab-inhabited lands. Only Saudi Arabia gained independence; France received Syria and Lebanon, and Britain won Palestine, Transjordan, and Iraq, all as mandates.

Loss of territory to the Greeks was too much for Turkish nationalists. General Mustapha Kemal carried out a coup, overthrew the decrepit government of the sultan, and established a republic. Turkish troops soon began to drive the Greeks out of their Asian foothold. Stability did not return to the area until the powers reached another agreement in 1923, the Treaty of Lausanne, which deprived the Greeks of most of their original gains. It also prepared the way for a massive transfer of the Greek population from Asia Minor to Greece and the Turkish minority from Greece to Turkey.

REACTIONS TO THE NEW ARRANGEMENTS

Although Wilson, Clemenceau, and Lloyd George all expressed satisfaction with the Peace of Paris, not everyone agreed with them. Germany's republican government only accepted the Treaty of Versailles because it had no alternative. But Germans who subscribed to the "stab in the back" legend blamed the republic for what they considered a humiliating dictated peace.

Germans in general reacted to the treaty with hostility. They believed that they had entered World War I to defend themselves from the encircling Allied powers and considered the "war guilt" clause a gross distortion of reality. Their anger over this made them highly resentful of the large reparations bill. But it was not so much the total that antagonized them as the obligation to pay anything. From the start, the government was determined to avoid paying the full amount. The Germans also found the disarmament provisions unfair and degrading to a great power, especially one in which the army had enjoyed such enormous prestige. Their forces were now hopelessly inferior in numbers and equipment even to those of Poland and Czechoslovakia. They argued that only if the Allies undertook disarmament themselves could they justify the restrictions they had placed on Germany's armed forces, which were now inadequate even to defend the country.

But the Germans found the territorial changes most detestable of all, especially the loss of Danzig and the lands to Poland. Few Germans held any sympathy for the new state and were not impressed by arguments that the Poles, too, had the right to exist as an independent people. The Germans looked forward to the day when their country could revise these provisions. Both the refusal of the Allies to allow the union of Austria with Germany and the incorporation of the Sudetenland into Czechoslovakia struck the Germans as hypocritical. It seemed to them that the peacemakers were interested in the principle of self-determination only if they could use it against the Germans.

To the British, it also appeared that the treaty was too harsh. Many agreed with Keynes that Germany was incapable of paying the reparations bill. They came to view the French as vindictive and perhaps determined to establish their own domination on the continent. Opinion also turned against the prewar connection with France, which many believed had dragged Britain into the conflict at the cost of 750,000 dead and the undermining of the country's economic stability. The British were determined to avoid any kind of arrangement in the future that might have the same effect and preferred a policy aimed at reconciliation with Germany.

The war also resulted in greater independence for territories of the British Empire that had become self-governing dominions during the late nineteenth and early twentieth centuries. Canada, Australia, New Zealand, and the Union of South Africa had all gained control of their own domestic affairs before the war. But they had still been technically dependent on Britain in foreign affairs. All of them had joined Britain in the conflict and had suffered heavy casualties on various fronts. As a reward for their services, they had each received separate representation at the peace conference as well as in the League of Nations. The dominions, henceforth, were virtually independent. This fact played a prominent role in the transformation of the empire into the Commonwealth of Nations during the postwar period and meant that Britain could not be certain of the support of the dominions in case of another war. British awareness of this changed relationship furthered the pursuit of a conciliatory policy toward Germany.

The debilitating effects of the war had also made Britain less certain of its hold over parts of the empire that had not gained the right of self-government. In some of them, most notably India, nationalist movements favored independence. This, too, contributed to the cautious British policy in Europe.

Americans also became disillusioned, not only with the peace settlement but with the war itself. To many, it seemed that Britain and France had lured the United States into a typical European power struggle. It appeared that despite Wilson's idealistic rhetoric about a peace of reconciliation, the settlement represented a cynical division of spoils. With the Senate's refusal to approve entry into the League of Nations, America returned to its traditional policy of isolation from European political affairs. But it was never complete isolation. The United States continued to play an active role in efforts to solve the related economic problems of European war debts, reparations, and currency stabilization but remained totally opposed to participation in any collective security arrangements.

Despite criticism of their alleged vindictiveness from friend and foe alike, the French were not happy with the peace settlement either. France had survived, but the war had taken the lives of 1,300,000 of the nation's soldiers, in proportion to population the heaviest loss suffered by any of the Great Powers. The northern provinces lay in desolation after four years of trench warfare and massive artillery barrages. And the war had left deep psychological wounds on the national spirit. The compromise peace had not brought France the security it had sought. The nation's allies had reneged on their commitment to join in a collective security agreement, leaving France with a deep sense of betrayal. To the French, the peace, far from being too harsh, was much too lenient.

Not surprisingly, the French feared a revival of German power and remained acutely concerned about their own security. Their wartime losses compounded the problem of a declining birth rate, which had been a source of worry even before the war. France's population in 1921 totaled only 39 million compared to Germany's 60 million. France also suffered from deep divisions between social classes, which were reflected in the republican political system. The Third Republic had come into existence in 1870 as a result of the French defeat in the Franco-Prussian War. Instead of a system of two major political parties, such as characterized both Britain and the United States, the Third Republic had developed a multiparty system. This made the French cabinet dependent on maintaining the support of a majority coalition of parties in parliament. Since these coalitions usually did not hold together for long, cabinets also did not remain in power for long. As a result, the system became chronically unstable, making it extremely difficult to deal with controversial issues.

The failure to achieve an alliance with Britain and the United States led the French to turn to lesser countries for help. During the early 1920s, they secured defensive military alliances with Belgium, Poland, and Czechoslovakia, all of whom shared France's dread of a revived Germany. They also made agreements with Rumania and Yugoslavia, which bound the partners to consult in case of a threat to their independence. But this system of collective security was a poor substitute for the wartime relationship between France, Britain, and America, and its ability to deter aggression was highly questionable. As a result, France assumed primary responsibility for enforcing the peace settlement. It soon proved to be a task beyond the nation's capabilities.

Italy also bitterly assailed its wartime Allies for disavowing their promises regarding Italian compensation in the Adriatic, the Middle East, and Africa. A chorus of nationalistic disapproval forced Orlando out of office, and the desire to revise the peace settlement remained strong.

Russia, only marginally affected by the Paris peace settlement, harbored resentment over the territorial losses that had originated with the Treaty of Brest-Litovsk. But even when the civil war ended, the Russians were not in a position to do much about these changes. Nevertheless, like Germany and Italy, Russia hoped to revise this settlement sometime in the future. The Bolshevik government retained a deep distrust of the Western Powers, which had recognized the new countries of Eastern Europe. It also did not forget the Allied intervention in the civil war.

ECONOMIC REPERCUSSIONS

European recovery from World War I proved elusive during the 1920s. The continent's economy was far from healthy. The conflict had disrupted the old prewar patterns of trade, and European countries encountered difficulty regaining their former shares of the world market. Imports ran far ahead of exports, creating an unfavorable balance of trade. To compound their problems, the United States raised tariffs on imported goods, making it more difficult for the debtor nations of Europe to sell products in the American market. They retaliated by increasing import duties to protect their own domestic industries from foreign competition. This mutual protectionist approach increased the strain on the international economy.

With the exception of Britain, the belligerent countries had financed their war efforts in large part by printing paper money that did not have gold backing. This led to serious inflation while the war was in progress, but tighter government controls managed to keep it within reason. In the postwar years, however, the inflationary spiral increased. By 1926, the French franc had fallen to 10 percent of its prewar value. In Germany, the situation was far worse. Before the war, 4.2 German marks possessed a value equivalent to 1 U.S. dollar. When the Paris Peace Conference convened, it took almost 9 marks to equal a dollar. A year later, the mark had declined to 65 to the dollar. By January 1923, it had skidded to 18,000 to the dollar. And this was only the beginning of an even more disastrous slide.

The related problems of war debts and reparations added to the economic dilemma. The United States had refused a British and French request for a temporary suspension of war debt payments during the peace conference. But despite this brusque attitude, America actually demanded little more than token payments during the 1920s. The problem of reparations was more serious. The French were desirous of securing early and regular payment of reparations to aid them in rebuilding their devastated areas. But they obtained relatively little. At first, they received payment in commodities such as coal and timber, in a half-hearted manner. It is now clear that Germany was capable of paying the annual installment the Reparations Commission had specified—it would have amounted to about 6 percent of the country's yearly income. Though clearly requiring sacrifices, such payments did not represent an intolerable burden, had the Germans wanted to pay. But this willingness was conspicuously absent, and the German government did all it could to avoid meeting its obligation. Although the French protested, the British from the start sympathized with Germany and urged France to make concessions. The British hoped that a reduction of reparations payments would aid the German economy and stimulate trade. Finally, in late 1922, Germany defaulted on its obligation altogether.

In early 1923, French Premier Raymond Poincaré responded vigorously to this action. His government ordered troops into the Ruhr, Germany's most important industrial area, just to the east of the Rhineland. The French hoped to force German compliance on reparations and, in the meantime, planned to operate the mines and railroads of the Ruhr for their own use. But German workers resorted to passive resistance, including strikes and delaying actions. The republican government subsidized the workers, and the French accomplished little. This Ruhr crisis lasted for almost a year while Germany's inflation soared completely out of control. By November, the mark's value had fallen to the amazing figure of 4.2 trillion to the dollar. Salaries, savings, pensions, and insurance became worthless while debtors easily paid off loans and merchandise purchased on the installment plan. The economy was a shambles.

Germany had no choice but to abandon its policy of promoting passive resistance, but the French were in no position to capitalize on this. They were spending more on their occupation forces than they were gaining in reparations and agreed to submit the whole question to an international commission, chaired by the American banker Charles Dawes. In April 1924, the Dawes Commission agreed that reparations payments should be based on Germany's "index of prosperity." This had the effect of reducing payments by half with the prospect for gradual increases in the future. The Dawes plan also urged an international loan to Germany to help stabilize the currency and promote prosperity. American financiers provided more than half of the subsequent loan, which began a pattern of U.S. financial assistance to Germany during the next five years.

This influx of foreign capital contributed to a remarkable economic recovery in Germany during this period. German leaders also introduced a new currency based officially on gold, which halted the inflation. Before the spiral ended, however, the government reaped a profit by paying off its internal debts with money that was worthless. In 1929, another committee of international financial experts, headed by the American Owen Young, scaled down the total German reparations bill to a mere $9 billion. But Germany never came close to paying this amount because the nation soon felt the impact of a far worse economic catastrophe—the Great Depression. In reality, during the 1920s the United States and, to a lesser degree, the former European Allies provided more than twice as much money to Germany's recovery than Germany paid in reparations.

POLITICAL REALIGNMENTS

The failure of the Ruhr occupation to secure German compliance on reparations led to France's realization that the nation could not enforce the Paris peace settlement alone. So France turned instead to cultivating better relations with Germany while avoiding as few meaningful concessions as possible. Foreign Minister Aristide Briand was the architect of this policy. Germany's foreign minister, Gustav Stresemann, also followed a friendlier approach to France, hoping to gain a revision of the peace settlement in the process. The chief result of their efforts was yet another treaty in 1925.

They negotiated this agreement in the Swiss resort town of Locarno with British Foreign Secretary Austen Chamberlain serving as mediator. The Treaty of Locarno was a curious document. It merely reaffirmed the provisions of the Versailles settlement that applied to Germany's western boundaries as well as the future demilitarization of the Rhineland. But the treaty was silent on the question of Germany's eastern borders, which, in effect, indicated that Germany did not consider them permanent. In fact, Stresemann hoped that Germany could eventually gain a revision of the eastern settlement. He especially wanted to regain Danzig and the Polish corridor and consummate a union of Austria with Germany.

During the next few years, observers spoke of a "spirit of Locarno," which supposedly represented the beginning of a new, more peaceful era in European affairs. Other agreements followed. In 1926, Germany entered the League of Nations. In 1928, American Secretary of State Frank Kellogg and Briand drafted a treaty that renounced war as an instrument of national policy. Sixty-five nations, including Germany, eventually signed the Kellogg-Briand Pact. But since it provided no means of enforcement, it merely represented a pious declaration of intent. Finally, the Young Committee, in addition to lowering Germany's reparations bill, also provided for the end of the Rhineland occupation in 1930, five years ahead of schedule.

Meanwhile, throughout the 1920s, Germany had been violating the disarmament provisions of the peace settlement. General Hans von Seeckt, who served as chief of the army command from 1920 to 1926, led the way. Seeckt, the stereotypical monocled Prussian general, maintained the outlawed general staff in existence by dividing its functions among various governmental bodies. He also created a reserve of 70,000 men that he disguised as a special labor force and later as a security organization. Seeckt made an agreement with the Krupp munitions firm to provide designs for artillery as well as working models in the company's affiliated plants in Sweden. Other Krupp affiliates in Spain and the Netherlands produced submarine models and torpedoes.

Germany also cultivated closer relations with Russia in the early postwar period. Both countries hoped to escape from their diplomatic isolation. Seeckt started this process by making a secret agreement with the Russian general staff in 1921. It granted the German army permission to establish illegal tank and artillery units as well as aviation schools on Russian soil. Germany also gained the right to manufacture prototypes of aircraft, tanks, and artillery and to experiment with poison gas. Seeckt reciprocated by training Russian soldiers and providing a financial subsidy. In 1922, the two governments startled the world by signing a treaty of friendship in the Italian city of Rapallo. This agreement provided mutual diplomatic recognition and renunciation of war claims. Neither side really trusted the other, but both believed that they would benefit from the new relationship.

The Western Powers also came to the conclusion that their attempt to keep Russia in isolation was self-defeating. Although they feared the spread of communism, they also coveted the Russian market as an outlet for their hard-pressed economies. Britain took the initiative in 1921 by signing an agreement that reestablished diplomatic relations and trade between the two powers. Other Western countries followed a similar policy during the next few years. But despite these efforts, no real friendship blossomed, and distrust continued.

THE RISE OF THE LAND OF THE RISING SUN

The United States was not the only non-European power to benefit from World War I. Japan, the sole industrialized country in East Asia, had also taken advantage of the inability of European powers to supply their former markets with peacetime goods. Japan could not match American commercial expansion because of its less well developed industry, but the island nation did improve its competitive position significantly. The Japanese also gained strategically important territories on China's coast and in the Pacific at Germany's expense.

When the war ended, few obstacles seemed to prevent still greater Japanese expansion. Russia, a longtime rival for influence in China, suffered from the accumulated effects of World War I, the revolution, and the civil war. Britain and France possessed colonies in East Asia along with economic and political interests in China. But they, too, focused their attention on recovery and the multitude of European problems that followed the war. The United States, although deeply interested in trade with China, was far away. In fact, much of Japan's relative importance was due to the nation's remoteness from other major powers.

Although some Japanese leaders looked longingly on Russia's East Asian territories, Japan's primary interest lay in China. Inferior in size only to Russia and Canada, China possessed the world's largest population as well as vast natural resources. But it had long suffered from political weakness and economic backwardness. During the nineteenth century, China fell prey to various Western powers, which forced the Chinese government to grant concessions. These included economic privileges and the right of extraterritoriality for European residents in China. This right made them immune from Chinese law and subject only to the legal jurisdiction of their respective countries. Some of the European powers also leased ports along the Chinese coast.

When Japan experienced the startling transformation to a major world power in the late nineteenth century, it, too, began to encroach on China, gaining economic concessions and extraterritoriality for Japanese citizens. As a result of victory over China in the Sino-Japanese War of 1894–95, Japan obtained control of the island of Formosa (Taiwan), strategically located off the Chinese mainland. In the aftermath of this conflict, the Japanese competed with Russia for political and economic influence in Korea and the adjoining Chinese province of Manchuria. This rivalry culminated in Japan's stunning triumph in the Russo-Japanese War of 1904–5. In the peace that followed, Japan replaced Russia as the predominant power in both Manchuria and Korea and took over Russian leases on the ports of Dairen (Talien) and Port Arthur (Lüshun). Japan annexed Korea in 1910.

Japanese ambitions encountered opposition from a Chinese nationalist movement that had overthrown the decadent Manchu dynasty in 1911 and established a republic. But the revolution did not lead to Chinese unity or greater freedom from foreign exploitation. Rival governments came into being in the north and south and vied for authority, while warlords, who had little or no allegiance to either regime, dominated many Chinese provinces. It was not until 1928 that the southern regime, dominated by the Kuomintang party, emerged triumphant in this struggle. Led by Chiang Kai-shek, a skillful and ruthless young general and politician, the Kuomintang officially ruled most of China, but its actual control was tenuous.

The Kuomintang regime was a corrupt military dictatorship that rested on a narrow base of support among the landowning peasantry and wealthy banking and commercial interests. Landless agricultural workers, who comprised the country's largest social class and had long been subject to the merciless exploitation of the landlords, felt little allegiance to the government. Many of them found more in common with the Chinese Communist party. The Communists, under the leadership of the determined and brilliant Mao Tse-tung, had cooperated with the Kuomintang until Chiang tried to crush them in 1927. Although some of them fell victim to this purge, Mao and many others escaped to Kiangsi province in southeastern China, where they established a Soviet-style regime in defiance of the Kuomintang.

Chiang and the Kuomintang demanded foreign recognition of China's full sovereignty as well as an end to the privileges and immunities enjoyed by other powers. They also attacked the Treaty of Versailles' assignment of Germany's possessions in China to Japan. Chiang particularly hoped to tighten his authority in the northeastern province of Manchuria, where the warlord Chang Hsueh-liang had recognized his sovereignty. But the Japanese viewed this as a direct threat to their own strong economic and political influence in Manchuria.

Western powers shared Japan's fears over China's revisionist policy. Britain grew especially concerned because, along with Japan, Britain had the largest investments in China and the most to lose from the establishment of complete Chinese sovereignty. The United States was also deeply interested in China, but for reasons that were less well grounded than those of Britain and Japan. Although their trade with China had never been extensive, the seemingly unlimited potential of the Chinese market exerted a powerful attraction to Americans. The United States opposed the exploitation that other powers pursued in China and remained faithful to the Open Door policy proclaimed at the turn of the century. The doctrine sought to maintain equal access to the Chinese market for all nations while maintaining China's sovereignty and territorial integrity. But America always emphasized the free trade aspects of the policy rather than defense of China's sovereignty.

SEEKING BALANCE BETWEEN EAST AND WEST

When World War I ended, Japan and Britain were linked by a defensive military alliance that they had negotiated in 1902. Originally intended to resist Russian encroachment on Manchuria, the pact had also facilitated British and Japanese penetration of China. The United States disliked this agreement and opposed its renewal in 1921. America preferred multinational agreements that would maintain existing foreign interests in East Asia while upholding China's sovereignty and equal access to the Chinese market for all powers. British leaders especially desired to remain on good terms with America in the uncertain aftermath of World War I. Canada also strongly favored such an Anglo-American relationship and pressured Britain to drop the Japanese alliance.

But American leaders were also concerned about the growth of Japanese naval power. Although Japan's navy ranked third behind those of Britain and the United States, all of it operated in East Asian and Pacific waters. The American fleet, on the other hand, divided its attention between the Pacific and the Atlantic, as did Britain's Royal Navy, which also had obligations in the Mediterranean and the Indian Ocean. American proponents of a huge two-ocean navy demanded a great increase in battleship strength, and 15 new capital ships were already under construction. This program alarmed the Japanese, who responded by laying down the keels of eight powerful battleships. Many American leaders feared the economic and political consequences of a naval race and urged an agreement that would prevent this. Britain was still the world's leading naval power, but most of its battleships were aging. Entering into an ambitious new naval building program would place a tremendous burden on the already ailing British economy.

Mutual concern over the prospect of a ruinously expensive naval race led to the decision to convene a conference in Washington to seek limitation of battleship strength. But the Washington conference of 1921–22 also considered the questions of the Anglo-Japanese alliance and the future of China.

Representatives of the United States, Britain, Japan, France, Italy, and several lesser powers attended the conference, which resulted in three treaties. The first of these, a naval agreement, placed limitations on battleships and battle cruisers. It provided for a ratio of strength of 5 to 5 to 3 to 1.75 to 1.75 for the United States, Britain, Japan, France, and Italy, respectively. This ratio reflected the size of the navies at that time. The treaty also placed limitations on total tonnage of aircraft carriers but not of cruisers, destroyers, or submarines. Finally, it prohibited the building of additional fortifications and military bases in the Pacific.

In the second agreement, the Four-Power Treaty, the United States, Britain, Japan, and France vowed to respect each other's possessions in the Pacific and refer disputes to mediation. This arrangement replaced the Anglo-Japanese alliance. All the countries represented at the conference signed the final pact, the Nine-Power Treaty. This document upheld China's sovereignty and territorial integrity while recognizing the right of all nations to equal economic opportunity in the Chinese market. Britain and Japan also agreed to return their possessions on the Shantung Peninsula to Chinese control. The treaty represented formal acceptance of the Open Door policy, and the agreement to restore Shantung to Chinese sovereignty was clearly a hopeful sign.

The naval limitation treaty made sense at the time and prevented a capital ship construction race during the 1920s. But it met with bitter criticism from both U.S. and Japanese naval leaders. American admirals insisted that the restrictions threatened their ability to deter Japanese aggression. Some of their counterparts in Japan insisted that the limitations on their navy placed it at such a disadvantage that it could not successfully resist an American attack. As for Britain, acceptance of parity in capital ships with the United States ended a long tradition of supremacy on the high seas, a clear indication of Britain's diminished power.

Ironically, the failure of the naval treaty to agree on a formula for limiting cruiser construction opened the way for the major powers to build cruisers in large numbers. This in turn led to attempts to halt the new race, culminating in the London Naval Treaty of 1930. In this understanding, the United States, Britain, and Japan agreed to limit construction of both cruisers and destroyers.

A FRAGILE OPTIMISM

Despite the good intentions and positive aspects of the settlement regarding China, the long-term outlook was not promising. China remained unstable and victim to internal conflict, while rival Chinese and Japanese ambitions in Manchuria clearly posed the danger of a collision.

Nevertheless, by the late 1920s, it appeared that the world was headed for a more secure and prosperous future. The war was receding deeper into the past, and the worst of its impact seemed to be over. Europe's economy, though far from restored to health, had at least rallied encouragingly from the dark days of the immediate postwar era. The French and Germans had abandoned their mutual hostility in favor of a policy of cooperation. In the process, Germany had escaped from its role as an outcast and had become a member of the League of Nations. The League itself, while still not tested by a major crisis, had at least won general acceptance. And despite the United States' failure to join the League, the Americans had shown their willingness to work with European countries on economic problems. The early fears of a spread of communism over the continent had proved unfounded, and the Soviet Union concentrated on internal problems. In East Asia, most of China was at least nominally under one government. The treaties of the Washington conference had also created new hope in the possibility of cooperation among the Great Powers.

But the partial economic recovery and political reconciliation of Europe were extremely fragile, as was the great power cooperation and relative tranquility in East Asia. None of these hopeful developments proved capable of withstanding the economic catastrophe and political extremism that lay just ahead.

3

The Rise of the Dictators

In the aftermath of World War I, many observers believed that a new age of democratic government had dawned. Wilson had proclaimed that the war's great aim was to "make the world safe for democracy," and the democratic Western Allies had emerged victorious. All of the new states of Central and Eastern Europe became democracies. Even Germany, a former bastion of authoritarian rule, had adopted this form of government. In East Asia, Japan also appeared to be making the transition to democracy. Although the Bolsheviks had created a dictatorship in Russia, they supposedly intended it to be temporary, in keeping with Marxist doctrine. But during the 1920s the democratic flame began to flicker, and in the 1930s it threatened to die out almost completely. Instead of an age of democracy, the interwar years, to a large extent, became an era of dictatorship.

THE EMERGENCE OF TOTALITARIANISM

The immediate postwar atmosphere did not prove conducive to the survival of democracy in many countries. None of the new nations had any experience with this type of government, and cleavages between social classes soon became reflected in multitudes of quarreling political parties. The new governments proved unable to fashion solutions to the problems that confronted them, including severe economic distress. Disillusionment over the war and the peace settlement also gripped defeated Germany, Austria, and Hungary and even victorious Italy. After the brief interval of partial recovery in the late 1920s, the Great Depression plunged the continent once again into economic chaos. It also spawned a growing reaction against the democratic governments, which were helpless in the face of the new disaster. By 1938, almost all of the hopeful fledgling democracies of Central and Eastern Europe had become dictatorships, and Japan had followed a similar course.

In three countries—the Soviet Union, Italy, and Germany—the dictatorial regimes became totalitarian. Although autocratic governments had been in existence for many centuries, totalitarianism was a development of the twentieth century. Totalitarian political systems were much more thoroughgoing in their efforts to control the individuals and groups that made up their populations than was the case with older forms of autocracy. In each of the three totalitarian states, the catalyst of the dictatorship was a political party that viewed itself as an elite group devoted to the commands of a single leader. The party also paid allegiance to an ideology that rejected much or all of the previous social and political systems and projected a utopian vision of the future. The leader became so central to the party and system that there soon developed a "cult of personality" that portrayed the leader as larger than life and the virtual embodiment of the nation.

Although none of the three parties originally had the backing of a majority of its people, after securing power each of them rapidly gained a large measure of popular support. To some extent, fear underlay this acceptance, but in all three cases much of it was genuine. Control of the army and the creation of a secret police force provided the bases for fear. Domination of the means of mass communication and the development of a sophisticated system of propaganda, which preached the glories of the party, the leader, and the nation, contributed to the growth of popular enthusiasm. Exploitation of the educational system to indoctrinate the young with the party ideology provided the basis for extending this support into the future.

Each of the totalitarian states also proclaimed the need for a centrally controlled and directed economy. But in reality, only the Communist regime in the Soviet Union provided a totally state-dominated economy. In both Italy and Germany, the dictatorships came to terms with the established capitalistic system, though subjecting it to a certain amount of governmental direction.

Popular disillusionment with the previous political systems and despair over economic conditions helped ease the way for the acquisition of power by the totalitarian parties. All of them promised revolutionary change and, in varying degrees, made good on their pledges. Although they dealt harshly with political opponents, their projection of a glorious future convinced many citizens to overlook such measures. Even if some disliked this oppression, there was little they could do about it, and any attempt to try would jeopardize their own safety.

LENIN AND THE BOLSHEVIKS

Russia created the first totalitarian regime following the Bolshevik victory in the revolution. The Bolsheviks, though a small fraction of the population, gained control of the government because of their superior organization and Lenin's brilliant leadership. Lenin's real name was Vladimir Ulyanov. He adopted "Lenin," which probably referred to the Lena River in eastern Siberia, as a pen name after spending three years in Siberia as punishment for illegal political activities against the czarist regime.

Lenin believed strongly in a small, tightly organized party composed of professional revolutionaries. Lenin remained faithful to the Marxist doctrine of revolution when many others were turning to a more moderate type of socialism that sought reforms by working through the established system. But he departed from Marx's belief that a revolution would only come in a highly industrialized country when conditions were favorable for success. Clearly, Russia's industrialization had not progressed to a point that would make it a candidate for revolution by this standard. Lenin considered it possible to speed up the process, using the party as the vanguard of the revolution and mobilizing the discontented groups in society, including the peasantry.

When the Russian Revolution began in March 1917, Lenin was in exile in Switzerland. He returned to Russia in April with the assistance of the German government, which hoped that his presence would create a disruptive influence and impede the Russian war effort. Lenin believed from the start that the provisional government was weak and that if the Bolsheviks gained control of the soviets, they could topple it from power. By the fall of 1917, it was clear to Lenin that the time to strike was at hand. The Bolsheviks followed their quick seizure of Petrograd with the capture of Moscow, and within a month most of the cities of European Russia were under their control. But once they had overthrown the provisional government, the Bolsheviks faced the immense problems of consolidating their power and restoring Russia to some semblance of order and economic well-being after the years of war and revolution.

The outbreak of civil war in 1918 created still more chaos, which did not provide a suitable en-

FIGURE 3-1 Czarist troops disperse demonstrators in Petrograd early in the Russian Revolution. (*UPI/Bettmann Newsphotos*)

vironment for the development of a Marxist system, either in the political or the economic realm. To complicate matters still more, no one knew exactly how to go about this task. Karl Marx had written in generalities about the need to establish a temporary dictatorship of the proletariat (working class), to be followed by the creation of a classless society and ultimately the withering away of the state. But he had offered no plan on how to go about translating these generalities into actual policies.

Soon after coming to power, Lenin tried to establish strong popular support for Bolshevik rule by holding elections for the constituent assembly that the provisional government had promised. The elections proved a great disappointment to the Bolsheviks, who gained only 25 percent of the seats in the assembly. Lenin solved the problem by dissolving the assembly after its first meeting and creating a Bolshevik dictatorship. He and his comrades visualized a temporary dictatorship in keeping with Marxist doctrine. This regime would take over the means of production in the name of society as a whole and provide an equitable redistribution of wealth. It would also create a classless society in which all persons were equal and no one would prosper at the expense of others.

But the outbreak of civil war soon made the survival of the regime the first order of business, and for a time it appeared that the anti-Bolshevik (White) forces would actually win. At the low point of the Bolsheviks' fortunes, they controlled only the central portion of European Russia, including the cities of Petrograd and Moscow. (Lenin had moved the capital from Petrograd to Moscow early in 1918.) This desperate situation called for extreme measures. One of these involved the development of an effective military force to fight the White armies. Lenin's brilliant colleague, Leon Trotsky, who had started as a moderate socialist but joined the Bolsheviks during the revolution, was the driving force in the development of the new Red Army. He provided both organizational and leadership ability, and utilized the talents of former czarist officers and noncommissioned officers to train and direct the army.

The Bolsheviks benefited from a lack of unity among the Whites, who consisted of various groups with differing political views. Their military forces lacked coordination, and their generals frequently regarded one another as rivals.

Lenin and the Bolsheviks also faced a serious economic dilemma. The war had revealed the inadequacies of both Russian industry and the transportation system. With the coming of civil war, the situation deteriorated still more. The government had to provide weapons, equipment, food, and other supplies to the army while feeding the civilian population as well. Obviously, there was no time for long-range planning. Instead, the Bolsheviks resorted to emergency measures, which became known as "war communism." These included the forced requisition of grain, livestock, and other commodities from the peasants, who had taken over the holdings of the large landowners during the revolution, and the nationalization of industry.

Although these actions contributed to victory and the salvation of the regime, they also caused much confusion and even more dissatisfaction. The peasants resented the forced requisitions, and many of them preferred to burn their crops and slaughter their livestock rather than allow them to fall into the hands of the government. Workers also protested the stringent production demands and regimentation that the government had imposed on them.

By the end of 1920, the Red Army had effectively defeated the Whites, but the economy was in deplorable condition. Widespread devastation, rampant inflation, and shortages of all kinds were the order of the day. The peasantry and workers were so hostile that another rebellion seemed highly possible. To add to the critical situation, the combination of shortages created by peasant resistance to the requisition policy and crop failures led to an appalling famine in 1921, which took the lives of 3 million people.

Lenin recognized that he must relax controls in an effort to gain the support of the peasants and workers. In 1921, he instituted the New Economic Policy (NEP), which eliminated forced requisitions and enabled the peasants to sell their surplus crops on the open market. Lenin retained government control of large-scale industry but allowed smaller operations to revert to private ownership. The NEP created a mixed system that included elements of both private enterprise and government control. But Lenin viewed the NEP as a stopgap measure. As he said at the time, "It is sometimes necessary to take one step backward in order to take two steps forward."

In 1923, the Bolsheviks reorganized the country as a federation of republics—the Union of Soviet Socialist Republics (USSR or Soviet Union). Each republic represented an area whose population consisted primarily of a specific ethnic group. This action recognized the fact that the country contained various nationalities, although the Great Russians were by far the most numerous. Their republic, the largest, included not only European Russia but most of Siberia as well and dominated the others.

The Bolsheviks established a hierarchical system of soviets ascending from rural and urban localities through the levels of the territories and provinces to that of the republic itself. The soviet of each republic chose delegates to the All Union Congress of Soviets, which elected the Central Executive, renamed the Supreme Soviet in 1936. The Central Executive in turn chose still another body, the Council of People's Commissars, which conducted the actual business of the Union.

Despite this elaborate government structure, real power lay with the party, which officially became the Communist party in 1918. It was the only political party, and Lenin still viewed it as an elite group. The party's organization was similar to that of the soviets, with local, territorial, provincial, and republican levels. At its summit was the Party Congress, which met in Moscow. The Congress selected a Central Committee, which included three smaller bodies, the Politburo, the Secretariat, and the Organizational Bureau. In reality, the Politburo was the governing body of the country. But the Secretariat, headed by a general secretary, was also important. The general secretary became increasingly powerful. The Politburo made the decisions, and they were carried out at each level of the Union and party hierarchies.

As early as December 1917, still another party organization came into operation—the secret police. Its duty was to hunt down and eliminate enemies of the party and the state, and it carried out this mission with enthusiasm and efficiency. The name of the secret police changed periodically, but the organization remained of great importance.

THE STALINIST ERA IN THE SOVIET UNION

Lenin suffered a series of strokes, starting in May 1922, and died in January 1924. Long before his death, it became apparent that a power struggle was developing among Communist leaders for the right to succeed the architect of the Bolshevik dictatorship. The two principal figures were Trotsky and the general secretary of the party, Iosif Dzhugashvili, who had taken the name Stalin, derived from the Russian word for steel.

Stalin was born to peasant parents in the region of Georgia in the Caucasus Mountains. He had entered a seminary as a youth but soon turned to revolutionary socialism. Unlike Lenin and many other Bolshevik leaders, Stalin did not go into exile and, in fact, had never ventured out of Russia. He became involved in conspiratorial activity and in the process became an astute organizer. From an early age, he betrayed symptoms of ruthlessness, cruelty, and an excessive desire for power. Although overshadowed by Lenin, Trotsky, and others during the revolution, he emerged as a major figure in the civil war and its aftermath.

Trotsky and most other Soviet leaders were international in their outlook. They believed that the Bolshevik success in Russia would be followed by revolution in other parts of Europe. To promote this goal, they developed an organization that would coordinate Communist movements in other countries—the Communist International or Comintern. Stalin was much less dedicated to the exportation of revolution. He believed that the Communists had enough to do in Russia and favored a policy of creating "socialism in one country." He also considered his colleagues unrealistic in their belief that revolution would succeed outside Russia. The failure of Communist revolts in Hungary and Germany in the immediate aftermath of World War I had convinced him that no such development was likely for the foreseeable future. Stalin not only headed the Secretariat as general secretary but led the Organizational Bureau as well, which gave him control over the party machinery and personnel. He also proved exceptionally skillful at political infighting and repeatedly outmaneuvered his rivals.

Even before Lenin's death, Stalin had joined forces with two other opponents of Trotsky—Gregori Zinoviev and Lev Kamenev. By 1925, they had removed Trotsky from his position as war commissar and two years later expelled him from the Central Committee. But later in 1927, Stalin moved against Zinoviev and Kamenev, using his position as general secretary as a power base. He charged them with deviation from Lenin's views and gained their ouster from the Politburo. Soon afterward, he used similar tactics to purge other rivals from the party leadership.

With the ouster of Trotsky, Zinoviev, and Kamenev, Stalin felt strong enough to launch a massive program to nationalize the economy and transform Russia into a first-class industrial power as quickly as possible. Not only had Lenin's New Economic Policy veered away from the Marxist ideal, but it had not worked well. Industrial production did not reach 1913 levels until 1927, and a segment of the peasantry had become increasingly powerful. This group, the kulaks, consisted of peasants who had managed to gain relatively large holdings. Stalin decided to bring the entire economy under state control by nationalizing all industry and abolishing private ownership of land in favor of a system of collectivization. To accomplish this, he launched a series of five-year plans, the first of which went into operation in 1928. It set sharply increased production goals for both agriculture and industry.

In agriculture, peasants were required to merge their holdings in large collective farms that the state would supervise and provide with mechanized equipment. But the program soon encountered resistance from the kulaks, who burned their crops and slaughtered livestock. Stalin responded with ruthless measures. Secret police and army units intervened, killing large numbers of kulaks and rounding up many others for shipment to Siberia. Peasant resistance, coupled with a crop failure in 1932, led to another terrible famine in 1932–33. Although reliable statistics are not available, Stalin himself later admitted that 10 million persons died as a result of collectivization and famine. Contrary to Stalin's hopes, these problems prevented achievement of the First Five-Year Plan's ambitious goals. In fact, agricultural production did not reach the level of 1928 until as late as 1937. Stalin persisted in his program, however, and, by 1939, fully 95 percent of agricultural land had come under collectivization. But many peasants remained both unhappy and uncooperative, and production continued to fall short of his goals.

The First Five-Year Plan also emphasized the development of heavy industry—steel mills, power plants, chemical factories, and large-scale machinery. Although industrial output increased substantially, the concentration on quantity led to problems in quality control. It was not until the Third Five-Year Plan in the late 1930s that quality improved to a satisfactory level. Expansion of heavy industry was costly, and the state could finance it only by diverting capital away from other areas of the economy such as light industry and agriculture. Wages and the standard of living remained low. But many peasants, who had suffered from much worse conditions in the countryside, found jobs in industry and became relatively better off. Many women also secured employment and were able to supplement the incomes of their families.

Meanwhile, Stalin consolidated his own personal power, but his ruthless tactics increased opposition within the party as well as within the hierarchy of the army's officer corps. In the mid-1930s, Stalin moved against his enemies in a series of massive purges. He ordered many "old Bolsheviks" arrested and tried for various crimes against the state and party. Among those found guilty and executed were Zinoviev and Kamenev. Trotsky had fled the country, but an assassin tracked him down in Mexico and murdered him in 1940.

Not content with eliminating these leaders, Stalin cast his net much farther and ordered thousands of lesser party and military officials either shot or imprisoned in Siberian labor camps. In all, perhaps 800,000 party members died in the purges, which also decimated the officer corps of the army. Stalin replaced the purged officials and army officers with men whom he trusted.

Despite Stalin's ruthless policies and the dictatorial nature of his system, by the late 1930s a new generation had grown up under the Communist regime. Its members had no ties to the prerevolutionary era and were proud of the achievements of the Soviet Union. Many of them had received technical, administrative, or scientific training and had found attractive positions in industry, government, the party, and the professions. This new intellectual elite felt a deep sense of loyalty to the system.

But the system was far from the one that Karl Marx had envisioned in his dream of a classless society. Instead of each contributing according to his ability and being rewarded according to his needs, party and government officials, industrial managers, technicians, and professional people enjoyed much higher salaries and prestige than the majority of the population. Even workers received the promise of higher wages for greater efforts. And far from the state withering away, the dictatorship of the Communist party, under Stalin's iron control, had become permanent.

FASCISM IN ITALY

Soon after the victory of Communist totalitarianism in Russia, fascism triumphed in Italy with startling speed. When the Fascist movement began in 1919, it lacked both an efficient organization and a definite ideology. It did not even become a formal political party until 1921. Nevertheless, by October 1922, Benito Mussolini, the Fascist leader, had become premier of Italy and within a few years had created a dictatorship. A multitude of problems that afflicted Italy in the immediate postwar period contributed greatly to this remarkable success story.

These included a general sense of dissatisfaction in the aftermath of the war. Italy had gained little from the conflict, at the cost of almost 500,000 dead. Italian nationalists felt a special sense of frustration and betrayal. Returning war veterans were angry over a lack of appreciation for their services, and many of them found it difficult to obtain jobs. Their troubles reflected the dislocation that plagued Italy's economy. Many blamed the government for not achieving more at the peace conference and for failing to solve the economic dilemma.

Since the unification of Italy into one state in 1861, it had been a constitutional monarchy. Its two-house parliament was dominated by the elective Chamber of Deputies, which was characterized by a multiparty system. Traditionally, the premier had resorted to corrupt practices to gain support in the Chamber for his cabinet's policies. The government, in fact, had gained the reputation as the most corrupt in Europe. Until 1912, the electorate that chose members of the Chamber had been small, but in that year a new electoral law extended the right to vote to all adult males, transforming Italy into a democracy. But many of the newly enfranchised Italians failed to vote in the election of 1913, and the old system continued to function. When Italy entered the war, the cabinet ruled largely by decree in the interest of victory, while parliament remained in the background.

With the return of peace, the democratic parliamentary system returned to full operation, and an election took place in 1919. The three largest parties in the new Chamber of Deputies were the Socialists, the Catholic Popular party, and the Liberals, all three of which had difficulty cooperating. To create a majority coalition, the Liberals usually allied with various conservative parties. But the government provided no solutions to the persistent economic problems, especially reducing Italy's debts or curbing inflation. It also failed to carry out promises made by the wartime government to adopt a land reform program that would help the country's peasants. Similar pledges to aid the working class in various ways also went unfulfilled. These failures led to growing unrest both in the cities, where strikes became increasingly common, and in the countryside, where peasants frequently took matters into their own hands and seized land from the large landlords.

Economic unrest reached a climax in 1920 when industrial workers, inspired by the Socialist party, briefly occupied many factories in the industrial north by means of sit-down strikes. The takeover of the factories and the peasant revolts convinced many of the property-owning classes that there was a real danger of a Socialist revolution. The specter of the Bolshevik victory in Russia haunted them, and they feared that the government would be too weak to cope with such a development. Ironically, the Socialists had reached their peak during the factory takeovers and soon fell victim to internal divisions.

It was against this chaotic background that Benito Mussolini and the Fascists came to power. Mussolini was born in the central Italian region of the Romagna, famous for its rebellious past. His father, a blacksmith and a Socialist, named him after the Mexican revolutionary leader Benito Juárez. The young Mussolini acquired a deep resentment of the privileged classes and the clergy from his father. But his devout mother sent him to a Catholic school, which he soon came to hate. He especially disliked the upper-class students, and when he stabbed one of them with a pen knife, the administrators expelled him. After an unsuccessful career as an elementary school teacher, he turned to socialism and rose rapidly in the Socialist party leadership. Mussolini became editor of the official party newspaper and initially preached the Socialist doctrine of internationalism and opposition to war. But a few months after the outbreak of World War I, he suddenly urged Italy's entry on the side of the Allies. This heresy outraged his fellow Socialists and led to his ouster from the party. When Italy did enter the conflict, Mussolini joined the army and served capably, seeing action and rising to the rank of corporal before being wounded when a grenade launcher blew up, showering him with fragments.

In the immediate aftermath of the war, many disgruntled veterans and ardent nationalists organized a number of fighting groups in various parts of Italy. One of these bands was led by Mussolini, who gradually won the allegiance of the others and formed the nucleus of the Fascist party. His movement gained its name from the fasces, a symbol of authority during the Roman Empire, consisting of a bundle of rods surrounding an ax. The fasces also became the Fascists insignia. Mussolini combined the movement's fighting units into a paramilitary force known as the *squadristi* or Black Shirts.

The various Fascist groups had little in the way of a common policy, except for their superheated nationalism. At first, Mussolini favored cooperation with moderate Socialists, but other Fascist leaders opposed this approach. Instead, the movement assumed an anti-Socialist guise and posed as the great opponent of "Red revolution." The Black Shirts spent much of their time fighting Socialists and other opposing groups in the streets, frequently forcing large doses of castor oil down the throats of those who fell into their hands. But the Fascists were less adept at wining parliamentary elections, failing to gain even one seat in 1919 and capturing only 35 in 1921. Mussolini did not actually emerge as the unchallenged Fascist leader until the official founding of the party in November 1921.

Fascist leaders soon became more ambitious. Black Shirts forced many Socialists out of local government councils and even seized a number of railroad stations and telegraph offices. Despite the obvious illegality of such actions, the government refused to move against the Fascists and tended to look upon them as a bulwark against socialism. Considerable support for fascism also existed in both the officer corps of the army and the court of King Victor Emmanuel III. All of this encouraged Mussolini and other Fascist leaders to attempt to seize power by sending the Black Shirts to march on Rome in October 1922. The government finally awoke to the danger and urged the king to sign a declaration of martial law. But Victor Emmanuel refused, and the cabinet resigned. Instead, the king asked Mussolini to become premier in a coalition cabinet. He took this action in large part because he feared civil war, but he also remembered Mussolini's recent declaration that he favored continuation of the monarchy.

Technically, Mussolini had come to power through constitutional means, but his threat of force had cleared the way for his appointment. Although he intended ultimately to subvert the constitution and impose a dictatorship, he approached this task very cautiously. Mussolini indicated his willingness to preside over a coalition government in which the Fascists would have only three posts. In return, the democratic parties supported his request that he be granted full government powers for a year. During the following months, he appointed Fascists to key local and national administrative positions and transformed the *squadristi* into a national militia. In 1924, he secured passage of a new electoral law that provided that a political party gaining at least 25 percent of the votes would receive two-thirds of the seats in the Chamber. The democratic parties supported this measure because they thought it would weaken the Socialists. During the subsequent election campaign, the Fascists resorted to intimidation and violence. When the balloting ended, a list of Fascist and non-Fascist candidates that Mussolini had endorsed had won 65 percent of the vote.

Now armed with a massive two-thirds majority in the Chamber, the Fascists applied pressure to other political parties and the press. They even murdered the most outspoken critic of fascism, the moderate Socialist Giacomo Matteotti, in June 1924. This incident created a serious crisis.

A wave of revulsion gripped non-Fascist Italians, and Liberal, Popular, and Socialist party members walked out of the Chamber in protest. They hoped that their action might rouse the king to dismiss Mussolini, but Victor Emmanuel took no action. Despite his initial concern, Mussolini actually benefited from the crisis, because the withdrawal of the democratic parties from the Chamber eliminated the last source of opposition.

In 1925 and 1926, Mussolini forced non-Fascists out of the cabinet, dissolved all other parties, and imposed tight censorship on the press. He also banned trade unions and secured his total control over local government. A Fascist secret police came into existence in 1926 along with a special tribunal to deal with enemies of the state. By the end of 1926, Italy had become a one-party dictatorship.

Mussolini made relatively little change in the official structure of government. The parliament remained in existence but henceforth had little to do while Mussolini ruled by decree. Victor Emmanuel III remained head of state, but though technically superior to Mussolini, the king deferred to the premier. As in the Soviet Union, the party was the actual center of power. Mussolini preferred his party title, Duce (leader), to that of premier and dominated both party and state. He organized a vast array of party organizations, extending from the local to the national level, as well as associations for various aspects of Italian society such as youth, education, labor, the press, even leisure activities. At the party's summit, Mussolini established the Fascist Grand Council, consisting of 20 to 30 top party leaders, which loyally approved his decrees.

With power secured, the Fascists belatedly formulated an ideology that remained their official creed until the party's downfall in 1943. It denounced liberalism and socialism for promoting individual and class selfishness and portrayed democratic government as corrupt and inefficient. Fascism, according to this argument, protected the interests of the community as a whole through strong, efficient leadership that subordinated selfish interests to those of the state. The Fascists saw their party as an elite group that emphasized the traditional virtues of discipline and sacrifice and thus was clearly suited to rule. In reality, in the following years, members of the party proved quite attracted to self-interest and corruption.

The Fascists also adopted the doctrine of corporativism, which supposedly furthered understanding between industrialists and workers while eliminating the selfish individualism that had characterized the capitalistic economy. It provided for the division of economic activity into seven categories—industry, commerce, banking, agriculture, internal transport, the merchant marine, and the intellectual community. A corporation was to represent each of the seven, and a Ministry of Corporations came into existence in 1926 to coordinate them. In theory, this organization became the basis for a "corporative state." But in reality, corporativism was a fraud that masked a cynical deal between Mussolini and Italian industry in 1925. This arrangement granted the industrialists a privileged position in return for their support of the regime.

The Federation of Italian Industrialists, an ultra-conservative organization established in 1919, now became a self-governing body that regulated the economy. The industrial workers were not so fortunate. The government denied them the right to strike and forced them to join a Fascist-dominated organization. They came under the joint control of their employers, the party, and the state. The regime made similar preferential agreements with organizations of large employers in both commerce and agriculture, which the large landowners still dominated. The propertied classes had come to terms with the Fascist state, and Mussolini had suppressed his long-standing hatred of the privileged groups in Italian society.

Fascism also exalted the importance of nationalism, imperialism, and militarism. Mussolini spoke in grandiose terms of Italy's right to achieve its national destiny through the creation of a large empire in the Mediterranean and Africa. Clearly, a powerful war machine was mandatory to attain this goal. To instill a warlike spirit in the Italian people, the Fascists argued that pacifism was a cowardly doctrine, whereas war unleashed the noble human virtues—patriotism, self-sacrifice, and courage. Mussolini posed as a man of action, often appearing in uniform and given to much strutting and posturing.

Mussolini was both able and willing to do whatever was necessary to secure his power. Most important, he saw the need to come to terms with the Catholic church. The papacy had never recognized the right of the Italian state to exist because united Italy had seized territory formerly ruled by the pope. Although Mussolini and other party leaders were avowed atheists, they recognized the need to conciliate the church in a country whose population was overwhelmingly Catholic. Accordingly, he opened secret negotiations with the papacy that culminated in the Lateran Accords of 1929. The government recognized the pope's territorial sovereignty over Vatican City, reaffirmed that Catholicism was "the sole religion of the state," and made religious instruction compulsory in all secondary schools. In return, Pope Pius XI extended recognition to the Italian government. Although relations between church and state remained somewhat strained, the new arrangements proved of great importance in reconciling devout Catholics to the Fascist regime.

By the early 1930s, Mussolini's government had gained general acceptance. To many Italians, its emphasis on order and discipline was a welcome relief from the instability of the democratic system. The regime also appeared to be efficient. As foreign tourists remarked, Mussolini "made the trains run on time." But support for the Duce and fascism was actually passive rather than enthusiastic. There appeared to be no alternative, and if one conformed, it was possible to live with relatively little interference from the state.

It is actually questionable to what extent the Fascist regime was totalitarian. To be sure, it was a one-party state and abounded with organizations designed to bring all aspects of life under its scrutiny. But in reality, it had preserved much of the old system—the monarchy, the church, capitalism, and the large landowners. And each of these institutions and social groups enjoyed a certain amount of independence.

The Fascist dictatorship was much milder than the Nazi regime that came into existence in Germany in 1933. Like Italian fascism, Nazism was largely the creation of its leader, Adolf Hitler. And also as in Italy, conditions in Germany provided the opportunity for Hitler and the Nazis to come to power.

HITLER AND THE NAZIS IN GERMANY

Adolf Hitler rose from rather modest origins, though not as humble as those of Mussolini and Stalin. His father was a minor customs official in the village of Braunau, Austria, where Adolf was born in 1889. As a boy, Hitler was an indifferent student and dropped out of school at 16. He dreamed of becoming an artist or an architect but failed to gain admission to either the Vienna Academy of Fine Arts or the Vienna School of Architecture. He remained in the Austrian capital for six years, however, living an aimless life and making ends meet primarily on inheritance money and an orphan's pension. In 1913, Hitler moved to Germany, taking up residence in the Bavarian capital of Munich. When World War I broke out the following year, he joined the German army and served as a dispatch runner at the front. He was wounded twice and earned five decorations, including an Iron Cross, First Class, a rare honor for a common soldier. Despite his exemplary record, he never rose above the rank of lance corporal.

When the war ended, Hitler was in a hospital, recovering from the effects of a poison gas attack that had left him temporarily blinded. The news of the armistice filled him with a deep sense of shame. He readily accepted the "stab-in-the-back" story and felt intense hatred for the German republic that embraced the "dictated peace." After leaving the hospital, he returned to Munich, where he became a member of the German Workers' party, one of the many small extremist political groups that hatched in the aftermath of Germany's defeat.

Hitler soon revealed an exceptional gift for political oratory and an astonishing ability to dominate his fellow party members by sheer force of personality. He also demonstrated considerable organizational and leadership skill. In 1921, the party, now renamed the National Socialist Germany Workers' (Nazi) party, voted him the official title of Führer (leader) with virtually dictatorial powers. In its original form, the party drew most of its members from manual laborers, but it soon attracted many former soldiers as well as various adventurers and misfits. The Nazis were violently nationalistic, anti-Semitic, and totally opposed to the democratic republican government, which they considered guilty of treason.

Their nationalism was of a peculiarly German *völkisch* type. The English expression *the common people* only approximates the sense of the German word *Volk,* which describes a people united with their surroundings. Indeed,the environment shaped the culture of the *Volk*. The term became closely linked to race and emphasized racial distinctions identified with native landscapes. According to this approach, the German *Volk* originated in dark, mysterious forests and, as a result, were deep and profound seekers after the light. The Jews, on the other hand, originating in the desert of the Middle East, were supposedly an arid, shallow people who were neither profound nor creative.

A multitude of *völkisch* political groups came into being during the nineteenth century. Their members felt alienated from Germany's industrial society and the individualism that had motivated its development. They looked back to a time when the people lived on the soil and were united by a common blood, a mystical bond that they summed up in the expression *blood and soil.* About 40 *völkisch* groups existed in Bavaria after the war and soon merged with the Nazis. They looked upon the German *Volk* as superior to other "races" and believed the Jews to be a particularly inferior "race."

Many of the party's early members shared an attachment to a vague, non-Marxist type of socialism. They expressed antagonism to both big business and labor unions and sympathized with hard-pressed small businessmen. Hitler actually disliked socialism in all its varieties, but for many years he went along with the socialist theme to avoid alienating a substantial segment of the party. The Nazis also organized a paramilitary force, the *Sturm Abteilung* (SA), or storm troops, in 1921. Composed largely of former soldiers, the SA also came to be known as the Brown Shirts.

Although the republic that the Nazis so detested came into existence with the fall of the monarchy in November 1918, it did not receive its constitution until August 1919. Since the constitution was proclaimed in the city of Weimar, the government became known as the Weimar Republic. The constitution provided for an elected president as head of state, a cabinet led by a chancellor, and a two-house parliament. The most important parliamentary body was the democratically elected Reichstag. As in the parliaments of the French Third Republic and early postwar democratic Italy, the Reichstag came to be characterized by a multiparty system, and the cabinet was dependent on the backing of a majority coalition. The Weimar Republic was beset by a number of enemies—various ultranationalist and conservative groups on the right and the Communists on the left. The right-wing parties favored either a restoration of the monarchy or some other kind of authoritarian regime, while the Communists looked forward to a Soviet-type system.

During its first few years, the republic contended with the difficult economic problems that followed the war, especially the disastrous inflation. It also had to withstand a number of revolts. The earliest of these, a Communist uprising in January 1919, forced the government to seek protection from the army, which easily put down the revolt with the help of the *Freikorps,* unofficial bands of former soldiers similar to those that developed in Italy. The army proved less reliable in the case of right-wing revolts. In 1920, a conservative ultranationalist group used one of the *Freikorps* to seize Berlin for a time, but the army refused to move against it. Fortunately, the rebel forces were weak and collapsed entirely when the Social Democratic party and the trade unions called a general strike, which paralyzed the capital.

The last of these revolts came in 1923 and became known as the Beer Hall Putsch because its preliminaries took place in a Munich beer hall. It involves a Nazi attempt to seize the state government of Bavaria, to be followed by a march on Berlin, but it failed miserably. The authorities arrested Hitler and several other party leaders and tried them for high treason. Although it appeared as if this fiasco had dealt the Nazis a death blow, they had suffered only a temporary setback. In fact, during the trial Hitler became a national figure for the first time. He took full responsibility for the putsch and turned his defense into a dramatic appeal to German nationalism. The court was sympathetic and administered the most lenient possible sentence, five years, of which Hitler actually served only nine months.

While in prison, Hitler dictated the first volume of *Mein Kampf* (My Struggle), a poorly written, bombastic, and self-serving book in which he expressed his major views. Among the most important was his belief in the superiority of what he referred to as the Aryan race. During the nineteenth century, a number of theorists of dubious qualifications had expounded on the supposed existence of such a race, notably the Frenchman Count Arthur de Gobineau and the Englishman Houston Stewart Chamberlain. Generally, they referred to the Aryans somewhat imprecisely as the inhabitants of northwestern Europe and considered them superior to other races. Chamberlain saw the Germans as the purest form of Aryan. Hitler identified all the Germanic peoples as Aryan. In addition to the ethnic Germans, these included the Dutch, the Flemish-speaking Belgians, the Scandinavians, and the English. He believed that the Aryan Germans must avoid interbreeding with lesser peoples, which would pollute Aryan blood and weaken the race.

In Hitler's scheme of things, the most loathsome of these lesser breeds were the Jews. To him, they were not only inferior but a sinister influence as well. He associated them with Marxist socialism and the Weimar Republic, both of which he detested. Karl Marx had been a Jew, as had a number of other Marxist leaders, including some of the founders of the republic. Marxism, with its emphasis on the international solidarity of the working class, ran counter to his own nationalism, and, of course, he blamed the republic for selling out the army and making a shameful peace. Some historians contend that his intense anti-Semitism actually had its origin in his outrage over this "betrayal" by the "Jewish republic."

Mein Kampf was also full of scorn for democracy and parliamentary institutions. Hitler much preferred what he called the leadership principle, the rule of one man, and, of course, he visualized himself in this role. To him, leadership was primary and decisive, providing order, discipline, and purpose in contrast to the confusion and drift he saw in democracy.

Finally, *Mein Kampf* expressed Hitler's views on foreign policy, including his call for an end to the limitations that the peace settlement had imposed. He also insisted on the need for Germany to absorb the ethnic Germans of Austria, the Sudetenland, Danzig, and Poland. But his ambitions did not end there. His ultimate goal was the conquest of *Lebensraum* (living space) for the German people in the Soviet Union. He looked with special longing to the vast area of the Ukraine with its rich agricultural land and natural resources. Few people read *Mein Kampf* when it first appeared in 1925, and many of those who did refused to take it seriously.

While in prison, Hitler also acquired the conviction that the Nazis must come to power legally through the electoral process of the Weimar Republic. There would be no more attempts to overthrow the government by force. But to win power legally would necessitate appealing to larger segments of the population, thereby creating a mass following. To accomplish this, the Nazis, who were primarily a regional party, needed to create a nationwide organization and make skillful use of propaganda to attack the republic and offer a popular alternative. In the following years, Hitler completely reorganized the party's structure and established party departments to deal with foreign affairs, labor relations, the press, agriculture, and the economy.

Propaganda was particularly important to Hitler's approach, and in Paul Goebbels he found just the man to head the party's new propaganda division. Goebbels, who walked with a limp as the result of a deformed foot, had considered entering the priesthood but earned a Ph.D. from Heidelberg University instead. Ironically, he had originally been antagonistic to Hitler and had supported the Führer's rival, Gregor Strasser, who favored the socialistic aspects of Nazism. But Goebbels soon recognized Hitler's political genius and became a devoted follower. He proved a master of persuasion and the art of using the mass media for the greatest impact. Hitler and Goebbels shared a low regard for the intellect of the masses and believed that most people would respond to emotional appeals, particularly to their hatreds.

Another of Hitler's chief lieutenants was Hermann Goering, an air ace who had shot down 22 Allied planes during World War I. He had served as the last commander of the legendary Baron von Richthofen's Flying Circus and was essentially an adventurer who deeply coveted fame, wealth, and power but held few strong ideological convictions. Able but intensely vain, Goering had commanded the SA before fleeing the country following the Beer Hall Putsch. He returned in 1928 to assist the Führer in various capacities.

Despite the efforts of Hitler and other Nazi leaders, the party's outlook was far from bright. The prosperity that Germany enjoyed during the second half of the 1920s strengthened the republic, as did Gustav Stresemann's foreign policy achievements. Nazi membership rose steadily but unspectacularly from 27,000 in 1925 to 100,000 three years later. In the Reichstag elections of 1928, the party won only 12 seats. But Hitler remained patient throughout these trying years. He was confident that his chance would come.

Opportunity beckoned with the advent of the Great Depression in 1929. Despite the prosperity of the late 1920s, the world economy had not recovered completely from the disruptive effects of World War I. Britain never regained prewar production levels, and unemployment remained a chronic problem throughout the 1920s. Germany's remarkable economic comeback rested to a large extent on foreign loans. World agriculture did not share in the prosperity of the late 1920s because commodity prices remained low. The related problems of war debts and reparations also continued to be a source of concern.

In the postwar economy, the position of the United States was of special importance. Any sharp reversal in its economic fortunes was sure to have great impact on the rest of the world. Although prices on the American stock market began to rise dramatically in 1928 and continued upward during the next year, there was actually little reason for optimism. Not only was U.S. agriculture depressed, but industrial production edged downward during 1929.

In Germany, a recession began as early as the winter of 1928–29, and although conditions improved during the summer, recovery was short-lived. This was due largely to developments in America. When the spectacular rise of the U.S. stock market abruptly ended in October 1929, stock values skidded catastrophically. The crash ruined many investors and destroyed the confidence of others. Industrial production plummeted; banks failed and unemployment soared. Aftershocks of this disaster spread rapidly as American financiers cut off loans to Germany, creating a severe shortage of capital. German production declined precipitously, businesses failed, and unemployment rose alarmingly.

THE WEIMAR REPUBLIC IN CRISIS

The Weimar Republic found itself in a dilemma, with sharply declining revenues and increasing demands for unemployment assistance. Business interests opposed any increase in these payments, while organized labor refused to support any reduction. The cabinet, unable to agree on a solution, resigned in March 1930. The new chancellor, Heinrich Brüning, actually had strong reservations about the democratic republic and favored a restoration of the monarchy. His authoritarian views made him acceptable to a number of generals who were influential with President Hindenburg, the World War I military leader. Although a monarchist at heart, Hindenburg had remained loyal to the oath he had taken to uphold the republic when he became president in 1925. But he was 80 years old and susceptible to his military advisers, who had recommended Brüning's appointment.

Brüning adopted a program that called for tax increases and reduction of expenditures in an effort to restore the financial stability of the government. He rigidly refused to accept any compromise, and as a result, the Reichstag voted against his program. But Brüning asked Hindenburg to put the program into effect by decree. Under article 48 of the Weimar constitution, the president had the power to enact programs by decree in time of emergency. Brüning's action marked the end of parliamentary democracy in Germany and launched a three-year period of rule by presidential decree. The chancellor also called a parliamentary election for September 1930, hoping that he could convince the electorate of the soundness of his program.

Unfortunately, the election of 1930 proved a disaster for both Brüning's hopes and the republic. In the largest turnout since 1919, the extremist parties, the Communists and Nazis, scored major gains. But the Nazis were especially successful, winning 107 seats, which gave them the second largest Reichstag delegation. Brüning now had no chance of creating a majority coalition but refused to resign. Instead, he continued to rely on presidential decree powers and clung to his rigid fiscal policy while the depression worsened. Unemployment had hovered around 3 million when he came to power. By the end of 1930, it had risen to 4,380,000 and a year later reached 5,615,000. The popularity of Brüning, now referred to as the "hunger chancellor," declined steadily.

Hitler, convinced that his patient policy was about to bring him even greater success, made an attempt to win the presidency when Hindenburg ran for a second term in the spring of 1932. In the election campaign, Hitler did not criticize the revered president directly but attacked Brüning's policies and the republic in general. Despite Hitler's most vigorous efforts, Hindenburg emerged as the winner with 53 percent of the vote, while Hitler received almost 37 percent and a Communist candidate won 10 percent.

By the spring of 1932, Brüning was losing the confidence of both Hindenburg and General Kurt von Schleicher, the army's liaison man with the government. In May, the chancellor bowed to their pressure and resigned. Schleicher now persuaded Hindenburg to appoint Franz von Papen as his successor. The general thought that he could dominate Papen, a second-rate figure with no strong personal following. Both Papen and Schleicher hoped to lure Hitler into accepting Nazi participation in a coalition cabinet. They believed that the need to share responsibility for government decisions would undermine Hitler's appeal with the voters. But Hitler had no intention of falling into their trap. He did agree not to oppose Papen in the Reichstag, however. In return, the chancellor agreed to call another parliamentary election in July.

Hitler and the Nazis made a major effort to win a sweeping victory. They lashed out at the republic's foreign policy and failure to solve the economic dilemma. The Nazis also offered different solutions to various audiences. They promised workers a revitalization of the economy and an end to unemployment. At the same time, they vowed to promote agricultural prosperity and make the peasantry a key factor in their proposed new order. They also were successful in persuading lower-middle-class voters that Big Business, Socialists, and Jews were to blame for their problems. But the Nazis also appealed to the wealthier urban voters by coupling nationalistic and anti-Semitic rhetoric with scathing attacks against the republic as well as both communism and socialism.

While Hitler concentrated on more traditional campaigning, the SA, under the leadership of Ernst Röhm, engaged in a struggle for "control of the streets." Storm troopers battled Communists and Social Democrats and resorted to acts of terrorism. Röhm, an army officer during World War I, had recruited many members of the *Freikorps* into the SA in its early days. But he had abandoned the party after the failure of the Beer Hall Putsch, serving for a time as an officer in the Bolivian army. Hitler had enticed him back in 1930 to reorganize the SA. By the end of 1932, Röhm commanded a force of over 400,000 men.

Far less conspicuous at this time but destined for much greater importance in the future was the *Schutz Staffel* (SS), which began as Hitler's bodyguard and consisted of less than 300 men in 1929. In that year, Heinrich Himmler, a former operator of a poultry farm, took command of the SS and began to increase its size and functions. Himmler appeared to be anything but the ideal Aryan. Of modest stature with a flabby body, he wore pince-nez glasses, which gave him the appearance of a pedantic schoolmaster, and suffered from a chronic stomach ailment and headaches. But behind his unimposing facade lay burning ambition and totally ruthless dedication. He became a devoted disciple of Hitler but at the same time constantly sought to aggrandize his own power.

When the election took place, the Nazis captured over 37 percent of the vote and increased their Reichstag delegation to 230, making them the country's largest party, but they were still far from a majority. Hitler now felt strong enough to demand the chancellorship for himself, but Schleicher, Papen, and Hindenburg refused to go along with this. Papen offered him the vice chancellorship instead, but Hitler declined and withheld Nazi support for the government in the Reichstag. His action forced Papen to call another election in November, but this time the balloting resulted in a major setback for the Nazis. They lost 2 million votes, and their Reichstag delegation fell to 196, although they remained the largest party. It looked as if the Nazis had definitely passed their peak. They were also deeply in debt because of the expense involved in waging three major election campaigns in one year.

Papen now attempted to break away from Schleicher's tutelage and proposed a remarkably ill-advised scheme to solve the government's dilemma. He urged Hindenburg to use his decree power to revise the constitution and transform the government into an authoritarian regime dominated by the wealthy groups. The president, who had grown extremely fond of Papen, supported him at first. But when Schleicher pointed out that this plan would result in a general strike or perhaps even civil war, Hindenburg changed his mind, and Papen resigned.

In the absence of another acceptable candidate, Schleicher became chancellor himself, but his position was no stronger than that of his predecessor. In an effort to build a majority coalition, he attempted to split the Nazis by making a deal with Gregor Strasser. But his scheme misfired, and he now urged Hindenburg to ban both the Nazis and the Communist party. The president pointed out that such an action would cause as great a crisis as Papen's earlier proposal and refused.

Meanwhile, Papen had been active behind the scenes and worked out a deal with Hitler. Under its terms, Hitler would become chancellor while Papen would take the vice chancellorship. Papen also promised to use his connections with important bankers and industrialists to help the Nazis with their financial problems. In return, Hitler agreed that Papen and his associates could choose the great majority of the cabinet members. Hindenburg did not relish the prospect of Hitler in power, but he finally bowed to Papen's pressure. On January 30, 1933, he appointed Hitler chancellor. Papen was delighted. As he commented to a friend shortly afterward, "We have hired him!" He told another, "Within two months we will have pushed Hitler so far into the corner that he'll squeak!"

THE THIRD REICH TAKES FORM

Hitler had no intention of allowing Papen or anyone else to dominate him. Instead, he set out to outmaneuver Papen and the cabinet. His first step was to gain agreement for an immediate dissolution of the Reichstag and the calling of a new

FIGURE 3-2 Nazi party comrades salute Adolf Hitler in Harzburg, Germany. (*AP/Wide World Photos*)

election in March. He hoped to gain a two-thirds majority for the Nazis. This would enable him to secure passage of legislation that would authorize him to rule by personal decree for four years. Hitler also took measures to curtail freedom of the press throughout the country.

In February, Hitler's hopes rose still higher when the Reichstag building burned down. Clearly arson, it is still not certain who actually set the fire. The Nazis blamed the Communists and used this charge as a pretext not only to crack down on Communist party officials but to suspend civil rights as well. Armed with this authority, the Nazis interfered with the activities of opposition parties. But despite all these advantages, Hitler found the election results disappointing. Although the Nazis won 288 seats, they were still short of a bare majority, not to mention the two-thirds needed to pass the enabling bill. Hitler now resorted to intimidation to gain the necessary support. On the day that the vote took place, SS personnel surrounded the building in which the Reichstag met, while SA troopers stationed themselves inside and chanted, "We want the bill or fire and murder!" Under such pressure, only the Social Democrats had the courage to vote against the bill, which passed by a margin of 347.

Hitler was not yet the complete dictator of Germany, but he was well on his way. To finish the process, he embarked on a policy of *Gleichschaltung* (coordination). This included bringing the state governments under Nazi control and subordinating them completely to the central administration. Other measures purged the civil service of "unreliable elements" and subjected the legal profession to party domination. Hitler eliminated all other political parties, ousted unacceptable members of the cabinet, and merged the labor unions in a new, Nazi-directed German Labor Front. Industrial workers lost their rights to engage in collective bargaining and to strike. The Reichstag continued to exist, but only as a Nazi-dominated assembly that listened to Hitler's decrees and roared back its total, slavish approval.

Soon after coming to power, the Nazis encroached on education and cultural affairs. They brought the curriculum from the elementary through the university level in line with Nazi ideas and stressed the *völkisch* aspects of Nazism, character building, and physical skills. The Nazis absorbed all the country's many youth organizations into the Hitler Youth. This movement fostered love of the Führer, idealization of the *Volk,* obedience to the party and state, and exaltation of warlike virtues. The party also sponsored mass book burnings in which university students committed many great humanistic works, especially those by Jewish authors, to the flames. Nazi officials rapidly regimented artistic and literary endeavor, stressing *völkisch* themes that glorified Germany's past and present.

Hitler referred to Nazi Germany as the Third Reich, the Third German Empire. The first Reich had been the medieval Holy Roman Empire, the second the imperial system that World War I had destroyed. Hitler predicted that the new Reich would last for a thousand years.

Despite the party's original hostility to large-scale industry and its pledge to help small businesses, the regime granted preferential treatment to big industrialists. Hitler realized that his plans for rearmament and expansion depended on heavy industry. Although the government regulated wages, prices, working conditions, and allocation of materials, it left ownership and management in private hands. Clearly, in view of Hitler's ambitious plans and his alliance with big industry, no possibility existed for the return to the soil envisaged by the *völkisch* element in Nazism. Relatively little change took place in the structure of agriculture, although farmers did receive a regulated market, price subsidies, and protection against foreclosures.

As soon as they gained power, the Nazis began to move against the Jews and political opponents. They purged Jews from the civil service and universities and subjected them to discrimination and violence. At first, these measures were unofficial and somewhat random in nature, but in the following years they became much more formal and increasingly restrictive.* A secret police organization, the Gestapo, relentlessly tracked down enemies of the regime. In 1933, the Nazis also established three concentration camps, the first of many, and by 1937, some 10,000 political prisoners languished in internment centers.

By 1934, Hitler had essentially completed his revolution. Only two potential sources of opposition still existed—the army and the SA. Military leaders were not unsympathetic to the creation of the Nazi dictatorship and listened with pleasure as Hitler promised to increase the size of the army and provide it with modern equipment. But the generals were alarmed by the rapid expansion of the SA, whose ranks had swollen to over a million men. They also were troubled by reports that Röhm hoped to merge the army with the SA. Hitler shared their concern over Röhm's intentions and feared that the SA leader might attempt to seize power. In June 1934, at the urging of both the army and Himmler, Hitler ordered the purge of the SA. SS troopers took Röhm and many other SA leaders by surprise and executed them without trial. For good measure, they included a number of Hitler's old enemies, including Strasser and Schleicher, among the victims.

Shortly after this purge, remembered as the "Night of the Long Knives," President Hindenburg died, and Hitler assumed his duties. But he refused to take the republican title of president and instead adopted the new designation of Reichsführer. The army agreed to support his acquisition of the presidential powers and swore an oath of allegiance to him. In return, Hitler affirmed the army's position as the sole bearers of arms in the nation. But while the army officers felt honor-bound to remain loyal to their oath, Hitler soon violated his part of the bargain. He recognized the SS as the SA's replacement with the right to form actual combat troops. The SS also took over the SA's responsibility for staffing the concentration camps. In the following years, the SS grew rapidly and, under Himmler's leadership, became the chief instrument of internal Nazi power. By 1936, Himmler had gained control over all German police, including the Gestapo. Later Himmler created special military units, the *Waffen SS* (armed SS), which were separate from the army.

*Nazi persecution of the Jews is covered in greater detail in Chapter 11.

THE FÜHRER AT THE HELM

Hitler now wielded absolute power over both party and state and contended that he embodied the aspirations of the entire German people. Whatever their original misgivings, a majority of Germans soon began to accept the Führer's rule as beneficial. When Hitler gave the people an opportunity to express their attitude toward his assumption of Hindenburg's power in a plebiscite, almost 85 percent voted in favor. While they were confronted by an intense propaganda campaign and in some cases even intimidation, the balloting took place in secret and appears to have been a reasonably accurate indication of his support.

Hitler also received credit for Germany's economic recovery from the depression and the great reduction in unemployment. Although recovery actually began before he came to power, his policies certainly contributed significantly to the process and gave the people a new sense of pride and achievement. They included an ambitious program of public works and rearmament. But all of this proved quite costly, and since the government lacked sufficient funds, it resorted to deficit financing. Under the leadership of Economics Minister Hjalmar Schacht, the Reichsbank extended the necessary credit to the government. Hitler also hoped to make Germany as self-sufficient as possible in foodstuffs and other commodities. But the emphasis on these economic policies resulted in a sharp decline in German exports. By 1936, Germany faced a severe shortage of hard currency, and despite an even more intense effort toward self-sufficiency during the next few years, progress was disappointing.

By the end of 1937, the initial enthusiasm for the regime was wearing thin. Continuing regulation, repression, and terror had transformed much of the early support to mere tolerance. In some circles, the first stirrings of an opposition movement had already begun. But it was never destined to gain a mass following.

Despite the power wielded by Hitler and the Nazis, the system lacked the complete coordination of all levels of government from the top that is usually associated with totalitarianism. Instead, a good deal of confusion, duplication of effort, and competition characterized relations between party and state. Hitler retained the governmental departments of the republic as well as most of their personnel, who tended to be of high quality. The most notable new department, the Propaganda Ministry, staffed by Nazis and headed by Goebbels, performed its functions of spreading lies and promoting hatred with chilling efficiency. But Hitler provided no systematic machinery for coordinating the policies of the departments. The cabinet had fulfilled this function during the republic, but under Hitler, it went into eclipse. Although he established his own Reich Chancellery, this body did not really take over the cabinet's responsibilities. It merely served Hitler personally.

The Führer also had a fondness for creating special authorities and agencies to deal with problems that existing ministries could have handled with greater efficiency. These bodies proliferated alarmingly and tended to compete not only with the ministries but also with each other. The same sort of duplication of effort took place at the state and local levels, where government officials experienced competition from party functionaries.

In part, this duplication and the resulting jurisdictional rivalries and lack of coordination stemmed from Hitler's own deliberate efforts. By dividing his underlings, he maintained unquestioned ascendancy over all of them. But despite this confused reality, Nazi propaganda effectively portrayed the regime as one of totalitarian order and efficiency to the German people and the outside world.

THE TRANSFORMATION OF JAPAN

In East Asia, dictatorship also came to Japan, but the form of oppression and the manner in which it developed differed from the models of Russia, Italy, and Germany. The driving force behind this transformation was not a political party or a single leader but the army. Japan possessed an ancient military tradition that had originated in a period of civil war between rival feudal clans, starting in the twelfth century and continuing until the 1500s. Throughout this period, a succession of emperors presided over the Japanese government. Although the emperor claimed divine origin as the descendant of the Sun Goddess, he actually played a minor role in the political system. Imperial power, such as it was, lay in the hands of the shogun, a military regent who ruled in the name of the emperor.

Despite the turmoil of those centuries, Japan maintained a highly developed civilization and a thriving commercial economy. The prestigious landowning clans, supported by armed retainers called samurai, dominated Japanese society, followed at a respectful distance by the wealthy merchant class. The landlords mercilessly exploited the peasantry, which comprised the overwhelming majority of the population. One of the clans, the Tokugawa, gradually gained control over Japan in the late sixteenth and early seventeenth centuries and acquired the office of shogun. For the next 200 years, Tokugawa shoguns governed the country as a military dictatorship.

The Tokugawa feared foreign influence and isolated the country from most contacts with the West. But in 1853, an American fleet, under the leadership of Commodore Matthew Perry, forced its way into Yedo (later Tokyo) Bay. Perry demanded that the Tokugawa enter into commercial relations with the United States and other Western powers. In the years that followed Perry's brusque visit, Japan agreed to a series of treaties with various Western countries. These were similar to the ones that China had made with European powers, complete with trade concessions and grants of extraterritoriality. But many Japanese resented the growing foreign domination and created a movement for national revival. In 1867, they overthrew the shogun and restored the emperor to his authority, at least in theory. The rebels adopted Western technology and organizational methods in an effort to resist Western domination. In keeping with this approach, they reorganized the administrative and legal systems and encouraged industrial and financial modernization. Japanese business groups invested in manufacturing enterprises and rapidly increased production whil, seeking foreign markets.

The new regime created a modern army, patterned after Prussia's military establishment, and transformed the samurai into an officer corps. Somewhat later, a navy, modeled after Britain's, also came into existence. By the early twentieth century, Japan had shaken off Western domination and had emerged as an important power. Its new war machine won victories over China in 1894–95 and Russia in 1904–5. Secure in their newly established position, the Japanese engaged in the same type of imperialistic activity in China that they had resisted in their own country.

Despite this startling transformation, Japan's traditional social structure continued largely unchanged. Landlords retained their importance and their control over the peasantry. The industrial and commercial groups had grown wealthier, but a few great families dominated the economy through giant trusts. And although an industrial working class had come into being, it remained thoroughly subordinate to management. Japan's culture also continued in its age-old form, except for the government's deliberate campaign to reduce the power of the Buddhist religion and to encourage the Shinto cult, which worshiped the emperor as the Son of Heaven.

Japan based its government on a constitution that drew inspiration in part from the political system of imperial Germany. Drafted in 1889, it vested authority in the emperor, but in reality, the premier and his cabinet ruled in the emperor's name, while the Son of Heaven existed in a state of exalted aloofness. A small electorate, based on property ownership, chose the members of the Diet, the Japanese parliament. Cabinet ministers were responsible to the emperor rather than to the Diet, but since the emperor remained above political affairs, they ruled with virtual freedom from civilian limitations. But they did have to contend with the army and the navy, which wielded enormous influence. High-ranking officers on active duty headed the war and navy ministries, and either minister could bring down the cabinet by resigning. The services could also block the formation of a cabinet not to their liking by refusing to designate officers to fill these positions. Both services even refused to provide information to the cabinet on the pretense of the need to protect military secrets.

Despite the traditional importance of the military, a movement toward liberalization of the system produced remarkable results during the 1920s. Western-style political parties and trade unions developed, and in 1925 Japan adopted manhood suffrage as the basis for parliamentary elections. There was even an attempt to reduce the influence of the army and navy in the realm of foreign affairs. The most notable examples of this were the commitments that Japanese officials made at the Washington and London conferences to limit naval strength. These agreements came over the vehement protests of many navy leaders. To a large extent, the liberalization movement found its strength in the relative economic prosperity that Japan enjoyed during the 1920s. But beneath the surface, the traditional social system still remained largely unchanged, and powerful forces objected to the innovations in the political system.

With the coming of the Great Depression, Japan encountered severe economic problems that discredited the civilian government and provided the opportunity for the military to reassert its power. Army leaders took the lead by insisting that the country must seek expansion on the Asian mainland as a way out of the economic dilemma. In particular, they demanded aggressive measures in Manchuria. Junior officers became active in secret organizations that resorted to the assassination of government officials. Their first victim was Premier Yuko Hamaguchi, whose government had negotiated the London Naval Treaty in 1930. These violent tendencies culminated in an attempted coup by a group of fanatical army officers in 1936. Although they failed in their bid for power, the rebels did succeed in assassinating several cabinet ministers.

The actions of these junior officers reflected the paradoxical nature of the Japanese army. Despite the ability of top-ranking generals to manipulate cabinets, they were not successful in controlling their own subordinates, who often acted in a startlingly independent manner. This was in keeping with the Japanese tradition of *gekokujo,* which involved open defiance of senior officers by juniors, a frequent occurrence in Japan's history. Army authorities often overlooked such glaring breaches of military discipline or merely imposed meaningless punishments. In large part this was due to the fact that senior officers often sympathized with the motives of their subordinates. Even when they did not, they admired their spirit. Indeed, Japanese military doctrine considered fighting spirit the decisive element in war and regarded cautious officers as cowards. All of this was indicative of an irrational element in the army's outlook, which focused on a willingness to undertake military action without due regard for the consequences or the strength of Japan's forces. It also took the form of fanatical devotion to military honor, fighting to the death in hopeless circumstances, and an insistence on suicide rather than surrender.

Japan's military leaders encroached steadily on the government during the 1930s, and the promising liberalization movement of the 1920s withered away. Civilian authorities buckled under to the army's demand for territorial expansion in China, and the more conservative civilian political groups shared this desire. Japan gradually took on the characteristics of a military dictatorship. But in many respects, the transition was more subtle than in Italy or Germany. There was no mass political movement, no charismatic leader, no revision or suspension of the constitution. But there was steady erosion of civil liberties, encroachment on freedom of the press and other forms of expression, and imprisonment of critics of the regime. The government undermined the powers of the Diet and gradually outlawed opposing political parties. In 1938, it promulgated the National Mobilization Law, which greatly increased the authority of the state.

The ascendancy of dictatorship in Germany and, to a lesser extent, in Italy foreshadowed the adoption of aggressive foreign policies by those countries that culminated in World War II. In Japan, the consolidation of dictatorship was largely a product of a war that the Japanese unleashed against China as early as 1931 and ultimately became a part of the global conflict.

4

The Road to War

World War II, far more than World War I, deserves to be called a global conflict. Although the 1914–18 war involved operations in Africa and the Middle East, in East Asia, and on the high seas, Europe remained its focus from start to finish. Europe also felt the war's impact much more profoundly than any other part of the globe. But World War II really consisted of two parallel though interconnected conflicts of major proportions—one in Europe and the Atlantic, the other on the Asian mainland and in the Pacific.

The earlier war plainly began in 1914; the start of the second struggle is not as easy to determine. Most accounts state that it commenced with the German invasion of Poland in September 1939. But others contend that it really began when Japan and China launched their prolonged hostilities in July 1937. Still others move the date as far back as September 1931, when the Japanese embarked on the conquest of Manchuria. Clearly, the European hostilities led to far greater immediate complications and the eventual joining of the two conflicts. Just as certainly, the first shots were fired in East Asia at least two years before.

JAPANESE AGGRESSION ON THE ASIAN MAINLAND

The first crisis, which jarred the world out of what was left of the optimism of the 1920s, came almost two years after the start of the Great Depression and less than 18 months before Hitler became chancellor of Germany. It began when soldiers of the Japanese Kwantung Army blew up a small section of railway track near the Manchurian capital of Mukden. The damage was negligible, but the effects were not. This incident triggered Japan's escalating involvement on the mainland of Asia, which ultimately led to the outbreak of World War II in the Pacific.

In the late 1920s and early 1930s, Japanese military leaders grew increasingly concerned about the northward expansion of Chiang Kai-shek's Kuomintang regime in China. They were especially distressed when the Manchurian warlord Chang Hsueh-liang recognized the Kuomintang's authority over Manchuria. Chiang also demanded an end to extraterritoriality and trade concessions to foreign powers. Manchurian officials had even gone so far as to boycott Japanese goods and interfere with the activities of Japanese citizens. If these developments were not bad enough, the Chinese had built competing railroads that challenged the monopoly on rail transport that Japan had enjoyed in Manchuria since the end of the Russo-Japanese War in 1905.

All of this clearly threatened Japan's political and economic position in Manchuria at the same time that the Great Depression had unhinged the economy at home. Officers of the Kwantung Army, which defended Japanese interests in Manchuria, were not impressed by arguments that the Chinese had the right to do as they chose in their own country, especially in view of the nebulous hold they maintained over Manchuria. It appeared to them that drastic measures were necessary.

Accordingly, in 1930 the leaders of the Kwantung Army and the war ministry agreed on a three-stage solution to the Manchurian question. They proposed government pressure on Chang Hsueh-liang's regime to guarantee Japanese rights in Manchuria. If Chang refused, efforts should be made to secure a pro-Japanese government in Mukden. If this proved impossible, the issue would be settled by force. The only disagreement arose over the deadline for military action. The war ministry preferred the summer of 1932; the Kwantung leadership wanted to strike by the fall of 1931. When no progress developed on the diplomatic level, the Kwantung officers decided to take matters into their own hands.

After blowing up the railway track, they blamed Chang's troops for the blast and used the incident to attack his forces. These actions represented a classic example of *gekokujo* and were taken without the war ministry's approval. The Japanese government quickly moved to put an end to the incident and received the army high command's support. But the Kwantung Army ignored instructions to cease operations and continued to advance. When confronted by this defiance, the army leaders in Tokyo gave in and approved the actions in Manchuria. The cabinet now realized that it had no choice but to go along with the army.

With all restraints removed, the Kwantung Army completed the conquest of Manchuria by January 1932. It was an easy victory because the Chinese did not seriously resist. Chiang realized that Chang's forces could not defeat the Japanese, but he had reserved his own troops for a showdown with the Chinese Communists. Although Chiang was not oblivious to the threat posed by the Japanese, he considered it less serious than the internal challenge of the Communists. He also recognized that his own control over Manchuria was tenuous at best and that his army was weak. Chiang preferred to invoke the support of the League of Nations, but the League merely urged an end to hostilities and called upon the Japanese to withdraw their troops. It avoided sanctions of any kind, although it did create a commission to investigate the situation. The United States, Britain, and France deplored Japan's aggressive actions, although they agreed that Chinese encroachments on Japanese treaty rights in Manchuria had provoked this extreme response. The Soviet Union was concerned about these developments on its eastern border but was in the midst of the internal struggle with the kulaks and in no condition to intervene.

In September 1932, the Japanese established a puppet state in Manchuria, which they renamed Manchukuo. Japan retained control over the country's military and foreign affairs, however. Soon afterward, the League commission issued its report, which called for an autonomous Manchurian government under Chinese sovereignty but with safeguards for Japan's special interests. Although the report was quite moderate, Japan withdrew from the League in protest. Almost simultaneously, the Kwantung Army moved into China's Jehol province, southwest of Manchuria. Again the Chinese government offered no serious resistance, and the Japanese incorporated Jehol into Manchukuo. In May 1933, Kwantung forces invaded China's Hopei province, and Chiang, with his attention focused on the imminent start of a new military campaign against the Communists, agreed to a truce. Under this arrangement, China recognized Japanese control over Manchuria and Jehol and also granted Tokyo extensive rights in Hopei. The failure to prevent Japan's conquest of Manchuria and Jehol represented a severe blow to the League's prestige and clearly revealed its basic weakness.

During the next four years, East Asia was relatively quiet, but the atmosphere remained tense. Chinese nationalists resented Japan's efforts to dominate the economy of northern China and undermine Kuomintang political authority in this area. But Chiang continued to view the Communists as the primary enemy and tried repeatedly to eliminate their stronghold in Kiangsi province. Although these efforts failed, they weakened Mao's forces. The Communist leader feared that another offensive would be fatal, and in 1934 he ordered his troops to seek refuge in the remote northern province of Shensi. To accomplish this, the Communists carried out an agonizingly difficult fighting withdrawal of 6,000 miles. Only 20,000 of the 90,000 men who started this legendary Long March reached Shensi, but once there, they took advantage of the mountainous terrain, which shielded them from Chiang's forces.

Many Chinese nationalists believed that Chiang was prepared to sacrifice the country to Japanese domination while he pursued his obsessive desire to crush communism. The forces of Chang Hsueh-liang, which had fled from Manchuria in 1931, were especially resentful and fell under the influence of Communist propaganda calling for war against Japan. Reports of this disaffection alarmed Chiang and prompted him to visit Chang's headquarters in December 1936 to seek a reconciliation. While he was there, a group of Manchurian officers took him prisoner. In return for his release, Chiang reluctantly agreed to end his anti-Communist crusade and cooperate with Mao Tse-tung to strengthen China against the Japanese. Chiang was never really committed to this agreement, however, and continued to be reluctant to risk war with Japan.

War came nevertheless. It began in July 1937 with a skirmish at the Marco Polo Bridge south of the major city of Peiping (now Beijing) in Hopei province. Although it is not clear which side actually initiated hostilities, neither government really desired a full-fledged conflict at that time. But heavy fighting followed, and the war quickly escalated. By the middle of August, the Japanese were in control of Peiping. Soon afterward, they besieged the great port city of Shanghai at the mouth of the Yangtze River far to the south. After a bitter struggle lasting seven weeks, Shanghai fell, and the Japanese advanced up the Yangtze Valley. In December, they captured Nanking, the Kuomintang capital. An orgy of rape and murder followed, and when the horror finally ended over a month later, the Japanese had killed at least 200,000 of Nanking's inhabitants and had burned down one-third of the city.

Alarm increased in the West as it became clear that the Japanese intended to dominate China, a development that threatened European and American economic interests. Japan also aroused disgust by the bombing of open cities and especially the rape of Nanking. Tension mounted in December as the Japanese seized a British gunboat and sank the American gunboat *Panay,* both on the Yangtze River. Although London and Washington protested, they were reluctant to take any steps that might lead them into war. Nazi Germany had cultivated close relations with both belligerents and agreed to act as intermediary for Japanese efforts to secure a negotiated peace. But the attempt failed when Japan demanded what amounted to economic and political domination of China. With the collapse of his peacemaking efforts, Hitler dropped the role of mediator and endorsed Japan's ambitions.

Stymied in its efforts to dictate a settlement, Japan resumed the quest for military victory in 1938. Japanese troops seized China's remaining seaports and continued their offensive up the Yangtze. Despite these setbacks, Chiang refused to capitulate and moved his government to the ancient city of Chungking much farther up the Yangtze. Chungking was so remote and surrounded by such rugged mountains that the Japanese realized an advance in its direction was impractical. Chiang now prepared to wait until the enemy agreed to negotiate a reasonable peace or other powers came to China's aid. By the end of 1938, Japan held almost all of China's major cities and the railroads that linked them. But it could not control the vast countryside, where Communist guerrillas became increasingly active. Clearly, the Japanese had embarked on a task that was beyond their capabilities. They could neither destroy the enemy nor end the war through negotiation.

FIGURE 4-1 Japanese troops guard a bridge during an engagement with Chinese forces. (*AP/Wide World Photos*)

Meanwhile, relations between the Kuomintang and the Communists deteriorated. The agreement, which Chiang had made under duress in 1936, remained officially in effect. But in reality, there was little cooperation, and frequently armed clashes broke out between the two rival forces. As the years passed, the Kuomintang regime became more corrupt, and its army did little actual fighting against the Japanese. At the same time, Mao's troops increased in strength and offered considerably more resistance to the invader. While the war dragged on into 1939, 1940, and beyond, the Chinese people, no strangers to suffering, continued to endure the horrors of enemy occupation and intermittent fighting. Many of them were homeless, destitute, and victims of recurring famine. The economy was in disarray, and the traditional structure of Chinese society and civilization began to break down.

HITLER'S PLANS FOR EUROPE

Despite the importance of the violent events unfolding in East Asia, to a large extent world attention during this period focused on Europe, where another drama was taking shape and led to the outbreak of war in 1939. Although many factors contributed to the coming of this conflict, the foreign policy of Hitler's Germany was the catalyst. The aims of this policy were far different from those of the Weimar Republic, which had tried to revise the peace settlement through negotiations. Most notably, Hitler added the concepts of racism and *Lebensraum*.

Some historians contend that Hitler had no long-range foreign policy goals and was essentially an opportunist who took advantage of the weakness of other countries and the lack of resolve and unity of the Western Powers and the Soviet Union. They dismiss the views that he expressed in *Mein Kampf* as daydreams not to be taken seriously. Relatively few observers agree with them. The signs of continuity between *Mein Kampf* and Hitler's later policies were simply too great. Indeed, the Nazi leader reaffirmed and elaborated on his *Mein Kampf* program in a second book manuscript, which he wrote in 1928 but never published. Its existence came to light only after the war, when it appeared under the title *Hitler's Secret Book*. Numerous statements, which the Führer made to Nazi officials both before and during the war, also remained faithful to his original statement of intent.

To be sure, Hitler was an opportunist and a skilled liar. If it served his immediate purpose, he would make agreements with countries he ultimately planned to destroy. He also repeatedly assured the Western Powers that he merely desired a revision of the peace settlement to correct injustices to Germany. But it is difficult to avoid the conclusion that he planned from the start to dominate Europe, to create *Lebensraum* for the German people in Eastern Europe, and to accomplish this ultimately by resorting to war. He also planned to solve the "Jewish question," although the ultimate nature of that solution does not appear to have taken final form until well after the outbreak of the war.

Hitler was, of course, violently anti-Semitic. The exact origin of his intense hatred of Jews is not clear. He claimed that he became an anti-Semite during his stay in Vienna. But many observers contend that this transformation occurred only after Germany's defeat in World War I and the establishment of the Weimar Republic. His anti-Semitism was of a *völkisch* type, probably reinforced by purely personal biases and a strong belief in the superiority of the Aryan race. In his view, only the Germanic peoples possessed pure Aryan blood, and he warned that they must not interbreed with inferiors, particularly the Jews but also the Slavs. He was less certain about the Latins (the French, Italians, Spanish, Portuguese, and Rumanians). He considered them to possess some Aryan blood, but unfortunately, the mixture of other blood lines had seriously reduced the Aryan content.

Closely identified with Hitler's racism was his view that the meaning of history lay in a struggle for existence among peoples or nations. He saw the object of this struggle as the acquisition of land, which was both limited and necessary to sustain the nation. Although he was certain that the Aryan Germans were the strongest nation and would ultimately win this struggle for *Lebensraum,* he saw the Jews as a potential obstacle. Hitler considered the Jews to be a special case because they were a people with no territorial base of their own, no real homeland. Thus they were international in outlook rather than nationalistic. In Hitler's view, they sought to denationalize the world through the process of the interbreeding with and the bastardization of other peoples. He saw this as an interference with the struggle for existence, and if history were to unfold as he thought it should, it was necessary to crush the Jews. This would enable the German people to pursue their struggle for *Lebensraum* to a victorious conclusion.

His concept of *Lebensraum* focused on the need to acquire land for the German people in the Soviet Union and found its inspiration in geopolitics. Geopolitics, which involves the application of geographic principles to political problems, became quite influential in the early twentieth century. Although geopolitical theories abounded, Hitler took special interest in those of Karl Haushofer, which stressed the importance of the Eurasian landmass. Haushofer believed that the nation that controlled what he referred to as the "heartland" of that vast area would be the dominant power in the world. The heartland included most of the Soviet Union.

Hitler warned that Germany was in a highly vulnerable position because of its location in the center of Europe, with a hostile France to the west and the Soviet Union on the east. Although he considered the Slavic Russians to be *untermenschen* (subhumans) and much inferior to the Germans, he believed that they were capable of using German technology and organizational methods to strengthen the Soviet Union. This, combined with the USSR's enormous landmass and huge population, would eventually enable the Soviets to crush the German people, with their limited population and territory. To prevent such a catastrophe, Hitler insisted that Germany must greatly increase its population, but he warned that there was a limit to the number of people that the country could support within its present borders.

Thus Germany had to expand its geographic base. The first step would involve taking over bordering territories that contained ethnic Germans—Austria, the Sudetenland, Danzig, Memel, and the areas ceded to Poland. Hitler assumed that to carry out even this limited expansion, it would be necessary to wage war against France. The Führer hoped to persuade Britain to remain neutral or even to entice the British into friendship with Germany. He also desired an alliance with Italy, which, despite its dubious Latin racial credentials, harbored ambitions in the Mediterranean and Africa. But Hitler contended that Germany's ultimate salvation lay in expansion eastward into the USSR. The Germans must colonize this area while enslaving most of the Slavs and deporting or exterminating the remainder. He also visualized the ouster—possibly the liquidation—of the Jews from both Germany and the areas to be conquered.

How could he accomplish this grandiose scheme in view of German weakness? Obviously, Germany would have to rearm in violation of the Treaty of Versailles. But if Britain and France intervened militarily to prevent this, the result would be disastrous. Hitler felt confident that they would not resort to such drastic action, however, and for a long time his optimism proved well founded.

REACTIONS OF NEIGHBORING NATIONS

The British and French were far from united in their attitude toward Hitler and Nazi Germany. Indeed, their own peoples were not in agreement on this question. In both countries, substantial numbers saw Hitler as a bulwark against the spread of communism and westward expansion by the Soviet Union. In France, many conservatives, including army officers, looked with special concern at the development of a large Communist party in their own country. And although the French government viewed any increase in German power as a threat to national security, they remembered the failure of their unilateral intervention during the Ruhr crisis in 1923. They were reluctant to undertake any similar action without British cooperation, but they realized that there was little chance of obtaining this. In fact, many members of the dominant British Conservative party still sympathized with the German desire to revise the peace settlement and did not believe that this could be avoided for long. A strong current of pacificism was also present in both countries.

The pressing economic problems created by the Great Depression also distracted the British and French. Although Britain began to make a partial recovery in 1933, France, with a more diversified economy, did not really feel the full impact of the depression until 1934, and recovery did not start until late 1938. The governments of both countries were reluctant to embark on rearmament programs that would be enormously expensive and would place a tremendous strain on the financial stability of their governments. Britain was especially sensitive to the wishes of the self-governing dominions, which also suffered from the depression and wanted desperately to avoid war. The Western Powers also knew that they could not count on the United States to contribute to the collective security of Europe.

At first, the Soviet Union also continued a policy of aloofness from European affairs but when the Russians did offer to cooperate with the West, starting in 1934, they made little progress. Britain and France were dubious about the seriousness of the Soviet commitment to collective security and were not certain that they wanted to ally themselves with Moscow under any circumstances. Stalin, for his part, continued to fear the possibility of a deal between the Western Powers and Hitler that might turn Germany's ambitions eastward at the USSR's expense. When Stalin launched his great purges in the mid-1930s, the British and French looked on with horror. Italy appeared a much better prospect for an alliance in the early 1930s. Mussolini developed a strong dislike for Hitler and feared the possibility of German expansion into Austria and the Balkans, where the Italians also had interests. But Italy's ambitions in Africa soon turned Mussolini away from the Western Powers and toward closer relations with Germany.

British and French leaders also misinterpreted Hitler's intentions. They tended to believe that he merely desired to end the restrictions that the peace settlement had placed on Germany. It was not until 1939 that they began to comprehend that his ambitions went beyond this and that he actually might contemplate the domination of Europe.

Hitler did not have to contend with one of the most detested legacies of the peace settlement. The problem of reparations had disappeared before he came to power. In 1931, the United States had granted a one-year moratorium on Allied war debts because of the depression, and soon afterward Britain and France agreed to a similar arrangement for German reparations. This moratorium actually marked the end of these payments.

PLOYS AND COUNTERPLOYS

The first major problem that confronted Hitler in foreign affairs was the question of how to circumvent the disarmament provisions of the Treaty of Versailles. An international conference had convened in Geneva in 1932 to consider the possibility of general disarmament. After coming to power, Hitler set out to sabotage this conference by demanding the end of all restrictions on German armaments. When France refused to agree, he withdrew Germany's delegation from the conference in October 1933. He used the same occasion as a pretext for terminating German membership in the League of the Nations. Up to this point, Hitler had been reluctant to engage in rearmament on a large scale because he feared French opposition, but when the Western Powers reacted meekly to his withdrawal from the disarmament conference and the League, he became less cautious.

He secretly ordered a sharp increase in arms production during 1934 and by 1935 was finding it difficult to disguise these violations. Early in March, Hitler decided to gamble by announcing that Germany already had an air force in being. A week later, he revealed his intention to reintroduce conscription and increase the German army to 550,000 men. The French and British could have responded by sending troops into Germany or by imposing an economic blockade. They did neither. Instead, they merely protested and took the matter before the League of Nations, which condemned Germany for violating the treaty but took no further action.

Even before Hitler announced rearmament, the first cracks began to appear in France's system of collective security in Eastern Europe. Polish leaders were concerned about their country's precarious geographic position between Germany and the Soviet Union and questioned France's willingness to honor its commitment to Poland if a crisis should arise. They decided that Poland would benefit from better relations with Germany while maintaining the French alliance. Hitler welcomed the opportunity to weaken the Franco-Polish alliance. In January 1934, Germany and Poland signed a ten-year nonaggression pact.

Hitler was less successful with regard to Austria. He looked forward to the eventual union (*Anschluss*) of his native Austria with his adopted Germany. But prospects were not bright. Austrian chancellor Engelbert Dollfuss, who had established a dictatorship in March 1933, strongly opposed *Anschluss*. He was also antagonistic to the Austrian Nazi party, which had close ties to its German namesake. France was certain to be hostile to any attempt at union, and it was by no means certain that Britain would approve. Italy looked on Austria as a client state and was also opposed to *Anschluss*. Dollfuss had even incorporated certain aspects of Italian fascism into his regime.

Despite these obstacles, the Austrian Nazis attempted to overthrow the government in July 1934. Although the putsch failed miserably, it did result in the assassination of Dollfuss. It is not clear to what extent Hitler was actually involved in the plot, but once it failed, he denied any complicity. The assassination outraged Mussolini, who dispatched troops to the Austrian border as a deterrent to any German attempt to intervene. Hitler now recognized that *Anschluss* would require much more thorough and extended preparation, and he restrained the Austrian Nazis during the next few years. Kurt von Schuschnigg succeeded Dollfuss as chancellor and continued his predecessor's dictatorship as well as his dedication to maintaining Austrian independence.

Contrary to their initial passive response to Hitler's rearmament announcements, Britain, France, and Italy soon took steps toward what appeared to be a system of collective security. Representatives of the three powers met in the Italian resort town of Stresa in April 1935 and agreed to work together to oppose future treaty violations. Observers spoke of a "Stresa front" against Hitler.

The situation looked even more encouraging when France and Russia signed a defensive military alliance in May 1935, but Franco-Russian solidarity was more apparent than real. French foreign minister Jean Louis Barthou had launched negotiations for the alliance in 1934 and had tried to breathe new life into France's Eastern European alliance system, with the USSR as the chief bulwark. But he had fallen victim to assassination in the fall of 1934. His successor, Pierre Laval, was not enthusiastic about close relations with the Soviets. But simply to drop negotiations might be embarrassing. Instead, Laval made the pact virtually inoperable by adding stipulations that required the approval of the League of Nations as well as Britain and Italy before France could take action in cooperation with the Soviets. In this form, the pact never became a factor of any importance in the power politics of the 1930s.

Russian willingness to make an alliance with France was indicative of a new Soviet policy that Stalin put into effect in 1934. Hitler's ruthless treatment of the German Communist party and his nonaggression pact with Poland had convinced Stalin that Nazi Germany posed a threat. He now attempted to build a collective security system that would seek to block German aggression. As the first step, the Soviet Union accepted membership in the League of Nations, and Foreign Commissar Maxim Litvinov became an outspoken advocate of collective security. In addition to the Franco-Russian alliance, Russia signed a mutual defense pact with Czechoslovakia in 1935. But the Soviets revealed their distrust of the French by stipulating that they were only obligated to aid the Czechs if France honored its alliance with Czechoslovakia first. The Comintern also instructed Communist parties in Western Europe to cooperate with the socialists and liberals in "popular fronts" against the Nazi menace. In 1936, popular front governments came to power in both France and Spain.

Despite these promising developments, Britain weakened prospects for a meaningful system of collective security by making a naval agreement with Germany in June 1935 without consulting either France or Italy. The British hoped to limit Germany's naval construction, which they expected Hitler to accelerate along with his military and air power. Under this arrangement, Britain recognized Germany's right to build up to 35 percent of British surface tonnage and 60 percent of British submarine strength. But in view of Germany's naval weakness, Germany could not reach either level for years and thus, in the meantime, could build without any limitations.

Mussolini's expansionist ambitions dealt the Stresa front its final blow. Continuing economic problems and increasing working-class unrest contributed to his decision to seek a cheap victory in Africa. He hoped that this would distract attention away from internal discontent. The Duce had been planning an invasion of the East African country of Ethiopia since 1932. Ethiopia had managed to remain independent while European powers had taken over most of Africa during the nineteenth century. Italy had attempted to conquer Ethiopia in 1896 but had suffered a humiliating defeat. The memory of this disgrace had rankled Italian nationalists for 40 years. In late 1935, Mussolini sent his troops across the border from neighboring Italian Somaliland and Eritrea. The ensuing Italo-Ethiopian War ruined relations between Italy and the Western Powers and opened the door to Italian cooperation with Germany.

Initially, the British government of Prime Minister Stanley Baldwin and Premier Laval's French cabinet supported sanctions by the League of Nations against Italian aggression. But they did not relish a breakdown of relations with Italy, and British foreign secretary Sir Samuel Hoare and

Laval worked behind the scenes to arrange a solution acceptable to Mussolini. The Hoare-Laval plan proposed that Ethiopia cede territory along the borders of Eritrea and Italian Somaliland to Italy and grant significant economic concessions as well. But when news of this proposal leaked to the press, it triggered an outburst of popular indignation in both countries, and Hoare and Laval felt compelled to resign soon afterward. Sobered by this experience, Britain and France reaffirmed their support for the League's policy of sanctions. Unfortunately, these sanctions did not extend to the sale of such vital commodities as oil and proved inadequate to prevent the Italians from completing their conquest of Ethiopia in 1936.

Mussolini reacted angrily to what he considered a breach of faith on the part of Britain and France. Hitler had been cool to Italy's invasion and had done relatively little to aid the cause, but at least he had not participated in sanctions. Perhaps even more important in Mussolini's mind was the feeble quality of Anglo-French opposition, which cast doubt on their strength as allies. All of this contributed to a reappraisal of Italian foreign policy, and in February 1936 Mussolini informed Hitler that the Stresa front was dead. The failure of sanctions also delivered a serious blow to the League's prestige. Little faith remained in its ability to deter aggression.

Hitler believed that with their attention focused on Ethiopia, Britain and France would be less inclined to resist a German attempt to remilitarize the Rhineland. He knew that Italy would not interfere. Accordingly, he sent troops into the Rhineland on March 7. The Führer pointed to the French parliament's ratification of the Franco-Russian alliance in late February as justification for his action. He contended that the pact was a direct provocation and abrogated the Locarno Treaty. His generals had advised him against the operation. They felt certain that the French, who were still militarily superior to Germany, would resist. But France did not intervene. French army leaders, who were in a strongly defensive frame of mind, advised the government of Premier Albert Sarraut against military action. They believed that the German force was much stronger than it really was and insisted that France would have to mobilize a million reservists if it were to intervene. Sarraut's cabinet, which had taken over when Laval resigned, was reluctant to resort to such a drastic measure as mobilization. Foreign Minister Pierre Flandin did consult with the British, but Baldwin's government opposed military intervention, considering it out of the question to prevent the Germans forcibly from occupying their own territory. The British and French contented themselves with referring the matter to the League, which again condemned Germany for its treaty violations but took no further action. Once again, Hitler's gamble had succeeded.

It probably would have been more difficult for France to oust the Germans from the Rhineland than was once believed, and such an attempt would likely have meant war. But the French were certainly strong enough to have accomplished the task. Vigorous military action on their part also could have dealt a serious blow to Hitler's prestige. By failing to act, the French conceded Germany a victory of crucial importance. The occupation of the Rhineland deprived France of a buffer zone against German aggression and badly undermined faith among France's allies in French determination to resist German aggression. Shortly afterward, Belgium renounced its defensive treaty with France and declared neutrality.

CIVIL WAR IN SPAIN

Four months after the Rhineland occupation, civil war erupted in Spain. This conflict had its origins in Spain's internal divisions and recent turbulent history. Revolutionaries had overthrown the Spanish monarchy in 1931 and had established a democratic republic. But the new republic encountered some of the same problems that democracy had faced in Italy and Germany—lack of a democratic tradition, economic problems, and an even more chaotic array of political parties, complete with extremists on the left and the right. A revolt in Spanish Morocco by troops under the command of General Francisco Franco triggered the civil war.

Oddly enough, Franco had little in the way of strong political convictions and was a latecomer to the military conspiracy that fostered the revolt. Prior to this, he had been totally absorbed in his army career and had served both the monarchy and the republic with distinction. The son of a naval officer of modest means, Franco had emulated his disciplined mother rather than his hard-drinking, womanizing father. He had seen action against Moroccan rebels and gained a reputation for bravery as well as caution. Although originally shy, introverted, and unpopular, he rose rapidly in rank, becoming one of the youngest generals in Europe and eventually chief of staff. His decision to assume command of the revolt was due to his growing concern over the breakdown of order under the popular front government, which took power in 1936, and the growth of radical leftist activity.

Franco's hopes for the conquest of Spain depended on the availability of aircraft to transport his troops across the Strait of Gibraltar. He appealed for aid to both Mussolini and Hitler, who, recognizing the advantage of another dictatorship on France's southern flank, agreed to supply the necessary planes. Although Franco hoped to extend his power rapidly over all of Spain, the republic proved stronger than he had expected. Franco's Nationalist troops managed to gain control over roughly the western half of the country while Republican forces held the remainder. Both Italy and Germany soon contributed manpower and other aid to the Nationalists. By early 1937, almost 50,000 Italian troops were serving in Spain. Hitler sent the so-called Condor Legion, which consisted primarily of planes and pilots, and some soldiers and tanks. Hitler deliberately limited aid to Franco in an effort to prolong the conflict. He wanted to keep British and French attention focused on Spain while he built up his military strength at home.

Stalin countered Hitler and Mussolini by dispatching aid to the popular front government. But he sent no troops, only military advisers and equipment, including tanks and aircraft. The Comintern also sponsored the creation of volunteer units from various countries, which came to be known as international brigades. At their peak, these forces may have reached 18,000. The largest influx of Soviet assistance came during 1936 and early 1937. But in late 1938, Stalin terminated his efforts, apparently sensing the defeat of the Republicans. Britain and France refused to support either side. Despite the fact that a French popular front government had come to power in May, it was split over the question of aid to the republic. Baldwin and his British colleagues were totally opposed to intervention, although they actually favored the Nationalist cause and feared the leftist tendencies of the republic. To prevent escalation of the war, Britain and France sponsored the Nonintervention Committee. This organization consisted of representatives from 27 countries, including Italy and Germany, which cynically participated despite their policy of aid to Franco. The committee accomplished little and became a symbol of hypocrisy.

Although the Republican forces fought gallantly against increasing odds, they lost ground steadily during most of 1938, and their last strongholds capitulated in March 1939. Franco had benefited greatly from Italian and German support, but his interests did not necessarily coincide with those of Hitler and Mussolini. During the conflict, he had identified his regime with the Falange, a fascist party that had sided with the Nationalists. But this connection was never more than a disguise for what was essentially a traditional authoritarian government. Franco was also determined to maintain his freedom of action in foreign affairs.

GERMANY ON THE OFFENSIVE

Their participation in the Spanish civil war inevitably brought the Germans and Italians into closer cooperation. Hitler had expected the conflict to make Italy more dependent on Germany, and his assumption proved correct, although Mussolini still hoped to make his way without becoming too closely tied to Berlin. It was the

Duce, nevertheless, who promoted the drafting of a vaguely worded agreement in October 1936 that provided for general cooperation between the two countries in the future. On November 1, Mussolini referred publicly to the existence of a "Rome-Berlin Axis."

Hitler also moved in the direction of closer relations with Japan in 1936. Despite the obvious fact that the Japanese were not Aryans, they won the Führer's admiration. He viewed them as a people in quest of *Lebensraum* on the Asian continent and also respected their opposition to communism and antagonism toward the Soviet Union. In November 1936, Germany and Japan signed the Anti-Comintern Pact, which bound the two countries to a policy of benevolent neutrality if one of them became involved in a war with the Soviet Union. A year later, Italy adhered to the pact.

During 1937, Hitler made no aggressive moves, other than to continue his aid to Franco. But in November, he summoned Foreign Minister Konstantine von Neurath and his chief military leaders to a high-level conference. The Führer informed them that his long-range goal was the creation of *Lebensraum* in Eastern Europe and warned that this would eventually mean war with France and Britain. He indicated that his first goals were *Anschluss* with Austria and the destruction of Czechoslovakia.

Hitler's bluntness worried Field Marshal Werner von Blomberg, the war minister, and General Werner von Fritsch, the commander in chief of the army. Both men pointed out that Germany was far from strong enough to provoke a war, and Neurath also expressed doubts. Their lack of enthusiasm disturbed Hitler, and early in 1938 he replaced Neurath with Joachim von Ribbentrop. A member of the Nazi party since 1932, Ribbentrop was slavishly devoted to the Führer's ideas. He had started his career as an importer of wine and spirits and had no training in foreign affairs. But he endeared himself to Hitler because of his knowledge of languages and air of self-assurance. Although elegant in appearance, he developed a tactless approach, which he pompously referred to as a uniquely National Socialist diplomatic style. With the exception of Hitler, virtually all German leaders detested Ribbentrop.

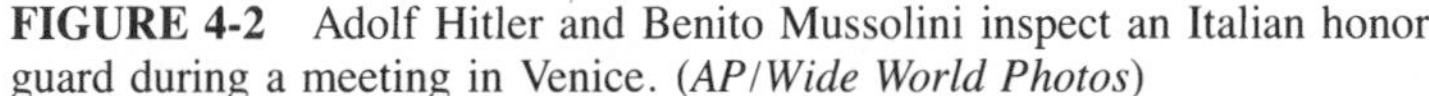

FIGURE 4-2 Adolf Hitler and Benito Mussolini inspect an Italian honor guard during a meeting in Venice. (*AP/Wide World Photos*)

Blomberg and Fritsch also gave up their posts under intense pressure. Instead of replacing Blomberg, Hitler abolished the war ministry and replaced it with the High Command of the Armed Forces (*Oberkommando der Wehrmacht,* abbreviated OKW). General Wilhelm Keitel headed the OKW with General Alfred Jodl as his chief of staff. Keitel, a particularly spineless individual, had earned the contempt of his fellow officers, who referred to him as a lackey and a lickspittle. Jodl was a man of considerable ability who fell under Hitler's spell. As Fritsch's successor, the Führer chose another officer who was not likely to stand up to him—General Walther von Brauchitsch.

It was also in February 1938 that Hitler invited Austrian chancellor Schuschnigg to his retreat at Berchtesgaden in the Bavarian Alps to discuss relations between their two countries. At this meeting, he subjected Schuschnigg to unbearable pressure and threats, demanding that he appoint a number of pro-Nazis to his cabinet. The most important of these, Arthur Seyss-Inquart, would become minister of the interior with control over the police. Schuschnigg realized that this would be a prelude to a Nazi takeover of Austria but finally yielded. After his return to Vienna, he resorted to a desperate gamble that he hoped might foil Hitler's plans. On March 9, he announced his intention to hold a plebiscite four days later in which the Austrian people could vote for or against *Anschluss.* Schuschnigg expected the plebiscite to result in a sizable majority in favor of continued independence.

Hitler apparently agreed and realized that such an outcome would undercut any contention that the Austrians desired absorption by Germany. The Führer reacted quickly and decisively. His first step was to promote demonstrations by Austrian Nazis. He also demanded Schuschnigg's resignation and the appointment of Seyss-Inquart to the chancellorship. The alternative would be an immediate German invasion. Schuschnigg, realizing that he had lost his gamble, complied. Seyss-Inquart became chancellor and, in his first official action, requested that Germany send troops into Austria to assist in the restoration of law and order. German forces crossed the border on March 12, and Hitler annexed Austria to Germany the following day.

These ruthless actions confronted British and French leaders with an accomplished fact. They could only change the situation by war and were not willing to resort to such drastic measures. In fact, both had assumed for some time that *Anschluss* would come eventually. The British believed that there was nothing intrinsically wrong with the merger of the two German peoples, but they were not happy with the tactics Hitler had employed.

Soon after the *Anschluss,* Hitler turned his attention to his next victim, Czechoslovakia. The issue, at least initially, was the German minority that lived in the Sudetenland. On March 28, he instructed Konrad Henlein, the leader of the Sudeten German party, to seek talks with the government in Prague on the question of autonomy for the Sudeten Germans within the Czech state. Czechoslovakia had outlawed the Nazi party, but Henlein's organization shared the Nazi goal of uniting the Sudetenland with Germany. Hitler did not want these talks to culminate in an agreement but planned to use them to create a crisis. He instructed Henlein to keep increasing his demands if the Czechs offered concessions. Once Henlein had convinced President Eduard Beneš and the Czech government to begin negotiations, Hitler launched an elaborate propaganda campaign that charged that the Czechs were mistreating the Sudeten Germans. He inferred that if this continued, Germany would have no choice but to intervene. In May, Hitler told his top generals of his "unalterable decision to smash Czechoslovakia by military action in the near future." In June, he selected October 1 as the day of reckoning.

THE DILEMMA OF CZECHOSLOVAKIA

The crisis posed serious problems for the Western Powers and the USSR. Both France and the Soviets had military alliances with Czechoslovakia. Britain had no obligation, but British leaders feared that if war came, they would become involved on the side of France. Both of the Western Powers considered the possibility of war with the utmost reluctance. They had little faith in Czechoslovakia's ability to repel a German invasion, despite the fact that the Czechs possessed a strong defensive line in the Sudetenland as well as an army of 35 divisions. Of greater importance to them was the ominous fact that since the *Anschluss,* German territory flanked Czechoslovakia on three sides.

France, as the power with the most definite commitment to Czechoslovakia, felt a special sense of dilemma. French leaders were particularly concerned about the weakness of their economy. It was still suffering from the belated effects of the depression, and the country was in poor condition to embark on a major rearmament program. French generals also indicated that the army would not be able to undertake any offensive action against Germany for another two years.

Premier Edouard Daladier, who came to power in April 1938, felt a keen sense of commitment to Czechoslovakia. But he was convinced that France could not undertake a war without British support and had little faith in the possibility of such aid. Daladier had been premier twice before and had served as war minister since 1936, a position he continued to hold as premier. The son of a baker in southern France, he had been a university history professor before entering politics. Daladier was the leader of the Radical Socialists, who despite their name were a moderate, middle-of-the-road party. Though honest and energetic, he was a heavy drinker and earned the reputation for possessing greater skill as a politician than as a statesman. His foreign minister, Georges Bonnet, believed even more firmly that France could not contemplate war.

Daladier was quite right in expecting no help from Britain. Neville Chamberlain, who had succeeded Baldwin as prime minister in May 1937, favored a policy of appeasement. In effect, Britain had been appeasing Germany since the early 1920s, when British leaders sympathized with German criticism of the Treaty of Versailles. Certainly, the British had been highly conciliatory toward Hitler's early violations of the peace settlement. But it was only with Chamberlain's advent to power that appeasement took on the guise of a thoroughgoing policy. Chamberlain was a member of a famous political family. His father, Joseph, had been a prominent industrialist and a power in the Liberal party and later the Conservative party. His brother, Austen, had served as foreign secretary at the time of the Locarno conference. A veteran of several cabinets, Chamberlain had been primarily involved in domestic matters. Despite his lack of experience in foreign affairs, he was determined personally to mold Britain's policy toward Hitler. He approached his task with a self-confidence bordering on arrogance.

The prime minister and most of his cabinet prided themselves on being realists. They felt that the peace settlement had artificially relegated Germany to the role of a third-rate power and that Hitler was merely attempting to restore his country's former greatness. They also sympathized with his desire to absorb fellow Germans into the Reich. In fact, when Chamberlain first came to power, he had been willing to negotiate a general agreement that would have given Hitler a virtual free hand in Austria, the Sudetenland, and Danzig. Chamberlain thought that such a settlement would preserve peace and satisfy Hitler. Chamberlain also believed that the areas in question were not vital to British interests and thus hardly a suitable cause for war. He shared France's economic concern and did not want to jeopardize Britain's partial recovery by approving huge defensive expenditures. British service chiefs also produced gloomy appraisals of the country's military and naval capabilities and greatly exaggerated German strength.

As for the USSR, soon after the *Anschluss,* Maxim Litvinov appealed to Britain and France to cooperate with the Soviet Union in case of continued German aggression. But Chamberlain viewed the proposal as an impediment to his appeasement policy and turned it down. Daladier also took no action in response to the overture from Moscow. The Western Powers were suspicious of Soviet intentions, particularly because the USSR did not border either Czechoslovakia or Germany. The Russians could aid the Czechs only by moving troops through Poland, but the Poles, who also had territorial claims on Czechoslovakia, were hardly likely to grant permission.

Ironically, German generals dreaded the prospect of war with the Western Powers and believed that France was far superior militarily to Germany. They also feared the formidable Czech defenses in the Sudetenland. When it became clear that Hitler planned to take military action, General Ludwig Beck, chief of staff of the Army High Command (*Oberkommando des Heeres,* abbreviated OKH), protested in the strongest terms. He even tried to persuade his colleagues to join in a general strike if the Führer persisted. Although Brauchitsch, the army's commander in chief, shared Beck's misgivings, he was not the man to challenge Hitler. In July, Beck resigned in frustration. General Franz Halder, who succeeded him as chief of staff, also was appalled by the prospect of war. Halder joined with Beck and several other generals in a conspiracy to arrest Hitler if he carried out his war plans and if the Western Powers resisted. To what extent the conspirators were determined to carry out their plans will never be known because the necessary prerequisite, Western intervention on behalf of Czechoslovakia, did not materialize.

Negotiations between the Czechs and Sudeten Germans dragged on without progress throughout the spring and summer. But matters came to a head in early September, when the British pressured Czechoslovakia to grant administrative autonomy to the Sudeten Germans. Hitler now changed his strategy. He ordered Henlein to break off the talks and delivered a bellicose speech in which he denounced the Czechs and emphasized his willingness to go to war to settle the Sudeten issue.

At this point, Chamberlain intervened in an attempt to reach a settlement with Hitler through personal diplomacy. He flew to Germany and asked the Führer what he really desired. Hitler for the first time specified German annexation of the Sudetenland. Chamberlain agreed to this in principle and returned to London, where he gained the support of his own government. Next he persuaded Daladier, Bonnet, and the French cabinet to agree. Beneš and the Czechs, recognizing that a refusal would leave them to confront Germany alone, also reluctantly consented. Chamberlain returned to Germany to report the good news to Hitler, but the Führer had now decided that this generous settlement was not enough. He insisted that the Czechs must also satisfy Polish and Hungarian demands for border revisions as well as a Slovak request for autonomy. Finally, he required the immediate German occupation of the designated areas.

Chamberlain's first response was anger, but by the time he had returned to London, he had decided that it would be necessary to accept Hitler's terms, however insulting they might be. But he had not reckoned on his own foreign secretary, Lord Halifax, who believed that Britain could not ask the Czechs for any additional sacrifices. Daladier also insisted that France would not accept these demands, and a number of British newspapers now attacked Chamberlain's policy. With his support dwindling, the prime minister reluctantly agreed to aid France militarily if that nation honored its commitment to Czechoslovakia. War appeared imminent.

But Chamberlain had not abandoned his peacemaking efforts. He now sought Mussolini's help in arranging another conference. The Duce realized that Italy was not prepared for war and was more than pleased to play the role of peacemaker. Hitler also had second thoughts and decided that it would be best to accept a bloodless conquest. This time, a four-power meeting convened in Munich on September 30, with Hitler, Mussolini, Chamberlain, and Daladier all in attendance. Neither Czechoslovakia nor the Soviet Union received an invitation. During the conference, Chamberlain and Daladier essentially accepted Hitler's original demands. They approved German annexation of the Sudetenland with a brief postponement of the actual occupation of some of the territory. Czechoslovakia had no choice but to accept the agreement. Hitler had won total victory; in addition to absorbing 3 million Germans, he had acquired important natural resources and industrial centers, including the huge Skoda armament works. Poland gained the border city of Teschen, and Hungary obtained a strip of southern Slovakia shortly thereafter.

A CHANGE OF POLICY IN THE WEST

Despite Chamberlain's boast that he had secured "peace in our time," he had merely postponed the coming of war for 11 months. Hitler had no intention of allowing the rump Czecho-Slovak state to survive and merely waited for the right opportunity to strike. It came in March 1939 in the form of squabbling between the Czechs and the Slovaks. Hitler urged Slovak extremists to demand independence and pressured the Czechs to agree to this as well as to accept a German protectorate over Bohemia and Moravia. The alternative was an immediate invasion. The Czechs gave in on March 15, and German troops quickly occupied the two provinces. Hitler now recognized the independence of Slovakia, which agreed to become a German protectorate. Hitler also granted Ruthenia, the extreme eastern portion of Czechoslovakia, to Hungary. The Czecho-Slovak state had ceased to exist, and Hitler had fallen heir to vast quantities of military equipment that substantially augmented his still incomplete rearmament program.

The destruction of Czechoslovakia proved a great blunder, the first serious mistake Hitler had made. If he had shown more restraint, he might have secured Western approval for German annexation of Danzig and Memel and perhaps modification of the borders with Poland. Certainly Chamberlain did not oppose this in principle. In fact, he had looked forward to a general European settlement with Hitler soon after Munich. But by ruthlessly destroying the remnant of Czechoslovakia, Hitler clearly revealed that his goal was not merely to absorb fellow Germans into the Reich. He increased tension still more by seizing Memel on March 23. Chamberlain now reluctantly changed his policy, and on March 30 Britain extended a guarantee to Poland that assured the Poles that if Germany attacked them, they could count on British support. France joined in this guarantee and also reaffirmed its original alliance.

Chamberlain's action represented a startling reversal in British policy. The prime minister was convinced that Britain must take a much firmer approach to Hitler. But he had not ruled out the possibility of a negotiated settlement over Danzig and Poland. It appeared to him that a show of determination would be more likely to bring Hitler to the bargaining table. But if such an approach were to have any chance of success, it required significant preparations for war and immediate efforts to coordinate military planning with the Poles. Little of this followed. Although the British introduced conscription on a limited basis, and both Britain and France strengthened their forces, they took only the most halting measures to cooperate with the Poles. None of this was sufficient to persuade Hitler that they were really serious about supporting Poland.

Actually, Hitler had originally hoped to achieve an alliance with Poland for use against the USSR. He had broached such an arrangement as early as 1935 and again in 1937. In return for concessions to Germany on Danzig and the Polish corridor, he held out the prospect of territory for Poland in the Ukraine. The Poles declined. They feared both Germany and the Soviets and were reluctant to become too closely associated with either. Instead, they tried to maintain a precarious balance between the two.

Ribbentrop, the Nazi foreign minister, revived this proposal in October 1938 and again in January 1939. He requested Polish approval for German annexation of Danzig and the construction of an extraterritorial road and railway across the Polish corridor to link East Prussia with Germany proper. He also asked that Poland adhere to the Anti-Comintern Pact. The Poles refused, fearing that acceptance would convert their country into a German satellite and lead to additional German demands. In April, soon after the Anglo-French guarantee to Poland, Germany brusquely renewed these demands. Again the Poles refused. This signaled the start of a new crisis, which continued throughout the spring and summer while the Germans launched another propaganda barrage, accusing the Poles of mistreating the German minority in Poland. In April, Hitler also ordered preparations to begin for an invasion of Poland in September.

CRISIS OVER POLAND

Hitler looked to Mussolini for support as German relations with Poland and the Western Powers deteriorated. Although the two dictators had grown closer since the outbreak of the Spanish civil war, it appears that the Duce was not altogether happy about this. He had attempted to improve relations with Britain as a counterweight to the Rome-Berlin Axis, but nothing substantial came from his efforts. The Italian dictator also resented Hitler's escalating importance and his own relegation to junior status in the Axis. On April 7, 1939, Italian forces seized little Albania, across the Adriatic Sea from southern Italy. This change was less dramatic than it appeared because the Italians had exercised strong political and economic influence over Albania since 1926. Many historians have long considered Mussolini's action a spiteful response to Hitler's seizure of Bohemia and Moravia, but the Duce had actually approved that operation in late 1938.

Despite Mussolini's dream of pursuing a middle course in foreign policy, he concluded an actual alliance, the "Pact of Steel," with Germany on May 22. This agreement bound the two partners to provide full assistance to each other in case of war, regardless of the circumstances. But Mussolini recognized that Italy would not be ready for war until 1943, and his foreign minister, Count Galeazzo Ciano, had so informed Ribbentrop during the negotiations. But the text of the pact made no reference to this. Hitler apparently assumed that Italy would enter the war when he attacked Poland, even though he kept his ally in the dark regarding his plans until late in the crisis. When he did finally confide in the Duce that a military showdown was imminent, Mussolini surprised him with the news that Italy could not join in hostilities for the foreseeable future.

With the deepening of the Polish crisis, the role of the Soviet Union loomed especially large. As Poland's neighbor on the east, the USSR was in a position either to aid the Poles in the defense of their country or to side with the Germans in its destruction. Clearly, both the Western Powers and Germany, not to mention Poland, were concerned about the Soviets' course of action. Britain and France recognized that an alliance with the Soviet Union would be the best way—perhaps the only way—to deter Hitler from attacking Poland. They began diplomatic discussions with the Russians as early as April, but the three powers could not agree on the type of agreement desired. Military staff talks did not start until early August and then quickly broke down when Poland announced that it would not allow Russian troops to enter Polish territory. The Poles feared the Russians at least as much as the Germans.

The whole enterprise took on an aura of unreality. Both Britain and France found it difficult to abandon their long-standing distrust of the Russians, and Stalin was perhaps even more suspicious of the Western Powers. He feared that if the Soviets agreed to an alliance and war came, the British and French would remain on the defensive while the USSR and Poland faced the full force of the German onslaught. Stalin was also wary of a possible Western deal with Germany that would enable Hitler to turn east without interference from Britain and France. The memory of the Munich agreement was still fresh in his mind.

Even before the start of the talks with the Western Powers, Stalin had turned to the possibility of an agreement with Hitler that would provide for Russian neutrality in case of war. He made his first approach to Berlin in April and in May replaced Foreign Commissar Litvinov with Vyacheslav Molotov, his oldest and closest associate. Litvinov, a Jew with an English wife, symbolized Soviet support for collective security. Molotov, by contrast, blessed with nerves of steel

Europe on the Eve of World War II, August 1939

and an imperturbable temperament, was devoted to Stalin. He was also a clever, ruthless, and absolutely determined negotiator.

Despite his aversion to the Soviet Union and communism, Hitler could see the obvious benefits to be gained from an agreement. In late May, talks began on economic issues and proceeded at a leisurely pace before culminating in an agreement on August 19. Under its terms, Russia was to supply Germany with raw materials in return for German credits for war materiel. But what Hitler wanted most was a political arrangement, and he pressed Stalin to receive Ribbentrop on August 23 to discuss such an understanding. The result was the Nazi-Soviet Nonaggression Pact, which Ribbentrop and Molotov drafted that same day. Under its terms, the two powers vowed to remain neutral if either of them became involved in a war. They also concluded a secret protocol that provided for a fourth partition of Poland. Under the latter agreement, the USSR conceded German occupation of the western half of the country while the Soviets claimed the eastern portion. Germany also recognized the predominance of Soviet interests in Finland, Estonia, Latvia, and the Rumanian province of Bessarabia, reserving Lithuania for its own sphere of influence.

When Germany and Russia announced the signing of the nonaggression pact, the news created a sensation throughout the world and came as a great blow to the British and French. It meant that Hitler would be free from the need to fight a two-front war once he had defeated Poland. But despite this great advantage, Hitler viewed the pact primarily as a mechanism for assuring the neutrality of Britain and France. Without Russian support, he expected the Western Powers to back down and desert Poland as they had abandoned Czechoslovakia. This would enable him to deal with the Poles in a localized war. Much to his surprise, however, the British and French did not back down. Despite this inconvenience, Hitler was determined to destroy Poland, and at dawn on September 1 he sent his forces across the border. The Western Powers declared war on Germany two days later. The conflict, which Hitler had hoped would be an unequal struggle between Germany and Poland, had become World War II.

5

Blitzkrieg in the East, *Sitzkrieg* in the West

During the opening period of World War II, from September 1939 to November 1941, Germany won a series of spectacular victories and conquered much of Europe. These successes stunned the world and gave the illusion of overwhelming strength. The Germans failed only in their attempt to crush Britain in 1940, but this defeat came in the air. They remained invincible on land.

DIFFERING APPROACHES TO WAR

Despite appearances, Germany's triumphs were not due to overwhelming strength, at least not in comparison to their primary land enemies—first France and later the USSR. Hitler's army was formidable, but considering his ambitious war aims, it was not enormously large. German soldiers were among the finest in the world, but much of their equipment, including their tanks, was not of the highest quality and not especially plentiful. Ironically, the Germans, who revolutionized warfare through mechanization during the 1930s, were short of motorized transport. Only a few of their infantry divisions were motorized. They also faced a serious shortage of trucks for supply purposes, and the mass of their army depended on horse-drawn vehicles to transport supplies. The actual keys to Hitler's success during the first two years of the war were not the size of his army or the quality of his equipment. They were the ways in which German leaders used their forces and took advantage of their opponents' mistakes.

Germany's approach to war was in large part predicated on Hitler's intention of dominating Europe and creating *Lebensraum.* He could accomplish this only by taking the offensive. But despite Hitler's dedication to offensive warfare, most German generals in the period between the wars were conservative and unimaginative. They initially expected to fight the next conflict as they had waged World War I—with mass infantry attacks. They were by no means convinced that the tank and the airplane were the weapons of the future.

During the interwar years, most French and British generals were also conservative and unimaginative in their outlook, but unlike the Germans, they were committed to defense and, in particular, fixed fortifications. They had learned what seemed to be the major lesson of World War I—the fact that victory had been won in large part by defensive firepower. Indeed, they had learned it too well.

Ironically, the French had been enthusiastic advocates of offensive warfare before and during World War I. The more optimistic of them believed that fighting spirit was the most important

European Theater, 1939–42

factor in war and that an army that possessed sufficient spirit could defeat any defensive force, no matter how powerful. The French put this suicidal doctrine into practice during World War I and tried repeatedly to break the stalemate by means of mass attacks. Each time, they failed while suffering huge casualties. This experience led to a revulsion against this type of warfare among postwar French leaders, especially Marshal Henri Pétain, who had opposed the prevailing offensive creed even before 1914 and commanded the French forces that stopped Germany's repeated attacks against the fortress city of Verdun in 1916. In the postwar era, he continued to champion defensive warfare and believed strongly in the ability of heavy artillery to destroy offensive formations as the French had done to the Germans at Verdun. British military leaders shared the French devotion to the defense. They also had undertaken massive offensives during World War I that had resulted in meager gains at a terrible price in lives. Like the French, they were repelled by this carnage.

But there was one lesson of World War I that most French and British generals had not learned—even though the defense had been supreme during most of the conflict, it was offensive power that eventually won the war. The Germans had failed to stop the Allied offensive during the summer and fall of 1918 and had fallen back steadily, although they had prevented a breakthrough. The Allies had employed large numbers of tanks in this operation. Unfortunately, these armored vehicles, ponderous and slow, had suffered heavy losses, convincing many French and British leaders that the tank would never be a decisive weapon.

Not all French and British military men were wedded to static defensive warfare in the postwar period, however. In France, General J. B. E. Estienne, the creator and leader of the French World War I tank force, believed that the key to the next war would be fast-striking offensive operations featuring large tank formations supported by aircraft. Estienne influenced a young colonel, Charles de Gaulle, who expounded similar views in a book he published in 1934. The politician Paul Reynaud shared their belief in the importance of mobile offensive warfare. Unfortunately, Estienne, de Gaulle, and Reynaud won few followers, and the static defensive mentality remained dominant. In Britain, General J. F. C. Fuller, who had served as chief of staff of the Royal Tank Corps in 1918, insisted that the tank, operating in large formations, was the weapon of the future. His most important convert was B. H. Liddell Hart, an infantry captain whose army career had ended when he was gassed during the Battle of the Somme. Liddell Hart developed the "expanding torrent" theory of deep, swift penetration by armored units as the key to breaking a static defensive line. But he was also a strong believer in defense and contended that powerful tank forces should be used in a defensive role to counterattack enemy offensive formations. Fuller and Liddell Hart failed to convince Britain's senior military leaders of the crucial role of armor, but Liddell Hart's views on the importance of defense served to reinforce the British defensive bias.

Ironically, it was the Germans who learned from the Western advocates of armored warfare. They had been slow to appreciate the value of the tank in World War I, but during the 1930s they created large armored (panzer) formations, which France and Britain ignored. The man most responsible for this transformation was Heinz Guderian, a relatively junior officer who did not become a general until 1938. While serving as an intelligence officer in World War I, Guderian had witnessed the appalling slaughter at Verdun. This experience convinced him that Germany must avoid the horrors of such static warfare in the future. During the 1920s, he fell under the influence of British advocates of armored warfare, especially Liddell Hart. Guderian concluded that powerful concentrations of fast-striking, well-armored, and heavily armed tanks, closely supported by aircraft and other motorized troops, would determine the outcome of the next conflict. Guderian found it difficult to overcome the resistance of the more conservative generals who held positions superior to his, but he did win Hitler's support as early as 1933. He published a book in 1937 that explained his theory of armored warfare and presented what amounted to a blueprint for the future *Blitzkrieg* (lightning war).

FIGURE 5-1 Adolf Hitler takes the salute of ecstatic Reichstag members after announcing the invasion of Poland. (*UPS/Bettmann Newsphotos*)

The intent of the *Blitzkrieg* was to gain victory as quickly, as decisively, and with as few German casualties as possible. To accomplish this, powerful panzer forces would smash through opposing border defenses and encircle large concentrations of enemy troops. "Motorized infantry," traveling in trucks or tracked personnel carriers, would follow behind the armor and consolidate the initial gains while the tanks dashed deeper into the interior. Next, the traditional mass of infantry, marching on foot, would relieve the motorized infantry, allowing it to keep pace with the panzers. Meanwhile, the Luftwaffe would destroy the enemy air force, ideally catching many planes on the ground. Once they had accomplished this, German aircraft would attack enemy communications and troop formations. Tanks, motorized infantry, and airpower would all work in harmony to crush the enemy.

But while the Germans staked their future on the *Blitzkrieg,* the French carried their defensive doctrine to its ultimate manifestation, the construction of the Maginot line, the greatest system of fixed fortifications ever built. France's shield against a German attack, the Maginot line consisted of massive concrete and steel forts housing guns of tremendous range and power, casements and pillboxes containing smaller guns, and shell- and bombproof underground facilities. Although the line was incredibly strong, it had one glaring weakness: it extended only from the Swiss frontier to a point just beyond the convergence of the borders of France, Luxembourg, and Belgium. Unfortunately, the likely route for a German invasion was through Belgium to the northwest of the Maginot line. This would enable the enemy to outflank its powerful fortifications.

Several factors contributed to the French failure to continue the line along the Belgian border to the sea. Such an extension would have been extremely expensive and would have run through heavily industrialized urban centers, creating a serious disruption of economic activity. The high water table in the extreme western portion of the border area also posed problems for underground construction. And France was concerned that the Belgians might consider the extension of the line an indication that the French would not aid their country against a German invasion but would merely wait behind their defenses. Finally, the French visualized the Maginot line as only a partial defense. In case of a German attack by way of Belgium, they intended to send troops to aid the Belgians. They hoped that these forces, anchored on the Maginot line to the south, would be sufficient to stop a German offensive before it reached French soil. By pursuing such a defensive strategy, France hoped to fight a war of "limited liability" and avoid a repetition of the horrible casualties of World War I.

Britain, too, had opted for a war of limited liability, to an even greater degree than France. The British armed forces clearly reflected this decision. As an island power, Britain's first line of defense was the Royal Navy, which, despite reduction in size during the interwar years, was still by far the largest in Europe. The Royal Air Force received second priority but only slowly increased in strength during the 1930s. The army came in a poor third, even after the introduction of conscription shortly before the outbreak of war. Although Britain sent an expeditionary force to France in the fall of 1939, it numbered only 250,000 men and contained just one armored division.

Despite his aggressive foreign policy and determination to take the offensive, Hitler actually had also committed Germany to a war of limited liability. He was confident that he could gain victory through a series of swift, decisive *Blitzkrieg* offensives that would not require full mobilization of the economy. Contrary to the view that prevailed in Britain and France, the Führer had not carried out a sweeping reorganization of the German economy; in reality, much of German industry still concentrated on the production of consumer goods.

Hitler believed that Germany could have both military success and many of the comforts of peacetime life. The Führer had chosen a policy of rearmament "in breadth." In other words, he wanted to provide the armed forces with sufficient weapons of various kinds to enable them to win a series of lightning campaigns. He did not anticipate a long war and thus did not favor an intense mobilization of the economy to provide rearmament "in depth." Such an approach would have concentrated first on expansion of Germany's heavy industry—a vast increase in steel production and construction of additional facilities to enable the manufacture of huge quantities of war materiel. A policy of this type would have necessitated postponing war until at least 1943 and would have assumed a lengthy conflict.

A PATCHWORK OF STRENGTHS AND WEAKNESSES

In 1936, Hitler established the Four-Year Plan, under Goering's leadership, aimed at making Germany as self-sufficient as possible and ready for war within four years. The plan had only indifferent success. It did not expand German industry; it merely brought existing production facilities up to full capacity. As for the proposed limited self-sufficiency, the results were disappointing. Hitler and Goering had hoped to make Germany independent in materials that the nation could produce. This would enable them to conserve foreign currency reserves for the purchase of raw materials that the Germans could not produce domestically and food. The Four-Year Plan emphasized production of synthetic materials. Goering projected that by 1939 German synthetic production would provide 100 percent of its oil needs and half of its rubber. But in 1939 it actually accounted for only 20 percent of Germany's oil and less than 15 percent of its rubber. Two-thirds of Germany's total raw materials still came from foreign countries. The Germans also had to import 20 percent of their food.

Germany did have some economic advantages, however. It had the potential to expand its industrial capabilities greatly if necessary, although this would clearly take time. With the absorption of Austria and the Sudetenland, Germany's population had reached 80 million, providing a good manpower pool for both industry and the armed forces. And the Russo-German economic agreement of August 1939 promised a steady flow of food, oil, and other raw materials. Hitler also expected to extract ample booty from the countries that fell under German control as a result of his *Blitzkrieg*.

Britain, with a population of 46 million, could not match Germany either in manpower or in its industrial base, but Britain did possess access to the resources of the rest of the world. The Commonwealth itself was a storehouse of raw materials. The British colony of Malaya alone produced 58 percent of the world's rubber. Britain, of course, could cut off Germany from overseas sources of supply by virtue of superior naval strength. Whether this would be sufficient to cause Germany critical problems was questionable in view of the 1939 Russo-German trade agreement. Hitler also had access to the resources of southeastern Europe, including Rumania's oil fields.

Britain's Achilles' heel was its dependence on large-scale imports of food and raw materials. To pay for them, the British had to maintain a high level of exports and services, such as shipping and insurance, as well as overseas investment. World War I had seriously disrupted all of these economic activities. Clearly, the outbreak of war in 1939 promised even more disastrous, perhaps fatal, injury to the failing economy. In view of this dilemma, it is not surprising that the British were reluctant to embark on an ambitious rearmament program during the 1930s. Although they finally accepted the need to make belated preparations for the likelihood of war, the results were far from impressive. The creation of new cabinet posts for supply, shipping, and food in 1939 helped lay the framework for a thoroughgoing war economy but led to little initial progress in this direction. Of more immediate importance, the British had begun to produce two excellent new fighter planes, the Hurricane and the Spitfire, which held out the promise of a greatly improved air defense.

France, too, suffered from economic problems. Like Britain, France in the late 1930s still felt the impact of the Great Depression. The French population of 42 million was much smaller than Germany's and even less than Britain's. France's industrial base was also much smaller than that of both countries, but the French had made some progress. Premier Daladier had appointed Paul Reynaud minister of finance in November 1938, and Reynaud had eased restrictions on investment credit and stimulated rearmament. Industrial production rose by 20 percent during the next ten months. It is indeed remarkable that France was able to enter the war on an equal basis with Germany in some respects, most notably in tanks and artillery. But the key to Anglo-French hopes for winning the war was time. If they could force Germany into a long war, their chances of victory would increase greatly. It soon became apparent, however, that time was a luxury that their alliance did not enjoy.

THE FIRST *BLITZKRIEG:* GERMANY'S INVASION OF POLAND

Germany first tested the *Blitzkrieg* in the invasion of Poland in September 1939, with spectacular results. The Poles never had a chance. Their antiquated army was at a great disadvantage in both men and equipment. The Germans committed 52 divisions (roughly 1 million men) to the campaign, including 6 panzer and 4 motorized divisions. German armor, for the most part, was not of high quality. The most numerous tank was the Panzer I, but its armament consisted of only two machine guns. The next most plentiful armored vehicle was the Panzer II, which carried a weak 20-millimeter cannon. Some higher-quality Panzer IIIs and Panzer IVs were available, but in small numbers. The Panzer III mounted a 37-millimeter gun, while the Panzer IV wielded a 75-millimeter weapon. In all, the Germans used 1,500 tanks, not a particularly large force, but together with their relatively few motorized divisions, it was more than sufficient to overwhelm the Poles.

On paper, Poland, with a population of 35 million, was capable of fielding an army of over 2 million men, but the Poles delayed mobilization until August 31 to avoid providing the Germans with an excuse for aggression. When the invasion began the following day, only 600,000 men were available. Most of this force consisted of infantry and cavalry. Poland's military leaders were exceptionally proud of their cavalry, but it was hardly a match for German armor. The Poles had only 310 tanks, most of them obsolete. They reduced their striking power still more by scattering them among infantry divisions. The Polish army had little else in the way of mechanized forces. Germany enjoyed a big advantage in air power, with 850 bombers and 400 fighters. Poland could muster a total of only 400 first-line planes, just 36 of which were modern.

Since the destruction of Czechoslovakia, German troops flanked Poland on three sides. This placed the Poles in a highly vulnerable position because they lacked the strength to defend the entire length of their borders. Logic seemed to dictate that Polish forces should take up positions to the east of the barrier created by the Narew, Vistula, and San rivers. But this would necessitate abandoning much of western Poland, including the country's most important industrial areas. Polish leaders refused to take such drastic action. Instead, they concentrated one-third of their strength in the general area of the Polish corridor and another third in reserve between the capital, Warsaw, and the industrial city of Lodz to the southwest. They stretched the rest of their forces dangerously thin to protect the remaining border areas.

Germany divided its invading forces into Army Group North, which included two armies under the command of General Fedor von Bock, and Army Group South, consisting of three armies commanded by General Gerd von Rundstedt. Bock and Rundstedt were both Prussian aristocrats and the sons of generals. Each had served capably during World War I. At 64, Rundstedt was the senior general in the German army and highly respected for his ability as a field commander. He had actually retired in 1938 but returned to active duty a few months later. Bock's most noteworthy qualities were determination and hard work rather than brilliance. An extremely arrogant man, he was utterly devoted to the army and contemptuous of civilians. General Halder's OKH staff drafted the operational plan for the invasion, which was given the code name

The German and Soviet Invasion of Poland, September 1939

Case White. It called for the destruction of the bulk of the Polish army to the west of Warsaw by means of a pincers movement in which elements of Army Group North would swing southeastward to link up with Army Group South, which was to strike northward. Additional troops from Army Group North were to smash across the base of the Polish corridor into East Prussia, cutting off the enemy forces to the north.

The *Blitzkrieg* began on September 1. German armored forces quickly broke through Poland's border defenses and penetrated deep into the interior. Meanwhile, the Luftwaffe annihilated the Polish air force within two days, most of it on the ground. This enabled the invading army to maneuver without threat of enemy air attacks while German medium bombers and Stuka dive bombers attacked Polish troops and communications. Although actually a mediocre plane with poor speed, flimsy armor, and limited range, the Stuka worked well in this type of unopposed operation. With its fixed landing gear, the Stuka resembled a bird of prey. It was outfitted with a siren that unleashed a shrill, blood-curdling shriek as it swooped down on its victims. These features added to its impact as a weapon of terror.

Germany's most remarkable progress came in the south, where an armored corps, commanded by General Erich Höpner, sliced northeastward, reaching the outskirts of Warsaw on September 8.

Another panzer corps, commanded by General Guderian, severed the Polish corridor and moved into Easst Prussia on September 3. The Poles fought gallantly but faced overwhelming odds. At times, when surrounded, Polish cavalry, armed with lances, actually charged German tanks rather than surrender. The outcome of such encounters was never in doubt. Confronted by these disasters, the Polish high command belatedly ordered a withdrawal of all remaining units to the Narew-Vistula-San river line.

The Germans received only one major scare. It came on September 9, when the Poles directed a determined counterattack against the flank of Rundstedt's forces to the west of Warsaw. But after heavy fighting, the Germans blunted the Polish thrust and drove on to meet Bock's forces pushing southward. This union encircled 170,000 Polish troops, completing the pincers movement outlined in Case White.

The final phase of the Polish campaign began on September 9. It took the form of another pincers movement, which closed near Brest-Litovsk on September 17 when Guderian's panzers, swinging southward from East Prussia, met armored forces, commanded by General Ewald von Kleist, that had dashed northward from southern Poland. On the same day, Russian troops attacked the beleaguered Poles from the east and quickly overran the remainder of the country. A total of 90,000 Polish troops escaped into Hungary and Rumania, many of them eventually making their way to France and Britain, from where they carried on the fight.

Polish resistance continued for some time at various isolated points, including Warsaw. After reaching the suburbs of the capital on September 8, the Germans soon discovered that the narrow confines of street fighting were not well suited for attacks by armor. They resorted instead to artillery and aerial bombardment and finally launched an infantry assault on September 26. The exhausted Polish garrison surrendered the following day. A few pockets of resistance held out in other parts of the country until early October.

The Germans had destroyed Poland with astonishing speed and thoroughness. But surprisingly, the Western Allies did not fully recognize the degree to which the *Blitzkrieg* had revolutionized warfare. They blamed Poland's inadequate military forces and faulty defensive plan for the disaster and assumed that it would be different when the Germans attacked in the west. The French began to have second thoughts about the potential of tanks, however, and hastily embarked on the creation of four armored divisions.

In keeping with their defensive strategy, France and Britain made no effort to stage an offensive against Germany while the *Blitzkrieg* was destroying Poland. The French launched only a minor probing action, which penetrated a few miles into the Saar before their troops withdrew to the safety of the Maginot line, despite the fact that Germany had only 25 weak reserve divisions in the west and a defensive system, the West Wall, which was far from complete and of negligible strength. But it was sufficient to impress the Western Powers, who persisted in calling it the Siegfried line after the legendary warrior of German mythology.

Ribbentrop and Soviet foreign minister Vyacheslav Molotov met on September 28 to partition Poland. The Soviet Union gained slightly more than half of the country and about a third of the population as well as the oil fields. Germany, though receiving a smaller amount of territory, acquired roughly two-thirds of the people, the major industrial centers, the mining regions, and the best farmland. Hitler annexed approximately half of his share, as well as Danzig, directly to Germany. He designated the remainder the "Government General" and kept it under total German domination. This arrangement gave the Germans slightly more territory than the secret protocol of August 23 had provided, but in return the Soviets received a free hand in Lithuania, which the original agreement had conceded to Germany.

Stalin had mixed emotions about the destruction of Poland. To be sure, the USSR had avoided involvement in the war against Germany and had gained over half of Poland and a claim to the

FIGURE 5-2 German tanks support advancing infantry in the Polish capital of Warsaw. (*AP/Wide World Photos*)

Baltic states. But the awesome display of German military power had disturbed the Soviet dictator. He quickly set out to create as much of a buffer zone between the Soviet Union and Germany as possible. In the next few weeks, he pressured Lithuania, Latvia, and Estonia into signing treaties that authorized the Russians to establish military, air, and naval bases on their territory.

A PHONY WAR OF REAL DANGER

In stark contrast to the horror of the *Blitzkrieg* in Poland, Western Europe remained strangely quiet during the first eight months of the war. This inactivity prompted observers to conclude that the conflict was really a fraud. Americans called it the "phony war." To the French it was the *drôle de guerre* (literally, "odd little war"), and to the Germans the *Sitzkrieg* (sitting war). But the war was not as phony as it appeared. Hitler, in fact, was determined to attack in the west in the fall of 1939 and quickly shifted his forces from Poland for this purpose.

The French fully expected the Germans to attack and placed their hope in the Maginot line and their other defensive forces. Britain's military leaders agreed that Germany would strike, but Chamberlain did not expect Hitler to launch a major offensive and felt that time was on the Allies' side. The prime minister believed that the war would hurt the German economy and lead to a collapse of civilian morale. He failed to recognize that Hitler was also fighting a war of limited liability that would not require full mobilization of the economy. Germany also negotiated a second and more far-reaching economic understanding with the Soviet Union soon after the conquest of Poland. The Soviets agreed to provide Germany with grain, oil, and other raw materials in return for manufactured goods, including armaments. The Russians also supplied the Germans with rubber, tin, and other commodities that they imported from Southeast Asia.

In line with Chamberlain's vision of the fragile nature of Germany's economy as well as traditional British policy, the Allies instituted a naval blockade. But the blockade proved less effective than in World War I because of Germany's economic relationship with the USSR. The Germans countered the blockade with submarine attacks on Allied shipping, but their U-boat fleet was too small at this time to be much more than a nuisance. The British also used the period of the "phony war" to strengthen the Royal Air Force, especially their fighter planes.

Brauchitsch, Halder, and other leading German generals were deeply concerned by Hitler's decision to attack in the west during the fall of 1939. They believed that Germany should remain on the defensive at least until spring. Under no circumstances could an offensive begin before November, and this would mean a winter campaign, which the generals viewed as an invitation to disaster. Brauchitsch and Halder protested against the proposed offensive, but Hitler asserted his authority and won the argument.

Hitler's intransigence led to a rebirth of the conspiracy against him that had flourished during the Sudetenland crisis only to go into eclipse as a result of his triumph at the Munich conference. Once again, members of the military agreed that they must remove Hitler from power for the good of Germany. This time they went so far as to plan his assassination. The conspiracy had its nerve center in the Abwehr (Armed Forces Intelligence) and its driving force in Colonel Hans Oster, an aide to Admiral Wilhelm Canaris, the Abwehr's chief. Canaris protected Oster in his efforts while keeping his distance from the actual plot. Oster gained the support of Halder, who again consented to lead a military coup following the assassination. In fact, for a time Halder carried a pistol in his pocket, intending to shoot Hitler, but he could not quite bring himself to kill an unarmed man.

As in 1938, Brauchitsch sympathized with the conspirators but refused to become directly involved. Other leading generals, including Bock and Rundstedt, also offered sympathy but declined to implicate themselves, contending that they were only soldiers, not politicians. But Halder, too, eventually lost his nerve, fearing discovery of the plot, and took no action. Indeed, as time passed, he became more optimistic about prospects for an offensive in the west. With his defection, the conspiracy failed for a second time.

Despite Hitler's insistence on an early offensive, bad weather forced repeated postponements, and in January 1940 an event occurred that cast doubt on the entire enterprise. A German courier plane, which carried documents pertaining to the plan of attack in the west, flew off course and made a forced landing in Belgium. Belgian authorities seized some of the documents before the Germans on board could destroy them. This bizarre episode caused confusion on both sides. The Allies could not decide whether the documents were genuine or a German trick. The Germans feared that the incident had compromised the security of their operation, and this concern, along with continuing bad weather, resulted in postponement of the offensive until May.

The capture of the documents also contributed to a decision to scrap the original invasion plan and adopt a substitute that proved infinitely superior and played a vital role in Germany's ultimate success. The old plan, code-named Case Yellow, did not promise a decisive result and held out the possibility of a renewal of the stalemate of 1914–18. It provided for primary concentration of strength, including most of the armor, in Army Group B, commanded by General von Bock. His forces were to drive through the Netherlands and Belgium into northern France before halting at the Somme River. Army Group A, under General von Rundstedt, was to drive through southern Belgium and Luxembourg in support of Bock's spearhead.

The revised plan for Case Yellow owed its inspiration primarily to General Erich von Manstein, Rundstedt's chief of staff. Cold in manner, hawklike in appearance, and extremely outspoken, Manstein won little acclaim for his personality, but he was undoubtedly the most brilliant of the German generals. Like Guderian, he had served at Verdun in 1916 and had developed a similar horror of static warfare. He offered his alternative plan as a means of avoiding a repetition of such a dilemma on the western front. It called for the spearhead of the offensive to be provided by Army Group A, which would receive additional strength, especially armor. Rundstedt's panzer forces were to drive through Luxembourg and southern Belgium and break into France near the fortress city of Sedan. Once they had accomplished this, they could pursue any of three options: swing eastward behind the Maginot line, drive toward Paris, or dash for the English Channel with the intention of cutting off Allied forces in northern France and Belgium. When the Germans finally launched their offensive in May 1940, they chose the third alternative, with amazingly successful results.

Manstein's plan also called for Bock's Army Group B to move through the Netherlands and northern Belgium as part of the overall forward movement and as a feint to lure the Allies into Belgium and away from the German spearhead. Brauchitsch and Halder originally resisted Manstein's plan as too bold. They feared an Allied counteroffensive against the German flank as Rundstedt's forces penetrated into northern France. But Hitler supported the idea. The Führer, in fact, was toying with a similar plan. His endorsement assured adoption of Manstein's variant of Case Yellow, which gained formal approval on March 15.

While the Germans debated the change in Case Yellow, the Allies put the finishing touches on their own plan, with which they intended to counter the expected attack. This was Plan D, or the Dyle Plan, referring to the Dyle River in Belgium. It provided for the advance of strong French and British forces to a line based on the Dyle and Meuse rivers in central Belgium. The Allies assumed that the main German attack would come, as in 1914 and as intended in the original Case Yellow plan, through the plains of northern Belgium. They dismissed the area of Luxembourg and southern Belgium as offering no serious threat because it contained the rugged Ardennes Forest. The French believed that armored forces could not maneuver successfully in this hilly, heavily wooded terrain. As a result, Plan D stipulated that the two strongest French armies and the British Expeditionary Force would advance to the Dyle and the Meuse in Belgium while two weaker French armies took up positions opposite the Ardennes. When Hitler unleashed his attack in May, the Allies thus unwittingly sent their best troops into the jaws of the German trap and left second-rate forces in the path of Rundstedt's spearhead.

While these developments were taking place in the opposing headquarters, the "phony war" continued along the Franco-German border. There were good reasons for inactivity. The Allies were waiting for the German offensive, and the Germans, while planning to attack during the fall and winter, were unable to do so because of the weather and the change in plan. Neither side could see any point in border skirmishes that would cause casualties without being decisive.

6

Complications in the North: Finland, Denmark, Norway

While the *Sitzkrieg* was in progress on the western front, world attention focused on northeastern Europe, where a new conflict erupted.

THE RUSSO-FINNISH WAR

The Russo-Finnish War (Winter War) raged from November 30, 1939 to March 14, 1940. Though something of a side show, it had some important effects. The hostilities resulted from Finland's refusal to grant certain concessions that the Soviet Union demanded in the fall of 1939.

These demands reflected Stalin's fear that Finland might fall under German influence. Leningrad, Russia's second largest city, lay only 20 miles from the Finnish border on the Karelian Isthmus, a narrow neck of land that separated the Gulf of Finland on the west from Lake Ladoga on the east. It was within range of Finnish artillery. The Soviets insisted that the Finns cede a portion of the Karelian Isthmus to Russia, thus freeing Leningrad from the threat of artillery bombardment. This revision would have left Finland's chief defensive system, the Mannerheim line, in Finnish hands. The Soviets also requested other changes, including a 30-year lease on the port of Hangö for use as a Russian naval base. Hangö was less than 100 miles from Helsinki, the Finnish capital. In return for these concessions, Moscow offered to give Finland twice as much territory to the north of Lake Ladoga.

The Finns agreed to most of the Soviet demands but refused the Hangö lease, contending that it was incompatible with their independence and neutrality to allow a foreign base on their territory. Some Finnish leaders considered the Russian position reasonable, however, and later maintained that the war could have been avoided if Finland had agreed.

Stalin responded to the Finnish refusal by sending an initial force of 30 divisions and six tank brigades across the border against a total of only nine Finnish divisions. Before the campaign ended, the Russians committed a total of 45 divisions. An overwhelming Soviet victory seemed certain. But the Russians had not anticipated their own bungling or the astonishingly heroic and effective Finnish resistance under the leadership of 72-year-old Field Marshal Carl von Mannerheim. Mannerheim had actually begun his career as a cavalry officer in the army of the Russian czar, seeing action in both the Russo-Japanese War and World War I. But he took advantage of Russia's weakness in 1918 to lead Finland to independence and defeated the Soviet-backed Red forces in a Finnish civil war. As chairman of the Council of National Defense in 1933, he was responsible for constructing the fortifications that bore his name.

FIGURE 6-1 Finnish ski troops move forward on the Karelian Isthmus front. (*National Archives*)

Finnish troops not only halted the Russian offensive but actually annihilated five Soviet divisions. The Russians had committed the blunder that the Germans had managed to avoid on the western front—an attack in the dead of winter. Although the Mannerheim line was not especially strong and many of its defenses were obsolete, the Red Army encountered difficulty with the forests, swamps, and lakes that abounded in the Karelian Isthmus, and its efforts to achieve a breakthrough failed miserably.

But far greater disasters befell the Russians when they attacked at several points to the north of Lake Ladoga in areas characterized by dense forests, thousands of lakes, few roads, and heavy snow. Soviet commanders failed to safeguard their supply lines and ordered their troops deep into the frozen wastes. Russian mechanized forces, which were quite unsuited for this type of warfare, had to move forward on the few crude tracks that passed for roads. They became strung out in long columns extending for many miles that offered inviting targets for Finnish troops wearing white uniforms and operating on skis. The Finns cut Soviet supply lines and proceeded to ambush and annihilate the isolated enemy forces. Russian troops also suffered terribly from the cold as temperatures fell as low as 50 degrees below 0 Celsius. They even lacked "trigger finger" mittens and had to bare their hands to fire their weapons. When the Finnish attacks ended, thousands of frozen Russian corpses littered the roads and forests of eastcentral Finland.

By early January 1940, it was clear that the Russian juggernaut had failed. Stalin now appointed Marshal Semyon Timoshenko to command the Finnish front and invested him with responsibility for resurrecting the battered Soviet cause. A Ukrainian, Timoshenko had served as a noncommissioned officer in the czarist army during World War I but became a Red Army officer in the Russian civil war. Though not a brilliant commander, he was far superior to the inept Marshal Klementi Voroshilov, one of Stalin's close associates, who had directed the abortive operations against Finland in December. Timoshenko abandoned the ill-advised attacks north of Lake Ladoga and concentrated on breaking through the Mannerheim line. He carried out a massive buildup throughout January and finally opened his offensive on February 11. The Russians outnumbered the Finns 50 to 1 and had an enormous advantage in equipment. They subjected the Finnish defenses to the most intensive artillery bombardment since the Battle of Verdun and pushed slowly forward. By early March, they had broken through the Mannerheim line. The Finns, realizing that they were at the end of their resources and fearing an imminent Soviet drive on Helsinki, asked for an armistice on March 12. All fighting ceased two days later.

The peace terms were more severe than the original Russian demands. Most important, they required the Finns to cede the entire Karelian Isthmus as well as all their other territory along the shores of Lake Ladoga. Finland also granted the lease on Hangö. But the Soviet Union, a great power of 175 million people, had little reason for jubilation. Though ultimately victorious, it had suffered repeated humiliations at the hands of a nation of barely 4 million. Respect for Soviet military capacity plummeted dramatically throughout the world. Hitler, who had been dubious about Russian power all along, was now convinced that his neighbor to the east was no match for the Wehrmacht. The Winter War contributed significantly to his underestimation of the USSR as an enemy a year later.

The Finnish campaign had an important by-product—the opening of all of Scandinavia as a potential theater of operations. British and French leaders were filled with admiration for the gallant Finnish resistance and actually contemplated sending a small military force to help Finland. They also pondered other means of striking at the Russians, including a proposal to bomb the oil fields of the Caucasus Mountains. In view of the Western Powers' reluctance to take military action to help Poland, it is really quite astonishing that they should have considered such an ambitious and foolhardy undertaking on behalf of Finland. It would have meant war with the USSR at the same time that the Allies faced the threat of a German offensive in the west. Furthermore, such limited aid would not have made the slightest difference in the final outcome of the Winter War. The Allied attitude revealed the extent of anti-Soviet feeling in both Britain and France.

If they were to provide direct assistance to Finland, the Allies needed to secure passage for their troops through neighboring Norway and Sweden, but the Norwegians and Swedes refused to grant permission. The Allies' interest in Scandinavia extended beyond their desire to aid the Finns, however. They also planned to occupy the mines of northern Sweden, which provided the Germans with high-grade iron ore vital to their war effort. Much of the ore reached Germany from the port of Lulea on the Gulf of Bothnia, an arm of the Baltic, but the gulf froze during the winter, necessitating shipments by rail to Narvik on Norway's Atlantic coast. From Narvik, the precious ore went by ship through the Norwegian Leads, a sheltered passage between the highly indented coast and the open sea. Winston Churchill, Britain's first lord of the admiralty, had urged the mining of the Leads to interfere with German ore shipments as early as September 1939.

FOCUS ON SCANDINAVIA

Although the conclusion of the Winter War ended the possibility of sending troops to Finland, Churchill and other Allied leaders persisted in plans to mine the Leads. They also assumed that such action would provoke Hitler to undertake an invasion of Norway, and at the first indication of this, they planned to occupy Narvik and the other major ports on Norway's Atlantic coast. But in all of their various schemes for intervention in Scandinavia, the Allies seriously underestimated the number of troops they would need to carry out such an operation. They were also skeptical of Germany's ability to invade Norway successfully in the face of superior British naval power. Britain especially assumed that the Germans could not risk operations against Norway's Atlantic seaboard but would simply send their invasion fleet across the Skagerrak, the relatively narrow body of water between Denmark and Norway.

Hitler worried about Allied intentions in Scandinavia during the Winter War and became especially concerned about the potential disruption of Swedish iron ore shipments to Germany. In De-

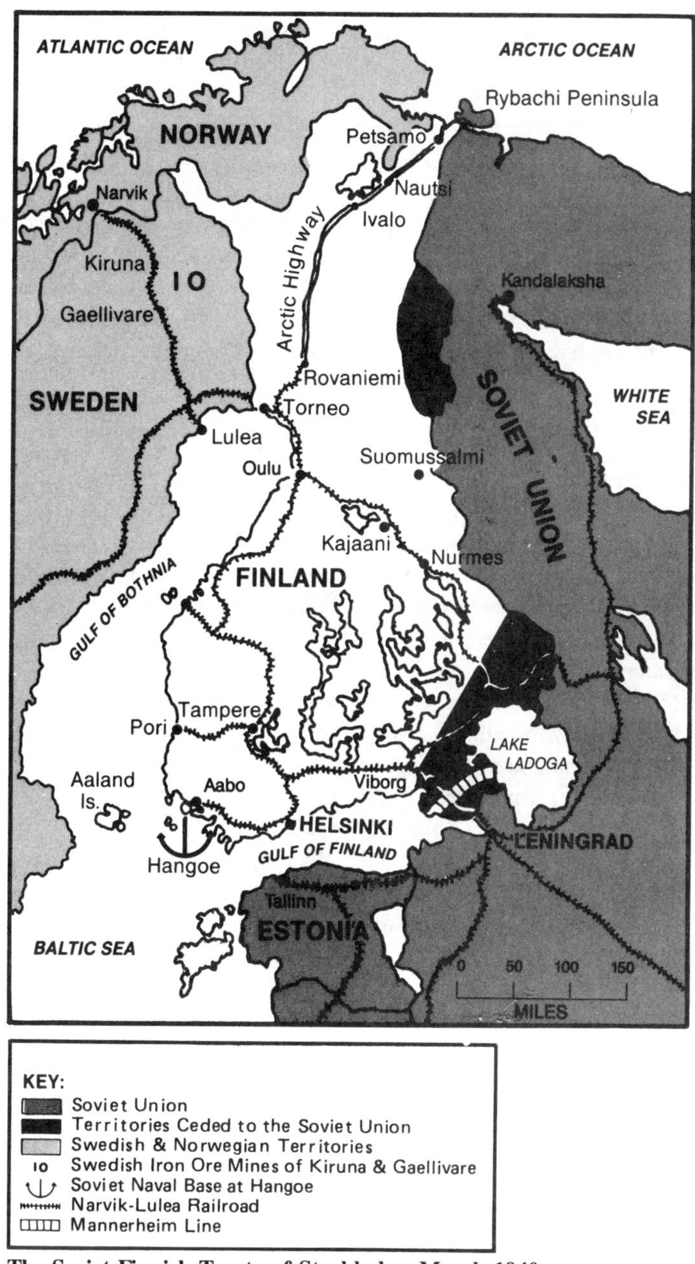

The Soviet-Finnish Treaty of Stockholm, March 1940

cember, he ordered preliminary planning for the possibility of a preemptive German invasion of not only Norway but Denmark as well. He decided to include Denmark because it lay between Germany and Norway and possessed important airfields that could be used in connection with an attack on Norway.

An incident occurred in February that helped persuade Hitler that a Scandinavian operation was necessary. On the night of February 16, the

British destroyer *Cossack* intercepted the German tanker *Altmark* in Norwegian territorial waters. A party from *Cossack* boarded *Altmark* and rescued 300 British prisoners, the survivors from a number of ships that the German surface raider *Graf Spee* had sunk during the first few months of the war. *Graf Spee*'s commander had transferred the prisoners to *Altmark*. The *Altmark* affair convinced Hitler that Britain would not respect Norwegian neutrality. Two days later, he ordered invasion preparations to be accelerated, and on March 1 he issued a formal directive for an attack on Denmark and Norway.

Hitler gave the OKW sole responsibility for the Scandinavian enterprise, and the OKH had no part in its development. It was the only major German campaign of the war that combined land, sea, and air operations and in which the navy played a decisive role. Hitler appointed General Nikolaus von Falkenhorst, who had commanded a corps in the Polish campaign, to direct the invasion. He chose Falkenhorst because the general had served in Finland for a few months in 1918. Although this hardly made Falkenhorst an expert on Scandinavia, it was enough for Hitler. With the bulk of German strength earmarked for the invasion of Western Europe in May, Falkenhorst had only limited forces at his disposal. But he used them boldly and skillfully when the Scandinavian operation began on April 9.

THE CONQUEST OF DENMARK AND NORWAY

Denmark's meager army of 15,000 men was no match for the Germans, who caught the Danes completely by surprise, despite the fact that Danish agents in Germany had provided their government with warnings of an impending attack. Danish officials failed to take them seriously, and the Germans overran the country in a matter of hours. Norwegian leaders in Oslo refused to believe similar warnings, and once again the Germans enjoyed the advantage of surprise when they landed in Norway. The Norwegian defensive forces were small and seriously deficient in modern equipment, especially aircraft. They were also totally lacking in experience because Norway had never fought a war since becoming independent from Sweden in 1905.

The invasion of Norway was an extremely risky undertaking. It involved transporting troops not only across the Skagerrak but into the Atlantic as well in the face of British naval supremacy. The German plan called for landings at all major Norwegian ports—Oslo and Kristiansand on the Skagerrak and Bergen, Stavanger, Trondheim, and Narvik on the Atlantic coast. Allied naval units had laid mines in Norwegian coastal waters the day before the invasion and were still nearby. The British could also intervene with their home fleet, which was stationed at Scapa Flow to the north of Scotland. In addition, they maintained a small military force that was to seize Norway's major Atlantic ports if the Germans showed any indication of retaliating for the British minelaying operation.

When the Germans actually launched their invasion fleet, British planes spotted German naval forces heading northward as early as the morning of April 7. But when the home fleet sailed seven hours later, its commander decided to leave the military force behind despite the plan to seize the Norwegian ports. British naval units were also uncertain of the exact location or destinations of the German invasion forces. To make matters worse, a savage storm impeded their search for the elusive enemy. Although elements of the rival fleets engaged in isolated skirmishes, no all-out battle took place, and the Royal Navy did not seriously interfere with the German landings.

Speed, precision timing, and luck all contributed to Germany's success. The OKW scheduled each landing to take place at approximately the same time. The first troops to land traveled on fast warships, which penetrated quickly into each port, and disembarked in most cases before the Norwegians could react. Reinforcements followed in slower transports. The initial invasion forces did not total more than 10,000 men, and the largest number at any one port was approximately 2,000. The Germans did not use panzer units, which were not well suited for the moun-

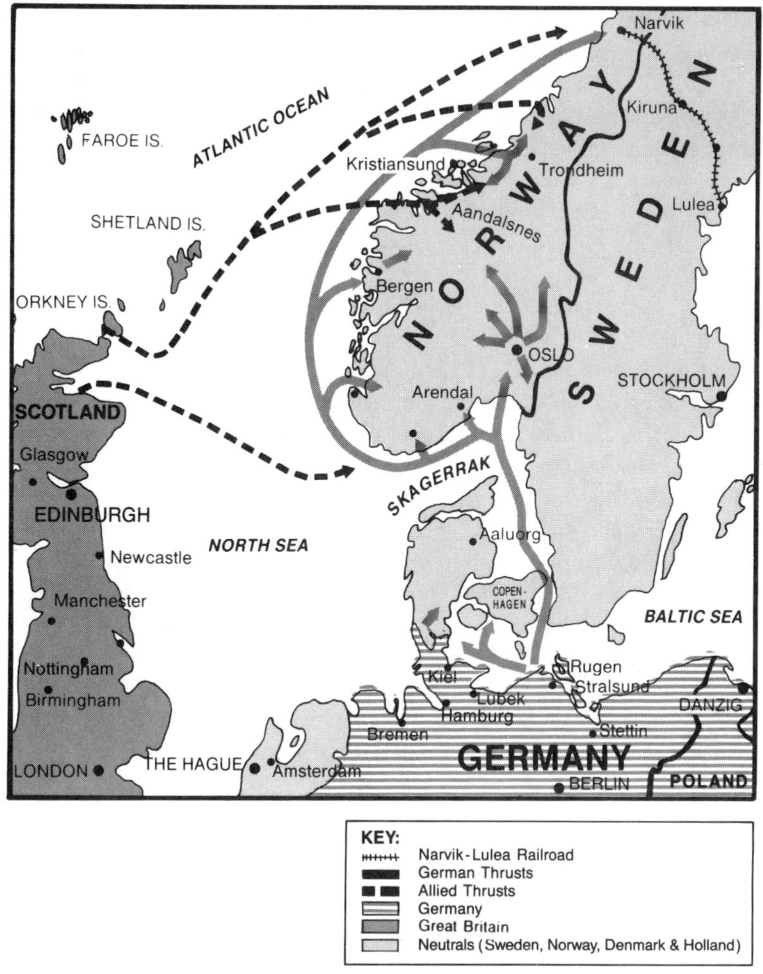

The German Invasion of Denmark and Norway, April 9, 1940

tainous Norwegian terrain. But they did employ small numbers of tanks to support the infantry, and the armor performed well in this role.

The only serious threat to the invasion came at Oslo, where for a time the fate of the entire operation seemed to hang in the balance. Oslo lay at the northern end of Oslofjord, the body of water that linked the capital with the Skagerrak. At the fjord's narrowest point, the old but formidable Oscarsborg fort guarded the approach to Oslo with 11-inch guns and torpedo defenses. These weapons combined to sink the new German cruiser *Blücher* when the invasion flotilla attempted to penetrate beyond the Oscarsborg. Confronted by this disaster, the other German ships turned back and disembarked their troops about 20 miles from Oslo.

The success of the assault now depended on a projected airborne seizure of the airfield outside the capital. Once the Germans had accomplished this, they planned to strengthen their initial force with troops ferried in by transport planes. But fog over southern Norway prevented them from carrying out the airborne operation. If the Norwegians had made a vigorous attempt to defend the capital and its airfield at this crucial point, they might have badly disrupted the German timetable. Instead, they abandoned the city without a fight. A small unit did try to hold the airfield, but a few German fighter planes managed to land, and the pilots, using their machine guns, held the defenders at bay until transports arrived with reinforcements. These troops quickly marched on Oslo and occupied the city.

Oslo was the key to the invasion. The Germans quickly moved out from the capital to link up with troops at the other ports, who were simply to hold their positions until the relief expeditions arrived. With the exception of the force at Narvik, all carried out their missions successfully. Narvik lay too far north. In the days following the landing there, British destroyers sank eight German destroyers and gained complete control of the neighboring waters. British troops landed near the town on April 14, but their commander proceeded with excessive caution, and they did not force the Germans out of Narvik until May 28. By then the Norwegian campaign was almost over.

Anglo-French forces also landed at two small ports in the general area of Trondheim—Namsos 125 miles to the north on April 14 and Åndalsnes 100 miles to the south three days later. They hoped to capture Trondheim and gain control of central Norway. But they launched this enterprise much too late and with a lamentable lack of planning. Although the Allies originally outnumbered the Germans in the Trondheim area by 13,000 to 2,000, they lacked heavy equipment, including artillery and tanks. The French found it particularly embarrassing when they had to leave most of their equipment aboard a cruiser that proved too long to penetrate into the small harbor at Namsos. The Allies were also well beyond the range of fighter planes based in Britain. The Germans, by contrast, used transport planes to reinforce their Trondheim garrison and provided strong tactical air support for their forces in the field.

Trondheim now became the key to Norway's fate. The Allies hoped to dislodge the German garrison by a pincers movement from north and south. It was not to be. They had to divert British forces from Åndalsnes to aid hard-pressed Norwegian troops that were trying to prevent the Germans from penetrating up two narrow valleys to-

FIGURE 6-2 German troops take shelter behind a tank during the Norwegian campaign. (*National Archives*)

ward Trondheim. But the British proved much too weak, and the Luftwaffe pounded the Allied troops mercilessly. Superior German strength forced them to fall back on Åndalsnes. Meanwhile, Allied units pushing south from Namsos toward Trondheim made little progress due to the mountainous terrain and heavy snow cover. It proved necessary to evacuate all British and French troops from the two little ports early in May. Despite continued fighting in the Narvik area, the campaign was virtually over. The British evacuation from Narvik early in June sealed the Allied defeat.

The "ramshackle Norwegian campaign," as Churchill called it, had revealed woeful deficiencies in Allied strategic planning and tactical execution. German forces, in their first real engagement against the British and French, had outthought, out-maneuvered, and out-fought their enemies. The entire Allied effort had been "too little, too late." It was widely believed at the time that the disaster had been due largely to wholesale treachery among the Norwegians themselves—the so-called Fifth Column led by Vidkun Quisling, a man whose name became synonymous with *traitor.* This was not true. To be sure, Quisling, the leader of a Nazi-type political party, had visited Berlin in December 1939 and had invited Hitler to take over his native land. But the Führer had not seen fit to take him into his confidence regarding the projected invasion, and Quisling was as surprised as any other Norwegian when the Germans actually struck. Quisling did move quickly to set up a collaborationist government in Oslo, but his regime proved so distasteful to most Norwegians that Hitler, after a brief flirtation, withdrew his support.

Germany had won another startling victory, adding to the developing myth of Wehrmacht invincibility. The triumph also secured concrete advantages for Germany. It removed any threat to the nation's northern flank and safeguarded access to Swedish iron ore. Germany had sealed off Sweden from the west, and the Swedes were in no position to be other than obliging suppliers of Germany's needs. The conquest of Norway also provided bases from which German bombers, submarines, and surface raiders could attack British ships. Finally, it hampered the British naval blockade by greatly expanding the area of water that the Royal Navy had to patrol

The campaign was not without its disadvantages for Germany, however. Most crucially, the German navy suffered serious losses, including the sinking of half its 20 destroyers and three of its eight cruisers. In addition, Germany's two battle cruisers, *Scharnhorst* and *Gneisenau,* and the pocket battleship *Lützow* were disabled for months. Some observers have argued since the war that had these naval forces been available after the fall of France, they would have greatly enhanced German prospects for an invasion of Britain. But in view of Britain's continued naval supremacy and the threat posed by British air power, it is doubtful that the addition of these ships would have been a critical factor in enabling the Germans to cross the English Channel.

7

The Fall of France

Hitler launched his long-awaited offensive in the west on May 10, while the Norwegian campaign was still in progress. The Wehrmacht put Manstein's variant of Case Yellow into effect, and the Allies responded with Plan D. The result was a spectacular success for the Germans, who smashed their enemies with such speed and ease that even they were astonished.

COMPARATIVE MILITARY STRENGTH

Germany's overwhelming triumph led to the widespread belief that its forces were much stronger in numbers and equipment than those of the Allies. This was not true, at least not at the start of the campaign or in regard to all types of equipment. The Germans had 136 divisions on the western front, but they assigned 19 of these to General Wilhelm Ritter von Leeb's Army Group C, which remained in a defensive position opposite the Maginot line. This left 117 divisions, including 42 that the OKH held in reserve. Seventy-five divisions took part in the initial assault. Of these, 30 comprised Bock's Army Group B and 45 formed Rundstedt's Army Group A. Allied strength totaled 144 divisions: 101 French, 11 British, 22 Belgian, and 10 Dutch. These troops varied in quality, however, and were under four separate commands, although the British and French maintained considerable cooperation between their forces. France also tied down 36 divisions in the Maginot line, which the Germans did not attack until it was hopelessly outflanked. The Allies, nevertheless, committed 81 divisions to meet the attack.

One of the great myths, which persisted throughout the war, was the belief that Germany enjoyed vast superiority in armor. The French estimated that the Germans possessed as many as 7,500 tanks, but in reality they had only 2,500, well over half of them inferior Panzer I and Panzer II models. The remainder consisted of relatively small numbers of Panzer III and Panzer IV models and about 350 Czech tanks similar to the Panzer III. France had about as many tanks as Germany, perhaps more. Many of them, especially the Somua medium tank and the Char B-1 heavy tank, were superior in armor and firepower, although they tended to be slower and had a limited range and poor communications. Britain had almost 300 tanks in France, including the Matilda, which was better armed and armored than any German tank except the Panzer IV. The fatal flaw was the Allied failure to concentrate their tanks in armored divisions. Instead, they parceled out most of them in support of infantry. The Germans, of course, used their tanks in armored units. Bock had three panzer divisions as well as one motorized division in Army Group B. Rundstedt's Army Group A deployed seven panzer and three motorized divisions, which formed the powerful spearhead of the German attack.

Most historians of the 1940 campaign have contended that Germany completely outclassed France in the air. Recent research indicates that this is somewhat misleading. In fact, the French possessed a total of 4,360 planes to 3,270 for the Germans, and for the most part France's fighters and bombers were comparable to or better than those of the enemy. Unfortunately, France deployed only one-fourth of its air strength against Germany. This was due in large part to a shortage of both air and ground crews. A prolonged disagreement between leaders of the armed forces over the mission of France's air power contributed to this problem. The army insisted on close tactical support of ground troops, but the air force favored a strategic role, stressing long-range heavy bombers. Guy La Chambre, who held the post of air minister from 1938 to 1940, agreed with the army and ordered preparations for the development of such a tactical force. But the air leaders failed to cooperate in implementing this policy. Thus when the Germans struck in 1940, the French had only 583 fighters and 84 bombers actually assigned to the northeastern front. The remainder were in the process of being reequipped or were stationed in France's colonies. Additional Allied strength, most of it British, included 197 fighters and 192 bombers. But the Royal Air Force held back the bulk of its aircraft for the defense of Britain. Under the circumstances, the Luftwaffe did enjoy a considerable advantage with 1,264 fighters and 1,504 bombers.

THE POLITICS OF MILITARY LEADERSHIP

France also suffered from a cumbersome army leadership structure. General Maurice Gamelin was the supreme commander of land forces. He had gained his reputation during World War I, first as chief of operations for Marshal Joffre, the French commander in chief during the first two years of the conflict, and later as a capable divisional commander. Though highly intelligent, he tended to be overly contemplative and indecisive. Gamelin also had a low regard for the potential of Germany's panzer forces. Despite his lofty position, Gamelin delegated operational control of the forces in northeastern France to General Alphonse Georges, who made most of the actual decisions. Georges had served as a staff officer in World War I and in a variety of staff and command positions during the interwar years. He still suffered from severe wounds inflicted by the same assassin who had killed King Alexander of Yugoslavia and French Foreign Secretary Barthou in 1934. Many French and British officers believed that Georges would have made a better supreme commander than Gamelin. The division of authority between Gamelin and Georges created confusion, and to make matters worse, the two men disliked each other. Communications between their respective headquarters were totally inadequate, and Gamelin was often ignorant of the exact situation at the front.

Both France and Britain faced the German offensive under new political leadership. Premier Daladier had provoked a crisis in the French parliament because of his failure to aid the Finns during the Winter War and had resigned in March. His successor was Paul Reynaud, whose voice had been one of those crying in the wilderness during the 1930s regarding France's need for armored divisions. A courageous, combative, and independent politician of small stature and somewhat Asian appearance, Reynaud had also criticized French foreign policy prior to the war. He had urged more vigorous measures against Germany and, as finance minister since 1938, had been largely responsible for increasing arms production. Unfortunately, Reynaud lacked a large personal following in parliament, while Daladier continued to have a strong base of support. Reynaud needed to maintain Daladier's backing and felt compelled to keep him in the cabinet as minister of war even though the two men detested each other.

In Britain, Chamberlain also ran into trouble with Parliament as a result of his handling of the

Norwegian campaign and resigned on the very day that the Germans attacked in the west. The new prime minister, Winston Churchill, was a descendant of the famous Duke of Marlborough, who had won glory in the early eighteenth century as one of Britain's greatest generals. Churchill had been prominent in British politics for four decades. He had held a variety of important cabinet posts, including first lord of the admiralty early in World War I. But Churchill had spent most of the 1930s as a political outcast, at first as the result of his opposition to the government's plan to extend limited self-government to India. Later he compounded his unpopularity by his outspoken criticism of Chamberlain's appeasement policy, especially the Munich agreement. But when the policy ended in failure with the outbreak of war in 1939, Churchill won vindication, and Chamberlain appointed him to his former position at the admiralty. Blessed with boundless self-confidence and determination as well as great charisma, a quicksilver mind, and a restless imagination, Churchill clearly had the potential to be a far better wartime leader than Chamberlain.

But the circumstances that prompted the change were ironic because Churchill, more than anyone else, had favored Allied intervention in Norway and, as first lord of the admiralty, held ultimate responsibility for the Royal Navy's failure to prevent the German invasion. At first, Churchill's position was similar to Reynaud's. He had no large parliamentary following of his own, while Chamberlain actually remained leader of Churchill's Conservative party and continued in the cabinet with effective control over domestic policy until October.

Reynaud had great contempt for General Gamelin. As he put it, Gamelin "might be all right as a prefect or a bishop, but he is not a leader of men." He was so dissatisfied with the army commander's conduct of the Norwegian campaign that he tried to dismiss him early in May. But Daladier and others in the cabinet opposed this action, and Reynaud resigned in disgust on May 9. During this crisis, Gamelin learned of Reynaud's criticism, and he, too, resigned. Thus when the Germans attacked the next day, France technically had neither a government nor an army commander in chief. Under the circumstances, both men withdrew their resignations.

Gamelin shared the belief that the Ardennes Forest was not a dangerous sector and was determined to send Allied troops deeply into Belgium, if and when Germany attacked. The general clung to this intention despite intelligence reports that indicated as early as March that the Germans were building up strength along the border opposite the Ardennes. He refused to take any measures to stiffen his forces in this area even after receiving a warning on April 30 that the enemy would strike through the Ardennes, with Sedan as the main objective, during the period May 8–10.

SWEEP THROUGH THE LOW COUNTRIES

Hitler unleashed his *Blitzkrieg* in the early hours of May 10, striking the Netherlands, Belgium, and Luxembourg simultaneously and making rapid progress everywhere. The Dutch were no match for Bock's Army Group B and received little aid from the Allies. Germany completely dominated the air over the Netherlands and made extensive use of paratroops to capture bridges over the many rivers and canals, key to the Dutch defense system. Knifing through the country, the Germans forced the Dutch to capitulate within five days. An especially ugly incident occurred while negotiations were under way for the surrender of Rotterdam, the Netherlands' leading port. German bombers leveled the center of the defenseless city and killed 980 civilians. This raid became symbolic of German ruthlessness, but it now appears that due to a breakdown in communications, the Luftwaffe units involved actually were not aware that the surrender talks were taking place.

Bock's attack on Belgium encountered fiercer resistance because the Belgian army was larger and its defenses stronger than those of the Dutch.

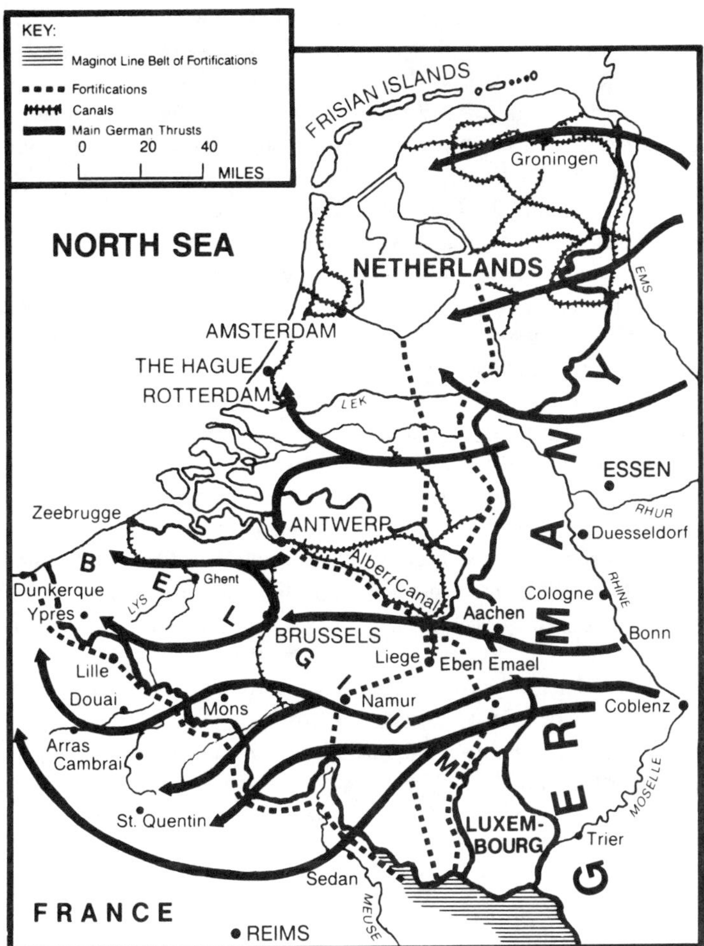

The German Invasion of Holland, Belgium, and Luxembourg, and the Penetration of the French Northern Defense Line, May 10–20, 1940

The Germans made rapid progress, nevertheless, and their capture of the supposedly impregnable Fort Eben Emael on the Albert Canal in eastern Belgium was especially impressive. An airborne force of only 85 men, transported by gliders, landed unmolested on the spacious and undefended roof of the fortress. The Belgian garrison totaled 750 men, but all of them were inside the fort. Once the Germans had consolidated their position, they used special explosive charges to blow up the guns and neutralize the defenders. Soon afterward, Bock's main forces pushed through to link up with the airborne troops and then advanced to the Dyle.

Meanwhile, French and British forces swept rapidly into Belgium to their prearranged positions along the Dyle and Meuse rivers. As a result, they had unwittingly placed themselves in a perfect position to be outflanked by Rundstedt's Army Group A. Three panzer corps, which formed Rundstedt's spearhead, slammed through Luxembourg and the Belgian Ardennes in two days against slight resistance. By May 13, each of them had crossed the Meuse in northern

France and by nightfall had torn open a gap 50 miles wide in the French front. Panic on the part of some French troops and hasty orders to withdraw from the Meuse contributed to the German success. The southernmost and strongest of the panzer corps, commanded by Guderian, made the crucial crossing near Sedan. Three well-trained and experienced panzer divisions attacked just one second-class French infantry division composed of inadequately prepared and poorly equipped reservists. The French assumed that the Germans would not try to cross the Meuse until their artillery arrived. Rather than wait, however, Guderian ordered repeated attacks by medium bombers and Stukas, which pinned down and demoralized the defenders, allowing German infantrymen to cross the river in rubber boats. They secured a bridgehead, and soon afterward, engineers constructed a pontoon bridge that enabled Guderian's tanks to cross and exploit the breakthrough.

Guderian's armor now dashed toward the sea and reached the Channel coast on May 20 near the mouth of the Somme, trapping the Allied forces in Belgium and northern France. Progress would have been even more rapid had it not been for the fears of Guderian's immediate superior, General von Kleist, that he was advancing too fast and might be cut off by French counterattacks. Kleist ordered him to halt briefly on two occasions to allow the following infantry to catch up to the panzers or at least narrow the gap. Descended from a long line of generals in a famous old Prussian military family, Kleist was a former cavalry officer who had not yet come to terms with the swift pace of armored warfare. Even Hitler, who had demonstrated an uncharacteristic lack of nerve in the aftermath of the breakthrough, urged caution, as did General von Rundstedt. But the French mounted little in the way of serious counterattacks, largely because of the speed of Guderian's advance and their own commitment of so many troops to Belgium and the Maginot line. They did attack with their few armored divisions but committed them on a piecemeal basis, which diluted their striking power. The Germans destroyed them one by one.

As Guderian closed the trap on the Allies, Bock's troops forced them to abandon the Dyle line and retreat into western Belgium. The Allies found themselves in a steadily shrinking pocket between the two German army groups. They searched desperately for some way to break through the encirclement, but all their efforts failed. Three alternatives now confronted them: surrender, continue fighting until annihilated, or attempt to evacuate as many troops as possible by sea. Ultimately they chose the third option, largely at the insistence of General Lord Gort, the British commander, who recognized long before the other Allied leaders that this was the only way to escape from the trap.

During World War I, Gort had gained a reputation for bravery that few could approach, being wounded four times and winning the Victoria Cross, Britain's highest military decoration. He had served as chief of the Imperial General Staff before taking over leadership of the British Expeditionary Force (BEF) in 1939. Although his fellow officers considered him a man of the highest integrity, many of them believed that he was out of his depth in commanding a large force. But Gort proved to be the savior of the BEF when, on his own initiative, he ordered his troops to fall back toward the English Channel on May 23.

Some authorities, including Gort himself, later contended that he made his decision largely because of intelligence reports that indicated that the Germans planned to sweep behind the BEF and cut it off from the Channel. The British, with major assistance from the Poles, had broken the German military cipher, which enabled them to read intercepted enemy radio messages. This achievement became the best-kept secret of the war and earned the code name Ultra. Confident that their cipher could not be broken, German leaders never realized what had happened.

Ultra reports may have reinforced Gort's decision to retreat, but it appears that he reacted primarily to the obvious German threat and the deteriorating position of the Belgian army, which supported his left flank. Although Ultra proved tremendously valuable later in the war, it was in its infancy and of marginal importance at this time. Churchill, who was slower to recognize the seriousness of the Allied dilemma, did not formally authorize a withdrawal until three days after Gort's decision to fall back toward the sea.

The Allies' chances of a successful evacuation did not appear promising. Guderian, after reaching the coast, turned north toward the French Channel ports—Boulogne, Calais, and Dunkirk. He hoped to take all three by a quick thrust. Elements of his force rapidly surrounded Boulogne and Calais while others moved toward Dunkirk, but on May 24 Rundstedt ordered him to halt his armor less than 15 miles from his destination. Guderian, Brauchitsch, and Halder all protested, but Hitler supported Rundstedt's decision. He also assigned to Bock's troops, with their preponderance of infantry, the task of capturing Dunkirk despite the fact that they were over twice as far away from the city as Guderian's faster-moving tanks.

This decision became one of the most controversial of the entire war. Some critics have charged that Hitler halted the armor in a deliberate effort to allow the British to escape, hoping that their gratitude for this favor would result in a willingness to make peace. But this argument does not square with the facts, especially since Rundstedt, not Hitler, originated the order. It appears more likely that both Rundstedt and Hitler were convinced that the Allies could not carry out a large-scale evacuation, and thus they could not see any need to press on to Dunkirk with Guderian's armor. This is not as surprising as it might seem. The British were initially pessimistic about their chances. Even Churchill did not believe that they could hold Dunkirk for more than two days or that the Royal Navy could save more than 45,000 troops. Reynaud and his military leaders had no faith at all in an evacuation, and French forces were slow to fall back on Dunkirk. Many of them never made it. To make matters worse, the Belgian army surrendered on May 28. Rundstedt and Hitler were also concerned about the heavier tank losses that the Germans had sustained in recent days. Both men wanted to conserve their armor for the next step in the offensive, a drive southward toward Paris. Finally, Luftwaffe commander Hermann Goering insisted that German air power could destroy the Allied forces at Dunkirk, and for a time Hitler accepted this as a possibility.

At least one observer has questioned whether Guderian's panzers would have been able to prevent the evacuation due to the fact that the area around Dunkirk was intersected by canals and was not well suited for armor. But Guderian's spearhead was so close to the city and the Allied defensive positions in the area were so weak that his chances for success were promising despite the water obstacles. Clearly, the decision to halt was a serious mistake.

By May 26, it had become obvious that Bock's infantry was making extremely slow progress toward Dunkirk, and Guderian received permission to resume his advance. But it was too late. In the intervening two days, the Allies had strengthened their defensive perimeter around the city, and the panzers could make little headway. At this point, Guderian himself called for an end to attacks by armor.

The Dunkirk evacuation began on May 26 and proved amazingly successful. Britain still ruled the sea, and the German navy, badly mauled in the Norwegian campaign, was not able to intervene in any substantial way. The Royal Navy recruited hundreds of small civilian pleasure craft to ferry troops from the beaches to the larger naval ships waiting offshore. While the tenacious Allied rear guard prevented the Germans from breaking through the defensive perimeter, the Luftwaffe attempted to thwart the evacuation by bombing and strafing. To this point in the campaign, the army's sensational breakthrough and dash to the sea had eclipsed Goering's efforts. But if the Luftwaffe could achieve a dramatic victory at Dunkirk, he could recoup much of his lost prestige. Unfortunately for him, the task proved far more difficult than he had expected. Although the Luftwaffe inflicted considerable casualties, it could not prevent the evacuation. The Royal Air Force did its best to hamper the German air attacks but failed to gain control of the air over Dunkirk and the surrounding beaches. The British carried out the evacuation despite German air superiority.

When the operation ended on June 4, a total of 338,000 Allied soldiers had escaped, 224,000 of them British, but they had to leave behind or destroy all of their heavy equipment. Despite the brilliance of the achievement, Dunkirk certainly was not a victory, as Churchill recognized, but the climax to an epic defeat. It gave Britain a badly needed psychological lift, but it did nothing to prevent the fall of France. Moreover, the British forces that escaped from Dunkirk did not contribute directly to the salvation of Britain from German invasion. Naval and air power, along with the limitations of Germany's armed forces, saved the British in the summer and fall of 1940. But it is true that had the British lost their expeditionary force at Dunkirk, this disaster might have destroyed their will to continue the war. The evacuated troops also provided the nucleus for the British army of the future.

THE CONQUEST OF FRANCE

When news of the German breakthrough at Sedan reached Paris on May 13, it caused near panic in the French government. Reynaud telephoned Churchill and sobbed, "We are beaten. We have lost the battle." Although the campaign had barely begun, Reynaud's words were prophetic. The disaster also led to Gamelin's dismissal on May 18. His successor was General Maxim Weygand, who had won renown as chief of staff to Marshal Foch during World War I. Weygand had succeeded Marshal Pétain as commander in chief of the French army in 1931 and retired four years later. Gamelin persuaded him to return to active duty in 1939 as military commander in Syria. He was still there when Reynaud called upon him to replace Gamelin. A devout Catholic, whom Clemenceau had once referred to as being "up to his neck in priests," Weygand was an ultraconservative in politics who disliked both the Third Republic and Reynaud. Although 73 years old, the general remained amazingly fit and still ran wind sprints. Weygand recognized from the start that he had inherited a hopeless situation.

Another change, and a fateful one, was Reynaud's appointment of Pétain, now 85, as vice premier. Reynaud took this step in an effort to inspire his people with memories of Pétain's stirring defense of Verdun in 1916. But Pétain, like Weygand, did not believe that it was possible to stop this German offensive. Instead, he used his position to undermine Reynaud and work for a separate peace.

While the fighting at Dunkirk was still in progress, Weygand tried to establish a defensive system along the Somme and Aisne rivers. But the "Weygand line" had no permanent fortifications and was manned by only 61 French divisions and one British, all of them infantry. At this point, the Germans did possess overwhelming superiority, both in men and armor. Weygand did not expect to stop the enemy but intended to fight one last battle to salvage French military honor. Starting on June 5, the OKH unleashed 95 divisions against the Weygand line and quickly broke through its weak defenses. Bock sent two spearheads toward Paris and another into Normandy to the northwest. Rundstedt directed his armor around the rear of the Maginot line.

As the Germans plunged deeply into the heart of France, Mussolini belatedly entered the conflict. Traditionally, historians have assumed that the Duce made the decision to stab his unfortunate neighbor in the back more or less on the spur of the moment. But recent research indicates that Mussolini had decided as early as April to declare war on France and Britain if and when Hitler struck in the west. He apparently expected another stalemate as in World War I and hoped for a negotiated peace in which Italy would be one of the participants. Instead, the unexpected success of the German *Blitzkrieg* convinced Mussolini

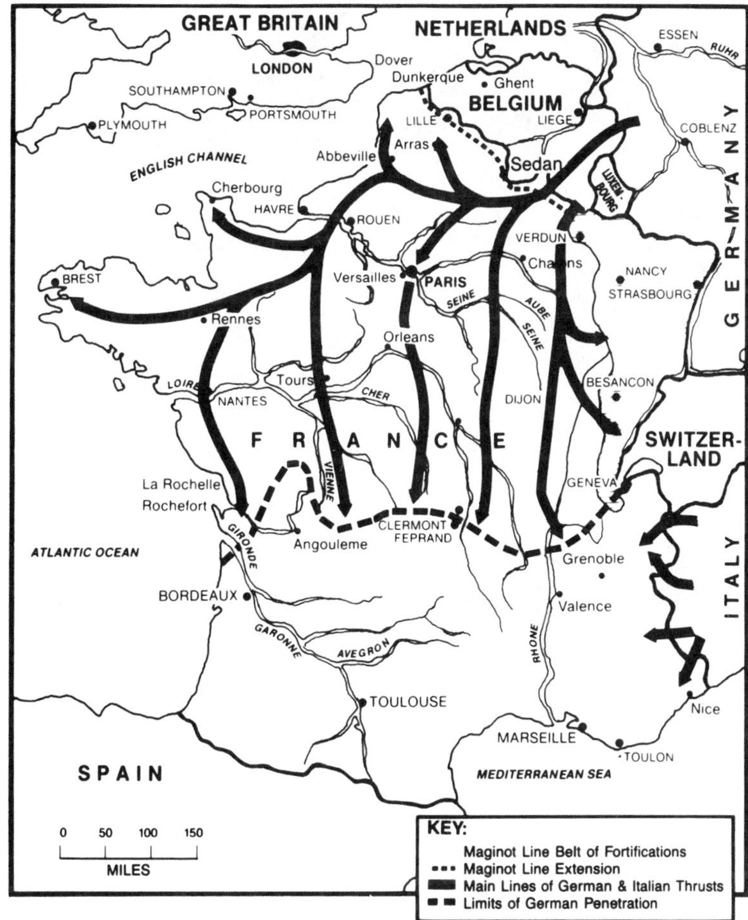

The German and Italian Invasions of France, May 10–June 24, 1940

that unless he acted, the conflict would end before Italy could claim any of the spoils. He declared war on June 10 but made no immediate attack.

Soon afterward, the French declared Paris an open city to spare it the horrors of Warsaw and Rotterdam, and on June 14 it fell to the Germans. The French government fled southward to Tours and shortly afterward to Bordeaux. German spearheads raced on. While Rundstedt's armor swung behind the Maginot line, General von Leeb's Army Group C attacked the line frontally. Leeb, a rather cautious and unimaginative Bavarian who was noted for his skill in defensive warfare, had commanded Army Group C since before the start of the war. His forces had remained on the defensive along the Rhine while the army groups of Bock and Rundstedt had won glory in Poland and had smashed the Allies in Belgium and northern France. But now his troops drew the unenviable assignment of testing the vaunted French defensive system, which proved exceedingly formidable. Despite heavy shelling, it held out until the end of hostilities without the loss of a single major fortress.

With the Germans rapidly overrunning the country and the French army disintegrating, France's government split on the question of fur-

FIGURE 7-1 Adolf Hitler expresses his joy on hearing of Marshal Pétain's request for an armistice. (*National Archives*)

ther resistance. Reynaud and his supporters wanted to fight on from the French colonial empire in North Africa, but Pétain and Weygand insisted on an armistice and gained the backing of a majority in the cabinet. Pétain succeeded Reynaud as premier on June 16 and quickly asked for a cease-fire, but almost a week elapsed before the armistice talks convened. In the meantime, the Germans continued to push southward. It was not until after the French request for an armistice that Mussolini actually ordered his troops into action. The Italians struck at two points—in the Alps and along the Mediterranean coast—but made little headway against meager French forces.

Hitler imposed his armistice in the exact spot where Germany had submitted to the Allies in 1918—near Compiègne, to the northeast of Paris. He even ordered the same railway car, which had been the site of the earlier capitulation, moved from a museum for the occasion. After attending the preliminaries of the surrender ceremony, he journeyed to the French capital, where, in silent contemplation, he viewed the tomb of Napoleon, his great predecessor in the art of conquest. Hitler's terms provided for German occupation of two-thirds of France, including Paris and the entire Atlantic coast. The rest of the country remained under French control, as did France's colonial empire and fleet. Italy continued to occupy the few bits of territory it had captured but received nothing else. All of these arrangements were temporary, the final peace treaty being left until the end of the war with Britain.

The fall of France marked the end of the democratic Third Republic, which had been the French form of government since 1870. Pétain and a number of his colleagues disliked the republic, with its unstable multiparty system. In its place they created an authoritarian regime with Pétain as head of state. They also selected the small health resort city of Vichy as the capital of unoccupied France. Vichy contained a number of large hotels and casinos that could serve as government buildings with relatively little modification. Stunned and humiliated by the speed and thoroughness of their defeat, the French faced the

FIGURE 7-2 Hitler and his entourage visit Paris following the French capitulation. (*AP/Wide World Photos*)

future with little hope that their country could survive as anything more than a satellite of an all-powerful Germany.

But one Frenchman chose not to capitulate. Charles de Gaulle, who had won promotion to general during the campaign and had served Reynaud briefly as undersecretary of war, refused to accept either the armistice or the Vichy regime. Instead he escaped to London, organized his own government in exile, and pieced together a "Free French" military force, primarily from troops in France's Central African colonies, which accepted his leadership.

France had fallen in just 35 days, but German armor had actually settled the issue within the first week of the campaign. Although it appeared at the time as if the Germans had pulled off an audacious gamble, in retrospect it hardly seems a gamble at all. If France had possessed a large force of armored divisions for defensive use, the situation might have been different. Guderian's flank would have been vulnerable to counterattack as he dashed for the sea. A powerful thrust by French tanks might have resulted in a German disaster. But the French lacked the necessary armored forces and misused those they did have. Once the Germans broke through at Sedan, there never was any real danger of a German failure. This, of course, was not readily apparent at the time, as evidenced by the nervousness of Hitler and some of his generals during the drive to the sea. But once they realized the magnitude of their victory, doubts about armored warfare vanished, and an almost blind faith in the potential of the *Blitzkrieg* took their place.

8

Britain Is Still an Island

In the aftermath of Germany's crushing victory over France, Hitler dominated the continent of Europe to an extent unmatched since the peak of Napoleon's power in the early nineteenth century. But he had not yet won the war because the British had not joined the French in seeking an armistice. Furthermore, Britain was still an island, separated from the continent by the English Channel and the North Sea, and thus could only be invaded by a difficult amphibious assault.

WHAT TO DO ABOUT BRITAIN?

In the euphoria that prevailed in the summer of 1940, however, Hitler and other German leaders were convinced that the British would have to make peace, eliminating the need for an invasion. Many observers around the world shared this view. Certainly the leaders of Vichy France did not expect Britain to survive for long. During the last days before the French capitulation, Churchill had made a grandiose offer of union between Britain and France, including joint citizenship for the peoples of both countries, if the French would continue the struggle. But the proposal met with little support in the French cabinet, and General Weygand remarked that France had nothing to gain from union with a country that would soon have its neck "wrung like a chicken's."

Even in Britain, contrary to popular myth, there was considerable support for a negotiated peace, particularly during the period between the French debacle at Sedan and the successful evacuation from Dunkirk. Chamberlain and Lord Halifax, the foreign secretary, both favored such a policy, and Churchill seriously considered this approach during May and June. He speculated on giving up Gibraltar and Malta in the Mediterranean, if necessary, to extricate Britain from its dilemma. But as time passed, Churchill veered away from the idea of a negotiated settlement, and support for such a solution faded among other British leaders, although it did not vanish for some time.

Germany put forth a number of peace feelers through neutral intermediaries, but the British ignored or rebuffed them all. Hitler finally made a personal appeal on July 19 in which he indicated that if Britain returned the German colonies it had received under the Versailles treaty and recognized Germany's domination of the continent, he would spare the British Empire. But to Churchill it appeared that Hitler visualized Britain as nothing more than a German satellite. He was not willing to consider peace on this basis.

Britain's reluctance to end the war left Hitler with no recourse but to force submission. But how was he to accomplish this? Although his fellow Germans sang the popular song "We Sail against England," it was not that easy. The Germans had failed to develop even the most rudimentary plan for an invasion. They also lacked the ships required to transport an army of sufficient size to undertake such an operation. Even if they were able to remedy this shortcoming, the German navy was totally inadequate to protect an invasion force against the formidable British fleet. And despite the awesome power that the German army had displayed in defeating France, none of its troops possessed the training necessary to carry out such a highly specialized undertaking.

Admiral Raeder, the commander of the German navy, was highly pessimistic about the chances for a successful cross-Channel invasion. Clearly, the Royal Navy was greatly superior to the German fleet, and the Royal Air Force (RAF) would make an all-out effort to prevent Germany from gaining control of the air over the Channel and any potential landing grounds. Without air supremacy, Raeder insisted, an invasion was not feasible. He believed that Germany would be wiser to attack Britain at other points that might be vulnerable—the naval base at Gibraltar on Spain's southern coast and the Middle East. But such a dispersal of effort would mean a long war, and it is unlikely that these objectives would have been as easy to accomplish as Raeder thought. Such a strategy had little appeal to Hitler. The German generals were confident that they could win another quick victory if they could get across the Channel. But they were not optimistic about the chances of attaining this prerequisite.

Hitler was hesitant, too. He was essentially continental in his thinking and feared the destruction of his army by the Royal Navy and the RAF. As he confessed to Raeder in a remarkably candid observation: "On land, I am a hero. At sea, I am a coward." He would authorize an invasion only if the Luftwaffe first eliminated British air power, thus allowing unhindered German air attacks on the Royal Navy. Although for a time he directed all German resources to the task of winning control of the air and preparing for an invasion, his heart was never really in either project. In fact, from as early as July, his mind was not focused solely on Britain. Instead, he turned his thoughts increasingly to the possibility of an attack on Russia. Whatever disadvantages such an operation might pose, it would at least not require the Germans to cross any substantial water barrier.

PLANNING THE ATTACK

Despite all these misgivings, on July 16, Hitler authorized the OKH to draft an invasion plan, which was given the code name Operation Sea Lion and the target date of August 15. In its original form, the plan was quite unrealistic and called for landings by 500,000 men on a front over 200 miles wide along Britain's southern coast. It designated the conquest of southeastern England as the operation's first objective. The OKH formulated Sea Lion without sufficient coordination with the navy, and Admiral Raeder was horrified when he saw the plan. He pointed out that the navy could provide neither the ships to carry the necessary troops nor sufficient warships to protect an invasion force on this scale. It would require vigorous effort even to scrape together enough vessels to transport a much smaller force. General Halder believed that such a reduced operation would be suicidal. As he put it, "I might just as well send the troops that have landed straight through the sausage machine." But he could hardly argue with Raeder's facts. Reluctantly, he revised the plan by reducing the landing area to the extreme southeastern corner of England and sharply cutting the number of troops. Halder and Brauchitsch also agreed to delay the invasion until September 15 to enable Raeder to assemble an improvised fleet of ships, barges, and tugs.

Before an invasion could start, of course, the Luftwaffe had to gain control of the air over the Channel and landing areas. Hitler, the army, and the navy were in agreement on this. But could the Luftwaffe succeed, and if so, could it finish the job quickly enough to allow the invasion to take place on schedule? Goering was extremely confident that he could carry out this assignment and even considered it possible to bomb Britain into submission without an actual invasion. The Luftwaffe's primary mission was to destroy the RAF fighter plane force. Once it had accomplished this, German bombers could attack British naval ships, coastal installations, and troops without fear of RAF interference. All German leaders considered the destruction of the British fighter force to be the absolutely essential prerequisite for an invasion.

Despite Goering's confidence, the Luftwaffe proved inadequate for its task. Essentially a tactical air force designed to support the army, it was undertaking a strategic mission that was beyond its capabilities. Also, the superiority of the Luftwaffe over the RAF was not as great as many believed at the time. Its chief strength consisted of two air fleets that operated from France, Belgium, and the Netherlands under the command of Field Marshals Albert Kesselring and Hugo Sperrle. Both men had started their careers in the army and had served in World War I. Kesselring participated in secret planning for the Luftwaffe during the 1920s and, after its creation, served as chief of staff from 1936 to 1937. Sperrle led the famous Condor Legion, which fought on Franco's side in the Spanish civil war. The combined strength of their air fleets included 1,200 high-level bombers and 280 Stukas, but the latter proved so vulnerable to British fighters that Kesselring and Sperrle quickly withdrew them from combat. For the first time, the Stuka faced fighters that could take advantage of its inadequate speed, armor, and armament.

The Luftwaffe also lacked long-range heavy bombers. Instead it had to make do with aircraft that had inferior bomb-load capacity and range. This weakness was the result of a combination of accident and deliberate choice. When the Luftwaffe came into existence in 1933, its first chief of staff, General Walter Wever, was convinced that in any future war, Britain would be among Germany's enemies. He recognized that Germany would need a strategic air force using long-range heavy bombers that could successfully attack British cities, especially those in the more remote areas. But Wever died in a plane crash in 1936 before he could carry out his plans. His successor, Kesselring, and other Luftwaffe leaders did not share Wever's enthusiasm for heavy bombers and questioned their accuracy from high altitudes. They preferred to concentrate instead on production of the Stuka and medium-range bombers—the Dornier 17, Heinkel 111, and Junkers 88—which could also serve as dive bombers. These were the aircraft that the Luftwaffe unleashed against Britain in the summer of 1940. They were too poorly armed to beat off British interceptor attacks and thus had to depend on fighter escorts during daylight. This meant that they could not advance much beyond London because of the limited range of the best German fighter, the Messerschmitt (Me) 109. Bombers could penetrate more deeply into British air space at night, without fighter escort, but night bombing was highly inaccurate.

The two air fleets combined had 760 Messerschmitt 109s and 220 twin-engine Messerschmitt 110 fighters. Although the Me 110 had greater range than the Me 109, it proved a big disappointment because it was too heavy and unmaneuverable. All things considered, the Me 109 was superior to the British Hurricane and on even terms with the best British fighter, the Spitfire.

A third and smaller German air fleet operated from Norway and Denmark, which were too far away from Britain for this force to be effective. Its bombers depended on unwieldy Me 110s for escort because their British targets lay beyond the range of the Me 109. The RAF also received early warnings of their approach. As a result of these problems, this air fleet made only one major daylight attack, which the British repulsed with heavy losses.

DEFENDING AGAINST THE LUFTWAFFE

When the Luftwaffe launched its offensive, RAF Fighter Command possessed a total of 650 operational aircraft, mostly Hurricanes and Spitfires, but also including 100 obsolete models. The

FIGURE 8-1 Royal Air Force Spitfires patrol the English Channel. (*AP/Wide World Photos*)

commander of this force was Air Marshal Hugh Dowding, whose reserved manner had earned him the nickname "Stuffy." Though lacking in charisma, he was popular with the fighter pilots, whom he affectionately called his "chicks." Dowding proved to be one of the major heroes of the Battle of Britain. Before the war, he had fought to increase the size of the fighter force against the opposition of the government and strategic air power enthusiasts in the RAF who had favored concentration on the production of long-range bombers. He had also been instrumental in the development of the Hurricane and the Spitfire. But despite his efforts, Dowding was concerned about Fighter Command's numeric inferiority in the summer of 1940. He feared the destruction of his force if he committed too many planes too early. To prevent this, he insisted on keeping a large number of fighters in reserve in northern and central Britain beyond the range of the Me 109.

This policy placed primary responsibility for fending off the Luftwaffe on Air Vice Marshal Keith Park's Fighter Command Group 11, which protected southeastern England, including London. A New Zealander by birth, Park saw action in the artillery during World War I and suffered severe wounds while fighting on the western front. He later became a fighter pilot and served as chief staff officer to Dowding before taking over as commander of Group 11. Park shared Dowding's insistence on conserving Fighter Command's strength. He refused to commit his entire force against German formations approaching England and kept many fighters in reserve. As a result, the British planes that intercepted the enemy were usually badly outnumbered. Not surprisingly, this approach drew strong criticism, but Dowding and Park remained adamant until mid-September, when they finally increased the number of fighters committed to combat. Despite its unpopularity at the time, their cautious policy contributed significantly to Fighter Command's salvation and ultimate victory.

British aircraft production increased greatly during the summer of 1940 and actually outdistanced German output by a considerable margin. This achievement was due primarily to the unrelenting efforts of Lord Beaverbrook, whom Churchill had appointed minister for aircraft production on May 14. Born in Canada, Beaverbrook was the publisher of the London *Daily Express*. He antagonized some RAF leaders, who criticized his single-minded emphasis on production of finished fighter planes at the expense of spare parts and other types of aircraft. But Beaverbrook insisted that national survival depended on the construction of Spitfires and Hurricanes.

The British had another distinct advantage—radar, which they had pioneered as early as 1935. Radar gave the RAF advance warning of the approach and direction of German planes. Much of its success was due to the efforts of scientist Robert Watson-Watt, who experimented with bouncing radio waves off distant planes and using the resulting echoes to detect their approach. Watson-Watt carried out his work with the help of a committee of scientists headed by Henry Tizard. Dowding recognized the importance of radar to Fighter Command and cooperated in developing a chain of 21 radar stations along England's southern and eastern coasts.

Tizard was also active in the creation of an effective ground control system that directed fighter planes to intercept German aircraft on the basis of radar warnings. To supplement the radar stations, the British developed an observer corps, consisting of hundreds of aircraft spotters who alerted the ground control operation centers of the estimated number, altitude, speed, and bearing of incoming enemy forces. The combination of radar, observers, and ground control eliminated the need to maintain constant air patrols to detect German planes and enabled British units to avoid being caught on the ground. The Germans had participated in the early development of radar but, failing to recognize its great value, neglected their own program.

Ultra reports were also available. They revealed that Hitler had ordered preparations for Operation Sea Lion and that the Germans encountered some problems in gathering tugs and barges for the projected invasion. The reports also provided information on the strength of the Luftwaffe and the location of its bases. But they often failed to indicate clearly actual bombing targets or exact timetables. In short, though useful during the Battle of Britain, Ultra was not of great value until considerably later.

With the threat of invasion now seemingly imminent, a startling transformation took place in the attitude of the British people, who were determined to defend their homeland. Churchill's leadership was a significant factor in this change. His masterful speeches and bulldog manner inspired confidence to a degree that Chamberlain could not remotely approach. Among his most memorable words were these, which he delivered soon after the fall of France:

> The Battle of France is over. I expect that the Battle of Britain is about to begin. Upon this battle depends the survival of Christian Civilization. Upon it depends our British life, and the long continuity of our institutions and our Empire. . . . Let us therefore brace ourselves to our duties, and so bear ourselves that, if the British Empire and its Commonwealth last for a thousand years, men will still say, "This was their finest hour."

THE BATTLE OF BRITAIN

Germany's preliminary air operations began on July 10 and continued until August 6. They consisted of raids against British shipping and resulted in relatively little combat between the two fighter forces. It was not until August 8 that the Germans switched to attacks on British airfields with the intention of destroying the RAF fighter force. This shift marked the actual start of the Battle of Britain. The Luftwaffe also unleashed heavy assaults against radar stations on August 12 but seriously damaged only one. It failed to undertake any important follow-up raids against these installations, which must be considered a blunder of the first magnitude.

Despite the fact that the Germans had been conducting major raids against RAF fighter bases for almost a week, they did not officially launch their grand air offensive until August 13. They hoped to win mastery of the skies over Britain and the Channel within four weeks to enable the invasion to commence by September 15. Intense aerial combat followed. Fighter Command absorbed considerable punishment, but it remained strong and replaced lost planes with new aircraft coming off the assembly line. Pilot losses were serious but perhaps not as critical as some ob-

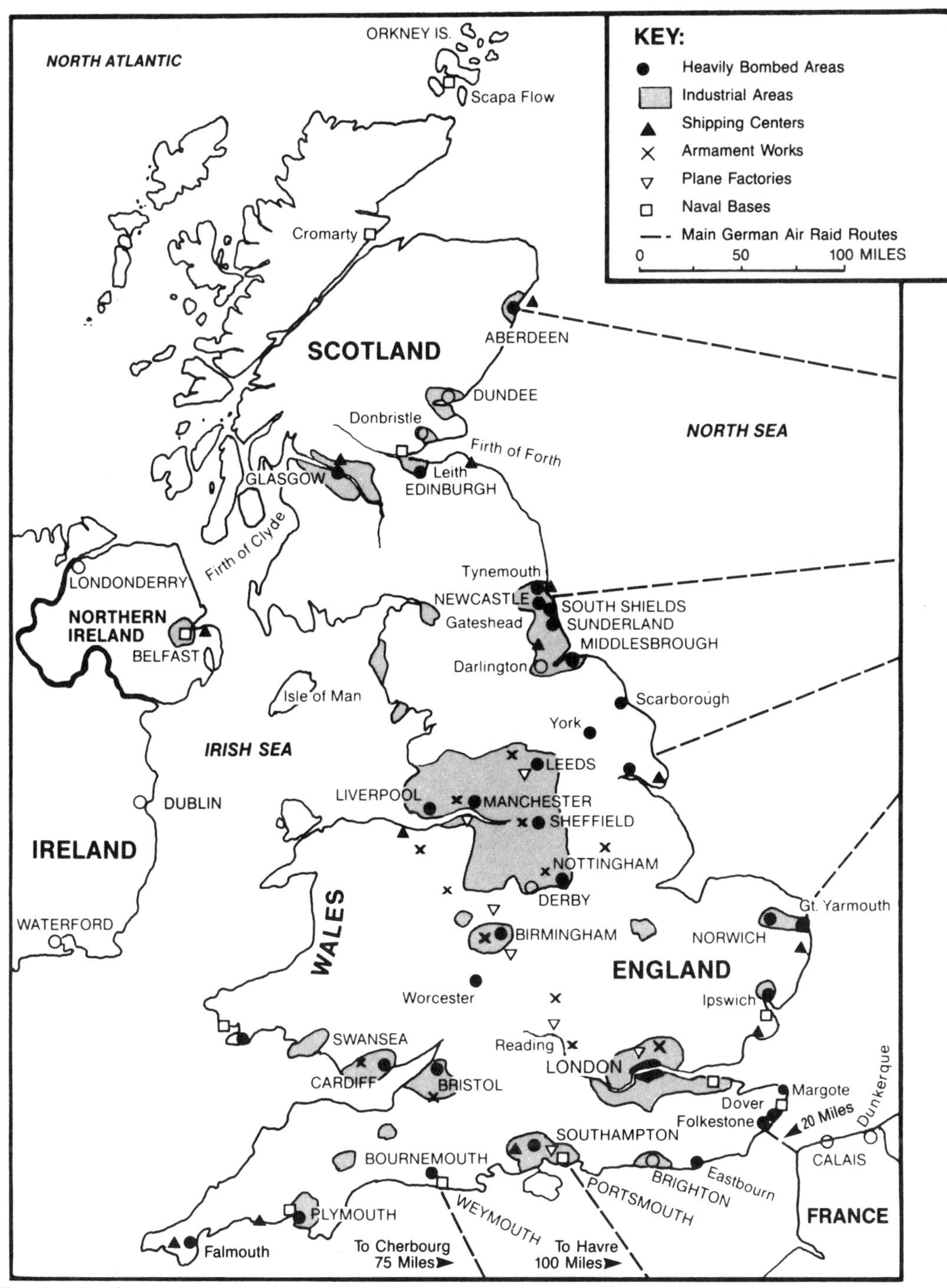

The Battle of Britain, July–December 1940

servers have contended. The British secured replacements who performed well. And since the battle took place over Britain, many pilots were able to bail out of their planes and return to action. German losses were also high. During the crucial months of August and September, the RAF lost 832 fighters, and 532 more were damaged. The Luftwaffe suffered fewer fighter losses—668 destroyed and 436 damaged—but it also lost 500 bombers and 67 Stukas. The heavier toll of British fighters was due partly to the Me 109's superiority over the Hurricane. But the RAF's policy of making German bombers its primary target was also an important factor. This left British fighters more vulnerable to Me 109 attacks than would have been the case if they had concentrated on attacking German fighters.

The Battle of Britain entered its second phase on August 24, when the Germans unleashed even more intense raids on Fighter Command bases. During the next week, the Luftwaffe shot down so many British fighters that the RAF losses actually outstripped production of replacement aircraft. The trend was dangerous, but the Germans also suffered significant losses and began to relax pressure on RAF airfields as early as September 4, when Goering diverted some strength to assaults on industrial cities and other targets.

Phase 3 of the Battle of Britain began on September 7. It featured a drastic change in tactics by the Germans, who abandoned their attacks on Fighter Command bases in favor of direct raids on London. Goering made this decision with the support of both Hitler and Kesselring over the protests of Sperrle, who feared the change would ease pressure on Fighter Command just as its losses were reaching a critical point. The shift was due in part to Goering's concern that the Luftwaffe was not making rapid enough progress toward air supremacy. He believed that attacks on London would lure more British fighters into the sky over the capital, where they could be destroyed. Hitler was also eager to punish London in retaliation for recent RAF bombing raids on Berlin, which did little damage but killed a few civilians. Finally, the German leaders hoped that the bombing of London might weaken British civilian morale.

Critics have pointed to this change in tactics as the turning point in the Battle of Britain because it supposedly gave Fighter Command a new lease on life just as it had reached the verge of exhaustion. This is a highly questionable thesis. To be sure, the diversion ended the damage that the Germans had inflicted on Fighter Command airfields, but it did not lessen the number of RAF fighter engagements with the Luftwaffe, and British losses remained high. The raids on London certainly did not destroy the RAF, but it is unlikely that continued attacks on Fighter Command bases would have had this effect either. Goering pressed his assault on London for a week, climaxed by two especially heavy raids on September 15. But they did little serious damage and resulted in heavy German losses.

While the Luftwaffe and RAF battled for control of the air, Admiral Raeder and his staff did a remarkable job of assembling the ships and barges necessary to transport the invasion forces across the Channel. But they could do nothing to ease the alarming shortage of escort vessels. Meanwhile, the British increased the strength of their army, and by the first week in September, 16 divisions guarded the landing areas. They were not at full strength in weapons, but they did have 800 tanks. RAF bombers also carried out raids during mid-September against German invasion craft in the French and Belgian Channel ports and caused considerable damage.

The failure of the Luftwaffe's attacks against London on September 15 convinced the Germans that their efforts to destroy RAF Fighter Command had failed. They had not achieved the all-important prerequisite for an invasion. On September 17, Hitler postponed Operation Sea Lion indefinitely. His decision really sounded the death knell for the project, because he soon shifted his attention away from Britain in favor of an invasion of the Soviet Union.

Luftwaffe attacks against Britain continued but without clear purpose. After September 15, the emphasis gradually shifted to night raids on

London. This reflected the fact that RAF fighter attacks were hurting the Luftwaffe. Night raids made it more difficult for the RAF to shoot down German bombers and enabled the Luftwaffe to penetrate deeper into British air space by sharply reducing the need for fighter escorts. But the shift also made it harder for German bombers to hit their targets and to destroy British fighters. Night attacks increasingly took on the guise of terror bombing, designed to undermine Britain's will to fight.

In November, Goering extended his raids to other cities and ports, starting with an attack that destroyed much of Coventry in the industrial Midlands. Over 400 bombers devastated the center of the city with incendiary and high-explosive bombs, killing more than 500 people and destroying a beautiful fourteenth-century Gothic cathedral. RAF Group Captain F. W. Winterbotham, who played a major role in the development of Ultra, stated after the war that the British had intercepted a message that indicated clearly that an attack on Coventry was coming. According to Winterbotham, Churchill refused to evacuate civilians from the city because he feared such an action would alert the Germans to the fact that the British had broken their cipher. But it is now clear that although Ultra revealed that the Luftwaffe was planning a heavy attack, it failed to determine the actual target. Available evidence indicated that London was the likely site until shortly before the assault began. The question of sacrificing Coventry to protect Ultra never arose.

The assault on cities continued until late December, followed by a comparative lull during the winter. One of the worst of these raids struck London on December 29. Although only 136 bombers took part, their incendiaries set almost 1,500 fires, which destroyed a large area bordering St. Paul's Cathedral. Despite being hit by 28 incendiaries, the cathedral itself suffered only minor damage. The Luftwaffe resumed its offensive in earnest when better weather returned in March 1941 and carried out a series of heavy attacks for the next two months. This time, in addition to London, the Germans concentrated on the port cities of Liverpool, Bristol, Plymouth, and Hull and the industrial centers of Birmingham and Manchester. But in May, the skies over Britain fell strangely silent as most of the Luft-

FIGURE 8-2 The dome of St. Paul's Cathedral still stands after a devastating Luftwaffe raid on London. (*UPI/Bettmann Newsphotos*)

waffe headed east to participate in the invasion of the USSR.

Both sides made wildly inflated estimates of enemy losses during the Battle of Britain, officially the period from July 10 through October 31. The British claimed a total of almost 2,700 enemy aircraft destroyed, while the Germans believed that they had accounted for slightly over 3,000 RAF planes. In reality, the Luftwaffe lost 1,882 fighters and bombers, the RAF 1,017 fighters, 118 bombers, and 130 Coastal Command aircraft for a total of 1,265.

Germany's air offensive had caused considerable damage and taken many lives, but it had not achieved its objectives of destroying RAF Fighter Command, preparing the way for invasion, or breaking the morale of the British people. This failure offered two lessons for those who were willing to learn. It demonstrated that a cross-Channel invasion could not be improvised but had to be prepared well in advance with ample troops, equipment, landing craft, warships, and control of the air. Britain and the United States learned this lesson well—perhaps too well. The German failure also revealed that there were definite limits to the effectiveness of bombing cities, something that Britain and the United States were exceedingly slow to learn. Obviously, the Luftwaffe was not suited for such a mission, but the British and Americans later experienced disappointing results from strategic bombing of German cities, carried out by long-range bombers that they had designed especially for this purpose.

It is now clear that Germany's attempt to destroy RAF Fighter Command in the summer of 1940 was probably doomed from the start. The inadequacies of the Luftwaffe, the weakness of its planning, and the inconsistency of its approach combined to diminish greatly the possibility of success. And if these obstacles were not enough, Fighter Command was a formidable opponent. The gallant British pilots who flew the Spitfires and Hurricanes denied control of the air to the Luftwaffe, and without this vital prerequisite, a cross-Channel invasion was out of the question. Churchill's memorable words immortalized their contribution: "Never in the field of human conflict was so much owed by so many to so few."

9

The Plot Thickens: The Mediterranean and the Balkans

Germany's failure to defeat Britain in the fall of 1940 dulled the luster of the Wehrmacht's reputation for invincibility and posed the likelihood of a long war. The conflict between Germany and Britain had become a stand-off. Although Germany could not invade Britain, the British were in no position to undertake an invasion of the continent. As time passed and both sides increased in strength, there would be little chance that this situation would change unless Britain gained allies. And when Hitler turned his attention in the fall of 1940 to planning his attack on the Soviet Union, he relegated Britain to second place in Germany's strategic considerations.

Hitler did want to exert some pressure on the British, however. To accomplish this, he turned to Admiral Raeder's proposal that Germany attack Britain's strongholds in the Mediterranean. But he did not want to commit too many resources to this task and always viewed the Mediterranean as a sideshow. As the war continued, however, he nevertheless became increasingly involved in this area as complications not of his making embroiled him in new commitments.

EXTENDING THE WAR SOUTHWARD

In the fall of 1940, the Führer's attention focused to a considerable extent on the western Mediterranean as he negotiated with three countries—Italy, Vichy France, and Spain. Hitler wanted to stay on good terms with all three, but this proved difficult because of their conflicting territorial ambitions. Mussolini was interested in a number of French possessions—the island of Corsica, the city of Nice on the French Mediterranean coast, and the Alpine province of Savoy as well as Tunisia and other French colonies in North Africa. But Hitler did not want to make any promises to his fellow dictator, because this would antagonize the Vichy French, whom he hoped to entice into active cooperation, perhaps even an alliance, with Germany. As for Spain, Franco had his eyes on Gibraltar, a British enclave on the Spanish coast, but he, too, coveted French colonies—Morocco, Algeria, and West Africa. Although Hitler had no objections regarding Gibraltar, he again was reluctant to agree to the Spanish acquisition of French possessions.

A German alliance with France seemed a real possibility in the fall of 1940 because of strained relations between the French and their former ally, Britain. Vichy leaders believed that the British had not provided France with sufficient support during the agonizing days of May and June and were outraged when elements of the Royal Navy actually attacked French ships in Algerian ports on July 3.

Churchill had become anxious that the French fleet might fall into German hands and ordered an

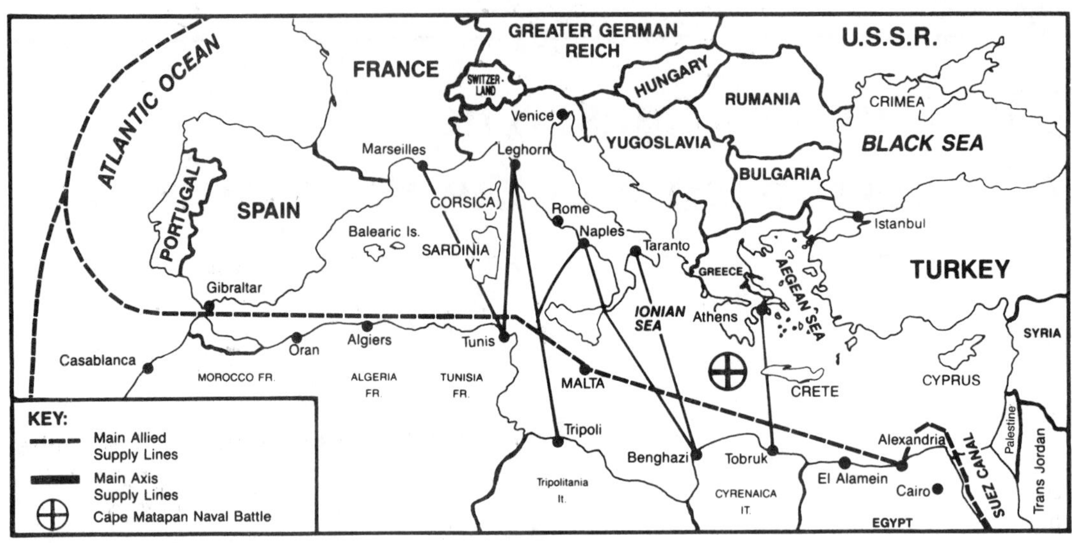

The Mediterranean Theater of Operations, 1940–43

FIGURE 9-1 Winston Churchill gives his famous "V" salute outside the prime minister's residence in London. (*UPI/Bettmann Newsphotos*)

operation against the large French naval force at Oran and the neighboring base of Mers-el-Kebir. He made this decision over the heated objections of British naval leaders, who warned that such action would have a disastrous impact on Anglo-French relations. Churchill instructed Admiral James Somerville to offer the French commander, Admiral Marcel Gensoul, the opportunity to join the British or take refuge in a distant colony. If he refused, Somerville's naval force was to attack. Gensoul chose to resist, and the British reluctantly opened fire, sinking one battleship, disabling three other capital ships, and killing over 1,000 French sailors. This incident triggered discussion in the French government of a possible declaration of war against Britain, but cooler heads prevailed, and France limited action to breaking diplomatic relations. The French also avoided an alliance with Germany, although they did follow a policy of collaboration on many issues.

The portion of Raeder's Mediterranean strategy that appealed most to Hitler was his proposal to attack Gibraltar. In October 1940, Hitler pressured Franco to join the Axis and allow the passage of German troops through Spain preliminary to an assault on the British stronghold. Franco indicated his willingness to join the Axis but asked for extensive compensation in French North Africa, a price that Hitler was unwilling to pay. In the end, Germany gained neither Spain's adherence to the Axis nor permission for the passage of German troops. Franco was by no means convinced that the Germans were going to win the war, especially in view of the failure of their air offensive against Britain.

NORTH AFRICA: THE DESERT WAR

Instead of attacking Gibraltar, Hitler ultimately embarked on operations in the eastern Mediterranean, where he had not originally planned to become involved. This entanglement was due to Italy's attempts to conquer Egypt and Greece in the fall of 1940 and the disastrous failure of both. Mussolini was eager to move out of Hitler's shadow and demonstrate the prowess of his armed forces. He struck first in Africa, where prospects looked bright. Italian troops in Libya greatly outnumbered the British in neighboring Egypt, while Mussolini's East African army in Eritrea, Ethiopia, and Italian Somaliland dwarfed Britain's forces in British Somaliland, Kenya, and the Sudan. Although Egypt had been officially independent since 1922, Britain had retained a strong influence in this desert country as well as military, naval, and air bases.

Things started out well enough as Italian troops overran British and French Somaliland in August. Mussolini planned to follow this success by sending his Libyan army into Egypt with Marshal Rodolfo Graziani in command. Graziani was no stranger to the North African desert, having commanded Mussolini's forces in Libya during the early 1930s. A staunch Fascist, he had also led one of the armies that overran Ethiopia in 1935–36 and served as viceroy of Italian East Africa for two years before returning to the Libyan command in the summer of 1940. But Graziani was pessimistic about the proposed offensive. He recognized that even though his troops outnumbered the British, they were deficient in armor as well as other motorized equipment. The Italians clearly suffered from a lack of mobility, a serious shortcoming in the desert.

Graziani was painfully aware that Italy was not prepared for war. The nation's industrial base was the smallest of any of the industrialized powers, and it had to import most raw materials. The Italians received no material aid from Germany, which, of course, also relied heavily on imports. In fact, the two allies actually competed for such commodities as Rumanian oil. Mussolini had hoped that the war would soon end in victory for the Axis. Instead, he found himself in a struggle that gave every indication of being a long one. As it persisted, the weakness of the Italian economy became ever more apparent.

General Archibald Wavell led Britain's forces in Egypt as well as East Africa and Palestine. Wavell had seen action in both the Boer War at the turn of the century and World War I. He had lost an eye on the western front and had also fought against the Turks in the Middle East. Respected for his considerable intellect, he had also gained a somewhat dubious reputation as a man of very few words. But despite his taciturn personality, he had won great popularity with his troops, who appreciated his frequent visits to front-line positions. In 1939, Wavell had undertaken the thankless task of organizing a Middle East command with limited resources but had managed to gain some reinforcements from India, New Zealand, and Australia.

Wavell tried to compensate for his numerical inferiority by dispersing his forces in packets along the Egyptian-Libyan border to give the impression that he was strong enough to cover the entire frontier. His troops also resorted to hit-and-run raids against the Italian positions. The bluff worked, and Graziani did not move across the border until September 13. But even then his heart was not in the enterprise, and he halted after reaching Sidi Barrani, 50 miles into Egypt. He established a series of fortified camps at this point and proceeded to build up a huge supply base for the next phase of the operation, an offensive toward Alexandria, Cairo, and the Suez Canal. But the Italian attack never came.

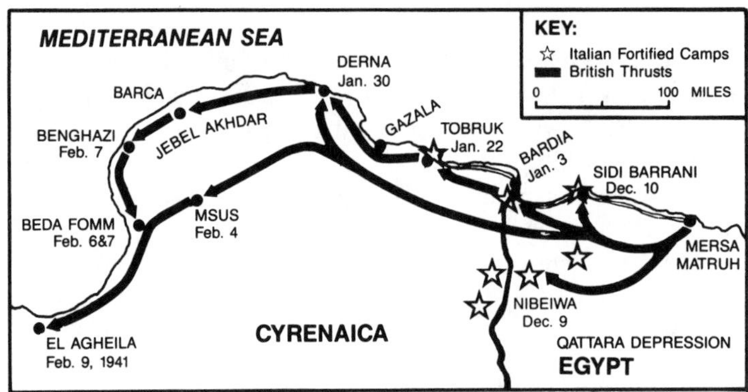

Western Desert Force Offensive against the Italians, December 7 and 8, 1940–February 9, 1941

Instead, Wavell went over to the offensive himself on December 9. The British commander originally planned only a large-scale raid because he estimated that the Italians outnumbered his forces 80,000 to 36,000. He did enjoy an advantage in tanks, however, with 275 to only 120 for the Italians. The British tanks included 50 heavily armored Matildas, which proved impervious to the Italians' inferior antitank weapons and played an especially important role. After one battle, the British counted 38 dents in the armor of a single Matilda, but none of the Italian shells had penetrated the tank's heavy skin. Italian tanks, by contrast, were death traps equipped with armor barely worthy of the name. British shells riddled them with holes. Wavell's forces were also much stronger in motorized transport.

Wavell was fortunate to have General Richard O'Connor as his field commander. Short and slight, O'Connor was far from flamboyant. But he won the complete confidence of his men, and with good reason. He had gained valuable experience commanding troops that fought Pathan tribesmen on India's Northwest Frontier as well as Arab guerrillas in Palestine. By 1940, he enjoyed a reputation for bold, imaginative tactics and soon proved that he was also a master at handling mobile forces in the desert.

O'Connor used his tanks to exploit a gap between two of the Italian fortified camps. He then attacked each camp from the rear, catching Graziani's forces completely by surprise and capturing 40,000 men. Those Italians, who managed to escape, fled back into Libya, where they took refuge in the coastal fortress of Bardia. But O'Connor's troops seized this stronghold early in January 1941 and took another 45,000 Italians prisoner. Anthony Eden, who had succeeded Halifax as British foreign secretary, greeted the fall of Bardia with a new version of Churchill's famous tribute to the RAF: "Never has so much been surrendered by so many to so few." The British moved on to encircle the port of Tobruk, which they captured on January 22 along with 30,000 more prisoners.

Despite these disasters, Graziani still had 20,000 men in eastern Libya, and they now fell back along the coast. In an effort to prevent their escape, O'Connor split his forces. One column pursued the retreating Italians, while a second spearhead of tanks and motorized infantry attempted to outflank them by cutting the coastal road at Beda Fomm. It did so by striking boldly across a 170-mile expanse of largely uncharted and extremely rugged desert. The soldiers who made this trek encountered terrible hardships, including sandstorms and freezing rain, but they reached Beda Fomm before the enemy. When the Italians arrived, the British attacked them from concealed positions and, after a desperately fought battle, captured another 20,000 prisoners. The British then moved on to El Agheila, about a third of the way across Libya. But on February 12, Churchill ordered Wavell to cease his offensive and divert part of his forces to Greece, where a new situation had developed as a result of Italy's invasion of that country.

Wavell's offensive had been amazingly successful. At the cost of fewer than 2,000 British casualties, it had accounted for a total of 130,000 prisoners. Britain's victory and Italy's disaster had been due in large part to differing approaches to the campaign. The British had recognized that the desert was similar to the ocean with its vast expanse of desolation. In such an environment, there really was no such thing as a continuous front. The key to victory was mobility, with tanks operating much as ships at sea. The far less mobile Italians had to rely on static defense in the form of fortified camps, such as those near Sidi Barrani, or fortress towns such as Bardia and Tobruk. They tied down their forces in these strongholds, which proved vulnerable to the encircling maneuvers of the more mobile British.

As the full scope of the Italian defeat became apparent, Hitler decided to intervene to save what was left of Libya. But with plans already under way for the invasion of the Soviet Union, he had few troops to spare—only one light and one panzer division, both understrength. He chose General Erwin Rommel to lead this meager force.

Born in southern Germany to middle-class parents, Rommel had won acclaim during World War I for his personal heroism as a young officer who specialized in tactics of infiltration behind enemy lines. Hitler's willingness to adopt new and unorthodox military ideas quickly won Rommel's admiration, and Rommel's relatively humble origins endeared him to the Führer, who often felt uncomfortable in the company of aristocratic generals. Hitler appointed Rommel to command his personal bodyguard in 1938. Until 1939, Rommel had always been an infantry officer, but the success of the *Blitzkrieg* in Poland made him a true believer in armored warfare. Soon afterward, Hitler helped him obtain command of a panzer division. Despite his lack of previous experience with tanks, Rommel mastered armored operations in a remarkably brief time. Indeed, his division performed with conspicuous success during the 1940 campaign in Western Europe. Like Guderian, he believed in the swiftest possible exploitation of a breakthrough. This continued to be his philosophy when he took over his new command in Libya.

Ultra reports alerted Wavell of Rommel's arrival and the strength of his forces. But Wavell misinterpreted the seriousness of the threat that Rommel posed. He was convinced that the Axis would not be able to launch an attack until at least May, especially in view of supply problems. In fact, the OKH ordered Rommel not to attack the British under any circumstances and to remain on the defensive. But Rommel was not one to play a passive role, and he decided to attack late in March, even before his full force had arrived. He recognized that the British were also weak. To give the impression of greater German strength, Rommel used dummy tanks mounted on Volkswagen chassis. He also retained five Italian divisions and enjoyed superiority in the air. His attack caught the British by surprise, and his troops defeated them in a series of brief encounters, forcing them to fall back in confusion all the way to the Egyptian frontier. The British suffered a severe blow when the Germans captured General O'Connor, their leading tank tactician, during the retreat. But Rommel was not able to pursue the British into Egypt because his forces were now in a vulnerable position at the end of a precarious supply line. The British also succeeded in holding Tobruk, which the Axis forces had bypassed in their drive to the Egyptian border. Tobruk posed a threat to Rommel's flank and deprived him of port facilities close to the front. It was now clear that the desert war had become a deadlock.

Meanwhile, the British enjoyed much greater success in East Africa, where they took the offensive against the Italians in January. One force pushed into Eritrea and Ethiopia from the Sudan, while a second invaded Italian Somaliland from Kenya. Although the Italians initially outnumbered Wavell's British, Indian, and native forces,

FIGURE 9-2 A German field artillery piece fires against a British position during the desert fighting. (*National Archives*)

they lacked modern equipment and were cut off from any hope of supply from Italy or Libya. The Allied forces moved with remarkable speed against weak resistance in Italian Somaliland and southern Ethiopia. In the north, the Italians put up a much tougher fight, but relentless British pressure forced them to retreat. By the end of May, Wavell's troops controlled virtually all of Italian East Africa and had also reconquered British and French Somaliland.

THE BALKAN CAMPAIGNS

Although Hitler could do nothing to save Mussolini's East African Empire because of its remote location, he did come to his fellow dictator's aid in the Balkans, where Italy had undertaken another ill-advised invasion in October 1940. This time Greece was the victim, but once again the operation turned into an Italian fiasco, one that jeopardized Hitler's own encroachment on the Balkans. During the previous summer, the Führer had resorted to diplomatic pressure to safeguard his Balkan flank and protect German access to Rumania's oil fields prior to the invasion of the USSR. Hitler was also concerned about Russian expansion into the Balkans, which followed Germany's victory over France. With the French defeated, Stalin realized that his country was more vulnerable to a German attack. The Soviet dictator moved to extend the buffer zone between Russia and Germany by annexing Lithuania, Latvia, and Estonia and seizing the Rumanian provinces of Bessarabia and Northern Bukovina. The occupation of Bessarabia brought Red Army troops within 100 miles of the Rumanian oil fields at Ploesti.

At about the same time, Hungary demanded the return of the province of Transylvania, lost to Rumania in the 1919 peace settlement. Bulgaria also insisted that the hard-pressed Rumanians cede the province of Southern Dobruja to them. Hitler feared that these disputes would lead to war between the Balkan states and that the Soviets might take advantage of this instability to extend their influence still more. To prevent this, he assumed the role of mediator in these disputes while pressing all three Balkan powers to join the Axis. He awarded Hungary a large part of Transylvania and granted Southern Dobruja to Bulgaria. In return, he guaranteed Rumania's remaining territory and received the right to station German troops on Rumanian soil.

Hitler had accomplished all this without firing a shot, but the failure of Italy's invasion of Greece posed a new threat to the stability of the

Balkans. The Führer had warned the Duce against taking action against Greece, and the Italian supreme command, which recognized the army's weakness in modern equipment, was equally opposed. But Mussolini was determined to strike and launched his attack from Italian-occupied Albania on October 28, despite the approach of winter and ominous weather forecasts. The Italians made good progress at first but were headed for trouble. Torrential rain fell as they penetrated down the mountain valleys of northwestern Greece. The small, poorly equipped but tough Greek army waited until the opportune time and then counterattacked. The Italians found themselves in an overextended position and exposed to murderous fire from artillery in the mountains above them. Greek attacks cut the Italian columns to pieces and forced the survivors back into Albania. By the end of the year, the Greeks were in control of almost one-quarter of Albania, but their offensive bogged down in January and the struggle degenerated into a stalemate. Mussolini had suffered another humiliation, and the Greeks had won the admiration of much of the world, just as the Finns had done the previous winter.

Hitler feared that Mussolini's "regrettable blunder" would lead to the diversion of British forces from Egypt to help Greece. But with his attack on Sidi Barrani approaching, Wavell could not spare any troops, although he did send a small military mission and some aircraft in November. It was not until after the British had smashed the Italians at Beda Fomm that they considered it possible to send an expeditionary force. Churchill was dubious about the chances for success, but Eden, who had undertaken a fact-finding trip to Greece, favored intervention, as did Wavell. The prime minister took their advice and dispatched 58,000 British, Australian, and New Zealand troops to Greece. The force was much too small for the task and desperately weak in both tanks and aircraft.

Even before Britain's intervention, Hitler had decided to invade Greece to rescue his Italian ally and protect his Balkan flank. To facilitate this operation, he persuaded Bulgarian leaders to allow German troops to enter their country on March 1, 1941. With Rumania, Hungary, and Bulgaria all safely in the Axis camp and the invasion of Greece looming in the near future, the position of Yugoslavia became crucial. Hitler had been pressuring the Yugoslavs to join the Axis ever since the start of Italy's invasion of Greece, and the Belgrade regime finally agreed on March 25. But certain Yugoslav officers opposed this decision and staged a coup that ousted the pro-German government. This heroic but rash act enraged Hitler, who now expanded his forthcoming operation against Greece to include Yugoslavia as well.

Germany unleashed *Blitzkriege* against both countries on April 6. They proved remarkably effective, especially the attack on Yugoslavia, which the OKH improvised on short notice. Hitler sent 650,000 troops against the Yugoslavs, including the Second Army, which pounced from Austria and Hungary, and the Twelfth Army, which struck from Rumania and Bulgaria. Seven panzer divisions played a crucial role in the operation despite the rugged mountain terrain. On paper, Yugoslavia could assemble an army of more than a million men, but the rapid German onslaught prevented full mobilization. The Yugoslavs were also woefully lacking in modern equipment, including tanks and aircraft. German columns quickly sliced through the stricken country. The invasion also glaringly revealed the fundamental flaw in the Yugoslav state: the inability of the two main national groups, the Serbs and the Croats, to get along. They had squabbled since the founding of Yugoslavia. Now many Croats refused to join in what they considered to be a Serbian fight, and some cooperated with the Germans. Belgrade fell on April 12, and five days later the Yugoslavian army surrendered.

Although the Greek campaign took a little longer, the outcome was never in doubt. Greece was in a hopeless position, with the bulk of its army engaged in Albania. Ultra gave the British an accurate picture of German troop dispositions and operational plans. But the Allied forces were

The Axis Invasion of Yugoslavia and Greece, April 6, 1941

far too weak to prevent enemy panzers from slashing through the country. The Greeks also insisted on keeping most of their remaining forces along the Metaxas line, a defensive system opposite the Bulgarian border. But the British urged them to withdraw from both the Metaxas line and Albania to the strong natural position of the Aliakmon River farther south. British leaders recognized that the Metaxas line was vulnerable to a flanking attack by German troops penetrating into Greece from southern Yugoslavia. Unfortunately, the Greeks held fast to the Metaxas line and Albania, and when the Germans struck, they quickly penetrated behind both positions and cut off the Greek defenders. The remaining Allied forces were badly outnumbered and had to retreat southward toward Athens. The British had no choice but to carry out a Dunkirk-type evacuation. Again it was successful, and 43,000 troops escaped during the period April 23–May 1.

THE QUICK CONQUEST OF CRETE

The Germans followed their conquest of Greece with an invasion of the Greek island of Crete, which lay 100 miles southeast of the mainland, on May 20. Originally, Hitler had not seriously considered an operation against Crete. But Goering convinced him of the need to undertake an airborne assault to prevent Britain from maintaining a base on the island. The Allies had over 30,000 men on Crete, including 20,000 who had been evacuated from the mainland. But they were critically deficient in equipment and totally lacking in air support.

Germany's conquest of Crete was one of the most remarkable campaigns of the war because it employed only airborne troops. This was not the original intention, however. The Germans planned to carry out a seaborne landing at the same time as the assault from the sky. But British naval units intercepted two flotillas of small Greek ships that carried 7,000 German troops. They sank 14 of the ships and forced the remainder to flee back to their ports in Greece. The airborne operation might have failed, too, because the Allied commander on Crete, General Bernard Freyberg, commander of the New Zealand Division, received detailed information from Ultra of the impending seaborne and airborne landings. Unfortunately, Freyberg, a man of incredible courage who had won the Victoria Cross in World War I, drew the wrong conclusions. He was primarily concerned about the amphibious operation, which, of course, never took place. As a result, he failed to defend adequately the all-important airfields that the Germans needed to capture if they were to reinforce their original airborne landing force.

Even so, it was a close call for the Germans. Goering and the other German planners had underestimated the size of the Allied garrison and deployed only 22,000 men to take the island. The first wave of parachutists and gliderborne troops numbered a mere 3,000, and the Allied defenders inflicted heavy casualties on them. But they pressed on relentlessly, with the help of complete air supremacy, and by the second day had captured the airfields that were their primary objectives. Once they had accomplished this, transport planes quickly flew in reinforcements. The British had to resort to another evacuation and succeeded in rescuing 16,000 men. But the Germans paid a heavy price for Crete: 3,674 killed and over 2,000 wounded. Indeed, Hitler considered the casualties so severe that he never again tried an airborne mission of such magnitude.

THE GERMANS IN CONTROL

As a result of his various Balkan operations, both diplomatic and military, Hitler had gained complete control of southeastern Europe and had secured his flank for the invasion of the Soviet Union. As for the British, their intervention had been reminiscent of the Norwegian campaign and represented another forlorn chapter in the continuing saga of "too little, too late." The decision to divert troops from North Africa to Greece had been a mistake. The forces involved had been too weak to prevent the German conquest and were sorely needed in Libya when Rommel appeared on the scene.

The spring of 1941 also witnessed dramatic events in the Middle East. In Iraq, the pro-German politician Rashid Ali and a group of army officers carried out a successful coup in April. Hitler promptly dispatched arms shipments to the new regime and received approval from Vichy France for German planes to land in neighboring Syria to refuel before moving on to Iraq. But Britain reacted to the coup by sending troops to Iraq from India and Palestine, forcing Rashid Ali to flee to Iran. The British proceeded to restore a friendly government to power in Baghdad.

Meanwhile, Britain had become concerned that the Germans might send troops into Syria. Actually, Hitler had no intention of doing so and quickly withdrew his aircraft. This really eliminated the need for Allied intervention, but Churchill was insistent. On June 8, British and Free French troops moved into Syria from Palestine and Iraq, and the Vichy government ordered its troops to resist. Fighting lasted for five weeks before the Vichy forces capitulated on July 14. Britain now controlled the entire eastern end of the Mediterranean with the exception of neutral Turkey. But after holding the world spotlight for several months, the Mediterranean now lapsed back into its true sideshow status. The war's main event had already begun on the plains of Russia.

10

Operation Barbarossa: Dream of *Lebensraum*

Hitler's invasion of the Soviet Union in June 1941 was his greatest blunder. The undertaking proved beyond Germany's capacities and thus was probably fatal in itself, apart from the fact that it created a two-front war. Hitler's only chance was a quick victory, but he lacked the power to accomplish this. The Soviets were almost certain to win a long war because of their greater resources in manpower, raw materials, and industrial potential.

THE DECISION TO INVADE THE USSR

Given Hitler's basic objective of creating *Lebensraum* in the east, it was virtually inevitable that he would attack the Soviet Union eventually. But why did he strike in 1941 when Soviet neutrality assured him of peace in the east, as well as important supplies, while he continued his war against Britain? It appears that he decided to attack because he believed that the Soviets were too weak to prevent him from realizing his cherished dream. At the same time, he recognized that Britain was no threat to invade the continent in the west.

But Hitler justified his decision on the grounds that he could not trust the Soviets. His concern was not entirely fabricated. Hitler never felt completely secure from a Soviet attack while he was dealing with the Western Powers, and his fears increased in the summer of 1940 when the Soviets seized the Baltic states and the Rumanian provinces of Bessarabia and Northern Bukovina. Why the takeover of the Baltic states and Bessarabia should have come as any surprise is difficult to understand. Germany had agreed in 1939 that they lay within the Soviet sphere of influence. But Northern Bukovina was another matter. It had never belonged to Russia, and the Germans had not conceded this territory to the Soviets. Reports of Soviet troop concentrations in the newly annexed provinces increased the Führer's paranoia regarding a Soviet attack.

Germany's dependence on the Soviet Union for raw materials also worried Hitler, especially because Stalin insisted on payment in the form of armaments. In fact, shortly before the start of operations in Scandinavia and Western Europe in 1940, Hitler had ordered that arms deliveries to the Soviets receive priority over those to the German army. He considered this drastic measure necessary to assure the continued flow of raw materials from the Soviet Union. By the summer of 1940, supplies from the Soviets comprised 22 percent of Germany's total imports.

Finally, Hitler feared that Stalin might enter into an alliance with Britain and, in fact, suspected that Stalin was responsible for the British refusal to make peace after the fall of France. His concern increased as a result of Foreign Commissar Molotov's visit to Berlin in November 1940. Molotov angered Hitler by his unwillingness to renounce Soviet interest in the Balkans.

Despite Hitler's fears, there is no indication that the Soviets planned to attack Germany at any time in 1940 or 1941. It is true that in May 1941 Stalin expressed concern about deteriorating Soviet-German relations and warned of the possibility of a German invasion. He hoped to stave off such action by diplomatic means but feared that war would be inevitable by 1942. At that point, he believed that the Soviets would be strong enough to face Germany and might even have to initiate hostilities. But he clearly based this speculation on fear of German intentions and certainly did not plan to strike without provocation.

Hitler's own thoughts were straying eastward well before the start of the Battle of Britain. As early as July 1940, he ordered Brauchitsch and Halder to submit plans for a possible campaign against the Soviets. Hitler declared that "to all intents and purposes the war is almost won" and added that Britain's only hope lay with the Soviet Union and the United States. He warned of the need to destroy the Soviet Union, thus depriving the British of their last potential continental ally. In his view, the defeat of the Soviets would also discourage the Americans from entering the war.

Despite the emphatic tone of this pronouncement, Hitler's decision was not yet irrevocable, and the Germans continued to plan Operation Sea Lion, albeit halfheartedly, and sent the Luftwaffe against Britain, albeit unsuccessfully. But increasingly the option that appealed to Hitler most was an invasion of the Soviet Union. He was convinced that such an undertaking would result in an easy victory. Never impressed by Soviet military power, he became thoroughly contemptuous of the Red Army after its dismal performance against Finland. He also believed that the Soviet government was unpopular and would collapse with the first few military defeats. As he proclaimed later, "You have only to kick in the door, and the whole rotten structure will come crashing down." His contempt reflected his racial theories, which, of course, represented the Slavs as *Untermenschen*.

Whatever misgivings Hitler's generals might have had, neither the OKW nor the OKH opposed the invasion. They shared Hitler's view of Soviet weakness and were particularly scornful of the Red Army's showing in the Winter War. After studying the situation, Halder concluded that the Soviets would not be able to resist for more than eight to ten weeks. Oddly enough, Goering was the most outspoken opponent of the invasion and tried unsuccessfully to change Hitler's mind.

MILITARY STRENGTHS AND WEAKNESSES

Both Hitler and his generals were guilty of two serious errors. They woefully underestimated the obstacles involved in a Russian campaign and the strength of the Soviet armed forces. They also overestimated Germany's own power. The obstacles should have been obvious. The Soviet Union comprised an area greater than North America, and its huge population provided vast reserves of manpower. Its infamous winter weather mandated that the Germans would have to win the campaign between May and October. The inadequate Soviet roads and the fact that Soviet railway gauge was wider than that of Western Europe posed staggering logistic problems. The Germans faced the dilemma of converting the rail system to the narrower Western gauge. Germany's shortage of motorized transport also would create far more difficult supply problems in the vast expanse of the Soviet Union than in the less spacious areas of Poland, France, and the Balkans.

The Soviet armed forces had some serious weaknesses, but they also possessed remarkable strength, especially in manpower and quantity of equipment. Although estimates vary, the Red Army appears to have had the equivalent of 230 to 240 divisions, including 170 infantry divisions, as well as 33 cavalry and 46 armored and motorized brigades. The USSR had enormous numbers of tanks, with estimates ranging from 10,000 to 24,000. Unfortunately, most of them were obsolete, but the Soviets had developed some outstanding new tanks—the heavy KV and the medium T34—that were superior to the best German models. The T34 was especially formidable. It was fast, armed with a 76-millimeter gun, and well armored. The Soviet air force contained at least 8,000 planes, including 2,000 fighters and 1,800 bombers, but only 800 in each category were modern.

The chief Soviet weakness was in military leadership. This was due largely to Stalin's extensive purge of the officer corps in the late 1930s. He had resorted to this action in an effort to destroy any possibility of army resistance to his rule. As a result, many of the top generals in 1941 were more notable for their political reliability than for their military prowess. There were some fine officers, but for the most part they did not rise to positions of authority until after the Red Army had experienced appalling disasters in the summer of 1941.

Two exceptions to this were Marshal Timoshenko and General Georgi Zhukov, who had actually assumed important posts shortly before the war. Zhukov, the son of a peasant shoemaker in a small village near Moscow, began his military career as an enlisted man during World War I. His bravery twice won him the Order of St. George, Czarist Russia's highest military decoration. With the coming of the revolution, he joined the Red Army and saw action as a cavalry officer in the civil war. He won Stalin's favor in the following years, rising swiftly in rank and becoming a specialist in armored warfare. Timoshenko had salvaged victory in the Winter War and, with Zhukov's help, had launched a desperately needed modernization of the Red Army that focused on the development of armored divisions. But their efforts encountered strong opposition among the less progressive elements in the Soviet leadership.

The Red Army's recent battle experience was not limited to the fiasco in Finland. The Soviets had fought Japanese troops along the disputed border between Manchuria and Soviet East Asian territories in 1938, and shortly before the outbreak of the European war, Zhukov had led a massive tank force to a resounding victory in the Battle of Khalkhin-Gol. Not surprisingly, after this experience, the Japanese did not share the German view of Soviet military weakness.

Stalin exercised supreme authority over the army and insisted that much of it be stationed far forward in the buffer area of Lithuania, eastern Poland, and Bessarabia. This placed the main Soviet armies in positions that were dangerously vulnerable to a German armored attack.

German strength in 1941 was not appreciably greater than it had been during the campaign in the west in 1940. The OKH assembled 145 divisions for the invasion, including 102 infantry, 19 armored, and 14 motorized. Although the number of armored units had almost doubled from May 1940, this was deceptive because the quantity of tanks per division had actually declined by half. The change was due to Hitler's infatuation with numbers. He found comfort in the fact that Germany possessed twice as many divisions, even though overall tank strength, 2,500, remained the same as in 1940. The Luftwaffe had 2,770 planes, including 1,085 bombers and 920 fighters. Its strength in both categories was actually lower than at the start of the Battle of Britain, although quality was somewhat higher.

OBJECTIVES AND STRATEGY

Hitler and the OKH disagreed over objectives. To be sure, both considered the destruction of the Red Army in the shortest possible time as the primary aim. But the OKH believed that German forces should concentrate on the capture of the capital, Moscow, which also was an important industrial center and the hub of the Soviet rail network. Hitler gave priority to the conquest of the Baltic states and Leningrad in the north as well as the Ukraine, with its huge supplies of grain and iron ore, and ultimately the Caucasus oil fields in the south. The Führer was also anxious for German forces to link up with the Finnish army in the Leningrad area. Finland had allowed a small German force to enter its territory as early as September 1940 and agreed to join in the campaign against the Soviets to regain the land lost in the Winter War.

Despite the divergence in views of German leaders, Hitler approved a compromise operational plan on December 18, 1940. It was given the code name Operation Barbarossa, in honor of the medieval German emperor Frederick Barbarossa, and provided for participation by three army groups. Army Group North, commanded by Field Marshal von Leeb, was to slash through the Baltic states toward Leningrad. It consisted of two infantry armies of 27 divisions and a panzer group of three armored divisions. Army Group Center, under Field Marshal von Bock, was to penetrate into Soviet-occupied Poland and Belorussia in the direction of Moscow. It was the largest army group with two infantry armies of 42 divisions and two panzer groups of nine armored divisions. Army Group South, led by Field Marshal von Rundstedt, was to drive through the Ukraine. Its strength included three infantry armies of 38 divisions and a panzer group of five armored divisions. Two Rumanian armies and a Hungarian corps were also to take part in the southern operation.

Army Group Center was to destroy the enemy in Poland and Belorussia and then shift its panzer forces to help Army Group North smash the enemy in the Leningrad area. After accomplishing this objective, the armor would return to the central front to resume the drive on Moscow. The campaign's ultimate objective was an extremely ambitious one—to reach a line running from Archangel in the far north to Astrakhan near the Caspian Sea in the south. The OKH intended to start Operation Barbarossa on May 15, but the *coup d'état* in Yugoslavia and Hitler's decision to crush that country forced postponement until June 22. Original German plans had called for an invasion of Greece without using forces earmarked for Barbarossa, but the Yugoslav complication necessitated a diversion of strength. Even without the intervention in Yugoslavia, however, it is doubtful that the Russian campaign could have started in May. The spring of 1941 was extremely wet, and the rivers in eastern Poland were at flood stage until early June. Shortages of equipment, especially motor transport vehicles, also contributed to the delay.

THE SPECTACULAR INVASION BEGINS

When Hitler finally unleashed his attack on June 22, the Germans caught Soviet troops in the forward areas totally off guard, even though Soviet agents had repeatedly warned Stalin of the impending invasion. The Soviets had an outstanding intelligence service, which included Richard Sorge, a German Communist who operated in Japan and had gained the complete trust of both German and Japanese officials in Tokyo. He not only alerted Stalin to the impending attack but even included the date of the invasion. Another Soviet agent in Switzerland, referred to as Lucy, confirmed the date and added details of the German operational plan. Churchill also sent Stalin personal warnings based on messages intercepted by Ultra and other sources. But the Soviet dictator refused to alert any of his commanders in the forward zone. Stalin apparently believed that Britain had instigated the warnings to stir up trouble between Russia and Germany and wanted to avoid any activity that might provoke the Germans. Although he finally allowed an alert to be sent early on June 22, it came far too late.

Germany also gained complete surprise from the air. The first bombers took off before the start of hostilities, flew at high altitudes to avoid detection, and then swooped down on unsuspecting Soviet air bases just as German troops crossed the border. More devastating air attacks followed. The Soviets lost an estimated 1,200 planes on the first day.

Operation Barbarossa made spectacular early progress. After the first week, the German propaganda ministry announced bombastically: "In seven short days, the Führer's offensive has smashed the Red Army to splinters. . . . The

FIGURE 10-1 German soldiers charge past an armored half-track vehicle and a burning farmhouse during the invasion of the USSR. (*Library of Congress*)

eastern continent lies, like a limp virgin, in the mighty arms of the German Mars." Leeb's Army Group North drove 155 miles through Lithuania and into Latvia in the first five days, spearheaded by a panzer group commanded by General Höpner. Although Höpner had been active in the conspiracy against Hitler before the war, he had demonstrated great skill as a panzer corps commander in both the Polish and Western European campaigns. By July 10, his armor was within 80 miles of Leningrad, but at this point the drive bogged down due to heavily wooded terrain and supply problems.

Bock's Army Group Center also scored massive gains. Two panzer groups, one commanded by General Hermann Hoth on the left and the other by Guderian on the right, carried out two successive encirclements of large Russian forces. Unlike Höpner, Hoth was a loyal supporter of Hitler, but he, too, had led panzer forces with considerable flair in Poland and Western Europe. He shared Guderian's fervor for swift exploitation of an armored breakthrough. Together they closed the first trap near Minsk in the area of the prewar Soviet-Polish border on June 26. They completed the second envelopment near Smolensk, 200 miles to the east, in mid-July. In all, Bock's troops captured 480,000 prisoners, and the Soviets suffered disastrous losses in armor. But as impressive as these victories were, they were less decisive than the Germans thought because many Soviets were able to escape before the pincers closed. Others eluded capture even after that because the panzers were so far ahead of the mass of infantry following on foot that the flanks of the encirclements were weakly held. Still, the Germans had covered 440 miles in 23 days and were only 200 miles from Moscow.

Progress was slower in the south as Rundstedt's forces moved toward Kiev with a panzer group, commanded by General von Kleist, in the vanguard. Although Kleist had worried over the rapid pace of Guderian's dash toward the English Channel in 1940, he had become a convert to armored warfare and had led a panzer group during the conquest of Yugoslavia. But he and Rundstedt encountered fierce Soviet resistance in the Ukraine as well as severe supply problems.

Germany's enormous success and the desperate condition of Red Army forces in the forward areas convinced Soviet leaders of the need to overhaul their command structure. Stalin created the State Defense Committee (GKO), which consisted of five members of the ruling Politburo with Stalin as its chairman. It now assumed overall direction of the war effort. Stalin also established Stavka, the general headquarters of the Soviet supreme command, which was directly subordinate to the GKO. The army general staff came under Stavka's supervision, and its chief of staff, General Boris Shaposhnikov, received a key position in Stavka. Henceforth, Stavka conceived basic strategy, while the general staff developed actual operational plans for the conduct of the war.

It was not until August 5 that the last resistance ended within the Smolensk pocket on the central front. Even before this it had been necessary for Bock's troops to halt their forward progress and establish an advance supply base. Army Group Center had outdistanced its supply line, and most of the infantry was still strung out far behind the armor. Meanwhile, the preinvasion dispute over strategy, which the compromise plan for Operation Barbarossa had temporarily settled, returned in a more virulent form on July 19. Hitler proposed to divert Hoth's panzer group from Army Group Center to help in the drive on Leningrad as the original plan had stipulated. But now he also wanted to shift Guderian's panzer group to the south, where the possibility of another huge encirclement loomed. Brauchitsch and Halder insisted that it would be wiser to keep the armor in the center for a drive on Moscow. Bock and Guderian agreed. They all contended that since Moscow was the decisive objective, the Soviets would commit their greatest strength to its defense. This posed the possibility of destroying much of the Red Army, which was the chief objective of Operation Barbarossa. The quarrel continued while Army Group Center fought off fierce Soviet counterattacks, but on August 20 Hitler ordered Hoth's armor northward and Guderian's to the south.

Critics have long contended that the generals were correct and that Germany may have lost the campaign and the war because of Hitler's refusal to allow an immediate drive on Moscow. But evidence now indicates that German supply problems were so severe that a major attack on the capital was probably not feasible until mid-September. It might have been possible to send Guderian's panzer group in a single thrust toward Moscow without any immediate support by the mass of Army Group Center. But there is some question that the Germans could have supplied even this force over the 200-mile distance. It also is unlikely that a single panzer group would have been strong enough to defeat the Soviets and take Moscow. Guderian's flanks would have been vulnerable to counterattacks that might have cut off his armor.

Hoth's panzers contributed to the encirclement of Leningrad, but Hitler did not intend to storm the city. He planned instead to starve it into submission. The siege began in September, and the suffering of Leningrad's population soon reached epic proportions. Perhaps as many as a million Leningraders worked incessantly to build a crude defensive perimeter around the city, including earthern walls, tank traps, pillboxes, and barbed wire entanglements. Many others volunteered for a paramilitary force, the People's Army. Despite having almost no training and few weapons, they received the grim assignment of plugging gaps in the army's defensive line. Some of them were armed only with containers of boiling water, which they threw at the enemy. Others ignited kerosene in an effort to slow the German advance. They suffered appalling casualties.

Although the Soviets were not able to lift the siege until early 1944, the worst of the ordeal occurred during November, December, and January of 1941–42. Food was in such short supply during this period that over 200,000 people died of starvation and diseases caused by malnutrition. The city depended on supplies that came by train from Moscow to Lake Ladoga and then by boat to the small port of Osinovets. From there the precious cargoes traveled another 35 miles by rail, a route within easy range of German artillery. But the Germans cut the Moscow-Leningrad

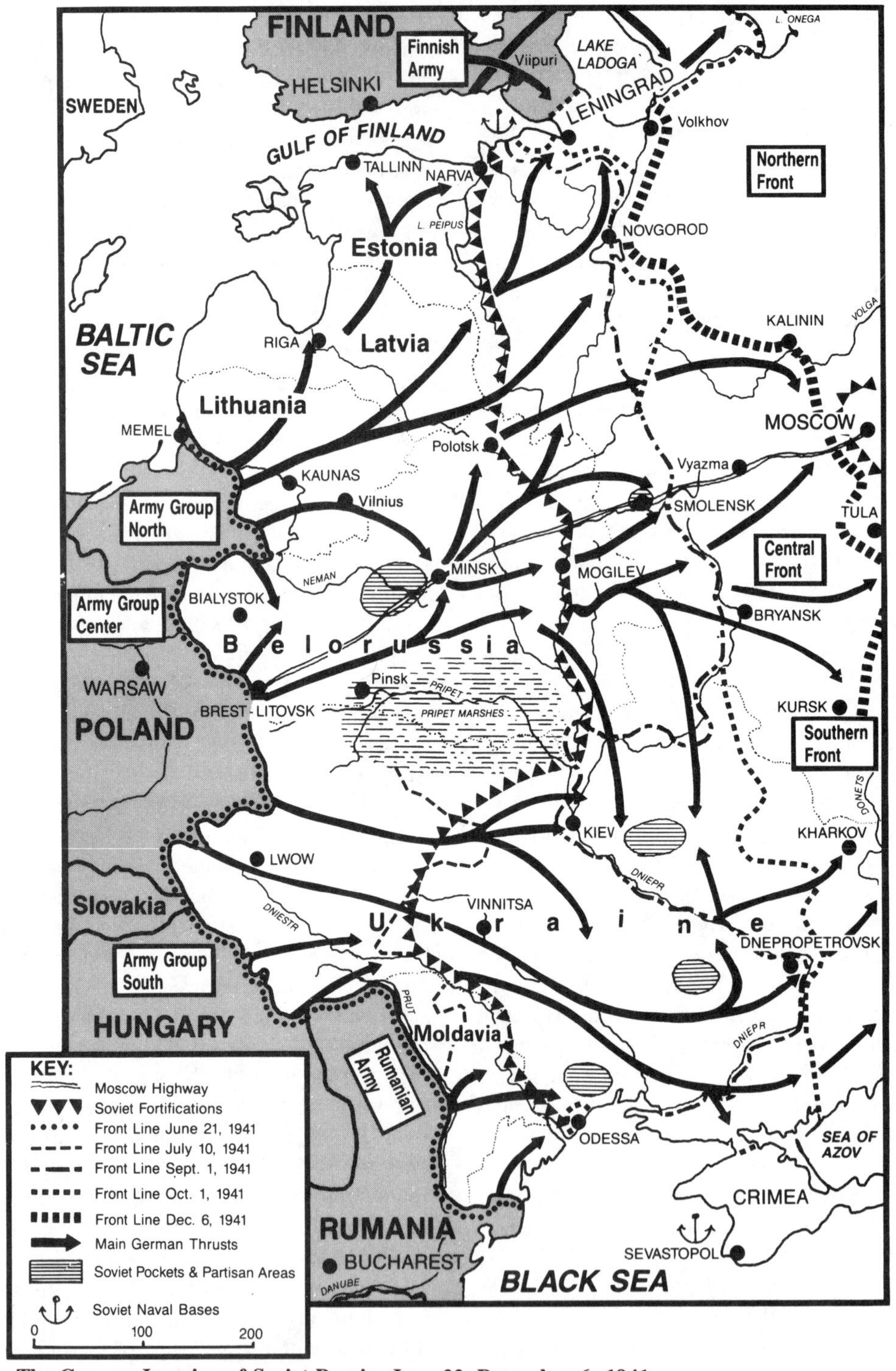

The German Invasion of Soviet Russia, June 22–December 6, 1941

railroad on November 9, and the Soviets did not regain control until a month later. Even after restoring the rail link, it was necessary to haul supplies across the frozen lake in trucks, many of which broke through the treacherous ice. Food became so scarce during the worst months of the siege that people resorted to devouring dogs, cats, rats, melted-down wallpaper glue, and a horrible jelly made from sheep intestines. Some also resorted to cannibalism, eating the flesh of corpses that they found in the streets or makeshift morgues.

Meanwhile, Guderian's panzer group took part in the encirclement of massive Soviet forces under the command of Marshal Semyon Budenny near Kiev, the capital of the Ukraine. Kleist's panzer group, which had driven to the southeast of Kiev, hooked north to link up with Guderian's armor, which was thrusting southward. Some have blamed Budenny, whom one observer described as a man "with an immense mustache but a very small brain," for the Soviet disaster. Certainly Budenny left much to be desired as a military leader. He had started his career in the czarist army, serving in both the Russo-Japanese War and World War I as a noncommissioned officer before becoming an officer in the Red Army cavalry. Budenny made his reputation in the civil war and became a close associate of Stalin, rising to high rank through favoritism. But despite Budenny's meager qualifications for command, the real culprit in the debacle at Kiev was Stalin, who ordered Budenny not to withdraw his forces from their exposed position. This decision enabled the Germans to capture over 600,000 Russians. Hitler was ecstatic and called the encirclement the "greatest battle in the history of the world." It was certainly a brilliant victory, but it did not assure a triumphant outcome to the campaign.

The Germans did not complete the Kiev operation until September 26. While it was in progress, Hitler decided that the time had come for an attack on Moscow with the greatest possible strength. He restored the panzer groups of Hoth and Guderian to Army Group Center and also shifted Höpner's armor from Army Group North to take part in the offensive. At the same time, Hitler ordered Army Group South to advance toward Kharkov, the Donetz Basin industrial area in the eastern Ukraine, and Rostov, the gateway to the Caucasus oil fields.

Bock launched his drive toward Moscow on September 30. It featured armored thrusts by Hoth on the north, Höpner in the center, and Guderian on the south that quickly produced two new encirclements and the capture of another 600,000 prisoners. Hitler was convinced that the enemy would "never rise again." His optimism appeared well founded. Soviet forces remaining to the west of Moscow were outnumbered and lacking in heavy equipment.

The Soviets had suffered huge losses of war materiel since the start of the invasion. They had managed to offset this to some extent by a drastic effort to increase production between July and October. But as the Germans swept eastward, Soviet leaders had no choice but to dismantle industrial plants and evacuate them to safer locations. These included the region of the Volga River hundreds of miles east of Moscow as well as much more remote destinations—the Ural Mountains, Western Siberia, and Central Asia. This was a formidable task that required exceptional planning and placed a tremendous strain on the railroad system. In all, the Soviets moved over 1,500 industrial enterprises to the east between July and November. Once they had completed this great evacuation, it was necessary to reassemble the industries as quickly as possible, under often very difficult conditions. Millions of workers had to make the long trek to the east, where they labored as many as 15 hours a day and experienced deplorable living conditions.

German troops also overran many of the Soviet Union's best food-producing regions, especially the Ukraine. As a result, the same areas that provided havens for the uprooted industries had to increase their food production drastically. This often involved the cultivation of crops that had never before grown in these regions. Once again, the results were remarkable.

In the aftermath of the great battles of en-

FIGURE 10-2 White-clad Red Army troops pause for a moment of relaxation during their winter offensive. (*Library of Congress*)

circlement, it seemed certain that Moscow would fall to a giant pincers movement. Hoth's panzers were to swing around the northern flank of the capital, while Guderian was to turn the southern flank. Höpner would continue his advance directly on the city. But now complications arose. Rain fell steadily during much of October, and in many places the advance mired in mud until November. Although the Germans were within 40 miles of Moscow at one point, they debated whether it might be wise to go over to the defensive.

WEATHER AND THE SOVIETS TURN THE TIDE

There was good reason for caution. The winter was about to start, German forces were depleted, and the supply situation was badly snarled. Yet some German generals believed that an all-out effort might crush the Red Army and feared that breaking off the offensive would result in a World War I–type stalemate. After much debate, the OKH finally proposed to resume the drive on Moscow, and Hitler agreed. The Germans based this decision, however, on inadequate knowledge of enemy strength. The Soviets had been moving in fresh divisions including many Siberian units from East Asia. Stalin felt secure in weakening his East Asian forces because of Sorge's reports from Tokyo that Japan would not intervene against Russia but intended to attack the United States. He also appointed Zhukov to take command of the Moscow front. Zhukov had no intention of committing his newly arrived troops to defend against a resumption of the German offensive. Instead, he hoarded them to the east of the capital and planned to wait until the enemy drive had lost its momentum before unleashing a powerful counterstroke.

In the meantime, the troops that had survived the earlier German offensive had to hold the flanks to the north and south of Moscow. Again officials recruited hundreds of thousands of civilians to build three rings of defenses around the city. They also committed units of the People's Army to fill gaps in the line, and as at Leningrad, these poorly trained and ill-equipped auxiliaries fought bravely and suffered heavy losses. While the desperate struggle unfolded, Stalin delivered stirring speeches in which, instead of resorting to the usual Communist slogans, he appealed directly to the patriotism of the army and the people. He implored them to rally to the defense of Holy Mother Russia, and they responded with grim determination.

Army Group Center launched its final onslaught on November 15, but the drive made limited progress and ground to a halt by the end of November. The weather had deteriorated even before the start of the offensive, with temperatures dropping as low as 35 to 40 degrees below 0 Celsius, and heavy snow fell later in the month. Because of the lack of antifreeze, the Germans kept small fires burning under their tanks when they were not in use to prevent freezing. The men were without winter clothing and had to make do with what they could seize from the Soviets. During this operation, the Wehrmacht lost more soldiers to frostbite than to the Soviets. Dysentery created additional dangers. Many men suffered congelation of the anus while squatting to relieve themselves in temperatures as low as −60 degrees Celsius. The stabbing cold also froze food so solid that butter had to be cut with a saw, and horse meat proved impervious to the ax. If hot soup were not eaten promptly, it became cold in seconds and frozen in minutes.

The stage was set for the Soviet counteroffensive. The Red Army's first initiative came in the south. Timoshenko had replaced Budenny as commander on this front after the Kiev encirclement, and his troops forced Rundstedt to abandon Rostov on November 28. Zhukov also launched far heavier attacks against the enemy flanks to the north and south of Moscow on December 5. Army Group Center now faced an ugly choice: resort to a major withdrawal or hold fast and fight for every inch. Halder favored a retreat to a more or less prepared line. But Hitler insisted that the troops must form a number of strong points, called hedgehogs, around advanced supply depots and fight on even if surrounded. His decision has been a source of controversy ever since. After the war, Halder blamed it for the heavy losses that the Germans suffered during the winter of 1941–42. But a number of other generals contended that Hitler actually saved the army from what would have been a rout if it had attempted a large-scale withdrawal.

The situation was precarious for a long time, and at one point there was a real danger that the Red Army might encircle Army Group Center. The Soviets did cut off some German troops, but they continued to hold out, and the Luftwaffe supplied them by air throughout the winter. Zhukov wanted to concentrate the bulk of the Red Army for an all-out assault on the Moscow front, which he believed might deal Army Group Center a fatal blow. But Stalin insisted that Soviet forces continue to attack on all fronts. This weakened Zhukov's striking power and helped the Germans to hold out. The Red Army also suffered heavy losses. This was inevitable against such a tenacious enemy, but it was also indicative of Zhukov's philosophy of war. He believed in hammering relentlessly at an objective, no matter what the cost in lives.

When the Soviet counteroffensive finally ground to a halt in March 1942, it was clear that the war on the eastern front had become a stalemate for the time being. It was also apparent that the struggle for the Soviet Union would be long and bloody.

Failure in the campaign led to a wholesale shake-up of Germany's military leadership. Rundstedt resigned in protest when Hitler refused to allow an additional withdrawal following the loss of Rostov. Soon afterward, Hitler dismissed both Guderian and Höpner for ordering unauthorized retreats. He lashed out with particular fury against Höpner, whom he stripped of his rank and ousted from the army. Bock gave up his command because of illness, and Leeb resigned early in 1942. An even higher luminary added his name to the roster of fallen generals when Brauchitsch asked to be relieved as commander in chief. His health had deteriorated steadily under the strain of the campaign. Rather than appoint a successor, Hitler took over as commander in chief himself. Halder was the sole survivor in the army's top echelon.

Hitler's assumption of Brauchitsch's duties represented a serious encroachment on army responsibilities. Henceforth, he restricted the OKH to planning operations on the eastern front only and even there frequently intervened in command decisions. Elsewhere, the OKW exercised operational authority, and the OKW was, of course, very much under the Führer's control. The success of Hitler's "hold fast" policy before Moscow during the winter of 1941–42 also increased his belief in his own destiny. It set a dangerous precedent. In the future, when confronted by even more serious situations, he repeatedly relied on the same policy, with catastrophic results.

The Wehrmacht's failure to crush the Red Army in 1941 was fatal to Hitler's dream of *Lebensraum* and ultimately to the existence of the Third Reich. His invincible army had been stopped, its power blunted. It would never again be as formidable as it had been in June 1941. Even if it had been possible for Army Group Center to capture Moscow, there is little likelihood that the Germans would have won the campaign. There is no reason to believe that the Soviets would not have continued to fight on. The crucial mistake was the decision to attack the Soviet Union in the first place. The task was simply beyond Germany's resources.

11

Hitler's New Order in Europe

Russia's unexpected counteroffensive had dealt Hitler's vision of *Lebensraum* in the east a shattering blow. But the dream was not yet dead. Indeed, efforts were under way to establish what Hitler called the New Order, not only in the areas of the Soviet Union that had fallen under German control but in the remainder of Nazi-dominated Europe as well. Hitler intended the New Order to apply ultimately to all the peoples of Europe, in ways that differed according to his view of the merits of each group.

THE GREATER GERMAN EMPIRE

The Germans were the chosen people in the New Order. But Germandom, in Hitler's mind, included not only the Germans of the Reich and the ethnic German minorities of Central and Eastern Europe but also the other Germanic peoples—the Scandinavians, the Dutch, the Luxembourgers, the German-speaking Swiss, the Flemish Belgians, and the English. He envisaged most of these peoples as members of a Greater German Empire. The English were the one possible exception to this. Hitler apparently intended to allow them to maintain their independence as an affiliated state, provided that they demonstrated a sufficiently positive attitude.

Hitler's approach to the Germanic peoples of Scandinavia and the Low Countries varied from area to area, but his final intent was to absorb all of them into the Greater Reich. When his troops overran Denmark in April 1940, he allowed the Danish government to continue administering the country, subject to German supervision. But he began to tie Denmark more closely to the Reich in 1942, and after a wave of strikes gripped the country in 1943, German domination became complete.

Hitler initially planned a similar policy of moderation for Norway, but Norwegian resistance to the German invasion shattered this hope. Instead, he recognized Quisling as head of a puppet regime, but Quisling proved so unpopular that the Germans quickly withdrew their support. Quisling regained Hitler's favor in 1942, however, and returned to the office of prime minister. He retained his position until the end of the war, even though Hitler found him increasingly tiresome. Despite Quisling's admiration for Nazi Germany, he visualized Norway as an independent client-state of the Reich. Hitler had no intention of allowing this. But Quisling was never more than a front man for the chief German official in Norway, Reich Commissioner Josef Terboven, who remained the dominant figure throughout the entire occupation. Norway's neighbor, Sweden, maintained its freedom from

Nazi occupation, but if Hitler had won the war, it seems likely that it, too, would have disappeared into the Nazi empire.

The Führer originally intended to grant preferential treatment to Luxembourg, but Grand Duchess Charlotte and her government fled into exile and refused to cooperate. As a result, the Germans absorbed the country into the Reich administratively and economically.

In the Netherlands, Dutch officials continued to handle routine administration but took orders from Reich Commissioner Arthur Seyss-Inquart, who had been Hitler's instrument in the destruction of Austria's independence. Seyss-Inquart soon encountered a number of rivals for authority, however. These included the SS, the Foreign Ministry, and various economic organizations. Hitler intended ultimately to incorporate the Netherlands into the Reich, and as the first step in this direction, German officials attempted to integrate the Dutch economy with Germany's. While considerable progress resulted, the competition between rival Nazi agencies also led to a great deal of inefficiency and confusion.

Belgium posed a special problem because of its mixed population. Hitler recognized the Flemish-speaking people of northwestern Belgium as Germanic and thus worthy of absorption into his Greater Germany. The French-speaking Walloons, who lived in the southeast, had highly questionable Germanic credentials. But Leon Degrelle, an extreme Walloon nationalist and admirer of the Nazis, actually persuaded Hitler that his people were Germanic. It is clear that Hitler planned to annex all of Belgium as well as the Flemish-speaking portions of northwestern France after the war. Unlike the Netherlands, Belgium remained under military authority during most of the German occupation and as a result experienced less competition for power among the various Nazi organizations.

Switzerland, like Sweden, remained free from occupation throughout the war. Hitler held the German-speaking Swiss in low esteem. He saw them as the black sheep of Germandom because of their democratic government and what he viewed as their single-minded devotion to business. To him, Switzerland was "a pimple on the face of Europe," but it appears that he intended, nevertheless, to annex at least the German-speaking areas after the war.

THE "JEWISH QUESTION"

If the Germanic groups were the chosen people in the New Order, the Jews were the damned. From the time he came to power, Hitler clearly planned to expel the Jews from Germany and other territories that fell under his control. Whether he intended from the start to exterminate them is less clear.

The early Nazi approach focused on the imposition of numerous restrictions aimed at making life miserable for the Jews and encouraging their emigration from Germany. Some Jews did leave, but the majority stayed. Many simply lacked the financial means to flee. Others disliked the thought of abandoning their homeland and hoped that the persecution might be temporary. The situation deteriorated in 1935 as Nazi thugs attacked Jewish shops and beat up Jews in the streets. This trend culminated later that year in the promulgation of the Nuremberg Laws, which deprived Jews of German citizenship and prohibited marriage and sexual relations between Jews and ethnic Germans.

Persecution became more intense in November 1938 when a Jew assassinated an official of the German embassy in Paris. A wave of terror followed in Germany. The Nazis murdered 100 Jews, arrested 30,000 others, and engaged in the wholesale burning of synagogues and the destruction of Jewish shops. They broke so much glass in the process that this pogrom became known as *Kristallnacht* (Night of Crystal Glass). In the aftermath of *Kristallnacht,* the Nazis forced the Jewish community to pay a heavy indemnity, seized Jewish businesses, and forced firms to dismiss Jewish employees. All of this led to a great increase in emigration during the remainder of 1938 and into 1939. But the refugees encountered resistance from other countries, which were reluctant to allow them to settle within their borders. Approximately 150,000 of Germany's 515,000 Jews had emigrated by 1938, but the annexation of Austria added another 200,000 Jews to the population. The Nazis established a special agency to facilitate emigration in early 1939, but despite their efforts, 350,000 Jews still remained when war erupted later that year.

With the outbreak of hostilities, Jewish emigration became extremely difficult, and the Nazis eventually resorted to deportation. At first they did little to implement this policy, other than to speculate on where to send the Jews. The most bizarre solution involved a plan to take over the island of Madagascar, a French possession off the southeast coast of Africa, and convert it into a permanent Jewish homeland. But the Germans were never able to gain control of Madagascar. Instead, they designated Poland as the dumping ground for Jews, but the process did not begin until the fall of 1941, when the Nazis launched a large-scale deportation program.

Hitler and his associates ultimately chose extermination as the "final solution to the Jewish question," a concept that appears to have taken shape gradually. They put the preliminaries into effect in 1939, when 2 million Polish Jews came under German domination. The SS, under the direction of Reinhard Heydrich, the head of Himmler's security service (SD), rounded up Polish Jews and concentrated them in ghettos in large cities. It is not clear whether the original intention was extermination or expulsion. Death camps, as such, did not come into existence until much later. The task of concentration proved a formidable one, however, and the SS eased the problem by shooting many Jews, a practice that continued when the Germans invaded the Soviet Union in 1941. Special murder squads carried out this policy in the USSR on a much greater scale than in Poland. The most notorious massacre featured the shooting of 33,000 Jewish men, women, and children in a wood called Babyi Yar near Kiev. In all, the SS killed approximately 1.4 million Jews in this manner by the end of 1942.

The next logical step, starting in December 1941, was the establishment of actual death camps, using gas. Most of these were located in the Government General of Poland, but the largest was centered at Auschwitz in an area of southwestern Poland that Hitler had incorporated into the Reich. At first the camps used carbon monoxide, but they soon switched to the more efficient hydrogen cyanide. Heydrich assumed responsibility for the extermination program, although Himmler retained overall supervision, and Adolf Eichmann handled the actual task of arresting and transporting Jews to the camps.

Heydrich and Eichmann were among the most sinister members of the Nazi hierarchy. Blond, tall, and well built with strong, indeed cruel features, Heydrich was one of the few party leaders who looked the part of the true Aryan. Ironically, this paragon of the Nordic "Blond Beast" was probably not "racially pure." He allegedly had a Jewish grandmother. This did not prevent him from executing the Final Solution with cold-blooded efficiency. No less an authority than Hitler admiringly referred to him as "the man with the iron heart." Eichmann, though German-born, had grown up in Austria under the care of a domineering stepmother. He lacked Heydrich's physical attributes but shared his devotion to duty. Eichmann rose gradually through the SS ranks and presided over the program that encouraged Jewish emigration and later enforced deportation. Many years after the war, he was still able to describe his role in the Final Solution without the faintest trace of regret:

> I did not take on the job as a senseless exercise. It gave me uncommon joy. I found it fascinating to have to deal with these matters. . . . My job was to catch these enemies and transport them to their destination. . . . I lived in this stuff, otherwise I would have remained only an assistant, a cog, something soulless. . . . To be frank with you, had we killed all of them, the 10.3 million, I would be happy. . . .*

---

*Yehuda Bauer, *A History of the Holocaust* (New York: Franklin Watts, 1982), p. 207.

FIGURE 11-1 Jews look forlornly from a truck while en route to perform forced labor for the Germans. (*YIVO Institute for Jewish Research*)

SS leaders referred to the killing of Jews euphemistically as "special treatment." At first they murdered only those who were unfit for work, but in the spring of 1942 they extended the principle to all Jews in Eastern Europe. In March 1943, the Nazis attempted to speed up the deportation of the remaining Jewish population from areas under direct German control as well as satellite states. Civilian authorities cooperated eagerly in some countries, while in others officials and ordinary citizens attempted to foil the Nazi policy. Most of the small Jewish population of Denmark and over half of the Norwegian Jews escaped to neutral Sweden. About 50 percent of Belgian Jews, again a small number, and more than two-thirds of the 300,000 French Jews were also able to elude Nazi efforts to capture them, as were most of Italy's 50,000 Jews.

The Jewish populations of other countries were less fortunate. Nazi death camps took the lives of most of the surviving Jews of Poland and the German-occupied areas in the Soviet Union as well as the majority of those from the Netherlands, Yugoslavia, and Greece. Despite the resistance of the Hungarian government, the Germans ultimately secured the deportation of 500,000 Jews after Germany occupied Hungary militarily in 1944. Most of them died at Auschwitz. In all, perhaps as many as 5.8 million Jews perished during the Holocaust. Their only crime was the fact that they were Jewish.

Although some commentators have expressed bewilderment that the Jews accepted their fate so docilely, resistance to the Nazi murderers was an exceedingly difficult undertaking. But many Jews did resist. The most notable example was the Warsaw Ghetto Uprising of April 1943, but revolts also took place in other Polish ghettos, and there were even uprisings in the Auschwitz and Sobibor death camps. All of them failed, but they at least allowed those who participated to die with far more dignity than was the case in the gas chambers. Other Jews fought as partisans in Poland and the Soviet Union, and many joined the French resistance forces.

One of the horrible ironies of World War II was the timing of the Final Solution. The Nazis launched their extermination policy at almost the same time that the German army was suffering its first reverse in Russia and accelerated the killing in 1943 when it should have been clear even to Hitler that chances of a German victory were extremely remote. They were determined to finish the task before the war ended.

Many survivors have related accounts of ghastly incidents that took place during the Holocaust, but the following eyewitness description by a German stoker at Auschwitz perhaps best captures the nightmarish horror of the crime against the Jews. It refers to a situation caused by the arrival at Auschwitz of over 400,000 Hungarian Jews in July 1944. Approximately 75 percent of them went to their deaths immediately, creating a serious problem for the camp's crematoriums, which lacked the capacity to process such a glut of bodies. The stokers had to burn many of the victims in open pits, which also created problems:

> While in the Crematorium ovens, once the corpses were thoroughly alight, it was possible to maintain a lasting red heat with the help of fans, in the pits the fire would burn only as the air could circulate freely in between the bodies. As the heap of bodies settled, no air was able to get in from outside. This meant that we stokers had to constantly pour oil or wood alcohol on the burning corpses, in addition to human fat, large quantities of which had collected and was boiling in the two collecting pans on either side of the pit. The sizzling fat was scooped out with buckets on a long curved rod and poured all over the pit causing flames to leap up amid much crackling and hissing. Dense smoke and fumes arose incessantly. The air reeked of oil, fat, benzole and burnt flesh.*

Despite Nazi efforts to keep the extermination of Jews secret, as early as 1941 news of the mass murders began to penetrate into Germany as well as Allied and neutral countries. At first, the reports were greeted with disbelief. Even Jews in the United States and Britain were skeptical. Gradually, as it became increasingly clear during 1942 that the Nazi regime was actively pursuing genocide, disbelief gave way in Allied countries to indifference, hesitation, and a callous focus on purely military objectives. The Soviet Union remained totally disinterested in the plight of the Jews. Although some Western leaders voiced sympathy, their record was not much better. To be sure, outsiders had limited potential to help the Jews, but the Allies did not vigorously pursue the options that did exist. They vetoed proposals to bomb the railway lines leading into Auschwitz and even the camp itself, ostensibly because Auschwitz was not a military target. Late in the war, German authorities made proposals to "sell" Jews in return for trucks and other equipment, but the Allies did not respond. They also failed to apply more than token pressure on the satellite states to resist the deportation of Jews. Even public declarations attacking the Nazi policy of extermination were few and muted.

The approach of both Churchill and Roosevelt was at best one of virtual indifference. The United States generally deferred to Britain in regard to policy toward the Jews until 1944, but Churchill and the British Foreign Office were in no mood to be distracted from pursuit of the war effort. The U.S. State Department also showed little interest in the plight of the Jews, and the same was true of Congress. In addition, the non-Jewish majorities in both countries did not appear overly concerned and contained strong anti-Semitic undercurrents. Elements of the Jewish-American population did attempt to exert pressure on the government as well as public opinion to help rescue the Jews. But divisions between Zionists, who favored the creation of a Jewish homeland in Palestine, and non-Zionists hampered even these efforts.

GERMAN TREATMENT OF OTHER NON-ARYANS

The Jews were not the only people to feel the fury of Hitler's hatred. He condemned the Gypsies to the same fate. The Gypsies apparently originated in India and over the centuries became dispersed

*Filip Müller, *Eyewitness Auschwitz: Three Years in the Gas Chambers* (New York: Stein & Day, 1979), p. 136.

FIGURE 11-2 Jewish prisoners await execution during the Nazi liquidation of the Warsaw Ghetto Uprising in 1943. (*YIVO Institute for Jewish Research*)

throughout the world. They wandered about in small groups and refused to settle in one place. Hitler considered them "trash" fit only for extermination. The death camps claimed the lives of approximately 200,000 out of a total of 700,000 European Gypsies.

Hitler also looked upon the Slavs with utter contempt. For them, the New Order ultimately held only the prospect of expulsion from their homelands, enslavement, or death. But during the war, Nazi policy toward the Slavs varied from country to country.

The Czechs of Bohemia and Moravia were the first Slavic people to fall under German domination. Hitler initially followed a moderate policy toward them because he valued their efforts in producing war materiel and because they cooperated with the Germans. The Czechs did so because they hoped to ensure their continued existence. They developed little in the way of a resistance movement, although former president Beneš did maintain an exile government in London. In Bohemia and Moravia, the Czechs carried out routine administration, but the real power remained in the hands of the German official who held the title of "Reich protector." Konstantine von Neurath, the former German foreign minister, was the first to hold this position. Himmler's protégé Karl Hermann Frank, a Sudeten German, served as Neurath's deputy but quickly built up his own rival power base.

At first, Hitler opposed any attempt to "Germanize" the Czechs, but Neurath and Frank persuaded him that Czechs who possessed "Germanic" characteristics were deserving of such an "honor." The majority of the Czechs, who were not eligible for Germanization, would face expulsion to the east when the convenient time came. Although the Germans developed this policy in secret, the Czechs soon became aware of its general intent and grew restless. Hitler considered Neurath too weak to control the situation and replaced him with Heydrich early in 1942. Heydrich followed a carrot-and-stick policy that combined specific benefits to workers and peasants with harsh repression of any dissent. The incentives included increased wages for workers and higher crop prices for peasants. His approach proved effective, and the Czechs became increasingly docile.

These developments alarmed the Czech government in exile and the British, who engineered a plot to assassinate Heydrich. They expected his death to provoke German vengeance, which would in turn kindle Czech resistance. The plot was successful; Heydrich fell victim to an ambush, and Nazi reaction was at least as brutal as expected. They totally destroyed two villages after shooting all the men and sending the women and children to concentration camps. The name of one of the stricken villages, Lidice, became a symbol for Nazi brutality. Contrary to the hopes of the British and the Czech exile regime, the German reprisals so thoroughly frightened the Czechs that resistance did not develop. Bohemia and Moravia continued to be remarkably quiet until the end of the war.

Slovakia, which had won a dubious position as a satellite state by cooperating with the Nazis in the destruction of Czechoslovakia, became an ally of Germany and even sent troops to fight in Russia. As a reward, Hitler allowed the Slovaks to keep their own government. But despite Slovak collaboration, German economic and military influence increased and in 1944 provoked a revolt that the Germans crushed with some difficulty. Hitler now imposed complete German domination, although the puppet Slovak regime continued to function. He apparently planned expulsion to the east or extermination as the ultimate fate of the Slovaks.

The Germans treated the Poles much more harshly than either the Czechs or the Slovaks. Poland had resisted, and Hitler was in no mood to be lenient. In an effort to deprive the Poles of a potential ruling class, the SS shot Polish intellectuals and clergy in the areas that were annexed to Germany. They planned to transfer the remainder of the Poles from the incorporated territories to the Government General and replace them with German settlers. The Nazis actually began this process during the war with the deportation of 300,000 Poles. Former German residents of the Baltic states took their place and were joined later by large numbers of ethnic Germans whom the Nazis shifted from Russia, Rumania, and Yugoslavia. A great deal of confusion snarled the process, and both the Poles and many of the ethnic Germans did not relish their arbitrary transfer. Although Hitler originally did not intend to Germanize any Poles, Himmler carried out a policy that called for the Germanization of Poles with "Germanic characteristics."

In addition to absorbing Poles who had lost their homes in the incorporated territories, the Government General had to accept large numbers of Jews and Gypsies. This huge influx of people created staggering administrative problems for Nazi officials and tremendous pressure on the already shattered Polish economy. Although the Nazis shipped many Poles to Germany to serve as laborers, the bulk of the population remained in the Government General. Hitler looked upon the Poles as "slaves of the Greater German Reich." SS units in the Government General also shot Polish intellectuals, clergy, and army officers.

Hitler appointed Dr. Hans Frank to head the administration of the Government General. Long an associate of Hitler, Frank had been a member of the SA and participated in the Beer Hall Putsch of 1923. A lawyer of considerable skill, he had served as head of the Nazi party's legal department and was responsible for reforming Germany's legal system in the spirit of Nazism. As governor general of Poland, Frank affected a pompous show of authority but in reality possessed little strength of character. He alienated both the Poles and his German associates, and various Nazi agencies soon challenged his power. Himmler and the SS dominated racial policy and supported a program of settling German colonists in the more favorable parts of the Government General while moving Poles to less desirable areas. Hitler apparently intended the final solution to the Polish question to include absorption of the entire Government General into the Reich, the resettling of the area with Germans, and the expulsion or extermination of Poles. The harsh nature of the German occupation led to the growth of resistance groups, many of which merged into the Polish Home Army later in the war.

Yugoslavia, like Czechoslovakia, was a Slavic country that experienced varying types of treatment at the hands of the Germans. Hitler partitioned the country soon after completion of the German conquest in April 1941. He divided the northwestern area of Slovenia into German and Italian occupation zones and established the puppet states of Croatia and Serbia.

Many Croats had refused to resist the German invasion and thus became the most favored Yugoslav group. Hitler greatly enlarged Croatia by granting the Croats territories inhabited by Serbs. Ante Pavelich, the leader of the extremist Croatian nationalist movement Ustaše, became head of the new state and followed slavishly pro-German policies. He even tried to convince Hitler, apparently with some success, that the Croats were actually Germanic. Pavelich had founded Ustaše in 1929, when King Alexander proclaimed a royal dictatorship over Yugoslavia and went into exile in Italy. Ustaše became notorious by carrying out the assassination of Alexander in 1934. Pavelich returned to his homeland after the German conquest of Yugoslavia, and he and Ustaše set out to expel or exterminate both the Serbs and the Jews within their territory. But despite Pavelich's subservience, Hitler had actually designated Croatia as an Italian satellite and allowed Mussolini's forces to occupy Croatian territory along the Adriatic Sea. Hitler also maintained German troops in the eastern portion of the country, and when Italy abandoned the war in 1943, Wehrmacht units replaced the Italians in the coastal strip.

The Serbs, who had been the predominant ethnic group in Yugoslavia, fared much worse under Nazi domination. Not only did they lose Serbian-populated territory to Croatia, but additional areas went to Italy, Hungary, and Bulgaria, leaving a state smaller than pre–World War I Serbia. Hitler allowed a Serbian government under the leadership of General Milan Nedich, but the country remained subject to overall German military supervision. Nedich, a former Yugoslav minister of war, cooperated with the Germans because he feared the alternative might be the extermination of his people.

Soon after the German conquest, Colonel Draja Mihailovich, a former member of the Yugoslav general staff, organized a resistance movement, the Chetniks, that remained loyal to King Peter's government in exile. But his organization was primarily a Serbian patriotic front and failed to transcend the prewar Serb-Croat rivalry, even though it won the support of the British and later the Americans. Indeed, Mihailovich was especially bitter toward the Croats, whom he blamed for the disintegration of Yugoslavia and for the Ustaše atrocities against Serbs. He visualized a restoration of a Serbian-dominated Yugoslavia after the war. The Partisans, a Communist resistance movement led by Josip Broz (better known as Tito), proved much more important.

Tito, who was born in Croatia, fought in the Austro-Hungarian army early in World War I. But the Russians captured him in 1915, and he remained a prisoner of war until the Russian Revolution. After his release, he remained in Russia, became a Communist, and saw action in the Red Army during the Russian civil war. When Tito returned to his homeland in 1923, he joined the outlawed Communist movement and later organized volunteers who fought on the republican side in the Spanish civil war. Tito became general secretary of his party in 1937. Due to the Nazi-Soviet Nonaggression Pact, he did not take the field against the Germans until after Hitler's invasion of the USSR. Tito had no links to the royalist government, and unlike Mihailovich, he strove to create a national movement that would embrace all Yugoslav ethnic groups.

The Partisans also posed a much more serious problem for Hitler than the Chetniks. Mihailovich became concerned that by fighting the Germans, he would expose the Serbian people to reprisals. He also feared that if Tito grew too strong, Yugoslavia would become a Communist state after the war. Bedeviled by these two specters, Mihailovich cooperated with the Germans against Tito, but his policy proved disastrous. Not only did it fail to save his compatriots from savage repression, but it also weakened the Chetniks in the eyes of the Western Allies, who shifted their support to Tito during 1943. When the war ended, Tito controlled large areas of Yugoslavia. Mihailovich fell into his hands, was tried for treason, and was executed. Tito went on to rule Yugoslavia until his death in 1982.

OCCUPATION POLICIES IN THE SOVIET UNION

Hitler's occupation policies in the Soviet Union were at least as ruthless as those he directed against the Poles and Serbs. He contended that Germany had but one obligation: "to Germanize the country by immigration of Germans, and to look upon the natives as Redskins." His reference to "Redskins" was an allusion to the United States's treatment of the Native Americans, a policy he greatly admired. The Nazis pursued this approach not only toward the Russians but also the Belorussians, Ukrainians, and at least some of the inhabitants of the Baltic states. This policy cost Germany the cooperation of these peoples, especially the Ukrainians, many of whom had greeted the Germans as liberators from Soviet tyranny. Hitler ordered the elimination of all potential leaders as well as Jews and Gypsies, and for good measure he suggested that anyone "who looked in any way suspicious" should be shot.

Much German-occupied territory in the Soviet Union remained under military administration because of its proximity to the front. Civilian authorities controlled only areas far enough to the rear to be considered safe. As in other occupied countries, German administration was a jumble of competing jurisdictions.

Officially, Alfred Rosenberg, the self-styled theoretician of the Nazi party, exercised full authority over the occupied areas. Although Rosenberg was of German descent, he had been born in the Baltic city of Tallinn in Czarist Estonia and had fled to Germany to escape the revolution. Rosenberg became an associate of Hitler and appears to have influenced his ideas to some extent in the early 1920s. But he had lost the Führer's confidence long before 1941, and other Nazi leaders held him in contempt. Hitler may have decided to appoint Rosenberg to his post because of his knowledge of the USSR—limited though it was, it was superior to that of most other Nazi leaders. But from the start, Rosenberg was able to exert little real control while various Nazi rivals challenged his authority.

Himmler and the SS especially operated as a law unto themselves and imposed a policy of terror in an attempt to cow the population into submission. Goering also assumed a lofty role that supposedly gave him control over economic exploitation. But others soon intruded and undercut Goering's position. These included Fritz Sauckel, the head of the slave labor program, and Dr. Fritz Todt, the minister of armaments and munitions.

Sauckel, previously a provincial Nazi party leader (*Gauleiter*) in Germany, became plenipotentiary general for labor in 1942. Technically, he remained under the authority of Goering as director of the Four-Year Plan, but in reality he wielded virtually unlimited power over recruiting laborers in Germany, in occupied territories, and among prisoners of war. Todt began as another of Goering's nominal subordinates under the Four-Year Plan and had been responsible for construction of the West Wall along Germany's western border and other defenses. But when he became minister of armaments and munitions in 1940, he was no longer responsible to Goering and eventually began the process of converting Germany's economy to a full wartime basis. When he died in a plane crash in 1942, Albert Speer succeeded him and greatly accelerated the transformation. In the face of all this competition, Goering's actual control over the Russian economy was never extensive.

To increase the confusion still more, the Germans established two special regional administrations. The first of these supervised the Ostland, an area consisting of the Baltic states and western Belorussia; eastern Belorussia remained under military rule. Hitler selected Hinrich Lohse as

Reich commissioner of the Ostland. Like so many other Nazi leaders, Lohse had been an early party member and a *Gauleiter* in Germany. He also had been a close associate of Rosenberg who had counted on Lohse's loyalty. But Lohse's primary aim was to build up his own power. In pursuit of this goal, he attempted to play off Rosenberg, Himmler, and Goering against one another.

Each of the Baltic states as well as Belorussia received its own subcommissioner who operated under Lohse's supervision. Wilhelm Kube, the subcommissioner of Belorussia, had served for many years as a Nazi member of the Reichstag as well as a *Gauleiter* and provincial administrator. He had lost the latter position and even spent a short time in jail because of a series of scandals, including attempted political blackmail. But this did not lessen his value in Hitler's eyes. Kube strove to increase his administrative autonomy and quarreled frequently with Lohse. He was fond of fair-haired Belorussian women and developed a virtual harem of "blondies," as he called them. He did not win their love, however, and one of them eventually killed him by means of an antipersonnel mine that she concealed in his bed.

The other special administration, under the direction of Erich Koch, supervised a large part of the Ukraine. The eastern Ukraine remained under military control. Still another *Gauleiter* and provincial administrator, Koch for many years had favored cooperation with the Soviet Union and had strongly supported the Nonaggression Pact of 1939. But once he received his appointment as Reich commissioner, he quickly changed his attitude. Described as a man of "monumental stupidity and arrogance," Koch followed relentlessly brutal policies and cooperated enthusiastically with the anti-Jewish campaign and slave labor program.

German occupation policies helped enlarge the Partisan movement in the Soviet Union, but this process took time. In 1941, most of the Partisans were soldiers who had been bypassed by the German advance and had managed to hold out in forests and swamps. It was not until 1942 that their numbers became notable, and a highly organized mass movement did not develop until 1943. This slow growth was due largely to the fact that the Soviet government and army were unable to devote much time to organizing Partisan warfare because of more immediate problems.

One of the most hideous aspects of Nazi policy toward Russia was the treatment of Soviet prisoners of war. Ironically, many Red Army soldiers, especially minorities, disliked the Soviet regime and went over to the Germans more or less voluntarily. But the SS subjected them to brutal treatment. Many starved, froze to death, or died from other causes. Almost 3.3 million Soviet prisoners perished in Nazi camps or in transit. When the war began to go against the Reich, the Germans changed this barbarous policy and used Soviet prisoners for labor. They even recruited some of them as soldiers, primarily members of minorities who still harbored grievances against the Soviet government. Although the number of such troops eventually reached substantial proportions, they never played an important role in Hitler's war effort.

Germany did not hold its Russian conquests long enough for Hitler to put his long-range program into effect, but he clearly intended to dominate the Soviet state at least as far east as the Ural Mountains. He also planned to annex the Baltic states, Belorussia, much of the Ukraine, and the Crimea. German colonists would have become the master race in this vast area, and the Nazi regime would have enslaved the native populations.

NAZI POLICY TOWARD OTHER EUROPEANS

Nazi policy toward the Latin peoples of Europe was less clear-cut than that pursued in regard to the Jews and the Slavs. Hitler considered them to possess some Aryan blood but, alas, not enough to qualify as Germanic. Although Italy was a Latin country, Hitler admired Italian culture with its roots in the civilization of ancient Rome and the Renaissance. He also had desired an alliance with Italy from an early date, and to obtain that goal he was even willing to submerge his nationalistic fervor somewhat. He refused to pressure Mussolini to cede the former Austrian territory of the South Tyrol, which contained a substantial German minority. Italy had obtained the South Tyrol in the 1919 peace settlement. He persisted in this policy throughout the 1930s and into the war, much to the chagrin of many of his fellow Nazis. His bond of friendship with Mussolini also extended to designating most of the Mediterranean as an Italian sphere of exploitation. But Italy's defection from Germany's side in 1943 put an end to Hitler's generosity. Henceforth, he thought in terms of annexing not only the South Tyrol but all Italian territory formerly belonging to Austria-Hungary and, perhaps, everything north of the Po River.

Hitler's attitude toward the French, another Latin people, was initially far less forbearing, as his plan to annex the Flemish-speaking areas of northwestern France would indicate. He also forced France to return Alsace-Lorraine in the 1940 armistice and planned to acquire a strip of French territory extending from the mouth of the Somme to the Swiss border. Until November 1942, Germany's relations with the French differed from those with other defeated peoples because the armistice of 1940 had left part of France unoccupied. Technically, the Vichy regime continued to administer the entire country, but in Occupied France, primary control lay with the Germany army. As usual, the SS and various Nazi economic agencies challenged this authority. Again this led to considerable chaos.

During 1940–41, Vichy leaders, such as Pétain and his chief minister Pierre Laval, considered a final German victory inevitable and thought that realism required French adjustment to a German-dominated Europe. Laval had overcome his humble background as the son of a small-town innkeeper and butcher to become a lawyer and politician. Although originally a Socialist, he later became an independent who opposed communism, supported Franco-German reconciliation, and hated war. Laval served four times as premier, but during his last term his attempt to concede Mussolini a virtual free hand in Ethiopia caused such a backlash that he resigned in early 1936. For the next four years, he receded into the political wilderness and grew extremely bitter toward the Third Republic. Pétain rescued Laval from near oblivion in June 1940 when he appointed him to be his deputy.

Admiral François Darlan succeeded Laval as the key man under Pétain during most of 1941 and early 1942. During the late 1920s and early 1930s, he served in the naval ministry and in 1937 became navy chief of staff. Darlan was especially skillful in obtaining funds, and when the war began, the fleet was stronger than ever. Due to the absence of major sea battles, it emerged from the conflict almost unscathed. Even after the British attack on Oran and Mers-el-Kebir in the summer of 1940, it remained an important factor in European power politics. Britain's action against the fleet also helped bring Darlan's latent anti-British sentiments to the surface. Darlan followed a strongly collaborationist policy until Germany's fortunes began to fade in Russia. When he shifted to a less pliant approach, the Germans pressured him out of office. Laval returned to power and remained the dominant leader in Vichy until the end of the regime in 1944. The Germans sent troops into formerly unoccupied France in November 1942 in response to the Allied invasion of French North Africa, and the usual competing German authorities quickly followed.

Most of the French people at first adjusted remarkably well to the capitulation of 1940. Many had feared the possibility of a Communist revolt and saw the rule of Marshal Pétain as infinitely preferable to such a development. Although a number of resistance movements soon came into existence, they did not become important or form a united front until several months after the German occupation of all of France. Germany's forced labor program proved to be the most important factor in their growth. The Germans sharply increased the number of French people required for labor service in 1943, but many of their prospective conscripts evaded this fate by joining the Resistance. The Resistance took the name Maquis (French for "underbrush") and adhered to de Gaulle's Fighting French movement.

Early in 1944, it created a unified military force, the French Forces of the Interior (FFI). Though poorly equipped, the FFI reached a numerical strength equivalent to 15 divisions and succeeded in liberating much of central France after the Allied invasion in June.

Spain, still another Latin country, was also in a unique position. Although the Spanish government had professed friendship to Germany, it had skillfully avoided an alliance. Hitler never forgave Franco for his duplicity. Even Franco's decision to dispatch a Spanish military force, the Blue Division, to fight on Germany's side in the Soviet Union did not eliminate his animosity. If Germany had won the war, Hitler probably would have pressed for the ouster of Franco and his replacement by a more pliable Spanish leader.

The Greeks were not related to the Germans, Slavs, or Latins, but they, too, suffered terribly. After the conquest of Greece in 1941, Hitler placed the country primarily under Italian and Bulgarian occupation while retaining German control over certain strategically important areas. Germany also established a puppet Greek government that proved highly unpopular and ineffective. When Italy left the war in 1943, German forces occupied the Italian-held area of Greece. A Greek resistance movement of considerable scope developed early in the occupation. It consisted of various rival groups, the most important of which was the Communist National Liberation Front (EAM). The Germans responded to Greek resistance by shooting large numbers of hostages and annihilating entire villages. But an even greater horror came in the guise of famine due to persistent food shortages. More Greeks succumbed to starvation than to German firing squads.

RESISTANCE MOVEMENTS

One of the recurring themes in Allied propaganda during the war was the tremendous importance of the resistance movements in occupied European countries. To a large extent, this reflected wishful thinking and distortion instead of reality. To be sure, some of the resistance movements had noteworthy achievements to their credit, especially the Yugoslav and Russian Partisans, the French Maquis, and the Polish Home Army. But in most cases, the hopes entertained for European resistance were far greater than the actual accomplishments. Churchill and the British were particularly sanguine about the possibilities of European resistance. In the dark days of 1940, they created the Special Operations Executive (SOE) to encourage and coordinate resistance on the continent. Churchill spoke of the need to "set Europe ablaze."

The blaze was slow in coming. Anti-Nazi activity remained of minor importance until 1941 and even later. The entrance of the USSR and the United States into the war provided the first big stimulus by inspiring the realization that a German victory was now unlikely. Germany's attack on Russia also brought Communists into opposition after more than a year and a half of adherence to the Soviet pro-Nazi line. They became prominent in most resistance movements and the dominant factor in those of Yugoslavia and Greece. But even after this escalation of activity, resistance forces confronted many obstacles. It was extremely difficult to organize operations of this type. Weapons were scarce, and the average person was afraid to participate in such a dangerous enterprise. The flat, open terrain of the Netherlands, Denmark, Poland, and much of Belgium and the Ukraine offered little protection, while Nazi reprisals were severe. Germany's forced labor policy provided the second great impetus to the growth of opposition in occupied countries. As in France, many persons joined the resistance to avoid becoming slave laborers in the service of the Reich.

Resistance usually took the form of sabotage, gathering information on German activities, aiding the escape of prisoners of war, and cooperating with Allied agents. Actual uprisings did not take place for the most part until late in the war, except in Yugoslavia and the Soviet Union. But the contribution of Soviet Partisans to Russia's early victories was less than is often portrayed, and the Germans actually forced Tito's troops to take refuge in remote mountain areas during much of the war.

The greatest contribution of European resistance was its ability to help tie down German forces that might otherwise have fought against Russian or Anglo-American troops. This was especially the case with Tito's Partisans. The Germans also kept 300,000 troops in Norway, but their presence was due less to the small-scale Norwegian resistance than to Hitler's fear that the Western Allies would attempt an invasion there. In the later stages of the war, Russian Partisan and French Maquis activities interfered significantly with German communications and troop movements.

HORROR AS STATE POLICY

Theoretically, at least, the Nazis inflicted their multiple horrors on Europe on behalf of the German people. Their actions were in keeping with Hitler's basic aims—domination of Europe, creation of *Lebensraum,* and the expulsion or extermination of Jews and other "undesirables" from Nazi-occupied areas. Whether the German people were in favor of such hideous policies was irrelevant to Hitler. He neither confided in them nor sought their opinions. And while they thrilled to the Wehrmacht's early victories and were not ignorant of much of what followed in the wake of these conquests, many Germans were not aware at least of the extent of the atrocities being committed in their name. As the war continued, more and more of them came to realize the enormity of these crimes. With this growing awareness, fear of retribution haunted them, strengthening their will to fight on in hope of delaying the day of reckoning. Even with the passage of decades it remains difficult to comprehend that one of the world's most culturally advanced nations could have perpetrated these horrors as a deliberate policy of state. But it did.

12

America Enters the War

If the German military disaster in Russia were not enough, at the very time that the Red Army unleashed its massive counterstroke, Hitler committed his second blunder. He declared war on the United States, opening the prospect of a really serious two-front conflict. Hitler's decision marked the culmination of steadily deteriorating relations between the two countries since the outbreak of the war. This process of erosion unfolded at the same time that Japan and America had embarked on a collision course that led to hostilities in the Pacific.

FRANKLIN ROOSEVELT

The administration of President Franklin Roosevelt had grown increasingly supportive of Britain in the struggle against Nazi Germany. But the president was reluctant to push matters too far, especially without assurance that American public opinion would be receptive to his policies. This approach was characteristic of Roosevelt's keen political instincts, which had been largely responsible for his unusually successful career. A member of a wealthy New York State family and a distant cousin of former President Theodore Roosevelt, he possessed boundless charm, good looks, and an effective speaking style. Roosevelt had served as assistant secretary of the navy during Woodrow Wilson's administration and had the misfortune of being the Democratic party's vice-presidential candidate in the disastrous election of 1920. Despite an attack of polio that left both his legs crippled, he became governor of New York in 1928 and gained reelection by a landslide margin two years later. His great success earned him the Democratic presidential nomination in 1932, and he scored an overwhelming victory over President Herbert Hoover.

When he assumed office, Roosevelt had little in the way of either strongly held political principles or a concrete program. Nevertheless, his administration gained congressional approval of a vast array of legislation designed to bring about recovery from the Great Depression while not interfering too greatly with the capitalistic economy. Although the country did recover to some extent, the depression continued throughout the 1930s. Roosevelt won reelection in 1936 by a huge majority.

In foreign policy, the president looked with concern at the expansion of German and Japanese power but followed a cautious policy toward both. The growth of American isolationism contributed to his reluctance to undertake any measures that might be interpreted as threatening to lead the country into war. For a time he attempted to win congressional acceptance of his right to impose embargoes on the sale of arms and other strategic materials to aggressor nations. But ultimately he accepted a series of three neutrality acts that Congress passed between 1935 and 1937. This legislation called for an immediate embargo on arms sales to all belligerents. But Hitler's seizure of Bohemia and Moravia and Mussolini's occupation of Albania in 1939 alarmed Roosevelt, and he made appeals to both dictators to refrain from further aggression. His attitude toward neutrality legislation also changed.

A CAUTIOUS APPROACH

When the European war broke out in September 1939, the American Neutrality Act of 1937 went into effect, placing an immediate embargo on arms sales, much to the distress of Britain and France. Their blockade prevented Germany from buying arms from the United States, but the embargo had the same effect on them. Roosevelt recognized this and appealed to Congress to revise the Neutrality Act. Congress responded in November by repealing the embargo provision and authorizing the sale of arms on a "cash and carry" basis. This action allowed the Allies to buy American arms and munitions and transport them in their own ships. But it barred U.S. vessels from carrying war materiel to Allied ports in an effort to avoid German submarine attacks on American shipping such as those that had brought the United States into World War I.

The fall of France and the German threat to Britain in the summer of 1940 inspired fear in the minds of many Americans that Germany might attack the United States if the Nazis should defeat Britain and gain control of the British and French fleets. This concern led to growing support for the extension of aid to Britain. But many still favored an isolationist approach and urged a policy of scrupulous neutrality. Very few Americans actually favored U.S. entry into the conflict, but the isolationists feared that by extending aid to Britain, America would eventually stumble into war. This difference in opinion led to a spirited debate between interventionists and isolationists. Roosevelt agreed with the interventionists that the United States should extend aid to Britain and increase its own defensive preparations. But he continued to be extremely cautious and did not take the lead in these matters. Instead, interventionists in Congress secured passage of a whole series of measures to strengthen the armed forces. This legislation culminated in the establishment of the first U.S. peacetime draft in the fall of 1940.

America also extended aid to Britain. Roosevelt and Churchill, who had met briefly during World War I, began to correspond soon after the outbreak of war. Their friendship became closer in the following months. The first fruit of this transatlantic relationship came when Roosevelt agreed to provide Britain with 50 overage U.S. destroyers for convoy duty. In return, Britain granted 99-year leases for American naval and air bases in British possessions in the Western Hemisphere, ranging from Newfoundland to British Guiana. This arrangement actually had limited immediate impact because many of the destroyers required repair before they were serviceable for convoy duty. The British also lacked experienced crews to operate them. But the agreement had great symbolic importance because it signified the start of closer cooperation between the United States and Britain.

Roosevelt reverted to a highly cautious approach during the presidential election campaign of 1940. But after winning reelection to an unprecedented third term, he felt able to offer greater aid to Britain. The key to this approach was the Lend-Lease Bill, which Congress passed in March 1941 over bitter isolationist opposition. The British had been buying war materiel from the United States since the fall of 1939, but by the end of 1940, it appeared that they would soon exhaust their financial reserves. The Lend-Lease Act came to the rescue by authorizing the president to lend or lease arms and munitions to Britain with payment deferred until after the war.

The immediate impact of lend-lease was not spectacular. It accounted for only 1 percent of the arms and munitions used by Britain during 1941, although America provided much needed shipments of food, fuel, and other supplies. But ultimately the program extended $27 billion in assistance. The United States also authorized aid to the Soviet Union soon after the start of the German invasion. Lend-lease was consistent with the attitude of a majority of Americans. In January 1941, a public opinion poll indicated that 70 percent favored aid to Britain, even at the risk of war.

While the debate over lend-lease took place, American planners revised their strategic priorities in case of war. As early as June 1939, a joint army-navy board had formulated the so-called Rainbow plans to provide for various contingencies in case of war. These included Rainbow 5, which covered the possibility of U.S. involvement on the side of Britain and France in a war against Germany. Shortly after Roosevelt's reelection in 1940, navy planners drafted Plan Dog, which contended that America's chief priority was the defeat of Germany. This document stated that U.S. intervention in the European war was necessary to achieve this aim. At the same time, it insisted that American forces would have to assume a defensive stance against Japan in the Pacific. Both the president and the army accepted the navy proposal.

GROWING U.S. SUPPORT FOR BRITAIN

In January 1941, American military and naval leaders met with their British counterparts in Washington to explore contingency plans in case the United States should enter the war. These American-British conversations (ABC) took place in the greatest secrecy and lasted for two months. They came to the same conclusions as Plan Dog and emphasized the importance of the Atlantic lifeline between America and Britain. Officially, the ABC-1 agreement concerned only hypothetical developments, but it forged still another link in the tightening relationship between the two countries. It also contributed to the transfer of U.S. naval units from the Pacific to the Atlantic.

Throughout the summer and fall of 1941, America's role in support of Britain increased significantly. In April, U.S. forces occupied the Danish territory of Greenland after an agreement with the Danish ambassador in Washington. In July, American troops also took over Iceland, another Danish possession. They relieved British troops, which had occupied the island soon after the German seizure of Denmark. Both Greenland and Iceland became bases from which U.S. air and naval units could patrol the Atlantic.

In August, Roosevelt and Churchill met in a secret rendezvous on the British battleship *Prince of Wales,* off the coast of Newfoundland. There they drafted the Atlantic Charter, which, as a joint declaration of policy by a belligerent power and a technically neutral nation, was a remarkable document. Its idealistic terms upheld the right of all peoples to choose their own governments, affirmed Anglo-American dedication to peace "after the final destruction of the Nazi tyranny," and rejected any territorial aggrandizement as a result of the war. The Atlantic Charter was important because it symbolized growing Anglo-American solidarity. It also had propaganda appeal to the conquered peoples of Europe, encouraging them not to lose hope.

During July 1941, Roosevelt ordered U.S. naval and air units to patrol the Western Atlantic to warn Britain of the presence of German submarines, again hardly a neutral act. Although Hitler instructed his submarine commanders not to retaliate against American ships, some of them became so outraged by the effectiveness of these patrols that they did respond in anger. Early in September, a German U-boat became involved in an engagement with the U.S. destroyer *Greer,* which had been tracking the submarine for several hours. It is not clear which vessel actually initiated hostilities, but neither suffered any damage. Roosevelt responded to the incident by authorizing U.S. destroyers to attack German submarines on sight. In October and November, U-boats attacked two other American destroyers and sank one of them, with the loss of 115 lives. Roosevelt reacted this time by persuading Congress to authorize the arming of U.S. merchant ships and allowing them to carry cargoes to Allied ports. Clearly, by the fall of 1941, the United

States was, for all intents and purposes, a participant in the war, although on a limited basis. And each incident in the North Atlantic increased the likelihood of a full-fledged American commitment.

DETERIORATION OF U.S.-JAPANESE RELATIONS

But war came to America not through developments in the Atlantic but because of growing friction between the United States and Japan in the Pacific. It was the culmination of a long history of fluctuating tension that began with the advent of the United States as a world power during the Spanish-American War in 1898. In the ensuing peace settlement, America forced Spain to cede Guam in the Central Pacific and the Philippines in East Asia. The acquisition of the Philippines created an American presence close to China, which at that time appeared to be at the mercy of the European powers and Japan. The United States feared that these countries would bar American commercial interests from China. In response to this concern, in 1899 Secretary of State John Hay formulated the Open Door policy, which sought to maintain U.S. access to the China market and, as modified in 1900, to preserve China's territorial integrity and independence.

At first, America viewed Germany and Russia as the chief threats to the Open Door, but when Japan defeated Russia in the Russo-Japanese War of 1904–5, the Japanese loomed as the greater peril. In 1911, U.S. leaders demonstrated their concern about the possibility of a conflict with Japan when they drew up War Plan Orange. This provided for American forces to hold out in the Philippines against a Japanese attack until the navy steamed across the Pacific to provide relief. The plan remained the basic U.S. strategy for a potential war with Japan until the adoption of the Rainbow plans in 1939. But even then it continued in existence in a modified form as Rainbow 3. Unfortunately, it failed to give sufficient consideration to the enormous logistic problems posed by the huge distances involved in such an operation. Its prospects became even more dubious when the Japanese seized the Caroline, Mariana, and Marshall islands from Germany during World War I. Japan's presence in the Central Pacific posed a serious threat to America's lines of communication with the Philippines.

The establishment of the Anglo-Japanese Alliance in 1902 also alarmed the United States. This agreement allowed Britain to shift most of its East Asian naval ships to their home base, and with the destruction of the Russian fleet in the Russo-Japanese War, Japan held the dominant position in Asian waters. In 1915, the Japanese took advantage of this situation to issue a series of demands that would have transformed China into a virtual Japanese dependency. But strong American and British pressure forced Japan to back down.

In the aftermath of World War I, the United States persuaded Britain to give up the Japanese alliance in favor of the various agreements associated with the Washington conference of 1921–22. Although relative tranquility prevailed in U.S.-Japanese relations during the 1920s, Japan's conquest of Manchuria in 1931 and invasion of China proper in 1937 caused growing American concern. Brutal incidents such as the rape of Nanking and the attack on the U.S. gunboat *Panay* also increased tension, as did Japanese interference with American and European trading rights. America extended some aid to China in the form of loans, arms sales, and eventually lend-lease supplies. The Chinese also won the hearts and minds of numerous Americans, especially the pressure group that came to be known as the China Lobby. Comprised of persons involved in Far Eastern trade, politicians, missionaries, and various admirers of the Chinese, this group pressured Congress to increase support for the Kuomintang regime. But until 1940, Washington tried to avoid any action that might lead to war with Japan, particularly in view of the deteriorating situation in Europe.

When the European war began in September 1939, Japan had been fighting in China for over two years, and hostilities continued there while

Hitler won his spectacular victories in Poland, Norway, and Western Europe. With the conquest of the Netherlands and the fall of France, Japan set out to take advantage of these countries in Southeast Asia, where Dutch authorities continued to rule the East Indies and the Vichy French administered Indochina. The Japanese pressured the Dutch to grant trade concessions in the East Indies and demanded that the French close supply routes through Indochina to China. They also gained Churchill's temporary agreement to prohibit aid from reaching Chiang's forces through Burma, the British colony that bordered China on the southwest. The United States viewed these actions as a prelude to greater Japanese penetration into Southeast Asia and adopted a much tougher policy. In July, America imposed an embargo on exports of aviation fuel and the highest grades of iron and scrap steel to Japan. The Japanese refused to be deterred by these measures, however, and in September they extorted the Vichy regime's reluctant agreement to the stationing of Japanese troops in northern Indochina. The United States responded by imposing a complete embargo on the export of all grades of iron and steel scrap to Japan.

Washington's alarm increased still more when Japan joined Germany and Italy in signing the Tripartite Pact in September. This agreement provided that the three powers would assist each other "with all political, economic, and military means" if one of them were attacked by a power not involved in the European war or the Sino-Japanese conflict. The three powers specifically exempted the Soviet Union, which still enjoyed friendly relations with Germany at that time, from the terms of the pact. But it appears that Hitler regarded this stipulation as a cover to disguise his growing interest in attacking the Soviets. But however the Führer may have viewed the pact, other governments saw it as a deterrent to America's entry into the war, either in Europe or Asia.

Japan continued to encroach on Indochina and established a protectorate over the entire colony in July 1941. This action clearly posed the likelihood of Japanese expansion into other parts of Southeast Asia and led to the most serious crisis to date in U.S.-Japanese relations. Roosevelt, acting on the recommendations of his top advisers, froze Japan's assets in the United States and enforced a trade embargo that went far beyond the 1940 restrictions. Britain and the Dutch took similar measures. Most important, the embargo cut off oil exports, which hit the Japanese particularly hard because they imported 88 percent of their oil. Without this vital commodity, Japan's war machine would grind to a halt. But Japan could solve this problem by gaining control of the Dutch East Indies which contained rich oil fields. If they seized British Malaya as well, they would gain four-fifths of the world's rubber supply and two-thirds of its tin.

JAPANESE INTENTIONS IN ASIA

The Japanese believed that they would have to choose one of three alternatives: (1) abandon their ambitions in Southeast Asia and perhaps China as well; (2) work out a compromise with the United States that would involve resumption of trade at the price of some Japanese concessions; or (3) attack Dutch and British possessions in Southeast Asia and, probably, American bases in East Asia and the Pacific. If they struck at the Dutch East Indies and Malaya without neutralizing the Philippines, their supply lines would be vulnerable to air interdiction by U.S. bombers based on the principal Philippine island of Luzon. It thus appeared that the third option would necessitate attacks on the Philippines as well as the U.S. Pacific Fleet at Pearl Harbor on Oahu in the Hawaiian Islands.

Admiral Isoroku Yamamoto, commander in chief of the Japanese Combined Fleet, insisted that if Japan were to have any chance of success in a war with the United States, it must destroy the Pacific Fleet by a surprise assault. There was a precedent for such an attack. At the start of the Russo-Japanese War in 1904, Yamamoto's hero, Admiral Heihachiro Togo, had dealt a severe blow to a Russian fleet at Port Arthur, destroying two battleships and several cruisers. This operation had been the prelude to an even greater Japanese victory, the Battle of Tsushima, in which Togo's forces sank almost all of a second Russian fleet. Yamamoto, who had lost two fingers in that struggle, was among the first Japanese naval officers to recognize the importance of air power. He had overcome resistance from more conservative admirals to the development of aircraft carriers and now proposed use of carrier-based planes to attack American naval power in the Pacific.

Ironically, Yamamoto had long been an opponent of war with the United States. He had studied at Harvard University and served as a naval attaché in Washington, and he clearly recognized America's enormous industrial potential. But he believed that aggressive Japanese policies made war inevitable. Thus he considered a lightning stroke to destroy or seriously cripple the Pacific Fleet absolutely mandatory. He believed that this would secure a period of six months during which Japan could establish a powerful position in Southeast Asia and the Western Pacific. This should convince American leaders that they could dislodge the Japanese only through a long, bloody struggle. Confronted by such a dismal prospect, perhaps they would settle for a negotiated peace that would confirm Japan's dominant position in East Asia. His plan was initially much too bold for most of the other top Japanese naval leaders, but he eventually won them over by persuasion and sheer force of personality.

The Japanese army favored war, but Premier Fumimaro Konoye preferred negotiations with the United States. Konoye was a member of a distinguished family that had been influential in Japan for centuries and was a close friend of Emperor Hirohito. An exceptionally cultured man, Konoye had served as premier at the time of the Japanese invasion of China but had resigned in 1938. He formed a second cabinet in the summer of 1940. Although a moderate, Konoye recognized the army's dominant influence over the government and the restricted nature of his own power. He shared the army's desire for Japanese hegemony in East Asia but doubted that war with America would facilitate this. The army leaders agreed to let Konoye seek a diplomatic solution, but only with the stipulation that if diplomacy did not secure a settlement by mid-October, Japan would resort to hostilities.

In return for American relaxation of the trade embargo, Konoye offered to withdraw Japanese troops from Indochina after the conclusion of the war with China. He did not specify any terms for ending the conflict but did propose a meeting with Roosevelt to discuss a general settlement. His overtures inspired little enthusiasm in the American government, and both Secretary of State Cordell Hull and Secretary of War Henry Stimson favored a hard line, fearing that any sign of weakness would only encourage Japan in its expansionist designs.

A former Tennessee lawyer, congressman, and senator, Hull had gained his position in Roosevelt's cabinet largely because of his popularity with southern Democrats and his influence in Congress. Hull's approach to foreign policy rested on a bedrock faith in the importance of reducing foreign trade rivalry as the key to world peace. Stimson had served as President Taft's secretary of war early in the century and as Hoover's secretary of state at the time of the Manchurian crisis. He had long been suspicious of Japanese aims in East Asia. A Republican, he had received his appointment in 1940 as a result of Roosevelt's desire to gain bipartisan support for his foreign policy. Washington responded to Konoye's initiative on October 2 by informing Japan that a meeting between the president and the premier would be possible only after the Japanese had clarified their obligations under the Tripartite Pact. The Americans also asked for a clear-cut indication of Japan's intent to withdraw its troops not only from Indochina but from China as well.

Konoye's diplomatic initiative had failed, and when the army's time limit for negotiations expired on October 15, he resigned. The war minister, General Hideki Tojo, became premier. Although his personality was far from magnetic, Tojo was hardworking, honest, and intelligent. Indeed, the sharpness of his mind so impressed his fellow officers that they called him "the Razor." But his intellect suffered from a narrow focus. He tended to view issues from the perspective of the army only, and had little knowledge of the rest of the world, a low regard for the United States, and a willingness to take risks. Before becoming war minister in 1940, he had served as chief of staff in the Kwantung Army and had been a brigade commander in the Sino-Japanese War. Unlike many generals, Tojo had no use for *gekokujo* and believed that junior officers should remain under the firm discipline of their superiors. This attitude won him the respect of conservative generals and civilian leaders alike. But not all members of the Japanese hierarchy were pleased with his appointment as premier. Yamamoto complained that he tended to act in an overly bold manner without a clear idea of the dangers that a conflict with America would pose for Japan.

Tojo favored war, but Emperor Hirohito insisted that the government "go back to blank paper" in its continued pursuit of an agreement with the United States. The cabinet bowed to his request and approved a new two-step approach. The first step, Plan A, called for a long-range agreement to guarantee economic equality for all powers, not only in China but throughout the world. It also offered to interpret the Tripartite Pact defensively if the United States refrained from taking advantage of this to enter the European war. Finally, the Japanese agreed to withdraw their forces from Indochina and parts of China. If the United States rejected Plan A, Japan would resort to the short-term Plan B, which proposed suspension of American aid to China and an end to economic sanctions. In return, Japan would launch peace talks with China. If the United States rejected this offer, Japan would consider war the only option.

AMERICAN DIPLOMATIC REACTIONS

Roosevelt and especially Hull reacted coolly to both proposals but agreed to continue negotiations, if for no other reason than to gain time to strengthen U.S. forces in East Asia. Indeed, both General George C. Marshall, the army chief of staff, and Admiral Harold Stark, chief of naval operations, warned of the inadequacy of American forces and urged that the United States make a counterproposal.

Marshall, a graduate of Virginia Military Institute rather than West Point, had served as a staff officer on the western front in World War I. He became chief of staff in 1939 and proved a masterful organizer with special skill in the difficult but vital art of logistics. Cold and aloof with few personal friends and almost no sense of humor, Marshall possessed an exceptionally keen mind that could cut to the heart of any issue. Although willing to listen to the views of his subordinates, once he decided on a course of action, he adhered to it with steadfast determination. Among his many strong qualities was his ability to choose the best people for key positions. He had no patience with failure but was unusually loyal to those who accepted responsibility and produced results.

Stark became chief of naval operations the same year that Marshall assumed his post. He had held a number of command positions, both on the high seas and as a staff officer in Washington. His naval colleagues still referred to him as "Betty," an unlikely nickname that he had acquired during his Annapolis days. Stark was an excellent planner but tended to be indecisive and lacking in forcefulness. He had two major achievements to his credit, however—drafting Plan Dog and securing congressional approval of a substantial increase in funding for the navy.

Hull responded to the pressure from Marshall and Stark by offering token economic concessions in return for Japan's withdrawal from threatening positions and a halt to all aggressive action. But this plan found little support among other American leaders and encountered British, Dutch, and Chinese opposition. Hull accordingly scrapped it in favor of a much tougher proposal that called for Japan to withdraw from both Indochina and China as a prerequisite for American agreement to unfreeze Japanese assets and resume trade. The Japanese viewed this as an ultimatum and on November 29 made their final decision for war.

American leaders had stiffened their attitude toward Japan during the summer and fall of 1941 in large part because they had obtained information from U.S. cryptanalysts who had broken Japan's diplomatic cipher and were thus able to intercept secret messages. As a result, Roosevelt and his advisers were aware of Japanese proposals well before they received them officially. They also knew that Japan intended to go to war to achieve its aims if the United States did not accept Japan's terms. The process of intercepting and deciphering Japanese messages was codenamed Magic. Unlike Ultra, Magic could only reveal diplomatic secrets. The Americans had not yet broken Japan's naval and military ciphers. Roosevelt, Stimson, and especially Hull grew increasingly cynical about the possibility of negotiating a settlement as a result of the information they obtained from Magic. They became convinced that war was virtually inevitable when they read a particularly ominous message that pinpointed November 29 as the final deadline for negotiations and added that thereafter, "things are automatically going to happen."

PREPARATIONS FOR WAR IN THE PACIFIC

The key factors in the forthcoming conflict in the Pacific were air and sea power, especially the ability to launch air strikes from aircraft carriers and attacks by submarines against enemy shipping. Although the British had used carrier-based planes against the Italian navy in the Mediterranean, the full extent of the revolution that air power posed for naval warfare did not become clear until the outbreak of the Pacific conflict. The Japanese had ten aircraft carriers, while their enemies had only three available in the Pacific, all U.S. carriers based at Pearl Harbor. In other aspects, the combined American, British, and Dutch naval forces in the Pacific nearly matched Japan's strength, but they were under three different commands and widely dispersed, and many of the Allied ships were inferior in quality. American and British remoteness from East Asia also made it exceedingly difficult for them to supply and reinforce their garrisons.

By far the strongest Allied naval force was the U.S. Pacific Fleet at Pearl Harbor. In addition to its three carriers, it included eight battleships, seven heavy cruisers, and numerous smaller craft. If the Japanese could destroy this force, especially the carriers, they would gain naval supremacy in the Pacific. Their plan also called for simultaneous attacks on other Allied strongholds—the U.S. outposts of Wake Island and Guam in the Pacific and the British possessions of Malaya and Hong Kong on the Asian mainland. Additional attacks would follow against the Philippines, the Dutch East Indies, and the British colony of Burma.

To deliver the blow against Pearl Harbor, Japanese planners provided a striking force of six carriers with a complement of 360 planes. These consisted of high-level bombers, dive bombers, torpedo bombers, and fighters. Two battleships, three cruisers, and eight destroyers escorted the carriers. Admiral Chuichi Nagumo commanded this formidable armada. Nagumo had received the honor by virtue of seniority despite the fact that he had no previous experience with air power. He had spent most of his career at sea aboard destroyers, cruisers, and battleships. The admiral had won renown for his skill in delivering torpedo attacks as well as affection for his kindness to his officers and men. Ironically, Nagumo had initially opposed the Pearl Harbor attack as too reckless. Indeed, Yamamoto's plan contained extremely dangerous elements. It required the striking force to travel 3,500 miles, without being discovered, according to a rigidly precise timetable. To avoid detection, the Japanese imposed absolute radio silence and charted the approach to Hawaii through a vast, lonely expanse of sea far from inhabited areas and regular shipping routes.

The Japanese also adopted certain technical innovations that they hoped would enhance their prospects for success. One of these arose out of concern over the shallow waters of Pearl Harbor. They feared that torpedoes might sink so low that they would detonate on the bottom. To prevent this, the Japanese borrowed a method developed by the British—the use of more buoyant wooden fins, which prevented torpedoes from falling too far below the surface. They also attached fins to naval gun shells, which they substituted for bombs. The fins made the shells fall like bombs, but the shells could pierce the armor of warships much more effectively than bombs.

When the Japanese unleased their attack on Pearl Harbor and nearby air and military installations on December 7, they took the Americans completely by surprise. This led to the birth of a conspiracy theory that still has its adherents who contend that Roosevelt and his associates deliberately provoked Japan into attacking the United States. These critics claim that by pursuing a hard-line policy during the summer and fall of 1941, American leaders gave the Japanese no option. They also charge that the president and his top advisers had access to Magic-intercepted messages, as well as other sources of information, indicating that Pearl Harbor was a likely target. However, according to this scenario, they refused to warn naval and military leaders in Hawaii because they wanted the attack to succeed. Proponents of this "back door to war" thesis insist that Roosevelt hoped the attack would create a wave of revulsion among the American people that would enable him to bring the United States into the war not only against Japan but, via the back door, Germany as well. The president supposedly pursued this devious policy because of popular opposition to America's entry into the European conflict by way of the Atlantic front door.

There is little evidence to support this conspiracy thesis. It is true that Roosevelt was becoming more actively involved in the Atlantic and in support of the British and Russian war efforts. By late 1941, he also probably thought American entry into the European conflict was necessary, but it is likely that incidents in the Atlantic would have accomplished this eventually without help from Japan. It also is true that messages intercepted by Magic showed clearly that Japanese attacks were likely in early December, but the question was where. Naval intelligence had also begun to penetrate the Japanese navy's cipher well before the attack on Pearl Harbor. But U.S. cryptanalysts were able to decipher only about 10 percent of intercepted messages at the time. They did not complete the breaking of the cipher until early 1942. Various pieces of information, if considered in isolation, hinted of Japanese interest in Pearl Harbor, but they were too few and too unspecific to indicate that the Pacific Fleet was a Japanese target. Roosevelt and his aides instead considered the Dutch East Indies, Malaya, Hong Kong, and the Philippines to be the probable targets. Reports of a large Japanese buildup in Indochina bolstered this belief. If Nagumo had difficulty accepting the boldness of Yamamoto's plan to attack Pearl Harbor, it is not surprising that American leaders did not anticipate such a daring stroke.

But the fact that the Japanese caught Pearl Harbor completely by surprise does reflect negatively on American leaders. This is especially true with regard to their rigidly secretive attitude toward Magic. Intercepted messages were available only to the highest-level civilian and military leaders. To maintain security, these leaders kept the breaking of the Japanese cipher secret even from Admiral Husband Kimmel, commander of the Pacific Fleet, and General Walter Short, the army commander in the Hawaiian Islands. They did issue several communications to Kimmel and Short that warned of the general possibility of war, but they sent the last of these messages on November 27. Marshall and Stark feared that the dispatch of still more warnings might be too much like the boy who cried wolf. But Marshall did issue one final alert to Short on the morning of December 7, when Magic revealed Japan's intention to break diplomatic relations. Washington viewed this as a preliminary to war. A delay in transmission prevented this message from reaching its destination until after the attack on Pearl Harbor, however.

The roles of Kimmel and Short in preparing the naval and military forces in Hawaii for possible attack have also stirred controversy. Both men had taken over their commands in February 1941. Kimmel was an Annapolis graduate who had held numerous command and staff positions at sea and on shore. He had earned a reputation for efficiency and discipline, though without noteworthy imagination or creativity. Navy leaders thought so highly of Kimmel that they selected him to command the Pacific Fleet despite the fact that he was junior to many other admirals. Short had served in the infantry for almost 40 years and had proved himself in a variety of command positions, most involved with training. His fellow officers considered him capable and highly conscientious rather than brilliant.

Although coordination between the two commanders appears to have been less than satisfactory, Kimmel did undertake long-range aerial reconnaissance of the waters off Oahu, but he directed his efforts primarily to the west and southwest of the island. This was in keeping with intelligence reports indicating that, if the Japanese attempted an attack, it would likely come from that direction. He also sent some patrols north of the island but lacked sufficient long-range aircraft to carry out this mission on a daily basis. Unfortunately, December 7 was one of the days this could not be done. Kimmel's predecessor, Admiral James O. Richardson, had not provided antitorpedo nets for the warships anchored at Pearl Harbor because he feared that they would impede the fleet's ability to move quickly. When Kimmel succeeded Richardson, the navy department informed him that it also considered such defenses unnecessary because the shallow waters of Pearl Harbor would prevent a successful Japanese torpedo assault, a decision that proved disastrous. Kimmel did fail to issue a general alert after a U.S. destroyer reported that it had attacked a Japanese submarine near the entrance to Pearl Harbor on the morning of December 7. He believed that the incident was not serious enough to warrant such an action. Finally, Short's radar system was understaffed and lacked experienced personnel. Whatever their mistakes, it now appears that both men may actually have been primarily victims of bad luck rather than negligence. But both ultimately were held responsible for the disaster and relieved of command.

THE ATTACK ON PEARL HARBOR

On the morning of December 7, 1941, two enlisted men, who were operating a mobile radar unit on the north end of Oahu, detected an unusually large number of aircraft approaching from the northwest. But when they reported their finding to the information center, an inexperienced lieutenant told them not to worry. He assumed that the planes were a flight of 13 U.S. B-17 bombers scheduled to arrive from California later that morning. Within a half-hour, the first wave of Nagumo's aircraft descended on Pearl Harbor.

The Japanese launched their planes from a point 220 miles northwest of Oahu, and their attacks were devastating. This was especially true of the first wave of torpedo bombers. Of the eight U.S. battleships, the Japanese sank four and severely damaged the others. They also sank three destroyers and four small ships, inflicted damage on three light cruisers, and destroyed 160 aircraft and disabled 128 others. Short had ordered the planes to be drawn up in tight formation on the airfields to make them less susceptible to sabotage. Unfortunately, this disposition left the aircraft much more vulnerable to Japanese bombers, which caught most of them on the ground. More than 2,400 American personnel lost their lives. Japanese losses totaled only 29 planes destroyed, along with their crews, and 70 planes damaged.

Pearl Harbor was a disaster for the Americans, but it could have been far worse. Nagumo's planes had put much of the Pacific Fleet out of action, but the three American carriers were not among the stricken ships. Two of them, *Lexington* and *Enterprise,* had left for other destinations, and *Saratoga* was undergoing repairs on the West Coast. Seven heavy cruisers were also at sea. Had the cruisers and especially the carriers been destroyed or seriously damaged, Japan would have won total supremacy in the Pacific. Of the stricken battleships, only three—*Arizona,*

FIGURE 12-1 U.S. warships burn following the Japanese attack on Pearl Harbor. (*National Archives*)

FIGURE 12-2 The battleship *California* settles into the mud of Pearl Harbor after the December 7 attack. (*Library of Congress*)

Oklahoma, and *Utah*—were beyond hope of salvage, but the last was a target ship and would not have seen combat. The Japanese also failed to destroy the navy's submarine base, fuel storage tanks, and repair and maintenance facilities. The loss of the fuel would have been especially disastrous.

When it became apparent that the American carriers were absent from Pearl Harbor, Commander Minoru Genda, Nagumo's air staff officer, urged the admiral to pursue additional operations. Unlike Nagumo, Genda was an expert on air power and an ace fighter pilot. Genda believed that Nagumo should locate the carriers at sea and destroy them. He also pressed for a follow-up raid on the fuel storage tanks and dockyards at Pearl Harbor. But Nagumo was overjoyed with his success and feared losses to his own carriers. As a result, he refused to take any more risks and ordered his striking force to return to its home base.

Japan had won a remarkable tactical victory, but it had not scored the great strategic triumph Yamamoto had gambled on. The admiral had gained time for Japan to establish a dominant position in Southeast Asia and the Western Pacific. But instead of convincing America of the futility of a long war, the attack on Pearl Harbor had the opposite effect. It united the government and the people in the determination to pursue the conflict to a victorious conclusion and to destroy Japan's war-making potential. Roosevelt went before a joint session of Congress on December 8 to deliver a grim but stirring speech. He referred to the previous day as "a date which will live in infamy" and called for a declaration of war. The House responded 388 to 1 in favor, the Senate unanimously.

THE UNITED STATES AT WAR

But war had come only with Japan. Despite the "back door to war" thesis, Roosevelt had not asked for a declaration of war against Germany. To have responded to a Japanese attack on Pearl Harbor with such a request would have aroused considerable opposition both in Congress and among the American people. It was Hitler who decided the issue.

During the summer and fall of 1941, the Führer had become increasingly concerned that Japan might work out an agreement with the United States, thus freeing America to intervene in the European war. In an effort to prevent such an occurrence, Hitler had encouraged Japan to attack U.S. bases in East Asia and the Pacific. This would deflect American forces to that part of the world. He had even gone so far as to assure Japan that Germany would respond to such a Japanese initiative with a declaration of war against the United States. He also pressured Mussolini into extending a similar guarantee. These pledges of assistance went far beyond the obligations of either Germany or Italy under the Tripartite Pact. Hitler was ignorant of the fact that Japan intended to attack the United States, even without German support, because the Japanese did not see fit to inform him. Obviously it was to their advantage to keep him in the dark until he had committed himself to enter the struggle against America. But they refused to take him into their confidence even after he had given them his assurance.

Japan's assault against Pearl Harbor thus caught Hitler as much by surprise as it did the United States. But when the Japanese asked him to honor his pledge soon afterward, he complied without hesitation. On December 11, both Germany and Italy declared war. Hitler's decision provided the United States with the option of concentrating its strongest forces against either Japan or Germany. Roosevelt and his advisers chose Germany because they considered it to be the more formidable enemy, though of necessity they earmarked much of the navy for the Pacific.

It is quite remarkable that Hitler honored his commitment to Japan. He had certainly violated agreements in the past, and by ignoring this one he might have avoided a clash with America while the Japanese tied down U.S. forces in the Pacific. Apparently he declared war because he still expected the United States to concentrate its primary effort against Japan. It also appears that he anticipated American entry into the conflict in Europe in the near future because of escalating incidents in the Atlantic. Thus, from his perspective, it did not seem that he was actually risking much by a declaration of war. Some historians have argued that Hitler took this step because he underestimated the United States's potential strength, in part because of his belief that the Americans were a mongrel people. But this argument is not convincing in view of Hitler's insistence that German submarine commanders avoid any kind of provocation to the United States in the Atlantic and his efforts to embroil America with Japan in the Pacific.

However he rationalized his decision, it was still a blunder, second in importance only to his attack on the USSR. He had brought the United States, Britain, and the Soviet Union into a coalition against him. This alliance virtually assured that Germany would lose the war—provided that the Allies could overcome political and strategic differences, which soon appeared, and lingering distrust, especially between the Soviets and the Western Powers.

13

Japan Triumphant, December 1941–May 1942

Pearl Harbor was only the beginning. A series of even more disastrous Allied defeats followed in rapid succession. Yamamoto had promised that his surprise attack on the Pacific Fleet would gain six months for Japan to establish an impregnable position in Southeast Asia and the Pacific. The extent to which the havoc the Japanese had created at Pearl Harbor was responsible for their subsequent conquests is debatable. Nevertheless, their success did continue for almost six months. But Japan's newly won position did not prove impregnable. Once the United States had recovered from the shock of Pearl Harbor, it began to bring its enormous war-making potential into play. American resources were far greater than those of the Japanese, and even before they became a factor of massive proportions, the United States was able to turn the tide.

But the first six months belonged to Japan. Her victories were reminiscent in some respects of Germany's *Blitzkrieg* triumphs. They came with amazing speed and remarkable ease. Like the Germans earlier, the Japanese seemed invincible. The Allied response was also similar to the abortive efforts of Britain and France in the early months of the war—too little, too late.

JAPANESE MILITARY STRENGTH

Even more than Germany, Japan won victories with forces that were not particularly large. The Japanese army in December 1941 contained only 51 active divisions, although it possessed garrison troops and other units equivalent to 40 additional divisions. In all, Japan's available forces totaled 1.2 million men, and the military could draw upon an additional 2 million reservists, many of whom had seen service against the Chinese. But much of the army remained in China, leaving only 11 divisions for operations against Southeast Asia and the Pacific. The army also had its own air force, which included 2,000 first-line planes.

Japan's navy contained a formidable nucleus of ten carriers, six of which took part in the Pearl Harbor mission. Its 11 battleships included *Yamato,* whose 70,000 tons and nine 18.1-inch guns made it the world's largest and most powerfully armed ship. *Yamato* was so huge that each of its gun turrets was as large as a destroyer. Construction on a sister ship, *Musashi,* was nearing completion. Eighteen heavy cruisers, 21 light cruisers, 100 destroyers, and 63 submarines were

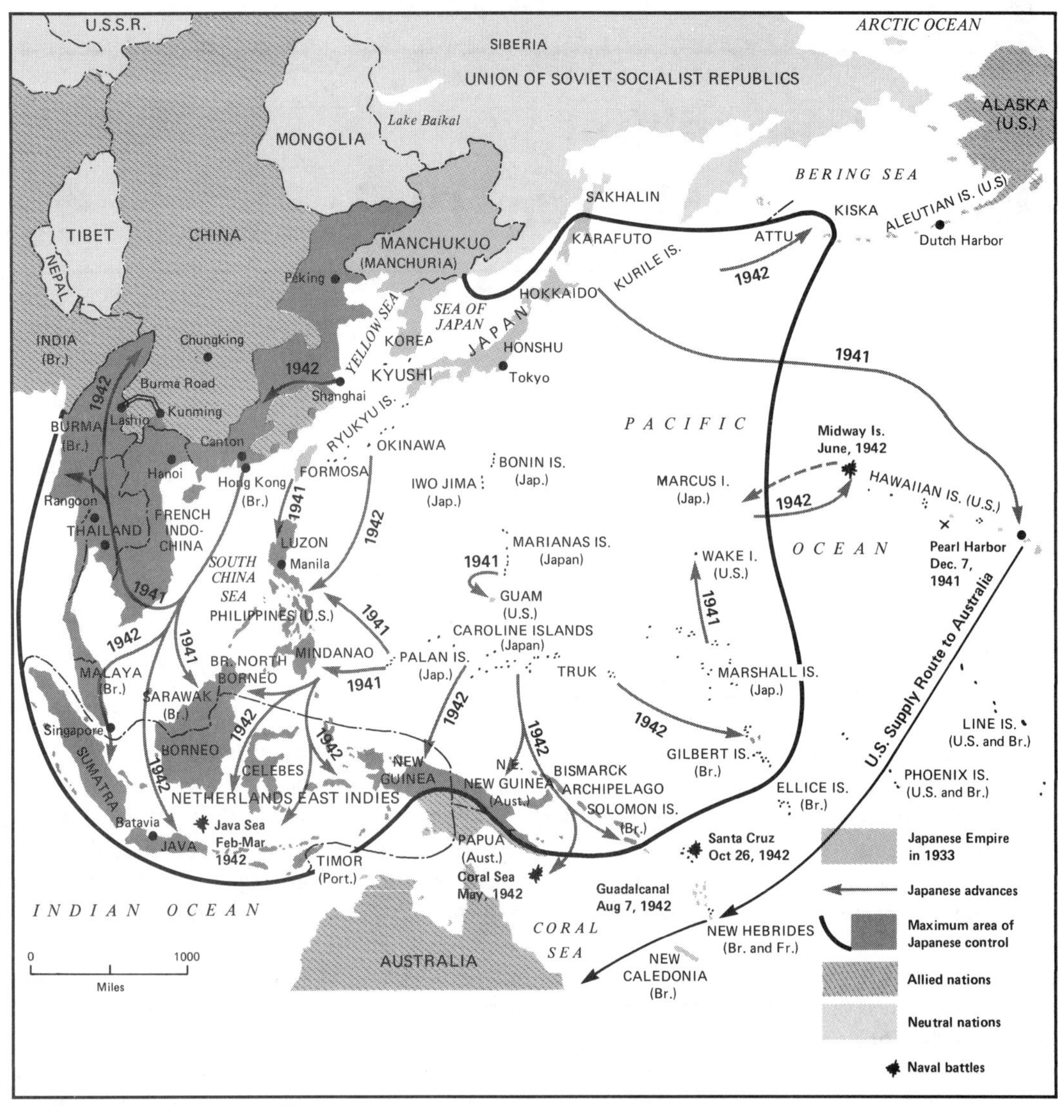

Japanese Advances, 1941–42

also available. The navy possessed an air force of 3,000 planes. Although most Japanese aircraft were not of outstanding quality, the Mitsubishi A6M fighter, which the Japanese called the Zero, was exceptional and saw service with both the army and the navy. During the early months of the war, it outclassed Allied fighters, but unfortunately for the Japanese, it remained their standard fighter long after the Allies had developed superior models.

The Japanese army differed greatly from the German. It had no armored divisions and emphasized light tanks, small guns, and mortars. These weapons suited the amphibious operations that characterized Japan's war effort in Southeast Asia and the Pacific. The Japanese also enjoyed the benefit of local air supremacy and the element of surprise as well as far greater experience and superior training. Allied blunders and slowness to respond to Japanese initiatives played important

FIGURE 13-1 A bamboo umbrella protects a scouting detachment from the sun during a Japanese advance. (*AP/Wide World Photos*)

roles, too, as did the Allies' marked tendency to underestimate the ability of Asiatic troops to stand up against Western forces.

WAR IN SOUTHEAST ASIA AND THE PACIFIC

In an effort to create some coordination among the widely dispersed Allied forces in East Asia, General Marshall urged the creation of a unified command structure. Roosevelt and Churchill agreed to his request at the Arcadia Conference in Washington during December. This was their first meeting since the entry of the United States into the war. With the help of their military staffs, they appointed General Wavell to direct the American, British, Dutch, and Australian Command (ABDACOM). The area under Wavell's jurisdiction included the Dutch East Indies, Malaya, Burma, and the Philippines. In reality, he had almost no control of the Philippines, which remained under the command of the American General Douglas MacArthur. By the time Wavell reached his headquarters in the Dutch East Indies on January 10, 1942, the outlook was gloomy, to say the least.

Japan struck at numerous other targets on the same day as the assault on Pearl Harbor. These attacks included air raids on Wake Island and the Philippines and land operations against Guam, Hong Kong, Malaya, and the Philippines. Guam was the first outpost to fall. Its weak defenses and close proximity to the powerful Japanese base on the island of Saipan in the Marianas made its position hopeless. After two days of air attacks, the Japanese landed and quickly overwhelmed the handful of defenders.

Over 1,000 miles to the east, Wake Island proved much harder to subjugate. Its 500-man garrison experienced three days of aerial bombardment followed by naval shelling on December 11. The Japanese planned a landing on the same day, but they underestimated the island's coastal defense guns and its few aircraft, which sank two warships and damaged three others. This remarkable setback required the Japanese to send for reinforcements, including two of the carriers that had taken part in the Pearl Harbor raid.

Admiral Kimmel, who still commanded the U.S. Pacific Fleet at that time, countered by ordering a task force, centered around the carrier *Saratoga,* to relieve Wake. But a series of problems delayed its progress, and soon after its departure, Admiral William Pye relieved Kimmel temporarily as fleet commander. Pye feared the possibility of losing *Saratoga* and called off the operation on December 23. The Japanese launched their final assault on Wake the same day, and after heavy fighting, the island surrendered. The failure of the Wake relief expedition, coming so soon after the Pearl Harbor debacle, represented another severe blow to the U.S. Navy's morale.

Hong Kong, still another isolated Allied base, fell before the end of December. Consisting of a group of islands and a small peninsula on the Chinese mainland adjacent to Japanese-held territory, Hong Kong's position, like Guam's, was hopeless. Japanese forces struck on December 8 and quickly drove the defenders off the mainland. They followed with an invasion of Hong Kong Island on December 18, captured its water supply, and split the garrison into two pockets. One of them surrendered on Christmas, the other the following day.

Japan faced a more formidable task in the Philippines, but the outcome was similar. American leaders had optimistically designated U.S. naval forces there as the Asiatic Fleet, but they actually consisted of only a few surface ships and 29 submarines. Although Allied ground forces were fairly numerous, they were of variable quality and poorly equipped. General MacArthur led 31,000 regular troops, including 12,000 Filipinos who functioned as a part of the U.S. Army, and the indifferently led, inadequately trained, Philippine army of 102,000.

MacArthur was a controversial figure before the war and has remained so ever since. The son of a Civil War hero, he graduated first in his class at West Point. During World War I, he won several decorations for bravery and became the youngest American general to command a division. He served as army chief of staff from 1930 to 1935. During the lowest point in the Great Depression, MacArthur committed a major public relations blunder when he led troops, using tear gas and tanks, to oust 2,000 World War I veterans from Washington. These men had been demanding early payment of their war service bonuses. In 1935, the general received an appointment as military adviser to the Philippines, which had become a commonwealth of the United States with limited self-government. He still held that post when Roosevelt recalled him to active service in 1941 and placed him in charge of the U.S. and Philippine forces. Although clearly an officer of great ability and inspirational leadership qualities, MacArthur was also intensely ambitious, extremely vain, and ardently fond of publicity. He habitually wore a gold braid–encrusted cap, carried a riding crop, and smoked a gigantic corncob pipe, all of which made him a prime target for photographers.

Concern over American air power on the main Philippine island of Luzon had been one of the primary reasons for Japan's decision to attack the United States. Actually, it was far less formidable than American leaders had intended. They had planned to station 165 heavy bombers on Luzon, but only 35 B-17 Flying Fortresses had arrived by the time the Japanese struck. A total of 104 P-40s, which were inferior to the Zero, and some obsolete models provided fighter support. Weak as it was, this air power remained the key to U.S. plans to hold the Philippines as well as to attack Japan's supply lines. But the Japanese quickly eliminated this threat through a combination of their own initiative, American mistakes, and fortunate timing.

THE PHILIPPINE DEBACLE

No one has ever satisfactorily explained why the Philippine disaster occurred. Since the war, the principal American actors in the drama—MacArthur; his able but domineering chief of staff, General Richard Sutherland; and the air commander, General Lewis Brereton—have all contradicted each other as to whom was actually to blame. It is clear that all three men had received ample warning of the Pearl Harbor attack. It is also certain that on that same day, Brereton planned to stage a bombing raid against Japanese bases on Formosa and attempted to obtain permission to do so from MacArthur. But Sutherland refused to allow him to see the general, contending that MacArthur was too busy. This caused a delay, and the raid never took place.

Instead, when Japanese planes struck targets in northern Luzon, the bombers at Clark Field near Manila went aloft to avoid being caught on the ground. The main fighter force attempted, unsuccessfully, to intercept the enemy. When the U.S. aircraft returned to refuel, enemy planes did catch them on the ground, destroying 18 B-17s and 53 P-40s. This calamity took place even though radar had warned of the Japanese approach. Despite the confusion over this unfortunate series of events, ultimate responsibility lay with MacArthur as commander of all forces in the Philippines. He failed to take the initiative in protecting his aircraft, and neither he nor Sutherland responded to Brereton's entreaties for prompt action. But it is also true that Brereton should have based his aircraft in Mindanao in the southern Philippines, where they would have been beyond the range of Japanese aircraft.

More raids followed during the next few days, and by December 17 only a handful of American fighters remained, while the surviving B-17s sought refuge in Australia. Japan had won total air supremacy in the Philippines. Japanese air attacks also devastated naval installations in Manila Bay and forced the flight of much of the Asiatic Fleet to Australia and the Dutch East Indies.

Japanese troops executed their first landings on Luzon's northern coast on December 8, but the main invasion did not come until December 22 at Lingayen Gulf, 150 miles north of Manila. General Mashaharu Homma commanded the invading force, which consisted of only two divisions. Homma was an unusual Japanese general. His interests were much broader than those of most of his fellow officers, extending to poetry and the arts. He was even an amateur playwright. Homma also shared Yamamoto's opposition to war with America, an attitude tantamount to heresy in the Japanese army. Nevertheless, he carried out the invasion with considerable skill.

The prewar American defensive plan called for a withdrawal to the Bataan Peninsula, which flanked Manila Bay on the west. But MacArthur had anticipated a landing at Lingayen Gulf and hoped to defeat the Japanese on the beaches. He also expected Washington to send a major relief expedition to his aid. MacArthur badly underestimated the fighting quality of the Japanese and overestimated the ability of his own troops, especially the Philippine army. And clearly, after the Pearl Harbor disaster, any relief expedition to the Philippines was out of the question. The Philippine forces defending northern Luzon proved quite incapable of repelling the Japanese. By Christmas, the enemy was preparing to drive on Manila. The Japanese also made another major landing on the southeast coast of Luzon, which MacArthur had not anticipated. Manila now faced powerful Japanese invaders from both north and south.

MacArthur had only two options: withdraw into the mountains to concentrate on guerrilla activity or adopt the original plan and make a stand on Bataan. He chose the latter and ordered a fighting withdrawal. Despite great obstacles, his forces completed their retreat by early January 1942. But it was a dubious success because they were now bottled up on Bataan and the fortified islands near the entrance to Manila Bay. MacArthur's misguided decision to defend the beaches at Lingayen Gulf also created severe logistic problems. Instead of shifting food, medicine, and other supplies to Bataan, as stipulated in the prewar plan, he sent them north to the gulf. Most were lost, and the supplies that did reach Bataan were inadequate. The defenders of the peninsula soon found themselves on half-rations, and many of them fell victim to malaria and other tropical diseases. They might hold out for weeks or even months, but they could not evacuate and had no hope of obtaining either reinforcements or additional supplies.

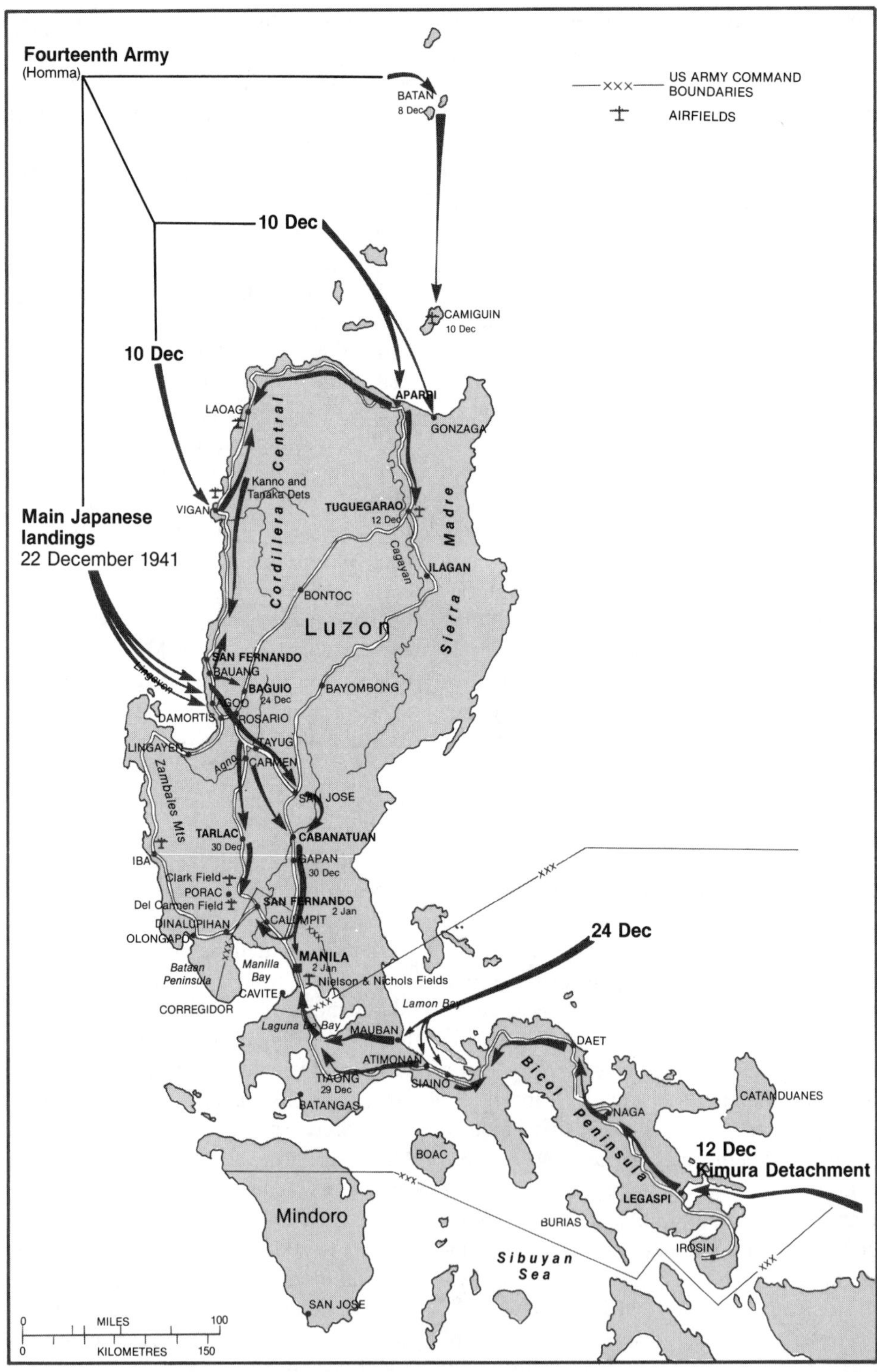

The Japanese Invasion of Luzon, December 1941–January 1942

MacArthur's troops were able to exploit the mountains and dense jungle of Bataan. They made their initial stand near the northern end of the peninsula along a line anchored on the forbidding peaks of an extinct volcano. But Homma's forces exerted intense pressure on the flat, swampy area to the east of this mountain bastion, and by January 26 were positioned to outflank the Allies. Another Japanese column crossed the supposedly impassable mountainous terrain to the west and threatened to cut off the defenders near the coast. MacArthur ordered a retreat and was able to stabilize the front 20 miles to the south. Malaria and other diseases now decimated the Japanese, who also received orders to divert a division to take part in operations against the Dutch East Indies. By early March, Homma had only 3,000 men in the line and feared an Allied counterattack. But the Americans failed to detect the extent of the enemy's weakness and were so plagued by illness and hunger themselves that they were in no condition to take offensive action. Instead, Japanese reinforcements arrived later in the month and rescued Homma from his dilemma.

MacArthur had been less than successful in his handling of the Luzon campaign. The disaster at Clark Field, the unfortunate decision to contest the beaches, and the problems it created for his forces when they reached Bataan provided ample justification for his dismissal. But he did not share the fate of Kimmel and Short. Instead, he emerged as a national hero. The ability of his troops to hold Bataan for over three months contrasted vividly with the succession of defeats that Allied forces suffered elsewhere. His publicity-oriented staff magnified his role, and the American mass media widely disseminated news of his achievements. Roosevelt and Marshall even recommended him for the Congressional Medal of Honor. The American people, thankful for any relief from the persistent gloom of the weeks after Pearl Harbor, eagerly accepted him as a larger-than-life figure.

Clearly, under the circumstances, dismissal and retirement were out of the question. To leave him to face capture and imprisonment seemed equally impossible. Instead, on March 12, Roosevelt ordered MacArthur to leave the Philippines and make his way to Australia. After a perilous journey by sea and air, he reached his destination and announced dramatically, "I came through and I shall return." General Jonathan Wainwright, an old cavalryman who had directed the retreat from Lingayen Gulf, succeeded MacArthur as commander, but his prospects were grim. Disease and short rations had weakened his troops, and MacArthur's departure had damaged their morale. On April 3, Homma opened his final offensive and quickly gained a breakthrough as Allied resistance disintegrated. Fighting on Bataan ceased on April 9. But Wainwright continued the struggle from the fortified island of Corregidor, which the Japanese subjected to heavy bombardment. On May 5, enemy troops landed on Corregidor and forced the final American capitulation.

One of the most horrible incidents of the Pacific war followed immediately after the surrender of Bataan—the Bataan Death March. It resulted in part from a breakdown of Japanese arrangements for transporting and feeding the captured Allied troops. They had expected to take no more than 25,000 prisoners, but the actual number was over 75,000. As a result, many of the captives had to walk the entire 55 miles to a railhead, where the Japanese directed them into overcrowded boxcars to complete the trip to the prison camp. The Allied soldiers were already weakened and malnourished, and many of them were ill. Japanese treatment of the prisoners varied greatly. Some showed kindness, but many others resorted to brutality, beating stragglers and bayoneting those who had fallen. Over 7,000 died on the journey, more than 4,000 of them Filipinos. This manifestation of brutality in part reflected Japanese contempt for troops who chose to surrender rather than die in battle or commit suicide. But brutality was also a way of life to Japanese soldiers, whose superiors often treated them savagely. Not surprisingly, they responded with even more violent treatment of those who fell under their jurisdiction.

THE CONQUEST OF MALAYA

Long before the end of resistance on Bataan and Corregidor, the Japanese had administered a defeat to the Allies that was far more devastating to their hopes and prestige: the conquest of Malaya and Britain's island fortress of Singapore at its southern tip.

British leaders had decided to build a naval base at Singapore in 1922, shortly after the Anglo-Japanese Alliance expired. They intended to base a fleet there as a deterrent to Japanese ambitions in Southeast Asia. To safeguard Singapore, they provided it with defenses that would repel any attack from the sea. But they built no fortifications on the north side of the island, despite the fact that this area offered little in the way of natural obstacles and lay across the narrow and shallow Strait of Johore from Malaya. The British did not consider such fortifications necessary. They assumed that the Japanese would not be so reckless as to try pushing their way through the supposedly impassable jungle of Malaya. Britain also established a number of airfields in Malaya that they intended to use as bases for the defense of Singapore. Unfortunately, funds were in short supply during the 1920s and 1930s, and with the outbreak of war in 1939, primary British concern focused on Europe and Britain. When Italy entered the conflict, the Middle East got second priority, leaving Singapore and Malaya a poor third on Britain's list of commitments.

Although British military leaders had asked for over 500 planes to defend Malaya and Singapore, only 158 were available when the Japanese struck, and most of them were obsolete. Despite their designation of Singapore as a naval base, the British were unable to supply it with a permanent fleet. In case of war in East Asia, they had originally planned to send a number of battleships and an aircraft carrier. As war approached in late 1941, however, the only ships they could spare were the battleship *Prince of Wales* and the battle cruiser *Repulse*. But without a carrier or adequate land-based aircraft, these ships were dangerously vulnerable to air attack. The Admiralty opposed the decision to send the ships to Singapore. But Churchill stubbornly insisted, and they reached their destination shortly before the Japanese attacked Malaya. Their commander, Admiral Sir Tom Phillips, known as "Tom Thumb" because of his diminutive stature, had a long and distinguished career. Unfortunately, he had little recent sea experience, and perhaps even more ominous, he continued to insist that "bombers were no match for battleships."

Despite the obvious inadequacies of the British position, the myth developed that Singapore, the "Gibraltar of the Pacific," was impregnable, and nowhere was this belief stronger than in Singapore itself. The effect of the Singapore myth was not unlike that of the "Maginot mentality" in prewar France. The British also badly underestimated Japanese military capabilities. But not all British leaders were blind to Singapore's vulnerability to an attack from the north. General W. G. S. Dobbie, the army commander in Malaya during 1937–38, and his chief of staff, General Arthur Percival, insisted that the real danger to Singapore would come from Japanese landings in Malaya. Their appreciation led to a decision to extend the defense of Singapore to the whole of Malaya, but little was done to provide adequate defensive positions other than to build the airfields. Percival became commander in Malaya during the spring of 1941. A tall, thin officer with a quiet personality, Percival had led troops in World War I with considerable bravery and served in France during the debacle of 1940. Upon his return to Malaya, he soon recognized the weakness of his position. Although he possessed 89,000 troops, they were deficient in training and lacked modern weapons. Of these, only 20,000 were British; the rest of the force consisted of 37,000 Indians, 17,000 locally recruited soldiers, and 15,000 Australians.

Percival's opponent in the struggle for Malaya and Singapore was General Tomoyuki Yamashita. Stockily built with a thick neck, large head, and expressionless face, Yamashita was perhaps the best general in the Japanese army. He was also highly controversial. Exceptionally pop-

FIGURE 13-2 Exuberant Japanese soldiers give a victory cheer. (*AP/Wide World Photos*)

ular in some circles, others suspected him of complicity in the 1936 coup that had attempted to seize the government. Tojo had long regarded him as a dangerous rival. Yamashita deployed 70,000 troops, but a shortage of sea transport limited his initial force to only 17,000 men. They were among the best in the Japanese army, however, and possessed superior equipment.

On December 8, Japanese troops landed on Malaya's northeast coast. The first landing actually preceded the Pearl Harbor attack by more than an hour, because Malaya lay well to the west of the International Dateline and thus was a day ahead of Pearl Harbor time. Later that day, Admiral Phillips put to sea with *Prince of Wales, Repulse,* and four destroyers to raid enemy ships taking part in the invasion. But Phillips made the fatal error of moving north without air cover. Japanese high-level bombers and torpedo bombers attacked the British squadron on December 10 and sent both *Prince of Wales* and *Repulse* to the bottom, along with Phillips and 800 crewmen. With one blow, the Japanese had won supremacy in the waters off Southeast Asia.

On land, Yamashita's troops pushed southward with remarkable speed despite the heavy jungle and mountainous terrain. British commanders overestimated Japanese strength and were so fearful of being outflanked that they frequently ordered retreats before they were really necessary. The Japanese quickly captured the northern airfields, turning the supposed key to Singapore's defense against the British and assuring Japanese supremacy in the air. One Japanese column knifed southward along the east coast, while two others moved along the western shore. They consistently outmaneuvered and outwitted the enemy by infiltrating around their positions and carrying out a series of landings behind British lines. To facilitate their mobility, many of the Japanese sped southward on bicycles. When their tires suffered blowouts from the intense heat, they simply continued to ride on the rims. In fact, the clattering noise of the rims caused panic among some retreating Allied soldiers, who assumed that tanks were pursuing them. By January 31, the Japanese had driven the British out of Malaya and into Singapore.

Even after the disasters in Malaya, Percival still had 85,000 troops to defend the island. But morale was low, and many of the troops and much of the leadership were of questionable quality. The Japanese, by contrast, displayed their usual dash and enjoyed domination of the air. Percival also mistakenly thought that the Japanese would land on the northeast coast and thus placed his strongest force there. Instead, on February 8, they crossed the strait and quickly established a large beachhead on the northwestern shore. Although the defending force was twice as large as the attackers, the Japanese again outmaneuvered and outfought their opponents. They captured the island's main water supply and penetrated the suburbs of Singapore itself.

The Japanese were now experiencing a shortage of ammunition, and Yamashita feared that if forced into street fighting to take the city, they would lose the battle. To prevent this, he brazenly demanded that the Allied forces surrender. At first, Percival wanted to continue the fight, but his principal subordinate commanders urged capitulation in view of the loss of the reservoirs. When confronted by the specter of fire, sickness, and death as a result of the water shortage, Percival agreed, and fighting ceased on February 15. The surrender was a humiliating end for the "Gibraltar of the Pacific." It also dealt a mortal blow to British and, indeed, Western prestige among the peoples of Southeast Asia. Singapore had become such a symbol of European power in Asia that its fall shattered the myth of Western invincibility. Another wave of atrocities followed as Japanese soldiers bayoneted prisoners, including the wounded, and massacred many Chinese residents.

THE EAST INDIES: DUTCH NO MORE

The Dutch East Indies did not feel the sting of invasion until well after the initial assaults on the Philippines and Malaya. Japanese leaders recognized that the Dutch were far weaker than the Americans and British and concentrated on their stronger opponents first. But by early January 1942, the campaigns in the Philippines and Malaya were clearly progressing toward victory, and the Japanese felt secure enough to strike at the East Indies and seize the long-coveted oil fields. They executed their first landings on January 11 on the northeastern coast of Borneo and a day later on the northern beaches of Celebes. In mid-February, Japanese troops landed on northern Sumatra. By the end of February, Japan controlled much of all three islands and had set the stage for an assault on Java, the principal island of the Dutch East Indies.

An Allied fleet of five cruisers and nine destroyers attempted to intercept the invasion convoy in the waters north of Java on February 27. The hastily assembled force included Dutch, U.S., British, and Australian ships and had no common tactical doctrine or signal code. It fell afoul of the enemy convoy's naval escort, consisting of four cruisers and 14 destroyers. Much of the ensuing Battle of the Java Sea took place after dark, and the Japanese were masters of night fighting. They sank two cruisers and three destroyers while suffering damage to just one of their own destroyers. The remaining three Allied cruisers managed to escape, only to succumb to other enemy naval units in the Battle of Sunda Strait off northwestern Java during the next two days. Japan had gained total supremacy in the waters around the island. Japanese troops landed at two points on Java's northern coast on March 1 and quickly overwhelmed the few defenders. Hostilities ended on March 8.

THE ALLIES TAKE A BEATING IN BURMA

While Japan was overrunning Malaya, Singapore, the Philippines, and the Dutch East Indies, its forces were also engaged in the conquest of Burma. This Texas-size British colony was strategically important because it bordered northern India on the east. Its seizure would place Japan in a position to strike at the industrial area around the great Indian city of Calcutta. Burma also contained the supply line to Chiang Kai-shek's Chinese forces. This route extended by rail and road from Rangoon, the capital and chief port, to Lashio 600 miles to the north and from there, via the Burma Road, to China. Japan's first penetration into Burma came as early as December 10 from neighboring Thailand. An independent country, Thailand had offered no resistance to the entry of Japanese troops two days earlier. But the main invasion of Burma began 400 miles farther north on January 20 with a thrust toward Rangoon. Although Japanese forces were scanty, the British, Indian, and Burmese defenders were even weaker. Once again, the Japanese fought masterfully in the jungles, outmaneuvered the Allies and encircled Rangoon. But the defenders were able to evacuate and escaped through a gap in the Japanese forces. Rangoon fell on March 6.

The Japanese received reinforcements later in March and pursued the Allies northward up the country's three great river valleys. Chinese forces arrived in early April to help the British make a stand 150 miles south of Mandalay in central Burma. But a rapid Japanese advance up the Irrawaddy River and its tributary, the Chindwin, prevented this. Another Japanese column dashed toward Lashio. Allied forces now had no choice but to fall back toward the border of India, while the Japanese advanced up the Chindwin in an effort to cut off their withdrawal. The Allies won the race and reached the sanctuary of India by the middle of May, ending their 1,000-mile retreat from Rangoon.

As the Japanese advanced from Rangoon to Mandalay, their navy carried out a raid against the British naval base on the island of Ceylon (now Sri Lanka) off the southeastern coast of India. Ceylon was vital strategically. If it should fall, the Japanese would menace not only southern India but also British supply lines around the southern tip of Africa to the Middle East, India, and Australia. To prevent this, Britain protected Ceylon with a substantial naval force, including three aircraft carriers and five battleships. Early in April, Admiral Nagumo led a Japanese task force, which featured five carriers and four battleships, into the Indian Ocean. He hoped to repeat his Pearl Harbor success, but British patrol planes warned Ceylon of the enemy approach. Although Nagumo's aircraft damaged port facilities and sank two cruisers, most of the British fleet withdrew to safety.

The raid nevertheless convinced the British that their fleet at Ceylon was vulnerable to Japan's superior strength, and they diverted their ships to bases on the west coast of India and as far away as East Africa. They also feared that the Japanese might send naval forces into the western Indian Ocean and threaten South Africa. To guard against such a possibility, they seized the port of Diego Suarez on French Madagascar in May and occupied the remainder of the island in September. The Japanese never again ventured even as far west as Ceylon.

By May 1942, Japan had reached the zenith of its power. Japanese forces dominated Southeast Asia and the Western Pacific. They threatened the Indian Ocean, Australia, and the Central Pacific. They had proved more than a match for their Western adversaries. But their days of victory were almost at an end.

14

The Tide Turns in the Pacific

The tide of battle in the Pacific turned dramatically when Japan suffered a series of setbacks between May and December 1942. The most spectacular of these took place at sea—the Battle of the Coral Sea in May, the Battle of Midway in June, and a series of bitter engagements in the waters off the Solomon Islands from August to November. Japanese fortunes on land also began to fade during the same period—on New Guinea and on Guadalcanal in the Solomons. By the end of the year, Japan was clearly on the defensive.

JAPANESE STRATEGY

Most of these encounters began with Japanese initiatives that the army and navy high commands agreed to carry out only after a heated and prolonged debate over strategy. These arguments took place while Japan was winning victories in early 1942 and focused on proposals for possible operations in the late spring and early summer. Army leaders, who had insisted that Japan go to war with the United States in 1941, now were reluctant to engage in any major new offensives against America or Britain. They were more interested in an attack on the USSR if, as they expected, Germany's projected summer offensive dealt the Soviets a mortal blow. To facilitate such an operation, they maintained powerful forces in Manchuria.

Naval leaders, who had been much more reluctant to go to war with America, now were eager to extend Japan's domination. But they did not agree on where to strike. Some urged the conquest of Ceylon, which would enable Japan to control the Indian Ocean and threaten India. Others preferred to thrust southward to eliminate Australia as a base for a possible Allied counteroffensive. Still others insisted on striking eastward to seize Midway, an atoll over 1,000 miles northwest of Pearl Harbor. Admiral Osami Nagano, chief of the naval general staff, favored the second alternative. Admiral Yamamoto much preferred the third. Nagano was Yamamoto's superior and possessed the authority to overrule him. He had served as vice chief of staff, navy minister, and commander in chief of the combined fleet before becoming chief of staff in 1941. Nagano had originally opposed the plan to attack Pearl Harbor, but after its success and the enormous prestige that it brought to Yamamoto, he was reluctant to push too forcefully his objections to the Midway proposal.

Predictably, Yamamoto eventually won the argument, and Nagano agreed to an operation against Midway. He also abandoned thoughts of an invasion of Australia but nevertheless decided to seal off that continent partially before the Midway undertaking. He planned to accomplish this by capturing Port Moresby, on the southeastern coast of the island of New Guinea, and Tulagi in the southern Solomons. Japanese forces had landed at various points along the northern coast of New Guinea during the winter and spring and had seized the Admiralty Islands, New Britain, and New Ireland to the northeast as well as the northern islands of the Solomon chain. Once in control of New Britain, they took advantage of the outstanding natural harbor at Rabaul to build a powerful naval base. By extending their domination over the airfield at Port Moresby, the Japanese could protect Rabaul from air attack while securing a base from which to bomb northern Australia. By establishing a seaplane base on Tulagi, they could patrol the eastern waters of the Coral Sea between the Solomons and both New Guinea and Australia.

AMERICAN OPERATIONS

Meanwhile, American leaders had reorganized the U.S. Navy's command structure. Shortly after Pearl Harbor, Admiral Ernest J. King became commander in chief of the U.S. Fleet, and Admiral Chester W. Nimitz took over as commander of the Pacific Fleet. King, like his army counterpart, General Marshall, was far from an endearing person. Clearly a brilliant planner and administrator, he was also arrogant and aloof. Few people felt any affection for him. A veteran of the Spanish-American War, he had served as chief of staff in the Atlantic Fleet during World War I. While in this position, he developed a strong dislike of the British that, unfortunately, he never lost. King had commanded the Atlantic Fleet with distinction during 1941.

Despite his obvious qualifications for command, the admiral viewed the war from a narrow focus that almost always favored the navy's interest. He disagreed with the "Europe first" strategy and urged greater emphasis on the Pacific. Such an approach would certainly enhance the navy's role because naval power was the key to victory over Japan. Just as obviously, the army would be of primary importance in Europe. Indeed, King's insistence on the significance of the Pacific contributed greatly to the fact that it never became as secondary a theater of operations as Roosevelt and others had originally planned.

Nimitz, by contrast, was quiet, easygoing, and well liked. He was a team player who shunned publicity. Although his hair had turned completely white, he was still youthful-looking and handsome at 57. An Annapolis graduate, Nimitz had served in a variety of seagoing and staff commands. Roosevelt chose him over 28 senior officers to lead the Pacific Fleet, certainly one of his most inspired decisions. Nimitz's first task was to revive the fleet's shattered morale after the Pearl Harbor disaster, and he achieved this with remarkable speed. He did so largely by refusing to dismiss most of the members of Kimmel's staff and instead expressed complete confidence in them. They in turn gave him their complete loyalty. Nimitz proved to be a brilliant leader of men as well as a skilled strategist and tactician.

The new commander faced the awesome responsibility of holding a line from Midway to Australia against further Japanese encroachments with the relatively meager forces remaining after the Pearl Harbor attack. Their chief strength lay in the carriers *Saratoga, Lexington, Enterprise,* and *Hornet*. But a Japanese submarine damaged *Saratoga* in January 1942 and forced it to return to the U.S. West Coast for repairs. As its replacement, Nimitz received *Yorktown* from the Atlantic Fleet. Fortunately for him, the Japanese navy was busy in the waters off Southeast Asia in the first few months of 1942 and made no move against his fleet.

Nimitz soon came into possession of another weapon that proved of tremendous value in the upcoming operations: navy cryptanalysts had broken the Japanese naval code. This was quite distinct from the Japanese diplomatic cipher, which had already fallen victim to American codebreakers before Pearl Harbor. By May, Nimitz possessed detailed information that made it clear that the Japanese intended to attack Midway as well as Port Moresby and Tulagi in early June. Starting in the summer of 1942, it became stan-

FIGURE 14-1 A U.S. naval gun fires during a night action in the Pacific. (*U.S. Navy Photo/National Archives*)

dard practice to refer to information derived from the Japanese naval codes by the British name, Ultra. When the Americans broke the enemy's army code in the spring of 1943, this source of intelligence also came under the Ultra umbrella. The name Magic applied only to diplomatic ciphers.

While the Allies were suffering their depressing series of defeats during the first few months of 1942, Nimitz carried out minor offensive operations against the Japanese, with little success. Carrier-based planes from a task force commanded by Admiral William Halsey raided Wake and islands in the Caroline chain during February and Marcus Island, less than 1,000 miles from Tokyo, in March but inflicted only minor damage.

By far the most ambitious undertaking during this period was an air attack by 16 army air corps B-25 bombers on April 18. This force, under the leadership of Lieutenant Colonel James Doolittle, took off from the carrier *Hornet* 700 miles to the southeast of Japan and bombed Tokyo and several other Japanese cities. Doolittle had already won fame for his daring peacetime exploits as a pilot. He had been the first person to fly across the United States in 12 hours and at one time held the world's record for air speed. The raid did little damage but provided a much needed psychological lift for the American public.

BATTLE OF THE CORAL SEA

Japanese leaders began their operations against Port Moresby and Tulagi in early May. They allotted strong naval forces to cover the landings, but this time the Americans were in a position to challenge them. Once his cryptanalysts had alerted Nimitz to the Japanese plan, he ordered a task force, under the command of Admiral Frank Jack Fletcher, to contest the enemy attempt to take Port Moresby. Fletcher's force included the carriers *Yorktown* and *Lexington*.

Fletcher had gained valuable sea experience aboard destroyers, cruisers, and battleships but had no connection with carriers or airplanes before the war. He had this shortcoming in common with many of his colleagues, however, and it did not prevent him from gaining command of a carrier task force. Although immensely popular with his fellow officers, he encountered criticism for poor seamanship and indecision during the abortive attempt to relieve Wake Island. One of Nimitz's staff officers later referred to him as "a big, nice, wonderful guy who didn't know his butt from third base."*

The Japanese occupied Tulagi without opposition on May 3. Meanwhile, the major invasion expedition headed southward from Rabaul toward Port Moresby under the protection of the light carrier *Shoho* and other naval units. At the same time, a more powerful task force converged on the Coral Sea from the Japanese base of Truk in the Carolines. It included the heavy carriers *Zuikaku* and *Shokaku,* which had both participated in the Pearl Harbor attack. The overall commander of the operation was Admiral Shigeyoshi Inouye, whose Fourth Fleet had overpowered Guam and Wake in December. Inouye expected American naval units to intervene but assumed that his slightly stronger force would prevail. The Battle of the Coral Sea followed on May 7–8. It was the first naval engagement in history in which the opposing ships never came within sight of each other. Carrier-based planes provided all the firepower. The Japanese lost *Shoho,* and *Shokaku* sustained severe damage. On the American side, *Lexington* survived the effects of Japanese torpedoes and bombs but succumbed when a spark from a generator ignited gasoline fumes and caused a series of explosions. Japanese planes also seriously damaged *Yorktown.*

Tactically, the battle was a draw because the opposing fleets inflicted roughly equal punishment. But the United States won a strategic victory because Inouye became so concerned about his losses that he called off the landing at Port Moresby. Even more important, both *Shokaku* and *Zuikaku* had to return to Japan, the former for extensive repairs and the latter for fresh planes and pilots. Neither was available when Yamamoto's forces steamed for Midway. The Battle of the Coral Sea was not decisive, but it clearly marked a shift in momentum, one that continued.

*Gordon W. Prange with Donald M. Goldstein and Katherine V. Dillon, *Miracle at Midway* (New York: Penguin Books, 1983), p. 97.

BATTLE OF MIDWAY

The really decisive battle came at Midway. Yamamoto assumed that American naval forces would intervene in strength if Japan threatened Midway. This would provide the opportunity for the Combined Fleet to finish the job it had started with the Pearl Harbor attack—the destruction of the U.S. Pacific Fleet, especially its carriers. Yamamoto based his strategy on the premise that Japan would not be secure until it had eliminated the Pacific Fleet. His thinking was undoubtedly sound, but his plan was faulty.

Its most serious flaw was the provision for too many objectives. This diluted Japanese strength. Yamamoto called for a secondary assault on two of the Aleutian Islands, Attu and Kiska, which lay many hundreds of miles to the west of Alaska. Although he hoped this operation would divert U.S. ships and planes away from the Midway area, it shifted Japanese strength from the major objective as well. And his insistence on the occupation of Midway also distracted attention from the main purpose of the plan: to lure the Pacific Fleet into a showdown battle. His forces could accomplish this by their mere presence in the waters near Midway.

Yamamoto also failed to concentrate the strength he had earmarked for the Midway operation. His plan provided for Admiral Nagumo's carrier striking force to perform two missions: an air strike against Midway's land-based aircraft and an attack on the Pacific Fleet when it intervened. Yamamoto was convinced that U.S. forces would not move westward until after the Japanese had taken Midway. But if the Americans should intervene earlier, they might catch Nagumo's force while his planes were assaulting Midway and his carriers were most vulnerable to air attack. Other Japanese naval units were to provide close support for the Midway invasion force. Meanwhile, Yamamoto himself planned to remain far to the rear with what he referred to as the Main Body, consisting of three battleships and supporting vessels. He intended to bring this force into action against the Americans when the opportune time came. But he placed the Main Body so far to the west that the showdown battle might be over before it could act.

Nagano and his naval staff pointed out many of these weaknesses. They discounted the importance of occupying Midway and warned that it was unlikely that the Japanese could again catch the Americans by surprise. But Yamamoto enjoyed such massive prestige that his plan won approval. The admiral also pointed to the Doolittle raid on the home islands as evidence that there was a gap in Japan's defenses. He argued that the seizure of Midway would eliminate this weakness. The army's contention that it could not provide troops for operations against either Ceylon or Australia also helped determine the outcome. The navy set early June as the target date for the attack on Midway.

Yamamoto and other Japanese naval leaders also suffered from what they later described as "victory disease." They had grown so accustomed to winning one great triumph after another that they became arrogant and assumed that they would overcome all obstacles. Even the members of the naval staff who criticized Yamamoto's plan most vehemently never doubted that their forces would succeed despite the problems they cited.

Despite the flaws in Yamamoto's plan and the breaking of the Japanese naval code, Nimitz's forces were considerably weaker than those of the enemy. Yamamoto's total strength included four heavy carriers—*Akagi, Kaga, Hiryu,* and *Soryu,* all veterans of the Pearl Harbor attack—and two light carriers as well as seven battleships, 15 cruisers, and 44 destroyers. To counter this huge armada, Nimitz had three carriers, eight cruisers, and 15 destroyers under the command of Admiral Fletcher. Two of the carriers, *Enterprise* and *Hornet,* formed the core of a task force under the command of Admiral Raymond Spruance. The hastily patched-up *Yorktown* provided the nucleus of a second small task force under Fletcher's direct control.

Nimitz had selected Spruance as a last-minute replacement for Halsey, who had to be hospitalized because of a severe skin condition. At first glance, Spruance might seem a poor choice. His prior sea experience had been as commander of destroyers, cruisers, and a battleship. He was thus a member of what naval aviators referred to disparagingly as the "gun club." Spruance shared Nimitz's antipathy for the limelight and, unlike the effervescent Fletcher and Halsey, had gained a reputation among other officers as cold and humorless. But he remained calm and cautious in action while demonstrating a flair for making the right decisions and taking advantage of opportunities. His performance in the forthcoming battle ended any doubts as to his ability.

Whereas Nimitz was aware of Japanese intentions and deployed his strength accordingly, Yamamoto was ignorant of the location of the Pacific Fleet. He assumed that Nimitz knew nothing of his plans and would not be able to intervene until after Midway had fallen. The Japanese also incorrectly believed that they had sunk *Yorktown* in the Battle of the Coral Sea, and Yamamoto expected to face, at most, two American carriers. His plan called for Japanese submarines to provide early warning of the Pacific Fleet's westward movement. However, due largely to the misconceived certainty that the Americans would not move prior to the Midway attack, the submarines were slow to take up their designated positions to the west of Oahu. When they finally did, U.S. naval forces had already passed far beyond that point and were awaiting the arrival of the enemy carrier striking force.

Nagumo's fleet penetrated to within 250 miles of Midway on June 4. It launched an attack on the atoll while sending out reconnaissance planes to search for any U.S. ships that might be in the area. But the Japanese carried out their search with neither a sense of urgency nor their usual efficiency, and hours elapsed before they discovered the presence of American vessels. Meanwhile, Japanese planes damaged installations on Midway and destroyed 17 aircraft. They were preparing for a second attack when a search plane finally spotted elements of the Pacific Fleet. Before Nagumo could react to this unwelcome news, wave after wave of American torpedo planes attacked the Japanese carriers. But they failed to damage their targets and fell victim to Japanese Zero fighters and withering antiaircraft fire. They managed, nevertheless, to disperse the Zeros, and when U.S. dive bombers pressed home their attacks soon afterward, they scored several direct hits on *Soryu, Akagi,* and *Kaga,* turning them all into blazing hulks.

Only *Hiryu* remained, and its planes took off in search of the American carriers. They found Fletcher's flagship, *Yorktown.* The first wave of dive bombers scored three hits, and the second assault by torpedo bombers added two more. Even now *Yorktown* might have survived, but two days later, an enemy submarine fired another pair of torpedoes into its side. This time there was no escape. But *Hiryu* was doomed, too. American dive bombers attacked and set it ablaze. Within a short time, the last of Nagumo's heavy carriers joined the three others on the bottom.

When Yamamoto received news of the Japanese disaster, he belatedly attempted to intervene with the battleships of his Main Body. He hoped to attack the Pacific Fleet in a night engagement. The Japanese had proved themselves masters in this type of encounter. But Spruance, who had succeeded to operational control of the Pacific Fleet when Fletcher had to abandon *Yorktown,* refused to risk his carriers and withdrew to the east. When Yamamoto discovered this, he, too, reluctantly pulled back. His Main Body, which had not fired a shot, might just as well have remained in Japanese waters.

Midway was decisive for two reasons. It restored the naval balance in the Pacific, and it marked the end of Japan's initiative on the high seas. Not only had the Japanese squandered four carriers, but they had also lost 253 planes and their skilled pilots. Neither their carrier force nor their naval air power ever recovered from this blow. Japanese sea power was still an important factor, but henceforth it played a defensive role. To the Americans, Midway was the beginning of an inexorable progression toward total domination of the Pacific.

SMALL VICTORIES, BIG DEFEATS

Yamamoto's only success was the capture of Attu and Kiska in the Aleutians, but this was a dubious achievement. The Japanese forces, which occupied these remote and desolate northern islands, faced an ominous future now that Japan no longer dominated the sea.

On land, the Japanese had not yet relinquished the initiative, but their days of ascendancy were dwindling. After the failure of their plan to capture Port Moresby by a seaborne operation, they attempted to take it by land. This was no easy task. It involved pushing southward along a narrow, perpetually muddy trail, known as the Kokoda Track, which ran from Buna on New Guinea's northeastern coast across the rugged, rain-swept, and jungle-choked Owen Stanley Mountains. The Japanese pushed southward from Buna in late July and by August 26 had penetrated to within 30 miles of Port Moresby. But their drive bogged down due to supply problems, the difficult terrain, and stiffening resistance from Australian troops. In mid-September, they abandoned their attempt to take Port Moresby and went over to the defensive.

The Australians launched a counteroffensive on September 28 but encountered ferocious Japanese resistance and did not push the defenders back to the Buna area until mid-November. Australian and American troops now slowly hammered away at skillfully constructed enemy defenses, featuring bunkers made from coconut tree logs, in swampy country. The Japanese fought with fanatical determination, preferring suicide charges to surrender, but eventually the Allies prevailed. Buna fell on January 2, 1943. It was now clear that the tide had turned irrevocably against Japan in New Guinea.

BATTLES FOR THE SOLOMON ISLANDS

Even before the Japanese drive on Port Moresby had halted on the Kokoda Track, American forces had launched their first offensive in the southern Solomon Islands. Initially, U.S. leaders had merely intended to take Tulagi and neighboring Gavatu. But when they discovered that enemy

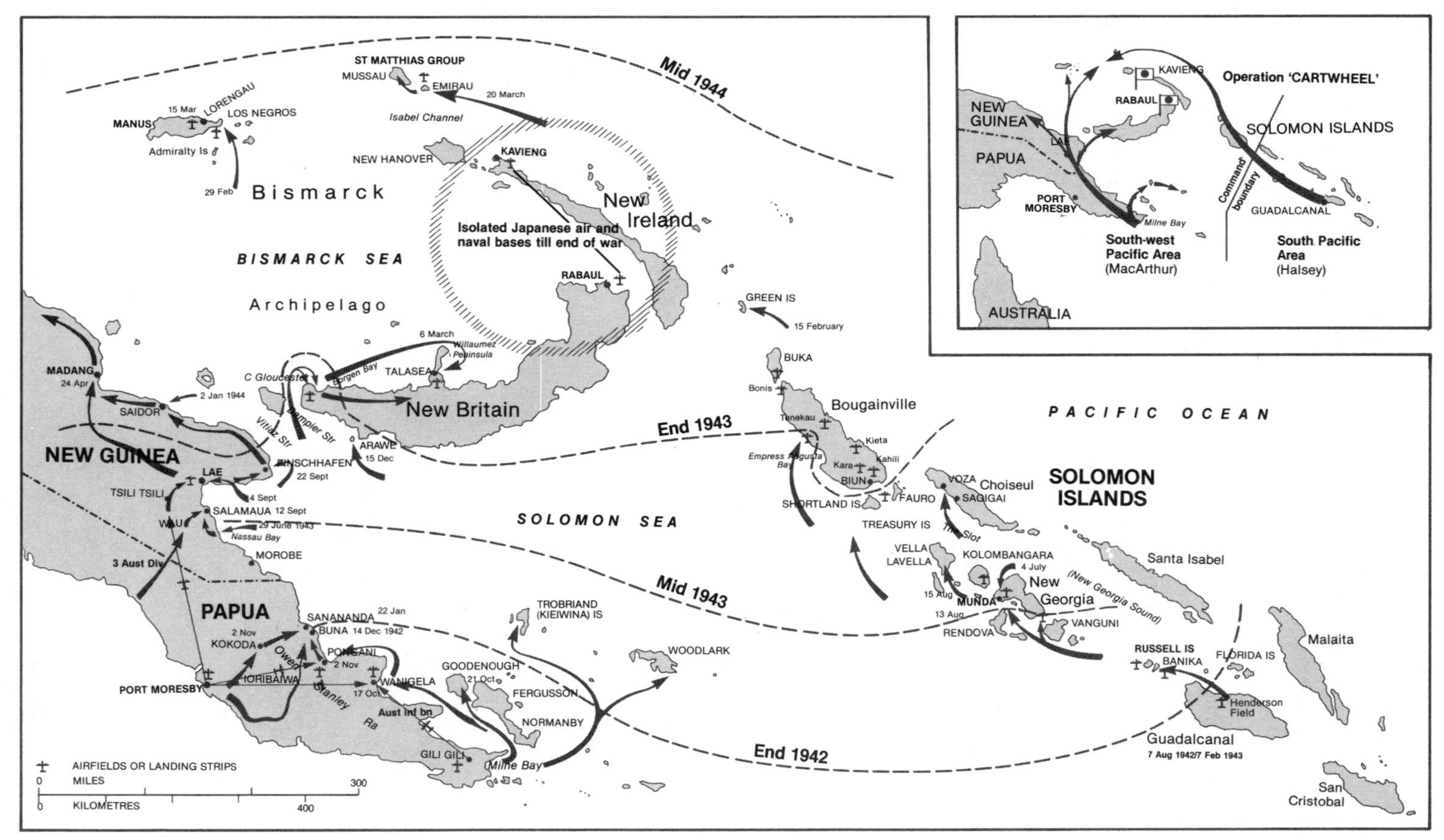

Eastern New Guinea, the Bismarck Archipelago and the Solomons

troops had landed on nearby Guadalcanal and were constructing an airstrip there, they decided to attack it as well. Although Guadalcanal had been something of an afterthought, this little-known island became the site of a desperate struggle that lasted for six months.

Admiral Robert Ghormley, the U.S. naval commander in the South Pacific, held overall responsibility for the invasion. A capable officer who had enjoyed a long and varied career, Ghormley had spent two years as chief naval observer in London and may have received the South Pacific command because of his diplomatic skills. They proved useful since he had to deal with Australian, New Zealand, and even French authorities. The site of Ghormley's headquarters was Nouméa, on the French island of New Caledonia, which had sided with de Gaulle. Although Nouméa lay 900 miles to the southeast of Guadalcanal, it was the nearest deep-water port with reasonably adequate facilities. Nouméa was also almost 6,500 miles from San Francisco. Its remote location from both the source of supplies and the fighting front, along with a chronic shortage of shipping, created a highly difficult logistic situation.

Ghormley had to make do with land and sea forces that were so slender and so hastily assembled that the undertaking earned the nickname Operation Shoestring. Eleven thousand marines, under the command of General Alexander Vandegrift, landed on Guadalcanal on August 7. A quiet, modest man known for his fatherly concern for his troops, Vandegrift had participated in various marine interventions in Central America during the interwar years. When first informed of his mission, he confessed that he had no idea as to the location of Guadalcanal. Smaller forces invaded Tulagi and Gavatu and by the next day had overcome the fierce resistance of their tiny garrisons. The Guadalcanal landing surprised the meager Japanese defenders, and they offered no opposition but withdrew into the jungle. They even abandoned their airstrip, which the Americans seized and christened Henderson Field after a marine pilot who had died at Midway.

Once Japanese leaders recovered from their initial shock, they set out to drive the marines into the sea and immediately dispatched reinforcements to Guadalcanal under the command of General Kiyotake Kawaguchi. A veteran of the Philippine campaign, Kawaguchi was noted for his bristling 10-inch mustache. He immediately recognized that Guadalcanal would become the crucial point in the Pacific war and was determined to dislodge the Americans.

In the following weeks and months, troop transports and supply ships repeatedly made night runs down the narrow channel separating the western Solomons from the eastern islands in the chain. The Americans called this body of water "The Slot" and referred to the nocturnal Japanese naval missions as the "Tokyo Express." Although the defeat at Midway had seriously weakened their carrier force, the Japanese still had a considerable advantage in battleships, cruisers, and destroyers. They used these vessels to escort their transports and supply ships as well as to bombard Henderson Field. At times they also attempted to interdict American reinforcements and supplies that converged on Guadalcanal during daylight hours.

The struggle for Guadalcanal became largely one of supply, and the side that maintained its flow while cutting off the enemy's would ultimately win. The issue remained in doubt for months. Kawaguchi's troops launched savage attacks against the defensive perimeter that the marines had established around Henderson Field. During the night of September 13, they tried repeatedly to break through a position that became known fittingly as Bloody Ridge. The marines repulsed them each time, killing over half the attacking force while suffering heavy casualties themselves. Early in October, General Harukichi Hyakutake, the Japanese commander in the Solomons, took personal control of the battle. But he was no more successful than Kawaguchi.

Guadalcanal was an abominable place to fight a war. Most of it consisted of rugged mountains, dense jungles, and malaria-ridden swamps. The heat and humidity were constant and oppressive.

FIGURE 14-2 Marine landing craft head for the enemy shore after a combined naval and aerial bombardment. (*Defense Dept. Photo [Marine Corps]*)

Both sides suffered from the appalling conditions and from some of the most ferocious fighting of the entire Pacific war. Despite continued fanatical Japanese attacks, which often featured suicide charges, the marines held out night after night, week after week, month after month. Fresh army forces finally relieved the exhausted garrison in December.

Meanwhile, the rival fleets fought a series of six major naval engagements and many minor ones between August and November in an effort to gain control of the sea and win the battle of supply. Most of these encounters took place at night and involved primarily cruisers and destroyers. The Japanese continued to demonstrate their mastery of night fighting and took a heavy toll of American ships, although they, too, suffered serious losses. But two of the clashes occurred in daylight and featured attacks by carrier-based aircraft. Savo Sound, the body of water between Guadalcanal and Tulagi, claimed so many ships from both fleets that the Americans nicknamed it "Ironbottom Sound."

The first of these encounters, the Battle of Savo Island, unfolded on the night of August 8–9, soon after the marine landings. It gained its name from the volcanic island at the entrance to "Ironbottom Sound" and ended in a Japanese victory. A Japanese cruiser squadron overwhelmed a somewhat makeshift Allied force, sinking one Australian and three American cruisers and severely damaging another as well as several destroyers. The Japanese lost only one cruiser to a submarine attack after the battle ended. It was one of the worst defeats ever suffered by the U.S. Navy. But the Japanese missed an opportunity to destroy the American transports off Guadalcanal and Tulagi. Instead, with the approach of dawn, Admiral Gumichi Mikawa withdrew his ships because he feared air attacks by carrier-based planes. But Admiral Fletcher, who had led U.S. forces in the Coral Sea and at Midway, had already pulled back his three carriers—*Saratoga, Enterprise,* and *Wasp*—because he feared a Japanese air strike. Their departure left the transports completely exposed to an attack, which fortunately never came.

Fletcher was less timid in the Battle of the Eastern Solomons later the same month. His carrier planes intercepted an enemy supply convoy and its supporting carrier force. They sank the light carrier *Ryujo,* but Japanese aircraft damaged *Enterprise.* Marine planes from Henderson Field also destroyed an enemy cruiser and a supply ship. Their losses convinced the Japanese that daylight runs were too risky, and they returned to the nighttime Tokyo Express. But Japanese submarines remained a constant menace. Torpedo attacks mortally wounded *Wasp* and put *Saratoga* and the battleship *North Carolina* out of action until November.

In the Battle of Cape d'Esperance on the night of October 11–12, U.S. warships used radar to detect the approach of an enemy convoy off Guadalcanal's northwest coast. They sank a destroyer and damaged two cruisers while losing a destroyer and suffering damage to a cruiser. Soon afterward, Admiral Nimitz concluded that the Guadalcanal operation required more aggressive and inspiring leadership than Admiral Ghormley was able to provide. He replaced him with Admiral Halsey.

The new commander was a man of action in the swashbuckling naval tradition, preferring to act quickly and boldly without too much thought for the consequences. He believed in carrying the fight to the enemy with unrelenting persistence and was, to put it charitably, an indifferent administrator. Unlike most of the leading American admirals at this time, Halsey was an aviator. He had won his wings in 1934 at the age of 52 after many years as a destroyer commander and naval attaché. When the war began, he was America's most experienced carrier task force commander. Tall and rather heavyset, he possessed a face almost bulldoglike in its ugliness. The media called him "Bull," but his many friends referred to him as "Bill." He was exceptionally outgoing and enjoyed the respect and love of his men. While Spruance, the victor of Midway, earned renown as "an admiral's admiral," Halsey was clearly "a sailor's admiral."

Halsey decided to bring the carriers into action again in an effort to gain the initiative. The result was another daylight encounter near the Santa Cruz Islands to the east of Guadalcanal on October 26. Aircraft from a task force commanded by Admiral Thomas Kinkaid, a veteran of the Battle of the Coral Sea, attacked and damaged the Japanese carriers *Zuiho* and *Shokaku.* But the Americans paid a heavy price as enemy planes sent the carrier *Hornet* to the bottom and damaged *Enterprise*'s flight deck. The battle ended in a tactical victory for the Japanese, but their heavy losses in planes and pilots tended to nullify their advantage.

The fifth and decisive clash, the Battle of Guadalcanal, took place on November 13–15 near the entrance to "Ironbottom Sound." A large Japanese force tried to protect a landing of reinforcements and supplies on Guadalcanal. A much smaller U.S. squadron rashly steamed forward to engage the enemy at close range. It sank the old battleship *Hiei* and two destroyers while losing two cruisers and sustaining damage to a third. The Japanese withdrew but returned the next night with the battleship *Kirishima,* four cruisers, and nine destroyers. This time they encountered two American battleships—*Washington* and *South Dakota*—and four destroyers. Another savage engagement followed as searchlight beams and the flashes of the big guns illuminated the sky. The Japanese crippled *South Dakota,* but *Washington* sent *Kirishima* to rest on the floor of Ironbottom Sound. The remaining Japanese units withdrew once again, leaving the U.S. Navy with control of the waters around Guadalcanal. American land- and carrier-based planes also destroyed an enemy cruiser and seven transports during the daylight hours of November 14.

Japanese forces tried again to land supplies on November 30, precipitating the sixth and final major battle. It took place off Guadalcanal's Tassafaronga Point. This time the Americans outnumbered the enemy. But again the Japanese demonstrated their skill in night fighting. They outmaneuvered the U.S. ships, sank a cruiser, and inflicted serious damage on three more at the cost of only one of their own destroyers. Despite this victory, during the weeks that followed Japanese leaders concluded that their navy could not continue to absorb losses like those they had been suffering since August and reluctantly agreed to abandon Guadalcanal. In early February 1943, they gradually and skillfully evacuated their forces despite U.S. naval superiority. By February 9, the Americans controlled the entire island.

Guadalcanal was in many aspects as much a turning point as Midway. The United States had taken the initiative on land, and although it had suffered heavy losses at sea, the U.S. Navy was able to obtain replacements and continued to press the attack in the following months. Japan was not so fortunate. The Japanese had staked a great deal on stopping this first Allied offensive and had failed. In the process, they had lost their reputation for invincibility in land warfare, and their naval power, so badly shaken at Midway, had suffered still another setback.

AMERICAN ATTITUDES TOWARD THE JAPANESE

The grim struggles on New Guinea and Guadalcanal as well as the "fight to the death" mentality of Japanese troops also increased American hatred of the enemy, which had been growing since Pearl Harbor. This took a different form from the animosity directed toward the Germans and the Italians. The nature of the attack on Pearl Harbor and the reports of atrocities that accompanied Japanese conquests played important roles in developing this attitude. But the Japanese were also members of a different race, and America had a long history of racial prejudice and hatred. Crude caricatures of short, bow-legged, buck-toothed "Japs" adorned posters for war bond drives and other patriotic appeals. Hollywood films portrayed Japanese soldiers as far more inhuman and sadistic than their German or Italian counterparts. Surveys indicated that many Americans, both soldiers and civilians, had little moral compunction about "killing Japs" and tended to equate them with subhumans, animals, or even reptiles.

American soldiers who actually fought against the Japanese, however, were often less hostile toward them than civilians and soldiers in training or in the European theater of operations. But the general stereotype of the enemy, coupled with the fanatical resistance of Japanese soldiers, assured that the Pacific war would continue to rage with a ferocity that American participation in the European conflict could not match.

15

The Tide Turns in Europe: Stalingrad and El Alamein

It is clear that 1941 was the crucial year of the war because of the failure of the German offensive in the Soviet Union and the entry of the United States into the conflict. But it was in 1942 that the war turned irretrievably against the Axis in both Europe and the Pacific. Yet during much of the year, Germany again held the initiative and won another series of victories in both Russia and North Africa. These triumphs proved to be a prelude to disaster, however, and the Wehrmacht was in full retreat in both theaters before the end of the year.

NEW GERMAN GOALS IN THE USSR

In the USSR, the Soviet winter counteroffensive bogged down by February 1942, and the Germans were able to recover from the sledgehammer blows that had sent them reeling in December and January. Hitler planned to wrest the initiative from the Russians by the summer. But the Germans lacked sufficient strength to attack on the scale of the 1941 campaign. Hitler decided instead to concentrate on the south and abandoned the possibility of a second attempt to capture Moscow. His primary aim in the 1942 campaign was economic—the capture of the Caucasus oil fields. This would cut off the Soviets from their chief source of petroleum and greatly increase German oil supplies. But it also meant that Hitler was abandoning the stated objective of Operation Barbarossa a year earlier—the destruction of the main Soviet forces, which still lay before Moscow.

The Germans planned a three-step operation. Phase 1 called for an encirclement of Soviet troops to the west of the Don River by two powerful components of Army Group South. Field Marshal von Bock, now recovered from the illness that had sidelined him during the winter, had taken over command in the south. General Hoth's Fourth Panzer Army provided the spearhead of the northern arm of the planned encirclement, with General Friedrich von Paulus's Sixth Army to its right. These forces were to drive toward Voronezh on the Don and then dash southeastward along the river's west bank toward the industrial city of Stalingrad on the Volga River. General von Kleist's First Panzer Army formed the southern spearhead and was to advance north of Rostov and link up with Hoth's column. After completing this encirclement, Hoth and Paulus would execute phase 2 by establishing a blocking position on the Volga near Stalingrad to protect the southern force, which would carry out phase 3, the drive to the Caucasus.

When Paulus took over as leader of the Sixth Army, it marked his first actual field command.

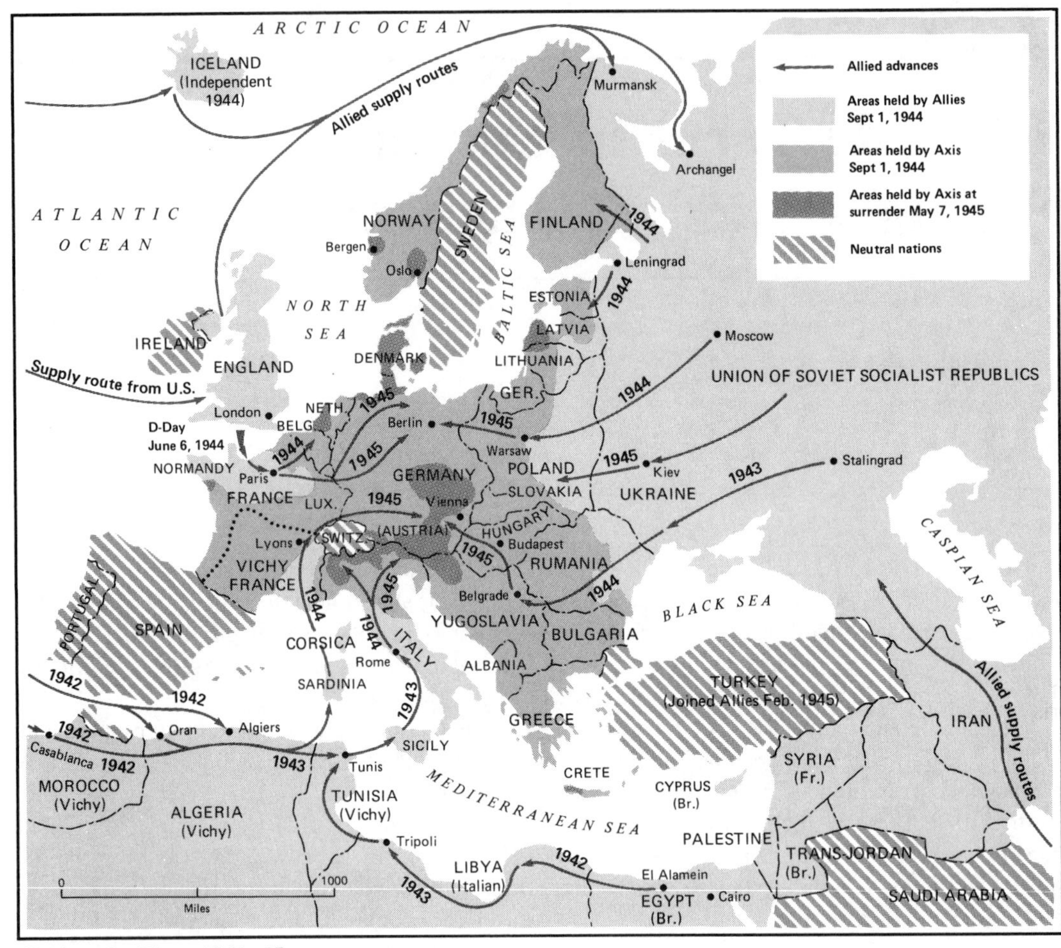

Closing the Ring, 1942–45

He had served as chief of staff of the Tenth Army during the campaigns in Poland and Western Europe. Paulus became Halder's deputy in October 1940 and participated in the planning for Operation Barbarossa. In fact, he had conducted war games prior to the 1941 invasion that demonstrated clearly that the *Blitzkrieg* would encounter severe supply problems and that German forces were barely adequate to capture Moscow. Halder had ignored his ominous warning. Paulus proved better suited to staff work than leadership in the field.

The German army on the eastern front had fallen below its strength at the start of the 1941 campaign by 350,000 men and now depended on Rumanian, Hungarian, and Italian units for support. These satellite troops were of lower quality and morale and lacked adequate equipment. Even the German troops were inferior to those of June 1941. The bitter winter fighting had taken its toll. Total tank strength was slightly less than at the start of the 1941 campaign, but the OKH had concentrated a large part of it in the south. Germany still had not developed a tank that was a match for the Soviet T34. The Soviets also had encountered difficulty in replacing their tremendous losses in armor, and they were not impressed by the arrival of U.S. and British tanks, which were inferior to both the T34 and KV. Soviet leaders sent most of this Western armor to quiet sectors of the front or to East Asia.

The Germans planned to eliminate a Soviet salient in their line south of Kharkov as a preliminary to the summer offensive. But before they could act, the Red Army staged an offensive from the salient with the intention of recapturing Kharkov, the hub of the German communications network in the south. This Soviet operation actually proved a boon to the Germans, who had been building up their strength along the flanks of the salient. Stalin and Timoshenko, the Russian southern front commander, had insisted on this offensive over the opposition of both Zhukov and Shaposhnikov, the chief of staff. Timoshenko launched his offensive on May 12. The Soviets advanced swiftly at first and made a deep penetration, increasing the vulnerability of their position. On May 17, the Germans struck the enemy flank from the south and within a few days had cut off the Soviet spearhead, capturing 240,000 prisoners and destroying over 600 tanks. Timoshenko had asked for permission to pull back before the Germans sealed off his forces, but Stalin and Stavka had refused.

FIGURE 15-1 Josef Stalin, the Soviet dictator. (*UPI/Bettmann Newsphotos*)

Another preliminary to the main German offensive came in the Crimea, the peninsula that juts into the Black Sea from the Ukraine. The Eleventh Army under General von Manstein, the chief architect of the Ardennes breakthrough in 1940, had conquered most of the Crimea during the fall of 1941. But Manstein's forces had failed to capture the Soviet naval base of Sevastopol, which remained secure behind three belts of powerful permanent defenses. The Soviets had also regained control of the Kerch Peninsula, the extreme eastern portion of the Crimea, in December. Manstein received reinforcements and strong air support in the spring and recaptured the Kerch Peninsula in May. On June 7, he unleashed another offensive against Sevastopol, but again the Soviets resisted furiously. Despite incessant air attacks, and shelling by two huge siege mortars, one of which hurled shells weighing over 2 tons, and a railway gun that fired 5-ton rounds, Sevastopol did not fall until July 3.

The disastrous failure of the Red Army's attempt to take Kharkov seriously weakened the Soviets in the south, and when the Germans opened their major offensive on June 28, they rapidly swept forward. Timoshenko's badly depleted forces, desperately short of armor, had to fall back quickly. Stalin remained convinced that the Germans intended to strike their major blow at Moscow and concentrated the bulk of his strength in defense of the capital. Once again he disregarded intelligence reports that the offensive would come in the south.

Hoth's Fourth Panzer Army drove 100 miles in eight days, reaching the Don near Voronezh, which the Germans planned to secure as the anchor for their eastern flank. But the Soviets defended Voronezh stubbornly, and Bock persisted in efforts to take the city before sending Hoth's panzers southward along the Don to form the northern pincer of the planned encirclement of enemy forces. This helped Timoshenko carry out a successful withdrawal toward Stalingrad. Several days elapsed before the Fourth Panzer Army abandoned the attack on Voronezh and headed south. Hitler became disenchanted with Bock's slow progress and replaced him with General Maximilian von Weichs. He also split Army Group South into two separate commands—Army Group B in the north under Weichs and Army Group A to the south under Field Marshal Wilhelm List. Weichs had been a corps commander in the Polish and Western European campaigns and led the Second Army in the invasions of Yugoslavia and Russia. List had commanded the Fourteenth Army in Poland and the Twelfth Army in both the Ardennes breakthrough and the Balkans.

Meanwhile, Kleist's First Panzer Army moved eastward to form the southern wing of the encirclement. But the Soviets withdrew here, too, and the Germans took few prisoners. Hitler assumed that the Red Army was fleeing in panic instead of executing an organized withdrawal and ecstatically proclaimed that "the Russian is finished," to which Halder responded, "I must admit, it looks like it." In his euphoria, the Führer decided that it was now possible to drive toward the Caucasus without first securing the German flank at Stalingrad.

In keeping with this new approach, Hitler ordered Army Group A to swing southward with the First Panzer Army in the lead. He also ordered the Fourth Panzer Army to abandon its drive on Stalingrad and assist Kleist's forces with their crossing of the Don east of Rostov. The less mobile Sixth Army, with its preponderance of infantry, received the task of capturing Stalingrad. The simultaneous pursuit of these two objectives and the diversion of the Fourth Panzer Army proved to be serious mistakes. If left to continue their drive on Stalingrad, Hoth's forces might have reached the city before the Soviets had consolidated their position there. And it soon became clear that the First Panzer Army did not need help crossing the Don as it made rapid progress against weak Soviet resistance. By August 9, it had streaked 200 miles southeast of Rostov and had reached the Maikop oil fields in the Caucasus foothills.

But now the Germans once again split their forces, one column moving east toward the Grozny oil fields and another hooking west in an effort to clear the Black Sea coast. Again it was a case of too many objectives. Both drives stalled because of a shortage of fuel, difficult mountain terrain, and stronger Soviet resistance. The Germans continued to try to break through during September, October, and November, without success. They had stretched themselves to the limit. Army Group South had originally been responsible for a 500-mile expanse of the front. As a result of the summer offensive, German forces in the south now had a dangerously long front stretching 1,300 miles.

A bizarre episode occurred while the Germans were fighting in the Caucasus. At one point, they reached the lower slopes of 18,481-foot Mount Elbrus, Europe's highest peak. A team of climbers actually braved fog and blizzard to scale the giant mountain and plant a German flag near its summit.

THE LONG STRUGGLE FOR STALINGRAD

While Army Group A was driving toward the Caucasus, the Sixth Army advanced slowly in the direction of Stalingrad. In the process, it created a long, vulnerable flank along the Don, which was guarded by weak satellite troops. The Soviets also retained a number of bridgeheads on the western bank of the river, and these provided strong positions for possible counterattacks. Hitler finally diverted the Fourth Panzer Army back to the Stalingrad operation, but it was too late for a speedy conquest. Soviet resistance stiffened as the Germans neared the city in late August, and the war of movement came to an end.

The Soviet position was still highly precarious. During August, Stalin made major leadership changes. He ordered General Andrei Yeremenko to form a new army group in the Stalingrad area from reserve divisions. Yeremenko was still another former czarist army soldier who had become an officer in the Red Army during the civil war. He had emerged as one of Stalin's chief trouble-shooters and participated in the defense of Moscow in 1941. Yeremenko, who was only 49, possessed bubbling optimism and an aggressive style of leadership. More important, Stalin called upon General Zhukov once again to come to the rescue. Although Timoshenko had conducted the retreat with reasonable skill, his name came to be associated with defeat. Zhukov, by contrast, had gained fame as the "savior of Moscow." In late August, Zhukov replaced Timoshenko as overall commander in the south.

General Vasili Chuikov was responsible for the actual defense of Stalingrad itself. Like Yeremenko, Chuikov was an optimist and acted with extreme decisiveness. He had been serving as a military attaché in China when the invasion began and did not return to the Soviet Union until March 1942. Since then, he had seen little action, but he had studied German methods closely. His observations convinced him that the enemy disliked close combat and would not perform well in street fighting. Upon taking up his new command, he notified his superiors that "we shall either hold the city or die there."

Chuikov organized a skillful defense, and the Germans resorted to battering-ram tactics as well as heavy bombing and shelling, which reduced much of the city to rubble. They gradually drove the Soviets back, street by street, block by block, building by building, sometimes room by room. The struggle became a colossal battle of attrition, and Stalingrad became a symbol for both sides. Stalin was insistent that the city that bore his name should not fall. Hitler became so mesmerized by the thought of taking Stalin's city that he lost sight of strategy and kept hammering away despite heavy casualties and the erosion of his armor, which was not well suited for this type of close-quarters conflict in support of infantry. Ironically, Stalingrad was not a vital objective. The Germans could have established their block on the Volga much more easily to the south of the city. Nevertheless, by early November they held nine-tenths of Stalingrad. But their position took the form of a salient with long, inviting flanks to the north and south.

The Soviets, too, suffered serious losses, but they were in a better position to replace them because of their greater manpower reserves. Soviet leaders had conscripted vast numbers of men after the invasion of 1941. By the fall of 1942, this policy had produced numerous fresh, well-trained divisions. Soviet war production had slumped drastically between October 1941 and the following spring as a result of the large-scale evacuation of industry to the Urals and other areas. But by early fall, factories were turning out a much greater flow of equipment. This was due in large part to concentration on only a few types of tanks, trucks, and artillery that could be easily mass-produced and round-the-clock manufacturing schedules.

Meanwhile, relations between Hitler and some of his top generals became increasingly strained. He dismissed List on September 9 and took over command of Army Group A himself. Even more significant, he ousted Halder as chief of staff late in September and replaced him with General Kurt Zeitzler, a younger, less experienced, and more pliable officer who had started the Russian campaign as a colonel. Zeitzler had gained a reputation as an expert in logistics and a dynamic problem solver. Rising quickly in rank, he won the

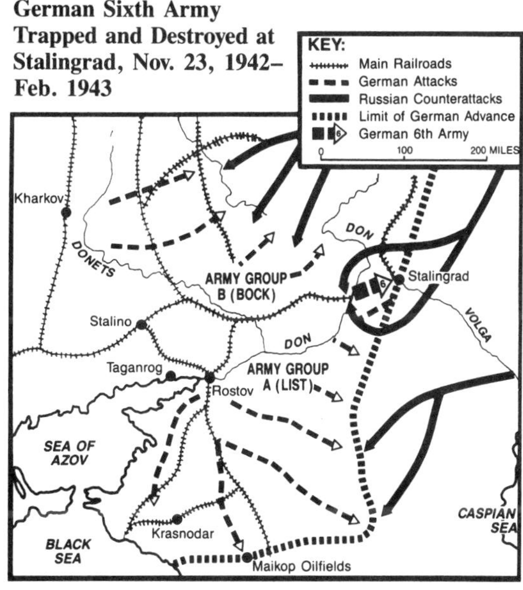

German Sixth Army Trapped and Destroyed at Stalingrad, Nov. 23, 1942–Feb. 1943

admiration of Hitler, who elevated him to chief of staff over many senior generals.

While the struggle for Stalingrad raged on into the fall, Zhukov followed the same approach he had used with success at Moscow a year earlier. He deliberately kept reinforcements for the Stalingrad garrison to a minimum in order to mass as much strength as possible opposite the weak Rumanian forces that held the flanks of the Stalingrad salient. On November 19, Zhukov launched his counterstroke.

An army group under General Nikolai Vatutin's command delivered the first blow against the Rumanian Third Army to the northwest of Stalingrad. Vatutin had started the war as deputy chief of staff and held field commands on the Moscow and Voronezh fronts. He had stymied Bock's attempt to seize Voronezh early in the 1942 offensive, helping to prevent the encirclement of Timoshenko's forces. Vatutin's troops struck the Rumanians from a large bridgehead on the west bank of the Don, quickly tore a gaping hole in their front, and then swung southeastward. The next day, a second army group, commanded by Yeremenko, shattered the Rumanian Fourth Army to the south of Stalingrad and raced northwestward. The Soviet spearheads came together 45 miles west of the city on November 23, sealing off the Sixth Army and one corps of the Fourth Panzer Army.

Paulus asked permission to abandon Stalingrad and attempt to break through the encirclement, but Hitler refused. Memories of his "hold fast" order of the previous year were still fresh. The Führer informed Paulus, "I am not leaving the Volga!" He thought of Stalingrad as a super hedgehog and ordered the Luftwaffe to supply the trapped forces by air, as it had done with isolated strong points called hedgehogs in the winter of 1941–42. But this time the Luftwaffe failed. To supply Stalingrad was a far greater task, and its earlier efforts had eroded both planes and pilots. Prolonged periods of violently stormy weather also snarled operations.

Hitler ordered Manstein, now a field marshal, to lead an expedition to reestablish contact with the Stalingrad garrison. Manstein launched his attempt on December 12 and made fairly good progress at first, but he could not possibly succeed unless the Sixth Army attempted to break out and link up with his forces. Hitler refused to allow this, and Paulus himself seemed to have had no confidence in his army's ability to carry out such a difficult undertaking at this late date. The whole question of the relief of Stalingrad became academic when the Soviets unleashed another offensive on December 16. This time they lunged from the Don toward Rostov with the intention of cutting off all German forces to the south, including Army Group A, which was still fighting in the Caucasus. Even Hitler could see the danger of a far worse disaster than Stalingrad. He ordered his troops in the threatened areas to retreat, and they managed to escape the impending trap.

German forces isolated at Stalingrad now found themselves in a hopeless position. They continued to hold out against increasing pressure, but the Soviets split them into two pockets in late January 1943. Hitler ordered the defenders to fight to the last man and promoted Paulus to field marshal as a bribe to continue the struggle. But the Germans were exhausted, were short of food and other supplies, and suffered horribly from the cold. Medical facilities were so inadequate that wounded men froze to death while awaiting treatment. They could not avoid surrender, and fighting ceased on February 2. Some Germans attempted to escape to the west. Only one of them actually succeeded; ironically, he fell victim to a mortar shell 24 hours after reaching the apparent safety of the German line. Hitler viewed the surrender as a betrayal. He railed against Paulus, vowing never to appoint another field marshal and complaining that it was shameful for him not to have committed suicide. The Führer also insisted that his troops should have shot themselves with their last bullets.

In all, the Germans lost over 200,000 troops at Stalingrad, including 90,000 prisoners. The disaster was one of the war's great turning points. Henceforth, Germany was almost continuously on the defensive on the eastern front.

THE "SIDESHOW" IN NORTH AFRICA

The war reached another turning point in October 1942, even before the start of the Soviet counteroffensive at Stalingrad. This one involved the defeat of Rommel's Axis forces at El Alamein in Egypt. Even though it came in a much less important theater of operations, it has received at least as much attention as the German debacle in Russia.

Hitler had always considered North Africa as a sideshow. Once he committed himself to the invasion of the Soviet Union, the North African campaign represented a drain on German resources, which he hoped to keep as slight as possible. Some observers have pointed to this as a great missed opportunity on Hitler's part. They argue that had he been willing to concentrate on North Africa, he might have conquered Egypt and the Suez Canal and driven on to seize the oil fields of the Middle East. In reality, even if he had been willing and able to allot greater resources to this theater, it is highly doubtful that the Germans could have conquered Egypt, not to speak of the Middle East, because of the huge logistic problems involved.

The distance from Tripoli, the main Axis port in western Libya, to the British naval base at Alexandria in Egypt is over 1,300 miles, more than twice the distance from the prewar Soviet-Polish border to Moscow. The port of Tripoli also had limited capacity, and the Germans had to transport supplies from there for hundreds of miles along a single road. To make matters worse, the German supply service was short of trucks. There were other ports east of Tripoli, but they were all far inferior in capacity. Coastal shipping was also in short supply. These logistic facts made it impossible for the Germans to supply large forces and extremely difficult for them to supply the troops they did have in North Africa. British air and naval forces, operating from the island of Malta south of Sicily, also harassed Rommel's supply line across the Mediterranean. The Axis considered an invasion of Malta to eliminate this threat, but nothing came of it. They did, however, subject the island to intense bombing and inflicted severe damage on British convoys attempting to supply Malta.

After Rommel's 1941 spring offensive bogged down along the Libyan-Egyptian border, he tried repeatedly to dislodge the British force that held Tobruk, the bypassed port on his left flank. But the British clung tenaciously to the town, in large part to prevent the Axis from obtaining a port close to the front. Although the acquisition of Tobruk certainly would have helped Rommel, it actually had limited importance because of the harbor's inadequate capacity and the Axis shortage of coastal shipping.

The British were anxious to regain the initiative, and General Wavell made an attempt to oust the Italo-German forces from their border positions and relieve the Tobruk garrison in May. But Rommel proved as skillful in defense as he had in offensive operations, and the attack failed. Meanwhile, Churchill had sent reinforcements, including tanks, to Egypt and prevailed upon Wavell to undertake a second and more powerful offensive in June. The British employed a flanking movement, which caught Rommel by surprise, but then followed up with direct attacks against Axis armor and antitank guns. Although they were at a considerable numerical disadvantage in tanks, the Axis forces handled their armor much better than the British, who still tended to group their tanks in packets rather than in large concentrations. The Germans also effectively adapted their 88-millimeter antiaircraft gun for use as an antitank weapon. British Matilda tanks, which had been so efficient against the Italians, proved vulnerable to the 88, as did their thin-skinned cruiser tanks. Rommel's troops forced the British to withdraw back to Egypt.

Churchill considered Wavell's handling of the operation to be overly cautious and replaced him with General Claude Auchinleck. Wavell actually exchanged positions with Auchinleck, who had been commander in chief in India. Auchinleck had spent most of his career in India, although he had fought the Turks in the Middle East during World War I. He had also commanded operations in northern Norway in 1940 and later organized the defense of southern Britain against the invasion that never came. Quiet and popular with his men, he was receptive to new ideas but, like most British generals at this time, knew little about armored warfare. Auchinleck soon obtained reinforcements and formed the new Eighth Army. But he bluntly resisted Churchill's insistent prodding for another offensive until he considered his forces strong enough to defeat Rommel and relieve Tobruk.

Auchinleck chose General Alan Cunningham to lead the Eighth Army. The brother of the Mediterranean Fleet commander, Cunningham came to Egypt from East Africa, where he had directed the great victory over the Italians earlier in 1941. But he had accomplished this famous exploit with much smaller forces and had no experience handling large armored units. He felt uncomfortable in his new assignment. During the following months British strength grew steadily, giving them a greater numerical superiority than they had enjoyed in their June offensive. British tanks were considerably more plentiful than those of the Germans, but they were inferior in quality to Rommel's Panzer III and Panzer IV models.

When Auchinleck finally launched his offensive on November 18, heavy fighting erupted along the border. Again the Axis forces outclassed their opponents in the use of armor. Rommel boldly directed a column around the British southern flank, hoping to shake Cunningham's confidence and force another withdrawal. He succeeded at first. Cunningham, whose morale had reached a low ebb, believed the battle was lost. But Auchinleck refused to break off the offensive. He replaced Cunningham with General Neil Ritchie and ordered the Eighth Army to hold its ground. Rommel, now in a highly vulnerable forward position and still at a disadvantage in strength, had no choice but to fall back. His flight continued throughout December all the way to El Agheila, the point from which he had launched his offensive the previous spring.

Meanwhile, the outbreak of war in East Asia led to the shift of two Allied divisions and an armored brigade as well as four fighter squadrons from North Africa to Southeast Asia. Rommel sensed that conditions were favorable for a counterattack, which he delivered on January 21. His forces outmaneuvered the British and forced them to withdraw to a fortified position running southward from Gazala, about 35 miles west of Tobruk. Here Rommel once more encountered supply problems, and a lull developed in the campaign while both sides built up their strength and prepared to take the offensive in the spring.

ROMMEL DRIVES INTO EGYPT

Rommel struck first. He unleashed a major offensive on May 26. Although he had obtained some reinforcements, he was still inferior to the British in armor but now had air superiority. He used another wide flanking attack in an attempt to swing north to the sea and cut off the British defenders. Auchinleck had received Ultra warnings of the impending assault, although they gave no help as to where the Axis would strike. He nevertheless guessed correctly that Rommel would combine an attack in the center with a thrust around the desert flank. Auchinleck recommended that Ritchie mass the bulk of his armor so that he could direct it in strength wherever it was most needed. But Ritchie ignored this advice and left his tanks scattered in various areas. Indeed, Ritchie lacked the experience to command in the field at this critical moment. He had served ably as a staff officer for 20 years but had not held a battlefield leadership role since World War I. Auchinleck had originally intended his appointment to be temporary and had actually directed field operations himself in the crucial days immediately following Cunningham's dismissal.

When Rommel opened his offensive, he soon

FIGURE 15-2 German soldiers ride atop a Panzer III tank in the desert. (*National Archives*)

realized that his forces were not strong enough to complete their initial thrust. Accordingly, he switched to a defensive position and lured Ritchie into attacking him. The Axis troops then made effective use of their antitank guns to wear down the British, who suffered such heavy losses in piecemeal assaults that Rommel was able to resume his offensive. Ritchie withdrew toward Egypt while one British force fell back on Tobruk. This time Rommel attacked the town before the British could consolidate their position. His troops quickly overran the defenders and captured 35,000 prisoners as well as vast quantities of fuel, food, and drinking water on May 21. These supplies enabled them to thrust deeply into Egyptian territory. They reached El Alamein, 60 miles west of Alexandria, on June 30. Hitler rewarded Rommel for his dramatic success by promoting him to field marshal.

Auchinleck was determined to make his stand at the El Alamein position. It was ideal for defense, taking the form of a 36-mile bottleneck between the Mediterranean to the north and the impassable salt marshes and soft sand of the Quattara Depression to the south. This meant that the Axis forces could not outflank El Alamein and thus could only take it by frontal assault. Auchinleck dismissed Ritchie and took over personal command of the Eighth Army. He was able to consolidate his defenses while Rommel encountered problems. The supplies, which the Germans had captured at Tobruk, were dwindling, and they were running short of armor.

Rommel tried, nevertheless, to break through at El Alamein in early July. But Auchinleck's forces held firm, although their subsequent counterattack failed to dislodge the Axis troops. This struggle, the First Battle of El Alamein, to a considerable extent marked the turning point of the North African campaign, even though Rommel remained dangerous until August. It represented a personal triumph for Auchinleck and a major contribution to the ultimate Allied victory. In the months that followed, Britain sent a stream of reinforcements and supplies to the Eighth Army, including many American Sherman and Grant tanks. The British also regained predominance in the air.

Despite Auchinleck's success in stopping Rommel in the First Battle of El Alamein, the disasters that had preceded this victory and the failure of his counterattack afterward led to his ouster. Churchill appointed General Harold Alexander commander of the entire theater and placed General Bernard Montgomery in charge of the Eighth Army. Alexander was a remarkably handsome and charming man with an aura of contagious confidence. At age 25, he had commanded a battalion on the western front in World War I, being wounded three times and winning numerous decorations for bravery. During the interwar years, he held a variety of commands and served on India's northern frontier. When World War II erupted, he led a division in Western Europe and guided the final stages of the Dunkirk evacuation. After directing the defense of southern Britain, he took over command in Burma just in time to supervise the long, arduous retreat to India. Although his new position made him Montgomery's superior, Alexander actually exercised little control over the headstrong leader of the Eighth Army.

Montgomery, like General MacArthur, possessed an outsized ego and loved to be the focus of publicity. But if anything, he was more arrogant, certainly far more abrasive, and clearly the most controversial British general of the war. The son of an Anglican bishop, he had served on the western front in World War I and almost succumbed to a sniper's bullet. The war's carnage convinced him of the need for organization, training, and caution in military operations. He also took a deep personal interest in his soldiers' welfare and, in return, earned their devotion. "Monty," as he became known to the public, commanded a division in the BEF during 1940 and later all forces engaged in the defense of southwestern Britain. He also shared MacArthur's fondness for unusual headgear, but he preferred an Australian slouch hat and later a beret to the American's gold-bedecked cap.

These changes occurred in mid-August, just before Rommel's last attempt to gain a breakthrough at El Alamein. His plan involved another "right hook" maneuver followed by a thrust northward toward the sea. In addition to his usual numerical disadvantage in armor, Rommel suffered from poor health. He directed his attack against the Alma Halfa Ridge, a position that, ironically, Auchinleck had strengthened with a deep belt of fortifications before his dismissal. Montgomery also used a defensive plan that Auchinleck had devised. When Rommel's offensive failed, Montgomery claimed that the plan was his own and refused to grant any credit to his predecessor. Montgomery also had the help of detailed Ultra reports that indicated where Rommel would attack and the forces he would use. This struggle ended Rommel's efforts to regain the initiative and forced his troops into a permanent defensive stance.

Montgomery was a master of the "set-piece" battle, an offensive in which the commander plans everything down to the last detail and amasses overwhelming manpower and materiel. If he had counterattacked immediately following the Battle of Alma Halfa, he might have cut off the German spearhead, which was in a highly vulnerable position. But Montgomery chose to eliminate any possibility of failure and refused to take action for almost two months. When he finally attacked in the Second Battle of El Alamein on October 23, his troops outnumbered the Axis forces 230,000 to 80,000. He also enjoyed an advantage in armor of 1,200 to 500, and only 210 of Rommel's tanks were of high quality. British command of the air was also overwhelming. Ultra reports continued to aid Montgomery as well. They provided information that enabled British submarines and aircraft to sink Axis shipping with cargoes bound for North Africa. Montgomery also gained a clear picture of Axis strength and morale, both before the offensive began and while it was in progress.

The British opened their offensive with an enormous artillery barrage that, though destructive, eliminated any chance of surprise. When the battle began, Rommel was not in Egypt. He had fallen victim to a severe case of boils, a common

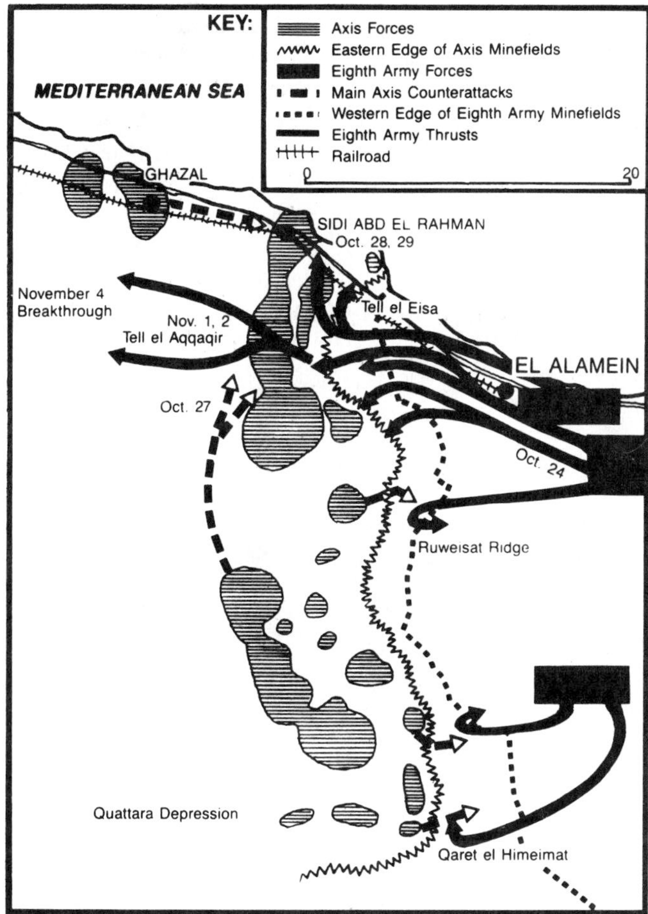

Second Battle of El Alamein, October 23–November 4, 1942

desert malady, and had flown to Germany for treatment. He did not return until two days after the start of the struggle. The bottleneck nature of the El Alamein position made it extremely difficult for attacking forces to maneuver under any circumstances. But Montgomery compounded the problem by concentrating most of his strength against a four-mile stretch of front near the northern end of the line. This enabled the Germans to bring firepower to bear against British armor, which also suffered heavy casualties in the extensive enemy mine fields. British tank losses were four times greater than those of their opponents, but the Axis could not afford even this ratio of attrition. By November 2, Rommel realized that he must retreat if he were to avoid total disaster. But Hitler, true to his "hold fast" mentality, delayed the withdrawal for two days.

Despite Rommel's earlier spectacular victories, his handling of this retreat was probably his greatest achievement. But he accomplished it only by taking over Italian motorized transport and ungallantly leaving most of his allies behind. Their sacrifice enabled 40,000 men to escape. The Eighth Army followed, but Montgomery was an exceptionally cautious general and his pursuit lacked boldness. If he had acted with more vigor, he might have destroyed Rommel's forces. He did make several attempts to outflank the fleeing enemy, but these were too tentative and did not penetrate deeply enough to get the job done. Instead, Rommel was able to retreat into Libya. Meanwhile, in early November, British and American forces landed in French Morocco and Algeria and moved toward Tunisia, threatening the Afrika Korps from the west. This time there was no halt at El Agheila as the Germans continued their flight across Libya to Tripoli and beyond.

By the end of 1942, Hitler's dream of victory in Russia and Egypt had faded into the nightmare reality of a major disaster at Stalingrad and the grim prospect of total expulsion from North Africa. He clung to his determination to win the war, but the new year offered little to stimulate optimism. To be sure, most of Germany's captive empire remained intact, but the cracks that had appeared in its outer ramparts as early as December 1941 now threatened to undermine the entire structure.

16

Problems of a Marriage of Convenience: The Second Front Question

The alliance of Britain, the United States, and the Soviet Union was just as much a marriage of convenience as the Nazi-Soviet Pact of 1939. It came into being in 1941 because all three powers had the same enemy, at least in Europe. Russia had not yet entered the war against Japan.

TWO'S COMPANY, THREE'S A COALITION

Britain and the United States enjoyed substantial agreement on basic war aims. And although the Western Allies frequently disagreed on strategy, they maintained a remarkable degree of cooperation. Both were democracies, detested the Nazi regime, and wanted to establish free governments in the countries that they planned to liberate from German rule. They also intended that those governments would be friendly toward them.

The Soviet Union, by contrast, had a totalitarian regime that harbored ambitions in Eastern Europe. To what extent Stalin had clearly thought out those ambitions in 1941, or for some time to come, is not clear. But he certainly intended to restore the Soviet borders that had existed prior to the German invasion. This, of course, would mean Russian control of eastern Poland, the Baltic states, Bessarabia, and Northern Bukovina as well as the territories that the Soviets had taken from Finland in the Winter War. However, ruthless as he was as dictator, Stalin was also a realist who recognized the limits of power and believed strongly in spheres of influence. As long as the Western Allies acknowledged the Soviets' right to fulfill their war aims in Eastern Europe, he appears to have been willing to extend the same recognition to Britain and America in Western Europe and the Mediterranean.

Coalitions are notoriously difficult to hold together, and this one contained the seeds of disintegration from the start. Stalin had been suspicious of the Western Powers throughout the 1930s, and he had made the 1939 pact with Hitler in the hope of watching Germany fight it out with the British and the French. As for Britain and the United States, they had deplored the Nazi-Soviet Pact, the Soviet seizure of eastern Poland and the Baltic states, and, most of all, the invasion of Finland. Yet when Hitler attacked the Soviet Union in 1941, Churchill offered cooperation to Stalin without hesitation. He considered alliance with Russia infinitely preferable to continued British isolation in the struggle against Germany, and he quickly diverted arms to his new ally. Roosevelt also extended lend-lease aid to Stalin even before the U.S. entry into the conflict.

Both Britain and the United States approached the war, at least in part, as a moral crusade against Hitler and Nazism. The Atlantic Charter reflected this attitude. But the two countries differed on their interpretations of the document. Roosevelt saw the Charter as having worldwide implications, including the right of British colonies to obtain independence. Churchill viewed it as applying only to nations that had lost their independence during the war. Stalin does not appear to have taken the Charter seriously.

In December 1941, Churchill and the British chiefs of staff traveled to Washington to confer with Roosevelt and the U.S. service chiefs in the Arcadia Conference. These leaders confirmed the "Europe first" approach to the war, which the Allies had laid down in January, and stipulated that the Pacific and East Asia would remain of secondary importance until the defeat of Germany. The Allies also agreed to form a unified Anglo-American high command that would operate in Washington. This combined chiefs of staff organization consisted of the top military and naval leaders of the two countries. But since the British chiefs would be in Britain most of the time, Field Marshal Sir John Dill, a former army chief of staff, would remain in Washington as London's permanent representative.

During the Arcadia Conference, the Americans noted the close coordination that existed among the British chiefs of staff compared to their own lack of cooperation. The British had established a chiefs of staff committee, consisting of Churchill's representative, General Hastings Ismay, and the heads of the three services—Field Marshal Alan Brooke (army), Admiral Sir Dudley Pound (navy), and Air Chief Marshal Sir Charles Portal (RAF). The United States had only the loosely linked Joint Board, which provided little real coordination.

In the aftermath of the conference, the Americans formed a joint chiefs of staff organization. It included General Marshall, Admiral King, and General H. H. Arnold, the head of the Army Air Corps, as well as Roosevelt's personal representative, Admiral William Leahy, a former chief of naval operations. This body henceforth provided overall direction to the American war effort, under Roosevelt's supervision.

Britain and America confronted a dilemma in the unmistakable fact that the Soviet Union carried the predominant burden of the war against Germany from 1941 to 1944. This proved embarrassing to Roosevelt and Churchill and was a deterrent to their hopes of modifying Soviet ambitions in Eastern Europe. They were hardly in a position to be demanding on this point, given the magnitude of the Soviet war effort.

The lack of a massive Western contribution in 1942 angered Stalin, especially during the summer and fall, when the Germans were driving toward Stalingrad and the Caucasus. To be sure, the British were fighting Rommel in North Africa, but this was a sideshow, involving relatively small numbers. The desert struggle was also far away from Germany and could bring little direct relief to the Soviet Union. Britain did begin heavy bombing raids against German cities in 1942, but despite extensive damage inflicted by these attacks, they had little impact on Germany's war industries.

ALLIED DIFFERENCES ON STRATEGY

Stalin insisted that Britain and the United States open a second front by undertaking a cross-Channel invasion of Nazi-occupied France in 1942. Such an operation would place them in a position to drive directly on Germany and force Hitler to divert troops from the eastern front. U.S. leaders, including Secretary of War Stimson and General Marshall, shared Stalin's interest in a cross-Channel assault. They argued that once established in western France, the Allies could thrust toward the heart of Germany by the shortest route. To them, every other potential theater of operations was of secondary importance. The British, however, preferred a more flexible approach, which recognized the need to invade Western Europe but also emphasized the exploitation of other opportunities, especially in the Mediterranean.

Churchill broached the possibility of an Allied landing in French North Africa during the Arcadia Conference. At that time, Auchinleck's

British Eighth Army was pursuing Rommel across eastern Libya toward El Agheila. Churchill proposed that Allied troops occupy the French colonies of Morocco, Algeria, and Tunisia, which bordered Libya on the west. This would threaten Rommel's rear and, it was hoped, lead to his expulsion from Africa. Roosevelt was sympathetic to such an undertaking, and the two civilian leaders and their military staffs agreed that this would be the major operation in 1942. They indicated that any invasion of the European mainland would have to wait until 1943.

But the failure of Auchinleck's offensive to gain decisive results and Allied setbacks in East Asia dashed hopes for an early invasion of French North Africa. The Japanese triumphs necessitated the diversion of more ships, troops, and planes to the Pacific than Allied leaders had expected and delayed the possibility of an assault against the French possessions until late in the year.

In the weeks that followed the Arcadia Conference, American military leaders became increasingly skeptical of the proposed North African operation. Stimson, Marshall, and General Dwight Eisenhower, the chief of the War Department's operations division, agreed that such an undertaking would only divert strength away from a cross-Channel invasion of Europe. They developed an alternative plan in March 1942 that called for an immediate buildup of Allied strength in Britain preliminary to a cross-Channel invasion in the spring of 1943 (Operation Roundup). But they also saw the possibility of a smaller landing on the coast of France (Operation Sledgehammer) as early as the fall of 1942. They recommended the latter if it proved necessary to divert German troops away from the Eastern Front or if other developments posed the likelihood of a successful undertaking of this type.

The initial British response was favorable, and Britain accepted the proposal in principle. But from the start, top British leaders, especially Field Marshal Brooke, had strong reservations about Sledgehammer. After studying the possibility of an invasion in 1942, Brooke came to the conclusion that the Allies were not strong enough to undertake such an operation. Specifically, he pointed to shortages of troops, equipment, and landing craft. Brooke had succeeded Dill as army chief of staff in December 1941, shortly before the Arcadia Conference. Previously, he had commanded a corps in France and had skillfully conducted the evacuation of BEF troops from Dunkirk. He also led Britain's home forces in the dark days following the fall of France. Brooke felt little confidence in the strategic sense or command ability of his American allies and quickly emerged as the foremost British opponent of a cross-Channel invasion.

Brooke gained Churchill's support for his opposition to Sledgehammer, and the prime minister pressed Roosevelt to abandon plans for a possible cross-Channel operation in 1942. In its place he urged a return to the original proposal to land in French North Africa. Although the debate continued for weeks, Roosevelt eventually accepted Churchill's argument. His decision angered Marshall, and the general now sided with Admiral King, who favored the concentration of U.S. strength in the Pacific rather than Europe. Marshall urged Roosevelt to resist the proposed North African operation and, if necessary, abandon the "Europe first" strategy and concentrate on the Pacific. It appears that he made this proposal as a bluff that might persuade the president to reconsider his support for a North African operation. But his effort failed. Roosevelt had definitely abandoned Sledgehammer and insisted that Western forces undertake an offensive somewhere in the general European theater in 1942. He could see no alternative to North Africa.

Roosevelt made his decision in part because of his desire to convince the Soviets that the Western Allies were determined to fight the Germans. But he also realized that many Americans favored gaining revenge for Pearl Harbor by concentrating on the Pacific, and he hoped to involve them emotionally in the war against Hitler. All these factors led to a compromise. Roosevelt ordered the military to go along with a North African invasion (Operation Torch), and he continued to view Europe as the crucial objective. But he also agreed to divert stronger forces to the Pacific, and during 1942 and most of 1943, more American forces operated in the Pacific than in the European theater.

Critics have contended since the war that Churchill was fundamentally opposed to any invasion of Western Europe, but this is probably an exaggeration. To be sure, the prime minister remembered the bloodbath on the western front in World War I and wanted to avoid another. Such fears certainly played an important part in his opposition to Sledgehammer. But his primary concern appears to have been to avoid a cross-Channel invasion until the Allies had become strong enough to ensure success. Considering the improvised nature of the German plan for an invasion of Britain in 1940, Churchill's opposition to Sledgehammer was not unfounded. But whether it was wise to shift strength to the Mediterranean instead of focusing all efforts on a buildup for an invasion of France in 1943 is another matter. Once Churchill and Roosevelt made the decision to intervene in French North Africa, prospects for a cross-Channel operation in 1943 plummeted, and the likelihood of the Allies' becoming bogged down in a Mediterranean strategy increased sharply.

Churchill believed that the West could plan both a Mediterranean and a cross-Channel strategy and exploit the one that offered the best chance of success. But American military leaders viewed Churchill's policy as one designed to secure Britain's political and economic interests in the Mediterranean. Certainly Churchill was a staunch believer in the need to maintain the British Empire on the strongest possible basis after the war. But it is unlikely that this motive alone sufficiently explains his actions. Critics have also argued that he was primarily interested in keeping British losses as small as possible and allowing the Soviet Union to pay the chief cost in blood. Again, it is clear that he was concerned about casualties on the scale of World War I. But he was also determined to keep the Soviets in the war and feared that Stalin might seek a separate peace if it appeared that Britain and the United States were not making a serious effort to defeat Nazi Germany.

British reluctance to undertake a cross-Channel invasion increased as a result of an abortive raid on the French Channel port of Dieppe in August 1942. The British planned this operation as an experiment to determine if they could capture an enemy port and hold it for a limited time. They employed a frontal assault by 6,000 troops, most of them Canadian. The German defenders

The Allied Pincers in North Africa (October 1942–May 1943)

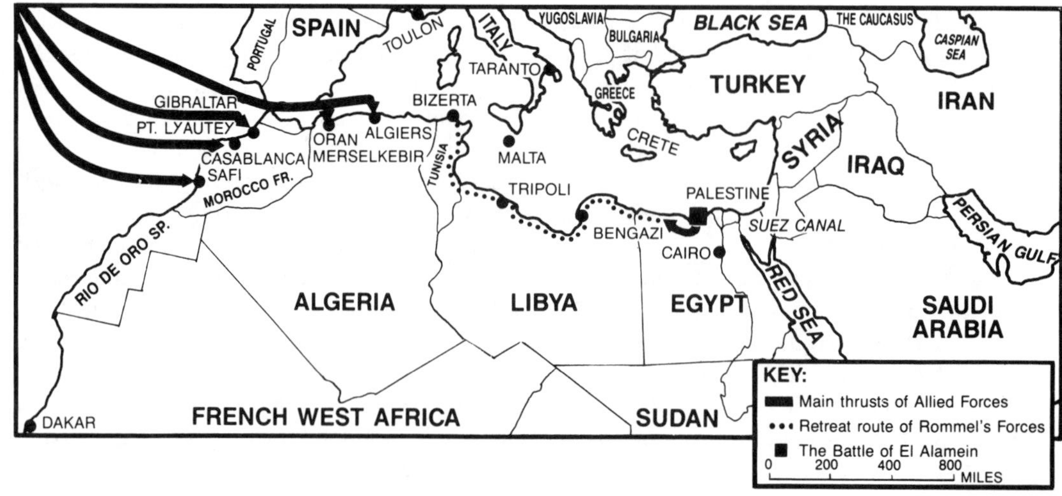

responded with withering fire, which killed more than half the attackers and forced the survivors to evacuate. Dieppe was an especially well-fortified point, and the Allies made the landing in daylight without preliminary bombardment. This bloody failure convinced the British that they had been correct about Sledgehammer and probably weakened their resolve to undertake Operation Roundup in 1943.

But the Dieppe raid also taught the Allies some valuable lessons regarding the conduct of amphibious operations. It proved clearly that they could not take a fortified port by direct assault from the sea. This realization led to the eventual creation of artificial harbors that ships could tow across the Channel. Dieppe also demonstrated the need to provide strong and continuous naval fire from close range against enemy coastal defenses. Finally, it led the British to devise specialized armored vehicles such as amphibious tanks that could be launched offshore and reach land under their own power. Other innovations included bulldozer tanks that could clear beach obstacles and tanks equipped with flails that could open paths through mine fields. These and other modified vehicles proved especially helpful when the cross-Channel invasion finally took place.

THE ALLIED INVASION OF FRENCH NORTH AFRICA

Once they had committed themselves to an invasion of French North Africa, the British and Americans appointed General Eisenhower to command the operation. Eisenhower had won Marshall's confidence and been given this lofty position despite being junior to many other Allied generals. This was quite remarkable, considering that he had never before held a field command. But he had gained a reputation as a first-class staff officer. Eisenhower had grown up in the small Kansas town of Abilene, where his father toiled as a creamery worker following his failure in an earlier business enterprise. Young Dwight pursued the same occupation until he won appointment to West Point by virtue of his strong performance in a competitive examination. "Ike," as his friends called him, missed the opportunity to see combat in World War I when the conflict ended just before his departure for France. During the interwar years Eisenhower served twice as an assistant to MacArthur. He became chief of the war plans division in 1941.

Eisenhower owed his selection as commander of the North African operation in part to his planning and organizational skills. Perhaps even more important, he possessed a rare talent for blending diverse personalities harmoniously in a common enterprise. First and foremost a team player, he proved particularly adept at securing cooperation between American and British officers who often did not like each other. His outgoing personality, twinkling eyes, and broad grin captivated everyone who met him. As General Montgomery later remarked, he had "the power of drawing the hearts of men towards him as a magnet attracts the bits of metal. He merely has to smile at you, and you trust him at once."*

The Allies soon disagreed on the scope of the invasion. Churchill wanted to restrict the landings to Algeria and to extend them as far east as the port of Bône, 75 miles from the Tunisian border. Some British leaders favored landings even farther east at Bizerta in Tunisia. But Marshall worried about the danger of Axis air power if an Allied task force ventured so deeply into the Mediterranean. He also feared German intervention in Spain, followed by a thrust to the Strait of Gibraltar. Such an operation would imperil the Allied supply line through the narrow passage between Spain and Morocco. Marshall proposed that landings be limited to Morocco's Atlantic coast. This would enable them to take place without fear of German air attack but would necessitate a long advance across Morocco and Algeria. Eisenhower agreed with the British and opposed Marshall on this question.

Eisenhower and the British were undoubtedly correct, but this dispute ended in a compromise.

*Field Marshal the Viscount Montgomery, *Memoirs* (New York: Signet, 1959), p. 483.

The Allies agreed to land at Casablanca in Morocco and at Oran and Algiers in Algeria. But they dropped plans to assault either Bône or Bizerta. The failure to land farther east eliminated the opportunity for a quick sweep into Tunisia. This ultimately prolonged the North African campaign for six months and precluded any chance for a cross-Channel invasion in 1943.

If the Allies could convince French military and naval commanders in North Africa not to resist the landings, they would gain a quick, bloodless victory. But many of the French officers were loyal to Vichy, which followed a policy of collaboration with Germany. Some also harbored a strong anti-British bias. This was especially true of naval leaders, who bitterly remembered the Royal Navy's attack on French warships at Oran and Mers-el-Kebir in July 1940. The British, accordingly, kept in the background as the Americans attempted to line up French support. But the Americans went about their task in an extremely cautious manner, fearing that they might alert the wrong people and jeopardize the invasion. And while some of the French leaders were sympathetic to the Allied cause, they worried about reprisals from their Vichy superiors and hesitated to commit themselves. Not surprisingly, the Americans failed to accomplish their mission.

Another vexing problem was the question of de Gaulle. Strong animosity existed between the military leaders loyal to Vichy and the Free French. The British and Americans excluded de Gaulle from any part in the planning and refused to use Free French forces in the landings. Roosevelt and the Americans especially considered de Gaulle to have little support in either France or North Africa. Instead, Allied leaders pinned their hopes on another French general, Henri Giraud, as the man who could rally the French once the landings had been made. Giraud, who had lost a leg in World War I, had commanded the French Seventh Army during the debacle of 1940. He had made a dramatic escape from a German prison early in 1942 and was living in southern France. To facilitate this scheme, an American submarine brought Giraud to Gibraltar. But he had no authority in North Africa, and French officers there felt no loyalty to him. To complicate matters still more, Admiral Darlan, the commander in chief of all French armed forces, was in Algiers when the invasion took place on November 8.

The French resisted all three landings, but opposition was strongest at Casablanca, where coastal batteries and the battleship *Jean Bart*'s 15-inch guns caused problems for both the invading troops and naval ships offshore. Resistance was weakest at Algiers, which surrendered on the first day. Eisenhower's deputy, General Mark Clark, quickly opened negotiations with Darlan in an attempt to halt hostilities, and his efforts culminated in a deal on November 10. Darlan agreed to order French forces to cease firing and join the Allies. In return, Eisenhower recognized the admiral's control over French administration in North Africa. Hitler responded to these developments by sending German troops into previously unoccupied France.

Darlan also "invited" Admiral Jean de Laborde, the commander of the French High Seas Fleet at Toulon on France's Mediterranean coast, to join the Allies in Algeria. Unfortunately, de Laborde hesitated, and when the Germans mined the entrance to Toulon harbor, he scuttled his fleet to prevent it from falling into their hands.

The decision to deal with Darlan embarrassed the Allies because he had been one of the most active collaborators in the Vichy regime and was intensely anti-British personally and a right-wing authoritarian politically. Eisenhower made the decision, with the backing of Churchill and Roosevelt, to save lives and speed the conquest of French North Africa. The cynical expediency of a deal with a man of Darlan's record nevertheless tarnished the Allied cause. But Darlan's ascendancy came to an end when he fell victim to an assassin's bullet on Christmas Eve.

Allied leaders recognized Giraud as his successor, but de Gaulle angrily challenged this decision. In frustration, Roosevelt and Churchill worked out a compromise that provided for the

FIGURE 16-1 American troops fire a howitzer during the North African fighting. (*U.S. Army Signal Corps Photo/National Archives*)

two generals to cooperate in a French Committee for National Liberation. Giraud proved totally inept politically, however, and de Gaulle easily outmaneuvered him. Within a year, Giraud had resigned, leaving de Gaulle in full control. The whole episode made de Gaulle highly resentful, and his relations with the British and Americans remained strained.

THE TUNISIAN CAMPAIGN

The Allied failure to land farther east than Algiers enabled Hitler to send troops across the 100-mile strait between Sicily and Tunisia to seize the major Tunisian ports of Tunis and Bizerta. The Germans quickly established a defensive perimeter. It extended from 25 miles west of Bizerta southward through mountainous terrain to the Mareth line, a defensive system that the French had constructed opposite the Libyan border. This enabled the Germans to provide a refuge for Rommel's troops, which were already in full retreat from El Alamein.

Meanwhile, the Allied forces that had landed at Algiers moved eastward. Airborne troops occupied Bône on November 12 and penetrated into Tunisia four days later. They reached a point within 12 miles of Tunis on November 28, but there the drive bogged down due to bad weather, a serious supply problem, and fierce German resistance. The Allied attempt to seize Tunis and Bizerta quickly had failed. Indecisive fighting continued throughout December and January.

Rommel ended his long retreat across the desert and reached the sanctuary of the Mareth line at the end of January 1943. He now prepared to defend southern Tunisia against Montgomery's pursuing Eighth Army while General Hans-Jurgen von Arnim commanded German troops in the north. Arnim, a sullen, hook-nosed man, had led a panzer division and later a corps on the eastern front. Hitler selected him for the Tunisian assignment because of his reputation for ruthlessness and his ability to get things done. But from the start, he and Rommel, who detested each other, engaged in jurisdictional disputes. Arnim opposed Allied forces under the leadership of the British general Kenneth Anderson, who had com-

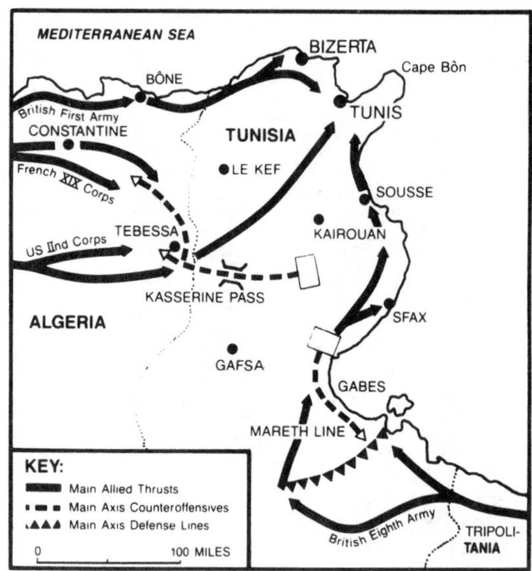

The Battle of Tunisia, December 1942–May 1943

manded a division in the Dunkirk evacuation as well as the unsuccessful attempt to capture Tunis and Bizerta. Noted for his stern and humorless manner, which did not endear him even to his own compatriots, Anderson soon encountered problems with his allies. The French objected to serving under a British officer, and General Lloyd Fredendall, the bombastic and posturing commander of the U.S. Second Corps, disliked the British in general and Anderson in particular.

Eisenhower had exercised little direct control over the campaign, being absorbed in a myriad of political problems stemming from the Darlan deal and relations with French authorities in North Africa. He did warn the commanders in the field against taking risks, however, and clearly intended no further offensive action until reinforcements and more equipment arrived. Criticism mounted over his failure to provide a firm hand and hasten the conquest of Tunisia. For a time it appeared as if General Alexander would replace him. But Roosevelt and Churchill agreed to retain him in command. They also made Alexander his deputy.

As soon as Rommel arrived at the Mareth line, he concluded that continued defense of Tunisia was hopeless. He flew to Germany to try to persuade Hitler of this, but the Führer refused to sanction an evacuation. The field marshal returned to Tunisia to await the arrival of Montgomery, who had encountered supply problems and had paused to clear the port of Tripoli before proceeding on to assault the Mareth line.

This enabled Rommel to attack U.S. forces in mountainous westcentral Tunisia during mid-February. If he could weaken them sufficiently, he could confront Montgomery without fear of an American attack on his rear. But he also hoped to gain a strategic victory by breaking through to the supply base at Tebessa in Algeria, just across the Tunisian border. He believed its capture would force the Allies to retreat into Algeria. If all went well, he even visualized an armored thrust northward to Bône to cut off the Allies in Tunisia.

In reality, Rommel's offensive fell far short of these ambitious goals. It failed in part because the Germans had not created a united command structure in Tunisia. Rommel had no jurisdiction over Arnim's forces in the north, and Arnim refused to provide additional armor to enable the attack to be delivered in full strength. Despite these obstacles, Rommel scored an impressive early success. Not only were the American forces in his path inexperienced, but they also suffered from unsatisfactory training, poor discipline, and indifferent leadership. Eisenhower had long harbored doubts about Fredendall's abilities but, unfortunately, had hesitated to replace him.

Although the Allies received Ultra reports indicating that a German offensive was coming, they expected an attack in the north only. Actually, Arnim did plan to carry out such an assault independent of Rommel's operation. This mistake coupled with lax American precautions enabled Rommel to catch them by surprise. The Germans easily brushed aside the forces defending Faid Pass, and Rommel prepared to strike directly at Tebessa. But his superiors were skeptical of such a daring plan. Instead, they ordered him to pursue a more limited objective by thrusting northwestward through the Kasserine Pass toward Thala and Sbiba. Ironically, if they had allowed Rommel to drive on Tebessa, he probably could have captured the supply base and threatened the entire enemy position in Tunisia. The Allies did not believe that he would be so bold as to advance in that direction. They expected him to do exactly as his superiors had ordered, and they arrayed their strongest forces in the path of his thrust toward Thala and Sbiba.

Rommel's panzers again broke through U.S. forces at Kasserine Pass, but they were not strong enough to overcome the Allied troops blocking his progress toward Thala and Sbiba. He had no choice but to retreat back through the pass. American forces had suffered a rude shock, but they had demonstrated their ability to rally from adversity and had contributed to the eventual failure of the German plan. Nevertheless, their initial setback had filled the British with concern about their combat ability. Alexander, who took over direction of field operations in Tunisia following the reverse at Kasserine Pass, believed that the Americans should play a secondary role during the remainder of the campaign. But Eisenhower refused to agree to this and insisted that they assume a major part in the final offensive.

Eisenhower also replaced Fredendall with General George Patton. He ordered Patton to tighten discipline and instill fighting spirit in the Second Corps. Patton, who had commanded the landings on Morocco's Atlantic coast, succeeded brilliantly in this task. The son of wealthy California ranch-owning parents, Patton's ego vied for prominence with those of Montgomery and MacArthur. He also shared their flamboyance and loved to wear two ivory-handled pistols. During World War I, he had served on Pershing's staff in France and later as commander of armored forces. General Marshall appointed him to lead an armored brigade in 1940, and he entered the war as America's most accomplished and vigorous exponent of armored warfare. Autocratic, outspoken, and controversial, Patton held extreme right-wing political views and was strongly anti-Communist and anti-Semitic. He also had little use for the British.

Rommel now hoped to divert his armor to the southeast for an offensive against the British Eighth Army before all of Montgomery's troops reached Medenine, opposite the Mareth line. But he encountered delays, and Ultra alerted Montgomery to the impending assault, including the exact date. The British rushed additional forces into position and prepared strong antitank defenses. When Rommel launched his attack on March 6, Montgomery's artillery inflicted heavy losses on enemy tanks and forced the Germans to fall back to the Mareth line. Once again, Rommel urged Hitler to evacuate Tunisia before it was too late. But the Führer had grown tired of Rommel's entreaties, which he considered defeatist. Hitler relieved him of his command, placing all Axis forces in Tunisia under Arnim's control.

THE FINAL PUSH IN TUNISIA

In the weeks that followed, the Allies increased their strength and prepared for the final push. Montgomery delivered the major opening assault on March 20. He began with an ill-advised frontal attack against the Mareth line, followed by a thrust around the right flank of the Italian and German forces. His direct action failed, but the flanking maneuver succeeded. The Axis troops found themselves in danger of being cut off. They abandoned the Mareth line and retreated northward along the coast while Patton's U.S. Second Corps applied pressure from the west.

By the middle of April, Allied forces had pushed the enemy back to a hilly perimeter around Tunis and Bizerta. Total Allied control of the air made it impossible for the Axis either to supply or evacuate their troops, which now were greatly inferior in numbers and equipment to their opponents'. Ultra provided such detailed and accurate information that Allied aircraft were able to destroy most of the German cargo planes that tried desperately to carry out supply missions. The combination of Allied air and naval power, Ultra, and the Italian navy's critical shortage of fuel also eliminated any possibility of rescue by sea. Although the Germans and Italians again fought tenaciously, by early May they

FIGURE 16-2 Field Marshal Erwin Rommel confers with two Italian generals in North Africa. (*AP/Wide World Photos*)

could no longer withstand the mounting Allied pressure. They abandoned both Tunis and Bizerta and withdrew into the Cape Bon Peninsula to the east. With virtually no fuel or ammunition, their position was hopeless. On May 13, the last Axis forces surrendered. A total of 170,000 prisoners went into captivity, a disaster that some Germans referred to with grim humor as "Tunisgrad."

Hitler's decision to send troops to Tunisia was in one sense a blunder because of the sacrifice of so many soldiers. But it also lengthened the Allied operation in North Africa to such an extent that the British and Americans were unable to shift forces to Britain in time for a cross-Channel invasion in 1943. Churchill and Roosevelt actually confirmed this outcome when they met in a conference at Casablanca in January 1943 while the struggle for Tunisia was still far from complete. Roosevelt accepted Churchill's proposal that the Allies concentrate on additional offensive operations in the Mediterranean during 1943, specifically, an invasion of Sicily. In return, Churchill approved a massive buildup for a cross-Channel invasion in 1944.

During the Casablanca conference, Roosevelt also announced, with Churchill's prior agreement, that the United States and Britain were resolved to accept unconditional surrender as the only basis for peace with all the Axis powers. The two leaders intended the declaration as a means of convincing the Soviets that the Western Allies were serious about the war with Germany. They also hoped that it would deter Stalin from possibly seeking a separate peace.

Critics have branded the unconditional surrender declaration a serious mistake. They have contended that it provided the Germans with a propaganda windfall. Indeed, Nazi propaganda minister Paul Goebbels did warn the German people that in view of this policy, they must continue to resist fanatically or be completely dominated by the vindictive Allies. The declaration may also have weakened the cause of a revived German conspiracy against Hitler. This included both civilians and military officers who hoped to kill Hitler, overthrow the Nazi regime, and seek a negotiated peace. Clearly, the demand for unconditional surrender made the conspirators' hope for a negotiated settlement highly dubious. But it is likely that even without the declaration, the Nazi regime would have maintained its absolute control over Germany, crushed the conspiracy's efforts to seize power, and fought the war to the bitter end.

One thing is clear, however. The declaration did not satisfy Stalin. The Soviet leader was furious when he heard that the Western Allies had postponed the cross-Channel invasion. Assurances of unconditional surrender did nothing to reduce his suspicions that Britain and America were content that the Soviet Union should continue to bear the brunt of the war against Germany. The decision to postpone the assault on Western Europe also weakened the ability of Churchill and Roosevelt to argue against Russian ambitions in Eastern Europe.

17

Probing the Underbelly: Sicily and Italy

The invasion of North Africa and the lengthy Tunisian campaign had inevitably drawn the Allies into a Mediterranean strategy. Unless their forces were to remain idle for a year, they would have no choice but to attack what Churchill inaccurately referred to as the "soft underbelly" of Europe. But initially, there was no agreement on where they should strike. Sicily was the obvious target. It lay only 100 miles from Tunisia and a mere two miles from the toe of the bootlike Italian peninsula. Its conquest would clear the central Mediterranean for Allied shipping. But some Allied planners favored an assault on Sardinia, which lay 150 miles north of Tunisia and 200 miles northwest of Sicily. Only weak Axis troops were present in Sardinia, and its capture would open the possibility of an invasion of the Italian mainland to the north of Rome or even a landing on the southern coast of France.

A number of factors persuaded Roosevelt and Churchill to choose Sicily over Sardinia. Allied fighter planes operating from Malta could provide air cover for a Sicilian operation, and the shorter distance from Tunisia to Sicily would make an invasion armada less vulnerable to enemy air and submarine attacks. Sicily also offered easier Allied access to mainland Italy. But the Allies made no decision regarding a follow-up operation against the Italian coast. The British favored such an enterprise, but the Americans were reluctant to commit themselves in advance to any undertaking that might endanger the promised buildup for the cross-Channel invasion of France in the spring of 1944.

THE ALLIED INVASION OF SICILY

Anglo-American planners paved the way for the invasion of Sicily with an elaborate hoax that later became the basis for a book and a film titled *The Man Who Never Was*. It involved the corpse of a British officer that washed up on a Spanish beach with a courier's briefcase chained to his wrist. The case contained false identity papers and an "official" letter indicating that the Allies planned to invade Sardinia or Greece. This information soon fell into the hands of German agents, who notified Berlin. Hitler responded by diverting troops to Greece. He had already sent reinforcements to Sardinia. Ultra quickly alerted Allied leaders that the enemy had taken the bait.

These diversions as well as the loss of so many Axis soldiers in Tunisia resulted in a shortage of manpower for the defense of Sicily. But Mussolini was reluctant to allow additional German divisions to come to the rescue. The Duce feared that such an influx would give Germany a commanding position in his country. He also

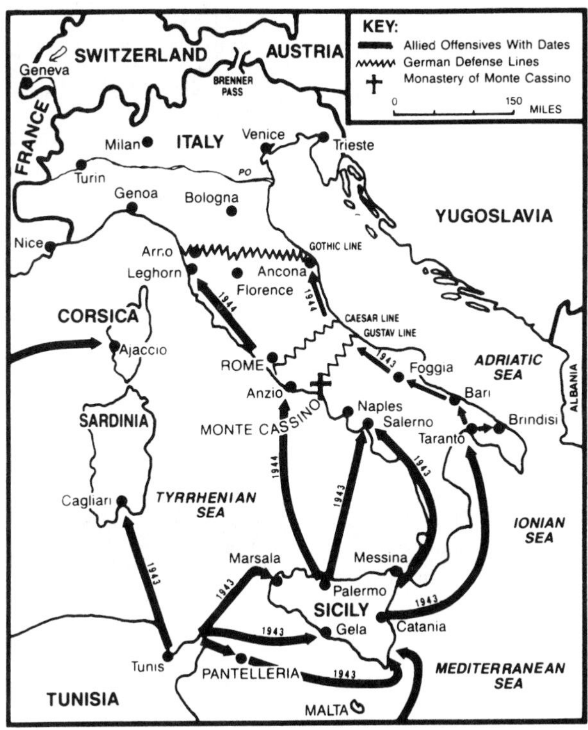

The Italian Campaign, July 1943 to the End of 1944

clung to a pathetically unrealistic desire to defend Sicily with Italian troops despite the demoralized condition of his army, which was especially weak in armor. When Hitler offered to send five panzer divisions to Italy, Mussolini indicated that he could manage with three. The Germans finally sent all five, two of them going to Sicily.

Churchill and Roosevelt agreed that Eisenhower would serve as supreme commander of the Sicilian operation, Alexander as actual field commander. Alexander led an army group that included Montgomery's British Eighth Army and the U.S. Seventh Army under Patton. The plan for the invasion (Operation Husky) provided for the Eighth Army to strike against the southeastern coast near the port of Syracuse while Patton's forces landed on the island's southern beaches. Ultra reports gave Allied leaders an accurate picture of Axis strength on the island and detected the arrival of the two German panzer divisions.

Eisenhower insisted on the capture of three small rocky Italian islands, which lay in the strait dividing Tunisia from Sicily, as a prerequisite for Operation Husky. The most important of these, Pantelleria, was a formidable bastion. It had no beaches and was so rocky that the Allies could only execute a landing by forcing their way through the island's narrow harbor. An invasion proved unnecessary, however. Six days and nights of bombing combined with naval bombardment persuaded the Italian garrison to surrender on June 11. The other islands capitulated two days later.

Italian troops defended the Sicilian coast while Field Marshal Kesselring, Hitler's commander in Sicily and southern Italy, held the less numerous but more mobile German forces in reserve. The Allies carried out the invasion on July

10 and caught the defenders off guard. Axis leaders had anticipated landings on the southwestern coast, which was nearer to Tunisia. They also did not expect the invasion to come when it did because of poor weather and high surf. The Italians were sick of the war, and their resistance rapidly disintegrated. Mass surrenders were frequent. Montgomery captured Syracuse and drove northward along the east coast toward the port of Messina on the Strait of Messina, which separated Sicily from the toe of the Italian peninsula. Patton's forces pushed inland toward the center of the island.

Operation Husky designated Montgomery's drive as the main spearhead because it was closest to Messina. If he could take the city quickly, he would make it difficult, perhaps impossible, for the Axis to evacuate to the Italian mainland. Kesselring was quite aware of this and prepared to make his stand south of Mount Etna, a huge volcano whose slopes lay in the path of the Eighth Army's advance. Montgomery also played into Kesselring's hands by pausing to regroup his forces before pushing northward. This enabled the Germans to strengthen their defenses, and when the British resumed their drive, they made slow progress.

The original plan called for Patton merely to protect Montgomery's left flank, but the American general chafed under this restriction and asked Alexander to authorize his forces to capture Palermo on Sicily's northern coast. Alexander reluctantly complied, and within four days Patton's troops swept through weak Italian resistance and seized the city on July 22. Despite this lack of opposition, the speed of Patton's advance made him a hero in America. The press hailed him as "Old Blood and Guts." Elements of the Seventh Army now pushed eastward along the northern coast toward Messina.

From this point, the campaign developed into a contest between Patton and Montgomery, who had already become rivals, to see which army could reach Messina first. But tenacious German resistance stalled Patton's advance as it had already foiled Montgomery. Kesselring nevertheless realized that his badly outnumbered forces could not hold the Allies for long. He prevailed upon Hitler to withdraw as many troops as possible to the mainland while his rear guard fought an effective delaying action. The evacuation began on the night of August 11 and continued under cover of darkness for the next week. Patton finally reached Messina on August 17, shortly ahead of Montgomery, but his entrance was anticlimactic. The Germans had gotten away.

FIGURE 17-1 A U.S. cargo ship explodes off the coast during the Allied invasion of Sicily. (*U.S. Coast Guard Photo/National Archives*)

Patton's elation over winning the "race" for Messina proved to be short-lived. This was due to an incident that occurred as his troops were advancing along the northern coast. While visiting a field hospital, the general encountered a soldier who suffered from a nervous disorder. Assuming that there was nothing wrong with the man, Patton lost his temper, accused him of cowardice, and slapped him twice. News reports of this incident reached America and led to demands for the general's dismissal. Eisenhower shunned such a drastic remedy, but he did reprimand Patton and ordered a public apology. Under the circumstances, there was no chance of Patton's participating in the invasion of Italy, and many believed that his career was over. These postmortems proved premature, but he did not command another army until the summer of 1944.

CONSEQUENCES OF ALLIED SUCCESS IN SICILY

Control of Sicily cleared the Mediterranean for Allied shipping and opened the way for an invasion of the Italian mainland. But the campaign also provided another vivid demonstration of German defensive brilliance and flair for executing fighting withdrawals. It should have been clear to Allied leaders that the enemy would be equally adept in defending Italy, where the terrain was even more difficult. Despite the success of the *Blitzkrieg* in the early years of the war, the power of a skillful defense still remained a factor of considerable importance.

The invasion of Sicily also led to Mussolini's fall from power. The war had been one long nightmare for the Duce, and the Italians had become ever more disillusioned with his leadership. With the expulsion of the Axis from Africa and the threat of an Allied invasion of Italy's home territory, opposition increased in the army and even within the Fascist party. The assault on Sicily convinced these dissidents that Mussolini must go, and on July 24 they moved against the once mighty dictator. King Victor Emmanuel III dismissed him as premier, and the police placed him under arrest. The aging and diminutive Marshal Pietro Badoglio took his place. A staunch monarchist, Badoglio had nevertheless prospered under the Fascist regime. He had served as chief of the Italian supreme command from 1925 until 1940, when he became the scapegoat for the failure of the invasion of Greece. Badoglio had also commanded one of the armies that conquered Ethiopia in 1935–36. But Mussolini was not yet finished. On September 12, a small German airborne force landed in gliders on the mountaintop where he was held prisoner, rescued him, and escaped by plane. Hitler now installed the Duce as ruler of a puppet Fascist state in northern Italy.

Although Badoglio had long been associated with Mussolini's regime, soon after becoming premier he dissolved the Fascist party and formed a government without political affiliation. He also opened secret negotiations for an armistice. This was no easy task. He wanted to switch sides and join the British and Americans in ridding Italy of the Germans, but the Allies, primarily at American insistence, clung to their doctrine of unconditional surrender. This divergence in aims slowed progress toward an agreement. At the same time, Badoglio tried to assure the Germans that he would remain loyal to the Axis cause. Hitler refused to be deluded by this stratagem. He sent additional German troops into northern Italy and the area around Rome to defend against the expected Allied invasion. To complicate the situation still more, American leaders did not agree to an invasion of the Italian mainland until July 20. The wholesale Italian surrenders in Sicily convinced them that they might be able to carry out a limited operation with relative ease. The late date of this decision meant that several weeks of preparation would be necessary before the Allies could act.

Negotiations with the Badoglio regime also sparked a controversy similar to the one that had erupted after the Darlan deal in North Africa. Both the new premier and King Victor Emmanuel III had close links to Mussolini. The king's continuation on the throne offended many people in Allied countries as well as in Italy. But Churchill saw the monarchy as a source of stability and a bulwark against communism. He strongly favored dealing with the new government, and Roosevelt acquiesced. Negotiations finally concluded in an agreement on September 3 that fell short of unconditional surrender. It provided for Italy to hand over its navy, merchant marine, and air force to the Allies. The Italians also agreed to become a cobelligerent against Germany.

ONTO THE MAINLAND

The decision to invade the Italian mainland marked the start of the final lengthy stage of the Mediterranean strategy that had begun with the invasion of North Africa. Despite his earlier commitment to a cross-Channel invasion, Churchill definitely appears to have lost his taste for such an enterprise by the summer of 1943. This was probably due in part to his concern over the defensive prowess the Germans had demonstrated in Tunisia and Sicily. The prospect of another World War I–type bloodbath in France, never far from his thoughts, now loomed larger. But he also believed that Allied operations in the Mediterranean had opened a much more promising strategy against the "soft underbelly" of Europe. He favored launching a vigorous offensive in Italy as well as providing aid to Yugoslav Partisans under Marshal Tito and attempting to bring Turkey into the war as an ally. The Americans did not share the British enthusiasm for an ambitious campaign in Italy, because they feared that this would divert strength from a cross-Channel invasion in 1944. They insisted on a limited commitment.

It now appears that the area north of Rome offered the best choice for an invasion site. Kesselring believed that an assault there would have resulted in a German withdrawal from the southern half of Italy. But the Allies considered an operation so far north to be too risky and chose to strike farther south. The invasion involved three landings. In the first of these, forces of Montgomery's Eighth Army crossed the Strait of Messina on September 3 and established a beachhead on the toe of the boot. Three days later, other elements of the Eighth Army went ashore near the Italian naval base at Taranto on the instep of the boot. At the same time, General Mark Clark's Anglo-American Fifth Army landed at Salerno, south of the great port of Naples.

Clark had recently enjoyed a meteoric rise from obscurity. A 1917 graduate of West Point, he fought briefly in France during World War I. His career had stagnated in the interwar years, but he attracted the attention of Marshall and Eisenhower shortly before America's entry into World War II. Clark became Ike's deputy for the North African campaign and made a secret mission to Algeria in an effort to win the support of Vichy officials prior to the landings. At age 46, he became the youngest lieutenant general ever to serve in the U.S. Army. Tall and lanky with a long, hooked nose, he possessed boundless energy and ambition. He also courted publicity and was frequently abrasive in his dealings with colleagues.

The Allies had chosen Salerno as an invasion site after a heated debate. Clark and other Americans preferred to outflank Naples by landing to the north of the city. This site would also reduce the distance to Rome, and its non-mountainous terrain posed the possibility of a rapid advance inland. The British insisted on Salerno because the area north of Naples lay outside the range of Allied fighter planes operating from Sicily. Unfortunately, the beaches near Salerno were ringed by mountains, which gave the Germans a strong defensive position.

Montgomery prepared the way for his landing on the toe of the boot with an enormous barrage from 600 guns based in Sicily as well as 120 naval guns. Although impressive, it proved totally unnecessary because the Germans chose not to contest the assault. But they did slow the British advance by skillful demolitions along the narrow roads leading north. The landing at Taranto also encountered no resistance. But the troops, which went ashore at Salerno, were not so fortunate. When the Germans heard the delayed announcement of Italy's surrender on September 8, their forces raced southward. They quickly disarmed Italian troops along the way and moved to block the Allied advance toward Naples and Rome. The Salerno operation ran into trouble initially from just one understrength panzer division. This unit held the mountains overlooking the beaches and rained down murderous artillery fire on the exposed Allied troops. A determined German counterattack threatened to force the invaders into the sea. Only the intervention of Anglo-American artillery, air power, and naval bombardment prevented a disaster and allowed Clark to consolidate his beachhead.

It was not until the advance elements of Montgomery's forces reached the Salerno area on September 16, after a slow advance from the south, that the Germans began to fall back toward Naples. The Allies had hoped to take Naples

FIGURE 17-2 Italian civilians look on as a wounded American soldier receives medical treatment. (*U.S. Coast Guard Photo/National Archives*)

three days after the Salerno landings but were not able to capture the city until October 1. British troops gained another important prize when they seized the major Italian air base at Foggia on the eastern side of the peninsula. Its capture enabled the Allies to dominate the skies over Italy and carry out bombing raids against targets as far away as Austria and the Balkans. German forces also evacuated Sardinia in late September and Corsica in early October.

Kesselring continued to make good use of Italy's ideal defensive terrain. The Apennine Mountains extended down the center of the peninsula, creating formidable barriers to the Allied advance. Innumerable rivers provided additional impediments, especially since heavy rains turned them into swollen torrents. The vision of "sunny Italy" soon faded from the minds of both Allied and German soldiers. The valleys oozed with ankle-deep mud that made progress painfully slow. In the barren, rock-strewn mountains, the men had to contend with cold, snow, and a lack of cover. At night they slept in caves if they could find them, behind piles of rocks if they could not. For supplies, they depended on mules, which carried them until the slopes became too steep, at which point soldiers took over and hauled them the rest of the way. In such conditions, armor was of little use. The struggle became one of opposing foot soldiers, often in hand-to-hand combat.

During the fall and early winter, the Allies slogged northward from one river to another until they bogged down before the main German defensive position less than 100 miles from Rome—the Gustav line—in January 1944. Kesselring anchored this powerful line on Monte Cassino, which dominated the Liri and Rapido river valleys. A famous medieval abbey crowned the summit of the mountain, and the town of Cassino sprawled on its lower southern slope. General Heinrich von Vietinghoff's Tenth Army defended the Gustav line. Vietinghoff had skillfully commanded a panzer corps in the Russian campaign and now proved a master of defensive warfare. He had led the German forces against the Fifth Army at Salerno and directed the retreat that had so effectively delayed the Allied advance.

CHANGES IN ALLIED COMMAND AND STRATEGY

A major change took place in the Allied command structure at the end of 1943. Eisenhower moved to London to become supreme commander of the long-delayed cross-Channel invasion, with Montgomery as his field commander. Alexander remained in charge of Allied forces in Italy, while General Oliver Leese took over the Eighth Army and Clark continued to lead the Fifth Army. Leese had studied under Montgomery at Staff College and became one of his closest associates. He had served as an Eighth Army corps commander at El Alamein as well as in Tunisia, Sicily, and Italy.

In a dramatic attempt to break the deadlock, the Allies made an amphibious landing behind the German front on January 22. They struck near the resort town of Anzio, which lay just 33 miles south of Rome. The operation took the Germans by surprise, and the attacking forces gained a beachhead against virtually no resistance. For a time, they imperiled the entire German position in Italy.

In planning the operation, General Alexander had intended that the invading troops advance rapidly to the Alban Hills 20 miles from the coast. This action would cut German communications between Rome and Cassino and force the enemy to abandon the Gustav line. But General Clark expected Kesselring to react quickly, as he had at Salerno, and ordered General John Lucas, the commander of the operation, to move inland only after building up strength in the beachhead. Lucas, a highly cautious and insecure man who lacked experience as a leader in the field, needed little encouragement to stand fast. Despite the remarkably successful landing, Clark refused to alter his decision. He stubbornly ignored Ultra intelligence, which revealed clearly that German reinforcements would not arrive for at least a week. Kesselring shifted forces as quickly as possible and prevented expansion of the beachhead. Instead of threatening the rear of the Gustav line, the Allies found themselves pinned down by incessant German artillery fire.

On February 19, Clark replaced Lucas with General Lucien Truscott. The new commander had trained the first American Ranger battalion, which he had modeled after the elite British Commando units. He had also led divisions in the North African, Sicilian, and Italian campaigns. Truscott provided much more vigorous leadership, but for the time being he and his troops had no choice but to remain on the defensive.

At the same time as the Anzio landing, Clark carried out a major attempt to gain control of the relatively wide valley of the Liri River. He and Alexander hoped that this would enable the Allies to outflank Monte Cassino on the southwest and link up with the beachhead. But American troops could not maintain a foothold across the Rapido River near its junction with the Liri and suffered heavy casualties. Later in January, Clark ordered the capture of Monte Cassino itself, which he believed was crucial if the advance were to continue. American units crossed the Rapido and penetrated the northern outskirts of the town of Cassino but failed to take the mountain.

In early February, a New Zealand corps under General Freyberg, who had led the unsuccessful defense of Crete in 1941, relieved the exhausted Americans. Freyberg's corps contained General Francis Tuker's Indian Division, which had won fame for its skill in mountain fighting. The acid-tongued Tuker urged an operation to outflank Monte Cassino rather than a frontal assault. But since his superiors insisted on a direct attack, he demanded that heavy bombers destroy Monte Cassino Abbey as a prerequisite. Allied soldiers firmly believed that the Germans were using the building as an observation post. Freyberg supported Tuker, and Alexander bowed to the New Zealander's pressure.

Alexander feared that unless the bombing took place, Freyberg would pull his corps out of the line. For some time, many people in New Zealand had been demanding that their troops return home. But General Clark, Freyberg's immediate superior, argued against bombing the abbey. He doubted that the enemy was using it for observation. Alexander insisted, however, and Clark finally agreed. On February 15, over 200 bombers pulverized the renowned structure—to no avail. The Indian attempt to storm Monte Cassino failed, with heavy casualties as the price. Ironically, the Germans had not used the building as an observation post, although they had maintained a presence nearby. But they now moved into its ruins, which provided effective cover for mortars and machine guns.

The Allies renewed their efforts in March. Again they placed their faith in air power. This time they sent 500 bombers against the town of Cassino as a prelude to a ground attack that would seize Cassino before the dazed German survivors could recover from the terrible pounding. One thousand tons of high explosives obliterated the town, but when the bombardment ceased, the German defenders repulsed the attacking troops. The bombing actually hindered Allied progress by blocking Cassino's narrow streets with huge heaps of rubble.

The deadlock did not end until May, when Alexander moved much of the British Eighth Army from the eastern end of the front to the Cassino area, where it worked in cooperation with the Fifth Army. The Allies now enjoyed an advantage of 20 divisions to only 7 for the Germans. Starting on May 11, they ground slowly forward, and this time they were successful. Soldiers from a number of Allied nations made major contributions.

French troops, under General Alphonse Juin, executed a crucial flanking operation through extremely rugged mountains southwest of the Liri. Kesselring and Vietinghoff had left this area lightly defended because they considered it impassable. Juin had long opposed the bloody attempts to take Monte Cassino by frontal assault. Despite a paralyzed right arm, a memento of World War I, he had led a division in the 1940 retreat to Dunkirk. He later commanded Vichy forces in North Africa. But his sympathies lay with the Allies, and he joined them after their landing in 1942. Juin now emerged as the man of the hour. His forces penetrated the Gustav line and threatened the entire enemy position. The Germans began to fall back. British forces took the town of Cassino, while a Polish corps outflanked Monte Cassino on the north. After another bitter struggle, the Poles reached the summit and captured the ruins of the abbey on May 18.

Five days later, reinforced American troops in the Anzio beachhead launched an attack that Alexander hoped would take the town of Valmontone and cut off the enemy retreat from the Gustav line. But Clark was thinking of another objective—Rome. He wanted American troops to have the honor of capturing the Eternal City. Clark ignored Alexander's orders, and his staff directed Truscott to move toward Rome, even though Ultra reports indicated that the capture of Valmontone would likely result in a disaster for the German Tenth Army. Truscott reluctantly complied. This decision allowed Kesselring to extricate his troops from danger, and he declared Rome an open city to spare it from destruction. American forces occupied the capital on June 4.

The Germans withdrew toward another prepared defensive position 150 miles to the north—the Gothic line, which stretched across the peninsula beyond the cities of Leghorn (Livorno) and Florence. They based this line on one of the last ridges of the Apennines to the south of the great plain extending northward to the Po River. By making skillful use of a series of strong mountain positions as he retreated, Kesselring prevented the Allies from reaching the Gothic line until late in August.

Allied leaders also weakened Alexander's striking power by diverting seven divisions to take part in an invasion of southern France (Operation Anvil-Dragoon). Churchill and Alexander were not keen on Anvil-Dragoon, preferring to push the offensive in Italy. Alexander insisted that if allowed to continue at full strength, he could capture the remainder of Italy and follow with a drive toward Vienna by way of the Ljubljana Gap in northern Yugoslavia. Since the war, critics of Anvil-Dragoon have contended that shifting these forces prevented Alexander from reaching Vienna and breaking into the Hungarian Plain ahead of the Soviets. This argument assumes a great deal. Although the retention of these troops might have resulted in the liberation of most of the remainder of Italy in 1944, it seems highly unlikely that a quick thrust toward Vienna would have followed. In view of the spectacular tenacity of German defensive efforts in the Apennines, it is difficult to see how the Allies could have expected anything other than excruciatingly slow progress through the various ranges of the Alps that blocked the route to the Austrian capital.

Despite their reduction in strength, Alexander's forces surprised Kesselring in September and fought their way through the Gothic line. But once beyond it, they continued to encounter difficult mountains as well as boggy terrain and an overabundance of rivers. German resistance stiffened, and although the Allies pressed their attacks throughout the fall, they made little progress. In late December, they decided to forgo additional offensive operations until the spring of 1945. Another grim winter in Italy's icy mountains lay ahead.

The Italian campaign remains extremely controversial. Its supporters contend that operations on the mainland pinned down 20 German divisions that might otherwise have opposed the Russians or the cross-Channel invasion. But was the heartbreakingly slow advance up the peninsula worth the price the Allies paid in blood and the destruction of so much of the country? An Anglo-American presence in Sicily, Sardinia, and Corsica alone probably would have forced the Germans to concentrate substantial strength in Italy to guard against an invasion. They maintained 24 divisions in the Balkans in large part to resist a potential assault on this area, which did not face as direct a threat as Italy. Certainly, once Anglo-American troops had gained control of the southern portion of the peninsula, the Germans could not have avoided a considerable commitment there. It is questionable whether the Allies showed good judgment in hammering away at such formidable defensive positions as the Gustav line. There was no strategic objective worthy of such an approach.

18

War in the Atlantic

Germany started World War II in a formidable position both on land and in the air, but its navy clearly suffered in comparison to the fleets of Britain and France. Indeed, the Allies' advantage on the high seas was greater than their margin of superiority in sea power during World War I. It became even more pronounced with America's entry into the conflict. But as the war continued, it became obvious that Germany's only chance of defeating the British lay in the Atlantic Ocean. This was due to Britain's dependence on the importation of vast quantities of food, raw materials, military supplies, and equipment. If the Germans could reduce that flow to a critical level, they might yet force the British to abandon hostilities. The key to such a possibility was the submarine (*Unterseeboot* in German—*U-boot* for short, which was adopted as *U-boat* in English). If Germany could produce enough of these U-boats and sink enough Allied ships, they might get the job done. Conversely, the key to Britain's survival was the development of antidotes for this submarine menace. The ongoing struggle to achieve these opposing aims became known as the Battle of the Atlantic.

THE BALANCE OF POWER AT SEA

When the war began, the Germans possessed 57 submarines, only 22 of them suitable for operations in the Atlantic. The remainder were intended for duty in coastal waters or for training. Admiral Raeder, the commander in chief of the German navy, and Admiral Karl Dönitz, commander of the submarine service, realized that such a meager force could not inflict decisive damage. And since both the army and the Luftwaffe received production priority over the navy, a large U-boat force would not be available for at least two years. In addition, Raeder hoped to strengthen his surface fleet, which also diverted resources from U-boat construction.

Raeder, who had received the navy's top post five years before Hitler came to power, was a veteran of the World War I naval battles of Dogger Bank and Jutland in the North Sea. Although formal and aloof in his personal contacts, Raeder was an excellent planner and an efficient organizer. The admiral was traditional in his views on the type of navy Germany should build in the prewar years. He wanted a balanced fleet that would include a large submarine force but would also possess a formidable surface component with numerous battleships. He was not convinced of the value of aircraft carriers but was willing to include some. There was one major flaw in his approach, however. Such a fleet would only begin to assume powerful dimensions in 1943 and would not reach completion until 1948. Much of the problem was due to Raeder's belief in Hitler's claim that there would be time for a major construction program before the outbreak of war. He also accepted the Führer's assurances that Germany could count on Britain's neutrality.

But since hostilities came in 1939, the German surface fleet, like the submarine force, was small. And because, contrary to Hitler's soothing words, Britain was arrayed against Germany, the surface fleet was also at a hopeless disadvantage in relation to the Royal Navy. It included three "pocket battleships"—*Deutschland, Admiral Scheer,* and *Admiral Graf Spee*. These vessels were products of the limitation of German naval construction under the Treaty of Versailles to warships of 10,000 tons or less. Although the pocket battleships actually exceeded this restriction by 2,000 tons, they were of light construction and possessed six 11-inch guns, which made them more powerful than most faster ships and faster than most vessels that were better armed. German naval leaders intended them as surface raiders that would prey on enemy merchant shipping. Other elements of the surface fleet included two battle cruisers of almost 32,000 tons—*Scharnhorst* and *Gneisenau*—as well as eight cruisers and 21 destroyers. Two 42,000-ton battleships of the latest design—*Bismarck* and *Tirpitz*—along with the heavy cruiser *Prinz Eugen* were under construction and would not be available until 1941. The Germans had also laid down an aircraft carrier, *Graf Zeppelin,* but due to other priorities, it was destined never to be completed.

By contrast, the Royal Navy had 15 capital ships and another five battleships under construction. The British also possessed 62 cruisers, seven aircraft carriers, 178 destroyers, and 56 submarines. France contributed five battleships, two battle cruisers, 19 cruisers, two carriers, 69 destroyers, and 75 submarines. With this discrepancy in their favor, the Allies instituted a blockade of Germany, but it initially proved less than successful because the Germans were able to obtain most of the raw materials they needed from the Soviet Union and Eastern Europe.

THE U-BOAT: KEY TO VICTORY?

Unlike Raeder, Dönitz had assumed all along that Britain would fight Germany in the next war and recognized that the submarine was the only weapon that could be decisive against the British in the North Atlantic. Although he had been an officer on a light cruiser when World War I began, he had served for two years on submarines during that conflict. This experience prompted him to push hard during the interwar years for the formation of a large U-boat force. When Hitler did away with the limitations of the Treaty of Versailles in 1935, Dönitz worked tirelessly to perfect submarine tactics that featured mass attacks on enemy convoys. Far more approachable than the austere Raeder, Dönitz enjoyed informal social gatherings with his staff officers and even engaged in light-hearted small talk. This made for extremely close relationships with his subordinates.

When the war began, Dönitz did what he could with his limited forces to launch a submarine campaign against the Allies. Its first victim was the British passenger liner *Athenia.* Although the facts are still not completely clear, the commander of a German U-boat apparently mistook the vessel for an auxiliary cruiser and torpedoed it. Loss of life was relatively light: Of 1,417 aboard, 112 perished.

The disaster touched off a propaganda duel. British leaders denounced the Germans for committing a deliberate atrocity, while Paul Goebbels, Hitler's propaganda minister, charged that the British had actually destroyed the ship in an effort to inflame anti-German sentiment and lure the United States into the conflict. Most people outside Germany believed the British account.

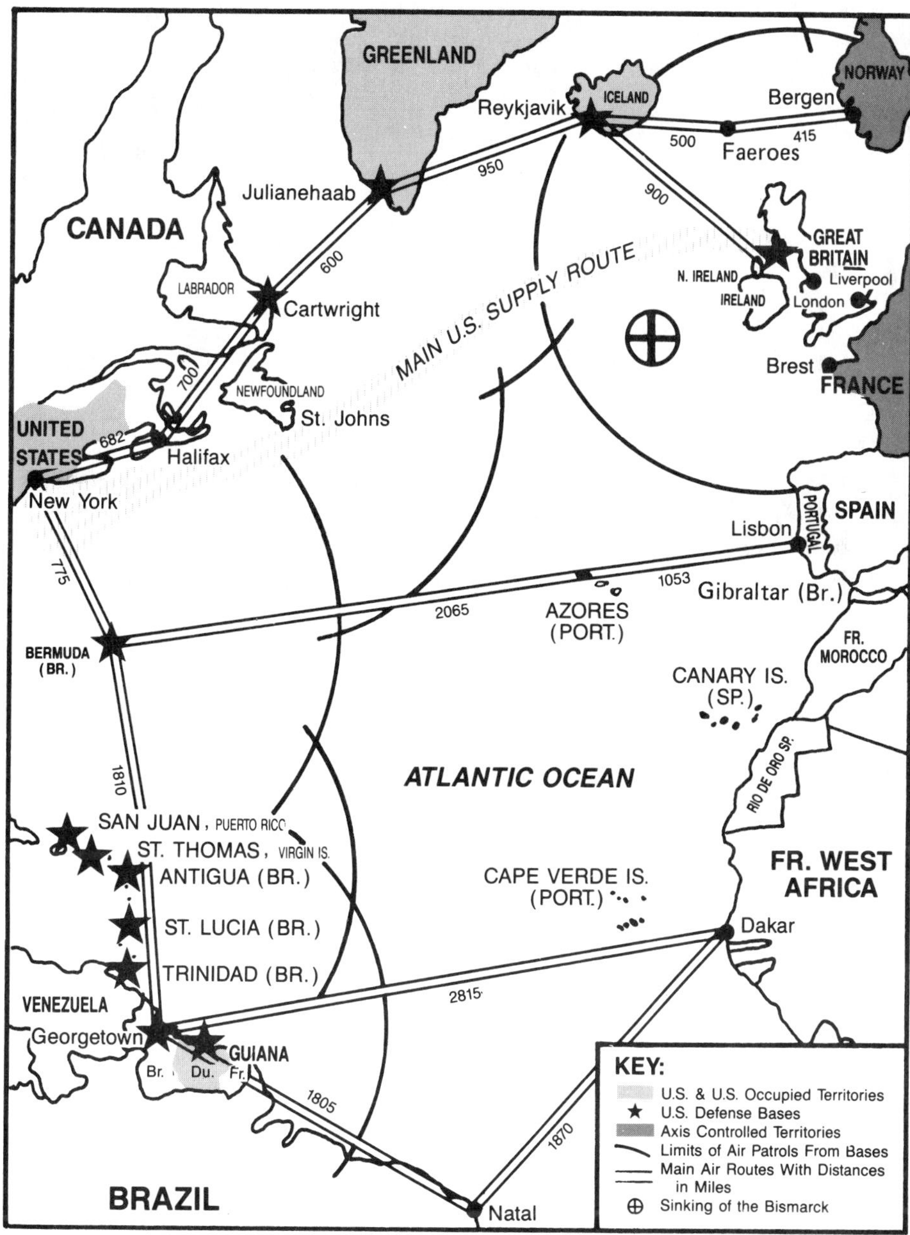

Battle of the Atlantic, 1940–43

Actually, Hitler deplored the sinking of the *Athenia,* and he ordered his submarine commanders to refrain from any further attacks on passenger ships. The Führer hoped to entice Britain and France to make peace once Germany had defeated Poland. This made him reluctant to precipitate any incidents that might provoke continued hostility on their part.

German U-boats scored a number of successes in the following months. The first of these came

FIGURE 18-1 A Royal Navy destroyer crewman looks out on the ships of an Atlantic convoy. (*Library of Congress*)

on September 17 with the sinking of the British aircraft carrier *Courageous*. The most spectacular occurred on the night of Friday, October 13, when *U-47,* commanded by Lieutenant Commander Günther Prien, penetrated the Royal Navy's main base at Scapa Flow in the Orkney Islands north of Scotland. The submarine sank the battleship *Royal Oak* and escaped without a scratch. U-boats also took a heavy toll of British shipping, considering their small numbers. By March 1940, they had sunk 222 ships, a total of 886,000 tons. But the Germans paid a stiff price, losing 15 of their precious few U-boats.

Germany enjoyed the advantage of having broken the Royal Navy's cipher before the war. This gave the Germans valuable information on British naval dispositions. Although the Admiralty developed protection for its cipher by the fall of 1940, the Germans compensated for this by breaking the British and Allied merchant ship code. This provided their U-boats with detailed intelligence on merchant traffic and contributed to many sinkings until the summer of 1943.

COMBATING GERMAN UNDERSEA POWER

The British resorted to the convoy system, which they had used to good advantage in World War I. This involved grouping large numbers of merchant ships and escorting them by warships, especially destroyers. But Churchill, as first lord of the admiralty and later as prime minister, was not convinced of the value of close escort of convoys. He preferred wide sweeps by naval ships to hunt down submarines. In line with his desires, warships split their duties between escorting convoys and running search-and-destroy missions. The results were disappointing. U-boat sinkings were few, while the skeleton escorts had difficulty fending off submarine attacks on convoys. Churchill proved hard to convince, however, and did not change his policy until 1942, when convoys received larger close escorts.

Escort vessels were fortunate to have the assistance of sonar (*so*und *n*avigation *a*nd *r*anging), a high-frequency device that could detect submerged U-boats. The British called this system asdic (*A*nti-*S*ubmarine *D*evices *I*nvestigation *C*ommittee). But asdic was not a miracle weapon. It could not detect submarines on the surface, and U-boats usually attacked while surfaced. It could detect the range and bearing of submerged submarines, but it could not determine their depth. U-boats were often able to escape destruction by diving to 400 feet, thus avoiding depth-charge patterns.

An additional 900,000 tons of Allied shipping fell victim to mines and surface raiders from the outbreak of the war to the end of February 1940. Indeed, for a time a new weapon, the magnetic mine, loomed as the greatest menace of all to the British. At first, it proved impervious to mine sweeping because, unlike conventional mines, which were extended from anchors by cables, the magnetic mines came to rest on the bottom in shallow water. When a ship's steel hull passed over such a device, it interfered with the earth's magnetic field and triggered the mine. Unfortunately for the Germans, the British soon discovered a remedy by attaching cables to their ships that set off electrical charges and desensitized the hulls of the vessels.

The most dramatic episode in the early days of the war at sea came in connection with attacks by surface raiders. Two of the pocket battleships, *Deutschland* and *Graf Spee,* had penetrated into the Atlantic shortly before the outbreak of hostilities. They received service from tanker supply ships that waited for them at prearranged locations in waters off the usual shipping routes. *Deutschland* operated in the North Atlantic but accomplished little. It sank only two vessels before returning to Germany in November. Hitler had worried about the propaganda effect of losing a ship named *Deutschland,* so after its return, he promptly renamed it *Lützow,* after the flagship of the German battle cruiser squadron in the Battle of Jutland.

Graf Spee was more fortunate, at first. Operating in the South Atlantic and the Indian Ocean, where there were fewer Allied warships, it found easy prey, sinking nine merchant ships. But in December, *Graf Spee* encountered a small British and New Zealand squadron consisting of the heavy cruiser *Exeter* and two light cruisers, *Ajax* and *Achilles,* off the coast of South America. Although the pocket battleship outgunned all three enemy vessels and thus could shell them safely from long range, its commander, Captain Hans Langsdorff, made the mistake of closing on his adversaries. In the ensuing battle, *Graf Spee* disabled *Exeter,* which had to break off the action, but Langsdorff's ship also sustained some damage. He decided to put in for repairs and refueling at Montevideo, the capital of Uruguay and a major port on the estuary of the Plate River. This proved to be his second mistake. The Uruguayan government responded to British diplomatic pressure by terminating the vessel's stay before the repairs had been completed.

In the meantime, the heavy cruiser *Cumberland* joined *Ajax* and *Achilles,* which were waiting offshore. Langsdorff now faced three options: internment for the duration of the war, another battle with the British cruisers, or scuttling his ship. He chose the third. After ordering timed explosive charges placed on the vessel, Langsdorff and his crew went ashore. At sunset on December 17, several explosions sent *Graf Spee* to the bottom of the Plate estuary. Langsdorff shot himself to death later that same night.

Despite the losses that the Germans had inflicted on Allied shipping during the first six months of the war, U-boat attacks were not yet more than a highly annoying nuisance. Moreover, the Scandinavian campaign distracted the German navy's attention away from the Atlantic sea lanes in April. Raeder's surface ships brilliantly carried out their role of transporting and protecting the invasion forces, which landed at the various Norwegian ports. But their heavy losses complicated planning for the proposed invasion of Britain after the fall of France in the summer of 1940. The failure of the Luftwaffe to win control of the air during the Battle of Britain eliminated any possibility of carrying out such an operation and assured that the war at sea would continue and, indeed, increase in ferocity.

Britain's prospects in that struggle received two serious blows during the summer of 1940: the fall of France and the entry of Italy into the conflict on Germany's side. Not only would the British lose the support of France's sizable navy, but Churchill feared that it would fall under Germany's control, greatly altering the balance of power on the high seas. It was this grim prospect that prompted Churchill to order the attack on French naval vessels at Mers-el-Kebir and Oran in July. Ironically, the operation, which naturally worsened relations between Britain and a recent ally, was quite unnecessary. Vichy leaders were determined to keep their fleet in French hands.

THE STRUGGLE FOR THE MEDITERRANEAN

The Italian navy was another matter. A formidable presence in the Mediterranean, it forced the British to divert naval strength to the new theater of operations. The Italian fleet included two modern 35,000-ton battleships, four old but modernized 23,000-ton battleships, 18 cruisers, more than 60 destroyers, a similar number of torpedo boats, and 100 submarines. This submarine force was the largest of any of the belligerents'. Italian surface ships generally were faster and possessed longer-range guns than their British counterparts. Their chief weakness was their relatively thin armor, which made them vulnerable to direct hits. Italy's numerical superiority was a source of deep concern to Admiral Sir Andrew Cunningham, the commander of Britain's Mediterranean Fleet based at Alexandria in Egypt, and Admiral Sir James Somerville, who commanded Force H based at Gibraltar.

Cunningham had gained a reputation as an aggressive destroyer commander during World War I but by 1937 appeared headed for retirement. The worsening international situation spared him this fate and led to his appointment to the crucial Mediterranean post before the outbreak of war. Somerville actually had retired in 1938 after a short illness but returned to service in 1939. He helped organize the Dunkirk evacuation and took over Force H after the fall of France.

On the night of November 11, 1940, the British carrier *Illustrious* launched an attack by 21 Swordfish bombers against the Italian naval base at Taranto. The Swordfish were antiquated fabric-covered, open-cockpit biplanes, and their lack of speed made them highly vulnerable to antiaircraft fire. They could deliver their strike only at night. Ten of the Swordfish dropped flares to illuminate the harbor and bombed shore installations. The remaining 11 launched torpedoes against the ships lying at anchor. They knocked one modernized old battleship out of action permanently and crippled two other battleships, including the new 35,000-ton *Littorio,* as well as two cruisers. The disaster forced Italian naval leaders to shift all remaining major ships to Naples and other, more remote ports on Italy's western coast, where they would be safe from British attack. In January 1941, German dive bombers, in their first action in the Mediterranean, gained a considerable measure of revenge for their ally's defeat at Taranto when they disabled *Illustrious* and forced it to withdraw from action.

Cunningham's fleet scored another triumph in March 1941, shortly before the German invasion of Greece and Yugoslavia. An Italian squadron, led by the new battleship *Vittorio Veneto* and comprising 8 cruisers and 13 destroyers, attempted to intercept a British convoy transporting ground forces to Greece. But British cryptanalysts had broken the Italian naval cipher and provided Cunningham with vital information on the enemy's intentions. In an engagement fought off Cape Matapan, the southernmost tip of the Greek mainland, British dive bombers damaged *Vittorio Veneto* and crippled the heavy cruiser *Pola*. British destroyers then finished off *Pola* as well as two other heavy cruisers and two destroyers.

Despite the disasters of Taranto and Cape Matapan, the Italian navy had far greater success escorting Axis troop and supply convoys to North

Africa. Italian submarines and light surface units, working in cooperation with German and Italian aircraft, also made it exceedingly difficult for British convoys to reach the island base of Malta. Lying only 70 miles south of Sicily, Malta posed a problem for Axis convoys because it lay astride their route to Libya. The British maintained a small number of cruisers and destroyers there as well as an air contingent. These forces attacked Axis convoys during the summer of 1941 and resulted in Raeder's decision to shift six U-boats to the Mediterranean. The submarines proved effective, sinking the carrier *Ark Royal* and the battleship *Barnham.* But the Italians carried out the most spectacular operation of that year when a submarine launched three slow-moving, electrically operated torpedoes near Alexandria in December. Two "frogmen" guided each torpedo through the harbor's defenses and deposited them under the battleships *Queen Elizabeth* and *Valiant* and a tanker. Explosions destroyed the tanker and seriously damaged both battleships.

At almost the same time, Malta's small naval force fell victim to a mine field, which sank a cruiser and a destroyer and damaged two other cruisers. German planes also began to attack Malta in January 1942, and the British reinforced the island's meager air strength in June. Many have hailed Malta as a critical factor in Britain's eventual victory in North Africa, but they may have exaggerated its importance. Approximately 86 percent of all materiel shipped to Axis forces arrived safely in Libya between 1940 and November 1942, and the British suffered heavily in their efforts to keep the island supplied. They paid their highest price in ships and lives in August 1942, when a large naval force escorted a convoy of 14 merchantmen from Britain to Malta by way of the Strait of Gibraltar. Axis submarines and air attacks sank all but five of the supply ships as well as one aircraft carrier, two cruisers, and a destroyer and severely damaged another carrier and two more cruisers. Malta may have been more of a liability than an asset.

By the end of 1942, Britain's victory at El Alamein, the Allied takeover of Morocco and Algeria, and the growth of Anglo-American air and sea power foreshadowed the eventual expulsion of the Axis from North Africa. By the spring of 1943, Allied control of the air over the central Mediterranean and a severe Italian fuel shortage made it impossible for Axis ground forces in Tunisia to receive supplies and doomed them to surrender.

THE BATTLE OF THE ATLANTIC CONTINUES

Meanwhile, Germany's victories in Norway and France in the spring of 1940 had provided bases on the Atlantic for submarine and surface raiders as well as aircraft. French bases proved superior to those in Norway because of the greater size of the harbors and their proximity to British shipping lanes. The Germans quickly built large concrete submarine pens that were impervious to air attack in ports along France's Atlantic coast. Air bases in France and Norway also provided Germany with its only opportunity to experiment with a long-range bomber, the Focke-Wulf 200 Kondor, which was actually a converted airliner and transport plane. Although the Kondor was slow and vulnerable to fighter planes, during 1940 and much of 1941 British convoys lacked such fighter support. This enabled Kondors along with medium bombers to destroy 580,000 tons of shipping in 1940 and over a million tons in 1941. With the advent of British escort aircraft carriers in September 1941, this threat quickly diminished.

Although U-boats were still not numerous enough to constitute a war-winning force, they sank over 1.6 million tons of shipping from June to November 1940, a period that U-boat crews referred to as the "happy time." These losses worried the British, whose naval resources were stretched dangerously thin. Escort vessels were at a premium, and the acquisition of 50 overage U.S. destroyers in October did not ease the situation immediately, because these ships were in need of refitting and trained crews. The development of the corvette, a small vessel of only 925 tons, was more useful. Britain produced large numbers of them in relatively short order. Though lacking the speed and punch of destroyers, corvettes greatly strengthened convoy escorts.

Sinkings tapered off during the winter of 1940–41 because of the difficulty that submarines encountered in bad weather but mounted again in the spring and summer. Dönitz made increasing use of "wolf pack" tactics, which employed a number of U-boats working together. Usually, one submarine would locate a convoy and alert other U-boats in the area by wireless. They would then attack the convoy at night while operating on the surface, where they had an advantage in speed over most escort vessels. Italian submarines also contributed to the Axis cause, and although their effort has received little recognition, they sank ships totaling almost 570,000 tons between 1941 and 1943.

Despite the persistent submarine and bomber menace, aid from North America helped brighten Britain's outlook. The Royal Canadian Navy created an escort force in June 1941 that provided protection for convoys between Newfoundland and Iceland. In April, the United States established air bases in Greenland, and in July, U.S. forces relieved British troops in Iceland. During July, Roosevelt ordered American naval and air forces to patrol the western Atlantic and warn British convoys of the presence of German submarines. The United States's lend-lease program also included constructing both naval ships and merchantmen for Britain as well as providing refitting facilities for British ships in American ports. In September, America undertook the responsibility of escorting convoys to a midocean meeting point where British escorts took over, and in November, Congress authorized the arming of U.S. merchant ships and allowed them to carry cargoes to belligerent ports.

Britain also benefited from Ultra. The German naval cipher had proved especially difficult to break, but in May 1941, a British destroyer crew captured a U-boat's cipher machine and code books. The destroyer had severely damaged the submarine, and the German commander had ordered his men to abandon ship after setting demolition charges. But these had failed to detonate. This stroke of fortune enabled the Royal Navy to amass a vast glut of information on U-boat strength and positions as well as plans for attacking convoys. Although this intelligence certainly did not end the submarine menace, it helped prevent the Germans from achieving greater success. But at this point in the war, the British still did not have enough naval craft, planes, or specialized weapons to make optimum use of Ultra.

During the period from April to December 1941, Axis submarines sank over 1.5 million tons of shipping, but only one-third of the victims were members of convoys. A definite decline in sinkings occurred between October and December, and it appeared that the British might be getting the better of the Battle of the Atlantic. But this improvement was short-lived.

It was also during the period 1940–41 that German surface raiding reached its peak. Disguised merchant ships led the way, starting in April 1940. These were equipped with 5.9-inch guns that gave them the firepower of most light cruisers. They also carried torpedoes and received supplies from ships that waited for them in quiet waters. Seven of these raiders sailed at various times between March 1940 and November 1941. They accounted for 65 merchantmen with a total tonnage of 435,000. But with the aid of detailed Ultra intelligence, British warships sank three of them and, starting in the summer of 1941, hunted down and destroyed most of their supply ships.

Ironically, the German surface warships were less productive, due largely to their shorter range and Hitler's reluctance to allow them to take risks. The pocket battleship *Scheer* enjoyed the most success. It sank 16 merchant ships totaling 99,000 tons as well as an armed British merchant cruiser between October 1940 and April of the following year. The cruiser *Hipper* carried out two raids in late 1940 and early 1941, sinking nine vessels of over 40,000 tons. And during the first three months of 1941, the formidable battle cruisers *Scharnhorst* and *Gneisenau* destroyed 22 ships with a total tonnage of 116,000 before taking refuge in the French port of Brest.

BISMARCK'S FIRST AND LAST VOYAGE

By far the most famous of these sorties, though certainly not the most successful, was that of the newly commissioned battleship *Bismarck* and the heavy cruiser *Prinz Eugen* in May 1941. Under the command of Admiral Günther Lütjens, these powerful ships left Bergen, Norway, on May 21 and ventured into the Atlantic. RAF reconnaissance planes discovered them the same day and alerted the British main fleet, which dispatched ships to intercept the enemy. The cruisers *Norfolk* and *Suffolk* sighted the German ships in the Denmark Strait between Iceland and Greenland on May 23, while the battle cruiser *Hood* and the new battleship *Prince of Wales* closed in for a showdown. *Prince of Wales* was still undergoing tests on her armament and, in fact, sailed with construction workers on board. *Hood* was Britain's largest ship but dated from 1920 and had poor armored protection. In the predawn twilight of May 24, the opposing ships opened fire at a range of 14 miles. A shell from *Bismarck* plunged through *Hood*'s weak deck armor and into a magazine. The ship immediately blew up, killing all but three of the crew of 1,400. Both *Bismarck* and *Prinz Eugen* also hit *Prince of Wales* with several shells, forcing it to break off action.

The two German ships continued on their way, with *Norfolk* and *Suffolk* shadowing them at a safe distance until the main British fleet, some 300 miles away, could arrive. But *Bismarck* had suffered damage from *Prince of Wales*'s shells, most notably an oil leak that forced Admiral Lütjens to abandon his raid into the Atlantic and head for the French port of St. Nazaire at reduced speed instead. Lütjens sent *Prinz Eugen* ahead, and that ship reached Brest on June 1.

Although *Bismarck*'s pursuers lost contract on May 25, a Catalina flying boat discovered the ship the following day. Soon afterward, Swordfish torpedo planes from the carrier *Ark Royal* attacked *Bismarck,* and one of the torpedoes jammed the ship's rudder, leaving the vessel helpless. When the British battleships *George V* and *Rodney* finally caught up with the stricken vessel, they pounded it with armor-piercing shells and left it a flaming hulk. The cruisers *Norfolk* and *Dorsetshire* attempted to finish the job with torpedoes, but they proved ineffective against *Bismarck*'s strong armor. The ship did not finally succumb until the crew scuttled it to prevent the pride of the German navy from being captured by the British.

Dorsetshire and a destroyer lingered after the great ship had vanished beneath the waves to pick up survivors. They had rescued 110 of *Bismarck*'s 2,300-man crew when *Dorsetshire* sighted a German submarine. The two ships looked to their own safety and steamed away at high speed. The U-boat's untimely appearance ironically condemned many German sailors who were still in the water to death. The submarine could save only three. The loss of *Bismarck* for all practical purposes ended the efforts of German surface craft to play a major role in the Battle of the Atlantic.

But *Scharnhorst, Gneisenau,* and *Prinz Eugen* all remained at Brest. Although well situated for additional sorties into the Atlantic, they were also vulnerable to Allied air and naval attack and remained immobilized until February 1942. By that time, Hitler had become convinced that the Allies planned to invade Norway and insisted that the three cruisers leave Brest and take up positions in northern waters. The only way in which they could possibly accomplish this was by a dangerous dash through the English Channel, where the British would almost certainly attack them. The Germans, accordingly, carried out minesweeping and radar-jamming operations in advance, and the cruisers left Brest with a destroyer escort on the night of February 11. When daylight came, they were only halfway through the Channel. Despite ample Ultra warnings that the Germans were planning a Channel dash, the British did not detect the ships until late in the morning. German fighter planes fought off RAF attacks, and the squadron continued its escape. Although both *Scharnhorst* and *Gneisenau* struck mines and suffered minor damage, all three ships found refuge in German ports.

Russia's entry into the conflict in June 1941, while clearly a major turning point in the war, added to the drain on British naval resources. Churchill shifted a large number of ships to transport war materiel to the hard-pressed Soviets. The transformation of the United States into a full-fledged belligerent in December 1941 also greatly enhanced Britain's prospects. But Japanese attacks on British possessions in East Asia compounded Britain's already heavy naval commitments and led to the loss of two more capital ships—*Prince of Wales* and *Repulse*—off the coast of Malaya in January 1942. Moreover, many American vessels, which had been cooperating with the British in the North Atlantic, now served their own country. And ships under construction in the United States that might otherwise have gone into the British navy or merchant marine joined the U.S. Pacific Fleet.

CRISIS AND RESOLUTION IN THE NORTH ATLANTIC

The Battle of the Atlantic reached its most critical stage during 1942. Admiral Dönitz estimated that sinkings of Allied shipping must average 700,000 tons per month if the Germans were to win the struggle on the high seas. They had averaged only 180,000 tons during 1941. In an effort to reach this goal, Dönitz sent as many U-boats as he could spare to American waters. Although the number actually operating there never exceeded a dozen, they accounted for almost half the tonnage that submarines sank between January and April and took an especially heavy toll of tankers. The chief reasons for this remarkable success were a shortage of U.S. escort vessels, which made it difficult to organize convoys, and American reluctance to take other precautions. Indeed, for some time the United States did not even impose a blackout on eastern seaboard cities. Merchant ships and tankers, silhouetted against this brightly illuminated background, provided perfect targets for U-boats operating at night. Submarine commanders later looked back on this period as the "second happy time" and the "American shooting season."

Allied losses during February, March, and April hovered near the 500,000-ton mark. In May, they rose to 600,000 and in June exceeded Dönitz's magic number of 700,000. The Germans also contributed to this success by changing the cipher used by their submarines in February. British cryptanalysts were not able to penetrate the new cipher until December, although they continued to detect other enemy naval messages. Belated American adoption of the convoy system and improved antisubmarine methods cut July sinkings to under 500,000 tons. The new techniques included a refined airborne radar that made it possible for aircraft to locate U-boats on the surface at night and attack them with the aid of searchlights. But the Germans adjusted to this by installing receivers in their submarines that could detect the impulses emitted by the radar of approaching enemy planes. This enabled the U-boats to dive before the aircraft arrived.

The Germans also increased their submarine strength to over 300 in August, about half of which were operational. These included larger vessels that had a range of 30,000 miles and could dive much deeper than earlier models. Sinkings once again climbed over 500,000 tons in August and continued to increase during the following months, reaching a high of over 700,000 in November. During all of 1942, the Allies lost a total of 1,664 ships with a tonnage of almost 7.8 million to all causes, over 80 percent to submarines. These losses ran almost a million tons ahead of new Allied shipping that came into service during 1942.

Early in 1943, Hitler angrily threatened to scrap all German surface ships after the failure of an attack by a force of cruisers and destroyers on a Russia-bound convoy. Admiral Raeder responded to this outburst by resigning as commander in chief of the navy, and Dönitz succeeded to his position. The new commander vowed to step up the U-boat campaign and also managed to persuade Hitler not to eliminate the surface fleet. After a lull during December 1942 and January 1943, due largely to bad weather, submarine attacks increased in February and reached alarming proportions during the first three weeks of March, when wolf packs accounted for over 600,000 tons.

But sinkings declined precipitously, starting in the last week of March and continuing into April and May. The key to this abrupt change was a new coordinated antisubmarine offensive instituted by British Admiral Sir Max Horton, who became commander in chief of Allied naval forces in the western approaches to the British Isles in November 1942. A submarine commander during World War I, Horton had been in charge of British home-based submarines since 1940. His knowledge of underwater craft as well as his great drive and willingness to experiment served him well in his new position. He devised methods that brought much greater pressure to bear on U-boats, and he proved more than a match for Dönitz. The restored ability of Ultra to decipher German messages flowing between U-boat captains and Submarine Command proved of crucial importance. Without it, Horton would not have been able to direct his offensive with such pinpoint accuracy. Ultra information also convinced the Admiralty that the enemy had penetrated its convoy code and led to the adoption of a replacement, which proved secure.

FIGURE 18-2 A depth charge explodes as a U.S. warship hunts an enemy submarine. (*U.S. Navy Photo/National Archives*)

Horton developed large support groups of destroyers and frigates, small warships that were faster than corvettes. These support groups aided convoy escorts by hunting down and destroying submarines operating in nearby waters. Horton also provided increased air support from both escort carriers and shore-based aircraft. These planes had the advantage of a new and revolutionary short-wavelength radar that German U-boats could not detect. Finally, improved depth charges and new rocket weapons also contributed to the remarkable reversal of fortunes. Not only did it become more difficult for U-boats to sink ships, but they found themselves hounded as never before. The climax came in May, when the Germans lost 41 submarines. This toll was so prohibitive that on May 23, Dönitz withdrew his forces from the North Atlantic. During the summer of 1943, the Allies built more ships than they lost. They had won the Battle of the Atlantic.

But the struggle was not yet over. Dönitz devoted himself to enlarging and improving the quality of his submarine force. He and his colleagues introduced the snorkel, a collapsible air intake and exhaust release mast that barely protruded above the surface and enabled submarines to remain continuously submerged. The homing torpedo, which was acoustically attracted by an enemy ship's propellers, also came into operation. But the Allies foiled this formidable weapon by developing the foxer, a device that a ship towed at a safe distance behind it. The foxer made more noise than the vessel's propellers and thus diverted homing torpedoes from their real targets.

The Germans also developed a formidable new submarine, the Walter type. This was a large U-boat that could remain underwater indefinitely and was capable of such high speeds when submerged that it could outdistance most escort vessels. But it encountered a multitude of "teething" problems that proved so difficult to overcome that none of this type of submarine ever saw action. Two other smaller models, both equipped with snorkels, did go into mass production during the winter of 1944–45. But by that time it was much too late.

Dönitz resumed the submarine offensive in September 1943, but it accomplished little, while the Allies destroyed 25 U-boats during the first two months. In early 1944, the Germans sank only three ships but lost 37 of their own craft. Dönitz found these results so discouraging that in March he halted operations against convoys until the new submarines would be able to go to sea in strength—a day that never came.

WAR IN THE ARCTIC OCEAN

From August 1941 to September 1943, a grim struggle also unfolded in the Arctic Ocean to the north of Norway and the USSR. Here, too, both German submarines and surface ships attempted to prevent British convoys from reaching their destinations—the Russian ports of Murmansk and Archangel. Because ice blocked access to Archangel during the winter, Murmansk was the more important of the two. German ground forces had attempted to capture the port during 1941 but had failed to make much headway in the barren wasteland of the Soviet extreme north. The Germans also had air and naval bases in Norway. In addition to submarines, by 1942 Germany had gathered most of its surface craft in Norwegian waters, including the battleship *Tirpitz,* the pocket battleships *Scheer* and *Lützow,* the battle cruiser *Scharnhorst,* and the heavy cruiser *Hipper.*

Allied convoys had to make much of the voyage to the Russian ports without benefit of air cover. The most severe German attacks came between March and July 1942, culminating in the tragic destruction of convoy PQ 17, which left Britain late in June. Admiral Sir Dudley Pound, the commander of the Royal Navy, received information that *Tirpitz* had put to sea with the apparent intention of attacking the convoy. Pound ordered the escorting cruisers to withdraw from the convoy, fearing that they would fall victim to the German battleship. He also ordered the merchant ships to scatter. But Hitler, fearing the loss of *Tirpitz,* insisted that the battle group return to base. German submarines and aircraft carried out the mission instead and did so with deadly efficiency, sinking 23 of the 36 merchantmen.

Sobered by this disaster, the Allies did not dispatch another convoy until September, despite Stalin's bitter protests. The next convoy, PQ 18, received a much stronger escort, and although German U-boats and aircraft sank 13 ships, they suffered heavy losses themselves. A few convoys also made the Arctic run during the winter of 1942–43. But in March, the British halted this traffic for several months due largely to the critical situation in the Atlantic. When convoys resumed in November, they received more powerful escorts than ever before, including carriers that protected the merchant ships and punished both German submarines and aircraft.

In late December, *Scharnhorst* and its supporting destroyers attempted to intercept a convoy. But the British battleship *Duke of York* and three cruisers received detailed Ultra reports of the German movements and laid a trap. They pummeled *Scharnhorst* with fire from their big guns. The battle cruiser proved extremely difficult to sink, however. It took direct hits from an estimated 25 shells and 11 torpedoes to send the vessel to the depths of the frigid Arctic. Only 36 of its crew of nearly 2,000 survived.

The last blow to German surface power came with the crippling and later the sinking of *Tirpitz.* In September 1943, British midget submarines damaged the huge battleship, which lay at anchor in northernmost Norway, putting it out of action for six months. Carrier-based planes attacked the vessel again in April 1944 and inflicted minor damage. RAF heavy bombers crippled it in September, and a second attack in November finally settled the issue. Six-ton bombs ripped into *Tirpitz*'s hull and set off a magazine. Soon afterward, the ship capsized, carrying almost 1,000 men to the bottom.

NO GUARANTEED VICTORY

In the last months of the war, German submarine strength continued to mount, reaching an all-time high of 463 in March 1945. But due to mechanical difficulties with the new and potentially revolutionary models, fuel shortages, and enemy strength on the high seas, they accomplished little.

Of the 1,170 submarines that Germany possessed during the whole of World War II, the Allies destroyed 784. In all, U-boats sank 2,828 Allied merchant ships, comprising a tonnage of over 14 million. Allied shipping losses in the Atlantic and European theater of operations from all causes totaled 21.6 million tons. Had the Germans been able to develop their new submarines earlier and bring them into action in large numbers, the outcome of the Battle of the Atlantic might have been different. If the Allies had been able to speed up their timetable and employ some of their ultimately decisive methods at an earlier date, their victory might have come sooner. Since neither development came to pass, it was, as the Duke of Wellington said of his victory over Napoleon at Waterloo, "a damned close-run thing."

19

Target Germany: The Allied Bombing Offensive

Of all the terrible new weapons that gained their baptism of fire in World War I, the one that most captured the popular imagination was the bomber. Although its actual importance was negligible during the 1914–18 conflict, it inspired a ghastly vision: the mass destruction of cities by a rain of bombs in a future war. The public was not alone in entertaining this apocalyptic view. Some military theorists also came to believe that the advent of the airplane had revolutionized warfare and that bombers would win the next conflict with little or no aid from other forces. They referred to this cataclysmic form of warfare as strategic bombing.

STRATEGIC BOMBING

A raid by 14 German Gotha aircraft on London in June 1917 had a special impact on British appraisals of the potential of strategic bombing. It had this effect even though, by later standards, it inflicted few casualties—162 persons killed and 432 wounded. Other raids of limited scope followed until May 1918. Together they helped convince some British military leaders that in the future, large formations of long-range bombers would be able to pound an enemy into submission.

This notion gained its strongest support in the fledgling Royal Air Force, which came into existence as a service independent of both the army and navy in April 1918. The RAF's first chief of staff, General Hugh Trenchard, became an outspoken enthusiast for strategic air power during the 1920s, and his associates developed theories on the objectives, methods, and probable results of precision bombing on a mass scale.

In America, General William ("Billy") Mitchell also championed the cause of strategic bombing during the same period, but he was less successful in gaining acceptance of his ideas. There was no independent air force in the United States; the army and navy retained their own air arms and tended to regard Mitchell as an irresponsible visionary.

The man who many later credited with having the greatest influence on the theory of strategic air power was the Italian general Giulio Douhet. In a book that appeared in 1921, Douhet preached that bombers held the key to victory in a future war. He visualized bombing raids that would paralyze industry and civilian morale and make continued resistance impossible. But his influence may not have been as great during the 1920s and 1930s as is commonly believed. A complete English translation of his work did not appear until 1942 in the United States and 1943 in Britain.

Although a German translation of Douhet appeared in 1935, theories of strategic bombing played little role in the Luftwaffe's approach to aerial war. To be sure, General Wever, the first German air chief of staff, saw the need for a large force of long-range bombers that could reach targets as distant as the Ural Mountains in the USSR. Indeed, he pressured the Dornier and Junkers aircraft firms to develop prototypes of such planes, but his death in 1936 ended progress in this direction. Instead, his successors devoted themselves to the creation of a tactical air force, consisting of dive bombers, medium bombers, and fighters, that would work closely with the army in its *Blitzkrieg* operations. Certainly, the Luftwaffe performed well in this role in the early campaigns of World War II. But its failure to develop a strategic bombing force was one factor that contributed to the futility of Germany's effort to knock Britain out of the war in 1940.

Even in Britain, where enthusiasm for strategic bombing ran highest, the RAF made little progress toward the development of an adequate bomber force prior to the war. This was due in part to the government's reluctance to provide the necessary funds. Disagreement also developed over the type of bomber that should be produced. As the war approached, the RAF still had a preponderance of light bombers that were unsuitable for strategic bombing. It also became obvious that Britain needed a strong fighter-plane force to defend the country against German air attacks. The simpler design of fighter planes also made it possible to produce them more quickly than the larger and more complex bombers. In 1939, the government gave priority to the creation of 18 new fighter squadrons, a decision that played a vital role in the RAF's victory over the Luftwaffe the following year.

When the war started, Britain was clearly at a numerical disadvantage in bombers, compared to Germany. This contributed to the realization that the RAF would be unable to inflict serious damage on German cities for the foreseeable future. British leaders concluded that it would be better to avoid provocative raids that might result in heavier retaliatory strikes on British cities. Nevertheless, the government went ahead with plans to develop four-engine long-range bombers. It had ordered prototypes of the future Sterling, Halifax, and Lancaster bombers as early as 1937. Although these planes were not available when the war began, they would devastate Germany later in the conflict. And despite this slow development, strategic bombing enthusiasts in the Royal Air Force never slackened in their faith regarding the war-winning potential of heavy long-range bombers. Their single-minded approach led them to downplay the benefits to be gained from the creation of a tactical air arm that would work in close support of the army and navy. The British and German air forces thus approached the war with completely different philosophies.

The RAF exponents of strategic bombing also greatly underestimated the difficulties that lay in wait for bombers. They thought in terms of precision raids in daylight and assumed that it would be relatively easy to find and destroy targets. To say the least, this was wildly optimistic. Indeed, accurate navigation to targets and the ability to hit them, if they were reached, proved difficult when World War II began.

In the early stages of the conflict, neither Germany nor the Western Allies engaged in any large-scale raids on the cities of their chief opponents. To be sure, the Luftwaffe attacked Polish cities, especially Warsaw, and later destroyed the center of Rotterdam. But both of these operations were, to some extent, extensions of the German doctrine of tactical support for the army.

British air activity during the period of the "phony war" consisted primarily of dropping leaflets over German cities at night and infrequent daylight bombing attacks on naval targets. The most ambitious of the latter raids occurred in December 1939. Twenty-two Wellington bombers attacked enemy shipping along Germany's North Sea coast. But the two-engine Wellingtons inflicted little damage, and only seven of them made it home. Heavy losses in other daylight attacks on similar targets led to a decision in April 1940 to restrict bombing to nighttime raids.

In May 1940, the RAF resorted to what many have described as the first strategic bombing raid in history: an attack by 99 bombers against the Ruhr on the night of May 15–16. Although they lost only one plane, the British did little damage to their targets.

During the Battle of Britain, Germany, of course, attempted to carry out a strategic mission with a tactical air force. It failed either to destroy RAF Fighter Command, the vital prerequisite for an invasion, or force Britain out of the conflict through bombing attacks alone. When German aircraft dropped a few bombs on London in August 1940, they caused little damage. But Churchill ordered a retaliatory strike on Berlin, and during the next few days, RAF Bomber Command carried out five raids on the German capital. They inflicted negligible damage. Indeed, only 29 of the 105 bombers that participated in the first raid actually found Berlin, a clear indication of the difficulties of aerial navigation. But the raids fulfilled their major mission: to make a gesture of Britain's willingness to strike back.

They also had an unexpected result. Hitler's anger over these violations of the sacred German capital contributed to the Luftwaffe's shift away from attacks on Fighter Command bases to direct attacks on London. The ensuing raids against the British capital and other cities during the next few months represented the most prolonged bombing assault in history up to that point, even though their results were disappointing.

German raids on cities also helped eliminate whatever squeamishness British leaders might still have harbored regarding the bombing of German cities. But the same problems persisted—an inadequate striking force as well as the technical problems of navigation and precision. An extremely inaccurate raid by 134 bombers against the railroad center of Mannheim on the Rhine in mid-December provided ample evidence of the lack of precision. Still, Bomber Command was the only British weapon capable of acting offensively against Germany.

During 1941, the British clung to the belief that they could carry out successful precision raids on such targets as German oil plants and railroads. But indications of woeful inaccuracy continued to mount. By the fall of that year, British air leaders, including Chief of the Air Staff Sir Charles Portal, came to the conclusion that area bombing offered the best opportunity to direct a decisive blow at Germany. This would involve striking at the center of German cities in an effort to inflict such heavy damage and casualties that enemy morale would crack, forcing an end to the war. Indeed, the air staff had been veering in this direction since late 1940, when Portal had taken over his duties.

Portal was a true disciple of Trenchard and had directed Bomber Command prior to assuming the RAF's top post. A man of great intelligence, efficiency, and capacity for work, he often preferred solitude to the company of others. Although Portal struggled with a shortage of aircraft during the first year of his appointment, he presided over a vast wartime expansion of the air force. This growth made possible the adoption of the strategic bombing policy in which he so strongly believed. Portal and other RAF leaders downplayed the failure of the Luftwaffe to break British morale in 1940–41. They attributed this in large part to the absence of strategic aircraft. To avoid a similar mistake, they visualized the creation of a British force of 4,000 heavy bombers capable of destroying Germany's will to resist within six months. They also assumed that enemy fighters would not be able to prevent night attacks any more than RAF fighters had stopped German night raids in 1940–41.

But Churchill doubted that area bombing would secure the desired result and warned that the Germans might improve their defenses against night attacks. He contended that only daylight bombing against industry held the possibility of real progress. This would only be feasible, however, if the RAF sharply reduced the size of the German fighter-plane force. In other words, control of the air was the key to a meaningful strategic bombing campaign. Unfortunately, the RAF could not accomplish this with its Hurricane and Spitfire fighters, which lacked the range to penetrate deeply into Germany.

Churchill's fear of stronger enemy defenses

proved prophetic. Improved radar enabled the Germans to detect the approach of British aircraft and direct night fighters to the attack. Luftwaffe aircraft now also used a precise short-range radar that allowed them to find their targets much more easily. British losses mounted, but the results of their bombing did not improve.

BRITAIN TAKES THE OFFENSIVE

Despite growing doubts about the potential of strategic air power, its supporters won out. Churchill found his own pessimism countered by the glowing optimism of his chief scientific adviser, Lord Cherwell, and the air staff opted for a policy of area raids against cities in February 1942. The appointment of Air Marshal Arthur Harris to the post of commander in chief of Bomber Command that same month provided the final ingredient. Harris had left home as a rebellious teenager to try his luck at farming and gold mining in Rhodesia. When World War I broke out, he enlisted in the army and served as a bugler in the campaign against the Germans in South-West Africa. Later he joined the Royal Flying Corps and won the Air Force Cross for bravery on the western front. Noted for his disdain of both the army and the navy, Harris became the high priest of strategic bombing.

Described as "ruthless, relentless, remorseless," Harris approached the war with total devotion to the principle of breaking civilian morale through 1,000-plane raids that would lay waste city after city. Despite mounting evidence to the contrary in the following months and years, "Bomber Harris" never faltered in this belief. He worked tirelessly to build up a huge force of four-engine bombers capable of carrying large bomb loads of ever-increasing destructiveness. His efforts were enhanced by the development of Gee, a radio device that aided navigation and enabled bomber crews to identify their targets with greater accuracy. Bomber Command also enjoyed access to a vast stream of information from Ultra. This intelligence proved useful in regard to the strength, location, and intentions of German fighter forces. It also provided details about weather over Germany and the enemy's radar system.

The first step in Harris's intensive campaign began in late March 1942, when 234 bombers attacked the German Baltic port of Lübeck. This raid featured the RAF's first use of large quantities of incendiary bombs, which destroyed the city's center, including many beautiful medieval buildings. But the attack resulted in little damage to either the port or industry. Raids against another Baltic port, Rostock, followed on four consecutive nights in April. Once again, incendiaries wiped out the medieval beauty of the old city but had a negligible impact on military targets. These assaults so enraged Hitler that he resorted to Luftwaffe attacks against a number of lovely historic English cities—Exeter, Bath, Norwich, York, and Canterbury.

In late May, the bomber offensive took a huge leap into the realm of destructiveness when Bomber Command carried out the first 1,000-plane raid against Cologne. Again, this massive force devastated the center of the city but had little effect on outlying industrial areas. The attackers lost 40 aircraft. Two days later, over 900 planes struck the great industrial city of Essen in the Ruhr, but heavy cloud cover prevented serious damage. Thirty-one bombers failed to return. Later that month, a force of comparable strength bombed the North Sea port of Bremen, but again bad weather conditions reduced the impact. The Bremen mission was the last of this scope until 1943. These raids had failed to break civilian morale.

Despite the disappointing results of these raids, British support for strategic bombing escalated during 1942. The number of planes involved and the tonnage of bombs dropped helped fire the imagination of leaders and common people alike. Hopes for the future of the bombing offensive also rose with an increase in the number of four-engine Lancasters, by far the best British bomber. Other promising developments included improved navigational capabilities and the use of Pathfinder, a force of planes that preceded the main body of bombers to find and illuminate target areas with flares. On a more ominous note, however, German fighter-plane production rose from 3,744 in 1941 to 5,515 during 1942.

THE AMERICANS JOIN IN

With America's entry into the war, the United States Army Air Force (USAAF) loomed as a new and potentially powerful addition to the bombing offensive. The first units of the U.S. Eighth Air Force arrived in May 1942 and began operations in August. Their contribution remained limited at first because American bomber strength was relatively small. U.S. planes did not penetrate beyond France, Belgium, and the Netherlands. But America possessed the capability to increase its bomber force drastically and also had two fine aircraft—the B-24 Liberator and, especially, the B-17 Flying Fortress. Both were four-engine heavy bombers that bristled with machine guns.

In contrast to their British allies, American leaders rejected area bombing of cities aimed at breaking civilian morale. They much preferred precision bombing of industrial and other military targets, using the superior Norden bombsight. Unfortunately, precision bombing required raids during daylight hours, which greatly increased danger to the attacking planes. Despite the unhappy British experience with daylight bombing, the Americans believed that their heavily armed aircraft could defend themselves against enemy fighter planes. They also expected to hit their targets much more accurately than the British. It soon became evident that they were overly optimistic on both counts. Although German fighter pilots were in awe of the B-17 at first, they quickly overcame their concern and inflicted heavy losses on U.S. bombers. Like the British before them, the Americans found that their raids were far less accurate than they had anticipated. Unlike the British, they persisted in raiding targets in daylight.

This approach dominated the thinking of the man who commanded the USAAF, General H. H. Arnold. One of America's pioneer aviators, Arnold had learned his flying from the Wright brothers. He became head of the Air Corps in 1938 and laid the groundwork for the vast wartime expansion of U.S. air power. Although Arnold's nickname "Hap" reflected a sunny personality, he was deadly serious in his belief that air power held the key to victory. His efforts had helped earn the air force equality with the army and navy, although technically it remained attached to the former. The first commander of the Eighth Air Force, General Carl ("Tooey") Spaatz, and General Ira Eaker, who succeeded him in late 1942, were also longtime fliers. Together they had set an endurance record when they remained aloft for almost 151 hours in 1927. They also shared an intense faith in daylight strategic bombing.

Ultra proved especially helpful to the USAAF's efforts. Daylight precision bombing required much more information on targets than did Bomber Command's nighttime area raids. Ultra not only provided vital details, which contributed to the actual missions, but also gave an accurate picture of damage inflicted and the progress of German repairs.

Roosevelt and Churchill agreed at the Casablanca conference in January 1943 that Allied air forces would continue both approaches to strategic bombing. American precision attacks would seek to destroy German industry, while RAF area raids would concentrate on undermining civilian morale. Starting in March and continuing until July, the British concentrated on bombing the industrial cities of the Ruhr. These raids, referred to collectively as the Battle of the Ruhr, caused widespread destruction but did not seriously impede German industrial production.

THE DESTRUCTION OF HAMBURG

By far the most devastating and horrible raids in this phase of the war took place during the period from July 24 to August 3, 1943, with Hamburg as the target. Almost 800 RAF bombers delivered the first attack on the night of July 24–25. Many factors conspired to bring ruin to Germany's greatest port and second largest city. The night was clear, the target was well marked by Pathfinders, and a new device, called Window, badly confused German radar signals. Window consisted of strips of tin foil that bomber crews dropped in bundles at intervals of one minute. So successful was this device that only 12 aircraft failed to return. The bombers dropped high-explosive, incendiary, and newly developed phosphorus bombs on the highly flammable center of Hamburg, causing widespread destruction.

Far worse disasters lay ahead for the stricken city, however. American bombers added to the devastation in the next two days, even though they suffered heavy losses from German fighter attacks. The greatest horror came on the night of July 26–27. The previous raids had virtually paralyzed Hamburg's firefighting capabilities. When RAF bombers returned to rain another deluge of incendiaries and phosphorus bombs on the city, they started innumerable fires, which all converged to form a firestorm. A 1½-mile-wide column of superheated air rose 8,000 feet into the sky, sucking in the air from the surrounding area and suffocating thousands of people. The conflagration's intense heat turned air raid shelters into ovens and literally baked alive thousands of persons who had taken refuge in them. Temperatures rose to over 1,000 degrees Celsius, and winds reached 150 miles per hour.

But of all the hideous forms of death that the citizens of Hamburg suffered, the most terrible fate befell several hundred who were spattered by showers of phosphorus. Phosphorus clings tenaciously to any surface it touches, including human flesh, and continues to burn as long as it remains exposed to oxygen. Even when smothered by sand or water, it flares into flame again once the cover is removed. Many victims of this horror threw themselves into the Alster River, where they had to choose between slowly dying in agony from flaming phosphorus or drowning.

A fifth attack followed on the night of July 29–30, and a final one took place on August 2–3 as a sort of melancholy postscript to this orgy of destruction and death. In all, the raids wiped out nine square miles of the city and killed at least 60,000 persons. Another 750,000 found themselves homeless.

Bomber Command struck at many other German cities during 1943, culminating in a series of 16 devastating raids on Berlin that began in November and continued until March 1944. But all of the terrible raids of 1943 and early 1944 had little impact on Germany's productive capacity, and despite the horror that gripped the country after the Hamburg raids, they failed to destroy civilian morale. Once the initial shock wore off, the German people steeled themselves to their fate. There was little else they could do.

Even more discouraging to the British were the increasing losses that their bombers suffered in the raids after Hamburg. The Germans developed an improved airborne radar, which was not subject to jamming by Window, as well as new night-fighting tactics. These innovations once again restored the balance in favor of the defense. To make matters still worse, the Germans increased fighter-plane production during the first half of 1943, reaching a peak of 2,316 a month by June. This accomplishment was largely due to techniques employed by Albert Speer, the minister for armaments and war production, including remarkably quick repair of bombing damage and dispersal of industry. German industry also concentrated on production of just two types of fighter—improved versions of the Me 109 and the newer Focke-Wulf 190.

The U.S. Eighth Air Force, to its credit, recognized the need to destroy the German aircraft industry, and during 1943 concentrated its daylight attacks primarily on targets related to the production of fighters or component parts. They did succeed in reducing German aircraft production to some extent during the second half of the year but suffered heavy losses in the effort. The most disastrous of these raids occurred in October, when 291 Flying Fortresses attacked the ball bearings factory at Schweinfurt in central Germany. Repeated German fighter attacks destroyed 60 bombers and damaged 138. It was now clear that daylight bombing could not succeed unless large numbers of long-range fighter planes escorted the bombers. Until late in 1943, Allied fighters lacked the range to penetrate deeply into Germany. Luftwaffe fighters simply waited until the escorts had to return to their base and then pounced on the bombers.

THE ALLIES REGAIN THE UPPER HAND

The answer to the Allied dilemma came in the form of fighter escort planes with vastly increased range. The first aircraft of this type was the P-47 Thunderbolt, which, with the aid of two disposable wing fuel tanks, was able to penetrate more deeply into Germany. Soon afterward came the even more formidable P-51 Mustang. Although the P-51 had been available since 1940, the USAAF had rejected the plane at first because of its underpowered engine. Now equipped with a new high-performance engine, it proved to be the finest prop-powered fighter plane of World War II. Superior to German fighters in speed and maneuverability, the Mustang also carried two disposable fuel tanks, which allowed it to penetrate to Berlin and beyond. The P-51 eventually replaced the P-47 as the premier escort aircraft. But the Thunderbolt continued to serve admirably in the role of fighter-bomber.

From April to September 1944, the Allies gave top priority to aerial attacks in support of the cross-Channel invasion. To accomplish this, they diverted heavy bombers from their strategic mission to aid the medium bombers and fighter bombers of General Lewis Brereton's U.S. Ninth Air Force and Air Marshal Sir Arthur Coningham's British Second Tactical Air Force. Their chief targets prior to the actual landings were the French railroad network and bridges leading to the projected landing site. These raids snarled the communications system so badly that when the invasion began, the Germans found it extremely difficult to move reinforcements and supplies to the beachhead. Once the Allied armies gained a foothold on the French coast, the air forces provided tactical support by attacking a multitude of targets at the front as well as in the German rear.

Brereton had been MacArthur's air commander in the Philippines and a central figure in the controversy over the destruction of most of the American planes on Luzon soon after Pearl Harbor. Since then, he had commanded forces in Java, China, and North Africa before taking over the Ninth Air Force in 1943. Brereton was the architect of the "bridge-busting" campaign prior to the invasion. Coningham had served as a

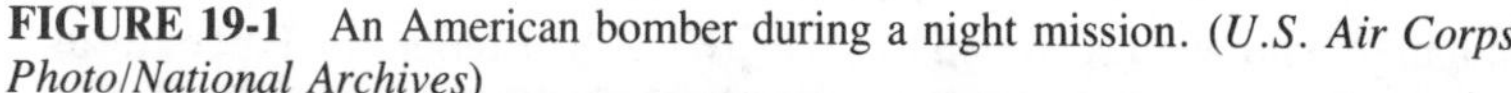
FIGURE 19-1 An American bomber during a night mission. (*U.S. Air Corps Photo/National Archives*)

fighter pilot on the western front during World War I and had been RAF commander in North Africa as well as leader of Allied air forces in Sicily and Italy. He believed strongly in close cooperation between air and ground forces but often quarreled with General Montgomery, who looked down on the RAF's contribution. General Elwood ("Pete") Quesada, who had gained prominence as a fighter commander in North Africa, served under Brereton as leader of the Ninth Tactical Air Command. Quesada was a much more avid believer in close support of ground troops than Brereton. He quickly won the admiration of army officers for his cooperative attitude and the brilliant success of his operations.

Meanwhile, the Germans concentrated on the development of new weapons that they hoped might turn the tide against the Allies. One of the potentially most useful of these was the Messerschmitt 262 jet-propelled fighter. It had been undergoing trials since 1942 and by the summer of 1943 was ready for mass production. With a speed in excess of 500 miles per hour, the Me 262 would have outclassed every Allied fighter, including the Mustang. It might have forced the Allies to abandon their mass bombing raids on Germany.

But Hitler thought in terms of offensive rather than defensive weapons. Despite the protests of General Adolf Galland, commander of the Luftwaffe's fighter arm, he insisted that the plane be converted into a fighter-bomber. Galland later commented that "one might as well have given orders to call a horse a cow!" Hitler hoped that large numbers of these aircraft would smash the Allied cross-Channel invasion when it came. But the Germans did not complete this conversion until after the Allies had successfully landed on the French coast. Even then, the aircraft were available in only small numbers. Finally, in September 1944, Hitler allowed some of the Me 262s to be used in their proper role as fighters. By then it was much too late, and there were too few of them to make an impact. This revolutionary plane never became a real factor in the war.

A week after the Allies began their cross-Channel invasion on June 6, 1944, Hitler unleashed the first of his "vengeance weapons" against Britain. This was the V-1, a pilotless jet-propelled plane with a warhead containing a ton of high explosives. During the next few weeks, the Germans launched thousands of these "flying bombs" from sites along the Channel coast against London and other British cities. Hitler sent an even more terrifying weapon, the V-2, against Britain from launching sites in the Netherlands, starting on September 8. The V-2 was an actual rocket and also carried a one-ton warhead. It reached a speed of 3,600 miles per hour and could not be intercepted. Both the V-1 and the V-2 were terror weapons as well as means of gaining some measure of vengeance for Allied bombing raids against German cities. Hitler hoped that they might have a decisive impact on the course of the war, but even though they killed almost 9,000 persons, their effect fell far short of expectations.

The V weapons did succeed in forcing the Allies to divert a large portion of their bombers to attacks on launching sites. Indeed, this had happened even before the V-1 became operational. The British believed that high-altitude attacks by heavy bombers were the best way to destroy the sites. The Americans, by contrast, feared that such aircraft would have difficulty hitting these relatively small and well-camouflaged targets. They thought that medium-level assaults by fighter-bombers offered a much better approach. But they deferred to their Allies because, after all, British cities were the intended victims of the V weapons. Nevertheless, medium bombers and fighter-bombers did supplement the heavier aircraft. Although these raids may have delayed the V-1 attacks for three or four months, they did not prevent the eventual onslaught. Raids against launching sites continued, but the Germans switched to smaller sites that were even more difficult to hit. Gradually the Allies came to realize that the only real remedy for V weapon attacks was to overrun the launching sites.

During the summer of 1944, a difference of opinion developed among Allied leaders over bombing targets. Air Chief Marshal Sir Arthur Tedder, the deputy supreme commander in Europe, favored raids on the German communications network. The great success of such attacks in France prior to the cross-Channel invasion convinced him of the value of this approach. But General Spaatz, the commander of all U.S. strategic air forces in Europe, believed that raids on Germany's oil supply would be even more effective. Spaatz had already directed American bombers to attack oil objectives during the spring of 1944. General Nathan Twining's U.S. Fifteenth Air Force bombed Rumania's Ploesti oil fields from its bases in Italy during April. The Eighth Air Force, now commanded by General James Doolittle, the hero of the 1942 raid on Tokyo, sent its bombers against German synthetic oil plants in May. These raids increased in frequency after the cross-Channel invasion and had a definite effect on German oil production. They were so successful that British bombers also began to strike at oil targets.

But the really crucial phase of the bombing offensive began in November 1944 with the establishment of oil plants as first-priority targets and communications as second-priority. Raids against synthetic oil production, coupled with the Russian capture of the Ploesti oil fields in August, caused an alarming drain on German oil stocks. Although Speer's ceaseless efforts resulted in some improvement, the overall trend was critical for both the Luftwaffe and the army. The formidable task of resisting Allied forces in Western Europe also vastly increased pressure on German fuel supplies. The Luftwaffe found it more and more difficult to obtain fuel for training flights, which sharply reduced its ability to put fighters into the air. This, coupled with the growing domination of the Mustang fighter, gradually resulted in Allied supremacy in the skies over Germany.

The assaults on German communications targets developed more slowly, but in February and March 1945, these operations became shat-

FIGURE 19-2 An aerial view of the devastation that Allied air power inflicted on Mannheim, Germany. (*U.S. Signal Corps Photograph*)

teringly effective. The flow of raw materials to German industry diminished to a trickle. With the Russian capture of eastern Germany's major industrial area of Upper Silesia in February, German dependence on the Ruhr became far greater. But raids on communications, along with RAF attacks on the Ruhr itself, virtually paralyzed the area's ability to produce war materiel. By April, Allied bombers were hard-pressed to find suitable strategic targets and devoted their efforts to tactical support of the ground forces that were overrunning Germany.

But terror raids continued to figure prominently in the bombing offensive throughout the period of Allied domination of the skies over Germany. Not only Bomber Command but the USAAF as well took part in devastating attacks on major German cities, including Berlin, Stuttgart, Nuremberg, Leipzig, and Munich. This wave of destruction culminated in a series of tragic raids on the beautiful city of Dresden. Renowned for its glorious Rococo architecture, Dresden had previously escaped devastation and contained little of strategic importance. The city's prewar population of 630,000 had increased dramatically with the influx of over 200,000 refugees fleeing from the Red Army, which had already penetrated eastern Germany. Several factors contributed to the decision to strike against Dresden. Churchill favored an attack as a means of impressing Stalin with the awesome power of Anglo-American air might as well as a demonstration of Western determination to cooperate with the Russian offensive. As an almost untouched urban center, Dresden also provided Allied leaders with a tempting target in keeping with the policy of smashing enemy cities.

On the night of February 13–14, over 800 British bombers dropped huge quantities of incendiaries and high-explosive bombs on the city, creating a hideous firestorm similar to the one that had tormented Hamburg a year and a half earlier. If this were not enough, 300 American planes rained additional devastation on the flaming target the following day, and 200 more U.S. bombers struck again on February 15. An estimated 35,000 persons died in the raids. Little remained of the once lovely city.

WAS IT ALL WORTHWHILE?

The Allied strategic bombing offensive has remained one of the most controversial episodes of World War II. Over 400,000 German civilians lost their lives as a result of attacks on targets within the Reich's pre-1938 borders. At least another 400,000 suffered injuries. By comparison, Britain lost only 65,000 civilians to German bombing attacks. Allied bombs destroyed 30 to 80 percent of 50 major German cities. But the price was high: 40,000 Allied planes destroyed and 160,000 airmen dead. Did all the destruction and slaughter visited upon Germany's cities really affect the war to an extent that justified such drastic measures? Did the results offset the heavy casualties suffered by Allied bomber crews? Were terror raids morally defensible under any circumstances?

Raids on German industry clearly did not destroy the Reich's ability to produce war materiel during 1943–44. In fact, German aircraft production rose from the previous high of 10,898 in 1943 to 25,285 in 1944. Tank production also increased sharply. To be sure, without Allied raids, Germany would have possessed the potential to increase production even more. The bombing offensive also forced the Germans to divert fighter aircraft from the fighting fronts to defend the Fatherland. Large numbers of men who might otherwise have seen combat against Allied troops also had to serve in antiaircraft gun crews and civil defense roles. All of these factors clearly helped the Allied cause, but they were far from decisive, and it still remains questionable whether they were worth the cost.

Whatever the benefits of direct attacks on industry, area bombing of cities certainly failed in its major purpose—to destroy German civilian morale and the will to resist. Terror raids, such as the savage attacks on Hamburg and Dresden, thus appear unjustified on practical as well as moral grounds. Indeed, they bring to mind Shakespeare's famous line, "It is a tale told by an idiot, full of sound and fury, signifying nothing."

It was not until the Allies focused on oil and communications targets late in the conflict that strategic bombing really had a major effect on Germany's ability to wage war. But by that time the outcome was no longer in doubt. It is possible that concentration on these targets earlier might have shortened the struggle, but such an approach was not feasible until the advent of long-range fighters in large numbers for escort duty. These were not available until early 1944. Without such escorts, large-scale raids deep into Germany against oil and communications targets would certainly have resulted in losses as prohibitive as those suffered in raids on cities.

Ironically, despite the infinitely greater emphasis on strategic bombing, tactical air power in support of ground troops probably made at least as significant a contribution to victory. But it, too, was sometimes guilty of overkill as in the massive attacks on Cassino and the French city of Caen. These raids actually caused more difficulty for the advancing Allied troops than for the German defenders. They created so much havoc that Allied tanks and supply vehicles could not penetrate through the huge mounds of debris that clogged the streets of the devastated towns. Allied air leaders often seemed incapable of restraint, at both the strategic and the tactical levels.

20

Total War and the Home Fronts

World War I had led to the creation of a new concept—total war. It had gradually taken shape after the initial dreams of speedy victory had died in the face of the reality of a prolonged and bloody conflict. Total war involved a close interrelationship between a nation's economy, its technology, and the mobilization of its civilian population for the purpose of winning the war. Although many aspects of total war had been present in earlier conflicts, World War I was the first instance in which governments attempted to integrate them all completely and in a most determined manner. The degree to which the various warring powers succeeded in securing the total mobilization of their economic and human resources varied considerably. World War II witnessed a similar attempt by the belligerents to harness their resources totally in the interest of victory. Again, the extent of their efforts and their achievements differed markedly.

GERMANY: FROM LIMITED LIABILITY TO TOTAL WAR

One might think that Nazi Germany, as a totalitarian state, would have been the most ambitious and the most successful in preparing its economy and people for total war. But the bureaucratic confusion that characterized the Third Reich, coupled with Hitler's dream of waging a war of limited liability, retarded its progress for years. In keeping with Hitler's long-standing fear of a breakdown of civilian morale similar to that which had occurred in Germany during World War I, he insisted that much of German industry concentrate on the production of consumer goods. But by the time that something approaching an all-out effort was underway, it was too late. The war was already lost.

Goebbels's propaganda ministry did quickly mobilize the press, radio, and film to foster support for the war, but the results were disappointing at first. Goebbels as well as Hitler and other Nazi leaders were disturbed by reports of Germans glumly watching their troops as they marched through Berlin soon after the invasion of Poland. Their reaction contrasted sharply with the almost ecstatic response to the outbreak of World War I. Memories of the horrors and privations of that awful conflict remained vivid to many and combined with fears of the unknown terrors that might lie in wait for Germany this time.

It was not until the Wehrmacht won its early victories and especially the spectacular *Blitzkrieg* triumph over France in the spring of 1940 that German confidence in an imminent end to the conflict flourished. The failure to knock Britain out of the war and, most notably, the invasion of the Soviet Union the following year, however, brought the return of doubt and fear. Once again, the early German successes on the eastern front, trumpeted so bombastically by Goebbels, only made the setback before Moscow more discouraging. A sudden increase in the number of wounded soldiers on the streets of German cities provided an especially sobering reminder that all was not well at the front.

With the resumption of German offensive activity during the summer of 1942, the propaganda barrage picked up in intensity, rekindling dreams of victory. But even Goebbels could not disguise the loss of the Sixth Army at Stalingrad. The advent of British bombing raids on German cities added an even greater blow to civilian morale, particularly the horrors of the firestorm that engulfed Hamburg in 1943. Goebbels took advantage of the Allied unconditional surrender proclamation in January of that year to try to stiffen civilian resolve to fight to the bitter end. The extent to which this propaganda windfall actually changed popular devotion to the war effort is by no means certain, however.

The German economy, geared to Hitler's rearmament "in breadth" approach, did not come close to total mobilization until 1942. By then, the growing difficulties on the eastern front gave Germany little option but to move in that direction. At this point Dr. Fritz Todt, minister of armaments since 1940, gained greater authority to deal with the overall economy, but he had only begun the process of converting industry to total war when he died in a plane crash early in 1942. Albert Speer succeeded him and immediately took up the task with exceptional energy and great success.

Speer loomed as a curious exception to most of the Nazi henchmen who surrounded Hitler and basked in his reflected glory while seeking their own aggrandizement. By contrast, Speer viewed himself as an artist and technician operating beyond the realm of politics. While clearly aware of the monstrous nature of Nazism and Hitler's policies, he considered them irrelevant to the sphere in which he worked and attempted to isolate himself from them. Speer had joined the Nazi party as a young architect in 1931 and soon came to the attention of the Führer, especially for his skill in designing and planning party rallies. He became Hitler's favorite architect and in 1934 received the honor of designing the facilities for the party's annual rallies in Nuremberg. Three years later, he became responsible for plans to transform Berlin into a capital worthy of a leader such as Hitler, complete with buildings that would last forever. Speer shared the Führer's love of an architectural style "in which pseudo-classical elements, excessive in size, and lack of charm combined to create a solemn emptiness."* His flair for organization and innovation prompted Hitler to choose him as Todt's successor at the age of 36, certainly one of the Führer's most inspired decisions. Speer quickly set out to increase production dramatically, develop new and better weapons, improve transportation, and eliminate waste. By 1943, he had placed the Reich's economy on what approached a full wartime level.

Despite Speer's efforts, much of German industry was still producing consumer goods. Speer also faced competition and obstruction from the many governmental and party organizations that played roles in the economy. His most notable adversary was Fritz Sauckel, who controlled industrial manpower in his capacity as plenipotentiary for labor mobilization. Sauckel successfully resisted Speer's attempt to take charge of all labor in Germany as well as in occupied countries in the interest of greater efficiency and a more thorough mobilization of resources. Speer and Sauckel quarreled in particular over the use of foreign labor. In Speer's view, it would be more effective to develop industries in occupied countries, thus creating a more contented work force by allowing foreign laborers to remain in their homelands. Sauckel would not have it. He insisted on rounding up foreign workers and shipping them to Germany as slave laborers,

*Joachim C. Fest, *The Face of the Third Reich: Portraits of the Nazi Leadership* (New York: Pantheon Books, 1970), p. 202.

a practice that provided little incentive for the workers and instilled in them an intense hatred of their Nazi masters.

As early as April 1942, Speer urged that women be recruited for industrial jobs. But Hitler and Sauckel both resisted, holding steadfastly to their belief that a woman's place was in the home. It was not until 1943 that women, 17 to 45 years of age, were required to register for compulsory labor. From that point, they became increasingly prominent in war industries and eventually were more numerous than male workers. But their wages continued to hover as much as 25 percent below those of men. Despite these and other problems, most notably the devastating Allied air raids, Speer produced remarkable results, increasing war production significantly.

In February 1943, soon after the Stalingrad debacle, Goebbels proclaimed a campaign of total war in an address to a crowd of Nazi enthusiasts in Berlin's Sportpalast. During his speech, he shouted, "Do you want total war?" His audience, carefully selected for its loyalty and zeal, thundered back, "Yes!" But the results of this attempt at total mobilization proved highly disappointing. Despite the ringing support expressed at the Sportpalast, party functionaries did not flock to the factories. Indeed, Martin Bormann, Hitler's deputy, refused to allow party workers to be recruited for work in war industries. In the crowning act of folly, the Nazis also continued to use thousands of able-bodied members of the SS to round up and transport Jews to death camps.

Goebbels tried again to mobilize Germany in a total war effort in July 1944. Now that it was much too late, he enjoyed more success. Stringent measures went into effect in an eleventh-hour attempt to cheat fate. The age limit for compulsory labor for women rose to 50, and all males, ages 16 to 65, were required to register, while younger children found themselves liable for agricultural work. But although Speer managed to eliminate many of the restrictions that had formerly hampered his efforts, he could not accomplish the impossible, and when Allied air power began to concentrate on attacking oil and communications targets, the increasing fuel shortage made attempts to increase production meaningless.

An anti-Nazi, antiwar opposition movement had developed in Germany well before the war, but in the existing police state conditions, it encountered tremendous obstacles. It began with civilian opponents on the left of the political spectrum. But both Social Democrats and Communists were so weakened by early Nazi moves against them that they accomplished nothing. A number of conservatives also opposed Hitler from an early date. These people disliked democracy and favored a traditional authoritarian government, but they detested the Nazi regime because of its extremism and Hitler's reckless foreign policy. Carl Goerdler, the former mayor of Leipzig, became the chief link between them and disaffected members of the army officer corps. Goerdler worked closely with General Beck, Halder's predecessor as chief of staff. Beck had led the unsuccessful military conspiracy at the time of the Sudetenland Crisis in 1938. After Beck's resignation in August 1938, Goerdler collaborated with Colonel Hans Oster, chief of the central division of army intelligence. Hitler's bloodless victory at the Munich Conference, of course, had cut the ground out from under the conspirators. Despite their opposition to Hitler, these conservatives believed that Germany had a right to its pre–World War I borders as well as Austria and the Sudetenland. They clung to their desire to retain these territories long after it should have been apparent that the Allies would never allow such gains, even if the resistance succeeded in ridding Germany of Hitler and the Nazis.

Another opposition group, consisting primarily of members of the aristocracy, was much less wedded to the conservative and nationalistic past and was more realistic in its approach. The Kreisau Circle, as it was called, disavowed German territorial gains and hoped to improve relations with both France and Poland. It even spoke of the possibility of a federation of European states. As time passed, however, some of its members also expressed a desire to retain the German-populated areas that Hitler had taken. Military involvement in the opposition waxed and waned according to the fortunes of war in the early years of the conflict but blossomed anew when the invasion of the Soviet Union soured. Starting in 1942, various plots to assassinate Hitler developed and led to an actual attempt on the Führer's life in July 1944.*

Less violent sources of opposition developed within the churches. Although they had originally rallied to the support of the Nazi regime following Hitler's rise to power, relations between the church and the state remained tenuous. The Nazis were fundamentally opposed to the Christian moral code, but, despite periodic outbursts of antireligious activity, Hitler was reluctant to push this hostility to the point of alienating Christians from his regime. Once the war began, he especially wanted to maintain both Protestant and Catholic support and ordered an end to anti-Christian activity, but tension mounted nevertheless. Bormann was especially outspoken in his contempt for the churches. Religious opposition to the regime eventually focused on the Nazi policy of extermination of the mentally ill and retarded. Clemens von Galen, the Catholic archbishop of Munster, delivered a sermon in 1941 that somewhat belatedly denounced the Nazi practice of euthanasia. Hitler was so concerned about antagonizing the Catholics that he terminated the program shortly afterward. Unfortunately, the Catholic church refrained from making similar attacks against the Nazi policy of exterminating Jews.

Some Protestant leaders also stood up to the Nazis when they attempted to interfere with the independence and theology of the churches. Among them was Martin Niemöller, a Lutheran pastor in Berlin. Niemöller, who had served as a U-boat commander in World War I, was arrested by the Gestapo in 1937 and languished for years in a variety of concentration camps. The theologian Dietrich Bonhoeffer became an active conspirator against Hitler and eventually lost his life in this cause. Both Niemöller and Bonhoeffer had spoken against the Nazis' anti-Semitic policies during the early days of the regime. The Jehovah's Witnesses were the most consistently anti-Nazi religious group, however. They steadfastly refused to cooperate with the regime and suffered severe persecution for their heroic opposition.

A small resistance movement also developed among some students at the University of Munich, who formed the White Rose group in the spring of 1942. Led by Hans Scholl, his sister Sophie, and Christoph Probst, the members of the White Rose printed and distributed pamphlets denouncing the Nazis and the war they had launched. Although characterized by perhaps the purest motives of any of the opposition groups, their efforts had no real effect. Their short history came to an especially poignant end when the Gestapo arrested the Scholls and Probst in the winter of 1943. They lost their heads to the guillotine soon afterward.

Although Goebbels appears to have recognized after Stalingrad that Germany was likely to lose the war, he never slackened his propaganda efforts to bolster civilian morale. He even sponsored the epic film *Kolberg,* which depicted the heroic resistance of the Prussian city of that name during the Napoleonic Wars. Intended to convince the German people that a united nation could overcome even the most overwhelming odds, the film took almost two years to complete. Despite the pressing need for troops at the front, Goebbels diverted large numbers of soldiers to serve as extras in this enterprise. A total of 185,000 eventually took part, although not all at once. When the film finally appeared, the Third Reich's days were numbered, as were those of Goebbels himself. Clearly, it did not fulfill its ambitious purpose.

Another Nazi stratagem that failed to fulfill the hopes placed in it was the *Volkssturm* (People's Storm), a paramilitary defense force. Made up of boys as young as 16 and men as old as 60, it

*See Chapter 22 for an account of the 1944 attempt on Hitler's life.

was viewed by Hitler as a last-ditch effort to stem the Allied tide. Created in November 1944, the few units that came into existence were poorly equipped, barely trained, and hardly composed of the finest fighting men. Those that saw action usually disintegrated quickly.

BRITAIN: TOWARD TOTAL MOBILIZATION

The responses of Britain and the United States to the challenge of total war posed a dramatic contrast to the confused and uneven German approach to the same task. Despite Hitler's accusation that they were soft and decadent, the Western democracies proved able to mobilize their resources far more completely, in a much more rational manner, and with exceptional dedication.

At first, however, Britain approached the conflict with less than an all-out effort. To be sure, Parliament passed an Emergency Powers Act in September 1939 that gave the government authority to control the economy in the interest of winning the war. But, in keeping with Chamberlain's vision of a war of limited liability, the British hoped to keep their military commitment to a minimum, placing their faith instead in the naval blockade, the strength of the French army, and the Maginot line. British war industries did not operate at full capacity for many months. In fact, much of British industry remained devoted to the production of consumer goods, and automobile dealers proudly displayed their new models for 1940. As late as the spring of that year, unemployment still hovered at 1 million, while the government had done little to stockpile food and raw materials. The strange atmosphere of the "phony war" did not stimulate a sense of urgency.

The greatest concern in Britain, as it had been during the interwar years, focused on the threat of aerial attack. Accordingly, the government adopted measures to strengthen British air defenses and to deal with damage caused by bombing and fires. It also launched a program of the evacuation of mothers and their children from the cities. Over 3 million of them quickly found refuge in rural areas and small towns, but most returned home when weeks and then months passed without air raids. The government also established new ministries for economic warfare, food, shipping, and information.

The real change in Great Britain came as a result of the debacle in France in 1940 and the looming threat of bombardment and invasion. The first step occurred with Churchill's ascent to power and his formation of a coalition cabinet as well as a war cabinet similar to those of World War I. One of Churchill's most important appointments was his selection of Lord Beaverbrook for the new post of minister of aircraft production. Beaverbrook, of course, greatly accelerated the production of Spitfire and Hurricane fighters during the Battle of Britain. His efforts also contributed significantly to the great increase in bomber production. During 1941, the British turned out a total of 20,000 aircraft, and the number continued to grow in the following years.

Under the direction of the famous economist John Maynard Keynes, the government embarked on a massive program to harness the entire economy to the formidable task of winning the war. It began with an ambitious survey of all the economic and human resources of the country. When completed in April 1941, this study provided massive data that the government utilized to make the most efficient use of national resources. Virtually the entire economy came under government direction, while railroads and ports were subject to actual government management. A nationwide system soon went into effect to provide for the allocation of all kinds of resources, the establishment of price controls, and the rationing of a large variety of commodities, including food. In late 1941, Parliament passed a National Services Act empowering the government to conscript all men, 18 to 50, for either the armed forces or industrial and other types of essential service. Before long, women were also subject to this provision, and over 2 million were eventually employed in war-related work. A vast expansion of war industries took place, and from 1940 to 1942 Britain produced more tanks and aircraft than Germany. Only with the beginning of the transformation of the Nazi economy in 1942 did this situation start to change. The amount of British land under cultivation also increased impressively, as every available patch of ground was soon transformed into a garden plot.

In keeping with the coalition nature of the government, Ernest Bevin, a Labour party and trade union leader, received the post of minister of labor. Bevin acted as a virtual dictator over labor allocation and regulation. But, despite stringent controls over the work force, Britain experienced little unrest among its workers. Patriotism, satisfaction over the end of unemployment, widespread respect for Bevin, provision for overtime pay, price controls, and a general improvement in the standard of living all contributed to relative tranquility.

Britain's massive investment in the war placed a serious strain on the country's financial resources. Half the national output of goods and services went into the war effort, while exports dropped dramatically and imports of food and other commodities accelerated sharply. In an effort to control inflation and avoid borrowing, the government sought to pay for as much as possible through increased taxation. By 1941, the basic tax rate reached 50 percent of earnings, and corporate excess profits were taxed at 100 percent. But this was not nearly enough. Britain had borrowed heavily from Commonwealth countries and the United States as its gold reserves dwindled alarmingly to pay for imports. The introduction of American lend-lease aid in 1941 did help to ease this problem but at a price.

The United States drove a hard bargain, gaining an end to restrictions on American trade with Commonwealth members, the acquisition of most of Britain's investments in foreign countries, and limitations on British exports. In 1942, the United States also obtained Britain's acceptance of a Reciprocal Aid Agreement, which established "reverse lend-lease." This required the British to provide material aid of various kinds to American forces stationed in Britain, ultimately amounting to $6 billion. In proportion to the British national income, this represented as high a figure as lend-lease did to the American national wealth.

Britain also used propaganda to build enthusiasm for the war effort at home as well as sympathy among neutral nations, especially the United States before its entry into the conflict. As in World War I, the British proved most adept at psychological warfare and were far more believable in other countries than the Germans. They benefited from the fact that, in the eyes of their own citizens as well as the peoples of many other countries, theirs was a just war against an evil enemy. It took little, if any, exaggeration on their part to portray the conflict in those terms. The Special Operations Executive (SOE), intended by Churchill as the means to "set Europe ablaze," fell far short of inspiring the immense resistance activity in occupied countries that he had envisaged. But it did provide encouragement and hope that an Allied victory would ultimately liberate the peoples of Nazi-dominated Europe.

The British civilian population suffered far less from bombing than did the Germans and was able to avoid the horrors of land warfare altogether. But it did sustain 300,000 casualties, including 65,000 dead, as well as widespread destruction from conventional bombing and the later V weapons. British civilians also had to put up with wartime austerity—shortages, rationing, and queuing to obtain items in short supply. Mutual experiences, such as waiting out air raids in crowded shelters, and shared responsibilities, such as serving as air raid wardens and fire spotters, helped bring people from various walks of life together and break down class divisions. For example, lower-class refugees from large cities often took up lodgings with middle-class families in small towns.

The recognition that all classes were sharing in the great crusade to defeat Hitler also led to a new interest among political leaders in social reform. The tremendous growth in the scope of state activities in running the war and mobilizing the economy opened the prospect of a greater role for the government in regard to social problems after the conflict. Churchill's Conservative party as well as the Labour and Liberal parties shared this interest in the welfare of society, although Labour was the most vocal.

But it was Lord Beveridge, a Liberal and long-time champion of reform, who was the driving force behind a famous report that appeared in 1942 calling for a system of insurance that would guarantee at least a subsistence level of income for all citizens as well as medical care and what amounted to "cradle to the grave" security. Although the Beveridge Report was widely publicized and highly popular, the government did not officially commit itself to such an ambitious program. Nevertheless, it did endorse many of the report's provisions the following year. In 1944, it also approved a proposal made by Beveridge in a second report for measures to reduce future unemployment to no more than 3 percent of the work force. Parliament passed legislation the same year to extend the right to a secondary education to all citizens.

In keeping with the precedent of World War I, the British postponed parliamentary elections until the end of the European war, although one should have been held as early as 1940. In the meantime, the coalition government provided a role for all parties in directing the country and the conflict.

THE AMERICAN GIANT AWAKENS

While Britain's mobilization for total war was remarkable as well as far more extensive and efficient than that of Nazi Germany, the British clearly did not have the huge economic resources or the vast population of the United States. Of all the belligerent powers, America was to perform the most prodigious feats in producing implements of war. Of key importance in its ability to accomplish this exceptional transformation was the fact that when the war began its industrial facilities were not being utilized to anything close to their full potential due to the lingering effects of the Great Depression. Despite the fact that it produced more steel than any other country on the eve of the outbreak of the European conflict, it was only using one-third of its capacity. Ten million men were still unemployed in 1939. But U.S. industry had become more efficient during the '30s with the introduction of new techniques and equipment. The government had also approved measures that set the stage for a great expansion in output by authorizing the doubling of the navy's strength in 1940 and planning to increase vastly the size of the air force. All of this meant that, once the United States entered the conflict, it could accelerate production without creating an undue strain on industry. At the same time, it would finally end the severe unemployment that had persisted for more than a decade.

Along with this immense industrial potential, the country became a full participant in the war with a totally united people. The Japanese attack on Pearl Harbor had seen to that. It ended the conflict between isolationists and interventionists that had grown increasingly heated during 1940 and 1941. Most isolationists quickly endorsed what they now accepted as a just war. Those who did not lapsed into silence. Large numbers of men rushed to the recruiting offices to volunteer for the armed forces. Before long, new patriotic songs such as "Remember Pearl Harbor" and "We Did It before and We Can Do It again" gained popularity. Somewhat later, "Praise the Lord and Pass the Ammunition" became a big hit. Anti-Japanese tunes proliferated as the war progressed, including "You're a Sap, Mr. Jap," while Spike Jones and his irreverent City Slickers lampooned Hitler in "Der Fuehrer's Face."

Unfortunately, as a part of this rush to unity, paranoia blossomed in the form of an irrational fear of the Japanese living in the United States. Soon after Pearl Harbor, this hysteria reached a crescendo in West Coast states. Fear of invasion and sabotage by an enemy "fifth column" led to demands that Japanese-Americans be interned in camps for the duration of the war. Few people argued against this shameful violation of the civil rights of U.S. citizens. President Roosevelt bowed to this pressure and in February 1942 approved an army order providing for the removal of 112,000 Americans of Japanese ancestry and

FIGURE 20-1 Mountains form a dramatic background for the grim reality of life in a war relocation camp for Americans of Japanese ancestry. (*National Archives*)

resident Japanese aliens from their homes. These unfortunate victims had no choice but to abandon their jobs, businesses, and farms and submit to internment in "relocation centers" in seven Western states. Although starting in 1943 the government allowed 35,000 Japanese-Americans to leave the camps in return for loyalty oaths and agreements not to settle on the West Coast, the camps remained in operation until January 1945.

The government did not take any measures against Germans and Italians who were American citizens except those charged with specific acts of disloyalty. But it did require enemy aliens to register, and those who were considered to be dangerous were also interned. Only 1,228 Germans and 232 Italians found themselves subjected to this kind of treatment, however. Most Italians gained their release within a few months of Italy's surrender, while the Germans remained confined until the end of the conflict. The government also made provision for men who refused to accept military service because of matters of conscience. Most of these conscientious objectors performed alternative service or were assigned to noncombatant positions in the armed forces. About 5,000 men refused either of these options and received prison terms instead. Perhaps the most famous person to claim conscientious objector status was the movie actor Lew Ayres, who had starred in the 1930 antiwar classic *All Quiet on the Western Front*.

The great sense of unity that the attack on Pearl Harbor had instilled in the American people soon manifested itself in various other forms of patriotic expression. And while the belief in a postwar world that would be safe for democracy, which had been so characteristic of the approach to World War I, was more subdued, it clearly was not absent. It was present in the war bond drives and civil defense preparations for the unlikely possibility of enemy air attacks and in scrap metal drives, which proved more useful for providing a sense of participation in the war effort than for any real material advantage. But perhaps the most strident example of this martial spirit came in the form of popular movies.

Films about the war in Europe usually portrayed Germans as boorish louts speaking guttural English. Sometimes this characterization took a humorous guise as in *To Be or Not to Be,* starring Jack Benny and Carole Lombard, who died soon after the film's release in a plane crash while on a war bond promotion tour. Among its best-remembered scenes was one in which an actor posing as Hitler ordered two Nazi soldiers to jump out of a plane without benefit of parachutes, which they gladly did while shouting "Heil Hitler!" Other films, such as *None Shall Escape,* took a much more serious view of the vicious reality of Nazi rule in occupied countries. The movie industry depicted Italian soldiers in most cases as likable buffoons, such as the general in *Five Graves to Cairo* who sang opera "but not Wagner," while clearly leaving much to be desired as a leader of men. In contrast, a common Italian soldier in the Humphrey Bogart film *Sahara* was a completely sympathetic character forced by Mussolini and the Fascists into fighting a war he hated.

It was the Japanese who provided the favorite targets for patriotic excess in films, however. They were invariably portrayed as bestial and devoid of any human feeling. Perhaps the most blatant example of this approach occurred in *Destination Tokyo* starring Cary Grant. In one scene, a surfaced American submarine shot down an attacking Japanese plane. Afterward, the pilot, who had escaped and was in the process of being fished out of the water by the benevolent submarine crew, proceeded to stab one of his rescuers in the back. His reward for this obviously stupid and suicidal act was to be dispatched by another crew member operating a machine gun. In a scene from *Objective Burma!* starring Errol Flynn, an American force discovered the mutilated bodies of another U.S. unit that the Japanese had massacred, clearly an atrocity not without precedent. But on this occasion, it provided the cue for an American war correspondent to denounce the enemy in an emotional outburst as "degenerate moral idiots, stinking little savages," who should be wiped off the face of the earth.

The number of men and women in the armed forces increased dramatically, eventually totaling 15 million. The draft had already increased the army's strength to 1.6 million by the time the Japanese attacked Pearl Harbor. This number rose to 8.3 million by the end of hostilities in 1945. The navy also grew from 325,000 to 3.4 million. General Lewis Hershey supervised the nationwide system of draft boards that carried out the formidable task of selecting the huge number of draftees who formed the overwhelming proportion of this manpower.

American industry saw to it that these vastly increased armed forces were equipped with enormous amounts of weapons and other materiel. Automobile plants soon converted their facilities to produce tanks, trucks, jeeps, and aircraft. Shipyards turned out staggering numbers of vessels of all kinds, from aircraft carriers and battleships to transports and merchantmen. The efforts of Henry J. Kaiser, a California industrialist who earned the nickname "Sir Launchalot," were especially notable. Kaiser built vast shipyards on the West Coast and greatly reduced the amount of time needed to construct ships. By 1945, tonnage had increased by 42 percent. Among the vessels produced was the Liberty ship, a new type of merchantman that could be built quickly in large numbers and at relatively low cost. Later, the larger and swifter Victory ships appeared. Also important were landing craft, such as the LSI (landing ship infantry) and LST (landing ship tank), which also came into service in abundance. Aircraft production rose from less than 6,000 in 1939 to over 96,000 in 1944.

Such a gigantic transformation of the economy required centralized direction on a significant scale, although the American system did not come close to matching that of Britain. The country's experience with a similar task in World War I provided a useful precedent, but this did not mean that all would go smoothly. Indeed, the vast scope of the war effort, coupled with Roosevelt's managerial style, led to a proliferation of agencies dealing with various aspects of mobilization. As in the earlier conflict, this resulted in considerable confusion and problems of divided authority. As early as 1939, Roosevelt had created a War Resources Board, which assumed responsibility for planning the conversion of industry to war production. Soon after Pearl Harbor, he appointed Donald Nelson, a Sears, Roebuck executive, to head the War Production Board (WPB). Subject only to the president's supervision, Nelson possessed the power to allocate resources and regulate production. Unfortunately, he proved so easygoing that he could not prevent the army and navy from bypassing the WPB and dealing directly with large corporations. Nevertheless, Nelson did ban the production of many items he considered nonessential, including automobiles for civilian use, refrigerators, and most other electric appliances. In addition, he halted housing construction except for homes for defense workers.

Roosevelt also created the Office of Economic Stabilization (OES), headed by his friend James Byrnes, a former senator from South Carolina whom the president had appointed to the Supreme Court only a few months before. Byrnes received the authority to control prices, wages, profits, and rents. In May 1943, Roosevelt elevated Byrnes to direct the newly formed Office of War Mobilization (OWM), which had vast powers over the entire home front. Byrnes proved a skillful administrator. Despite the mushrooming agencies, overlapping jurisdictions, and bickering that marked the American war effort, remarkable progress came with astonishing speed. During 1942, U.S. production equaled that of all Axis powers. In 1943, it was one and a half times as great and, in 1944, twice the output of Germany and Japan combined.

This sudden and spectacular expansion of industrial activity led to an urgent need for labor. With so many men going into the armed forces, opportunity beckoned for numerous people who had been previously unemployed or engaged in menial labor. Among them were large numbers of African Americans. They migrated from the South to seek jobs in the industrial cities of the North and on the West Coast. Unfortunately, they also encountered discrimination. A. Philip Randolph, an African American leader, gained some alleviation of the problem by threatening a march on Washington by 50,000 black citizens to protest racial discrimination in both industry and the federal government during the summer of 1941. To head off such an embarrassing development, Roosevelt issued an executive order establishing a Fair Employment Practices Committee, but the committee suffered from poor funding and a meager staff. Although some progress was made, especially in government employment, discrimination persisted in industry. The great influx of African Americans also increased racial tensions in the North and West and in some cases riots. The worst of these occurred in Detroit in June 1943, when an exchange of insults between blacks and whites led to violence that claimed the lives of 25 blacks and nine whites. National Guard units were needed to restore order.

Women also moved into jobs in war industries in large numbers. Often they were the wives of servicemen, although many were single. Their wages remained lower than those of male workers, however, and they often encountered hostility when they moved into positions previously reserved for men. Despite these problems, many women enjoyed their newly found independence. The overall increase in female employment was not as great as might be expected, however, rising from 25 to 36 percent of the work force. Women also entered the armed forces. During 1942, the government formed what became the Women's Army Corps (WAC), as well as equivalents in the navy (WAVES), coast guard, (SPARS), and marines. The latter contingent never received a nickname, and the marine corps reacted with hostility to the suggestion that they be called "marinettes." A total of 215,000 women eventually enlisted in the four branches of the military, 100,000 in the WACS and 86,000 in the WAVES. They served in a variety of noncombatant positions. Yet despite the contribution of women to the war effort, there was little change in the traditional male view that woman's place was in the home.

FIGURE 20-2 American women put finishing touches on the noses of bombers at Douglas Aircraft's plant in Long Beach, California. (*National Archives*)

In an effort to promote harmonious relations between management and labor, the government established the National War Labor Board (NWLB) in 1942. Both management and labor agreed to settle disputes peacefully in the interest of the war effort and to accept the mediation of the NWLB in cases that could not be settled through collective bargaining. While this system certainly did not eliminate work stoppages, for the most part strikes tended to be short. The most serious of them occurred in 1943, when the United Mine Workers, under the leadership of John L. Lewis, carried out a lengthy walkout. Although the government and unions agreed in 1943 to limit wage increases in most cases to 15 percent, workers enjoyed unprecedented prosperity, in large part because of overtime pay.

Farmers shared in this prosperity. With the help of unusually good weather during much of the war, they harvested the largest crops in history and achieved equally impressive results in meat production. Although farmers urged that prices for agricultural commodities be allowed to rise to their natural levels, Roosevelt warned that this would lead to runaway inflation. He insisted on price controls coupled with government subsidies to farmers instead. Farm income doubled between 1940 and 1943, while farm mortgage debt dropped significantly. Despite the upsurge in farm production, the demand for food in the armed forces and among America's allies as well as on the home front led to the imposition of rationing. The Office of Price Administration (OPA), established in 1942 to deal with the problem of imposing price ceilings, also was responsible for rationing. It used this power to limit the distribution of such items as meat, butter, sugar, coffee, and canned goods, as well as nonfood products such as gasoline and tires. The combination of price controls and rationing retarded inflation and facilitated a more equitable distribution of scarce commodities. Such measures could not overcome human nature and the desire for profit, however, and as in all other belligerent countries, some people sold rationed items on the black market for prices significantly higher than those established by the OPA. Shortages also developed in many unrationed commodities. Cigarettes especially were often in short supply, and lines grew to impressive lengths when they did become available. The American Tobacco Company changed the color of its Lucky Strike package from green to white, allegedly because the green ink contained metal needed for military production. Although the company's ads proclaimed that "Lucky Strike green has gone to war," cynics charged that this was a ploy to get rid of the old color because white was believed to be more appealing to women smokers. Whichever version was true, Lucky Strike green never returned from the war.

It was one thing to boost production to unprecedented levels, it was another to pay for it. World War II cost the government more than $300 billion, compared to only $32 billion for World War I. Roosevelt hoped to finance much of this through increased taxation but encountered opposition in Congress. Nevertheless, Congress did raise income and excise taxes. It also provided for a graduated percentage tax increase according to personal income, sharply higher corporation taxes, and a 95 percent tax on profits in excess of prewar expectations. In all, taxes paid for 40 percent of the war's cost. The government attempted to cover as much as possible of the remainder through the sale of war bonds to American citizens. A series of eight war bond drives ultimately accounted for about three-fifths of the total expenditures. Despite all of these measures, the federal deficit rose from $49 billion in 1941 to $259 billion in 1945.

Unlike Britain, which faced a much more direct threat, elections continued as usual in the United States. A congressional election in 1942 resulted in substantial Republican gains in both the House and the Senate. In 1944, Roosevelt, although weary and suffering from heart disease and high blood pressure, ran for a fourth term. He defeated Thomas E. Dewey, the Republican governor of New York, but the margin of victory, 3.6 million votes, was his smallest.

THE SOVIETS REBOUND FROM DISASTER

The Soviet Union shared some of the same weaknesses that plagued Germany in meeting the challenge of total war. Like the Nazi regime, the Soviet dictatorship in theory exercised total control over all aspects of life, but unlike Germany, this domination extended to the economy. Yet in reality, it too suffered from divided authority, inefficiency, and confusion. Although the state directed a centralized economy, the sheer size of the country and the excessive bureaucratic procedures characteristic of the system necessitated that many decisions be made on the local level. In the process, local officials often circumvented the cumbersome formal system. And, despite the Soviet Union's reputation for being a "garrison state" even in peacetime, it had devised no detailed strategic plan for dealing with a possible German invasion or mobilizing the economy for total war. When Hitler launched Operation Barbarossa in 1941, these weaknesses played a major role in the early Soviet disasters.

Just as Hitler often bore responsibility for German mistakes and defeats, Stalin contributed in no small way to the catastrophic setbacks of 1941–42. The Soviet dictator's disregard for human life in his ruthless pursuit of victory was perhaps the most important factor in the appalling losses suffered by the Red Army not only in the early months but in the later triumphant phases of the war as well. Stalin's refusal to heed the many warnings of a German attack, along with his insistence on maintaining so many troops close to the border, his obsession with reckless counterattacks, and his refusal to authorize evacuations from untenable positions, repeatedly placed Soviet troops in jeopardy. During the prewar period, he had also failed to provide for any kind of overall coordination of Soviet forces. This oversight created confusion and an almost total absence of centralized control during the first days of the invasion. It was not until the establishment of the GKO as a war cabinet and Stavka as a general military headquarters that coordination began to take the place of chaos.

Even then, Stalin dominated both bodies and played the major role in the deployment of troops that led to the disastrous encirclements at Kiev and Vyazma in 1941 and Kharkov in 1942. "But for Stalin," two authorities on the Soviet war effort have charged, "it may well be argued, the Germans would never have reached Moscow or Leningrad, the Caucasus or Stalingrad."*

Stalin and the Soviet government also made serious mistakes in their failure to provide plans to mobilize the Soviet economy for war. To be sure, much of the country's industrial resources were already producing war materiel, but no master plan existed for the coordination of the entire economy, and Soviet leaders had failed to disperse industries to areas in the deep interior. As a result, well over half of the Soviet Union's industrial capacity lay in the western and southern regions that fell to the enemy by the fall of 1941. Naïvely trusting in the Red Army's ability to stop an invasion quickly, the Soviets also did not devise a plan to evacuate industry from the threatened areas. They finally had to improvise such measures in the most unfavorable conditions and in many cases were unable to carry out the task before the arrival of the Germans. Nevertheless, the Soviets did achieve notable results from their evacuation program.

While the evacuation of industry played a significant role, it was certainly not the only factor in the process of placing the economy on a total war basis. The conversion of nonmilitary industry to war production was of key importance. This task also required speed and took place largely through local improvisation with relatively little centralized direction. Although this approach provided badly needed war materiel in the short run, the lack of overall planning led to excessive concentration on this kind of production. It had the unfortunate byproduct of dangerously restricting the output of steel, fuel, electrical power, and other resources necessary for continuing production of war materiel in the future. As a result, the economy fell into a serious crisis during the first half of 1942.

A severe shortage of labor also developed when many skilled workers entered the army. It grew even worse as the terrible losses in military personnel mounted, necessitating wholesale replacements, while many workers were trapped in enemy-occupied areas. It became necessary to recruit unskilled laborers to replace skilled workers, with a corresponding decline in quality and efficiency. This supply of labor came largely from teenage boys, men over 50, and women. A similar shortage of workers afflicted agriculture. The peasantry had provided by far the largest proportion of recruits for the army even before 1941. To fill the resulting void in farm workers, women became the major source of labor in the production of food. By 1944, they provided almost 75 percent of the rural work force and three-fifths of the industrial workers. But their tradition-minded male superiors denied them access to most administrative and managerial positions.

Prisoners also constituted a large portion of the labor force. These included both political prisoners and actual criminals, who worked as slave laborers in industry, construction, mining, and farming. Perhaps more than 250,000 of them labored in appalling conditions, and many died because of hunger and other privations as well as savage discipline. The Soviets used other prisoners in penal battalions attached to the Red Army. These unfortunate men performed especially dangerous duties and suffered the heaviest casualties of any Soviet military units.

As much of the best agricultural land, especially in the Ukraine, fell to the Germans, the Soviets faced a critical food crisis that was compounded by the shortage of labor. As a result, food production lagged far below prewar levels throughout the war. This decline reached bottom

*John Barber and Mark Harrison, *The Soviet Home Front, 1941–1945: A Social and Economic History of the USSR in World War II* (London: Longman, 1991), p. 54.

in 1943, as the Red Army recovered more and more territory formerly occupied by the Germans. For the time being, however, much of this land, devastated by either combat or the retreating enemy, could not be cultivated, while many more people had to be fed in the liberated areas.

During 1942, it became obvious that the economy was so badly disrupted and out of balance that the government had to adopt a more centralized system to coordinate all areas of production in pursuit of a more harmonious whole. The chief mechanism for this transformation was a subcommittee of the GKO called the Operations Bureau. Even at this point, much of the old, informal network of improvisation continued to function but with much closer supervision and a new system of priorities.

The magnitude of the danger created by the German invasion and the early disasters led to a change in policy regarding the role of the Communist party. During the prewar period, the government had identified the achievements of the regime with the party and downplayed nationalism. But soon after the outbreak of war, Soviet leaders portrayed the struggle in patriotic rather than ideological terms. They referred to the conflict as the Great Patriotic War and warned of the danger to Holy Mother Russia. Stalin addressed the country in stirring patriotic speeches and even cited the heroic deeds of heroes from the wars of the czarist period.

Stalin also sought a reconciliation with the Orthodox Church, which had been subjected to persecution and had been sinking more and more into oblivion since the revolution. In return for assurances of total allegiance to the state, the church gained the right to conduct services on a reasonably free basis throughout the remainder of the war. This had the effect of rallying devout citizens to the support of the regime and the war effort, but it also kindled a religious revival that survived even in the postwar years, when Stalin watered down some of the wartime concessions that had been granted to the church.

During the early months of defeat, Stalin tended to identify the war effort with the government as a whole rather than with himself. But when the Soviets began to gain the initiative and staged their increasingly successful offensives, he saw to it that he gained the lion's share of credit. Propaganda soon created a massive cult of personality dedicated to Stalin as a larger-than-life war leader and the symbol of victory. In the eyes of many Soviet citizens, he emerged as a popular hero for the first time. Indeed, despite his early catastrophic failures and continuing disdain for human life, Stalin did contribute significantly to the ultimate triumph. He learned from his mistakes and provided increasingly intelligent and undeniably firm leadership.

But the Soviet citizens played an even greater role in winning the final victory in supplying millions of people for both the armed forces and for industry and agriculture, where they produced the weapons and food that were essential for success. Most of them suffered from hunger and other privations as the standard of living plummeted. Many others, who languished for years under German occupation or in prison camps, fared far worse. Those unfortunate Soviet soldiers who fell captive to the Germans and survived this terrible ordeal found themselves treated as traitors after their liberation, because Stalin had decreed that surrender was tantamount to treason. During World War II, no country suffered as severely from start to finish as did the Soviet Union. While not all of its inhabitants rallied to the unconditional support of the regime, they all faced one glaring truth: the terrible fate that awaited them if the Germans won the war. This helped unite them in an effort that often took the form of a genuine crusade against the hated invader.

Not all Soviet citizens viewed the war as a patriotic crusade, however. This was especially true of members of the many national minorities. Large numbers of Ukrainians, Belorussians, and inhabitants of the former Baltic states initially welcomed the Germans as liberators. The brutal reality of Nazi racial policy soon turned many of them against the invaders, but some continued to collaborate, including substantial numbers who served in military units formed by the Germans. Among these armed formations was the Russian Liberation Army, led by the disillusioned former Soviet general Andrei Vlasov. But most of its soldiers were Russian prisoners of war who preferred the prospect of serving the Germans over dying from starvation or exposure in Nazi prison camps. Despite its lofty name, Vlasov's army accomplished nothing, and Vlasov himself eventually fell into Soviet hands and was executed.

The most notable example of cooperation between non-Russians and Germans took place in the Caucasus during its relatively brief period of occupation in 1942. Here the German army remained in control of administration because of the area's proximity to the front and ruled with moderation, while keeping the SS and other Nazi agencies at bay. This enlightened approach led to close relations between the invaders and various small ethnic groups. When the Germans withdrew, however, the Soviets quickly instituted a reign of terror, executing prominent collaborators and deporting the remainder of these minorities to Central Asia. Deportation to Central Asia or Siberia was also the fate of the Volga German minority of eastern Russia as well as the Tartars of the Crimea. Most of these unfortunate people were victims of "guilt by association" rather than actual collaboration.

JAPAN: CONFLICT OF INTEREST

If Germany and the Soviet Union suffered from the problems of lack of coordination, bureaucratic inefficiency and confusion, Japan was plagued even more by such difficulties. Its army and navy engaged in an extreme case of interservice rivalry at the expense of the overall war effort. Thus while attempting with considerable success to press the entire population into total war, Japan ironically found its progress toward full mobilization stymied by those who were most determined to fight the war to a victorious conclusion. It also faced a number of limitations on what it could accomplish under any circumstances. Japanese industrial resources, while considerable, paled by comparison to those of the United States. This was the case when the war began and continued to accelerate as it progressed. In 1941, the United States possessed a population almost twice as large as Japan's, an industrial potential at least seven times greater, and raw materials perhaps 78 times more plentiful. And while America enjoyed immense productivity in agriculture, Japan still featured small plot cultivation, making it at least as dependent on food imports as Britain.

Although people in the United States and Britain looked upon Japan as a dictatorship in which Tojo's authority was as great as that of Hitler, in reality the Japanese premier probably wielded less direct power than did either Churchill or Roosevelt. While he also served as war minister and at times as foreign minister as well as minister of commerce and industry, he always had to compete for power with a number of influential former premiers and aristocrats close to the emperor. Most important, the army general staff continued to exercise its traditional independence. In his new roles, Tojo was only a political leader, and real authority in Japan still lay with the army hierarchy. When Tojo finally attempted to bridge the gap by assuming the post of chief of staff of the army in February 1944, it was far too late to prevent Japan from spiraling ever closer to defeat. But it was not only the army that followed an independent course, for the navy also operated as a law unto itself.

The most critical factor in weakening Japan's war effort was the ongoing feud between the army and navy, which resulted in an almost total lack of coordination between them. The officer corps of each had utter contempt for the other, and hatred between the families of military and naval leaders in many cases dated back for generations. The two branches of service were more interested in competing with each other than in joining forces against the common enemy. The results were catastrophic. This vicious rivalry had an especially baneful effect on attempts to mobilize industry for the maximum and most efficient production of war materiel.

Officially, the ministry of commerce and a cabinet planning board were to work with industrial leaders to develop policy for the production and distribution of supplies to the army and navy. Their efforts came to nothing, however, because neither service would cooperate. Each withheld information and dealt directly with industrial firms to fulfill its needs without any consideration of the overall conduct of the war. Soon after the conflict started, the government established civilian agencies for each industry in an effort to control and coordinate production, but they proved no more successful in preventing the army and navy from going their separate ways. Later a new munitions ministry, headed by Tojo himself, tried to bring order to this chaos and failed just as miserably.

The most lamentable examples of this destructive rivalry developed in the aircraft industry and in regard to oil supplies. Bickering over the design and production of planes as well as duplication of effort led to the underutilization of available industrial facilities. In 1943, Japan produced only 10,000 aircraft despite having the potential to turn out more than 50,000. The army managed to gain control over 85 percent of the oil supply from the East Indies, even though its needs were limited. This confronted the navy, which was dependent on oil to fuel its ships, with a critical shortage that seriously hampered its operations. The army even built its own tankers and later started to construct submarines, allegedly for the purpose of supplying its far-flung garrisons, a decision that accomplished nothing.

As in other belligerent countries, labor shortages plagued Japanese industry. The army's insistence on drafting skilled workers, especially from industries producing materiel for the navy, did nothing to improve the situation. Students, Korean laborers, and women replaced these vital workers despite the strongly held view that women should be restricted to producing children and caring for their families. In 1942, government leaders, including Tojo, expressed empathic opposition to employing women in war work, but in 1943, they had no choice but to make women liable for labor service. In 1944, over 14 million women were employed in various occupations and played important roles in factories and mines, working in some cases as much as 16 hours a day. Although clearly intended as a temporary expedient, the release of women from their traditional role helped to instill in them a new attitude that prepared them for important changes in their position in the postwar era.

Despite the interservice rivalry, the lack of overall coordination of economic planning, and the shortage of labor, Japan built up its heavy industry. It also reduced the number of small and medium-sized firms, which strengthened the big industrialists. In the process, the Japanese increased their total industrial production by one-fourth between 1940 and 1944. Unfortunately for them, this did not begin to approach the massive rise in American industrial output. Between 1941 and 1944, for example, the Japanese turned out almost 59,000 aircraft, while the United States produced 262,000. Japan's per capita productivity actually dropped significantly as a result of the loss of skilled workers to the services.

The shortage of labor also took its toll in agriculture. Again, women along with old men and young boys and girls stepped into the breach. They managed to prevent a decline in domestic rice production until 1945, but imports fell off alarmingly due to crop failures in Korea and the growing impact of American submarine and air attacks on shipping. Fish, another important element in the Japanese diet, also became increasingly scarce as fishermen entered the service and fishing became more dangerous as American forces moved ever closer to the Japanese home islands. Hunger rose accordingly, as did the prevalence of disease associated with malnutrition. To encourage greater food production, the government reduced the rents of tenant farmers, who improved their position relative to landlords, a change that helped prepare the way for postwar land reform. The Japanese also used every available bit of land to grow food, much as the British were doing. Rationing, which was a major factor throughout the war, increased in stringency with the worsening of shortages of virtually everything. As in other warring countries, the black market flourished, and those in charge of its operations were able to obtain scarce commodities and sell them for huge profits.

The final death blows to Japan's economy came in the form of the massive fire bombing of the country's major cities in 1945 and the escalation of the American submarine campaign, which strangled the Japanese supply line to Southeast Asia. By the summer of 1945, many thousands of Japanese civilians had paid the ultimate price for the attack on Pearl Harbor, and millions of others were homeless and suffered from mounting privations and bleak prospects.

While Japan did not utilize concentration camps such as those of Nazi Germany or forced labor camps such as those of the Soviet Union, various types of civilian as well as military police maintained close surveillance of the activities of the people. Paranoia over dissent and possible espionage also increased, although almost no overt resistance to the war existed. The government also subjected newspapers and other publications to rigid censorship and engaged in an ambitious propaganda effort to glorify Japan's early victories, while either ignoring or distorting the rising number of defeats. For example, survivors of Japanese ships sunk in the Battle of Midway found themselves placed in seclusion upon their return to Japan to prevent dissemination of the news of the disaster. For years the people received a steady diet of bombastic proclamations insisting that ultimate success was assured. Eventually, however, it became impossible to disguise the scope of the debacle that was befalling Japan. As city after city fell victim to destruction from fire bombs, the Japanese people needed no confirmation from the government that the end was near. Japan had descended into the "Valley of Darkness" long before the atomic bombs devastated Hiroshima and Nagasaki.

21

Russia Moves West, 1943–44

After the disaster at Stalingrad and the retreat from the Caucasus, no real hope remained that Germany could achieve an offensive victory over the Soviet Union. The Wehrmacht had twice shown itself unable to overcome the twin obstacles of the USSR's vast distances and Soviet staying power. By early 1943, it was clear that the Red Army was superior in materiel as well as in numbers.

THE GERMANS ON THE DEFENSIVE

The Germans had managed to escape the trap that the Russians had tried to spring on their armies in the Caucasus, but Soviet forces had pushed them back to the starting point of their 1942 offensive and for a time drove well beyond this line. Two factors had prevented an even more catastrophic defeat. As the Soviets moved west, they faced the same problem that the Germans had encountered during the 1941 and 1942 offensives. Their supply lines became badly overextended while the enemy fell back on his main supply bases. Also, Field Marshal von Manstein proved himself a master of defensive warfare. He succeeded in holding Rostov long enough to enable large German forces to escape the Red Army spearhead that threatened to cut them off. Then, in February 1943, just as the Soviets appeared to be on the verge of dealing a death blow to the whole German position in the south, he delivered a brilliantly conceived counterattack. The Red Army had captured Kharkov and was driving toward the Dnieper River, but in the process it had created a deep salient with long, vulnerable flanks. Manstein sensed his opportunity and thinned out his forces in the path of the Russian advance while massing his panzers to the south and north of the overextended Soviets. He then attacked the enemy flanks and forced the Soviets to retreat. His troops recaptured Kharkov and drove beyond.

Other developments bolstered the German cause. One of the most important was Hitler's appointment of Albert Speer to the position of minister of armaments in 1942. Within a year, Speer had placed German industry on a basis approaching a full wartime footing, and his efforts greatly accelerated production of tanks and other weapons until well into 1944. Hitler also brought General Guderian back to active duty as inspector general of armored troops in February 1943. Speer and Guderian worked together to increase the quantity and improve the quality of German armor. Their efforts led to the adoption of two new models, the Tiger and the Panther. The Tiger was a heavy tank with thick armor, wide tracks, and a powerful 88-mm gun. The Panther, a medium tank, was faster and more maneuverable than the Tiger and eventually was equal or superior to the Soviet T34. Unfortunately, it suffered from various mechanical problems at first, including an alarming tendency to catch fire. It was not until the winter of 1943–44 that the Panther's designers overcame these "teething" problems.

German numerical inferiority after Stalingrad not only sounded the death knell for an offensive strategy but cast serious doubt on the possibility of a static defense as well. The Wehrmacht simply lacked the strength to defend the entire front, which sprawled from Leningrad to the Black Sea. The only hope for a successful strategy lay in an elastic defense. Such an approach required extensive withdrawals to shorten the front. As the Germans pulled back, they hoped to be able to lure the Soviets into an overly aggressive pursuit. This could create the opportunity for counterattacks similar to the one that Manstein had used to such good effect in February. Both Manstein and Guderian favored this approach. They believed that it offered the only chance to wear down the Soviets to a point that might erode their will to continue the war and open the way to a negotiated peace.

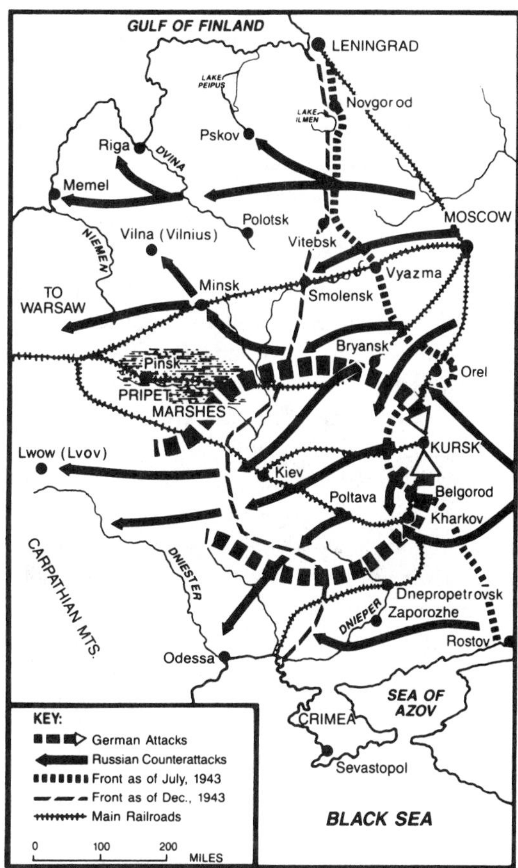

The Battle of Kursk, July 1943, and the Subsequent Soviet Offensive

OPERATION CITADEL

Manstein proposed such a strategy for the spring of 1943. The southern portion of the front in the Ukraine took the form of a large German bulge that jutted precariously eastward, well beyond the northward extension of the battle line. Manstein assumed that the Soviets would try to cut off this salient in the spring and urged that the Germans fall back toward the Dnieper when the Soviets struck. He hoped to entice the Soviets into overextending their advance. Then, when they were most vulnerable, he would attack their flank near Kiev. If all went well, the Red Army would suffer a disastrous defeat. But such an operation would necessitate abandoning the mineral-rich Donetz Basin, and Hitler was unwilling to give up this valuable territory.

Instead, the Germans adopted an alternative and much less imaginative plan that ultimately proved catastrophic. It focused on another salient, this time an enemy bulge that extended around the city of Kursk to the north of Kharkov. The OKH feared that the Soviets would stage their spring offensive from this position and urged that it be eliminated by simultaneous attacks against its northern and southern flanks. Manstein had actually suggested such an undertaking soon after his victory at Kharkov. He had insisted that the assault begin in April, before the Soviets could build up their defenses in the salient. But a series of delays forced postponement of the offensive until July.

The German plan, Operation Citadel, called for Field Marshal Günther von Kluge's Army

Group Center to attack the salient from the north while Manstein's troops struck from the south. General Zeitzler, the chief of staff, and Kluge were the foremost advocates of Citadel. Guderian was dead set against it from the start, and Manstein's enthusiasm cooled when it became clear that delays would be involved. Hitler had strong misgivings but eventually bowed to the arguments of Zeitzler and Kluge. Kluge and Guderian were old and bitter rivals. Before succeeding Bock as head of Army Group Center, Kluge had commanded the Fourth Army in Poland, France, and the 1941 Russian campaign. He considered Guderian to be bold to the point of recklessness and once charged that the panzer leader's operations "always hang by a thread." At one point Kluge challenged Guderian to a duel, but Hitler ordered the two generals to reconcile their differences.

Unfortunately for Hitler and his generals, the Russians soon learned about the entire plan from their spy network and took elaborate defensive measures. Marshal Zhukov, the hero of Moscow and Stalingrad, once again directed Soviet planning. He intended to follow his usual approach: wear down the attacking Germans and then direct powerful counterstrokes against their flanks. To facilitate this plan, the Soviets laid deep mine fields, behind which they concentrated vast quantities of artillery and antitank guns as well as large reserves of armor. Their efforts created a prodigiously strong defensive position that extended 65 miles in depth.

An army group, under General Konstantine Rokossovsky's command, defended the northern portion of the salient, while General Vatutin, one of the heroes of the Stalingrad encirclement, directed another army group along the southern flank. Rokossovsky belonged to the rising generation of generals that was supplanting the old guard in the Red Army. The son of a Polish father and a Russian mother, he became an orphan at 14 and served as a construction worker before being drafted into the czarist army in World War I. Rokossovsky joined the Red Army during the civil war and rose swiftly in rank. In 1937, it appeared as if his career were over when he landed in prison as a result of Stalin's purge of the officer corps. But he gained his release in 1940 and went on to command a corps in the Ukraine, an army in the Battle of Moscow, and an army group at Stalingrad.

FIGURE 21-1 Marshal Georgi Zhukov, the architect of the Red Army's victory. (*Sovfoto*)

When the Germans finally launched Operation Citadel on July 5, they unleashed an exceptionally powerful force of 17 panzer divisions. Despite the magnitude of their effort, the Red Army outnumbered them in manpower 1.3 million to 900,000 and enjoyed an advantage in tanks of 3,300 to 2,700. Soviet superiority in artillery was even more marked—20,000 to 10,000. The Germans soon encountered heavy losses in the mine fields, which the Soviets had situated in such a way as to channel enemy armor directly into artillery and antitank fire.

The struggle became a great battle of attrition along a front that seldom exceeded 15 miles in width. It was the greatest clash of armor of the entire war, with almost 3,000 tanks on the field at the peak of the fighting. The Germans did little more than dent the Soviet defenses. Both sides suffered exceptionally heavy losses, but whereas the Soviets could sustain theirs, the Germans were less fortunate. For them, Kursk was fatal. On July 12, Hitler ordered his generals to break off their attacks.

His action did not come a moment too soon, because the Red Army opened a powerful counteroffensive the same day. They attacked the enemy flank to the north of the Kursk salient and threatened to cut off the German forces, which had been advancing southward. On August 3, the Soviets delivered another blow against the Germans to the south of the salient and thrust toward Kharkov. The great industrial city changed hands for the fourth and last time on August 22 as General Ivan Konev's troops drove the enemy westward. Konev was another general who rose to prominence during the war. His fame ultimately became second only to that of Zhukov. Konev, whose broad face betrayed his peasant origin, had followed the usual route of future Soviet commanders. A non-commissioned officer in the czar's forces, he joined the Red Army in 1918, winning renown for his guerrilla exploits in Siberia during the civil war. He had assumed command of the Moscow front just in time to take the blame for the disasters of October 1941. For a time he appeared headed for oblivion, but Zhukov came to his rescue and made him his deputy. He became an army group commander in 1943. Despite Zhukov's kindness, Konev later became his chief rival.

The Soviets rolled on toward the Dnieper and crossed the river near Kiev at the end of September. Instead of halting their advance to organize a conventional crossing, their spearhead units simply stormed across the river with the help of small boats and improvised rafts. They established several bridgeheads on the west bank before the Germans could consolidate their defense. By early November, the Red Army had recaptured Kiev.

THE GERMANS BEGIN TO CRUMBLE

If the failure at Stalingrad had ended all hope for a German offensive victory, the disaster at Kursk and the subsequent Soviet counteroffensive eliminated any chance for a successful defensive struggle. Hitler's panzer forces never fully recovered from the triphammer blows of the summer and fall of 1943. And despite Speer's amazing achievement in increasing German tank production, it did not keep pace with Soviet output of armor. During 1944–45, Germany produced 8,400 tanks, a figure almost three times greater than the entire armored force that had launched the Russian campaign in 1941, but the Soviets produced 10,000 T34s alone during 1944. Russian industry turned out vast quantities of other arms as well, including greatly improved aircraft, guns, mortars, and automatic infantry weapons.

By this time, American industry had also made the transition to a full wartime basis. In addition to providing a steadily increasing flow of materiel to their own armed forces, the Americans sent much more lend-lease aid to Russia. This included all types of equipment, food, and other supplies. Most significant, abundant U.S. trucks, jeeps, and other motorized vehicles gave the Red Army much greater mobility. Although America continued to send tanks as well, even the best of them, the Sherman, proved inferior to the T34.

In the aftermath of the Kursk debacle, Germany also found it impossible to replace its manpower losses, whereas the Soviets were able to draft large numbers of men from the areas they recaptured. The Red Army also absorbed partisan units that had been operating behind enemy lines. If the Soviets harbored any doubts about their ability to win the war before the Battle of Kursk, they had none afterward.

The staggering defeat at Kursk struck Hitler with tremendous impact. He now withdrew in relative isolation, with only a few people in attendance, and found refuge in his own dream world. The catastrophe increased his distrust of the generals. After all, Kursk had been their idea, not his. The OKH had planned the operation, and Zeitzler had talked him into overcoming his own doubts. In the future, he relied more and more on his own intuition. But even though he had been right about Kursk, he now returned to the rigid "stand fast" mentality that had led to the Stalingrad encirclement and soon contributed to new

FIGURE 21-2 Soviet partisans in action behind the German front. (*Library of Congress*)

disasters. The first of these occurred when the Führer rejected Manstein's plea that he evacuate the Seventeenth Army from the Crimea. His refusal enabled the Soviets to cut off this force in November.

THE SOVIETS ROLL ON

Meanwhile, the Red Army continued to drive westward. In January 1944, it penetrated into the southeastern corner of prewar Poland. The same month also witnessed the lifting of the 900-day siege of Leningrad. In early February, Soviet troops, operating from bridgeheads west of the Dnieper, attempted to cut off a German salient around the town of Korsun. Konev sent a spearhead slashing northwestward, while Vatutin swung to the southeast. The two forces came together on February 3, trapping almost 75,000 Germans. Konev received a promotion to the rank of marshal as his reward. Vatutin was not so fortunate. He died of wounds inflicted by a band of Ukrainian nationalists soon afterward.

In March, Konev launched an incredible operation, his "mud offensive," which took place during the worst part of the spring thaw in the Ukraine. It provided ample evidence of the growing skill of Red Army commanders and violated all the rules of war. Playing on the advantage of complete surprise, it resulted in another great Soviet victory. The keys to this achievement were the wide-tracked T34 tank and the American four-wheel-drive truck; both were able to perform efficiently in the abominable conditions. Before the month was over, the Soviets swept into Bessarabia in prewar Rumania. These defeats so enraged Hitler that he dismissed both his army group commanders in the south, Manstein and Kleist. Despite their many brilliant contributions to Germany's efforts in Russia, they could not accomplish the impossible.

A lull set in on the eastern front in April. But the Soviets resumed the offensive with even greater vigor in Belorussia on June 23, a little over two weeks after the start of the Anglo-American cross-Channel invasion of France. Once again Marshal Zhukov held overall command. This time he enjoyed a 4-to-1 superiority in manpower and a 6-to-1 advantage in armor.

With the possible exception of the Battle of Kursk, this was the most carefully prepared Soviet offensive of the war. It caught Army Group Center off guard and stabbed deep into the German rear, destroying 25 divisions with a total of 350,000 men. The disaster was greater than Stalingrad. Soviet forces now proceeded to liberate the last remnants of Soviet soil from German control and threatened the Baltic states. They also overran most of eastern Poland. By late August, troops under Rokossovsky's command had reached the outskirts of Warsaw.

THE WARSAW UPRISING

The arrival of the Soviet spearhead in the vicinity of the Polish capital triggered one of the great tragedies of the war—the Warsaw Uprising. The Polish Home Army, an anti-Communist resistance force affiliated with the London-based Polish government in exile, attempted to seize Warsaw before the Red Army entered the city. This action represented the culmination of gradually deteriorating relations between the London Poles and Moscow.

General Wladislaw Sikorski had personally organized the Polish exile regime in Paris during the fall of 1939. Sikorski, who had commanded the forces that had halted the Red Army's attempt to capture Warsaw during the Russo-Polish War in 1920, had also recruited an 82,000-man military force, largely from Poles who had been working as miners in France. With the French capitulation in 1940, Sikorski moved his government and army to Britain.

Sikorski had established diplomatic relations with Moscow after the German invasion of the Soviet Union. Stalin had been eager to accept any offers of friendship at that time, but he was not willing to agree to Sikorski's plea for a restoration of Poland's prewar eastern border after the conflict. His refusal contributed to continuing tension between the Soviets and the Poles. This worsened dramatically in April 1943, when Germany announced the discovery of the bodies of 4,300 Polish army officers in the Katyn Forest of eastern Poland. The Germans charged that the Russians had murdered these men while this area had been under their control. Many Westerners believed that the Germans had actually committed the atrocity, but Sikorski's government asked for an inquiry by the International Red Cross. Stalin reacted to this by angrily breaking off relations with the Poles. There now appears to be no doubt that the Russians were indeed the culprits.

Shortly after the severing of relations, Sikorski died in a plane crash, and Stanislaw Mikolajczyk succeeded him as prime minister. Mikolajczyk was a moderate of peasant stock who had fought the Germans in 1939 before escaping to the West. He tried to persuade his colleagues that they had no choice but to seek an understanding with the Soviets. But he lacked Sikorski's prestige and authority, and anti-Russian members of his cabinet refused to follow a conciliatory policy.

When the Soviets smashed into Poland during their 1944 summer offensive, they recognized the Communist-dominated Polish Committee of National Liberation, which established itself as a provisional government in the city of Lublin. They also arrested members of the Home Army in areas that fell under their control. The Soviet presence and the existence of the Lublin regime badly undercut the London Poles' claim to be the legitimate government of Poland. It was this combination of events that led to the decision to launch the Warsaw Uprising. If the Home Army could gain control of Warsaw, it would provide Mikolajczyk's government with a power base in Poland. Whether it could maintain that position once the Red Army arrived in strength was another matter, however. At best, the operation was an act of desperation.

The Warsaw Uprising began on August 1, and General Tadeusz Bor-Komorowski's Home Army forces soon captured half the city. The general's name originally had been simply Komorowski, and he had served as a cavalry leader during the German invasion of Poland. Soon afterward, he had persuaded Sikorski to allow the formation of an underground home army and became its commander in 1943. The general had assumed the name Bor as a cover and subsequently retained it. Despite their initial success, the Poles could not defeat the German garrison without help from the Red Army, but Rokossovsky halted his advance along the Vistula River to the east of Warsaw.

Critics have charged that Stalin deliberately refused to allow his troops to come to the rescue and thus enabled the Germans to destroy the Home Army. Although it is true that the Soviet dictator had no sympathy for Bor-Komorowski's forces and was not sorry to see the Germans crush the revolt, the Soviet failure to act appears to have been due to less sinister factors. When Rokossovsky's troops reached the vicinity of Warsaw, they were suffering from exhaustion and severe supply problems. They were especially deficient in bridging equipment, which was necessary for a crossing of the Vistula. It appears that Rokossovsky had no choice but to halt. Indeed, the whole massive offensive into Poland had lost its momentum by this time. When the Soviets did attempt to force their way across the river late in September, the Germans repulsed the attack.

Anglo-American leaders hoped to drop supplies by air to the beleaguered Poles, but for several weeks Stalin would not allow their planes to land on Russian airfields to refuel for the return trip. When he finally granted permission for one such operation, it proved a dismal failure. By this time, the Germans had recaptured much of the city, and most of the supplies fell into their hands. Without outside help, the Poles were doomed, and on October 2 the survivors of the horrible ordeal surrendered. In the process of crushing resistance, the Germans committed savage atrocities against Warsaw's population. They set fire to buildings and shot down many thousands of men, women, and children. When the fighting ended, Hitler ordered the total destruction of what was left of the city. The Germans also shipped 150,000 civilians to the Reich as slave laborers and sent the remaining 550,000 to concentration camps. Not a single Pole remained in the wasteland of demolished buildings that had once been Poland's capital.

SOVIET SUCCESSES IN THE BALTIC STATES AND THE BALKANS

Zhukov's sweepingly successful offensive against Army Group Center had also threatened to outflank Army Group North in the Baltic states. But the Soviet high command left the actual task of clearing Estonia, Latvia, and Lithuania to other Red Army forces. A major offensive began on September 14 with the objective of breaking through to the Baltic coast near Riga, the Latvian capital. Field Marshal Ferdinand Schörner, the commander of Army Group North, was a staunch supporter of the Nazi regime as well as a tough and resourceful officer. He managed to evacuate his forces from Estonia and northern Latvia but encountered increasing pressure from General Ivan Bagramyan's troops, which were thrusting through Lithuania. Bagramyan had seen most of his previous service in the Ukraine. He had narrowly missed being captured in the 1941 Kiev encirclement and had commanded an army in the Battle of Kursk. His troops reached the Baltic to the southwest of Riga on October 10 and captured the city five days later. The bulk of Army Group North was now trapped in a pocket in the Courland Peninsula of western Latvia.

Guderian, who had succeeded Zeitzler as chief of staff in July, urged Hitler to evacuate Schörner's forces by sea. Hitler flatly refused, insisting that by staying in the Courland Pocket, Army Group North would divert Soviet strength away from other operations. Guderian pointed out that these troops would be far more useful in defense of the eastern approaches to Germany. As usual, Hitler won the argument. Although some units withdrew later, 26 divisions remained in Courland until the end of the war.

The collapse of Germany's position in the East led to the rapid defection of its satellites during the late summer of 1944. On June 10, Red Army troops had opened attacks against Finland in the Karelian Isthmus. By June 20, they had recaptured Viipuri, and the Finns asked for an armistice. But both the negotiations and the Soviet offensive bogged down for the next two months.

It was not until September 19 that hostilities finally ceased. The Soviet terms were roughly those that had ended the Winter War four years earlier, with some relatively minor changes. Finland's timely exit from the conflict allowed it to avoid occupation by Soviet forces.

Rumania, Bulgaria, Slovakia, and Hungary had all been seeking to desert the Axis for some time. Rumania was the first to succeed. On August 20, Soviet army groups, commanded by Marshals Rodion Malinovsky and F. I. Tolbukhin, converged on the Axis troops defending northeastern Rumania. They broke through to the Danube River and cut off 12 German divisions. The youthful-looking Malinovsky had won fame for his part in repulsing Manstein's attempt to relieve the German troops trapped in the Stalingrad pocket. This had required leading his army on a forced march that covered 125 miles in five days through a howling blizzard. As an army group commander, he had played a major role in expelling the enemy from the Ukraine. Tolbukhin had commanded an army in the encirclement of Stalingrad. Later his army group had contributed to the first sweep across the Ukraine and the reconquest of the Crimea.

When the Red Army began its offensive, Rumania's King Michael, with the support of army leaders, ousted the pro-German premier, Marshal Ion Antonescu, and announced the end of hostilities. In their surrender terms, the Soviets forced the Rumanians to return Bessarabia and Northern Bukovina to the USSR. But in return, they supported Rumania's claim for the restoration of Hungarian-occupied Transylvania to Rumanian sovereignty. A Rumanian coalition government, consisting of both Communist and non-Communist ministers, took office, but it was disunited and inefficient. By February 1945, the Soviets had pressured the formation of a new regime that was essentially Communist.

After their disaster in Rumania, the Germans faced a hopeless position in much of the Balkans. A vast open flank lay in the path of the Soviet juggernaut. Germany's remaining forces in Rumania fell back to the west and abandoned both the Ploesti oil fields and Bucharest, the capital, before the end of September. There was now nothing to prevent the Red Army from overrunning Bulgaria while other Soviet forces penetrated into Yugoslavia. On October 20, they joined with Tito's Partisans to capture Belgrade, the Yugoslav capital.

These developments made the position of the German troops in Greece even more precarious. Retreat northward was the only option if they were to avoid being cut off by the Soviet advance. They had to carry out their withdrawal over extremely poor roads, which Tito's forces subjected to repeated attacks. But they did escape. The German departure left a political vacuum in Greece, and Churchill dispatched British troops to fill it. They landed in Greece on October 4 and occupied Athens nine days later, just after the Germans had evacuated. A coalition Greek government took over administration of the country, but its prospects were bleak. Large guerrilla bands, including many Communists, roamed over much of the country. The regime could maintain itself in power only with British military support.

In Slovakia, disenchantment with the German alliance led to a revolt by Slovak partisans in September. The Slovaks hoped that Red Army troops would soon join them, but the Soviets had to cross the rugged Carpathian Mountains, which the Germans defended tenaciously, and did not reach Slovakia until October. By then the Germans had crushed the revolt.

Hungary, the last of the Nazi satellites, also looked for a way out of its dilemma. When the Soviets made their first penetration into Rumania in March 1944, Hitler sent German troops to stiffen Hungary's will to resist. But with the defection of the Rumanians from the Axis camp in September, Hungarian dictator Admiral Nicholas Horthy tried to secure an armistice. Hitler responded with his usual quickness. He dispatched the same SS unit that had rescued Mussolini to kidnap Horthy and recognized a new pro-Axis Hungarian regime. The Führer's efforts proved less successful in halting the relentless advance of the Red Army. The Soviets broke into the Hungarian Plain in October and reached the suburbs of Budapest on November 4. Axis forces defended the Hungarian capital stubbornly, but by late December, the Soviets had encircled the city, trapping one Hungarian and four German divisions.

The year 1944 had been one of unrelieved disaster for the Germans on the eastern front. The Red Army had ousted them from the USSR, most of the Baltic states, half of Poland, and all but the northern fringes of the Balkans. It had even occupied the extreme eastern border area of East Prussia, the first Soviet penetration of Germany's prewar territory. But Hitler's forces were not yet finished. By late December, the Soviet steamroller had ground to a halt. This lull was due less to German defensive efforts than to Russian logistic problems, however. And it was not destined to last for long. Stalin's forces were planning to unleash a new series of powerful blows early in 1945.

22

Cross-Channel Invasion at Last: D Day to the German Border

Controversy continues to this day on the question of whether the Western Allies could have carried out a successful cross-Channel invasion of France in 1943. Some observers contend that such an operation was definitely within Anglo-American capabilities. They argue that had Roosevelt and Churchill followed this approach and avoided embroilment in the Mediterranean, they would have shortened the war and Western troops would have liberated much more of Europe than they subsequently did in 1944–45. But most commentators insist that conditions were not conducive to a successful invasion before 1944. To support their position, they point to the German submarine offensive, which took a heavy toll on Allied shipping until the spring of 1943, as well as shortages of ships, landing craft, troops, and equipment. They also insist that the campaigns in North Africa, Sicily, and Italy provided valuable combat experience that many Allied troops, especially American, needed before starting a cross-Channel operation.

In rebuttal, proponents of a 1943 invasion convincingly argue that the Allies did possess sufficient ships and landing craft before 1944, but in the wrong places—the Mediterranean and the Pacific. They contend that the Allies could have avoided this dilemma had they remained faithful to their original plan to strike across the Channel. These critics also demonstrate that the Allies could have provided enough men and materiel for an invasion by the spring of 1943. Although they admit that many of these troops would not have had actual battle experience, they believe that German weakness in the west would have offset this deficiency. Hitler had only 49 divisions in France, most of them of second-line quality, and was especially short of tanks during 1943. A year later, he had assembled 58 divisions and was considerably stronger in armor. German defenses along France's Atlantic coast were also much weaker in 1943 than in 1944, and the Allies would have enjoyed air superiority. The chief question that casts doubt on the possibility of a successful 1943 operation was the threat posed by German submarines to Allied shipping in the Atlantic. Clearly it was still a serious problem in early 1943, whereas it had virtually ceased to exist in 1944. Whether it was critical enough to have prevented assembling sufficient troops and materiel for an invasion is by no means clear.

In the final analysis, it is impossible to answer definitively the question of whether an invasion in 1943 would have led to victory or a serious setback for the Allies. We do know, however, that when the invasion finally came in 1944, it took place despite the continued doubts of many British leaders. These included Field Marshal

Brooke, who had always favored a Mediterranean strategy, and Churchill, who had become a convert to Brooke's approach to the war. British interest in the Mediterranean had increased since the agreement at the Casablanca conference to undertake a cross-Channel invasion in 1944. Churchill reaffirmed his commitment to an invasion of Western Europe at both the Washington Trident Conference in May and the Quadrant Conference at Quebec in August. But he also argued for an extension of operations into northern Italy.

PLANNING ALLIED STRATEGY

Churchill's attachment to the Italian campaign contributed to American skepticism regarding British intentions. This concern did not finally subside until November 1943, when Roosevelt, Churchill, and Stalin agreed on the basic details of the cross-Channel invasion at the Teheran conference. This was the first face-to-face meeting of all three Allied leaders. It took place in the capital of Iran, a country that Russian and British troops had occupied jointly in the summer of 1941 to facilitate the transit of Western aid to Russia and to safeguard Allied access to the Iranian oil fields. The "Big Three" concluded that the cross-Channel invasion (Operation Overlord) would have top priority in 1944, while the Italian campaign would continue to have secondary importance. They also agreed that American troops would undertake an invasion of southern France to coincide with Overlord but on a lesser scale.

It was also at Teheran that Roosevelt made his decision to appoint Eisenhower supreme commander of the Allied expeditionary forces that would carry out the invasion. Western leaders had already agreed that an American would serve in this post because the United States would ultimately commit larger forces to the conquest of Western Europe than the British. But Eisenhower's appointment came as a surprise to Churchill and Stalin, both of whom would have preferred General Marshall. Roosevelt chose Eisenhower largely because he considered Marshall irreplaceable as chief of staff.

The decision proved especially beneficial to the Allied cause. Eisenhower possessed the ability to get along with both American and British leaders, including such "prima donnas" as Montgomery and Patton. These qualities were of vital importance in the man who was responsible for holding the Western coalition together and making it function smoothly. British Air Marshal Sir Arthur Tedder served as Eisenhower's deputy. Another team player, Tedder had developed a close and cordial relationship with Eisenhower in the Mediterranean. Earlier, he had commanded British air operations in North Africa, Sicily, and Italy, with impressive results. Although handsome and polished in manner, Tedder possessed a common touch that made him popular with his subordinates. Montgomery was given command of the Allied ground forces that were to make the landings on the French coast as well as responsibility for much of the planning for the invasion.

By 1944, the Western Allies had produced vast amounts of war materiel that were essential if the invasion were to be successful. This materiel was available not only for the cross-Channel invasion, but for the war effort in the Mediterranean and the Pacific as well. Nevertheless, Operation Overlord received first priority, and the buildup of equipment and supplies in Britain mounted throughout the months preceding the actual landings on the French coast.

PREPARING FOR THE INVASION

The Allies chose the coast of Normandy for the invasion site. Several important factors influenced their decision. Normandy contained two important ports—Cherbourg to the west and Le Havre to the east—either of which would be extremely valuable for supplying the invading troops. The projected landing areas also lay to the east of the Cotentin Peninsula, which jutted northward into the English Channel, protecting the beaches from the prevailing westerly winds. Ultra had informed Allied leaders that the Germans expected the invasion to come at the Pas de Calais, 200 miles to the northeast. This area lay

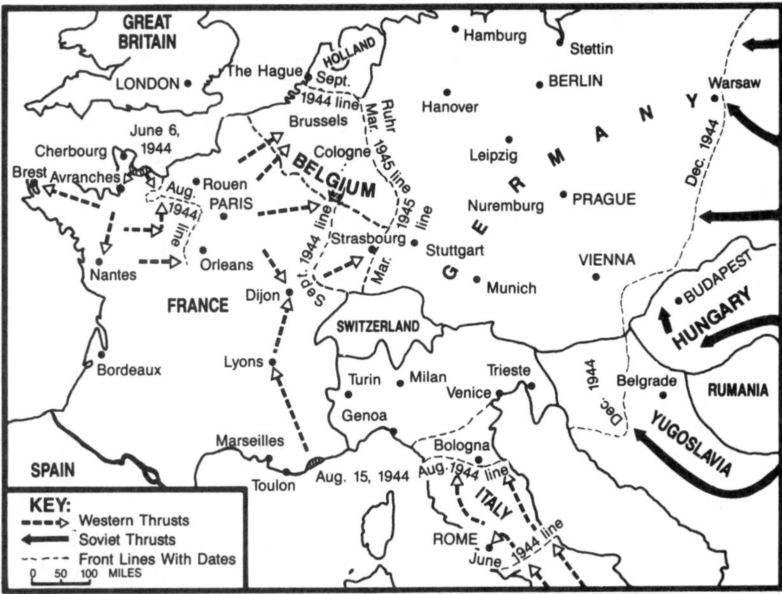

Allied Invasions of Europe, 1944–45

only 20 miles from England across the Strait of Dover. The Allies also knew that the Germans had erected stronger defenses and stationed a larger proportion of their troops there than in Normandy. Finally, the British ports across the Channel from Normandy were larger and could handle much greater ship and troop concentrations than those opposite the Pas de Calais.

Six divisions formed the initial seaborne landing force—three American, two British, and one Canadian. The Americans represented the nucleus of the U.S. First Army, commanded by General Omar Bradley, and were to land near the eastern base of the Cotentin Peninsula and drive toward Cherbourg. In stark contrast to the flamboyant Patton, Bradley was unassuming and colorless, but his quiet efficiency won the respect of his fellow officers. Bradley had been Eisenhower's classmate at West Point and, like him, had missed active service during World War I. He did not gain his first field command until 1941. When Patton took over the Seventh Army, Bradley replaced him as commander of the Second Corps in the last stages of the Tunisian campaign and in Sicily. Marshall and Eisenhower chose him for the First Army post largely because of his administrative ability.

The British and Canadians, the advance guard of General Miles Dempsey's British Second Army, were to land farther east near the mouth of the Orne River and capture the important road junction of Caen, which was to serve as the anchor point for the beachhead. Dempsey, like Bradley, was quiet but able. Long associated with Montgomery, he had served as a corps commander in Sicily and Italy. The tall, angular Dempsey was one of the few British generals who did not resent Montgomery's constant interference with operations in the field.

Shortly before these troops went ashore, two American airborne divisions were to land to the west of the U.S. beachheads to provide flank cover, while one British airborne division was to carry out the same mission to the east of the Anglo-Canadian landings. Reinforcements would arrive as soon as the assault units had secured a foothold on the coast.

Until Bradley's troops captured Cherbourg and repaired the damage that the Germans were certain to inflict on port facilities, the invasion force would rely on prefabricated concrete harbors called Mulberries. Allied ships were to tow the Mulberries across the Channel in sections and put them into place off the Normandy coast. They were also to lay pipelines that would provide badly needed fuel. Preparations for the invasion took many months to complete, including the transportation of 1.5 million American soldiers across the Atlantic and from the Mediterranean. Six hundred warships and over 4,000 transports and landing craft of various types formed the greatest invasion armada in history. A total of 12,000 planes were to provide support for the operation.

Meanwhile, the Germans made preparations to resist the expected invasion. Field Marshal Rundstedt had returned from the inactive list to command all German forces in the west. But the actual leader of the ground forces (Army Group B) in the northern third of France, Belgium, and the southern Netherlands was Field Marshal Rommel. The Germans did not agree as to where the invasion would come. Hitler guessed correctly that the target would be Normandy. But Rundstedt and Rommel expected the Allies to attack the Pas de Calais because of its proximity to England. This seemed consistent with the cautious Allied strategy in North Africa and Italy. The Pas de Calais was also closer to Germany and its industrial heartland, the Ruhr. But Hitler's concern about Normandy did lead Rommel to strengthen the defenses there.

Allied leaders also went to elaborate lengths to convince the Germans that a large concentration of American troops, under Patton's command, was present in southeastern England. The obvious objective of such a force, if it existed, would be the Pas de Calais. They even constructed a dummy headquarters, supply depots, and railroad sidings in this area. Bombing raids in the months preceding the invasion also avoided Normandy to help persuade the Germans that it would not be the invasion target. Again, Ultra reported that these deceptions had reinforced enemy certainty that the assault would come at the Pas de Calais. Meanwhile, air attacks concentrated on the French rail and road networks, including the bridges over the Seine River to the east and the Loire River to the south of Normandy. In the process, they sealed off the invasion site, which made it extremely difficult for the Germans to reinforce their Normandy garrison.

Eisenhower planned to launch the invasion on June 5, but stormy weather forced postponement and threatened to delay the operation for two weeks. German leaders in France were convinced that they had nothing to fear for the foreseeable future. This false sense of security prompted Rommel to visit Germany to celebrate his wife's birthday. Several other generals left their coastal commands to participate, ironically, in a war game simulating an Allied invasion. But on June 5, Eisenhower received a report that a lull in the bad weather would begin later that day and continue until the next morning. Ike decided to take advantage of this brief respite and ordered the invasion to take place on June 6.

THE INVASION BEGINS

German certainty that the weather would delay the invasion and the absence of so many commanders from their posts contributed to the surprise of the Allied landings. Even after they began, Rundstedt considered them to be only a feint and persisted in his belief that the main attack would come at the Pas de Calais. Ironically, Hitler, who had originally predicted that Normandy would be the invasion site, now agreed with Rundstedt. The relatively small number of Allied divisions that took part in the initial assault convinced him that stronger enemy forces would strike east of the Seine. Thus the German leaders at first refused to divert forces from the Fifteenth Army in the Pas de Calais to bolster the front in Normandy. Ultra, of course, kept Allied leaders apprised of this. Rundstedt did seek permission to shift two panzer divisions from reserve to Normandy. But Hitler was sleeping when his headquarters received this request, and no one was willing to wake him. Twelve precious hours elapsed before Rundstedt received approval, and several more passed before the divisions actually departed for the beachhead.

FIGURE 22-1 American troops head for the coast of Normandy on D day, June 6, 1944. (*U.S. Coast Guard Photograph*)

The Allies planned to carry out Operation Overlord in three stages. They referred to the first of these as the break-in, which included the actual landings and consolidation of the beachhead. The second was the buildup. This focused on expanding the beachhead and increasing the size of the invasion force. Finally came the breakout, which the Allies were to execute when the buildup was complete. It involved punching through the German defenses around the beachhead and breaking out in the direction of Paris and the German border.

Allied forces executed the break-in stage successfully, starting on D day, June 6. But they progressed much more slowly than anticipated, especially at Omaha Beach, the easternmost of the two American landing sites, where numerous problems developed. The navy launched many landing craft too far out, and the choppy sea swamped them, taking a heavy toll of men, tanks, and artillery. Once the invaders reached the shore, they encountered fierce resistance that pinned them down for hours. It was not until late in the day that they finally established a secure position. The Americans who landed at Utah Beach to the west encountered fewer obstacles, although here, too, they moved inland more slowly than expected.

British and Canadian troops landed at Gold, Juno, and Sword beaches to the east of Omaha Beach and advanced several miles with relatively little difficulty. But they failed to fulfill their major objective for the first day, the capture of the key communications center of Caen. This enabled the enemy to establish strong defensive positions to the north of the city. Once the Germans realized that Normandy was actually the main invasion target, they became convinced that the Allies planned to attempt their breakout from the Caen area. It does appear that Montgomery had originally considered an operation of this type. But strong German resistance and slow Allied progress prevented such a strategy. Instead, the final Allied plan called for the British and Canadians to maintain maximum pressure on the Germans at Caen to give the impression that the main breakout attempt would come there. The Americans were to execute the actual breakout at the opposite end of the beachhead.

Slightly over 100,000 Allied troops reached

shore during the first two days. General Friedrich Dollmann's German Seventh Army, which was responsible for the defense of Normandy, possessed six infantry divisions and one panzer division at first. Dollmann had commanded this army since the outbreak of the war. His forces had taken part in the conquest of France but had found themselves relegated to garrison duty during the following four years. Within ten days, Allied manpower in Normandy had increased to over 500,000, and by July 1, almost a million men were inside the beachhead. During the same period, the Germans built up their strength to 14 divisions, 9 of which were panzer divisions.

The first major American objective was to pinch off the Cotentin Peninsula and capture Cherbourg. Although they encountered strong German resistance, they finally took the city on June 27. But the Germans destroyed the port installations and blocked access to the harbor with sunken ships. As a result, the Allies were not able to use the port until July 16 and did not complete clearing operations until the end of September.

Not only did Rommel expect the British to execute the breakout attempt, but he was also especially concerned about the terrain on the eastern end of the beachhead. It consisted of a rolling plain, stretching from Caen to Falaise 25 miles to the south, and it was ideally suited for armored attacks. Rommel seemingly had less to fear from the Americans, who had to contend with the extremely difficult "hedgerow country" to the west of Caen. High earthen banks, topped by thick hedges, lined the fields and roads of this region, providing the Germans with a deep belt of perfect defensive positions. Heavy fighting followed for several weeks, especially at Caen and Saint-Lô, a small city that was the key point in the projected American breakout. Although the Germans resisted tenaciously, the Allies gradually wore them down.

The buildup of Allied strength in Normandy led to the creation of two army groups by the end of July. The Twenty-first Army Group, under Montgomery's command, consisted of Dempsey's British Second Army and General Henry Crerar's new Canadian First Army. Crerar, who had spent the interwar years strengthening his country's small army, established a Canadian military headquarters on British soil in 1939. He returned to Canada the following year to serve as chief of staff before taking over as commander of a corps that fought in Italy. The Twelfth Army Group, led by Bradley, included the First Army, now commanded by General Courtney Hodges, and the newly activated Third Army, headed by Patton, who by this time had overcome the disgrace of the slapping incident in Sicily.

Compared to Patton, Hodges provided an even greater contrast than Bradley. Likened by some to a small-town banker or businessman, his manner was extremely reserved. Hodges had gained high rank despite being dismissed from West Point because he failed geometry. Undeterred by this setback, he enlisted as a private and quickly gained a commission. After serving in the 1916–17 Mexican border expedition, he won the Distinguished Service Cross as leader of a machine-gun company in France during World War I. Although Bradley considered him a masterful tactician, some of his associates criticized him for not exerting enough control over his subordinates.

The German command structure experienced even more far-reaching changes. Hitler dismissed Rundstedt early in July when the field marshal expressed pessimism regarding the chance of pushing the Allies back into the sea. Rommel suffered injuries when a British plane attacked his staff car on July 17, ending his role in the defense of Normandy. The Führer called on Field Marshal von Kluge, the former commander of Army Group Center on the eastern front, to succeed both Rundstedt and Rommel.

AN ATTEMPT ON HITLER'S LIFE

These developments coincided with an unsuccessful attempt to assassinate Hitler on July 20, the final chapter in a conspiracy that had begun before the war and persisted into the conflict. When the tide turned against Germany in Russia, a number of staff officers had tried several times to kill Hitler during his visits to the eastern front, but all their efforts had misfired. On one occasion, a bomb had failed to detonate, and on another, Hitler had changed his schedule in the nick of time. It seemed that he had the devil's own luck.

The July 20 attempt on Hitler's life took place during a staff conference at his "Wolf's Lair" headquarters in East Prussia. The key figure in the plot was Colonel Claus Schenck von Stauffenberg, a young staff officer who had served in Poland, Western Europe, and North Africa. He had lost an arm and an eye when attacked by a fighter plane in Tunisia. Stauffenberg attended the July 20 meeting in his capacity as chief of staff of the Home Army, which had responsibility for training troops. After placing a briefcase containing a bomb under the conference table, he excused himself and made his escape. When the bomb exploded a few minutes later, it killed four men and wounded 20 others. But the table's heavy oak top and stumplike support absorbed enough of the blast to spare Hitler.

Stauffenberg and his fellow conspirators had planned to follow the assassination by seizing control of the government in Berlin and seeking an end to the war. But officers who remained loyal to Hitler received word that he was still alive and quickly arrested Stauffenberg and several others, effectively crushing the plot. They shot Stauffenberg and his immediate associates shortly thereafter. But most of the conspirators were not so fortunate. Hitler took his revenge on them in the weeks and months that followed. High-ranking officers and civilians had to endure thunderous denunciations from the rabid Nazi judge Roland Freisler, who presided over perfunctory trials and handed out predetermined sentences. Many of the condemned suffered horrible deaths, being slowly hanged by piano wire suspended from meat hooks. Hitler ordered the executions to be filmed so that he could view the victims' death agonies at his leisure. From all accounts, he found this entertainment immensely satisfying. Among those implicated in the conspiracy were Kluge and Rommel. Both committed suicide, Kluge a few weeks after the failure of the plot and Rommel two months later.

Hitler had already replaced Kluge with Field Marshal Walther Model, a veteran of the eastern front whose loyalty to the Führer had remained unshaken. A blunt, outspoken officer of middle-class background, Model led a panzer division in the 1941 invasion of the Soviet Union. He subsequently became known as "the Führer's fireman" for his ability to halt Soviet offensives. He commanded all three army groups on the eastern front in succession during 1943–44. Model was not afraid to stand up to Hitler and at times even ignored his orders.

Another important change took place at almost the same time as the attempt on Hitler's life, although there was no connection between the two incidents. General Zeitzler, the OKH chief of staff, had become so frustrated by his repeated confrontations with Hitler that he asked to be allowed to go on sick leave. The Führer was so enraged by this request that he dismissed Zeitzler from the army and refused to allow him to wear his uniform. He appointed General Guderian to succeed him.

The attempt on his life increased Hitler's suspicion of even generals who remained loyal to him. And the fact that he had cheated death added to his conviction that he was a man of destiny who would somehow overcome the enormous problems that confronted him.

THE ALLIES BREAK OUT

Meanwhile, back at the front, the Americans took Saint-Lô on July 18, and the British finally completed the capture of Caen two days later. The long-awaited breakout began on July 25. After an intense aerial bombardment, Bradley launched an offensive by the First Army along a narrow front south of Saint-Lô. The Germans, still convinced that the British would make the breakout attempt, persisted in keeping most of their panzer divisions in the Caen area, thus contributing to the American success. Ultra continued to keep Bradley informed of the relatively weak forces in the path of his troops. General J. Lawton Collins's Seventh Corps provided the First Army's spearhead. Collins had proved himself as a division commander on Guadalcanal, where he had earned the nickname "Lightning Joe." An exceptionally vigorous officer, he would not tolerate any lack of aggressiveness in his subordinates and became famous for his ability to move his troops quickly. He had skillfully directed the capture of Cherbourg and now scored a breakthrough at Saint-Lô. His forces cleared the way for a thrust to Avranches, at the western base of the Cotentin Peninsula.

The Third Army now exploited the gap that the First Army had created. Patton sent one corps sweeping westward into Brittany in the hope of capturing the Breton ports, while the rest of his army wheeled to the east and began to drive across France, against little opposition. The attempt to capture the Breton ports failed because the Germans defended them skillfully in an effort to deny the Allies the use of their facilities. The American breakthrough threatened the entire German position in Normandy and seemed to dictate a general withdrawal to the Seine. But instead of pulling back, Hitler ordered an assault against the American flank near Avranches. The attack failed, and the German Seventh Army now found itself in a highly precarious situation. Elements of the First Army were swinging eastward around its southern flank, while the British and Canadians were pressuring it from the north.

Bradley hoped to prevent an enemy retreat by sending elements of both the First and Third armies north through Argentan to link up with the Canadian First Army, which struck south by way of Falaise. But the trap did not close quickly enough. Although the Americans made rapid progress at first, Bradley ordered them to halt because he feared that they would collide with the Canadians in the open field. The Canadians, who encountered stronger resistance, also advanced more slowly than hoped, and Montgomery failed to reinforce them with British troops. This combination of factors enabled 35,000 enemy soldiers to escape before the pincers closed on August 19. Nevertheless, 10,000 Germans died in the Falaise pocket, and another 50,000 surrendered. The slaughter became so concentrated in the battle's final stages that Eisenhower referred to the pocket as a "killing ground." Even the German forces that had escaped fell back on the Seine mauled and demoralized.

Now, when it was too late, Hitler authorized the Fifteenth Army to move south from the Pas de Calais in an attempt to stabilize the front. But it accomplished little and became intermingled with the fleeing remnants of the Seventh Army, compounding the confusion. Meanwhile, Patton's forces threatened an even greater trap as they crossed the Seine and rolled to the northeast of Paris toward the German border. Their rapid progress eliminated any chance of a German stand along the Seine.

THE SOUTHERN INVASION: ANVIL-DRAGOON

While the Battle of the Falaise Pocket raged and Patton's troops rampaged almost unmolested through the French countryside, Allied forces landed on France's Mediterranean coast. Eisenhower originally intended this operation to take place at the same time as the invasion of Normandy, but a shortage of landing craft forced its postponement for over two months. The British opposed the operation, which originally had the code name Anvil, because the plan called for the diversion of troops from Italy. Eisenhower and other American leaders insisted, however, and the invasion began on August 15 with the new code name Dragoon. General Alexander Patch's U.S. Seventh Army went ashore between the French naval base of Toulon and the resort city of Cannes. A veteran of World War I, Patch had spent most of the interwar years training troops. He had commanded the army forces that relieved the marines at Guadalcanal and had been Collins's superior in that campaign.

The invaders made rapid progress against weak opposition, quickly established a beachhead, and moved inland. French troops, under General Jean de Lattre de Tassigny, landed soon afterward. De Lattre had served in the defense of France in 1940 and had refused to buckle under to either the Germans or the Vichy regime during the following months. His outspokenness cost him a ten-year prison sentence, but he escaped to Britain in 1943 and later commanded French troops in North Africa. De Lattre's forces joined with the Americans to capture Toulon as well as the great port of Marseille. The Allies soon received word from Ultra of Hitler's order for all German troops in southern France to withdraw northward. This information enabled them to pursue the enemy up the valley of the Rhone River with great confidence and vigor. Their progress was so swift that on September 12, they made contact with the U.S. Third Army north of Dijon in eastern France.

Few operations have received more criticism than Anvil-Dragoon. Most appraisals have insisted that it was unnecessary and prevented the exploitation of the situation in Italy. But the capture of Marseille alone made the undertaking worthwhile, especially in view of the failure to capture the Breton ports. From September through January, the Allies unloaded more supplies at Marseille than at any other port.

THE ALLIES' SWIFT ADVANCE

As the German position in Western France disintegrated following the breakout from Normandy and the Falaise pocket disaster, all Allied armies streaked forward against little resistance. Paris now lay in the path of the U.S. First Army, but Eisenhower planned to bypass the great city. He wanted to avoid street fighting, which might destroy the beautiful capital and cause heavy casualties. If Paris fell, the task of supplying its huge population with food would also confront the Allies with a serious logistic problem. The French, both within and outside the city, decided the issue. French Forces of the Interior rose in revolt against the Paris garrison, and de Gaulle demanded that Eisenhower hasten troops to relieve the poorly armed Resistance units. While the supreme commander hesitated, General Jacques Philippe Leclerc,* commander of the French Second Armored Division, acted.

Leclerc had been one of the first officers to rally to de Gaulle in 1940. He won fame in December 1942 by marching a Free French regiment from the central African colony of Chad through over 1,200 miles of desert to join the British at Tripoli. Now the independent-minded general defied orders and sent a force toward Paris. Bowing to the inevitable, Eisenhower approved his action. But Leclerc's troops progressed more slowly than expected, and Bradley dispatched American units to join in the liberation. Paris fell on August 25. Like Rome, the City of Light had escaped serious damage. Huge throngs of ecstatic Parisians plied the Allied troops with flowers, wine, and kisses and cheered as they marched in triumph down the famous Champs Élysées.

Soon after the liberation of Paris, the British Second, Canadian First, and U.S. First armies all knifed into Belgium while Patton's forces swung into northeastern France. By September 15, most of Belgium and Luxembourg had fallen into Allied hands, and the German border was only a few miles away. But this remarkable advance was not without problems. The Allies outdistanced their supply lines, and shortages, especially of fuel, began to develop. It became clear that all the armies could not continue their breakneck progress. Accordingly, Montgomery urged a single-thrust strategy with the British Second and U.S. First armies driving toward the Rhine and the Ruhr while the Canadians and Patton's troops halted to conserve supplies. But Eisenhower insisted on a broad-front strategy with both army groups moving forward more or less simultaneously. The supreme commander prevailed, and his decision sparked a controversy that still continues. Montgomery contended that it prevented not only the encirclement of the Ruhr but also a thrust all the way to Berlin.

---

*Jacques Philippe Leclerc was the name that Philippe de Hautecloque took to protect his family from reprisal when he joined de Gaulle's forces.

FIGURE 22-2 Allied Supreme Commander General Dwight Eisenhower (right) confers with Generals Ralph Royce (left) and Omar Bradley (center). (*U.S. Army Photograph*)

Evidence now indicates that Montgomery was probably correct regarding the feasibility of a quick drive to the Rhine. The Germans had little strength in the path of such an operation, and the Allies probably had sufficient supplies to service the forces of Dempsey and Hodges or, conversely, those of Patton. But it does not appear that a Rhine crossing was possible, and certainly Montgomery was wildly optimistic about prospects for an advance to Berlin. The Allies clearly lacked the capability to supply such an ambitious enterprise.

Although the capture of Marseille eased the supply problem, the Allies badly needed a major port close to the front. The obvious choice was the Belgian city of Antwerp, one of Europe's largest ports. Allied leaders were elated when Antwerp fell to the British on September 4 with its port intact. The British had advanced so rapidly that the Germans were unable to block the harbor or destroy its facilities. But to take the city was not enough. Antwerp lay on the Scheldt River, 60 miles from the North Sea, and the Germans still controlled the Belgian and Dutch territory that bordered the river's estuary.

Eisenhower and Montgomery obtained repeated warnings from Ultra that Hitler planned to hold the estuary and thus deny the use of Antwerp to the Allies. A quick British and Canadian thrust might have cleared the approaches to the Scheldt before the Germans were able to consolidate their defenses there. But despite the great value that Eisenhower placed on Antwerp, he did not order Montgomery to clear the estuary, and Montgomery made no effort to do so. His mind was on other objectives. Had he immediately swung to the northwest of Antwerp, he might also have trapped the remnants of the German Fifteenth Army. The speed of his advance had pinned the Germans into a pocket on the southern bank of the Scheldt's estuary. But Montgomery's failure to act allowed most of the enemy troops to evacuate across the river. This battered but substantial force was then able to participate in the defense of the Netherlands. A German rear guard also continued to hold the Scheldt estuary and prevented its clearing until November. Until then, Antwerp was useless to the Allies.

THE PUSH TO CROSS THE RHINE

After failing to convince Eisenhower of the need for a single thrust toward the Ruhr, Montgomery turned to the possibility of crossing the Rhine in the Netherlands. If the Allies could accomplish this, they would not only hurdle the formidable river barrier that guarded Germany but would also outflank the northernmost fortifications of the West Wall along the German-Dutch border. They would also be able to threaten German V-2 rocket-launching sites in the Netherlands. But the proposed operation would require the Allies to cross four other rivers and three canals before they reached the Lower Rhine at Arnhem. If it were to succeed, Anglo-American airborne troops would have to seize the bridges over these water obstacles while British land forces drove northward to relieve them. The distance to the most remote bridge at Arnhem was 64 miles.

This time, Eisenhower approved Montgomery's proposal, which was given the code name Operation Market-Garden. It was an exceptionally bold undertaking and required unusually precise timing. To compound the risk, Ultra detected the presence of two SS panzer divisions near Arnhem. But neither Montgomery nor Eisenhower was willing to call off the operation. The plan called for the U.S. 101st Airborne Division to capture the bridge across the Maas, the Dutch part of the Meuse, southernmost of the three major rivers, near Eindhoven. This force, nicknamed Screaming Eagles, also would take a number of bridges over lesser streams and canals. The American Eighty-second Airborne Division was assigned the task of seizing the span over the Waal River, a branch of the Rhine, farther north near Nijmegen. The British First Airborne Division, called the Red Devils because its men wore maroon berets, drew the most difficult assignment of all. It had to capture the northernmost bridge across the Lower Rhine at Arnhem.

When Market-Garden began on September 17, it encountered a multitude of problems, including bad weather that delayed the dropping of some of the paratroops. Even more serious, Ultra proved correct; the two German panzer divisions were indeed in the vicinity of Arnhem. This posed a serious menace to the First Airborne Division. The British compounded the dilemma by dropping their forces too far from the objective. This enabled the Germans to split them into two segments and prevent the capture of the bridge. One group of 500 men, commanded by John Frost, a 31-year-old lieutenant colonel who carried a fox-hunting horn into battle, managed to seize the northern approach to the span. But it was too weak to move across without aid from

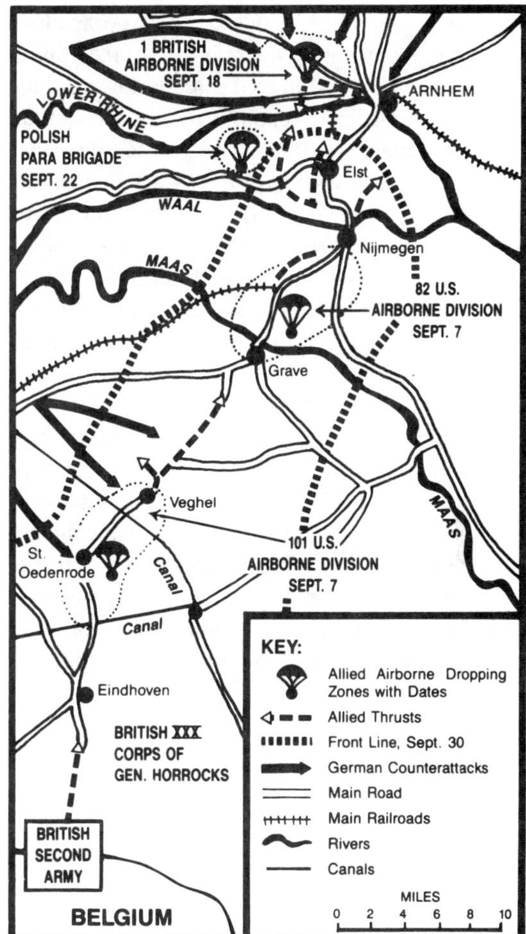

Operation Market-Garden, September 17–25, 1944

the main force. The Eighty-second Airborne also had difficulty capturing the bridge over the Waal. If the Americans had moved directly toward this objective immediately upon landing, they would have encountered only a few enemy sentries. Instead, they concentrated on taking the high ground near Nijmegen first. By the time they advanced toward the river, the Germans had sent reinforcements and held the bridge for three days. Only after a bloody crossing of the Waal in flimsy canvas boats was the Eighty-second able to secure the bridge.

Finally, the British Thirtieth Corps, comprising the relief force, had to move through swampy terrain along one narrow road that the Germans subjected to artillery fire. These obstacles, among others, prevented it from advancing as rapidly as anticipated. Ultimately, the relief force came to the rescue of all the airborne troops except those at Arnhem. The bridge there proved too far away. After nine days of heavy fighting, only 2,400 of the original 9,000 Red Devils managed to break through enemy lines and escape. The failure of Market-Garden ended Allied hopes of crossing the Rhine in 1944.

Shortly before the start of this operation, Hitler had reappointed Rundstedt to his former position as German supreme commander in the west. Rundstedt and especially Model, still in command of Army Group B, managed to scrape together enough forces to reconstruct the front. They did so not only in the Netherlands but also opposite Hodges, who was probing beyond the Belgian border into Germany, and Patton, whose drive had bogged down in the northeastern French province of Lorraine. The First Army drove to within a few miles of the German border city of Aachen on September 15 but was unable to complete its capture until October 21. Despite the great success of the Allied summer offensive, the Germans were not yet finished in the west any more than in the east.

23

The End of the Thousand-Year Reich

Allied frustration increased in the late fall of 1944 as German resistance stiffened all along the western front. The failure of Operation Market-Garden had stymied British progress in the Netherlands, and American forces also encountered problems. Hodges's First Army came up against the fortifications of the West Wall and the difficult terrain of Germany's Hürtgen Forest south of Aachen. The battle to take this dense and dismal forest became the bloodiest and most protracted since the hedgerow fighting in Normandy. To the south, Patton's Third Army had to struggle through the hilly country of Lorraine before reaching the West Wall in the coal-mining region of the Saar. Still farther south, Patch's Seventh Army and de Lattre's French forces contended with the Vosges Mountains, a long, low range along the western border of Alsace. But even though dreams of a quick triumph had vanished, certainty of ultimate victory remained high. Eisenhower and his commanders continued to prepare for the thrust to the Rhine and beyond.

THE BATTLE OF THE BULGE

But Hitler had one final trump to play—one last offensive. This counterstroke was strictly the Führer's idea, and its ambitious scope appalled both Rundstedt and Model. Hitler envisioned a variation on the theme of an earlier triumph. He chose to strike in the Ardennes once again, recognizing that it was the weak point in the Allied line, just as it had been the French Achilles' heel in 1940. But this time, rather than penetrating into France, he planned to send his armor across the Meuse River all the way to Antwerp. If he could accomplish this, he would isolate Montgomery's forces from the American armies to the south.

To fulfill his grandiose dream, Hitler rashly weakened German strength on the eastern front to provide a powerful striking force for the Ardennes operation. It included General Josef Sepp Dietrich's Sixth SS Panzer Army on the north, General Hasso von Manteuffel's Fifth Panzer Army in the center, and the refurbished Seventh Army of General Erich Brandenberger on the south. Dietrich was an authentic Nazi and a close associate of Hitler's since the early days of the party, when he had led the Führer's SS bodyguard. This hard-drinking butcher's son later commanded a panzer division on the eastern front as well as an armored corps in Normandy. Dietrich lacked the skill and imaginative leadership of the aristocratic Manteuffel who, though extremely short in stature, had gained an impressive reputation as a panzer corps commander in Russia. Brandenberger, another veteran of panzer warfare, had taken over the Seventh Army following the disasters of the summer. He had shown considerable ability in plugging weak points in the German line during the autumn fighting. In all, the OKW amassed 24 divisions, including 10 panzer, an armored force larger than the one that had executed the great Ardennes breakthrough in 1940.

Considering the ease with which the Wehrmacht had slashed through the Ardennes 4½ years earlier, it is remarkable that the Allies failed to take greater precautions to protect this portion of the front. Although the Germans had clearly shown that they were still dangerous in a defensive role, Allied leaders did not consider them capable of a major counteroffensive or foolhardy enough to try one. Surprisingly, they believed that Rundstedt was actually in charge on the western front. In reality, he merely carried out Hitler's orders.

Only four American divisions from Hodges's First Army held the Ardennes front, and Allied leaders were oblivious to the impending onslaught. The chief factor that contributed to their lack of concern was Hitler's insistence on complete radio silence in connection with the operation. Ultra was thus unable to read any messages indicating specifically that an assault was coming in the Ardennes. But Ultra and other sources did detect the transfer of panzer divisions and fighter planes from the eastern front to the west. Eisenhower, Hodges, and other generals interpreted this buildup as preliminary to a possible attack to the north of the Ardennes near Aachen. More significantly, Ultra intercepted numerous messages in which Model called for detailed aerial reconnaissance over the Ardennes. The Allies refused to give sufficient credence to these reports, an oversight that ranks as one of the great intelligence failures of the war. Again, the parallel to a similar French blunder in 1940 is striking.

Operation Autumn Fog, as Hitler called it, opened with a predawn artillery barrage on December 16. It was a complete surprise. English-speaking German commandos infiltrated behind U.S. lines and for a time caused great confusion. Dressed in American uniforms, they cut telephone lines, changed road signs, and killed mili-

The German Offensive in the Ardennes, December 16–31, 1944 (The Battle of the Bulge)

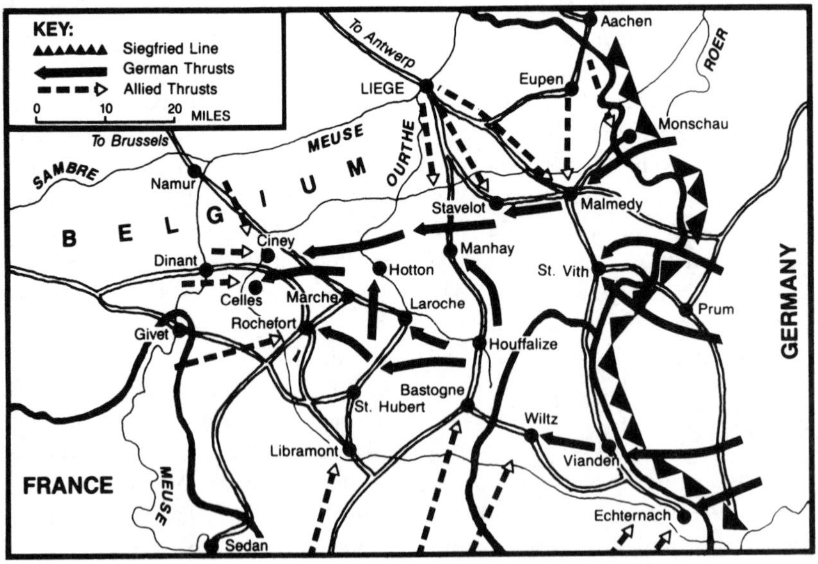

tary policemen in charge of directing troop convoys. Their presence spread fear among American personnel, who began to suspect everyone and subjected strangers to informal questioning. Queries ranged from asking the identity of major league batting champions to the names of state capitals. Although this approach proved reasonably successful, even genuine Americans didn't know all the answers. At one point, General Bradley had to confess ignorance when asked to identify the husband of popular movie star Betty Grable. But his interrogator let him pass anyway. On another occasion, Bradley responded correctly that Springfield was the capital of Illinois, only to be told that the answer was really Chicago!

Members of the First SS Panzer Division inspired still more fear by murdering Americans who fell into their hands early in the offensive. The most notorious massacre occurred near the town of Malmédy, where German machine-gun and pistol fire took 86 lives.

The Germans overwhelmed badly outnumbered American forces along a 70-mile front, and their armor rumbled on toward the Meuse. Allied leaders were slow to grasp the seriousness of the situation, and the enemy benefited from the low overcast, which prevented Anglo-American air power from intervening. But American units stubbornly defended two road junctions in eastern Belgium—St. Vith and Bastogne. Although St. Vith fell on December 22, Bastogne continued to hold out. When Eisenhower finally recognized that the German counterstroke was a major operation, he ordered the U.S. 101st Airborne Division to reinforce the town's garrison. German troops surrounded Bastogne and issued an appeal for the defenders to surrender. General Anthony McAuliffe, the American commander, limited his response to one word: "Nuts!" The struggle for the town continued.

When the skies finally cleared on December 23, Allied fighter bombers decimated enemy armored spearheads. The Germans, who were also experiencing a severe fuel shortage, had no choice but to break off their offensive the following day. Manteuffel's Fifth Panzer Army had penetrated to within five miles of the Meuse. It was now apparent that Hitler's dream of reaching Antwerp had been far too ambitious. The best his great counteroffensive could accomplish was to create a bulge in the Allied line 65 miles deep and 45 miles wide.

Meanwhile, for the purpose of greater efficiency, Eisenhower transferred the U.S. First and Ninth armies, which lay to the north of the bulge, to Montgomery's Twenty-first Army Group. The Ninth Army, commanded by General William Simpson, had entered the Allied line in November between the British on the north and the First Army on the south. Its first units had seen action in the bloody fighting that led to the capture of the Breton port of Brest in September. Simpson, a tall, slender officer with a completely shaved head, was austere in appearance but mellow in manner. Marshall selected him personally for the job. Although Eisenhower and Bradley would have preferred Collins, both soon came to appreciate Simpson's quiet, uncomplaining, and efficient professionalism.

This change left only Patton's Third Army to the south of the salient in Bradley's Twelfth Army Group. Although the decision contributed to much better coordination of U.S. and British forces in the north, Montgomery's arrogant attitude worsened already strained relations between him and American commanders. As one of Montgomery's own staff officers remarked, he "strode into Hodges's headquarters like Christ come to cleanse the temple."

Allied forces soon struck against the flanks of the bulge. Patton drove quickly northward and relieved the surrounded Bastogne garrison on December 26. To the north of the salient, Montgomery did not launch his attack until January 3, 1945. It soon became obvious to Manteuffel and Rundstedt that they must pull back their troops from the dangerously exposed salient. But Hitler, true to his "hold fast" mentality, refused. The Allies forced the Germans to give ground, nevertheless, and inflicted severe casualties. By the end of January, they had eliminated the bulge. More important, Hitler had sacrificed his last reserves and his greatest concentration of armor in an enterprise that never had a chance of success. True, he had delayed the final Allied offensive in the west, but he would have precious little strength left to meet the attack when it came in early 1945. His disastrous failure in the Battle of the Bulge also dealt a severe blow to German morale on the western front. And he had played into Russian hands by weakening his forces in the east.

THE STRUGGLE FOR THE COLMAR POCKET

Hitler did not limit his offensive operations to the Ardennes. Just before midnight on December 31, he unleashed seven infantry and three panzer divisions against General Jacob Devers's recently formed Sixth Army Group, consisting of Patch's U.S. Seventh and de Lattre's French First armies. Devers, who appeared much younger than his 58 years, had commanded U.S. forces in Britain prior to Eisenhower's arrival and then moved to the Mediterranean, where he supervised the invasion of southern France. Noted for his administrative ability and common sense, Devers possessed a smile that came close to rivaling that of the supreme commander.

The Germans delivered their attack from another salient, the so-called Colmar pocket, a large bridgehead that they had retained on the west bank of the Rhine. Containing the city of Colmar, it lay to the south of Strasbourg, the provincial capital of Alsace. This offensive had two major aims. Hitler hoped to force Eisenhower to divert Third Army troops away from their attacks against the southern flank of the Bulge. He also wanted to maintain a strong foothold in Alsace, which he considered part of Germany. Allied leaders received ample warning of the attack from Ultra as well as other intelligence sources. But the shift of Patton's army to the north had required Patch and de Lattre to stretch their forces thinly to protect a considerably broader front.

When the Germans struck, Eisenhower thought it would be best to retreat to the Vosges Mountains. But this would leave Strasbourg open to German occupation. General de Gaulle refused to allow de Lattre's troops to participate in such a withdrawal. Patch and de Lattre also questioned the need for such an extensive pullback. Confronted by a potential split in the Allied coalition, Eisenhower discarded plans for a major withdrawal. The German assault made limited progress, but the Americans held along the Moder River. By January 25, the Germans broke off their offensive and began to transfer some of their best divisions to the eastern front. It had not been necessary for Eisenhower to divert strength away from Patton to hold the line.

Meanwhile, French and American forces had opened a counterattack against the southern flank of the Colmar pocket five days before the end of the enemy offensive. Although progress was slow at first, the French captured Colmar on February 2, and the Allies eliminated the last vestiges of the pocket one week later. Once again Hitler had squandered resources and failed to gain any lasting advantage.

THE SOVIET ASSAULT ON POLAND AND BEYOND

Long before the Western Allies had eliminated the Bulge and the Colmar pocket, Soviet forces unleashed a gigantic offensive in Poland. The Red Army originally planned this operation to coincide with the major Anglo-American assault in the west. Hitler's Ardennes counterstroke had delayed the latter but in the process had thinned out German forces opposite the Red Army to a dangerously low point. In December, German intelligence reported a buildup of 225 Soviet divisions and 22 armored corps along the front from the Baltic to the Carpathians. Hitler refused to accept the validity of this information and insisted on continuing his Ardennes operation rather than shifting forces back to the eastern front. He even refused General Guderian's request for evacuation of the 26 German divisions that the Soviets had cut off in Latvia's Courland Peninsula.

Hitler's blindness to the danger in Poland led him to transfer two panzer divisions from there to take part in an attempt to break the Russian encirclement of Budapest. Although the Germans penetrated to within 12 miles of the Hungarian capital in late January, a Soviet counterattack forced them to abandon their offensive. After savage street fighting, Red Army troops completed their conquest of Budapest on February 14.

While Hitler focused on the relief of Budapest, the Soviet high command prepared to deliver its blow in Poland. Three army groups assembled along the Vistula River—Rokossovsky's Second Belorussian Front to the northeast of Warsaw, Zhukov's First Belorussian Front to the south of the city, and Marshal Konev's First Ukrainian Front in extreme southern Poland. To the north, additional Red Army troops were poised opposite the German province of East Prussia. In all, the Russians concentrated 1.5 million men, 3,300 tanks, 28,000 guns, and 10,000 aircraft. To defend against this overwhelming strength, the Germans could muster only 596,000 men, 700 tanks, 8,200 guns, and 1,300 planes.

The Red Army launched its massive offensive on January 12. Konev struck from a bridgehead on the west bank of the Vistula, about 100 miles south of Warsaw. Zhukov attacked just below the Polish capital and swung behind the city. To the north, Rokossovsky wheeled toward East Prussia and Danzig. The three spearheads tore open a 200-mile gap in the German front and rolled on relentlessly. Zhukov seized Warsaw on January 17, and Konev's troops penetrated into the province of Silesia, Germany's second most important industrial area, on January 20. Three days later, they crossed the Oder River near Breslau. Rokossovsky reached the Baltic east of Danzig on January 26, cutting off the German defenders of East Prussia.

After taking the Polish capital, Zhukov's armies captured the industrial city of Lodz and encircled Poznan, a communications center that controlled the major supply routes between Warsaw and Berlin. On January 30, they sliced into Germany and a day later reached Kustrin on the Oder. Within a week, they crossed the river and established two sizable bridgeheads, one only 33 miles from the suburbs of Berlin. Zhukov now encountered supply problems, which the Germans aggravated by holding out in Poznan until February 23.

Konev was more fortunate, at least for the time being. On February 9, his forces swung northeastward from their bridgeheads across the Oder and a week later reached the Neisse River, a tributary of the Oder. They were now just 60 miles from Berlin. But the Germans continued to hold out in bypassed Breslau, confronting Konev with supply problems as severe as those of Zhukov. Hitler also shifted several divisions from the western front to bolster his defenses on the Oder and the Neisse. To make matters worse for the Soviets, a sudden thaw turned many of the roads to mud and melted the ice on the Oder.

By pushing so rapidly to the Oder, Zhukov's armies had created a salient with a long, vulnerable northern flank. Relatively strong German forces still held much of the province of Pomerania, which lay between the Soviets and the Baltic. Guderian planned to stage a counterattack from this area in the hope of pinching off the advance Soviet units on the Oder. He urged that General von Weichs, a veteran of the 1941 and 1942 campaigns in Russia, lead the assault. Much to his astonishment, Hitler insisted on Himmler, who had neither military training nor skill. By this time, the Führer so distrusted army generals that he preferred a loyal Nazi as commander, whatever his qualifications. Guderian also requested that Sepp Dietrich's Sixth SS Panzer Army, which had broken off the Ardennes offensive, be shifted to Pomerania to take part in the counterattack. Again Hitler refused and instead sent Dietrich's forces to Hungary. Not surprisingly, when Guderian launched his counterstroke on February 15, it was far too weak to achieve his objective.

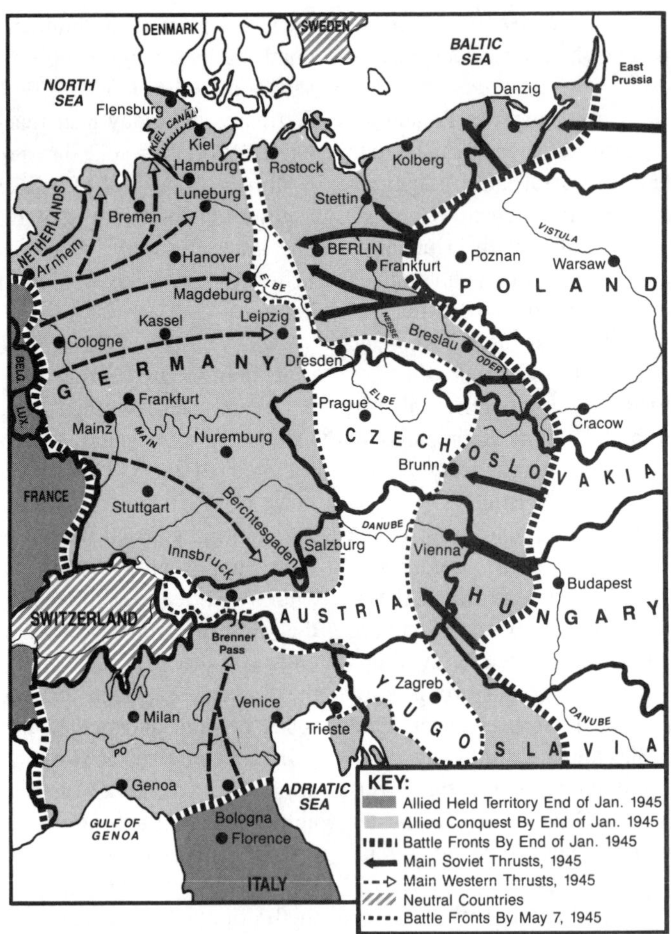

The Last Battles on Three Main European Fronts—Eastern, Western, and Southern—February 1–May 7, 1945

But the German attack made Stalin nervous, and he ordered Zhukov and Rokossovsky to eliminate the threat from the north before attempting to move farther west. German forces resisted the Soviet thrust as best they could but had to fall back to three strong points on the Baltic coast—Danzig, Gdynia, and Kolberg. It was not until March 30 that the last of them, Danzig, surrendered, and the Soviets moved into the smoking ruins of the great port, which had been one of the immediate causes of World War II.

Meanwhile, Hitler ordered his troops in Hungary, bolstered by the arrival of the Sixth SS Panzer Army, to launch the final German offensive of the war. He hoped to protect the oil fields in western Hungary by driving to the Danube River and threatening Budapest. The attack began on March 5 and made some progress but soon fell afoul of muddy conditions, a fuel shortage, and stronger Red Army forces. By March 15, the Soviets had regained the initiative, and Marshal F. I. Tolbukhin's army group started an offensive. The Germans resisted stubbornly for three days, but when Soviet troops threatened to cut off their escape route, they fell back precipitously. Their retreat became a rout, and Tolbukhin's forces pursued them across the Austrian border. The Soviets reached the outskirts of Vienna on April 4 and, after six days of street fighting, occupied the entire city. Although Vienna suffered damage to many of its famous historic buildings, much of the city survived intact.

As the Red Army penetrated into Germany and Austria, many civilians fled in panic. There was good reason for their flight, as Soviet political officers had exhorted Red Army soldiers to take vengeance on the German population. Many of the troops needed little or no persuasion. They were vividly aware of the atrocities that the Germans had perpetrated in the Soviet Union, and now, after years of savage fighting, they had finally reached the homeland of the hated enemy. But most of the German people did not flee and felt the invader's wrath. Soviet soldiers shot some of them and raped many women, including the very young and the very old. Although their actions were horrible, they were far more understandable than the crimes that the SS had inflicted against the Jews and other Soviet ethnic groups that had fallen under its merciless rule.

Amid all these disasters and growing chaos, Hitler decided to rid himself of Guderian. The general had always been outspoken and was never afraid of Hitler, qualities that the Führer actually admired. But in recent weeks, the quarrels between the two men had deteriorated into shouting matches. Finally, after a particularly heated conversation on March 28, Hitler sent Guderian on sick leave and replaced him with General Hans Krebs, a much weaker personality who had no thought of disagreeing with Hitler.

THE ALLIED DRIVE TO THE RHINE

While these dramatic events were taking place in the east, equally momentous developments were unfolding in the west. After the failure of Hitler's Second Ardennes offensive, logic dictated a German withdrawal to the Rhine. The Reich's only hope of holding out against Western Allied might was to defend the great river barrier. German forces were not powerful enough to attempt a stand west of the Rhine. Not only had they suffered from the fearful pounding in the Ardennes, but their leaders had shifted much of their remaining strength to try to stem the Soviet flood. Hitler nevertheless insisted that his troops contest every inch of German soil. They would fight to the west of the Rhine.

The Allied plan for clearing the Rhineland provided for three separate operations. In the north, Dempsey's British Second and Crerar's Canadian First armies would strike southward, while Simpson's U.S. Ninth Army was to thrust northward to meet them. In the center, Hodges's First Army, now restored to Bradley's Twelfth Army Group, would drive toward Cologne and Bonn on the Rhine and then pivot southward along the river. It was to link up with Patton's Third Army, which was to swing along the north bank of the Moselle River toward the Rhine. Farther south, Patch's Seventh Army would move northward to make contact with Patton's forces near Koblenz.

The British and Canadians opened this ambitious plan with an enormous artillery barrage on February 8. But they encountered bitter resistance as well as flooded terrain, which slowed their progress. They did not reach the Rhine until February 21. Simpson's forces suffered from even greater obstacles. They had to cross the Roer River to launch their attack, and the Germans opened the gates of a dam upstream, flooding the area. The Americans had to wait two weeks before the waters subsided sufficiently for them to negotiate the remaining barrier in assault boats. On March 4, they finally made contact with the Canadians.

The First Army opened its offensive on February 26 when Collins's Seventh Corps crossed the Roer with a dual mission: to protect Simpson's left flank and to capture Cologne. This great city, which had been one of the most frequent targets of Allied bombers, fell on March 5. Although much of Cologne lay in ruins, its great twin-spired Gothic cathedral, despite some damage, remained intact. Meanwhile, the First Army's Third Corps moved toward Bonn and Remagen, 15 miles farther south.

FIGURE 23-1 A convoy of U.S. Seventh Army trucks rolls past wrecked buildings in Augsburg, Germany. (*U.S. Army Photograph*)

At Remagen, a platoon of the Ninth Armored Division accomplished one of the most incredible feats of the war. It stormed the Hohenzollern railroad bridge on March 7 and, despite heavy enemy fire, succeeded in seizing its objective. The Germans had tried to blow up the span; two preliminary explosions had caused some structural damage, but the main charge had failed to detonate. The Americans quickly established a bridgehead on the west bank of the Rhine, and within 24 hours, 8,000 men were across the river. It was the only bridge along the entire course of the Rhine that the Germans failed to destroy. Ironically, its capture came on the ninth anniversary of the German occupation of the Rhineland. Hitler reacted to the Remagen disaster by dismissing Rundstedt as commander in chief on the western front for the second and last time. Kesselring, the commander in Italy, succeeded Rundstedt in this unenviable position. General von Vietinghoff took Kesselring's place in Italy.

Patton's Third Army was active, too. Its armored spearhead dashed 65 miles along the north bank of the Moselle and reached the Rhine in less than three days. On March 15, Patton sent his Twelfth Corps southward along the Rhine. The Germans had expected him to swing north to exploit the Remagen bridgehead, and his maneuver took them by surprise. At the same time, Patch's Seventh Army struck northward through the Saar to link up with Patton. By March 25, all organized resistance west of the Rhine had ceased. Hitler's decision to fight in the Rhineland had cost him dearly. The Allies had mauled his forces and had taken 290,000 prisoners. As the struggle for the Rhineland unfolded, German morale, which had been so strong for so long, also began to crack.

The Remagen bridgehead was located in one of the most rugged areas of the Rhine, one that the Allies had not intended as a major crossing point. But once the First Army gained its foothold there, Eisenhower moved quickly to expand it. In part, he did this to draw German troops away from other portions of the Rhine's east bank and ease the task of establishing additional bridgeheads. The Third Army gained the first of these when it secured a foothold southwest of Frankfurt on March 22. The Germans, who had managed to retreat across the river, had blown up the bridges but were too few, too disorganized, and too demoralized to offer any real resistance to Patton's crossing.

Ironically, Patton had secured his bridgehead while Montgomery was still planning an operation that Eisenhower had intended as the main crossing all along. The British commander had massed 25 divisions from the Second and Ninth armies as well as enormous supplies preparatory to an assault across the river to the north of the Ruhr. Before launching this pile-driver blow on March 23, he subjected the east bank of the Rhine to a colossal pounding from 3,000 artillery pieces as well as aerial bombardment. Considering the fact that only five weak German divisions guarded the landing area, this spectacular display of firepower proved more than adequate. The Germans offered little resistance. Allied airborne troops also dropped behind enemy lines once the operation began and contributed to its overwhelming success. By March 27, all seven Allied armies were across the great river, which had proved a weak barrier. The German position in the west was now clearly hopeless, and the way to the Reich's heartland lay open.

CRUSHING THE AXIS IN ITALY

Germany was not the only place where catastrophe beckoned the Nazi regime. In Italy, a three-month lull in Allied offensive operations came to an end early in April. Although the Germans and the Italian forces, which Mussolini had managed to recruit in northern Italy, actually had more divisions than the Allies, they were badly understrength. In reality, Allied fighting men outnumbered the enemy 2 to 1. They also enjoyed the same margin of superiority in artillery and a 3-to-1 advantage in tanks. In addition, they had recently received much up-to-date equipment and abundant supplies. Allied air power dominated the skies.

British troops opened their attack on April 9 with a frontal assault along the Senio and Reno rivers coupled with an amphibious operation across Lake Comacchio, a large body of water near the Adriatic coast. They secured a beachhead on the lake's western shore, which threatened the enemy flank and forced the Germans to withdraw. By April 18, the Eighth Army had broken into the broad plain that stretched toward the great Po River. Meanwhile, the Fifth Army opened its attack across the last remaining mountain ridges south of the plain on April 14 and achieved a breakthrough three days later.

Vietinghoff had committed most of his forces to the front line and was unable to establish a new defensive position. He urged Hitler to authorize a retreat to the Po, but the Führer, as usual, refused. Finally, on April 20, Vietinghoff ordered a withdrawal himself. But by that time it was too late. Allied armored forces swept toward the river and cut off many Germans. Some managed to swim across the Po, but they had to abandon all their equipment. The entire Axis position in Italy had collapsed. The industrial city of Bologna fell to the Americans on April 21; the British crossed the Po and captured Venice on April 28.

As the Axis disasters mounted, Mussolini made a desperate attempt to escape to Switzerland with his longtime mistress, Clara Petacci. But Italian Partisans cut short their flight on April 28 and shot them both to death. They brought their bodies to Milan and dumped them in a large square, where a mob of vengeful Italians trampled and spat on the corpses. One well-placed kick broke the former Duce's jaw. When this grisly ritual ended, Partisans strung wire around the forlorn couple's feet and hung them upside down from a steel girder, where they remained on display for some time. Thus, the man who had once dreamed of creating a new Roman Empire perished in total degradation.

All that remained was the surrender of the surviving Axis troops. Actually, General Karl Wolff, head of the SS in Italy, had opened secret negotiations for capitulation through neutral Switzerland as early as February. He had encountered a myriad of obstacles, however, and had been unable to conclude arrangements before the start of the final Allied offensive. Now, as it became obvious that nothing could prevent total defeat, Vietinghoff and Marshal Graziani, who commanded Mussolini's forces, joined Wolff in seeking an end to the struggle. German representatives signed an unconditional surrender agreement on April 29, and the document became effective on May 2.

THE ALLIES OVERRUN THE REICH

Meanwhile, the stage was set for the final German collapse in the Reich itself. The establishment of multiple Allied bridgeheads on the east bank of the Rhine accelerated the disintegration of German forces. There was no fortified line to which they could withdraw for shelter. The great North German Plain lay in the path of the Allied leviathan, and although occasional river barriers remained to be crossed, they were still a considerable distance to the east. The badly outnumbered, exhausted, and demoralized soldiers of the Wehrmacht were nearing the end of their tether. Equipment was breaking down, supplies were running low, and Allied planes roamed at will over the stricken Fatherland. Fuel shortages became so critical that tanks could not move and planes could not fly.

The next Allied objective was the Ruhr. Eisenhower planned to encircle it and then squeeze it into submission. Its neutralization, along with the loss of Silesia, would deal a death blow to German industry. Eisenhower sent elements of Simpson's Ninth Army on a dash around the Ruhr's northern flank, while units of Hodges's First Army swept around the sprawling industrial complex from the south. The two arms of the envelopment came together at Lippstadt on April 1, trapping all of Model's Army Group B and two corps of Army Group H, which defended northern Germany. Hitler characteristically proclaimed the Ruhr a fortress to be defended to the last man and the last bullet. But it was not a fortress, and its garrison was in no condition to carry out prolonged resistance. For the next two weeks, the encircling forces applied increasing pressure on the defenders, splitting them into two pockets on April 14 and securing their final capitulation five days later. A total of 325,000 Germans surrendered. Among those who did not was Model, who preferred suicide to captivity.

Even while the Battle of the Ruhr Pocket was raging, other elements of both Ninth and First armies were stabbing deeply into the heart of Germany. The creation of the Ruhr pocket had left a yawning void in their path with only scattered German units between them and the Elbe River far to the east. Simpson's spearhead reached the river on April 11 and by April 13 had secured a bridgehead on the east bank only 50 miles from Berlin. It appeared that the road to the German capital was open. Simpson, with "the bit between his teeth," urged that he be allowed to push on to Berlin. But Eisenhower ordered him to halt while Allied armies "cleaned up" the flanks to the north and south. The American advance now shifted to the southeast toward Leipzig, Chemnitz, and Dresden. It also focused on Bavaria and Austria, where Hitler supposedly planned to make a last stand in a National Redoubt centered in the Alps. On April 16, the Soviets launched their long-awaited final offensive against Berlin and encircled the city ten days later.

Eisenhower's decision to halt Simpson's advance became still another of the controversial issues of the war. Critics, especially Simpson and Montgomery, charged that had Ike allowed the Ninth Army to continue its drive, it would have reached Berlin before the Soviets. But only Simpson's spearhead had reached the Elbe, and its tanks were running low on fuel. Most of his forces were still far to the west. The situation was not unlike that of Germany's Army Group Center when it reached Smolensk in the summer of 1941. The Americans had fewer than 50,000 men and little artillery in their advance positions. The Red Army, by contrast, had been massing troops and supplies on the Oder for weeks and were only 33 miles away from the city. Had Simpson attempted to continue his push toward Berlin, the Soviets would almost certainly have speeded up the timetable for their offensive against the capital. With two bridgeheads to the west of the Oder and 1,250,000 men and 22,000 artillery pieces in position, it seems likely that they would have reached Berlin in force before the Americans.

When he made his decision to halt, Eisenhower was fully cognizant of the weakness of Simpson's advance forces as well as the far greater strength of the Soviets. He also knew that Roosevelt, Churchill, and Stalin had agreed to divide Germany into occupation zones after the war and that Berlin would lie within the Soviet zone. The Big Three had concluded this agreement in February when they met at Yalta on the coast of the USSR's Crimean Peninsula. The Allied leaders had also provided for the division of Berlin itself into occupation zones for each of the three major powers. Even if American forces had been able to take the city, this agreement would have required their withdrawal from the portion reserved for the Soviets as well as from territory east of the Elbe. At this point, Eisenhower also considered both the Leipzig-Dresden area and the National Redoubt more important military objectives for the Western Allies than Berlin, which he assumed would fall to the Red Army.

In reality, the National Redoubt was a myth. Although American leaders had long speculated on the possibility of a last-ditch stand by die-hard Nazis in the south, the Germans never planned such a desperate scenario. But Propaganda Minister Goebbels had learned of this American illusion in late 1944 and did everything he could to encourage his enemies in their belief. He was remarkably successful. Although U.S. intelligence wavered between skepticism and acceptance, Eisenhower became convinced that the possibility of a redoubt had to be assumed. Bradley was even more certain of its existence. Both men feared that unless American troops moved into this area quickly, SS forces and other Nazi fanatics might prolong the war for months, perhaps even years.

Allied forces were now lunging forward everywhere. Crerar's Canadian First Army liberated most of the remainder of the Netherlands and occupied the northwestern portion of Germany. Dempsey's British Second Army took the North Sea ports of Bremen on April 26 and Hamburg a week later. It also reached Lübeck on the Baltic on May 3, effectively sealing off Denmark to the northwest from the advancing Russian armies. In the south, the French First Army crossed the Rhine, captured Stuttgart on April 21, and penetrated into western Austria. Patch's Seventh Army drove across Germany's narrow waist; seized Nuremberg, site of the Nazi party rallies, on April 20; then hooked south to take Munich, the party's birthplace, ten days later. It captured Hitler's mountain retreat at Berchtesgaden on May 4.

Patton's Third Army drove into eastern Germany, reached the Czech border on April 25, and moved into the Sudetenland. With only weak German forces between his tanks and Prague, Patton asked permission to push on to the Czech capital. Eisenhower refused, indicating that it, like Berlin, was now a political rather than a military objective and lay in the path of the Red Army's advance. There seems little doubt that Patton could have reached Prague first, because the Soviets were considerably farther away and encountering stronger resistance. Instead, elements of the Third Army swung southward into Austria and soon discovered that there was no National Redoubt. Eisenhower now changed his mind and on May 4 offered to assist the Red Army in the capture of Prague. The Soviets, whose forces were closing in from the east, declined his overture. The Czech capital fell to the Red Army on May 9.

As Allied armies converged from east and west, they began to occupy the Nazi death camps in Poland and the concentration camps of the Reich itself. SS units attempted to destroy the evidence of their monstrous deeds in the Polish camps. Although not always successful in this endeavor, they did blow up the huge crematoriums at Auschwitz. SS guards herded many of the surviving inmates westward and shot large

FIGURE 23-2 The heaped corpses of political prisoners at the Belsen concentration camp symbolize the brutality of the Nazi regime. (*U.S. Army Photograph*)

numbers along the way. Others escaped and wandered about in the devastated countryside.

The rapid advance of Allied forces in the west engulfed the camps of Germany before the SS could destroy them. One by one they revealed their horrible secrets, confirming the half-believed reports that had been circulating for years. The hideous evidence was all there, including torture chambers and strangling rooms where guards hung prisoners with short nooses attached to rows of hooks. There were also lamp shades, purses, and gloves made from human skin as well as the victims of ghastly medical experiments. And, of course, there were the crematoriums, huge piles of corpses, and the living skeletons of the survivors. Photographs and films brought much of the impact of these horrors home to the people of Britain and America. The names of the camps became watchwords of shame—Buchenwald, Belsen, Dachau. The commandants and their associates—brutal sadists such as Josef Kramer, the "Beast of Belsen," and Ilse Koch, the "Bitch of Buchenwald"—became notorious.

But the greatest drama of all unfolded in Berlin. Hitler had shifted his headquarters to the capital from East Prussia when the Soviets opened their January offensive. With the approach of enemy troops, he took refuge in an underground bunker near the Reich's Chancellery building. The once mighty conqueror had become a physical wreck during the years of defeat. He had developed a stoop, suffered from tremors in his limbs, and dragged his left leg when he walked. His shattered dream of European domination, the pressure of directing the war effort, lack of sleep, and nervous exhaustion all contributed to this deterioration. He had also fallen under the influence of a quack doctor, Theodore Morell, who convinced him that the answer to his health problems lay in frequent injections of powerful drugs as well as a variety of pills. These remedies actually made his condition worse. The injuries that the Führer suffered in the attempt on his life in July 1944, though not serious, also weakened him.

Despite his failing health, Hitler remained the dominant figure of the Third Reich. He cowed his associates with the violence of his wrath and retained the power of life and death over every German from the highest generals to the lowliest members of society. His capacity for hatred and his morbid fascination with destruction grew more pronounced as the certainty of final defeat became ever greater. In March 1945, he ordered Speer to supervise the destruction of everything that might be useful to the Allies as they advanced into Germany. His list included bridges, dams, factories, railroads, mines, and rolling stock. He visualized a total scorched-earth policy. Speer balked at this and told Hitler that the war was lost and that nothing should be done to jeopardize the survival of the German people. The Führer was not impressed:

> If the war is to be lost, the nation also will perish. . . . There is no longer need to consider the basis for even a most primitive existence. On the contrary, it is better to destroy even that, and to destroy it ourselves. The nation has proved itself weak, and the future belongs to the stronger Eastern nation. Besides, those who remain after the battle are of little value; for the good have fallen.*

Appalled at the prospect of such senseless destruction, Speer set out to sabotage the Führer's orders and succeeded to a considerable degree. Although Germany emerged from the war in a thoroughly battered condition, the devastation was not as total as Hitler, the self-proclaimed embodiment of the German nation, had desired.

Hitler was still in the bunker when the Red Army launched its final offensive on April 16. The Soviet plan provided for Zhukov's forces to outflank Berlin from the north while Konev's troops swung around from the south. The assault began with the most intensive artillery barrage of the war, featuring a concentration of one gun every 13 feet. The Germans fought desperately, but within two days, the Soviets had broken through and poured like a torrent toward and around the capital. The two wings of the pincers met to the west of Berlin on April 25. Other Red Army forces dashed westward and on the same day met elements of the U.S. First Army near Torgau on the Elbe.

Although Hitler's aides had urged him to leave Berlin even before the start of the Red Army offensive, he refused and remained in his bunker after the Soviet jaws closed. Even now he visualized a miraculous turnabout in the war and continued to talk about counteroffensives using divisions that existed only on paper. He clutched at the few straws that still seemed available. The most notable example occurred when President Roosevelt died of a cerebral hemorrhage on April 12, four days before the Soviets opened their drive on Berlin. Both Hitler and Goebbels saw a parallel between Roosevelt's death and the demise of the Russian czarina Elizabeth in 1762 during the Seven Years' War, when Frederick the Great was king of Prussia. At that time, the Russians were threatening to capture Berlin, but following the czarina's death, her successor chose to make peace with Frederick instead. The Prussian king had always been a hero to Hitler, and now the Führer saw himself as a modern-day Frederick. He and Goebbels hoped that Roosevelt's successor, Harry Truman, might be the architect of a negotiated peace with Germany. Both men continued to believe that sooner or later the Western Allies would fall out with the Soviets and join Germany in an anti-Communist crusade. Their expectation proved totally unfounded. Truman was determined to fight the war to the victorious conclusion so close at hand.

Red Army troops penetrated into Berlin's suburbs on April 22, and the German capital, like Stalingrad, Budapest, and the Ruhr before it, won the dubious designation of "fortress" from the Führer. The struggle for the German capital became much like that for Stalingrad 2½ years earlier. The German garrison fought with fanatical dedication while Hitler did what he could to spur them on. But his cause was beyond redemption. The Soviets pushed forward, street by street and building by building. By April 26, they were less than a mile from Hitler's bunker. The city, already devastated by years of Allied air attacks,

*Quoted in H. R. Trevor Roper, *The Last Days of Hitler* (London: Pan Books, 1952), p. 88.

sank into total ruin from the effects of Red Army artillery and the savage fighting.

THE BITTER END

As the days passed, Hitler's last illusions about a miraculous turning of the tide slipped away. Realizing that the end was near, he lashed out with particular fury at those whom he held responsible for his defeat—the German officer corps, the Germany army, the German people. Then he received the unkindest cuts of all. The first came from Goering, who had moved his headquarters to the Bavarian Alps. Misinterpreting instructions from Hitler, Marshal Goering announced that he was assuming the power to negotiate with the Allies. This so enraged Hitler that he ordered Goering arrested. Soon afterward, he received a report that Himmler, who was in northern Germany, had attempted to open peace negotiations on his own authority. Even the man whom Hitler referred to as "*treue Heinrich*" (loyal Heinrich) had proved guilty of treachery.

By April 29, Hitler had resigned himself to death, but he still had unfinished business. First he married his longtime mistress, Eva Braun. Then he drafted his political testament in which he expelled Goering and Himmler from the party as traitors and appointed Admiral Dönitz president and commander in chief of the armed forces. The following day, Hitler bade farewell to the few remaining members of his staff and retired to his suite, where he and his bride committed suicide—she by poison, he by a pistol shot through the mouth. Aides burned their bodies in the Chancellery garden. Goebbels and his wife poisoned their six children soon afterward and then took their own lives. On May 2, the last fighting ended in Berlin. The shattered, flaming city was a suitable setting for Hitler's *Götterdämmerung* (twilight of the gods).

The war in Europe was not yet over, but it would linger only a few more days. American troops continued to knife through southern Germany and Austria and penetrated the Brenner Pass into Italy. In the process, they rounded up Goering and other Nazi leaders. On May 2, the same day that German forces laid down their arms in Italy, Dönitz asked for a separate peace with the Western Allies, indicating his intention to continue the war against the Soviets. The Americans and British refused. Unconditional surrender was the only option. It finally came in a schoolhouse in Reims, France, at 2:41 on the morning of May 7. A second ceremony followed in Berlin the next day as Allied and German military leaders met to ratify the earlier agreement. World War II in Europe was over, and with it Hitler's "Thousand-Year Reich" expired. It had lasted 12 years.

24

Island Hopping in the Pacific

From 1943 to 1945, while Allied forces in Europe moved relentlessly toward the final destruction of Nazi Germany, the war in the Pacific turned steadily against Japan. At first, Allied forces made discouragingly slow progress as they inched their way forward in the heartbreakingly difficult terrain of New Guinea and the Solomons. But they took an increasing toll of enemy resources on land and especially at sea and in the air. As time passed, America also transformed its vast industrial potential into actual production of ships, planes, and other weapons on a scale that Japan's smaller industrial base could not even approach. The gap between the capabilities of the two protagonists widened at a spectacular pace.

QUESTIONS OF STRATEGY AND LEADERSHIP

As this process unfolded, the United States and its allies grappled with vexing questions of strategy—where and how to strike at the enemy with greatest effect. They also confronted the problem of leadership. Should there be unity or division of command over operations in the vast Pacific? Since Britain devoted its strength overwhelmingly to the war in Europe and to a lesser extent to the defense of India and the proposed reconquest of Burma, the war in the Pacific became primarily an American responsibility. In view of this disparity, American interservice and personal rivalries assumed key importance in the development of strategy.

Early in the conflict, when the Japanese still held the initiative, Admiral King and other naval leaders looked forward to the time when the United States could take the offensive. They visualized Admiral Nimitz as the supreme commander of this great enterprise. But General MacArthur, the hero of Bataan, had other ideas. His defense of the Philippines, though in some respects disastrously inadequate, had captured the imagination of the American people. Even though President Roosevelt had originally proposed one commander for the entire Pacific, MacArthur's dramatic escape from the Philippines and his great popularity contributed to the decision to divide responsibilities between the general and Nimitz.

MacArthur became commander in chief of Allied forces in the Southwest Pacific, an area that included Australia, the Solomons, New Guinea, the Bismarck Archipelago, the Philippines, and all the Dutch Indies except Sumatra. Nimitz, in addition to retaining his command over the Pacific Fleet, became commander in chief of the North, Central, and South Pacific theaters of operations. He also assumed direct command over

Assault on Japan, 1942–45

the North and Central Pacific, while Admiral Ghormley carried out this duty in the South Pacific under Nimitz's overall direction. The Southwest Pacific thus became an army responsibility, with MacArthur subject nominally to the authority of General Marshall. The other Pacific areas became navy preserves, with Nimitz under the more direct supervision of Admiral King. Britain retained operational control over Burma and the rest of Southeast Asia, including Sumatra.

During the first two years of the war, planning focused on the great naval base that enemy forces had created at Rabaul on the island of New Britain. Control of Rabaul enabled the Japanese to support their forces, which had penetrated into New Guinea to the southwest and the Solomons to the southeast. Both these advances threatened Australia.

In March 1942, Admiral King proposed a counteroffensive that would feature simultaneous drives through New Guinea and the Solomons before converging on Rabaul. Soon after the Battle of Midway in June, MacArthur urged a thrust directly on Rabaul without the preliminaries in New Guinea and the Solomons. He spoke of accomplishing this in less than three weeks with the aid of a naval task force. Clearly such a daring stroke was far beyond American capabilities at this time, especially in view of Japanese strength in the area. MacArthur probably realized this, but his proposal catapulted him into the forefront of the strategic debate. Once confronted by the objections of naval leaders, he quickly agreed that a more gradual approach was indeed preferable. He insisted that since such an operation would take place in his Southwest Pacific theater, it was only just that he should assume command. But King contended that since the participation of large-scale naval forces would be absolutely essential, Nimitz should be the commander.

This divergence of opinion resulted in a heated argument that King and Marshall finally settled by dividing responsibilities between Nimitz and MacArthur. They shifted the boundary between the Southwest and South Pacific commands slightly to the west to bring the southern Solomons within the latter area. Their agreement called for an advance in the Solomons by forces under Ghormley's command while MacArthur cleared the northeastern coast of New Guinea. When the two commanders had successfully carried out these tasks, they would launch converging attacks against Rabaul. The opening phase of this ambitious undertaking culminated in the capture of Buna on the New Guinea coast in January 1943 and the Japanese evacuation from Guadalcanal a month later.

The navy also favored a thrust through the Marshall, Caroline, and Mariana island chains, which dotted the Central Pacific. King considered this the most direct and best route to the Japanese home islands. The key to the success of a Central Pacific strategy was the capture or neutralization of another major Japanese naval base, at Truk in the Carolines. Truk's large lagoon had the protection of surrounding coral reefs and provided an ideal anchorage. MacArthur much preferred a drive along the northern coast of New Guinea followed by a thrust through the Philippines to Japan. Such an approach would, of course, take place within his Southwest Pacific theater, enabling him to make good his pledge to return to the Philippines.

The navy was undoubtedly correct in its belief that the Central Pacific offered the superior route. It certainly was more direct and would facilitate concentration of resources for maximum effect. And because the Marshalls, Carolines, and Marianas consisted of over 1,000 far-flung small islands, the navy could pick its invasion targets. The Japanese clearly could not defend all these islands but would have to stretch their forces thinly to provide for the defense of as many as possible. Finally, the conquest of the Marianas would bring the cities of Japan within range of American long-range bombers while isolating the Solomons, New Guinea, and Rabaul, leaving them to "wither on the vine" in the rear of the American onslaught.

Once again, this dispute over navy and army objectives resulted in a compromise. In April 1943, the Joint Chiefs of Staff opted for a two-pronged strategy that employed both the navy's Central Pacific approach and MacArthur's route. They based their decision in part on the belief that the expenditure in blood, materiel, and effort in the Solomons and New Guinea had been too great simply to terminate these operations. But they designated the Central Pacific as the primary theater and proposed to devote the lion's share of naval strength to this area. In May, Roosevelt, Churchill, and the Allied Combined Chiefs of Staff approved this plan at the Trident Conference in Washington.

Both offensives employed an island-hopping technique. This involved capturing islands or parts of islands and then moving several hundred miles to other objectives, followed by another leap and then another. In the process, the two offensives bypassed many Japanese-held islands.

AMERICAN MOVES IN THE NORTH PACIFIC

There was also the less important matter of the North Pacific. Japanese troops still held the barren, unpopulated, fog-shrouded Aleutian islands of Kiska and Attu, which they had seized at the time of the Battle of Midway. These forces, however, were too weak to attempt additional landings in the eastern Aleutians or Alaska. The United States probably would have been wise simply to allow them to remain on their bleak outposts while seeking more important objectives elsewhere. But fear that the enemy garrisons might pose a threat to Alaska led to the decision to invade Attu, the more weakly defended of the two islands, on May 11, 1943.

With a 5-to-1 advantage in numbers, the U.S. Army's Seventh Division landed without opposition on two sides of Attu. But once ashore, the Americans found themselves subjected to savage artillery, mortar, and machine-gun fire. Snow and mud added to their difficulties as they slogged slowly inland. The two invading forces managed to link up five days later with the aid of intense naval shelling and drove the Japanese toward the northeastern end of the island. The defenders resisted grimly until the end of the month, engaging in repeated desperation charges. Almost the entire garrison of 2,600 men fought to the death or committed suicide. The Americans next turned their attention to Kiska. Bombers attacked the island repeatedly, starting in July. But when U.S. troops actually landed on August 15, they discovered that the Japanese had evacuated their garrison two weeks earlier under cover of fog.

ACTION IN THE SOUTHWEST THEATER

Meanwhile, following the capture of Buna and Guadalcanal in early 1943, the Joint Chiefs of Staff again took up the thorny question of command in New Guinea and the Solomons. Since the northern Solomons lay within the boundaries of MacArthur's Southwest Pacific theater, the Joint Chiefs agreed that the general would exercise strategic command over both areas. But Admiral Halsey would retain tactical control in the Solomons under MacArthur's general directives. Halsey had succeeded Ghormley as commander of Allied forces in the South Pacific during the Guadalcanal campaign. The Joint Chiefs also laid down guidelines for the strategy that MacArthur and Halsey were to carry out during 1943. The two commanders then hammered out a final plan, code-named Operation Cartwheel, in April. It provided for MacArthur to persevere in his advance along New Guinea's northern coast and ultimately to undertake a landing on New Britain's western shore. At the same time, Halsey's forces were to push into the northern Solomons.

Before these operations could begin, MacArthur's air commander, General George C. Kenney, led his Fifth Air Force to a rousing victory against a Japanese convoy in the Bismarck Sea to the north of New Britain. Kenney had taken over command in August 1942. An exceptionally dynamic man with intense drive and determination, Kenney insisted on maintaining complete control over air operations himself. When MacArthur's chief of staff, General Sutherland, tried to interfere, he informed him in the most emphatic terms that when it came to air operations, he was the expert and Sutherland was the novice.

Land-based bombers had accomplished little in either the New Guinea or Guadalcanal campaigns before Kenney took over. They had operated at high altitudes, in keeping with air force doctrine, but Kenney decided to experiment with low-level attacks by B-25 Mitchell two-engine medium bombers. These planes, named for the famous advocate of strategic air power, General William ("Billy") Mitchell, practiced bombing runs during the fall and winter of 1942–43 from altitudes as low as 150 feet. By the end of the winter, they had mastered this art and were ready to try it on the enemy.

Their opportunity came when Ultra reports indicated that a Japanese convoy of seven troop transports and eight destroyers had left Rabaul on March 1 bound for New Guinea. Kenney sent B-17s to bomb the convoy from high altitude in the usual manner. But after two such attacks, which sank two transports, B-25s and other medium bombers zoomed in at low level the next day and sank the remaining five transports as well as four destroyers. Almost 3,000 enemy troops lost their lives. For the first time, land-based bombers had destroyed a Japanese fleet without the aid of naval forces. This Battle of the Bismarck Sea placed a premium on such air power in the future and strengthened the American resolve to obtain advance air bases that would bring more remote Japanese strongholds within striking range of U.S. bombers.

Japan's defeat in the Battle of the Bismarck Sea also impressed Admiral Yamamoto with the unmistakable fact that the Americans were gaining air superiority in the Southwest Pacific. Yamamoto sought to reverse this trend by sending over 300 planes on a series of raids against Guadalcanal and Tulagi as well as Allied bases in New Guinea during April. But this effort proved ineffective, as the Japanese suffered aircraft losses at least equal to those that they inflicted on the Allies.

Some of the inexperienced pilots who took part in the operation believed that their efforts had been far more successful than was actually the case, however. Their overly optimistic reports misled Yamamoto, who decided to visit the northernmost island of the Solomons, Bougainville, to congratulate his supposedly victorious flyers personally. This proved a fatal mistake. American cryptanalysts intercepted messages containing detailed information on the admiral's trip. Eighteen twin-engine P-38 Lightning fighters were waiting for his bomber and its escort of nine Zeros as they approached southern Bougainville on April 18. One of the P-38s shot down the admiral's plane, which crashed in the jungle, killing the architect of the attack on Pearl Harbor. Yamamoto had chosen his own successor, Admiral Mineichi Koga, as commander of the Combined Fleet. Though capable and efficient, Koga lacked his predecessor's strategic ability and adopted a conservative and unimaginative approach to the war.

By June 1943, Halsey and MacArthur were ready to launch their new operations in the Solomons and New Guinea. The two key targets in the Solomons were New Georgia, which lay to the northwest of Guadalcanal, and Bougainville. Successful landings on these islands would enable Halsey's forces to bypass most of the remainder of the Solomons and provide air bases for raids against Rabaul.

The attack on New Georgia began with landings at two points along the island's southeastern coast late in June. Americans also went ashore on neighboring Rendova Island. Within artillery range of southwestern New Georgia, Rendova provided a convenient jumping-off point for the major invasion near the chief Japanese base at Munda on July 2. Although the inexperienced Forty-third Army Division went ashore without opposition, it soon encountered extremely rugged, jungle-choked terrain and made agonizingly slow progress against Japanese forces, who held the high ground before Munda. The division's morale became so poor and "combat fatigue" cases so prevalent that Halsey had to send in two additional army divisions.

The Americans were not able to make a concerted effort to take the airfield at Munda until July 25. Numerous well-situated coconut-log-and-coral pillboxes barred their way, and the Japanese fought with their usual grim determination. But incessant artillery, air, and naval bombardment gradually took a heavy toll on the defenders, as did that fearsome weapon, the flamethrower, which made its first extensive appearance in the Pacific war. By July 29, the highly capable and resourceful Japanese commander, General Noburu Sasaki, realized that additional resistance was futile and began to withdraw his forces to Kolombangara Island just to the northwest. Munda airfield fell to the Americans on August 5, but resistance continued elsewhere on New Georgia for another two weeks.

Kolombangara now posed a problem. With a garrison of 12,000 troops, it promised another bloody struggle, but Halsey opted to bypass it. On August 5, he sent 4,500 men ashore on lightly defended Vella Lavella, which lay to the northwest. These forces quickly occupied the island and confronted General Sasaki with the alternative of leaving his troops on Kolombangara to wither on the vine or withdrawing them to Bougainville. He chose the latter, and in late September and early October, the Japanese carried out a skillful nighttime evacuation.

As in the Guadalcanal campaign, rival naval forces fought a series of engagements while the battle raged on New Georgia. In the first of these on July 6, a Japanese destroyer force sank the light cruiser *Helena* while losing two of its own ships. In another encounter on July 13, the Japanese lost a light cruiser but damaged three Allied cruisers and sank a destroyer. The final engagement came on the night of August 6–7 in the waters between Vella Lavella and Kolombangara. In this Battle of Vella Lavella Gulf, six U.S. destroyers ambushed a squadron of four enemy destroyers and bested them at their own game, night fighting with torpedoes. They sent all but one of the Japanese ships to the bottom.

Halsey's final objective in the Solomons was Bougainville. If the Americans could gain a foothold there, they could establish airfields much closer to New Britain. This would enable fighter planes using these bases to provide protection for Kenney's bombing raids against Rabaul. Conversely, the key to a successful landing on Bougainville was to destroy Japanese air bases on the island. Planes operating from Munda carried out this task with great efficiency.

Halsey decided to bypass heavily defended southern Bougainville and strike at Empress Augusta Bay, about two-thirds of the way up the western coast. The Third Marine Division made the assault against weak opposition on November 1 and pushed inland. The Japanese commander, General Hyakutake, who had failed earlier to dislodge the Americans from Guadalcanal, had expected the landing to come in the south. He clung persistently to this belief even after the Americans had established a substantial perimeter at Empress Augusta Bay. His failure to send reinforcements to the landing site eased the marine advance, although Japanese counterattacks did result in some heavy fighting. By the end of December, the Americans held an enclave ten miles wide and five miles deep and had built three airstrips.

On the first night of the American landing, Admiral Sentaro Omori attempted to attack the transports disembarking troops. He used two heavy and two light cruisers as well as six destroyers for this purpose, but they fell afoul of an American force of four light cruisers and eight destroyers, commanded by Admiral M. Stanton Merrill. In the Battle of Empress Augusta Bay that followed, Merrill's ships denied the Japanese access to the transports while sinking one light cruiser and a destroyer. After this rebuff, the Japanese squadron retired to Rabaul.

Admiral Koga responded to Omori's defeat by dispatching seven heavy cruisers, one light cruiser, and four destroyers from Truk to Rabaul, preparatory to another strike. But U.S. cryptanalysts intercepted messages pertaining to the operation and alerted Halsey. The admiral had no surface ships capable of dealing with such a large number of heavy cruisers and faced a potentially critical situation. He decided to use the only weapon he had, Task Force 38, which he had borrowed from Nimitz to support the Bougainville operation. Admiral Frederick Sherman, who had been captain of the carrier *Lexington* in the Battle of the Coral Sea, commanded this force. It included the carriers *Saratoga* and *Princeton.*

The United States had never tried a carrier strike against a base as powerful as Rabaul. But on November 5, Sherman's planes swooped in for a surprise attack, which, with the aid of considerable good luck, scored a remarkable success. While clouds protected *Saratoga* and *Princeton* from Japanese aircraft, U.S. planes had the benefit of bright sunshine over Rabaul. They damaged three cruisers and the same number of destroyers. The Japanese never again attempted to use heavy cruisers in this theater.

PUSHING ALONG NEW GUINEA'S COAST

While Halsey's forces invaded New Georgia and Bougainville, MacArthur continued operations along the New Guinea coast. His objectives were the villages of Salamaua and Lae near the southern edge of the Huon Peninsula, about 175 miles north of Buna. Important preliminaries for this operation had started in January, when Allied aircraft transported an Australian brigade to strengthen Kanga Force, a guerrilla unit that had maintained an airstrip at the village of Wau, 25 miles southeast of Salamaua. These troops repulsed a Japanese attempt to capture the airstrip and in February began to push the enemy back toward Salamaua.

In late June, American forces carried out a seaborne landing at Nassau Bay, 15 miles south of Salamaua. This operation opened a supply route to the Australians at Wau and also helped convince the Japanese that the Allies intended to deliver their main thrust toward Salamaua. In reality, their primary objective was Lae, about 25 miles to the north. Lae was the gateway to the Markham and Ramu river valleys, which extended almost 400 miles to the northwest on the landward side of the Huon Peninsula. They formed a relatively easy route to the important Japanese base at Madang, just north of the peninsula's western edge.

The campaign to take Lae and Salamaua was a grueling affair that featured an abundance of mountains and thick, rain-soaked jungle. Extreme heat and humidity as well as a variety of tropical diseases were ever-present. Australian troops landed on the coast 20 miles east of Lae on September 4, and soon afterward U.S. forces carried out an airborne landing on the bank of the Markham River to the northwest. The two Allied units then pushed forward from both directions, forcing the Japanese to evacuate Lae and Salamaua by September 16.

During the remainder of September and October, Australian forces thrust up the Markham and Ramu valleys to outflank the Huon Peninsula and reached a point only 50 miles south of Madang. Other Australian troops encountered strong resistance along the peninsula's coast but in mid-November began slowly to push the enemy back. On January 2, 1944, U.S. troops landed at Saidor to the northwest of the peninsula in an effort to cut off the enemy retreat. Although the Japanese managed to avoid this fate by side-stepping the Americans with the help of inland trails, they lost almost a third of their original force of 7,000 men. Even those who survived suffered from disease and starvation. In late March, the Australians, who had been advancing up the Markham and Ramu valleys, reached the coast, linking up with the Americans near Saidor. On April 24, Allied troops finally occupied Madang, but its capture proved anticlimactic. The Japanese had already evacuated to Wewak, nearly 200 miles to the northwest.

While the Australians continued the thankless task of pushing along New Guinea's seemingly endless coast, MacArthur staged a series of leapfrog amphibious operations. The first of these took place on April 22 at Aitape, 75 miles from Wewak, and Hollandia, 125 miles farther west. U.S. forces took the Japanese by surprise and quickly gained control of both objectives. Another landing seized the small, weakly defended island of Wakde, 130 miles from Hollandia, on May 17. Ten days later, U.S. forces went ashore on the larger island of Biak, 190 miles to the northwest. Biak became a nightmare. Its garrison was much larger than the Americans had expected, and the Japanese had fortified a multitude of interconnecting caves in the island's steep cliffs. The invaders had to dislodge the enemy from each of these strongholds with the help of TNT, flamethrowers, and ignited gasoline. This bloody work continued until mid-August, when the last resistance ended.

A CHAIN AROUND RABAUL

In December 1943, while Allied forces were still struggling to conquer New Guinea's Huon Peninsula and Halsey's troops were establishing their perimeter at Empress Augusta Bay, MacArthur launched still another phase of Operation Cartwheel—the invasion of New Britain. Army troops executed an uncontested landing at Arawe, along the southern coast, on December 15 and, after securing a beachhead, successfully fought off Japanese counterattacks. On the day after Christmas, marines easily gained a foothold at Cape Gloucester, near the island's northwestern tip. But they had to overcome a Japanese force entrenched on a nearby hill as well as torrential monsoon rains before securing their position.

By the end of 1943, the Allies menaced Rabaul from the western end of New Britain as well as from Bougainville and New Georgia. They subjected the great base to repeated air attacks during the months which followed, but they abandoned their original plan for a seaborne assault. During the Quadrant Conference at Quebec in August 1943, Roosevelt and Churchill had accepted the Joint Chiefs of Staff proposal that the Allies bypass Rabaul. It had gradually become evident that an invasion was not necessary.

On February 29, 1944, American troops provided the last major link in the chain that the Allies were forging around Rabaul when they landed on Los Negros in the Admiralty Islands, almost 200 miles northwest of New Britain. Aerial intelligence had indicated that the island contained only a weak defending force, but in reality it totaled 4,000 men. Fortunately for the Americans, the enemy troops were on the opposite end of the island. By the time the Japanese were able to counterattack, the landing force had firmly established itself and repelled the enemy.

THE CENTRAL PACIFIC OFFENSIVE

Meanwhile, Nimitz had opened his Central Pacific offensive. He had been able to assemble far larger naval forces than were available for the various phases of Operation Cartwheel. By October 1943, the Fifth Fleet, under Admiral Spruance, consisted of eight carriers, seven battleships, seven heavy and three light cruisers, and 34 destroyers. Despite the loss of four carriers during 1942, *Saratoga* and *Enterprise* were still afloat and had recovered from assorted injuries. The navy had also received six new *Essex*-class carriers, which were faster, more maneuverable, and better armed than the older carriers. In addition, the Pacific Fleet was putting into service another half-dozen light carriers of the *Independence* class. Actually converted cruisers, these vessels were equal in speed to the larger carriers but could carry only half as many planes. Carrier aircraft had also improved. American designers had studied a captured Japanese Zero and had developed their answer to this famous fighter, the FGF Hellcat. Not only did the Hellcat possess better armor and armament, but it could both outclimb and outdive the Zero.

The original plan for the Central Pacific offensive called for American forces to bypass the Gilbert Islands, the southeasternmost point in the Japanese defensive perimeter, and strike directly at the Marshalls. But American strategists ultimately decided that it would be best to gain bases in the Gilberts first to provide steppingstones to the Marshalls.

Spruance held overall command of the operation in the Gilberts. Admiral Richmond Kelly Turner led the naval assault force, including the transports, landing craft, and supporting warships, which would actually be responsible for getting the troops ashore. Marine General Holland Smith would take command of the troops once they were ashore. Turner's marked tendency to try to control operations even after the ground forces went into action became the source of friction between himself and Smith. Both "Terrible Turner" and "Howlin' Mad" Smith were formidable personalities, and their jurisdictional squabbles contributed little to the smoothness of the operation.

THE TAKING OF TARAWA AND MAKIN

The objectives of the invasion were two small atolls—Tarawa, near the center of the Gilberts, and Makin, at their northwestern extremity. Plans called for attacks on both targets on November 20, 1943. Tarawa's defenses were much more formidable than those of Makin. They included a garrison of 5,000 men as well as eight-inch gun batteries housed in concrete and coconut log bunkers. Tarawa consisted of a number of islands and coral reefs surrounding a 15-mile-long lagoon.

The key point was the elongated island of Betio, which stretched for $2^1/_2$ miles but measured only 800 yards at its widest point. Betio contained the majority of the Japanese defenders and had the protection of a coral reef that surrounded it on all sides. Moreover, the November tides at Tarawa were unpredictable. In fact, an expert on the island's tides warned that the water would not be deep enough to allow landing craft to pass over the reef and urged postponement of the invasion until December. But other former residents of Tarawa insisted that there would be sufficient clearance. Spruance refused to postpone the invasion, a decision that proved to be a mistake.

Although warships and land-based aircraft blasted Tarawa with the heaviest bombardment ever to precede an invasion up to that time, the Japanese defenses withstood this frightful tattoo. Worse, the warning about the reef turned out to be true. New amphibious tractor landing craft (amphtracs), which were capable of climbing over the reef, carried the first three waves of marines to the beach with relatively little trouble. But the troops that followed were not so fortunate. Since there were too few amphtracs, they had to make do with deep-draft landing craft. These became caught on the reef, and the marines had to wade through shoulder-high water for hundreds of yards to reach the beach. Many of them fell victim to Japanese fire. Even those who had landed earlier found themselves pinned down on the beach. By nightfall, 5,000 men had landed, but 1,500 of them were dead or wounded. The marines clung to a beachhead that did not exceed 300 yards in depth.

More savage fighting took place the next day, but the marines, with the help of flamethrowers and TNT, gradually forced the defenders back. The tide also finally increased in depth, allowing the landing of artillery, while naval guns and carrier planes blasted the Japanese positions. By the third night, the marines had pushed the enemy back into the western end of the island. The Japanese now resorted to desperation attacks, which the Americans repulsed with heavy losses. Resistance ended on the afternoon of November 23.

"Bloody Tarawa" had been a rude shock, not only to the marines who experienced the battle and those who had planned it but to the American people as well. It had cost over 1,000 dead and more than 2,000 wounded, a terrible price for such a small atoll. The Japanese had suffered a far worse fate. Only 17 of them survived.

The assault on Makin also proved more difficult than expected. Although army troops, who greatly outnumbered the defenders, were able to establish a beachhead against little resistance, they found their progress inland slowed by snipers. The pace of the advance quickened the next day, but the Americans did not gain complete control of the atoll until November 23.

THE LEAP TO KWAJALEIN

Possession of Tarawa and Makin set the stage for the next operation, a thrust northwestward into the Marshall Islands. Spruance, Turner, and Smith, who were to repeat the roles they had played in the Tarawa operation, assumed that the invasion target would be in the eastern Marshalls, which lay closest to the Gilberts. All three men were horrified when Admiral Nimitz informed them that he intended to leap ahead 400 miles to attack the Kwajalein atoll in the center of the island chain. They warned that such a daring operation would expose both ships and landing force to bombing attacks from the many Japanese air bases in the Marshalls. But Nimitz's decision was not as wild as his dumbfounded subordinates thought. He had received Ultra reports that clearly indicated that the Japanese were expecting an attack against the outer Marshalls and were making their troop dispositions accordingly.

Nimitz did agree to Spruance's demand that Task Force 58, commanded by Admiral Marc Mitscher, carry out raids against airfields in the Marshalls with its carrier-based planes. Unlike most U.S. naval commanders at this time, Mitscher was actually an aviator and proved a master at handling carriers. He also took a keen personal interest in his men, who in turn held him in exceptionally high regard. But Mitscher's carriers had to return to Pearl Harbor for refitting and

FIGURE 24-1 Dead Japanese soldiers litter the ground near the entrance to a reinforced dugout on Tarawa. (*Defense Dept. Photo/Marine Corps*)

could not undertake their mission until January 1944. In the meantime, army and navy planes, operating from airstrips on Tarawa and Makin, began the process of pounding the enemy bases. When the task force returned, it made quick work of the remaining Japanese aircraft.

Kwajalein possessed defenses comparable to those of Tarawa, but the invading Americans outnumbered the Japanese 41,000 to 8,000. On February 1, two marine regiments landed on Roi and Namur, islands at the northern end of the atoll's lagoon, while two army regiments went ashore on Kwajalein island itself in the extreme south. The American forces encountered no problem with reefs this time, but a multitude of mishaps and mistakes delayed the landings on Roi and Namur for more than two hours. Nevertheless, the Japanese did not contest the landings, and the preinvasion bombardment was more prolonged and devastating than at Tarawa. The marines made rapid progress once they were ashore, and by the end of the second day, resistance had ended. In marked contrast to the initial muddle in the north, the landing on Kwajalein took place without difficulty. But once ashore, the troops advanced more slowly and did not complete their operations until February 4. The conquest of the atoll cost far fewer casualties than Tarawa—373 dead and 1,500 wounded.

THE NEUTRALIZATION OF TRUK

Nimitz's next objective was the Eniwetok atoll, at the far western edge of the Marshalls. His original timetable did not call for its capture until May. But the surprisingly easy victory at Kwajalein had justified the admiral's boldness and inspired a longing to take risks in other commanders. Spruance, Turner, and Smith urged an assault on Eniwetok as quickly as possible. They knew that the island was lightly defended but feared that this situation would not last long. Nimitz was in complete agreement. But one great danger confronted such an undertaking: Eniwetok lay within striking distance of Japanese air and naval forces at the great base of Truk in the

FIGURE 24-2 A marine (center) falls victim to a sniper as Japanese troops open fire on a U.S. patrol on Saipan. (*UPI/Bettmann News photos*)

Carolines. Even though Koga had withdrawn the major components of the Combined Fleet after the fall of Kwajalein, any attempt to take Eniwetok would be dangerous unless American air power neutralized Truk first. On February 17–18, Mitscher's task force attacked Truk, revealing the atoll's defenses as being far from impregnable. Carrier planes delivered repeated strikes, which destroyed 200 aircraft, sank eight warships and 24 merchant vessels, and damaged one carrier. The raids ended Truk's value as a major base.

In stark contrast to the ease with which Mitscher's flyers shattered the legend of Truk's invincibility, the conquest of Eniwetok proved a tougher task than anticipated. The Japanese had created a system of interlocking trenches, foxholes, and pillboxes that resembled a spiderweb. They greeted the invaders with heavy machine-gun and mortar fire, and as usual, the majority of the defenders fought to the death. Four days passed before resistance ended.

ASSAULT ON THE MARIANAS

The capture of Kwajalein and Eniwetok gave the Americans effective control over the Marshalls and left the remaining Japanese garrisons on islands in the chain to wither on the vine. Nimitz and Spruance now planned to bypass Truk and the other Caroline Islands and leap forward all the way to the Marianas, over 1,000 miles northwest of Eniwetok. Their objectives were Saipan, Tinian, and Guam, which contained the three largest Japanese garrisons in the Marianas. Unlike the atolls of the Gilberts and Marshalls, the Marianas were substantial islands that lay only 1,200 miles from Japan. Their capture promised to open a multitude of objectives to Allied planners: an assault on the Philippines to the west, a northward thrust toward the Bonin Islands, within 700 miles of Japan, and the establishment of air bases from which long-range bombers could attack Japanese cities.

In addition to his Fifth Fleet, Spruance had

127,000 troops available for the invasion, by far the largest force yet committed to any operation in the Pacific. Mitscher's task force attacked Japanese air bases for months prior to the invasion and virtually destroyed enemy air power in the Marianas.

Nimitz chose Saipan, the northernmost of the three major islands, as his first objective. Admiral Turner again commanded the amphibious force that made the assault, and General Smith led the ground forces. Mitscher's battleships hammered the island for two days before the actual invasion, and Turner's warships added their bombardment on the morning of the landings, but neither eliminated the enemy defenses. When two marine divisions landed on the southwest shore on June 15, they encountered fierce opposition and did not consolidate their beachhead until nightfall. During the next two weeks, with the help of army reinforcements, they fought their way northward to the main enemy defenses, which extended across the center of the island.

Admiral Nagumo, who had led the Japanese carrier striking force to its rousing victory at Pearl Harbor and its grim defeat at Midway, commanded the defending forces. Although the Japanese resisted desperately, the Americans ground slowly northward. On July 6, Nagumo and the island's army commander, General Yoshitsugu Saito, both took their own lives in an effort to encourage their troops to make a final attack. This assault came on the night of July 6–7 in the form of suicidal charges that decimated the remaining troops and virtually ended organized resistance. But one last gruesome chapter remained—the mass suicide of perhaps as many as 8,000 civilians in the last hours of the battle. They threw themselves off cliffs on the northern tip of the island, touched off grenades against their bodies, or simply walked into the ocean to drown.

While the marines were pushing northward on Saipan, an even more dramatic struggle took place in the skies over the Philippine Sea, the portion of the Pacific between the Marianas and the Philippines. Admiral Koga had died in an airplane crash in April, and Admiral Soemu Toyoda had taken over as commander of the Combined Fleet. A much more aggressive leader than Koga, Toyoda reacted to the news of the impending invasion of Saipan by ordering Admiral Jisaburo Ozawa to move from the Philippines with his First Mobile Fleet to destroy American naval units off the Marianas. Ozawa had started the war as commander of naval forces in support of operations against Malaya and in the Dutch East Indies. He had long been a leading advocate of carrier warfare. Next to Yamamoto, his American opponents considered him the most skillful Japanese admiral of the conflict. Both Toyoda and Ozawa hoped that this encounter would be the decisive battle.

When Spruance received reports of Ozawa's approach, he dispatched Mitscher's task force along with additional ships from the Fifth Fleet to repel the enemy challenge. American strength included seven heavy and eight light carriers and a large number of battleships, cruisers, and destroyers. The Japanese countered with five heavy and four light carriers and a smaller supporting force. Ozawa launched an air strike on the morning of June 19, but American radar alerted the task force to the enemy's approach. U.S. fighters intercepted the Japanese planes 50 miles to the west. The Americans enjoyed a big numerical advantage with a total of 956 planes, including 475 fighters. The Japanese had only 222 fighters out of a total of 473 aircraft.

To make the discrepancy even greater, American pilots were better trained and more experienced. They had alternated between periods of combat and intervals in which they had served as flight instructors. This practice enabled them to give new pilots the benefit of their experience and expertise. The Japanese, by contrast, had committed their veteran pilots to a steady diet of combat. By the summer of 1944, few of them were left.

Japanese aircraft carried out four mass attacks on Mitscher's task force, but few of them were able to penetrate the U.S. fighter screen. They inflicted minor damage to just one vessel, the battleship *South Dakota*. Their own losses were staggering—275 of the 373 planes actually engaged. Only 29 American aircraft failed to return safely to their carriers. The Battle of the Philippine Sea was so one-sided that it earned the nickname "the Great Marianas Turkey Shoot." To add to Japanese woes, two American submarines, *Albacore* and *Cavalla,* sank the carriers *Shokaku* and *Taiho*. *Shokaku* was a veteran of the Pearl Harbor raid; *Taiho* was the largest carrier in the Japanese navy.

Despite this great victory, the Americans did not discover the location of Ozawa's fleet until the afternoon of June 20. Unfortunately, it was 340 miles to the east, a distance that made it unlikely that many American planes would have enough fuel to return to their carriers after attacking the enemy ships. Those that did make it back would have to land in the dark, a most dangerous assignment. This predicament was due to Spruance's concern before the battle began that Ozawa might divide his fleet and send one force to attack the transports off Saipan. To prevent such a possibility, he had refused Mitscher's request to close in on the enemy. Instead Spruance had ordered the task force to fall back toward Saipan.

Despite the danger to his aircraft, Mitscher was determined to attack the Japanese fleet. Given the problems involved, the results were good. Dive bombers and torpedo planes sank the carrier *Hiyo,* badly damaged three others, and destroyed 65 enemy aircraft. But 80 U.S. planes failed to make it back to their carriers or crashed while landing. Mitscher, defying both navy doctrine and possible enemy submarine attacks, ordered all ships to turn on their lights to guide the returning pilots to their destinations. Rescue ships and planes recovered the majority of the crews who had ditched at sea the next day.

Spruance's decision to turn back toward Saipan rather than to keep Task Force 58 moving toward the enemy fleet has caused continuing controversy. Some have argued that had he sent Mitscher farther west, his planes might have virtually destroyed the enemy carrier force. Others have contended that under the circumstances, Spruance acted correctly. They point to the fact that by keeping their distance, no American ships were lost, while the Japanese sacrificed their aircraft in vain. Certainly there is something to be said for this viewpoint. Nevertheless, it would seem that the possibility of dealing the enemy a death blow was worth the risk to both the transports at Saipan and Mitscher's task force. But this debate should not obscure the fact that the Americans had administered a crippling defeat to Japanese naval air power, one from which it would never recover.

Even before the fall of Saipan, U.S. planes and ships pounded Tinian, which lay just to the southwest. The actual invasion came on July 24, when the same two marine divisions that had made the initial landings on Saipan went ashore on the north end of the island and encountered little opposition. The Japanese had expected the assault to come in the south, where they had massed the bulk of their strength. Again, the Japanese fought with blind heroism and resorted to their familiar suicide charges. But this time, the marines were able to overrun the island in only eight days.

Marine and army forces had actually landed on Guam three days before the start of the invasion of Tinian. They struck to the north and south of their main objectives, the harbor and airfields on the island's western shore. Unlike the situation on Tinian, the enemy resisted the landings, and the Americans moved inland only after heavy fighting. Later they also had to withstand a massive counterattack. But once again the Japanese failed and withdrew to the northern end of the island, where they made another suicidal last stand. Organized fighting ended on August 1, but mopping up operations continued in parts of the island until the end of the war. In addition to the honor of recapturing the first former U.S. possession to be liberated from the Japanese, the Americans acquired still another prize—a huge supply of liquor that the Japanese had stockpiled. It proved more than sufficient to quench the thirst of the victorious troops.

The loss of the Marianas and the disastrous Battle of the Philippine Sea represented a shattering blow to Japanese hopes of winning the war. Nine days after the fall of Saipan, Premier Tojo and his government accepted the consequences of defeat and resigned. General Kuniaki Koiso succeeded Tojo and formed a new cabinet, which shouldered the task of halting the American momentum. Prospects were far from bright. The United States was now in a position to strike at the Philippines, an action that would threaten Japan's oil supply from the East Indies. American engineers were already transforming the airfields of the Marianas to accommodate the new B-29 Superfortress bombers. The range and bomb capacity of these giant planes gave them the capability of bringing death and destruction on a massive scale to the crowded and inflammable cities of Japan.

25

War on the Periphery: China, Burma, India

While U.S. forces carried out their island-hopping operations in the Southwest and Central Pacific, fighting also took place in China, Burma, and even along the frontier of India. The Americans referred to this vast area as the China-Burma-India theater (CBI). But this designation gave the impression of greater unity in Allied operations in Southeast and East Asia than was actually the case. In reality, Chiang Kai-shek retained command in China, and the British exercised authority in India and in attempts to reconquer Burma. Starting in 1942, small American ground forces and larger air contingents operated from bases in India but remained strictly under U.S. jurisdiction. Cooperation among the three Allies was often far from close, and a great deal of mutual distrust prevailed.

American and British aims in the CBI also diverged on the question of the role that China should and could play in the war. Indeed, U.S. policy toward China strongly shaped Allied strategy and led to operations in Burma, which the British did not wish to undertake. And since the entire area lay on the periphery of the struggle against Japan and was far from crucial, the decision to devote so much effort to it was clearly a mistake.

THE CHINESE SITUATION

Although of secondary importance in the Pacific war, China had long held a strange fascination for American leaders and people alike, and this continued until well into the conflict. When the Japanese attacked Pearl Harbor in 1941, Chiang Kai-shek's forces had not fought a major battle since 1938. But the entry of the United States into hostilities convinced the Kuomintang leader that Japan would lose the war. He did not intend to risk his troops in fighting against the Japanese if he could avoid it. He preferred to conserve them for the postwar era, when he would face the formidable task of restoring his control over all of China. And he intended to settle his old score with the Communists.

At best, Chiang's army was a flimsy affair. Much of it was poorly trained and equipped and under the leadership of warlords whose allegiance to the government in Chungking was questionable. Chiang did maintain a substantial number of higher-quality divisions under his own control, but even they left much to be desired. He used many of his best troops to blockade the Communists in an effort to cut them off from the possibility of foreign aid. The Communists, ironically, were the only Chinese force that dedicated itself to fighting the Japanese. Their guerrilla tactics also proved effective in bringing much of the countryside under their control while restricting the enemy increasingly to the cities. The Kuomintang regime became more corrupt and inefficient during the interminable war. Its members devoted themselves primarily to advancing their own personal interests and paid little attention to the pressing economic and social evils that afflicted the Chinese people. Even had they possessed the will to deal with these problems, the pressures of war sharply limited their ability to do so.

Despite the depressing reality of China's situation, U.S. leaders pursued a policy toward that country that came close to wishful thinking. Roosevelt sympathized with China's desire to free itself from foreign influence—not merely Japanese but Western as well. He believed that the weakening of British, French, and Dutch colonialism in all of eastern Asia would facilitate this. But, nevertheless, the president looked forward to a close postwar relationship with China that would favor U.S. economic interests.

Roosevelt did not base his outlook solely on self-interest, however. He visualized China as a great power in the postwar era and believed that it deserved to be treated as one while the fighting raged. A great power must have a strong army, and Roosevelt intended to provide Chiang with U.S. military equipment, supplies, and advisers to help him make the best use of his abundant population. The president feared that if such assistance were not forthcoming, China might collapse or seek a separate peace. Lend-lease aid had begun to flow to the Chinese even before the attack on Pearl Harbor. It had traveled over the Burma Road from Lashio in eastern Burma to Chungking. But the fall of Burma in 1942 cut this route, and the United States resorted to an airlift of supplies over the world's highest mountain range, the Himalayas, which separated India from China. The Americans called this barrier "the Hump." Roosevelt and other U.S. leaders also saw China as a possible strategic objective after the conquest of the Philippines. It would provide a formidable jumping-off position for a seaborne assault on Japan as well as air bases for bombing raids against Japanese cities.

Many of the American people shared Roosevelt's sympathy for China and looked upon Chiang not as the dictatorial head of a corrupt regime but as a great national hero and the leader of a government that enjoyed strong support from the Chinese people. The "China lobby" helped create and perpetuate this distortion.

The establishment in China of a small air contingent, the American Volunteer Group (AVG), shortly before the attack on Pearl Harbor, contributed to the prevailing view. The AVG consisted of mercenary pilots whom Colonel Claire L. Chennault, a retired U.S. Army air officer, had recruited to fight in the service of China. After Pearl Harbor, it also participated in the defense of Burma and fashioned a remarkable record despite its dependence on obsolete P-40 fighters that were inferior to the Zero. Chennault minimized this disadvantage by using fighters operating in pairs and diving on their opponents from higher altitudes. The group soon earned the nickname "Flying Tigers" because of the painted tiger shark's teeth that adorned the noses of its planes. The AVG's exploits came as a relief to the American people, who were weary of a steady diet of defeat in the early months of the war. They even inspired a film, *Flying Tigers,* starring John Wayne. The AVG later became a part of the U.S. Fourteenth Air Force, operating from bases in southeastern China.

Not all Americans were uncritical of Chiang. Those who were most familiar with China warned that he and the Kuomintang regime were not what they seemed to be and that the Chinese army was not much better than a rabble. Churchill and the British, while not lacking in sympathy for China and the Chinese, also did not share the popular American view and were alarmed by Roosevelt's policies. They did not see China as a potential great power, a major factor in the war, or even a likely candidate for collapse or a separate peace.

In his effort to bolster the Chinese government, Roosevelt sent General Joseph W. Stilwell to China early in 1942. Stilwell, who otherwise might have commanded U.S. troops in Europe, received his appointment largely because of his extensive service in the U.S. embassy in China and his fluency in Chinese. Chiang appointed him to serve as his chief of staff. But in addition, the general received command of all U.S. forces in the China-Burma-India theater as well as serving as Roosevelt's personal representative to Chiang and the administrator of lend-lease aid. This multitude of responsibilities caused much confusion.

To make matters worse, Stilwell and Chiang did not get along. Chiang's suspicion of foreigners and his stubbornness were legendary, and Stilwell's acerbic personality had earned him the nickname "Vinegar Joe." Stilwell did not share Roosevelt's faith in the Chinese leader, to whom he referred in private as "Peanut." But he did take seriously his mission to transform the Chinese army into an effective fighting force and a major factor in the war. Since Chiang had no intention of cooperating in this impossible task, it is not surprising that the two men often quarreled.

Stilwell also found himself closely involved in developments in Burma, which bordered China on the southwest. He arrived in Chungking in March 1942 while the British were retreating northward from Rangoon. Chiang placed him in charge of Chinese forces that were assisting the British in Burma in an effort to keep open China's supply route from the West. Stilwell soon discovered that the Chinese operated with little regard for his orders. His troops became victims of the general Allied collapse, and the capture of Lashio cut the Burma Road, preventing their retreat into China. Instead they fled through the nightmarishly difficult mountains and dense jungle of northern Burma, eventually finding refuge in India. As Stilwell put it, they suffered "a hell of a beating."

BRITISH RAIDS ON BURMA

Once the Japanese had conquered Burma, they had reached the limit of their planned expansion in Southeast Asia. Despite Allied fears to the contrary, they had no intention of invading India. Stilwell, who disliked the British and had been highly critical of their direction of the Burma campaign, called for an offensive to oust the enemy from the country as soon as possible. The British commander in India was Field Marshal Wavell, who had driven the Italians out of Egypt in 1940 and had assumed the hopeless task of commanding Allied forces in Southeast Asia during the early days of the Pacific war. Wavell recognized that his resources would not allow for

The Burma Theater

such an ambitious undertaking. He did agree to launch a limited attack with British and Indian troops designed to capture the coastal area of Arakan, bordering India on the southeast.

But when the thrust into Arakan began in December 1942, it progressed slowly. Many of the Allied troops had little experience, were poorly trained, and suffered from both malaria and low morale. The British also resorted to frontal assaults, which accomplished little but caused heavy casualties. When the Japanese counterattacked, they forced the Allies back to their original line by May 1943.

One bright episode helped to reduce Allied gloom. In late 1942, Wavell established a commando force of 3,000 men under the leadership of General Orde Wingate. Eccentric and unorthodox, Wingate was an inspirational leader who had utter contempt for most of his superiors. Although he was given to sudden and extreme changes of mood and had once attempted suicide, he had conducted successful guerrilla operations behind Italian lines during the British conquest of Ethiopia. Wingate referred to his commandos as "the Chindits." He took this name from the Chinthe, a mythical beast, half-lion and half-eagle, whose likeness adorned many Burmese temples. To Wingate, this creature symbolized his belief in close ground-to-air coordination as the key to successful guerrilla operations. He divided his British and Indian forces into seven columns, which moved into northern Burma in February 1943 and, with the help of supplies dropped by cargo planes, raided enemy outposts and communications. Ultra reports on Japanese troop movements aided his undertaking.

The Chindit raids were more of a nuisance than a major problem for the Japanese. They also resulted in the loss of one-third of Wingate's men, and many of the survivors were so weakened by disease and malnutrition that they could never return to combat. But this exploit did show that British and Indian troops could hold their own in jungle fighting with the Japanese and enhanced Allied morale. The Chindits also devised jungle warfare techniques that Allied commanders successfully applied to later operations by larger formations. Wingate especially demonstrated that large-scale air supply was absolutely essential for troops operating in a vast wilderness such as Burma.

INDIA'S INTERNAL INSTABILITY

While struggling with the Japanese in Burma, Britain also had to contend with problems in India. A nationalist movement had developed there during the early twentieth century. Under the leadership of Mohandas Gandhi, it had pursued a nonviolent policy of civil disobedience and moral pressure in its quest for independence. Gandhi and his followers, most notably Jawaharlal Nehru, had formed the Congress party, which attempted to unite all Indians under one banner. Gandhi was more than a political leader, however. He also became a Hindu spiritual figure who devoted himself to a life of prayer, meditation, and fasting. Dressed in the loincloth and shawl worn by the lowliest Indians, Gandhi became known as "Mahatma" (Great Soul) and symbolized the struggle for freedom.

But as time passed, India's basic religious division between Hindus and Moslems created an impediment to the Congress party's pursuit of independence. Although the Hindus were by far the most numerous of the many religious groups that made up the population, the Moslems comprised the overwhelming majority in certain areas, especially in the northwest. The Moslems also found a leader of great ability and determination—Mohammed Ali Jinnah. Although Jinnah originally supported the aims of the Congress party, he eventually came to believe that if India gained independence as one state, the Moslems would find themselves in the position of a neglected, perhaps even persecuted minority. This concern led him to break with Congress and to assume leadership of another party, the Moslem League. Jinnah and the League favored divi-

FIGURE 25-1 Mohandas Gandhi, the spiritual leader of Indian nationalism. (*AP/Wide World Photos*)

sion of the country into a Hindu India and a Moslem Pakistan. Gandhi, Nehru, and the Congress party remained totally opposed to such a policy.

By the early 1930s, Britain recognized that it could not avoid granting extensive concessions to Indian nationalism. The Government of India Act of 1935 provided for a parliamentary government complete with Indian ministers, but control over foreign affairs and defense remained in British hands. The Congress party found this unsatisfactory and demanded full dominion status. Despite its objections, Congress went along with the legislation as a stopgap measure.

When World War II began in 1939, the British, with their control over foreign policy, declared that India was at war with Germany. While Gandhi, Nehru, and certain other Congress leaders shared Britain's outrage over the policies of Nazi Germany, they did not believe that India had sufficient cause to go to war. They also protested the manner in which the British had brought India into the conflict. Their ministers resigned from the government, while Gandhi, true to his pacifist beliefs, condemned participation in any war as immoral. Nevertheless, elements of the Indian army, much of which was Moslem, served with distinction on Britain's side in North Africa and the Middle East.

With Japan's conquest of Malaya and Burma, the war came to India's doorstep. And as evidence of British weakness mounted, nationalist agitation increased. Britain realized that further concessions were inevitable and in March 1942 appointed Sir Stafford Cripps as a special envoy to seek an agreement. Cripps proposed that upon conclusion of the war, a constituent assembly would draft a constitution for India with complete freedom to create an independent state. In return, Congress would rejoin the government and support the war. But the proposal also provided that if the Moslems expressed their desire to secede from India, they would be allowed to create a separate state of Pakistan. Congress found such a partition completely unacceptable, and Gandhi planned to call for a nationwide movement of civil disobedience.

Before Gandhi could act, the government arrested him and the other Congress leaders. They remained in custody for the duration of the war in relative comfort. Ironically, Gandhi, a man renowned for his humble lifestyle, found himself installed in a sumptuous palace. The Indian population accepted the arrests with remarkably little protest, and an unexpected calm settled over the country.

Nationalist opposition of a violent type came from outside India. The architect of this policy was Subhas Chandra Bose, a former Congress leader who had turned to extremism. Bose fled India early in 1941 and made his way to Germany, where he fell under the spell of Nazism. He believed that only an authoritarian system could create a unified Indian state. In 1943, he left Germany by submarine to assume leadership of a Free India movement that Japan was organizing among Indians in Southeast Asia as part of a plan for a "Greater East Asia co-prosperity sphere."

The concept of a co-prosperity sphere had originated before the attack on Pearl Harbor and visualized a new order for East Asia. Supposedly designed to free Asians from Western imperialism, in reality it was largely a propaganda device to mask Japanese domination of the region. Although Japan sponsored "free" governments in China, Indochina, Malaya, Burma, and the Philippines, these were nothing more than puppet regimes that never gained the allegiance of a majority of their respective populations. The tendency of the Japanese army to treat these peoples with contempt and often with brutality also helped undermine this endeavor. Upon his arrival in Singapore, Bose took over the leadership of a government for Free India as well as the small Indian National Army, which consisted mostly of prisoners of war who had enlisted to escape the miserable conditions in Japanese penal camps. Such motivation was hardly likely to fill them with fervor for Bose's cause.

ALLIED SQUABBLES OVER STRATEGY

It was against this troubled background that the Allies waged war in Burma while American and British leaders quarreled over strategy. To Roosevelt and his advisers, the reopening of a land supply route to China held first priority. To accomplish this, Allied troops must first reconquer northern Burma. This would enable the construction of a road from Ledo in India to China, facilitating the flow of supplies to Chiang and the buildup of Chennault's Fourteenth Air Force operating from Chinese bases. But the Americans also wanted to reopen the old Burma Road and to recapture Rangoon. Until the Allies controlled the port of Rangoon and the railroad that extended northward to Lashio, any land supply route to China would be inadequate.

British leaders doubted that reopening the land supply route was worth a full-scale operation in the jungles of Burma. Indeed, they questioned whether providing more supplies to China would really benefit the Allied cause. They much preferred amphibious operations against the East Indies, which would threaten Japan's oil supply. But neither sufficient naval forces nor landing craft would be available for such an enterprise until late 1944. American leaders tended to attribute the British position to an unwillingness to shoulder a rightful share of the war against Japan. Churchill and his advisers were especially sensitive to such criticism, given the scope of U.S. operations in the Pacific. This placed them at a disadvantage in the strategic debate, and they gradually yielded to American insistence on a major offensive.

As a major step in this direction, Allied leaders agreed on the need for a supreme commander in Southeast Asia. At the Quadrant Conference in August 1944, they chose Admiral Louis Mountbatten, who had been serving as Britain's chief of combined operations. A cousin of King George VI, Mountbatten was only 42 years old and combined dashing good looks with a gift for maintaining close personal relations with both his British subordinates and American officers. He also possessed a keen sense of public relations as well as administrative and strategic ability. In another change, General Auchinleck, who had succeeded Wavell in control of North African operations in 1941, now took over his post as commander in India. Wavell moved "upstairs" to the political office of viceroy in India.

In preparation for the impending offensive in Burma, Allied reinforcements reached India and resulted in the establishment of the Fourteenth Army with General William J. Slim in command. Slim, who had experienced the harrowing retreat from Burma in 1942, was perhaps the only British officer to earn the respect of both Stilwell and Wingate. Modest and approachable, he possessed a sincere concern for the welfare of his men, a trait that won him their wholehearted devotion. The Allies planned their major attack in the north, where engineers were to build the Ledo Road. Indeed, construction on the Indian portion of this supply route had begun as early as December 1942.

THE CAMPAIGN TO RETAKE BURMA

The offensive started in October 1943 as two Chinese divisions under Stilwell's command thrust down the Hukawng River toward the major communications center of Myitkyina on the Irrawaddy River. But Japanese resistance stalled their advance. In February 1944, in an effort to speed his drive, Stilwell sent an American guerrilla force, under the leadership of General Frank Merrill, to carry out a series of operations behind Japanese lines. This unit consisted of volunteers who had trained with the Chindits. It soon acquired the name "Merrill's Marauders." Wingate also launched a second Chindit operation in March but lost his life in a plane crash soon afterward. The Marauders captured the Myitkyina airfield in May, but both raider forces suffered heavy casualties while the Japanese and monsoon rains delayed the fall of Myitkyina until August. Its capture opened the way for the extension of the Ledo Road, and the herculean efforts of American engineers as well as Indian and Chinese laborers resulted in completion of the project in January 1945.

General Slim launched a second Arakan offensive in January 1944, only to be halted again by Japanese counterattacks that threatened to outflank the Allied troops. But this time Slim avoided a major retreat by withdrawing into a series of strongholds that received supplies by air. The new approach proved so successful that the enemy forces had to break off their assault.

Meanwhile, General Renya Mutaguchi's Fifteenth Japanese Army invaded India in mid-March. This operation was in part a delayed response to the first Chindit raids, which had persuaded the Japanese that their hold on northern and central Burma was precarious. Mutaguchi hoped to seize the communication centers of Kohima and Imphal near the Burmese border. An especially aggressive officer, Mutaguchi had been implicated in the coup that had attempted to overthrow the Japanese government in 1936. His regiment had also been involved in the Marco Polo Bridge incident that precipitated the Sino-Japanese War. Mutaguchi possessed vast determination but little common sense. He plunged into his invasion of India with woefully inadequate supplies and scant regard for the dangers that lay ahead. Nevertheless, his forces advanced quickly, and early in April they surrounded both Kohima and Imphal. Their success might have been still greater had Ultra reports not warned the British that the Japanese were planning an offensive. Slim ordered the two garrisons to hang on with the aid of airlifted supplies.

The badly outnumbered defenders of Kohima fought one of the most courageous battles of the war and managed to hold out for two weeks until a relief expedition arrived. Imphal's garrison was considerably larger but also confronted much stronger Japanese forces than those that attacked Kohima. The siege lasted 88 days while both sides, especially the Japanese, ran dangerously short of supplies. When the British finally broke the encirclement on May 12, the remnants of Mutaguchi's starving and disease-weakened troops fell back into Burma.

Bose's Indian National Army participated in the Japanese invasion. The nationalist leader hoped that the operation would result in a triumphal march that would lure thousands of Indians to his cause. But his troops displayed a dismal lack of fighting spirit and an alarming fondness for desertion.

Although the struggle for Kohima and Imphal took place in India, it was the most decisive engagement of the Burma campaign. It cost the Japanese 50,000 troops and severely weakened their ability to resist when Slim launched a major offensive in mid-November. The Allies now had the advantage of a greatly improved supply system, numerical superiority, and control of the air. Their forces moved across the Chindwin River, and the Japanese fell back toward the Irrawaddy. General Hoyotaro Kimura, the Japanese commander in Burma, hoped to smash the Allied forces as they crossed the Irrawaddy north of Mandalay. But Slim anticipated this and made his major crossing farther south against weak opposition on February 13. Once across, Indian troops dashed for Meiktila and captured the town on March 3, cutting road and rail communications to Mandalay, 75 miles to the north. Although Kimura shifted forces from Mandalay in a desperate effort to retake Meiktila, the Indians held on to the town. By the end of March, Kimura accepted the inevitable, abandoned Mandalay, and retreated southward from Meiktila.

The road to Rangoon now lay open. But Slim was encountering supply problems, and it appeared doubtful that he could reach the capital before the start of the monsoon season. On May 1, Mountbatten came to the rescue by launching Operation Dracula, which featured both amphibious and airborne landings south of Rangoon. Caught between these forces and the main Allied column to the north, the Japanese evacuated Rangoon. The Allies occupied the city on May 3.

Meanwhile, Stilwell had opened a drive southward from Myitkyina in October. But soon afterward he had one quarrel too many with Chiang, who demanded his dismissal. Roosevelt had no choice but to comply. He appointed the much more tactful General Albert C. Wedemeyer to take Stilwell's place. But before long, Wedemeyer was sending messages reminiscent of Stilwell's in which he complained of Chiang's deviousness and lack of cooperation. Nevertheless, his forces pushed forward and on March 7 captured Lashio, the western terminus of the Burma Road.

A CHANGE OF PLANS FOR CHINA

Ironically, now that the Allies had regained control of the original supply route, Roosevelt and his advisers abandoned their former high hopes for Chiang and China. America's swift advances in the Pacific had undercut the country's strategic importance, while events inside China had left U.S. leaders totally disillusioned with Chiang and his regime. All of this made it clear that the British had been right. The conquest of Burma and the supply route to China had not been worth the investment in blood and materiel.

Indeed, Japan's position in China became much stronger as the result of an offensive that its troops began in April 1944. This operation aimed at capturing the Fourteenth Air Force bases in the southeastern part of the country. Attacks by General Chennault's planes on Japanese shipping had become a source of growing concern to Tokyo. The Japanese offensive made remarkable progress and in June captured the important communications center of Changsha, which the Chinese abandoned without a fight. By the end of November, most of Chennault's bases were in enemy hands, and the Japanese at long last had created a land link between northern China and Southeast Asia. But, as always in China, the war dragged on—at least for a few more months.

26

The Collapse of Japan

By the late summer of 1944, there was no question that the war had turned irretrievably against Japan. Although most Japanese leaders were unwilling to accept this fact, they could find little reason for optimism. The Japanese were still in the ascendancy in China, but this hardly made up for the disastrous erosion of their position in the Central and Southwest Pacific and even Burma. Far worse disasters lay ahead. The Americans soon embarked on a series of new operations that left Japan on the brink of total collapse.

THE RETURN TO THE PHILIPPINES

MacArthur, after securing his series of bases along New Guinea's northern coast, focused his attention on the reconquest of the Philippines. He had originally planned to invade Mindanao in the southern part of the archipelago before moving northward toward the principal island of Luzon. But in September, Halsey executed a carrier strike against the Philippines that indicated that Japanese air power in the islands might be weaker than expected. Halsey now urged that American forces bypass Mindanao and instead capture Leyte on the eastern edge of the central Philippines. MacArthur and Nimitz both agreed, but the Pacific Fleet commander also insisted on a preliminary attack against the Palau Islands, which he desired as an advance base to support the Leyte landing. The Palaus lay 500 miles to the southeast of Mindanao. The Joint Chiefs of Staff endorsed the Leyte proposal and set October 20 as the invasion date. They also agreed to a September 15 attack on the Palaus, a decision that proved to be a mistake.

When the First Marine Division went ashore on the island of Peleliu, which contained the main airfield in the Palaus, they soon discovered that American planners had greatly underestimated the difficulties involved. The northern portion of the island consisted of a series of jagged coral ridges separated by precipitous gorges. These ridges were full of interconnecting caves that the Japanese had reinforced with concrete. They were virtually impervious to preliminary shelling and bombing. Even with the help of army reinforcements, the marines were not able to root out the last Japanese from this labyrinth of caves until November 26. In addition to the horrendous terrain, the heat was unbearable, with temperatures soaring as high as 115 degrees. Despite 6,000 American casualties, possession of Peleliu did not contribute significantly to the success of the Leyte operation.

Ten days prior to the invasion of Leyte, Halsey led his Third Fleet in a series of carrier raids against Luzon and Formosa as well as the

Ryukyu Islands, which stretched 600 miles from Japan toward Formosa. The Third Fleet was actually the Fifth Fleet under different command. During the summer of 1944, Nimitz adopted the practice of alternating the fleet's commanders and staffs. When Admiral Spruance was in charge, it was the Fifth Fleet, and Halsey and his staff planned their next operation. When Halsey took over, it became the Third Fleet, and Spruance and his staff prepared their next campaign. This procedure enabled Nimitz to get the most action out of the fleet.

Halsey's raids met a determined response from both land-based aircraft and Admiral Ozawa's carrier planes. But once again the Japanese fared badly, losing over 500 planes to only 79 for the Americans. Nevertheless, inexperienced Japanese pilots who survived the battle believed that they had actually sunk large numbers of U.S. ships and reported a great victory. In reality, they had damaged only two cruisers and a carrier. Although Japanese naval leaders later discovered that the pilots' claims were wildly inflated, they neglected to inform the army high command, which continued to believe that much of the U.S. fleet lay at the bottom of the Pacific. This delusion emboldened army leaders to change their strategy for meeting the invasion of the Philippines. They had planned to mass most of their troops in defense of Luzon. Now they decided that they could make a major stand on Leyte.

The Americans assembled an impressive force for the invasion of Leyte. Admiral Thomas Kinkaid commanded the Seventh Fleet, which was responsible for transporting and protecting the actual assault force, General George Krueger's Sixth Army. Halsey's Third Fleet provided the covering naval force, including Mitscher's task force with its core of 17 carriers. Kinkaid had led forces in the Coral Sea, Midway, and Guadalcanal actions as well as in the Aleutians. He took over the Seventh Fleet in late 1943. Krueger was born in Germany and moved to America with his parents as a boy. A veteran of the Spanish-American War, he had commanded troops in the New Britain and New Guinea campaigns.

On October 20, Krueger's forces landed at three points along the coast of Leyte Gulf, the body of water bordering the island on the east. They encountered little opposition and by nightfall had secured a substantial beachhead. Early in the afternoon of the first day, MacArthur and a small party waded ashore in knee-deep water after their landing craft ran aground a short distance from the beach. This scene provided photographers with one of the most famous pictures of the war. Soon afterward, MacArthur made a brief statement over a radio transmitter in which he announced, "People of the Philippines, I have returned!" By October 23, American troops had captured two airfields and liberated Tacloban, Leyte's capital.

THE BATTLE OF LEYTE GULF

But the real drama took place during the following days, not on Leyte itself but in the surrounding waters—the Battle of Leyte Gulf, the greatest naval struggle of all time. Despite its mauling in the Battle of the Philippine Sea, the Japanese navy still hoped to destroy the Pacific Fleet in the decisive battle it had been seeking since the start of the war. To accomplish this, Admiral Toyoda devised a master plan that provided for the entire Combined Fleet to converge on the Philippines.

Ozawa's Northern Force moved south from Japan as a decoy to lure Halsey's Third Fleet away from Leyte. Although it included Japan's four surviving carriers, they had a combined strength of only 110 aircraft. At the same time, two Japanese task forces rushed northward from the Singapore area, made their way through the congested waters of the Philippines, and headed for Leyte Gulf from two directions. Their mission: to destroy the American transports and supporting warships. One of them, Admiral Takeo Kurita's powerful Force A, contained the super-battleships *Yamato* and *Musashi* as well as three other battleships, 12 cruisers, and 15 destroyers. It was to penetrate San Bernardino Strait, which separated Luzon from Samar, an island just to the northeast of Leyte. At the same time, Admiral

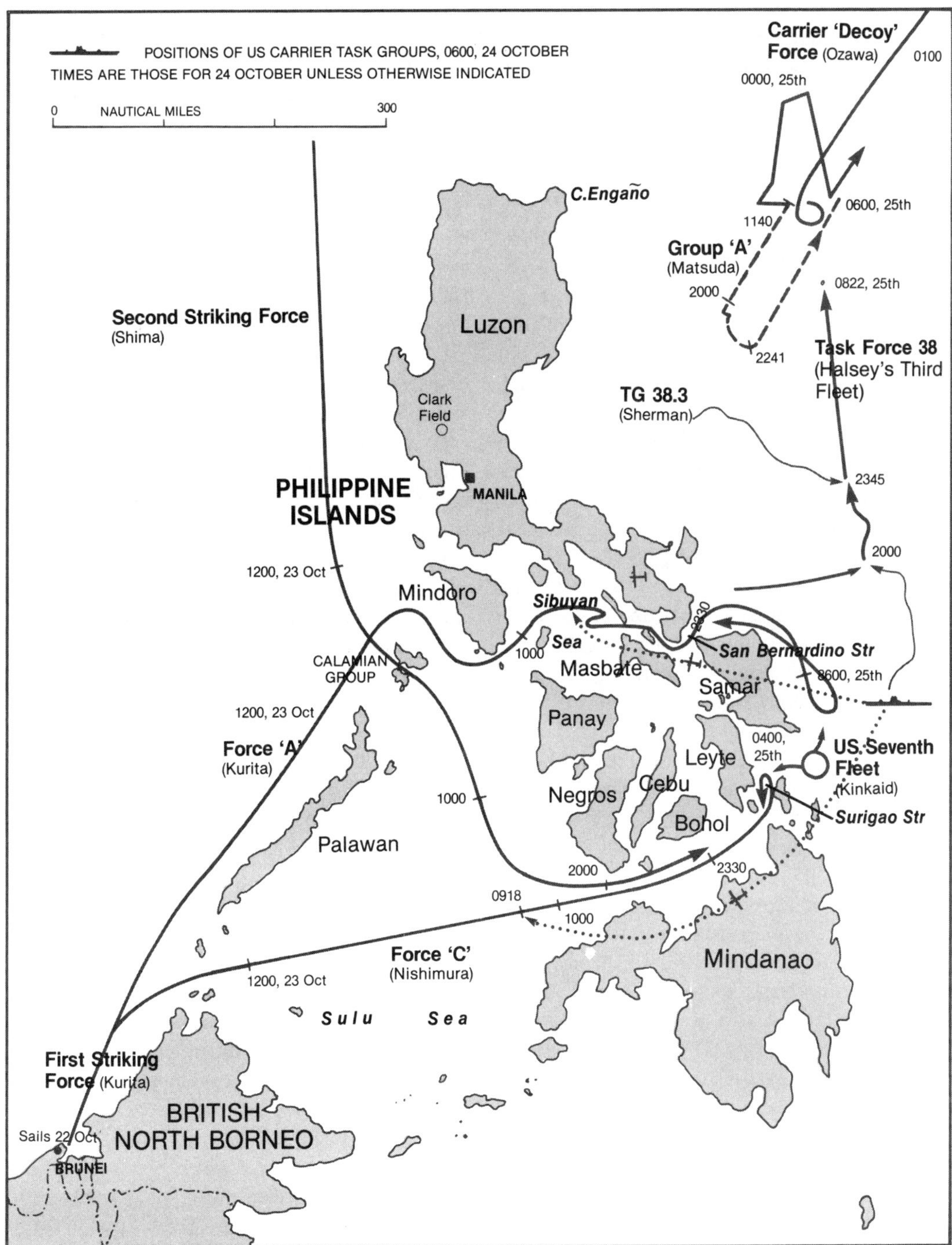

The Battle of Leyte Gulf, October 1944

Shoji Nishimura's Force C, including two battleships, a heavy cruiser, and four destroyers, would steam through Surigao Strait to the south of Leyte. Admiral Kiyohide Shima's Second Striking Force, consisting of three cruisers and four destroyers, was to push south from Japanese waters to assist Nishimura. Toyoda's plan was bold and imaginative but was also highly complex, required exceptionally precise timing, and exposed the Japanese fleet to great danger, especially in view of its lack of carrier-based planes. The forces converging on Leyte Gulf had to depend completely on land-based aircraft, which proved quite unreliable.

On October 23, two U.S. submarines sighted Kurita's force and alerted Halsey. They also sank two heavy cruisers and disabled a third. Kurita continued into the Sibuyan Sea to the south of Luzon, where planes from Mitscher's task force attacked *Musashi* the next day. The huge ship suffered no fewer than 19 torpedo and 17 bomb hits, which finally sent her to the bottom. Three other battleships sustained damage. After this rude reception, Kurita turned back to the west, and his maneuver convinced Halsey that he was giving up the struggle. But after dark, Kurita moved once again toward San Bernardino Strait.

U.S. carrier aircraft spotted Force C the same day, and Admiral Jesse Oldendorf set out to intercept it with six battleships, including five survivors of the Pearl Harbor attack, as well as eight cruisers and a large destroyer force. A night engagement followed in which Oldendorf arrayed his cruisers and battleships across the entrance to Surigao Strait while his destroyers and PT boats penetrated into the narrow body of water. The smaller craft made skillful use of their torpedoes, destroying one battleship and three destroyers and slightly damaging Admiral Nishimura's flagship, the battleship *Yamashiro*. Despite this disaster, Nishimura proceeded with his remaining three vessels in column formation. Oldendorf's waiting line of cruisers and battleships finished off *Yamashiro* and crippled both the cruiser *Mogami* and a destroyer. Soon afterward, Shima's force ventured into the strait, but when it encountered the blazing wreckage of several of Nishimura's ships, Shima wisely retreated.

Meanwhile, Halsey, assuming that he had nothing to fear from Kurita's Force A, shifted his Third Fleet northward to intercept Ozawa's carriers. He did not even bother to leave a covering force at San Bernardino Strait and failed to bring this to the attention of Admiral Kinkaid, the Seventh Fleet commander. Kinkaid, assuming that Halsey had left a rear guard, took no further action. As a result, only Admiral Clifton Sprague's weak force of five small escort carriers, three destroyers, and four destroyer escorts lay between Kurita and Leyte Gulf.

When Kurita emerged from San Bernardino Strait on the morning of October 25, he proceeded southward and discovered Sprague's ships off Samar. The little escort carriers were too slow to outrun Kurita's formidable armada but moved away as quickly as possible while launching air strikes against the pursuing enemy. Kurita mistakenly thought that he had fallen upon the big U.S. carriers and dashed forward to destroy them. He moved too fast. His ships became separated, and the engagement became a confused melee, reducing the tremendous striking power of his superior force. Torpedo attacks by Sprague's destroyers as well as planes from Admiral Felix Stumpf's escort carrier group, which lay to the south, also helped to disrupt the Japanese. Although Kurita's ships sank an escort carrier and two destroyers, three Japanese cruisers also went to the bottom. Nevertheless, Kurita continued to enjoy an overwhelming advantage in firepower and seemed on the verge of annihilating the Americans. But instead of moving in for the kill, he hesitated, apparently fearing intervention from Mitscher's task force, and finally decided to withdraw through San Bernardino Strait.

Contrary to Kurita's fears, Mitscher was still far to the north with Halsey, who refused to divert any ships to the south for some time after receiving news of the threat to Sprague's forces. He was determined to destroy Ozawa's carriers, and success eventually rewarded his persistence. Mitscher's planes sank all four, including *Zuikaku*, the last survivor of the Pearl Harbor striking force, as well as five other ships. Halsey finally did divert a carrier group to intercept Kurita's squadron, but the Japanese had already fled.

The Battle of Leyte Gulf had dealt a death blow to Japan's naval power. Four carriers, three battleships, six heavy and four light cruisers, and 11 destroyers littered the ocean's floor. The Japanese had also lost 500 planes. But, ironically, Toyoda's master plan had almost worked. If Kurita had continued his assault on Sprague's escort carriers, he almost certainly would have destroyed them as well as the transports and supply ships offshore. Halsey had blundered by not leaving a force to guard San Bernardino Strait. He had been fortunate that Kurita had placed discretion ahead of valor.

Shortly before the end of the three-day struggle, the Japanese introduced a new weapon, one that soon became terribly familiar to American sailors—the kamikaze. A suicide unit composed of pilots who deliberately crashed their bomb-laden planes into American ships, the Kamikaze Special Attack Corps owed its existence to the disastrous decline of Japan's air power. *Kamikaze,* meaning "divine wind," referred to the typhoon that had destroyed the fleet of the Mongol ruler Kublai Khan, saving Japan from invasion in the late thirteenth century. Admiral Takijiro Onishi, who commanded the First Air Fleet, believed that kamikaze attacks were the only way in which the Japanese could inflict meaningful damage on U.S. ships and morale. Such assaults posed special defensive problems. It was extremely difficult to stop a crash dive completely. Even if crippled, a kamikaze plane might still hit its target. Although the first suicide attack badly damaged an Australian cruiser on October 21, the main assault came four days later against the hard-pressed U.S. escort carriers. It caught the Americans by surprise, sinking the carrier *St. Lo* and damaging four others.

PROGRESS ON LAND

While the opposing fleets fought their desperate battle, American troops on Leyte continued to push forward. But they soon encountered stronger opposition. General Yamashita, who had gained the nickname "Tiger of Malaya" as a result of his brilliant conquest of that British colony, now commanded Japanese forces in the Philippines. He had favored massing his troops on Luzon for an all-out struggle there. But his superior, Field Marshal Count Hisaichi Terauchi, the commander for all of Southeast Asia, insisted that Yamashita shift as many men as possible to Leyte. This increase in strength delayed the American advance but did not save Leyte.

The Twenty-fourth Corps drove south from the beachhead and then swung inland, reaching the western coast on November 1. Almost simultaneously, the Tenth Corps swept through the Leyte Valley to the northern coast. The two forces were now in position to converge on Ormoc, the chief enemy base on the western coast. But General Krueger paused to consolidate his position in the north before thrusting into the mountains that protected Ormoc. This delay enabled the Japanese commander, General Sasaki Suzuki, a veteran of the Malaya and Singapore campaigns, to establish a strong defense in the rugged heights. Incessant rain also hampered the American advance. But on December 7, the third anniversary of the Pearl Harbor attack, the Seventy-seventh Division settled the issue by a surprise landing to the south of Ormoc and seized the town three days later. Although this maneuver really decided the fate of Leyte, Japanese units held out in various parts of the island until as late as May 1945. On December 15, MacArthur sent troops ashore on lightly held Mindoro, just to the south of Luzon. They made rapid progress, and engineers immediately began to construct airfields from which U.S. planes could support an operation against Luzon itself.

MacArthur chose Lingayen Gulf, near the site of the major Japanese landing in 1941, as his invasion target on Luzon. General Yamashita's hopes for an all-out struggle in defense of the island perished when Terauchi ordered him to divert so many troops to Leyte. Yamashita accordingly withdrew most of his remaining forces to the mountainous interior to fight a delaying action and did not contest the landings at Lingayen

Gulf, which took place on January 9, 1945. But kamikaze planes sank one escort carrier and damaged another as well as two battleships and five cruisers. These attacks were especially hard on American morale because the great Leyte Gulf victory had seemingly ended the enemy's ability to interfere with amphibious operations. Americans also found it difficult to comprehend the mentality that motivated suicide attacks. To them, they seemed the ultimate in fanaticism. In reality, not all kamikaze pilots were willing volunteers. Many of them joined only after experiencing intense pressure from their superiors.

After Krueger's Sixth Army had consolidated its beachhead, the First Corps pushed slowly north and east in mountainous terrain against the strongest concentration of Yamashita's forces. The Fourteenth Corps had an easier task driving southward through open country. It reached Clark Field on January 23 but did not secure the base until over a week later. Soon afterward, two motorized "flying columns" of the First Cavalry Division dashed for Manila and penetrated the city's suburbs on February 3. As U.S. forces moved into Manila, they occupied three prisoner of war camps and liberated 8,500 Americans. Many of the prisoners were on the verge of starvation and suffered from malaria, dysentery, and other diseases. In late January and early February, elements of General Robert Eichelberger's Eighth Army landed without resistance to the north of Bataan Peninsula and to the south of Manila Bay. Eichelberger was serving as commandant of West Point when the war began. He took over the task of capturing Buna in December 1942 and commanded troops in many of the subsequent operations along the New Guinea coast.

In contrast to the relatively easy thrust to Manila, the actual conquest of the capital became a long, arduous struggle. Yamashita had ordered his troops to abandon the capital, but Admiral Sanji Iwabachi, who commanded the naval forces there, refused to comply. Instead, navy and army units fought the Americans street by street, block by block, and building by building. In the process, Manila experienced widespread devastation, and its population suffered horribly. Almost 100,000 civilians died, including many who fell victim to Japanese atrocities reminiscent of the rape of Nanking. The last fighting did not end until March 3.

Meanwhile, the Americans who had landed north of Bataan sealed off the peninsula and, after overcoming heavy initial resistance, moved quickly southward. All of Bataan was under their control by late February. The Japanese also attempted to hold Corregidor in an effort to block access to Manila Bay, but the Americans surprised them with a combined amphibious and airborne assault on February 16 and captured most of the island within ten days. Now MacArthur's forces confronted the task of eliminating Yamashita's strongholds in the mountainous interior of Luzon. This necessitated another slow, bloody campaign, which continued with diminishing intensity until the end of the war.

Although the Joint Chiefs of Staff had not planned to waste time and lives invading the remaining Philippine islands, MacArthur had intended from the start to liberate all of them. Without official authorization from Washington, he ordered Eichelberger's Eighth Army to begin the process while the battle for Manila was still raging. By mid-April, Eichelberger had carried out 38 landings. His forces achieved their major objectives everywhere within two months, but resistance continued in many of the more remote areas until the war ended. While these operations were taking place, Australian troops carried out a series of landings in the East Indies, starting with the invasion of Tarakan Island, just to the east of Borneo, on May 1. Other Australian forces made two landings on Borneo itself in June and July.

THE AGONIZING FIGHT FOR IWO JIMA

Even before MacArthur's forces had taken Manila, Nimitz had launched another invasion in the Central Pacific. This time the objective was the small island of Iwo Jima in the Volcano group of the Bonin Islands. The Bonins stretched from near Japan to within 300 miles of Saipan. The name "Volcano" was apt. All of the islands were of volcanic origin and were, to say the least, uninviting. Iwo Jima, which means "Sulfur Island," was no exception.

Various writers have described Iwo, when seen from the air, as resembling either a misshapen pear or a pork chop. Mount Suribachi, a 550-foot dormant volcano, dominated the island's narrow southern end. The wider northern half consisted of a plateau that rose as high as 350 feet and contained a series of jagged volcanic ridges. Both uplands possessed innumerable caves. The Japanese had reinforced them with concrete, adding a large number of bunkers and blockhouses. They had fortified these positions with big naval guns, mortars, and machine guns. An intricate network of tunnels connected the caves and fortresses. Japanese engineers had also constructed underground quarters for the troops as well as other installations well below the surface.

Between the two upland areas lay a connecting stretch of lower-lying terrain that contained two airfields and the island's only beaches. These were no ordinary beaches. Instead of sand, they consisted of volcanic ash, so soft that men sank into it up to their ankles. This made walking difficult and running almost impossible. Just beyond the beaches, a series of volcanic terraces rose abruptly to a height of 15 feet. The combination of the soft ash and these steep obstacles created a serious problem for amphibious vehicles and tanks attempting to move inland. In addition, the Japanese had ringed the beaches with bunkers, blockhouses, and pillboxes. The island, less than five miles long and 2½ miles across at its widest point, also abounded with bubbling sulfur pits, which created a pervasive acrid smell. As one observer later remarked it was "like hell with the fire out."

American leaders coveted this dismal volcanic outcrop because it lay only 660 miles from Tokyo. Its capture would eliminate attacks by Japanese fighter planes operating from the island against B-29s en route from the Marianas to raid Japanese cities. American fighters could then use

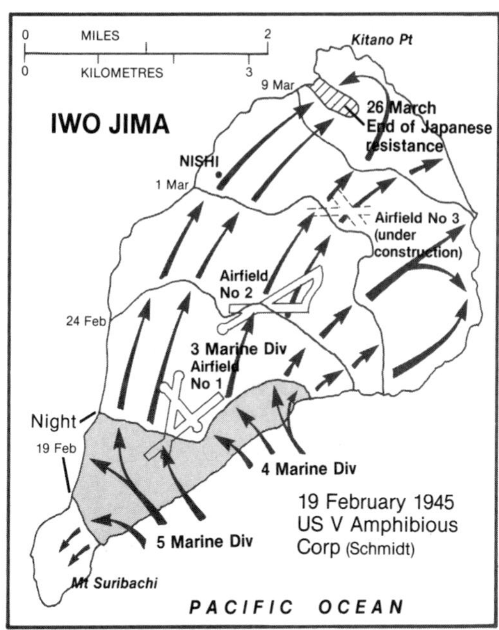

Battle of Iwo Jima, February–March 1945

the same bases to provide escort protection for the Superfortresses. Iwo also had potential as an advance base for the bombers themselves. Finally, the airfields would provide a useful haven for crippled aircraft that might not be able to make it back to their bases in the Marianas. The Joint Chiefs of Staff set the original invasion date for January 2, but the slow conquest of Leyte delayed the assault until February 19.

Months of bombing did little to soften up Iwo's defenses. But the postponement of the invasion enabled the Japanese to reinforce their garrison until it reached a total of 21,000 men. American leaders knew that the island was well defended, but they were not aware of how strong it really was. Three days of shelling by Spruance's Fifth Fleet failed to eliminate the island's well-protected defenses, although the barrage did knock out many of the installations around the beaches.

General Tadamichi Kuribayashi, the highly capable and realistic Japanese commander, had no intention of contesting the landing. He had learned from earlier defeats that such tactics did not work against an enemy that possessed naval and air supremacy. He preferred to wait until the Americans had landed and then rake the beaches with fire from the multitude of guns on the island. Thus when General Harry Schmidt's Fifth Marine Amphibious Corps went ashore on February 19, it initially encountered much greater difficulty from the soft volcanic ash and steep terraces than from the Japanese. But the marines, virtually unprotected on the exposed beaches, soon came under murderous fire, and their casualties mounted alarmingly as they inched forward. Nevertheless, by nightfall, the Fifth Division had fought its way across the narrowest part of the island, isolating Mount Suribachi. Kuribayashi had not started his barrage soon enough. Too many troops, tanks, and other equipment had landed. All he could do now was to exact as heavy a price as possible for the island.

Despite ferocious opposition, Schmidt's troops clawed their way slowly up the slopes of Mount Suribachi, and a patrol reached the summit on February 23. Soon afterward, Associated Press photographer Joe Rosenthal happened to be present as four marines hoisted an American flag and hastily snapped what became the most famous picture of the war.

The capture of Mount Suribachi lifted the spirits of the Americans, but the campaign had barely begun. With about half the island under their control, the marines now confronted the grim task of conquering the rugged terrain of the northern plateau with its myriad of fortified caves. Kuribayashi had also learned from Japanese experience on other islands that suicide charges were much more costly to their own troops than to the Americans. He was determined to avoid the temptation and insisted that his forces defend the island from their concealed positions. This proved highly effective in slowing the American advance and inflicting heavy casualties.

Again, as on Biak and Peleliu, flamethrowers and TNT proved the surest weapons against these powerful defenses. Some Japanese soldiers volunteered to be human booby traps, strapping explosives to their bodies and lying in the paths of unsuspecting flamethrowing tanks. The bloody struggle continued for weeks as the marines cleared all but two pockets on the extreme northern part of the island. Then, with all hope gone, the remnants of the Japanese garrison did resort to a series of suicide attacks. Fighting ended on March 23.

As Admiral Nimitz observed, "uncommon valor was a common virtue" on Iwo Jima. Thirty percent of the marines who saw action on the island became casualties. Almost 6,000 died and over 17,000 suffered wounds. Virtually the entire Japanese garrison perished, including General Kuribayashi. Iwo may not have been worth the price. It proved less effective as a B-29 base than American leaders had expected, and since the air force shifted to night bombing raids against Japan, fighter support was not really necessary. Iwo's primary value came to be as a base where many crippled B-29s found safety. But whether this benefit was worth the lives lost in taking the island remains questionable.

THE COSTLY STRUGGLE FOR OKINAWA

Iwo Jima was one of two enemy island bastions that Admiral Nimitz planned to take during the first half of 1945. The other was Okinawa, which lay in the center of the Ryukyu Islands, only 350 miles from Kyushu, the southernmost of the major Japanese home islands. Sixty-seven miles long and varying in width from 2 to 18 miles, Okinawa contained airfields as well as two excellent anchorages and would provide an ideal base for an invasion of Japan.

The island was beyond the range of American land-based planes but relatively close to enemy airfields on Kyushu, Formosa, and the other Ryukyus. This meant that Spruance's Fifth Fleet would be vulnerable to attack by Japanese planes. In an attempt to eliminate this threat, aircraft from Mitscher's carriers as well as a newly arrived British task force raided these bases prior to the invasion. But despite their efforts, the Japanese still had 700 planes available when the as-

FIGURE 26-1 A U.S. marine receives Communion from a Catholic chaplain after the capture of Mount Suribachi on Iwo Jima. (*National Archives*)

sault on Okinawa began on Easter Sunday, April 1.

Admiral Turner was in charge of the overall expeditionary force, while General Simon Bolivar Buckner, Jr., commanded the Tenth Army, which made the actual landing. Buckner, the son of a Confederate army general, had previously led U.S. troops in the Aleutians. His force of 180,000 men included both army and marine units. The Fifth Fleet provided the heaviest preinvasion bombardment of the Pacific war, but Japanese defenses survived almost unscathed. Nevertheless, the landings on the southwestern side of the island went extremely well against only token opposition. Marine forces reached the east coast the next day, cutting the island in two.

Things had gone so well on Okinawa during the first week that Admiral Turner radioed Nimitz, "I may be crazy but it looks like the Japanese have quit the war, at least in this sector." To which, the far less optimistic commander of the Pacific Fleet replied sarcastically, "Delete all after 'crazy.'" There was good reason for the lack of resistance. General Mitsuru Ushijima, the clever and determined Japanese commander, planned to employ the same strategy that Kuribayashi had used on Iwo Jima. He realized that he could neither prevent the landing nor defend all of Okinawa. Instead, he chose to abandon the northern three-fourths of the island and make his stand in the southern portion, which contained the two main towns, Naha and Shuri. The entire area abounded with limestone cliffs and ridges honeycombed with caves and pillboxes connected by tunnels and bristling with the strongest Japanese artillery concentration of the war. The garrison numbered 120,000 men, the largest that U.S. forces encountered during the entire conflict.

On April 9, army troops collided with Ushijima's powerful defensive line to the north of Naha and Shuri. Six weeks of desperate fighting followed before the Americans forced the enemy back to the last ring of defenses anchored on Shuri. During the next ten days, they made slow progress as 12 inches of rain drenched the island,

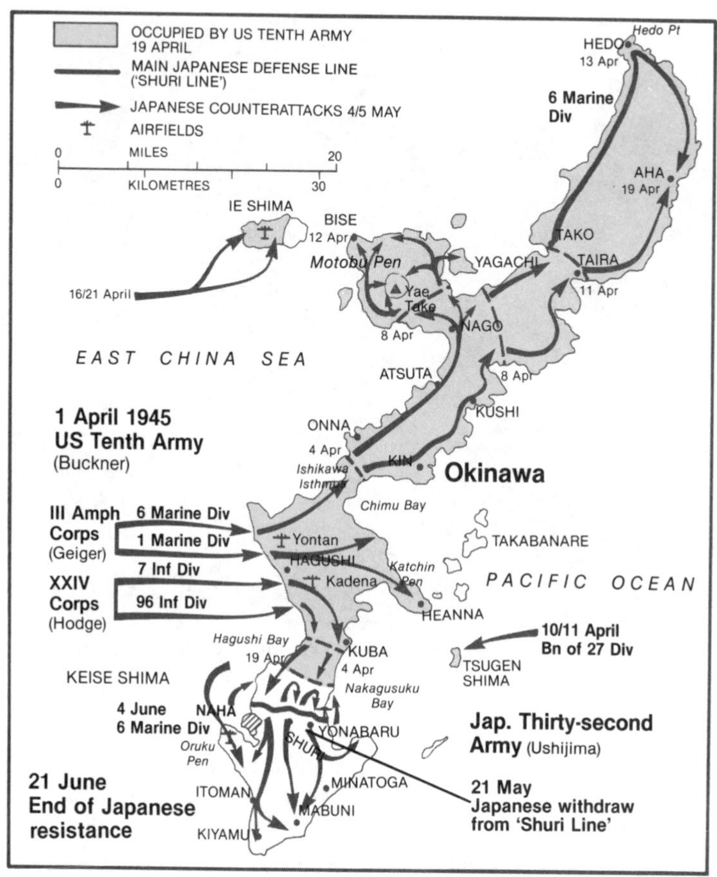

Battle of Okinawa, April–June 1945

but on May 31, Ushijima abandoned Shuri and withdrew for a final stand in the cave-studded ridges and ravines of extreme southern Okinawa. Another month of bloodshed lay ahead before the Americans overcame the last remnants of Japanese resistance. Again, U.S. forces paid a heavy price for Okinawa—over 12,000 killed and 36,000 wounded. As usual, most of the defenders lost their lives, but for the first time, several thousand Japanese soldiers actually surrendered. Both commanders were among the dead. Ushijima committed suicide; Buckner fell victim to a shell burst that sent a piece of coral ripping into his chest.

While this ordeal unfolded on Okinawa, the Japanese subjected the Fifth Fleet and offshore shipping to the war's most sustained and destructive kamikaze assault. Spruance arrayed large numbers of destroyers in an outlying arc around the island to detect Japanese planes on radar and alert the carriers and other units of their approach. The gallant crews of these "radar pickets" bore the brunt of the attacks. The Japanese timed the start of the kamikaze offensive to coincide with a sortie by elements of their surface fleet. On April 6, the superbattleship *Yamato* left Japanese home waters accompanied by a light cruiser and eight destroyers. They had only enough fuel for the voyage to Okinawa. *Yamato* was to attack the Fifth Fleet and then beach itself on the shore, where its 18-inch guns would support the island's garrison. It was a suicide mission and did not get far. U.S. submarines soon spotted the fleet and alerted Mitscher's task

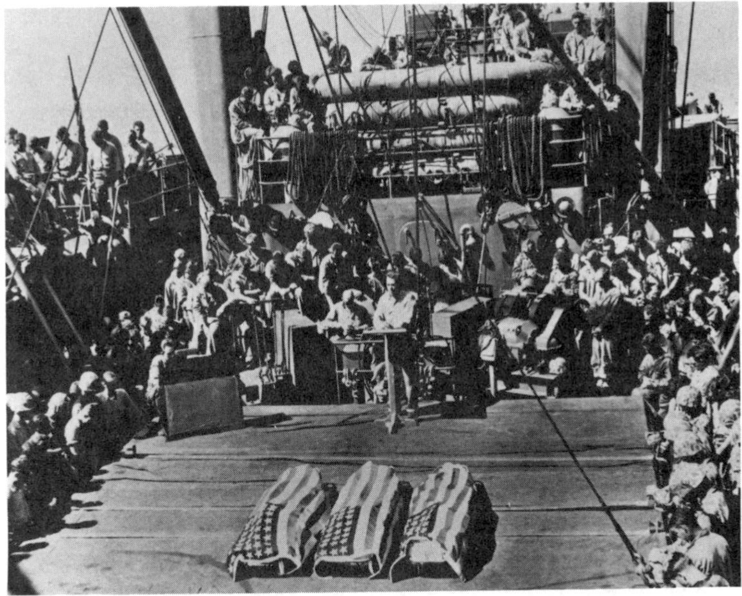

FIGURE 26-2 U.S. servicemen pay their last respects to three dead comrades during a shipboard memorial service. (*U.S. Marine Corps Photo/National Archives*)

force. Three hundred planes repeatedly attacked the Japanese ships to the southeast of Kyushu, sinking *Yamato,* the cruiser, and four destroyers.

Despite the failure of this final sortie of the Japanese navy, kamikaze and conventional air attacks continued for weeks. In all, they sank 34 ships and damaged over 350. Among those that sustained damage were the veteran carrier *Enterprise,* four other flattops, and ten battleships.

THE PACIFIC SUBMARINE WAR

Although American leaders considered the conquest of Okinawa as only a preliminary to the projected invasion of the Japanese home islands, it turned out to be the last major amphibious operation of the war. But another campaign had virtually drawn to a close as well. This was a submarine offensive against Japanese merchant shipping. Although it received few headlines, it ultimately made as great a contribution to victory as the exploits of the land forces and the surface fleet. Despite criticism of the unrestricted submarine warfare that Germany had employed in World War I, U.S. leaders adopted a similar policy soon after the attack on Pearl Harbor. But almost two years passed before this approach produced any important results.

For some time, Americans continued to think primarily in terms of submarine attacks on Japanese warships rather than on merchantmen and were slow to change their focus. As a result, during 1942 and early 1943, Japanese merchant traffic between Southeast Asia and the home islands encountered relatively little difficulty. Defective torpedoes also contributed to the American dilemma. It gradually became apparent that these weapons suffered from both inaccurate depth control and faulty firing mechanisms. Technicians solved the depth problem in August 1942, but they did not remedy the last of the firing-pin shortcomings until 13 months later.

Accumulation of Ultra reports on the movements of Japanese merchantmen and tankers gradually persuaded naval leaders that these ships would be easy prey for submarines. The Americans adopted "wolf pack" tactics, similar to those employed by the Germans, and these proved highly effective against such targets. In addition, much improved submarines became available in large numbers by late 1943. And the failure of the Japanese to provide adequate protection for their convoys also played into American hands. Even before the war, Japan's naval leaders had underestimated the potential of submarine attacks, and the poor showing of the Americans during 1942 and much of 1943 had done little to rouse them to action.

Sinkings by submarines increased during the second half of 1943, and by the end of 1944, half of Japan's merchant fleet lay at the bottom of the sea. Submarine attacks had virtually cut off the home islands from the natural resources of Southeast Asia. The interdiction of oil supplies was particularly disastrous for Japan's surviving air and naval units. When the war ended in August 1945, only 1.8 million tons of Japanese merchant shipping remained afloat, out of a total of 9.4 million used during the conflict. Submarines had accounted for 60 percent of the sinkings.

Curiously, the Japanese never made a concerted effort to cut American supply lines by submarine attacks, even though the links between the United States and the fighting areas of the Pacific were perilously long. They persisted in viewing submarines as weapons for use primarily against warships. Thus America's massive industrial and logistic achievements continued to provide the basis for victory without any real challenge in the sea lanes.

FIRE FROM THE SKY

Disaster also afflicted Japan from the air. Although it did not develop as soon as on the land and sea, when it finally struck, it did so with savage fury. The agent of destruction was the B-29 Superfortress, which was much heavier and faster than the B-17 and carried a far greater bombload. When B-29s became available for combat in early 1944, American forces were still far away from the Marianas, and the bombers could only operate from bases in China. A substantial number of them came under General Kenneth Wolfe's Twentieth Bomber Command. But Wolfe encountered many problems. His bases were totally dependent on air supply via "the Hump" and had to compete with Stilwell's ground forces and Chennault's Fourteenth Air Force for the rather meager supplies that made it to China. Persistent mechanical defects also kept many of the B-29s grounded.

Wolfe was not able to launch a raid against Japan until June 14, 1944, when over 60 B-29s struck the huge iron and steel complex at Yawata. They delivered their attack from high altitude, according to the prevailing doctrine of precision bombing, but the assault was far from precise and inflicted little damage. It did result in large headlines in American newspapers, which made leaders and the public alike eager for additional raids against the home islands. But due to his many troubles, Wolfe was slow to comply, and this led General "Hap" Arnold to replace him with General Curtis Le May, a veteran of the strategic bombing offensive against Germany.

At age 39, Le May was the youngest major general in the U.S. Army Air Force and had gained notoriety for his extreme outspokenness. Almost never without either a cigar or a pipe, which he clenched savagely between his teeth, he believed fiercely in the potential of high-level precision bombing. But all efforts to translate his faith into reality met with disappointment. B-29s continued to do little serious damage to Japanese industry. Strong winds and heavy cloud cover made precision bombing extremely difficult. In January 1945, Le May assumed leadership of the Twenty-first Bomber Command in the Marianas but continued to encounter the same disappointing results.

Reluctantly, the general concluded that he must change his approach. He decided to use incendiary bombs against enemy cities that contained many dwellings of flimsy wooden construction. The Japanese also housed much of their industry in small workshops in these highly inflammable residential areas. By this time, a particularly nasty type of incendiary was available.

It contained napalm, a jellied form of petroleum that exploded upon impact and spread like a torrent, engulfing all before it. To provide greater accuracy, Le May sharply reduced bombing altitude, and he stripped the B-29s of their machine guns to increase speed. Since the raids would take place at night, he believed that the faster-moving planes had little to fear from Japanese antiaircraft fire. The bomber crews did not share his confidence and approached the first large-scale mission of this type with great misgivings.

On March 9, 1945, over 300 B-29s dropped huge quantities of incendiaries on Tokyo from altitudes as low as 4,900 feet. Exploding napalm ignited rivers of fire, and strong winds whipped them into a vast inferno that destroyed 16 square miles of the city and incinerated almost 85,000 persons. The raid was even more destructive than those that had obliterated much of Hamburg and Dresden. The temperature of the holocaust reached an incredible 1,800 degrees Fahrenheit. The tremendous heat created such air turbulence that some bombers had difficulty maintaining control and were sucked into the fires. But overall, B-29 losses were light. More firebombing raids followed in rapid succession. Nagoya, Osaka, Kobe, Yokohama, and many other cities fell victim to the same type of horror. Ostensibly, these raids aimed at destroying Japanese industry, and, to be sure, they did knock out an ample portion, but they were clearly terror raids, designed to weaken Japanese morale.

BOTH SIDES WOO THE SOVIETS

By the spring of 1945, Japan's economy was a shambles, and at least some Japanese leaders realized that the country could not continue the war for long. Lack of raw materials had cut steel output to less than 100,000 tons per month. Production of aircraft had declined disastrously, and planes that did come into service were starved for fuel. Similar shortages also immobilized the remnants of the navy and verged on paralyzing the entire transportation system. Food stocks dwindled alarmingly.

Although Japanese Premier Koiso publicly supported a vigorous war effort, he secretly opened diplomatic contacts with the Soviet Union, hoping to secure an honorable peace. But Stalin was not interested in acting as mediator, and Koiso's government could not survive the multitude of disasters that befell Japan. In early April, Baron Kantaro Suzuki, a 78-year-old retired admiral and hero of the Russo-Japanese War of 1904–5, became premier. Suzuki apparently favored an end to the war, but many army and navy leaders still thought only in terms of fighting to the bitter end.

In the face of such opposition, the pursuit of peace was a tricky business. Like Koiso, Suzuki openly stated his support for the war, but behind the scenes his foreign minister, Shigenori Togo, looked for a way to end the conflict. Togo favored negotiations with the United States, but Suzuki insisted on reviving Koiso's indirect approach through the USSR. Again, Stalin declined to cooperate.

The United States and Britain had long sought Soviet participation in the war against Japan once the Allies had defeated Germany. Soviet intervention in Manchuria would make it difficult for the Japanese to shift forces from there to help defend the home islands. Stalin had given his promise to enter the East Asian conflict at the Teheran conference in November 1943 and had outlined the concessions he expected in return. He presented more specific demands, which Roosevelt and Churchill accepted, at the Yalta conference in February 1945.

These included acquisition of the southern half of Sakhalin, a large island just to the north of Japan, as well as the Kuriles, a chain of much smaller islands stretching northeastward from Japan to the Soviet Union's Kamchatka Peninsula. He also asked for a lease on Port Arthur and special rights in the nearby port of Dairen on the Manchurian coast. Russia had controlled all of these territories, except the Kuriles, until Japan seized them in the Russo-Japanese War. Finally, Stalin insisted on joint Soviet-Chinese administration of the Manchurian railroads. Since the war, critics have attacked this agreement as a betrayal of China and a boon to Russian expansionism. No doubt it was. But realistically, there is no question that Stalin was in a position to enforce his will on the areas involved, regardless of whether the United States and Britain concurred.

ADVENT OF A NEW AGE: THE ATOMIC BOMB

Ironically, the need for Soviet intervention as well as an invasion of the Japanese home islands became academic on the morning of July 16, 1945, when the United States detonated the first atomic bomb in the desert of New Mexico. The ensuing explosion created a huge fireball and a cloud of smoke that rose more than eight miles into the sky. Dr. J. Robert Oppenheimer, leader of the team of scientists that had been largely responsible for developing the bomb, watched the dawn of the atomic age with both fascination and horror. It reminded him of a passage from the *Bhagavad-Gita*, the great Sanskrit poem of India: "If the radiance of a thousand suns were to burst at once into the sky, that would be like the splendor of the Mighty One. . . . I am become Death, Shatterer of Worlds."

This dramatic spectacle marked the culmination of startling developments in physics that had begun early in the twentieth century and led to revolutionary progress in the late 1930s. Scientists discovered that splitting the nucleus of the uranium atom would produce enormous energy and release particles that would in turn trigger a chain reaction in other atoms, creating an even greater amount of energy. They also recognized that it was theoretically possible to harness this vast energy in a bomb of appalling power, but that the technical problems and expense involved would be prodigious.

German physicists were particularly active in this process of discovery, and some of them fled the tyranny of Hitler's regime. Fearing that Nazi Germany would produce an atomic bomb, they brought the matter to Roosevelt's attention in 1939. The president appointed a committee of scientists to study the problem, and in 1940, he and Churchill agreed to pool Anglo-American resources in this endeavor. But it was not until after America's entry into the war that a special unit of army engineers, headed by General Leslie Groves, assumed the devilishly difficult task of actually creating an atomic bomb. This top-secret undertaking was code-named the Manhattan Project. Groves worked closely with Oppenheimer's team, which also contained British scientists. The obstacles were staggering, but by the summer of 1945, the bomb was ready.

President Truman, who had succeeded to the presidency after Roosevelt's death in April 1945, received news of the successful test while he was in Germany, conferring with Stalin and Churchill at the Potsdam conference. This was the last of the Allied summit meetings, and, indeed, before it ended, only Stalin remained of the wartime Big Three. Churchill departed for home ten days after the conference began to await the results of Britain's first parliamentary election since 1935. He never returned. Instead, Clement Attlee, the leader of the Labour party, which won an unexpected landslide victory, took his place as prime minister and at Potsdam.

Roosevelt and Churchill had never informed Stalin of the Manhattan Project, and Truman was not prepared to do so now. He had watched with growing concern as the Soviets tightened their control over Eastern Europe and also worried about their intentions in Germany. However, he did tell the Russian leader that the United States possessed a new bomb of "unusual destructive force." Stalin blandly indicated his satisfaction but did not press for details. In reality, he was already quite knowledgeable about the bomb. Klaus Fuchs, a German scientist who had fled his homeland to become a British subject and later a member of Oppenheimer's scientific team, had supplied Soviet agents with extensive information on the project.

Stalin also belatedly informed Truman of the peace overtures that the Japanese had been making. But this came as no surprise to the president because Magic intercepts of Japanese diplomatic messages had kept him abreast of their efforts to obtain peace. It was quite clear that the combination of submarine and air attacks as well as Japanese defeats in the Pacific had weakened Tokyo's resolve to continue the war. But the Americans made no effort to pursue the question of negotiation and clung to their doctrine of unconditional surrender. Truman did agree, however, to issue a joint Allied declaration from Potsdam on July 26 that called on Japan to surrender or face "complete and utter destruction."

The Japanese reply to this appeal was vague, but Truman and his advisers interpreted it as a rejection and decided to go ahead with plans to drop an atomic bomb on a major Japanese city. They compiled a list of urban centers that had escaped firebombing and thus would provide a dramatic demonstration of the bomb's terrible power. The leading candidate was Hiroshima, a city of 340,000 located on the southeastern coast of Honshu, Japan's principal island.

With Colonel Paul Tibbets, Jr., at the controls, a B-29, named *Enola Gay* after the pilot's mother, took off from Tinian early on the morning of August 6, carrying a 9,000-pound nuclear bomb with the destructive power of 20,000 tons of TNT. The weather over Hiroshima was ideal as *Enola Gay* approached. Shortly before 8:15 A.M., an ungainly object hurtled out of her bomb bay doors. When it reached a point 660 yards from the ground, a blinding flash illuminated the sky, and a split second later, a gigantic fireball burst over the stricken city. Shock waves of unbelievable force followed, leveling almost everything in their path. The unearthly sight inspired copilot Robert Lewis to enter a terse, "My God!" in his log book. A tower of purple orange, gray, and black smoke churned upward, topped by a cloud in the shape of a mushroom. It ultimately reached an altitude of 55,000 feet. Below, 60 percent of Hiroshima had virtually disappeared. Perhaps as many as 100,000 persons died instantly and as many more perished in the following days, weeks, and years from injuries and the effects of radiation.

FORCING JAPAN'S SURRENDER

Later on that fateful day, Truman warned the Japanese that unless they surrendered, more cities would experience the same horror. The Suzuki government reacted to the disaster by stepping up its unrealistic efforts to persuade the Soviet Union to help arrange peace. Stalin's response was a declaration of war on August 8. Although he had been massing over 1.5 million men along the Manchurian border for months, the bombing of Hiroshima undoubtedly hastened his actual intervention. If he did not act, the war might be over. The once formidable Kwantung Army, which defended Manchuria, had seen much of its strength siphoned off to bolster the defense of Japan and other fronts. Three Soviet armies knifed swiftly into Manchuria from both east and west.

Secretary of War Stimson was troubled by the horror of the Hiroshima cataclysm and urged Truman to make a peace overture to Japan. But the president was determined to stand on the Potsdam Declaration, and since the Japanese had not agreed to surrender, he authorized the dropping of a second atomic bomb. This time the target was Nagasaki, a city of 250,000 on Kyushu's western coast. Although the second bomb was more powerful than the first, it produced less spectacular results. The explosion flattened Nagasaki's center and killed 35,000 people, but the surrounding hills limited the area affected.

The combination of the two atomic bombs and the Soviet Union's entry into the war convinced many Japanese leaders that they had no choice but to surrender. In fact, the Supreme War Council, which had overall responsibility for directing the military effort, was debating acceptance of the Potsdam Declaration even before the second bomb struck Nagasaki. But the council's military representatives voiced intense opposition. Emperor Hirohito broke precedent and the deadlock the day after the Nagasaki disaster by personally requesting that the council and cabinet consent to the declaration with the sole proviso that the emperor should retain his position. On August 10, the government relayed its acceptance on this basis.

Some American leaders still opposed the retention of the emperor, especially James F. Byrnes, who had recently become secretary of state. To Byrnes and others, the emperor symbolized the hated militaristic clique that dominated Japan. But Stimson realized how greatly the Japanese revered their emperor and believed that granting this concession was the only way to assure peace and avoid massive American casualties in an invasion of Japan. On August 11, the leaders reached a compromise that allowed the Japanese to keep their emperor but subjected his authority to an Allied supreme commander of occupation forces. The drama was not yet over however. Japanese military leaders still opposed surrender, and the supreme council debated the matter for three days. Once again, Hirohito decided the issue. He tearfully urged acceptance of surrender and asked that the cabinet prepare a message to this effect that he would record for broadcast to the nation the next morning. The cabinet members, almost overcome by emotion, agreed.

A group of young fanatical army officers made one last attempt to prevent surrender. They broke into the imperial palace grounds, seeking to destroy the recording of the emperor's message, and hoped to coerce the government into continuing the war. It was a final act of *gekokujo*. But this time there was too little support from higher officers. The coup failed.

When the announcement of Japan's surrender reached the United States, one of the most spontaneous celebrations in history erupted. Men, women, and children rushed into the streets and headed, as if by prior agreement, for the center of every town and city in America. They milled around in elated excitement for hours. The war was over. The mood in Japan was quite different—a combination of shock, shame, and relief. As the emperor had said in his address to the people, it was necessary to endure "the unendurable" and bear "the unbearable."

To the American people, August 14 was V-J Day, the moment of victory over Japan. But officially the war did not end until September 2, when the Japanese formally signed the document of surrender aboard the huge U.S. battleship *Missouri* in Tokyo Bay. General MacArthur, whom Truman had appointed Allied supreme commander, presided. During the ceremonies, he spoke these words, which reflected the feelings of everyone present as well as millions of people around the world:

> It is my earnest hope and indeed the hope of all mankind that from this solemn occasion a better world shall emerge out of the blood and carnage of the past—a world founded upon faith and understanding—a world dedicated to the dignity of man and the fulfillment of his most cherished wish—for freedom, tolerance and justice.

POSTMORTEM: WAS ATOMIC FORCE NECESSARY?

The question of whether it was necessary to use the atomic bomb to force Japan's surrender has remained probably the most controversial issue of World War II. Truman and other American leaders contended that they resorted to the bomb to shorten the war and save American lives. They also insisted that both the Hiroshima and Nagasaki bombs were necessary to convince the Japanese that further resistance was suicidal. From their perspective, dropping the second bomb might foster the mistaken belief among Japan's leaders that America had the bomb in mass production. These arguments formed the basis for the traditional interpretation of this question, which many historians still accept.

In later years, however, revisionist historians have charged that the bomb was not needed to end the war and that Japan could not have resisted for long. They contend that the United States not only should have paid more attention to Tokyo's peace overtures but should have taken the initiative by guaranteeing the emperor's throne. At the very least, they feel that Washington should have warned the Japanese of the bomb's existence and staged a demonstration of its destructiveness. Some also contend that U.S. leaders used the bomb not to force Japan's surrender but to impress the Soviets with America's awesome new power and to persuade Stalin to moderate his policies in Europe.

Some of these revisionist arguments are persuasive. There is strong evidence that Japan could not have long avoided surrender. The submarine blockade and the firebombing attacks had sharply reduced the country's ability to make war and had caused great suffering. Indeed, total casualties from the incendiary raids were far greater than those inflicted by the atomic attacks. The United States Strategic Bombing Survey after the war stated flatly that Japan could not have continued the struggle beyond the end of 1945, even without the use of the bomb.

It also is true that the United States made no effort to capitalize on Japanese overtures or to take any diplomatic initiative to secure peace. Truman and his advisers questioned the seriousness of the cautious Japanese feelers to the Soviets, especially since they consistently failed to make any headway. A direct approach to Washington might have had more impact. American leaders also doubted that the tentative peace initiatives really represented the position of the Japanese military. Indeed, there was good reason for this lack of conviction, because many of the enemy's top army leaders opposed acceptance of the Potsdam Declaration, and only the emperor's personal intervention settled the matter. Finally, the Japanese had consistently fought to the bitter end in the Pacific and American leaders expected even greater fanaticism and bloodshed in defense of the sacred home islands.

It is much more difficult to accept the contention that Truman and his advisers used the bomb to impress the Soviet Union rather than to end the war. Certainly, by the summer of 1945, they were concerned about Russia's position in Europe, and once the bomb was available, they lost their desire for Soviet intervention in the East Asian conflict. But since the Russians already dominated Eastern Europe, the bomb would have little impact on their policy there. Perhaps American leaders hoped that the weapon's awesome power might help restrain Moscow's actions regarding the remainder of Europe, but this is not clear. And there was no reason for them to believe that the bomb would persuade the Russians to refrain from invading Manchuria. Indeed, once the first bomb obliterated Hiroshima, it appears to have triggered that intervention. However unnecessary the bomb may have been in forcing the Japanese surrender, it does not appear that the leaders in Washington were convinced of this. They probably believed sincerely that their action would save American lives. But it is hard to avoid the conclusion that they acted with indecent haste in dropping the second bomb. They would have sacrificed nothing by giving the Japanese a few more days to overcome the resistance that still remained on the question of surrender.

Probably it is best to consider the decision to drop the bomb in the context of the steadily escalating vindictiveness and brutality that marked the Allied war effort. This was the case not only against the Japanese but against the Germans as well. Once the British resorted to area bombing of Germany's cities, it was only a step to the firebombing of Hamburg and Dresden. Even the Americans, despite their protests against such an approach, had joined in area bombing of German cities by 1945. Hatred for the Japanese was even more pronounced. It no doubt had its basis to some extent in racism. Wartime propaganda portrayed the "Japs" as vicious, bloodthirsty, even subhuman, a theme that every Hollywood film about the Pacific war featured during this period. Neither the American people nor their leaders could forget the attack on Pearl Harbor, the Bataan Death March, or the fanatical Japanese resistance on island after island. U.S. leaders also became increasingly dedicated to the cause of unconditional surrender, which they believed would prevent a resurgence of Japanese militarism. When conventional strategic bombing of Japanese cities failed, it was but another step to area bombing with incendiaries. It is by no means certain that inflicting death by napalm was more humane than incinerating with nuclear bombs. The decisions to destroy Hiroshima and Nagasaki would seem to have been the last logical elements in the growing crescendo of hatred and destructiveness—undoubtedly terrible, perhaps morally indefensible, but, unfortunately and tragically, understandable.

Aftermath

History's greatest war was over, but its effects lingered. Some actually had their origin in the legacy of World War I. Others were of more recent vintage. Much of the world felt their impact, even areas that had not been directly involved in the conflict. As is the case with most wars, many of the issues that provoked hostilities were not really solved. Others were.

THE PHYSICAL COSTS OF WORLD WAR II

World War II was the most costly conflict in history, in terms of both casualties and destructiveness as well as wealth expended. At least 17 million soldiers lost their lives in battle, and perhaps 18 million civilians also perished, among them the almost 6 million Jewish victims of the Holocaust.

Russia suffered by far the most grievous total losses—7.5 million military and more than 10 million civilian dead. Germany, too, paid a heavy price for Hitler's ambitions—at least 3.5 million soldiers killed along with 1 million civilians. Austria, which had been a part of the Reich during the war, lost 300,000. China also suffered horribly. Estimates of Chinese total losses vary from as many as 13.5 million to as few as 2.5 million. Japan's military and civilian fatalities numbered 2 million. France, Britain, and Italy each suffered over 400,000 deaths, including both military and civilians. Poland's losses were the greatest of any of the smaller powers, with 300,000 battle deaths and over 5 million civilian deaths, including almost 3 million Jews. Yugoslavia lost 400,000 soldiers and more than a million noncombatants. As in World War I, the United States remained free of destruction, but U.S. battle losses totaled 290,000.

The war had also uprooted perhaps as many as 30 million people from their homes in Europe, including those who had served as slave laborers or had survived the Nazi death and concentration camps. These unfortunate victims became known as "displaced persons" in the postwar era. In addition, the end of the war brought wholesale population shifts on a deliberate basis. Germans were the chief victims of this practice. Poland expelled 9 million of them from the territory east of the line formed by the Oder and Neisse rivers and from the southern two-thirds of East Prussia. The Poles had received these lands as compensation for the loss of eastern Poland to the USSR. Czechoslovakia also ousted the 3 million Sudeten Germans, thereby finally solving the Sudetenland question.

Total direct and indirect costs of the war in monetary terms may have reached as high as $4 trillion. Destruction was present almost everywhere in Europe, from Norway to Sicily and from Britain to Stalingrad, as well as in North Africa. Unlike the situation after World War I, Germany had suffered extensive devastation, and all its major cities lay in ruins. If World War I had disrupted the European economy, the conflict of 1939–45 had brought it to a virtual standstill. In many countries, the industrial complex, communications network, and natural resources were in a state of desolation. Prewar patterns of trade were in total disarray, as were the financial and monetary systems. Inflation was rampant. The fighting had sharply curtailed food production, and starvation and disease stalked large areas of the continent.

In Asia, China bore the scars of eight years of conflict, and another four years of civil war lay just ahead. But, except for Burma and the Philippines, much of Southeast Asia had experienced little direct destruction since 1942. Most of the fighting had taken place on islands with small populations and primitive economies. Japan had not been so fortunate. The rain of death from the skies had, of course, destroyed large portions of that nation's major cities.

PROSECUTING WAR CRIMINALS

The victorious Allies were determined to bring to justice the leaders who had been responsible for starting the war and the atrocities that followed. In the case of Germany, the two main culprits had escaped the ignominy of standing trial. Hitler, the man most responsible for the war and its horrors, was dead. So was Himmler, who like his Führer had resorted to suicide. But many German leaders were still alive, and most of them were in Allied custody. The United States, Britain, the Soviet Union, and France agreed in August 1945 to establish an international military tribunal to try the most important of them.

It convened in Nuremberg, the site of the former Nazi party rallies, in November 1945 and brought forth indictments against 24 German leaders. Among the best known were Goering, Ribbentrop, Speer, Generals Keitel and Jodl, and Admirals Raeder and Dönitz. They also included Alfred Rosenberg, the self-styled Nazi theoretician; Ernst Kaltenbrunner, who had succeeded Heydrich as chief of the Nazi security police; and Fritz Sauckel, the head of the slave labor program. The two men who had served as Hitler's deputies were on the list as well. The first of these, Rudolf Hess, had been officially the number three man in the Nazi hierarchy until May 1941. At that time, he had crashlanded an Me 110 fighter plane on British soil in an ill-advised attempt to negotiate peace. The second, Martin Bormann, had succeeded Hess and had disappeared in Berlin after Hitler's death. It is likely that he died trying to escape to the West.

The trial lasted until October 1946 and resulted in death sentences by hanging for 11 of the defendants, including Goering, Ribbentrop, Kaltenbrunner, Rosenberg, Sauckel, Keitel, and Jodl as well as Bormann *in absentia*. Hess and Raeder received life sentences, Speer 20 years, and Dönitz 10 years. Shortly before his scheduled execution, Goering cheated the rope by biting into a cyanide capsule that he had concealed on his person. A series of trials of less important Nazi officials also took place in the various occupation zones. The most important of these in the American zone resulted in 24 death sentences and 116 prison terms.

In Japan, another international tribunal tried 40 leaders on charges of war crimes. Seven of them received death sentences, including former Premier Tojo, who had failed in a suicide attempt prior to his arrest. Eighteen others received prison sentences. Fumimaro Konoye, who had preceded Tojo as premier, avoided arrest by taking poison. Other trials took place in various parts of Japan's former empire. Among the most notable defendants was General Yamashita. A court in Manila found the Tiger of Malaya guilty of condoning atrocities in the Philippines and sentenced him to death.

Despite the enormity of the crimes involved, the tribunals have received much criticism. Some have questioned whether international courts had any legal standing since there was no world state. They also pointed out that the defendants, despite their undoubted complicity in barbaric policies, had actually broken no existing international laws. The proceedings were thus of a retroactive or *ex post facto* type, which neither the British nor the American legal system recognized. There was also the question of Allied behavior during the war. Were the Russians not guilty of aggression against Poland, the Baltic states, and Finland? Did they not commit mass murder in the shooting of the Polish officers in the Katyn Forest as well as atrocities against the population of eastern Germany? Did they not attack Japan without provocation in the last days of the war? What of the Anglo-American terror-bombing raids against Germany and the American firebombing of Japanese cities? What about Hiroshima and Nagasaki?

Former occupied countries of Europe also took action against leaders who had collaborated with the Germans. In Norway, Quisling, the man whose name had become synonymous with treason, died before a firing squad. In France, Pierre Laval, the chief collaborator during much of the Vichy regime's existence, met a similar fate. A French court also found Marshal Pétain, the World War I hero and Vichy's head of state, guilty of treason and sentenced him to death. But Charles de Gaulle, France's provisional president, commuted the sentence to life imprisonment in recognition of Pétain's earlier service.

POLITICAL REPERCUSSIONS

The war also transformed the power structure of the world. World War I had started this process with the disintegration of Austria-Hungary. World War II banished five other countries from the ranks of the great powers—France, Italy, Germany, Japan, and even Britain. Although Britain had been one of the three major powers in the alliance against the Axis, it had become painfully clear that it was the junior partner and lacked the size, population, and resources of the USSR and the United States. Even though Great Britain had suffered less destruction than the Soviet Union or Germany or even France, the British had paid a fearful price for victory. Their economy, which World War I had so badly disrupted, was now a shambles. The nation was deeply in debt, its resources depleted, and its share of the world market but a memory.

Now only two great powers remained—the United States and the Soviet Union—and they were really superpowers, towering above all other nations and posing the possibility of a world split into two rival blocs. Furthermore, they were divided ideologically. America became the champion of capitalism and liberal democracy, the USSR of communism and totalitarianism. But as time passed, the United States came to support many countries that, though anti-Communist, were far from democratic. In the process, the distinction between the "free world" and the "totalitarian world" became fuzzy.

The war had created two vast power vacuums, one in Europe, the other in East Asia. In Europe, this was the logical conclusion to another legacy of World War I—the creation of a power vacuum in the central and eastern portions of the continent. For a time, Nazi Germany had filled that vacuum, but by 1945, the Red Army held most of Eastern and Central Europe by right of conquest.

Since 1945, many critics have attacked the United States and Britain, specifically Roosevelt and to a lesser extent Churchill, for supposedly allowing the Soviets to dominate Eastern Europe. As proof they have pointed to arrangements that the two Western leaders made with Stalin during the last months of the war. Indeed, it is true that they did grant certain concessions, but these were only in keeping with the reality of the Red Army's presence in Eastern Europe.

Churchill had essentially acknowledged the Soviet claim to eastern Poland at the Teheran conference in November 1943. Actually, the prime minister, like many other British leaders, had always been skeptical about Poland's claim to much of this area because the population was primarily Ukrainian and Belorussian rather than Polish. Churchill also recognized that there was nothing that either he or Roosevelt could do to keep the Baltic states out of Soviet hands. As for Roosevelt, he attempted to establish a close personal relationship with Stalin, which he hoped would persuade the Soviet leader to be reasonable about Eastern Europe. The president firmly believed that Soviet cooperation with the West was necessary for postwar stability in the world.

SOVIET INFLUENCE IN EASTERN EUROPE

By late 1944, Churchill was growing alarmed at the Red Army's increasing control of Eastern Europe. In an attempt to salvage something in this area, the prime minister posed the possibility of a division of influence in the Balkans during a visit to Moscow in October 1944. Stalin seemed receptive, and in a surprisingly casual manner, the two leaders agreed that the Soviets should enjoy 90 percent interest in Rumania and 75 percent in Bulgaria. The West would have to be content with 10 and 25 percent, respectively, in these countries but would hold a 90 percent advantage in Greece to the Soviets' 10 percent. Churchill and Stalin proposed a 50–50 division of interest in Hungary and Yugoslavia. To Churchill's chagrin, Roosevelt found this agreement a glaring example of the spheres-of-influence approach to power politics, which he detested.

Although the agreement did not extend to Poland, Churchill clearly realized that little could be done to save the cause of Mikolajczyk's Polish government in exile. Stalin's support for the Polish National Liberation Committee in Lublin and the failure of the Warsaw Uprising had sealed the fate of the London Poles. Mikolajczyk was in Moscow at the time of Churchill's meeting with Stalin and recognized the need to make concessions to the Soviet Union. But his colleagues in the government in exile refused, and he resigned as premier. Soon afterward, Churchill washed his hands of the stubborn London Poles and recognized the Lublin government the following January.

At Yalta in February 1945, Churchill and Roosevelt recognized the USSR's claim to eastern Poland and agreed that the border should run generally along the line that British foreign secretary Lord Curzon had proposed as Poland's eastern border in 1919. They also generally accepted Stalin's proposal that Poland and the Soviet Union divide East Prussia and that the Poles receive additional compensation to the east of the Oder. In return, the Western leaders won Stalin's agreement that the London Poles would be represented in the Polish Liberation Committee and that free elections would determine Poland's future government.

Despite Western concessions, the presence of the Red Army was the determining factor in Russian domination of Eastern Europe. The only way in which the United States and Britain could possibly have changed this situation was by resorting to military action. Neither country was prepared to attempt such a drastic solution. Indeed, until the advent of the atomic bomb, both the Americans and the British thought in terms of enticing the Soviets into the war against Japan. Even had they considered attempting to expel the Red Army from Eastern Europe, there was no assurance that they could have done so in a conventional war. At best, a stalemate would probably have resulted. It is true that by the summer of 1945, the United States had a monopoly on the atomic bomb, but only the lunatic fringe believed that nuclear war was the answer to the dilemma. Moreover, atomic weapons remained in short supply for several years.

Critics have also contended that Western troops could have liberated much of Eastern Europe before the Red Army. Some have charged that the United States and Britain made a fatal error by not invading the Balkans in 1943 or 1944. But such an operation would have been clearly political in nature, and U.S. leaders were eager to secure military victory by the quickest and most direct manner—a cross-Channel invasion of Western Europe. They were not interested in political objectives on Europe's remote southeastern periphery. Certainly their thinking was sound militarily. Any assault on the Balkans would also have encountered extremely mountainous terrain, which would have provided the Germans with ideal defensive positions similar to those in Italy.

Since the war, the myth has developed that Churchill actively urged such a policy from a relatively early date. In reality, he never proposed anything more than aid to Tito's Partisans in Yugoslavia, the occupation of the island of Rhodes in the Aegean Sea, and efforts to entice Turkey into the war. He did, of course, order British troops into Greece in 1944, but this operation took place only after the Germans had begun to withdraw from the country. Otherwise, Churchill supported General Alexander's questionable dream of a thrust through northeastern Italy toward Vienna and the Hungarian Plain. But such an operation could not have begun before early 1945, far too late to have had any real effect on the situation in Central Europe.

Some have also charged that Western forces could have beaten the Red Army to Berlin in April 1945. But this is highly questionable because the Soviets had massive forces less than 40 miles from the German capital at that time, while just the spearheads of General Simpson's U.S. Ninth Army were within striking distance. Only in the case of Czechoslovakia was there a real opportunity for U.S. forces to push farther east. Indeed, they probably could have taken Prague before the Soviets. Whether the Americans would have maintained a presence in the Czech capital and whether Czechoslovakia would have remained outside the Soviet orbit in the long run is by no means clear, however.

Soviet-dominated territories fell into two categories in the postwar era—those that the USSR annexed directly and those that became satellite states. The former consisted of the areas that Finland had ceded to the Soviets, the Baltic states, the northern third of East Prussia, eastern Poland, the eastern Czech province of Ruthenia, which contained a predominantly Ukrainian population, and the Rumanian provinces of Bessarabia and Northern Bukovina. The Allies concluded peace treaties with Finland and Rumania in 1946 that confirmed their territorial losses. Britain and America never officially recognized the annexation of the Baltic states, although informally both Roosevelt and Churchill had realized at least as early as 1944 that this was inevitable.

As compensation for the loss of its eastern territory, Poland received the southern two-thirds of East Prussia and the area of Germany east of the Oder-Neisse line. The Americans and British approved the Polish occupation of these territories at the Potsdam conference. But they insisted on deferring actual determination of Poland's borders until the Big Three could agree on a peace treaty for Germany. As it turned out, the Allied powers never drafted a treaty, and the territories remained under Polish control. In its new form, Poland was 20 percent smaller than it had been in 1939, but the land received from Germany was considerably more valuable than that lost to the Soviet Union. The added territory included the ports of Danzig and Stettin and the rich industrial area of Silesia.

Poland became a Soviet satellite, along with East Germany, Czechoslovakia, Hungary, Rumania, and Bulgaria. The subjugation of these countries occurred despite Stalin's agreement at Yalta to an American-sponsored Declaration on Liberated Europe. This document provided for the establishment of coalition governments, containing both Communists and non-Communists, in all liberated countries, as well as free parliamentary elections. Although coalition governments did come into existence, Communists held most of the key positions in these regimes. As time passed, they increased their control and gradually squeezed out the non-Communists.

The exact manner in which this took place varied from country to country, as did the tempo of change. But a Communist monopoly on the vital cabinet post of minister of the interior, which controlled the police, usually contributed to the process. Deteriorating relations between the Soviet Union and the Western Powers as well as between Moscow and one of the Communist states, Yugoslavia, also led to a tightening of Soviet influence. Although local Communists were primarily responsible for the transformation, the Red Army's presence in each country certainly served as a deterrent to any active resistance to the takeovers.

The Communists eventually modeled the regimes of the satellite states closely after the Stalinist system in the USSR. They allowed no opposition parties and kept tight control over all aspects of life, including state-controlled economies. Bowing to Soviet pressure, they granted concessions that enabled the USSR to exploit their countries economically. Each government also followed foreign policies that dovetailed closely with that of Moscow.

Yugoslavia was an exception to this pattern. Although Soviet troops had helped drive the Germans from the country, Tito's Partisans had carried out most of this task. Thus the Red Army never played the inhibiting role it had assumed in other countries. Instead, Tito and his Communist followers dominated Yugoslavia from the start. With the cooling of East-West relations, Stalin tried to increase Soviet influence over Tito's regime. But the Yugoslav leader refused to acquiesce. When the USSR applied economic pressure, instead of buckling under, Tito turned to the West for aid. The United States was eager to assist, and in the years that followed, Yugoslavia remained Communist but enjoyed independence from both blocs.

Little Albania represented another exception. When the Germans withdrew in late 1944 to avoid being cut off by the Red Army, local Communists with help from Tito's Partisans, fought Albanian non-Communists and established a provisional government. In the process, Yugoslavia's influence became so strong that it threatened to convert Albania into a satellite of Belgrade. To avoid this, Enver Hoxha, the Albanian Communist leader, turned to the USSR for support at the time of Tito's break with Stalin. The Soviet leader was happy to oblige. Hoxha accordingly proceeded to wipe out all opposition to his rule, established a thoroughly Stalinist system, and linked his country closely to Moscow.

Finland was still another exception. Not only did the Finns remain free from Soviet domination, but they continued as a non-Communist, democratic state. They owed this independence largely to their ability to make peace with the Soviets in 1944 before the Red Army could penetrate deeply into the country. Stalin was willing to allow Finland to enjoy its freedom, provided that it retain close relations with the USSR. Under the circumstances, the Finns followed a policy of economic cooperation and friendship with their huge neighbor to the east.

U.S. AID TO WESTERN EUROPE

During the immediate postwar years, while the USSR consolidated its control over Eastern Europe, most of Western Europe emerged with democratic governments and badly strained economies. The United States and Britain allowed the Western European countries to handle their own affairs. Indicative of this is the fact that in two of these countries, France and Italy, large Communist parties flourished. In view of the lagging economic recovery of Western Europe, non-Communists feared that continued distress might lead to growing Communist support. The French restored a form of government similar to the Third Republic. This Fourth Republic experienced many of the same problems, especially a multiparty system and chronic political instability. Cabinets fell with alarming regularity. The Italians abolished their monarchy in 1946 and established a republic that also suffered from a multitude of parties and an unstable parliamentary system. The United States viewed the situation in both countries with growing concern.

But the American government looked with far greater distress at developments in Greece and Turkey, which bordered the Soviet satellites. A civil war had plagued Greece intermittently since 1944. It featured a sizable group of rebels under Communist leadership who opposed the corrupt and reactionary Greek government. Neighboring Bulgaria, Yugoslavia, and Albania provided aid to the Communists. But Stalin scrupulously honored his 1944 arrangement with Churchill, which had given Britain a free hand in Greece in return for a similar Soviet advantage in Rumania and Bulgaria. British forces had propped up the Greek government since 1944, but in early 1947, Britain indicated that due to financial difficulties, it would have to withdraw its troops in the near future. Meanwhile, Turkey was having trouble with the Soviets, who demanded the return of border areas that had been Russian before 1918. They also asked for the right to share in the defense of the straits linking the Black Sea with the Mediterranean.

This combination of developments led President Truman to announce in early 1947 that henceforth the United States would "support free peoples who are resisting attempted subjugation by armed minorities or by outside pressures." In the same speech, the president proposed to provide economic aid to both Greece and Turkey as well as military advisers and equipment. The president's speech was tremendously significant because in proclaiming what came to be known as the Truman Doctrine, he launched an entirely new approach to foreign policy. America had definitely abandoned its traditional peacetime aloofness from European affairs. Truman clearly aimed his policy against the Soviet Union, even though Stalin had consistently refused to support the Greek rebels. The Truman Doctrine represented the official start of the American policy of containment, which attempted to prevent Soviet expansion and the spread of communism.

Later the same year, Secretary of State George Marshall, the U.S. army's wartime chief of staff, proposed a program for the economic rehabilitation of Europe. Officially titled the European Recovery Program, it was soon being referred to as the Marshall Plan. Concern over the economic woes of Western Europe and fear of increasing Communist strength in France and Italy motivated the program. In its inception, the plan offered economic aid to all of Europe, including the Soviet Union.

The USSR and its satellites actually responded to the offer with some interest, but when the United States demanded a survey of the economic resources of recipient countries, Moscow turned against the program and pressured the satellites to follow suit. Thus when the Marshall Plan went into effect in 1948, it was primarily a Western European enterprise, although it also extended to Greece and Turkey. The venture proved remarkably effective. Between 1948 and 1951, the United States provided credits and goods to European countries amounting to over $12 billion. This infusion of aid greatly stimulated recovery. Industrial production in Western Europe soon equaled prewar levels and by 1951 had surpassed them by 41 percent. The Marshall Plan also laid the basis for Western European economic integration. It required the recipient countries to cooperate in solving mutual economic problems as a prerequisite for aid.

THE COLD WAR

The expansion of Soviet domination in Eastern Europe and the American response in bolstering Greece, Turkey, and Western Europe divided the continent into rival power blocs. The increased tension between them became known as the Cold War. Both the Soviet Union and the United States contributed to the process.

It is not surprising that the growth of Soviet control in Eastern Europe inspired concern in the West, especially the brusque manner in which this took place. But it is also not surprising that the Soviets were determined to regain the territory they had taken from Finland, the Baltic states, Poland, and Rumania during 1939–40. Stalin had repeatedly insisted on this while the war raged. And it is understandable that he desired Communist governments in Poland, Rumania, and Bulgaria. Both Poland and Rumania had been hostile to the Soviet Union throughout the interwar years. Rumania had also participated in the invasion of the USSR and had even helped itself, with German consent, to a slice of Soviet territory adjacent to Bessarabia. Bulgaria, though never actually declaring war against the Soviet Union, had joined the Axis. Stalin's original intentions toward Czechoslovakia and Hungary are less clear. There is reason to believe that he might have been willing to maintain coalition governments in both, providing that they contained strong Communist representation. But local Communists took matters into their own hands and ruthlessly established their complete control.

Stalin believed that the USSR's sacrifices in the war against Germany, which were infinitely greater than those of the Western Allies, entitled it to a dominant position in Eastern Europe. It seemed to him that the Americans and British should realize this and not interfere. In return, he was willing to grant them a free hand in Western Europe and the Mediterranean. His attitude toward Greece was a graphic example of his belief in spheres of influence. There is no indication that he ever thought in terms of extending Soviet control into Western Europe. Certainly such an attempt would have resulted in war with America and Britain. The Soviets could hardly have benefited from a conflict against their former allies in the aftermath of the appalling struggle with Germany.

But the British and especially the Americans were not convinced that Stalin had no ambitions in Western Europe. They tended to view him as another Hitler bent on the subjugation of the entire continent. Again not surprisingly, they took measures to guard against the possibility of additional Soviet expansion. In the process, there appears little doubt that they overreacted to the perceived menace.

The Cold War in its early stages focused above all on Germany, where East and West were clearly at cross-purposes. According to the wartime and immediate postwar agreements, the Soviets and the Western Allies divided Germany into occupation zones. In addition to those of the Big Three, France received a smaller zone that bordered French territory. They also divided Berlin, but the German capital lay deep within the Soviet zone, making Western access dependent on Soviet cooperation.

Supposedly all four occupying powers were to cooperate on matters of mutual concern, including the drafting of a peace treaty that would determine Germany's permanent fate. But there proved to be little cooperation, except on such obvious issues as disarmament, punishment of war criminals, and elimination of Nazi influence.

The question of reparations proved particularly thorny. The USSR insisted on extensive reparations to compensate for wartime losses and to help rebuild the Soviet economy. The Western Powers considered these demands excessive. Stalin looked on the Western attitude as evidence of hostility and simply decided to take whatever he considered necessary from within the Soviet zone. This involved dismantling German factories and shipping machinery to the Soviet Union as well as exploitation of other German resources. The Soviets treated their zone as a self-contained economic unit. Britain, the United States, and France also disagreed with the Soviets on the type of German government that should emerge from the period of occupation. They desired a Western-style democracy with a capitalistic economy. The Soviets preferred a Germany in which Communist influence would be strong.

A number of conferences involving the foreign ministers of the occupying powers failed to resolve any of the major issues. By late 1946, the British and Americans abandoned all hope of cooperation with the Soviets and merged their zones under one administration. They also began to strengthen the western German economy. In March 1948, they pressured the French to merge their zone and announced the intention to create a federal government for all of West Germany. Preparations began for an assembly that would draft a constitution for the proposed state. In June, the Western Powers introduced a new West German currency. The Soviets objected strenuously to these actions and cut off Western rail and highway access to Berlin through the Soviet zone. The Western Powers resorted to an airlift of supplies by hundreds of cargo planes, which carried thousands of tons of supplies into Berlin every day.

This deadlock lasted for almost a year, but in May 1949, the Soviets admitted defeat by restoring Western land access to Berlin. The lengthy crisis represented the first serious confrontation between East and West in the Cold War and symbolized a hardening of positions on both sides. A West German state came into existence in May 1949, and the Soviets responded by creating a Communist East German republic in their zone. These actions confirmed the division of Germany.

Another symbol of the Cold War came into being while the Berlin blockade was still in effect. This was the North Atlantic Treaty Organization (NATO), a collective security alliance under American leadership aimed at defending Western Europe against a possible Soviet attack. Most of the Western European nations joined, as did Canada. The question of West German membership in NATO soon became the subject of strenuous debate. Clearly the new German state would greatly strengthen the alliance, but European NATO members, especially France, feared a rearmed Germany. Despite this concern, West Germany became a member of NATO in 1955 and received the right to develop an army, which became part of the alliance's military force. The USSR responded to West Germany's admission by creating the Warsaw Pact later in 1955. This was the Eastern European counterpart to NATO and included East Germany. Actually, the Warsaw Pact merely superseded earlier separate military agreements that the Soviets had made with the satellites.

The descent into Cold War became even more ominous when the Soviets tested an atomic bomb in 1949 and began to develop a nuclear arsenal. In the years that followed, the two sides entered into an arms race that eventually featured intercontinental ballistic missiles armed with nuclear warheads. These sinister weapons increased alarmingly, not only in number but also in striking power. The Hiroshima bomb, the equivalent of 20,000 tons of TNT, had shocked the world in 1945. But by 1954, the United States had tested a bomb with the force of 20 million tons of TNT. It also became painfully clear that fallout in the form of radioactive dust from these weapons could contaminate the entire globe, posing the prospect of a war without winners or even survivors.

THE SPREAD OF DEMOCRACY

Although Western observers in the postwar era tended to focus their attention on the triumph of communism in Eastern Europe, democracy also scored impressive victories in countries that had experienced dictatorship during the interwar and wartime years. The horrible examples of fascism in Italy and Nazism in Germany helped convince many people in both countries that there were far worse things than democracy. Despite their earlier lack of success with such governments, this time both countries made their new democratic systems work. Austria, too, overcame the legacy of the Dollfuss-Schuschnigg dictatorship and Nazi rule and fashioned a viable democracy.

The war also led to the establishment of a new world peacekeeping organization, the United Nations. To a large extent, President Roosevelt had provided its inspiration. Similar in many respects to the ill-fated League of Nations, the UN suffered from many of the same shortcomings. Except in unusual cases, it could take no action that either of the superpowers opposed. On the rare occasions when the United States and the USSR reached agreement on substantive issues, they usually did so outside the United Nations. But within its limitations, the organization performed useful work, especially in attempting to mediate disputes between lesser powers.

While the Cold War was taking shape in Europe, dramatic changes also occurred in Asia. Japan followed Germany and Italy into the ranks of the democratic powers under the tutelage of the United States and, specifically, General MacArthur in his capacity as supreme commander of the Allied Powers. The United States, which had played the major role in the Pacific war, had no intention of sharing the occupation of Japan with any other power. To be sure, the Americans agreed to the establishment of a four-power con-

FIGURE A-1 The grim specter of the nuclear mushroom cloud haunted the postwar world. (*U.S. Air Force Photograph*)

trol council, but MacArthur actually governed the country. The general's first task in converting Japan into a democracy was to transform the emperor from a god to a constitutional monarch, and he persuaded Hirohito to renounce his supposed divine origin. In April 1946, MacArthur authorized elections for a constituent assembly, which drafted a new constitution. This document did not meet with his approval, however, so he issued his own version, which the assembly dutifully ratified.

Parliamentary elections took place in 1947, and a Japanese government came into being shortly thereafter. Its decisions remained subject to MacArthur's veto until the occupation ended in 1951. Although the new democracy contained elements borrowed from the American constitution, it bore a greater resemblance to the British system, which was more in keeping with earlier Japanese parliamentary institutions. The constitution renounced Japan's right to make war or maintain armed forces. (In later years, the Japanese did agree to cooperate with the United States by establishing a small military force for their own defense.) MacArthur and his staff also presided over an ambitious land reform program that granted the former hard-pressed tenant farmers ownership of their land.

Japan's empire was a casualty of the war. In addition to the loss of the Kurile Islands and southern Sakhalin to the USSR, Japan returned Manchuria and Formosa to China and relinquished control of Korea. The United States received the Mariana, Caroline, and Marshall islands as trust territories under United Nations supervision.

CIVIL WAR IN CHINA

Change also came to China, but in a more violent way. Soon after the war, the old animosities between the Kuomintang and the Communists erupted once again in civil war. This time the Communists were in a much stronger position than before the Sino-Japanese conflict. They held extensive territory in the north, especially Manchuria, and their armies also operated in much of the countryside to the south. But they received little support from the Soviets. In the immediate aftermath of the war, Stalin still thought in terms of cooperation with the West. His association with Mao Tse-tung, the Chinese Communist leader, had never been close, and he disliked Mao's independent attitude. For the time being, he continued to recognize Chiang's regime and cooperated with the American airlift of Kuomintang troops, which had taken over the cities of Manchuria following Japan's surrender. However, he did nothing to prevent the Communists from acquiring Japanese war materiel.

Although the United States supplied arms and military advisers to Chiang, there was little it could do to prevent erosion of the Kuomintang position. Chiang tried to hold Manchuria after Soviet troops pulled out in 1946. But the Communists controlled the countryside and were able to recruit large numbers of peasants for their army, which fought with considerable enthusiasm. Chiang's own forces suffered from poor leadership and low morale, and the corrupt and inefficient Kuomintang regime failed to capture the allegiance of the masses. The Communists had conquered most of Manchuria by the spring of 1947 and possessed much of China north of the Yangtze River by the summer of 1948. They overran the remainder of the mainland during 1949, and Chiang withdrew to Formosa, accompanied by his best troops.

As was so often the case with China, a great deal of misinformation circulated in the United States. Much of it was due to propaganda by the "China lobby" as well as by Republican leaders, who charged that President Truman and his Democratic administration had betrayed China. In reality, nothing could have saved Chiang's decadent regime. Most Americans also believed that the Communist victory had been due primarily to Soviet aid, but in reality Stalin had hedged his bets until the last moment and had provided no direct support to Mao's forces. He did not even recognize the Communist regime until it had proclaimed itself as the People's Republic of China in October 1949. And although the Soviets did provide military aid to the Communists after that, relations remained cool. Mao resented the cautious Soviet attitude, while Stalin viewed the Chinese leader as a rival.

The Communists lacked the naval strength to carry out an invasion of Formosa. Instead, Chiang was able to maintain his dictatorial power over the island and with it the myth that somehow in the future he might be able to regain control over the mainland. Since the United States continued to recognize his regime as the legal government of China, this helped prevent the development of normal American relations with Communist China for many years.

EVENTS IN KOREA LEAD TO WAR

The drama in China soon became intertwined with events in Korea, which adjoined Manchuria. During World War II, Korean nationalists in exile had hoped to establish an independent Korea. But the United States did not consider the Koreans ready for self-government and favored a period of Allied occupation that would prepare them for independence. When the war ended, American forces occupied the country south of the 38th parallel while Soviet troops occupied the area to the north. Rival Korean regimes soon developed in each sector. In the south, Syngman Rhee, an authoritarian and quarrelsome politician, headed a government dominated by conservative landowners, many of whom had cooperated with the Japanese. In the north, a Communist regime came into existence under the leadership of the guerrilla leader Kim Il-sung. Unlike the situation in China, the Soviets trained and equipped a North Korean army.

A Soviet-American commission considered the problem of reunifying the country but could reach no agreement. By 1949, Soviet and American troops had withdrawn, leaving the two Koreas to fend for themselves. Rhee's government became more dictatorial and unpopular as it imprisoned many of its liberal political opponents. In the north, the Communist regime confiscated the estates of the large landowners and distributed the land to the peasants.

On June 25, 1950, North Korean soldiers crossed the 38th parallel and drove rapidly southward. Only the intervention of American troops, under United Nations authorization, prevented a Communist unification of the country. United Nations forces, under General MacArthur's command, clung to a perimeter around the port of Pusan on the southeastern coast. After substantial American reinforcements arrived, they took the offensive in September. MacArthur carried out a brilliant amphibious landing near Inchon, far to the northwest, that threatened to cut off the Communist troops near Pusan and forced them to retreat. Before the end of the month, American and South Korean forces had reached the 38th parallel. But instead of halting at the border, they pursued the enemy northward with the avowed intention of uniting all of Korea under Rhee's government. As they approached the Yalu River, which separated Korea from Manchuria, the Chinese Communists became alarmed by an American presence so close to their border. In late November, they launched a massive attack across the Yalu and sent the UN forces reeling back into South Korea. The war finally ended in a deadlock in July 1953, with the border between North and South fixed near the 38th parallel.

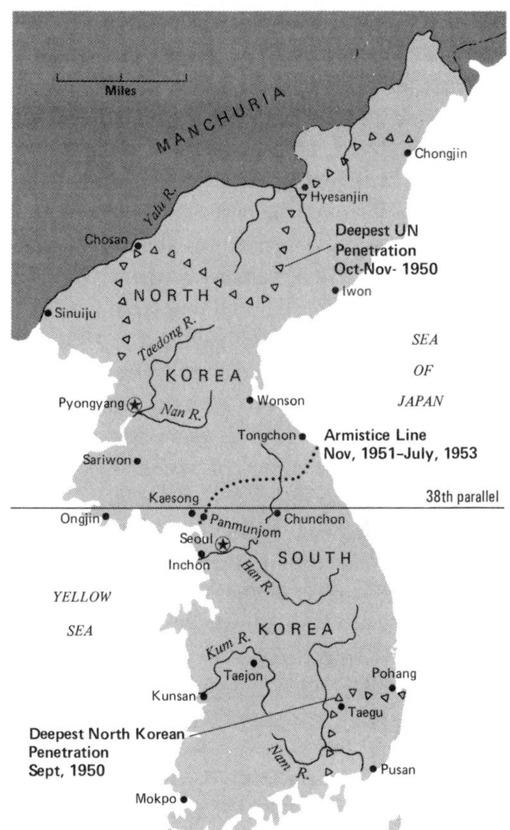

The Korean War, 1950–53

American leaders assumed that the Soviets were behind the original North Korean invasion and feared that this action might be the prelude to a similar operation against Western Europe. The decision to bring West Germany into NATO was a direct result of this concern. But it is by no means clear that the Soviet Union instigated the assault. The North Koreans may have acted on their own. Moreover, it was China, not Russia, that eventually intervened to save North Korea. There is no evidence to indicate that Stalin planned an attack in Europe. Events in Korea also led the United States to extend the protection of the Seventh Fleet to Chiang's regime in Formosa. This action completed the reversal of an earlier policy that had stated that neither Formosa nor Korea was vital to American interests. The Korean conflict, in addition to confirming the permanent division of Korea, signified the extension of both the Cold War and the American policy of containment to East Asia. U.S. relations with the Soviet Union and Communist China had suffered a serious setback.

WITHDRAWAL FROM EMPIRE

Elsewhere in Asia, and in Africa and the Middle East, the war fatally weakened European imperialism and led to the collapse of the British, French, and Dutch empires. Japan's invasion of China in 1937 and subsequent curtailment of Western economic influence there had started the process. The eventual Japanese defeat and the Communist victory in the civil war assured that neither the West nor Japan would ever again dominate China. Japan's seizure of French Indochina and conquest of the Dutch East Indies, Malaya,

Singapore, and Burma also dealt a severe blow to European prestige. Even though the French, Dutch, and British restored their administrations over these possessions after the war, none of them was able to maintain control.

Britain withdrew from India as early as 1948 after presiding over the partitioning of the country into two independent states—India and Pakistan. The Netherlands left the East Indies and recognized the new nation of Indonesia in 1949. France abandoned Indochina in 1954 after failing to defeat Communist guerrilla forces in a prolonged conflict. Even American military intervention in the following years could not prevent the consolidation of three Communist states—Vietnam, Laos, and Cambodia—in the former French colony. A myriad of new countries came into existence in other parts of Southeast Asia and in Africa. In the Middle East, Britain withdrew from Palestine as the new state of Israel gained its independence only to experience decades of hostility and intermittent warfare with its Arab neighbors.

THE END OF THE COLD WAR AND THE SOVIET UNION

The Cold War and the specter of a possible conflict between the superpowers haunted the world throughout the 1950s and beyond. Mutual fear and suspicion continued, and nuclear arsenals proliferated to levels that could destroy humanity many times over. Virtually everyone agreed that no one would be so madly irresponsible as to actually use these terrible weapons. And yet, the nightmare of a crisis, such as that of 1914, or a tragic mistake or misunderstanding triggering a fatal showdown persisted.

But all was not gloom. The death of Stalin in 1953 proved especially significant. Within two years Nikita Khrushchev, the new general secretary of the Communist party, had outmaneuvered several other leaders to become the dominant figure in the Soviet hierarchy. Under his direction, the Cold War experienced a thaw. The Soviet Union broke with its Stalinist image, softened the repressive nature of its system, and even loosened its hold over the satellite states to some extent.

Old suspicions died hard, however, and although East-West tensions generally slackened, they did not disappear and on occasion sparked new crises. The most notable of these was the Cuban Missile Crisis of 1962, which followed the American discovery of Soviet offensive missiles in Cuba, within 90 miles of Florida. Cuba had become an ally of the Soviet Union after a revolutionary movement, led by Fidel Castro, seized power in 1959. Castro soon established a Communist dictatorship. President John F. Kennedy imposed a naval blockade of Cuba to force the removal of the missiles. For a time, it appeared as if war between the superpowers was a real possibility. But, the crisis ended peacefully when Khrushchev buckled under and ordered the elimination of the weapons.

This humiliation, along with deteriorating relations between the Soviet Union and Communist China and persistent economic problems, led to Khrushchev's ouster by other Soviet leaders in 1964. Leonid Brezhnev succeeded Khrushchev as general secretary and remained in power until 1982. Under his leadership, the Soviets backed away from additional internal reforms and focused their economy on a massive military buildup, complete with huge stockpiles of nuclear weapons. This did not prevent a continuing dialogue between his government and the United States, however. In the early 1970s, President Richard Nixon pursued a policy of detente, which sought to improve East-West relations and succeeded to some extent. The superpowers even made periodic efforts during the following years to negotiate reductions in nuclear weapons, but progress remained painfully slow.

Meanwhile, both superpowers became embroiled in wars against rebel opponents in Asia that involved conventional weapons. During the 1960s, the United States entered the Vietnam War to prevent a Communist guerrilla movement from conquering South Vietnam. In the process, Washington propped up a weak, unpopular dictatorial regime because it was anti-Communist.

But, despite its armed might, the United States proved unable to win this struggle against well-trained and highly motivated forces that emerged from the jungle wilderness and melted back into it at will, often with the support of the surrounding population. This failure and the growing opposition to the conflict among elements of the American people led to the gradual withdrawal of U.S. troops between 1968 and 1973. Communist forces completed their conquest of South Vietnam in 1975. The conflict cost the lives of 57,000 Americans, while another 300,000 were wounded. In terms of money, it was the second costliest war in U.S. history.

Starting in 1979 and continuing into the 1980s, the Soviet Union became involved in its own "Vietnam" in Afghanistan. In this case, the Soviets tried to prop up a weak, unpopular Communist regime against guerrilla forces that utilized the mountainous wilderness of the country. Eventually, Moscow, too, had to recognize its failure and evacuate its troops. Clearly, there were limits to power, even for superpowers.

These limits were becoming obvious in other ways as well. While the United States and the Soviet Union concentrated so much of their industrial efforts on the production of war materiel and these unsuccessful conflicts, their national debts mushroomed. At the same time, the countries of Western Europe, especially West Germany, had recovered from their postwar problems and experienced remarkable economic progress. They also moved steadily in the direction of complete integration of their economies and, less surely, toward political union. Japan's rise from the ashes of World War II was even more spectacular. By the 1970s, Japanese industry had overtaken and passed the United States in the production of automobiles, ships, camera equipment, and appliances of various kinds. American productivity and quality steadily declined along with investment in research, development, and the modernization of industry. The United States also suffered from an increasingly unfavorable balance of trade. At the same time, Japan and Western European countries devoted relatively little of their wealth to military purposes. Even nations such as South Korea, Taiwan, and Singapore became increasingly competitive. Japan also replaced the United States as the world's leading creditor nation.

More and more the United States and the Soviet Union found that they were superpowers only in the realm of military strength, while the likelihood of an armed confrontation between them became ever more remote. The Soviet Union's problems were far greater than those of America, however. Its economy, focused on heavy industry and the production of war materiel, became increasingly inefficient due to obsolete methods, bureaucratic complications, and resistance to change. Soviet technology lagged far behind in such vital areas as computer science and telecommunications. The growth rate of agricultural production also dropped alarmingly throughout the 1960s and 1970s, forcing the Soviets to import large amounts of food. Not surprisingly, the satellite states of Eastern Europe shared many of the troubles that bedeviled the Soviet economy. Throughout the Eastern Bloc the standard of living remained low, which became an increasing source of popular discontent with the system.

When the reform-minded Mikhail Gorbachev came to power in the Soviet Union in 1985, he was convinced that something had to be done to remedy this myriad of economic ailments and restore popular support for the government. Being a good Communist, he hoped to accomplish this through the system by providing more effective management and incentives for effort, while eliminating complicated and ineffective methods. But, after two years, he realized that the problems were much more severe than he had thought and would require more far-reaching measures. His answer was to embark upon a policy of *perestroika,* a thorough restructuring of the system to be carried out by the Communist party. He recognized, however, that many members of the party bureaucracy would resist such an approach. To gain support for his program, he resorted to a second new policy—*glasnost.* This involved an unprecedented degree of freedom to discuss pressing problems and even to criticize the system and the party.

It also became obvious to Gorbachev that the Soviet Union could not afford the expense of its gargantuan military establishment and the arms race. As a way out of this dilemma, he sought better relations with the United States and offered to negotiate a wide-ranging nuclear arms limitation agreement. In 1987, he and President Ronald Reagan agreed to abolish intermediate-range missiles. This opened the way for additional reductions in other types of nuclear weapons as well as conventional forces during the next few years. Gorbachev recognized, too, that the Soviet Union had enough problems without continuing to force its will on the countries of Eastern Europe. He decided that it was best to allow them to determine their own fate and, thus, to reduce the distraction and expense of propping up their Communist regimes. It was now up to those governments to come to terms with their citizens. This proved an impossible task, however, and the peoples of the various countries began to demand not merely reforms but an end to Communist rule. The process began in Poland and Hungary, the two countries where unrest had been greatest and where attempts had already been made to modify the systems. The Communist regimes proved incapable of resisting the increasing demands for change, and both the police and armed forces proved unreliable. A chain reaction of swift and, for the most part, peaceful revolutions followed. By the end of 1989, the Communist governments had collapsed everywhere. Within a year, the East and West German states, for so long a symbol of the Cold War, had merged in a reunited Germany.

These swift and dramatic changes in the former satellite states inevitably led to demands for independence in some of the republics within the Soviet Union itself. Lithuania led the way by actually declaring its independence and establishing its own government in March 1990. But, Gorbachev was not willing to agree to independence for any of the republics because they, unlike the satellites, were actually parts of the Soviet Union. If he sanctioned Lithuania's breaking away, he would open the door to the disintegration of the union. He could not prevent another chain reaction, however, and other republics, including Latvia, Estonia, Georgia, Armenia, and the Ukraine, soon followed Lithuania's example.

To make matters worse, Gorbachev also encountered problems even among ethnic Russians, who were unhappy about the failure of the economy to improve and were impatient for greater political changes. These critics found a leader in Boris Yeltsin, the president of the Russian Soviet Republic and a former supporter of Gorbachev. Yeltsin went so far as to challenge the authority of the union government over Russia. Increasingly, Gorbachev found himself caught in the middle. While Yeltsin and leaders of the other republics demanded greater freedom from the Soviet government, party hard-liners felt that Gorbachev's reforms had paved the way to the total collapse of the Soviet system.

The hard-liners were correct, but ironically it was they who provided the final impetus when they resorted to a coup in August 1991 and placed Gorbachev under house arrest. Unfortunately for them, they took this drastic action with insufficient planning and without due consideration for the realities of power. Most of the leadership of the armed forces and the police refused to support the rebels, and a wave of popular opposition, much like that which had led to the revolutions in the satellite states, resulted in the speedy collapse of the coup. This failure sounded the death knell for the Soviet Union. Although Gorbachev tried desperately to preserve some kind of union, real power had passed to Yeltsin and the leaders of the other republics. In December 1991, they agreed to dissolve the Soviet Union and replaced it with a loose Confederation of Independent States. Gorbachev, the catalyst for change, now found himself the odd man out and went into retirement.

All of these momentous changes, culminating in the "Second Russian Revolution" of August 1991, were so dramatic that they caught everyone completely by surprise. They marked not only the end of the Soviet Union and its satellite empire, but, as one historian has noted, they represented, in the most fundamental sense, the last chapter of World War II. For decades, the Cold War between the superpowers had been by far the most persistent and ominous legacy of that conflict. After decades of gradual change, suddenly it was no more. Neither was the Soviet Union, one of the victors of World War II and one of the chief protagonists of the Cold War. And Germany, divided for 45 years in the aftermath of the war, was once again united and once again strong, even without the eastern territories it had lost to Poland and the USSR.

But, although the many changes initially created rapturous joy in the countries involved as well as much of the non-Communist world, many deeply rooted problems persisted. The always volatile Middle East remained a continuing threat to stability and peace. And, while nationalism steadily lost ground in Western Europe in favor of the movement toward greater economic and political unity, nationalistic rivalries became all important in parts of Eastern Europe as well as in some of the republics of the former Soviet Union. In 1993, the Czechs and the Slovaks severed their ties and created separate states. In Yugoslavia, never actually a part of the satellite bloc, old ethnic hatreds flared into an especially ugly conflagration. While the Slovenes were able to declare their independence peacefully in 1991, the attempts of the Croats and Moslem Bosnians to break away were not so fortunate. The Serbs resorted to open warfare to stymie their ambitions, leading to prolonged bloodshed, appalling atrocities, and widespread destruction.

Clearly the brave new world, which had dawned so unexpectedly, had failed to fulfill all the great expectations it had kindled. The future of Eastern Europe and the former Soviet Union remained uncertain. Only one unfortunate fact was clear: Widespread economic problems and political instability, always a dangerous combination, were likely to continue for the foreseeable future. And, the economic problems facing the United States did not go away. During the 1950s Khrushchev, in attempting to forge better relations with Yugoslavia, remarked that there were different roads to socialism. If the United States does not put its house in order, it may find that there are different roads to economic ruin.

Additional Reading

The literature on World War II and its origins is exceedingly vast. The following essay makes no pretense to being complete. It merely attempts to cite some of the more significant works that are available in English.

GENERAL

The United States government has published monumental official histories. These include Kent Roberts Greenfield and Stetson Conn, eds., *The United States Army in World War II* (Washington: Government Printing Office, 1944–1981), 75 volumes. More manageable is Samuel Eliot Morison's semiofficial 15-volume *History of the United States Naval Operations in World War II* (Boston: Little, Brown, 1947–1962); and the seven-volume *Army Air Forces in World War II* (Chicago: University of Chicago Press, 1948–1955), edited by Wesley Frank Craven and James Lea Cate. The British have also produced multivolume histories, including J. R. Butler, J. M. A. Gwyner, John Ehrman, and Michael Howard, *Grand Strategy* (London: HMSO, 1956–1972); Sir Charles Webster and Noble Frankland, *The Strategic Air Offensive Against Germany, 1939–1945* (London: HMSO, 1961); and Captain S. W. Roskill, *The War at Sea, 1939–1945* (London: HMSO, 1954–1961).

Winston Churchill's six-volume *History of the Second World War* (Boston: Houghton Mifflin, 1948–54) was one of the first major general works to appear, but it really constitutes the wartime prime minister's memoirs. Other full-scale histories include B. H. Liddell Hart, *History of the Second World War* (New York: Putnam, 1971), and J. F. C. Fuller, *The Second World War* (London: Eyre & Spottiswoode, 1948), both of which are highly interpretive. Gordon Wright, *The Ordeal of Total War, 1939–1945* (New York: Pantheon, 1990), surveys the social, economic, and intellectual aspects of the conflict in addition to the military and diplomatic developments. Peter Calvocoressi and Guy Wint, *Total War* (London: Penguin, 1972), is a lengthy but outstanding book that gives equal attention to both the European and East Asian conflicts. Other general works include Martin Kitchen, *A World in Flames* (London: Longman, 1990), James L. Stokesbury, *A Short History of World War II* (New York: William Morrow, 1980), and Louis L. Snyder, *The War: A Concise History* (New York: Dell, 1965). M. K. Dziewanowski presents a survey of the European war in *War at Any Price* (Englewood Cliffs, N.J.: Prentice-Hall, 1987).

Revelation of the breaking of the German cipher and the great importance of this achievement to the Allied victory came with the publication of F. W. Winterbotham, *The Ultra Secret* (New York: Dell, 1974). Soon afterward, Ronald Lewin's more extensive *Ultra Goes to War* (London: Hutchinson, 1978) appeared, followed by Ralph Bennett's *Ultra in the West* (London: Hutchinson, 1979) and David Kahn's *Seizing the Enigma: The Race to Break the German U-Boat Codes, 1939–1943* (Boston: Houghton Mifflin, 1991). Lewin also published the highly useful *American Magic: Codes, Ciphers, and the Defeat of Japan* (New York: Farrar, Straus, and Giroux, 1982).

CHAPTER 1: WORLD WAR I

Perhaps no subject has provoked more historical controversy than the origins of World War I. Among the most notable older books on this subject are two-volume works by Sidney B. Fay, *The Origins of the World War* (New York: Macmillan, 1928–30), and Bernadotte Schmitt, *The Coming of the War, 1914* (New York: Scribner, 1930). Luigi Albertini's three-volume *Origins of the War of 1914* (New York: Oxford University Press, 1952–57) is the most detailed account to appear since World War II.

By far the most controversial work on the conflict is *Germany's Aims in the First World War* (New York: Norton, 1967) by the noted German historian Fritz Fischer. With the help of vast archival material, Fischer charges Germany with chief responsibility for the outbreak of the war and traces the development of extensive German aims. Fischer's *War of Illusions: German Policies from 1911 to 1914* (New York: Norton, 1975) focuses specifically and in highly critical fashion on Germany's prewar policies. Although no one questions the extent of German war aims, some German historians dispute Fischer's appraisal of the degree to which civilian leaders were involved in developing them. They also consider his interpretation of prewar German policy too extreme. The foremost of these critics is Gerhard Ritter. In his four-volume work *The Sword and the Scepter* (Princeton Junction, N.J.: Scholar's Bookshelf, 1970–88), Ritter contends that Germany's military leaders were primarily to blame for the extent of the country's war aims. Other German historians, most notably Immanuel Geiss in *German Foreign Policy, 1871–1914* (London: Routledge & Paul, 1976), support Fischer's approach.

Good brief and readable accounts of the war's origins are Laurence Lafore, *The Long Fuse: An Interpretation of the Origins of World War I* (Philadelphia: J. B. Lippincott, 1965), and Joachim Remak, *The Origins of World War I, 1871–1914* (New York: Holt, Rinehart and Winston, 1967). Oron J. Hale, *The Great Illusion, 1900–1914* (New York: Harper & Row, 1971), and James Joll, *The Origins of the First World War* (London: Longman, 1984), focus on the broader background for the period before the war.

Books abound on the conflict itself. The most recent of the general studies is the forthcoming Michael J. Lyons, *World War I: A Short History* (Englewood Cliffs, N.J.: Prentice-Hall, 1994). Others include Bernadotte E. Schmitt and Harold C. Vedeler, *The World in the Crucible, 1914–1919* (New York: Harper & Row, 1984), and Marc Ferro, *The Great War, 1914–1918* (London: Routledge & Kegan Paul, 1973). René Albrecht-Carrié, *The Meaning of the First World War* (Englewood Cliffs, N.J.: Prentice-Hall, 1965), and Jack J. Roth, *World War I: A Turning Point in History* (New York: Knopf, 1967), are brief and instructive attempts to place the war in the broader perspective of the twentieth century.

CHAPTER 2: THE LEGACY OF WORLD WAR I

Many of the general works that deal with the period of the peace settlement and the 1920s cover the entire period 1919 to 1939. Among the best of these is Raymond J. Sontag, *A Broken World, 1919–1939* (New York: Harper & Row, 1971), which analyzes social, intellectual, cultural, and technological aspects as well as political and diplomatic developments. Other good brief general accounts include Laurence Lafore, *The End of Glory* (Philadelphia: Lippincott, 1970), and Keith Eubank, *The Origins of World*

War II, 2nd ed. (Arlington Heights, Ill.: Harlan Davidson, 1990).

A thorough account of the treaty that Germany forced on Russia is John W. Wheeler-Bennett, *Brest-Litovsk: The Forgotten Peace, March 1918* (London: St. Martin's, 1938). Several histories of the Paris peace settlement are available. Paul Birdsall's *Versailles Twenty Years After* (New York: Reynal & Hitchcock, 1941) is still useful but dated in some respects. Ferdinand Czernin's *Versailles, 1919* (New York: Capricorn Books, 1964) is unusual in structure, combining narrative with extensive documents. Arno Mayer's massive and controversial *Politics and Diplomacy of Peacemaking: Containment and Counterrevolution at Versailles, 1918–1919* (New York: Knopf, 1967) focuses critically on Allied attitudes toward Bolshevik Russia.

The famous economist John Maynard Keynes wrote a scathing analysis of the Treaty of Versailles, *The Economic Consequences of the Peace* (New York: Harcourt, Brace, 1920). Keynes was particularly critical of the reparations settlement, which he considered beyond Germany's capability to pay. Étienne Mantoux, in *The Carthaginian Peace, or the Economic Consequences of Mr. Keynes* (New York: Scribner, 1952), challenged Keynes's thesis and launched a reevaluation of the reparations issue that is still in progress. Marc Trachtenberg, *Reparations and World Politics* (New York: Columbia University Press, 1980), and Stephen A. Schuker, *The Financial Crisis of 1924 and the Adoption of the Dawes Plan* (Chapel Hill, N.C.: University of North Carolina Press, 1976), both argue that Germany did not suffer unduly from the reparations burden.

The best general work on the diplomatic history of the period from the end of the war to the advent of Hitler is Sally Marks, *The Illusion of Peace: International Relations in Europe, 1918–1933* (London: St. Martin's, 1976). Stephen A. Schuker, *The End of French Predominance in Europe* (Chapel Hill, N.C.: University of North Carolina Press, 1976), offers a valuable interpretation of the importance of the Ruhr crisis as a turning point in the interwar history of Europe. *Russia and the West under Lenin and Stalin* by George Kennan (New York: New American Library, 1962) covers the entire interwar period as well as World War II but is especially good on the peace conference and the 1920s. Adam B. Ulam's *Expansion and Coexistence* (New York: Praeger, 1968) also deals with Russian foreign policy during the 1920s. Robert P. Grathwol has produced an analysis of foreign policy during the prosperous years of the Weimar Republic in *Stresemann and the DNVP: Reconciliation or Revenge in German Foreign Policy, 1924–1928* (Lawrence, Kans.: University of Kansas Press, 1980). Francis L. Carsten, *The Reichswehr and Politics, 1918–1933* (Oxford: Oxford University Press, 1966), analyzes the role of the army and secret rearmament during the Weimar period.

Arnold A. Offner has fashioned an excellent analysis of U.S. policy relative to both Europe and East Asia in *The Origins of the Second World War: American Foreign Policy and World Politics, 1917–1941* (New York: Praeger, 1975). Akira Iriye's *After Imperialism: The Search for Order in the Far East, 1921–1931* (Cambridge, Mass.: Harvard University Press, 1965) is a thorough study of East Asian relations. Warren I. Cohen examines U.S. policy toward China in *America's Response to China: An Interpretive History of Sino-American Relations* (New York: Wiley, 1971).

CHAPTER 3: THE RISE OF THE DICTATORS

Books on totalitarianism in general include Hannah Arendt, *The Origins of Totalitarianism* (New York: Harcourt, Brace & World, 1966), and Carl J. Friedrich and Zbigniew K. Brzezinski, *Totalitarian Dictatorship and Autocracy* (New York: Oxford University Press, 1965). Works on the establishment and development of the Communist dictatorship in Russia are legion. The most ambitious is Edward H. Carr's multivolume work, *A History of the Soviet Union* (New York: Macmillan, 1950–71), which suffers to some extent from the author's overly sympathetic attitude toward Lenin. Robert V. Daniels, *The Nature of Communism* (New York: Random House, 1962), presents a useful analysis of Communist totalitarianism. The standard work on the revolution is William Henry Chamberlain's two-volume work, *The Russian Revolution, 1917–1920* (New York: Grosset & Dunlap, 1935). Theodore von Laue offers a brief interpretation of the revolution and its aftermath in *Why Lenin? Why Stalin?: A Reappraisal of the Russian Revolution, 1917–1930* (Philadelphia: Lippincott, 1964). Adam Ulam, *The Bolsheviks* (New York: Collier Books, 1965), is an in-depth study of Lenin's career. The best biography of Stalin is Adam Ulam, *Stalin: The Man and His Era* (New York: Viking, 1973).

Mussolini and Fascist Italy are now the source of considerable controversy. Massive studies by Renzo De Felice and Rosario Quartararo have challenged traditional interpretations of both the Italian dictator and his regime. Unfortunately, their books, which portray Mussolini in much more favorable terms than most accounts, are not available in English. De Felice's *Interpretations of Fascism* (Cambridge, Mass.: Harvard University Press, 1977) does provide a starting point for this approach, however. A good introduction to the general topic of fascism is Alan Cassels's *Fascism* (Arlington Heights, Ill.: AHM Publishing Corporation, 1975), which analyzes Italian fascism as well as Nazism and other forms of fascism. Ernst Nolte's *Three Faces of Fascism* (New York: New American Library, 1969), focuses on fascism in Italy, Germany, and France. Biographies of Mussolini include Denis Mack Smith, *Mussolini* (London: Weidenfeld & Nicolson, 1981), and Ivone Kirkpatrick, *Mussolini: A Study of Power* (New York: Hawthorne, 1964). Another useful work is Elizabeth Wiskemann, *Fascism in Italy: Its Development and Influence* (New York: St. Martin's Press, 1969).

Publications on Hitler and Nazi Germany are incredibly vast. Although poorly written, tedious, and self-glorifying, Hitler's *Mein Kampf* (London: Hurst and Blackett, 1938) remains an important historical document, along with *Hitler's Secret Book* (New York: Grove Press, 1961). Despite being dated in some respects, especially in regard to the Führer's early life, Alan Bullock's *Hitler: A Study in Tyranny* (New York: Harper & Row, 1964) is still the finest biography of the Nazi dictator. The best of many others is Joachim Fest, *Hitler* (New York: Harcourt, Brace, Jovanovich, 1973). Fest has also written *The Face of the Third Reich* (New York: Pantheon, 1970), which provides character sketches of top Nazi leaders. Albert Speer's *Inside the Third Reich* (New York: Macmillan, 1970) is a valuable firsthand account of life in Hitler's entourage. Various historians have attempted to psychoanalyze Hitler, but none of them is totally convincing. The most noteworthy are Robert Waite, *The Psychopathic God: Adolf Hitler* (New York: New American Library, 1977), J. P. Stern, *Hitler: Führer and People* (Berkeley: University of California Press, 1974), and Rudolph Binion, *Hitler among the Germans* (New York: Elsevier, 1976).

Karl Dietrich Bracher, *The German Dictatorship* (New York: Praeger, 1970), and Martin Broszat, *The Hitler State* (London: Longman's, 1981), are outstanding studies of the theory and structure of the Third Reich. Dietrich Orlow provides the best account of the Nazi movement in his two-volume *History of the Nazi Party* (Pittsburgh: University of Pittsburgh Press, 1969–73). Two books have tended to undermine the traditional view that Nazi voting strength was concentrated in the lower middle class. They are Richard F. Hamilton, *Who Voted for Hitler?* (Princeton: Princeton University Press, 1982), and Thomas Childers, *The Nazi Voter* (Chapel Hill, N.C.: University of North Carolina Press, 1983). R. J. Overy, *The Nazi Economic Recovery, 1932–1938* (London: Macmillan, 1982), is an excellent account of Hitler's economic policies. The scope of Nazi totalitarianism is clearly demonstrated in Edward N. Peterson, *The Limits of Hitler's Power* (Princeton: Princeton University Press, 1969), and Ian Kershaw, *Popular Opinion and Political Dissent in the Third Reich: Bavaria,*

1933–1945 (New York: Oxford University Press, 1985).

Books in English on Japan during this period are at a premium. Among the best general histories are Richard Storry, *A History of Modern Japan* (London: Penguin, 1960), Mikiso Hane, *Modern Japan* (Boulder, Colo.: Westview Press, 1986), and P. H. Clyde and B. F. Beers, *The Far East: A History of the Western Impact and the Eastern Response* (Englewood Cliffs, N.J.: Prentice-Hall, 1966). Saburo Ienaga, *The Pacific War: World War II and the Japanese, 1931–1945* (New York: Random House, 1978), is a highly critical account of the rise of dictatorship and the development of aggressive foreign policy in Japan. The first portion of John Toland's *Rising Sun: The Decline and Fall of the Japanese Empire* (New York: Random House, 1970) deals with the encroachment of the military on the Japanese government. Richard Storry, *The Double Patriots: A Study in Japanese Nationalism* (Boston: Houghton Mifflin, 1957), concentrates on the decade of the 1930s, as does Sharon Minichiello, *Retreat from Reform: Patterns of Political Behavior in Interwar Japan* (Honolulu: University of Hawaii Press, 1984).

CHAPTER 4: THE ROAD TO WAR

Both Toland and Ienaga discuss the Japanese conquest of Manchuria and invasion of China to some extent. James William Morley, ed., *Japan Erupts: The London Naval Conference and the Manchurian Incident, 1928–1932* (New York: Columbia University Press, 1984), focuses specifically on this crisis. Other useful studies include J. H. Boyle, *China and Japan at War, 1937–1945* (Stanford, Calif.: Stanford University Press, 1972), Parks N. Coble, *The Shanghai Capitalists and the Nationalist Government, 1927–1937* (Cambridge, Mass.: Harvard University Press, 1980), Paul K. T. Sih, *Nationalist China during the Sino-Japanese War, 1937–1945* (Hicksville, N.Y.: Exposition Press, 1977), and Akira Iriye, *The Origins of the Second World War: Asia and the Pacific* (London: Longman, 1987).

The best work on Hitler's ideas regarding racism and expansion is Eberhard Jäckel, *Hitler's World View: A Blueprint for Power* (Cambridge, Mass.: Harvard University Press, 1981). By far the most controversial interpretation of Hitler and his foreign policy is A. J. P. Taylor, *The Origins of the Second World War* (New York: Atheneum, 1961). Taylor contends that Hitler had no clearly formulated plans for conquest but was merely a typical German statesman and an opportunist. Although few historians have accepted this thesis, it has had the effect of focusing more critical attention on many aspects of the 1930s. The result has been a continuing stream of books that have substantially revised our view of the prewar period. Among the leading works that disagree with Taylor regarding Hitler's long-range goals are Norman Rich, *Hitler's War Aims: Ideology, the Nazi State and the Course of Expansion* (New York: Norton, 1973), Klaus Hildebrand, *The Foreign Policy of the Third Reich* (Berkeley: University of California Press, 1973), and Gerhard L. Weinberg's definitive two-volume work, *The Foreign Policy of Hitler's Germany* (Chicago: University of Chicago Press, 1970–80).

Martin Kitchen's *Europe between the Wars: A Political History* (London: Longman, 1988) is a good general account of the entire interwar period.

Denis Mack Smith examines Italian foreign policy critically in *Mussolini's Roman Empire* (New York: Viking, 1976), while Luigi Villari is highly sympathetic in *Italian Foreign Policy under Mussolini* (New York: Devin-Adair, 1956). Two good books focus on Soviet policy during the 1930s: Jonathan Haslam, *The Soviet Union and the Struggle for Collective Security in Europe, 1933–39* (New York: St. Martin's, 1984), and Jiri Hochman, *The Soviet Union and the Failure of Collective Security* (Ithaca, N.Y.: Cornell University Press, 1984).

Among the important works on the many crises of the 1930s are J. T. Emmerson, *The Rhineland Crisis, 7 March 1936* (Ames, Iowa: Iowa State University Press, 1977), G. W. Baer, *Test Case: Italy, Ethiopia and the League of Nations* (Stanford, Calif.: Hoover Institute Press, 1977),

Hugh Thomas, *The Spanish Civil War* (New York: Harper and Brothers, 1961), and Gordon Brooke-Shepherd, *Anschluss: The Rape of Austria* (London: Macmillan, 1963). The Munich crisis has provided the subject for numerous books, including Keith Eubank, *Munich* (Norman, Okla.: University of Oklahoma Press, 1963), and Telford Taylor, *Munich: The Price of Peace* (Garden City, N.Y.: Doubleday, 1979). Two of the best studies on the last two years of peace are Christopher Thorne, *The Approach of War, 1938–1939* (London: St. Martin's Press, 1967), and Williamson Murray, *The Change in the European Balance of Power, 1938–1939: The Path to Ruin* (Princeton: Princeton University Press, 1984).

CHAPTER 5: *BLITZKRIEG* IN THE EAST, *SITZKRIEG* IN THE WEST

Brian Holden Reid's *J. F. C. Fuller: Military Thinker* (New York: St. Martin, 1988) and Brian Bond's *Liddell Hart: A Study of His Military Thought* (London: Cassell, 1977) analyze the theories of Britain's two leading exponents of armored warfare. John J. Mersheimer presents a highly critical appraisal of Liddell Hart in *Liddell Hart and the Weight of History* (Ithaca, N.Y.: Cornell University Press, 1988). The best account of the Maginot line is Vivian Rowe, *The Great Wall of France* (New York: Putnam, 1959). Books that focus on economic planning for the war include Bernice A. Carroll, *Design for Total War: Arms and Economics of the Third Reich* (The Hague, The Netherlands: Mouton, 1968), A. S. Milward, *The German Economy at War* (London: Athlone Press, 1965), and Edward L. Homze, *Arming the Luftwaffe* (Lincoln, Nebr.: University of Nebraska Press, 1977).

Histories that deal specifically with the Polish campaign are Nicholas Bethell, *The War Hitler Won: The Fall of Poland* (New York: Holt, Rinehart and Winston, 1972), and Robert M. Kennedy, *The German Campaign in Poland, 1939* (Washington: Department of the Army, 1956). General Heinz Guderian's memoirs, *Panzer Leader* (London: Michael Joseph, 1952), provide an eyewitness account of the Polish campaign as well as most of the major operations from 1939 to 1941. Guderian's book is one of many that detail the relationship between Hitler and his generals. Among the most notable of these are Telford Taylor, *Sword and Swastika: Generals and Nazis in the Third Reich* (Chicago: Quadrangle Paperbacks, 1952), John W. Wheeler-Bennett, *The Nemesis of Power: The German Army in Politics, 1918–1945* (London: Macmillan, 1964), Walter Görlitz, *History of the German General Staff* (New York: Praeger, 1953), and Gordon Craig, *The Politics of the Prussian Army, 1640–1945* (New York: Oxford University Press, 1964). General Franz Halder attacked Hitler bitterly for his intrusion in the realm of military strategy in his brief *Hitler as War Lord* (London: Putnam, 1950). Harold C. Deutsch, *The Conspiracy against Hitler in the Twilight War* (Minneapolis: University of Minnesota Press, 1968), traces the development of opposition to Hitler's plans for the invasion of Western Europe.

Telford Taylor's *March of Conquest: The German Victories in Western Europe, 1940* (New York: Simon & Schuster, 1958), Alistair Horne's *To Lose a Battle: France, 1940* (London: Macmillan, 1969), General Errich von Manstein's *Lost Victories* (Chicago: Henry Regner, 1958), and Guderian's book all provide good accounts of the planning for the invasion of Western Europe.

CHAPTER 6: COMPLICATIONS IN THE NORTH

Few books are available specifically on the Russo-Finnish War. The standard work on this subject is V. A. Tanner, *The Winter War: Finland against Russia, 1939–1940* (Stanford, Calif.: Stanford University Press, 1957). Marshal Mannerheim's *Memoirs* (New York: Dutton, 1954) deals with this struggle as well as Soviet-Finnish relations in general. The Norwegian campaign has attracted more interest. Richard Petrow, in *The Bitter Years: The Invasion and Occupation of Denmark and Norway, April 1940–May 1945* (New York: Morrow, 1979), analyzes not just the campaign but the entire occupation. E. F. Ziemke, *The German Northern Theater of Operations, 1940–1945* (Washington: Department of the Army, 1959), focuses on this same period. Books that concentrate specifically on the 1940 operation are Bernard Ash, *Norway, 1940* (London: Cassell, 1964), T. K. Derry, *The Campaign in Norway* (London: H.M.S.O., 1952), and J. L. Moulton, *A Study of Warfare in Three Dimensions: The Norwegian Campaign of 1940* (Athens, Ohio: The Ohio University Press, 1967).

CHAPTER 7: THE FALL OF FRANCE

Taylor's *March of Conquest* provides an absorbing analysis of the German victory in Western Europe in 1940 and demonstrates that the French were hardly deficient in either men or tanks. Horne's *To Lose a Battle* and Guy Chapman's *Why France Fell: The Defeat of the French Army in 1940* (New York: Holt, Rinehart and Winston, 1968) concentrate specifically on the 1940 campaign but tend to overstate France's weakness. Horne particularly exaggerates the moral rot in French leadership circles, as does William L. Shirer in *The Collapse of the Third Republic* (New York: Simon & Schuster, 1969). General Sir Edward Spears's two-volume *Assignment to Catastrophe* (New York: A. A. Wynn, 1954) and Colonel Adolphe Goutard's *The Battle of France, 1940* (New York: Ives Washburn, 1959) provide firsthand accounts. Liddell Hart, *The German Generals Talk* (New York: Morrow, 1948), presents fascinating material based on interviews. Unfortunately, some of the generals' comments have tended to perpetuate the contention that Hitler deliberately allowed the British to escape from Dunkirk. Taylor and others have dispelled this myth and have implicated Rundstedt in the decision to halt Guderian's panzers. David Divine, *The Nine Days of Dunkirk* (New York: Ballantine, 1959), insists that Guderian could not have taken the port in a quick sweep because of the abundance of water obstacles in the area.

More recent works place primary responsibility not on French weakness or the unwillingness of civilian leaders to supply funds for weapons but on the faulty planning of military leaders. These include Jeffrey A. Gunsburg, *Divided and Conquered: The French High Command and the Defeat of the West, 1940* (Westport, Conn.: Greenwood Press, 1979), and Robert A. Doughty, *The Seeds of Disaster: The Development of French Army Doctrine, 1919–1939* (Hamden, Conn.: Archon, 1986). Faris R. Kirkland, in "The French Air Force in 1940: Was It Defeated by the Luftwaffe or by Politics?" *Air University Review* (September–October 1985), provides strong documentation to support his contention that French air power was much stronger in 1940 than has been believed.

CHAPTER 8: BRITAIN IS STILL AN ISLAND

The most controversial aspect of the Battle of Britain is the question of how close the Luftwaffe came to defeating the RAF in 1940. Traditionally, the German shift from direct attacks on Fighter Command airfields to attacks on London appeared to be a crucial mistake. This is Chester Wilmot's contention in *The Struggle for Europe* (London: Harper & Row, 1952). Churchill's *Their Finest Hour,* volume 2 of his *History of the Second World War,* also states that this decision provided a vital breathing spell for the RAF. Telford Taylor, in *The Breaking Wave* (New York: Simon & Schuster, 1967), presents convincing evidence that the decision to change targets was not a critical factor. Taylor also demonstrates the confusion and lack of resolve on the part of German leaders over the possibility of invading Britain. John Terraine, *A Time for Courage: The Royal Air Force in the European War, 1939–1945* (New York: Macmillan, 1985), treats the Battle of Britain in the context of the entire air war and is strongly supportive of the strategy of Air Marshal Dowding.

Numerous books are available on the actual air combat, including Derek Dempster and Derek Wood, *The Narrow Margin: The Battle of Britain and the Rise of Airpower, 1939–1940* (London: Hutchinson, 1961), F. K. Mason, *Battle over*

Britain (Garden City, N.Y.: Doubleday, 1970), and Constantine Fitzgibbon, *The Blitz* (London: Wingate, 1957). Three good studies concentrate on German plans and preparations for the invasion that never came: Peter Fleming, *Operation Sea Lion* (New York: Simon & Schuster, 1957), Ronald Wheatley, *Operation Sea Lion: German Plans for the Invasion of Britain, 1939–1942* (Oxford: Oxford University Press, 1958), and Walter Ansel, *Hitler Confronts England* (Durham, N.C.: Duke University Press, 1960). Robert Wright's *Dowding and the Battle of Britain* (London: MacDonald & Co., 1969) is the standard biography of the architect of the RAF's gallant defense. Randolph S. Churchill and Martin Gilbert, *The Life of Winston Churchill,* 8 vols. (Boston: Houghton Mifflin, 1966–86), is an impressive biography of the British wartime leader.

CHAPTER 9: THE PLOT THICKENS

The role of Spain receives attention in Dante A. Puzzo, *Spain and the Great Powers, 1936–1941* (New York: Columbia University Press, 1962). Mussolini's foreign minister, Count Galeazzo Ciano, in *The Ciano Diaries, 1939–1943* (Garden City, N.Y.: Doubleday, 1946), provides a fascinating firsthand account of Italian foreign and military policy. Robert O. Paxton's *Vichy France* (New York: Knopf, 1972) focuses on relations between the Vichy regime and Hitler during 1940 and the following years. There is a large number of books on the war in North Africa, including W. F. G. Jackson, *The North African Campaign, 1940–43* (London: Batsford, 1975), Alan Moorehead, *The Desert War* (London: Hamish Hamilton, 1965), Paul Carell, *Foxes of the Desert* (New York: Dutton, 1961), and D. W. Braddock, *The Campaigns in Egypt and Libya, 1940–1942* (Aldershot, U.K.: Gale and Polden, 1964). John Connell's *Wavell: Scholar and Soldier* (London: Collins, 1964) views the architect of the 1940–41 British offensive against the Italians in a favorable light, as does Correlli Barnett in *The Desert Generals* (London: Kimber, 1960).

Rich details German diplomatic maneuvering in the Balkans during 1940–41 in *Hitler's War Aims*. Charles Cruikshank, *Greece, 1940–1941* (London: Davis-Pointer, 1976), explores the background for the German invasion and British intervention in Greece as well as the actual campaign. Martin van Creveld, *Hitler's Strategy, 1940–41: The Balkan Clue* (Cambridge: Cambridge University Press, 1973), deals with the same topic. Anthony Heckstall-Smith and H. T. Baillie-Grohman, *Greek Tragedy, 1941* (New York: Norton, 1961), concentrates on military operations, as does Alan Clark, *The Fall of Crete* (New York: Morrow, 1962). Geoffrey Warner's *Iraq and Syria, 1941* (Newark, Del.: University of Delaware Press, 1976), analyzes both the background and military operations in these Middle Eastern countries.

CHAPTER 10: OPERATION BARBAROSSA

Although some have referred to the struggle between Germany and Russia as "the unknown war," it has inspired many impressive works. Gerhard Weinberg's *Germany and the Soviet Union, 1939–1941* (Leiden, The Netherlands: Brill, 1954) is especially good on the background for Operation Barbarossa. John Erickson provides an excellent analysis of Red Army leadership in *The Soviet High Command: A Military-Political History, 1918–1941* (London: Macmillan, 1962) and of the military campaign from 1941 to early 1943 in *The Road to Stalingrad* (New York: Harper & Row, 1975), which concentrates on the Soviet response to the German invasion. Alan Clark's *Barbarossa: The Russian-German Conflict, 1941–1945* (New York: Morrow, 1965) is less critical of Hitler and more negative toward German generals in the conduct of the war than most observers. Albert Seaton, *The Russo-German War, 1941–45* (New York: Praeger, 1970), downplays the ability of the Russians to defeat Germany without Western aid. Paul Carell wrote *Hitler Moves East, 1941–1943* (Boston: Little, Brown, 1954) from the German perspective.

Alexander Werth, who was a correspondent in the Soviet Union during the conflict, provides a dramatic account of *Russia at War, 1941–1945*

(New York: Avon, 1970). Bryan Fugate, *Operation Barbarossa: Strategy and Tactics on the Eastern Front, 1941* (Novato, Calif.: Presidio Press, 1984), deals only with the 1941 campaign. Harrison Salisbury has produced a horrifying picture of Leningrad's ordeal in *The 900 Days: The Siege of Leningrad* (New York: Avon, 1969). Georgi Zhukov, *Marshal Zhukov's Greatest Battles* (New York: Pocket Books, 1970), details the Russian military leader's conduct of four major battles, including the struggle for Moscow in 1941. Martin van Creveld emphasizes the enormous logistic problems confronting Army Group Center in the summer of 1941 in *Supplying War* (Cambridge: Cambridge University Press, 1977).

CHAPTER 11: HITLER'S NEW ORDER IN EUROPE

The best general account of German occupation policies is Rich's *Hitler's War Aims.* The literature on the Holocaust is vast. The most detailed and reliable work is Raul Hilberg, *The Destruction of the European Jews* (New York: Holmes & Meier, 1985). Also important are Lucy Dawidowicz, *The War against the Jews, 1933–1945* (New York: Holt, Rinehart and Winston, 1975), and Yehuda Bauer, *A History of the Holocaust* (New York: Doubleday, 1982). David Irving's *Hitler's War* (London: Hodder and Stoughton, 1977) argues unconvincingly that Himmler and the SS planned and carried out the Holocaust without Hitler's knowledge until 1943. Gerald Fleming has effectively demolished Irving's thesis in the extremely significant *Hitler and the Final Solution* (Berkeley: University of California Press, 1984). An excellent study of the various roles of the SS is Hans Buchheim, Martin Broszat, H. A. Jacobsen, and Helmut Krausnick, *Anatomy of the SS State* (New York: Walker, 1968). Walter Laqueur, *The Terrible Secret: Suppression of the Truth about Hitler's "Final Solution"* (Boston: Little, Brown, 1980), relates the Allied response to news of the Holocaust. David S. Wyman's excellent *The Abandonment of the Jews: America and the Holocaust, 1941–1945* (New York: Pantheon Books, 1984) offers a sobering assessment of the failure of the United States to take any effective action to help save the Jews until late in the war.

Petrow's *The Bitter Years* gives a good account of the German occupation of Denmark and Norway. Werner Warmbrunn, *The Dutch under German Occupation* (Stanford, Calif.: Stanford University Press, 1963), is also valuable, as are Vojtech Mastny, *The Czechs under Nazi Rule: The Failure of National Resistance, 1939–1942* (New York: Columbia University Press, 1971), Richard C. Lukas, *The Forgotten Holocaust: The Poles under German Occupation, 1939–1944* (Lexington, Ky.: University Press of Kentucky, 1986), and Jan Tomasz Gross, *Polish Society under German Occupation* (Princeton: Princeton University Press, 1979). Alexander Dallin's *German Rule in Russia, 1941–1945* (London: Macmillan, 1957) is an outstanding history of German policies toward the peoples of the Soviet Union. Bertram Gordon, in *Collaborationism in France during the Second World War* (Ithaca, N.Y.: Cornell University Press, 1980), ably portrays the extent of French collaboration and the appeal of fascism under the Vichy regime. Edward J. Homze, *Foreign Labor in Nazi Germany* (Princeton: Princeton University Press, 1967), describes the slave labor program.

Jorgen Haestrup provides an excellent general survey of *European Resistance Movements, 1939–1945* (Westport, Conn.: Meckler Publishing, 1981). Accounts of activities in specific countries include Polish General Thadeusz Bor-Komorowski's personal memoir, *The Secret Army* (London: Macmillan, 1953), Matthew Cooper, *The Nazi War against Soviet Partisans* (New York: Stein & Day, 1979), Valdimir Dedijer, *Tito* (New York: Simon & Schuster, 1953), and Charles F. Delzell, *Mussolini's Enemies: The Anti-Fascist Resistance* (Princeton: Princeton University Press, 1961). David Stafford, *Britain and European Resistance* (London: Macmillan, 1980), studies the often frustrating British efforts to organize opposition to Nazi rule. Roderick Kedward and Roger Austin have edited *Vichy*

France and the Resistance (New York: Barnes & Noble, 1985), an excellent collection of essays.

CHAPTER 12: AMERICA ENTERS THE WAR

One of the best general histories of U.S. policy in the twentieth century is Stephen Ambrose, *Rise to Globalism: American Foreign Policy since 1938* (New York: Penguin, 1983). For the period before America's entry into the war, two works by William L. Langer and S. Everett Gleason are standard: *The Challenge to Isolation, 1937–1940* (New York: Harper & Row, 1952) and *The Undeclared War, 1940–1941* (New York: Harper & Row, 1953). Somewhat more recent are Robert Divine, *The Reluctant Belligerent: American Entry into World War II* (New York: Wiley, 1965), and T. R. Fehrenbach, *FDR's Undeclared War* (New York: David McKay, 1967). Other excellent books are Arnold A. Offner, *American Appeasement: United States Foreign Policy and Germany, 1933–1938* (Cambridge, Mass.: Harvard University Press, 1969), and Robert A. Dallek, *Franklin D. Roosevelt and American Policy, 1932–1945* (New York: Oxford University Press, 1979). David Reynolds, *The Creation of the Anglo-American Alliance, 1937–1941* (Chapel Hill, N.C.: University of North Carolina Press, 1982), documents the growing concern over Germany and Japan, which enabled Britain and the United States to surmount considerable mutual distrust. Samuel Eliot Morison examines American involvement in the naval war in *The Battle of the Atlantic, September 1939–May 1943,* the first of his 15-volume history. Morison also provides a much more manageable one-volume account in *The Two-Ocean War* (Boston: Little, Brown, 1963).

The controversy over Pearl Harbor has inspired a vast literature. Gordon W. Prange's *At Dawn We Slept: The Untold Story of Pearl Harbor* (New York: McGraw-Hill, 1981) details the background and actual attack on the U.S. base. Prange effectively refutes the argument that Roosevelt and his advisers knew of Japan's plan to attack Pearl Harbor and deliberately refused to alert the military and naval leaders there. But the conspiracy thesis springs eternal. Shortly after the appearance of Prange's work, John Toland published *Infamy: Pearl Harbor and Its Aftermath* (Garden City, N.Y.: Doubleday, 1982). Toland contends on the basis of meager evidence that Roosevelt did know in advance and allowed the attack to take place without warning Pearl Harbor. Prange's *Pearl Harbor: The Verdict of History* (New York: McGraw-Hill, 1986) provides an even more substantial refutation of the plot theory. In *"And I Was There": Pearl Harbor and Midway—Breaking the Secrets* (New York: Morrow, 1985), Rear Admiral Edwin T. Layton, with the assistance of Captain Roger Pineau and John Costello, assails Washington's handling of intelligence reports prior to Pearl Harbor and contends that Admiral Kimmel was made a scapegoat for the December 7 disaster.

Other works that cover the background for the Pacific war are Arthur Marder, *Old Friends, New Enemies* (New York: Oxford University Press, 1981), Stephen Pelz, *Race to Pearl Harbor* (Cambridge, Mass.: Harvard University Press, 1974), and James R. Leutze, *Bargaining for Supremacy* (Chapel Hill, N.C.: University of North Carolina Press, 1977). Toland, *Rising Sun,* and Robert J. C. Butow, *Tojo and the Coming of the War* (Princeton: Princeton University Press, 1961), examine the outbreak of the conflict from the Japanese side. Ronald Lewin's *American Magic* provides an excellent account of the breaking of the Japanese diplomatic code.

CHAPTER 13: JAPAN TRIUMPHANT

The best general history of the Pacific war is Ronald H. Spector, *Eagle against the Sun* (New York: The Free Press, 1985). Other useful studies are John Costello, *The Pacific War, 1941–1945* (New York: Rawson Wade, 1981), and Charles Bateson, *The War with Japan* (East Lansing, Mich.: Michigan State University Press, 1968), as well as Toland's *Rising Sun,* Morison's *Two-Ocean War,* and Ienaga's *Pacific War.* Morison's *Rising Sun in the Pacific,* volume 3 of his 15-volume work, covers the period of Japan's victories, as does John Toland in *But Not in Shame: The Six Months after Pearl Harbor* (New York: Random House, 1961) and John B. Lundstrom in *The First South Pacific Campaign: Pacific Fleet Strategy, December 1941–June 1942* (Annapolis: Naval Institute Press, 1976). Paul S. Dull has provided a good one-volume study, *A Battle History of the Imperial Japanese Navy, 1941–1945* (Annapolis: U.S. Naval Institute, 1958).

The defense of the Philippines receives attention in Carol Morris Petillo, *Douglas MacArthur: The Philippine Years* (Bloomington, Ind.: Indiana University Press, 1981), Louis Morton, *The Fall of the Philippines* (Washington: Department of the Army, 1953), and D. Clayton James's outstanding two-volume biography, *The Years of MacArthur* (New York: Houghton Mifflin, 1972–75). The British disaster in Malaya amd Singapore has inspired numerous works, including Louis Allen, *Singapore, 1941–42* (Newark, Del.: University of Delaware Press, 1976), Noel Barber, *A Sinister Twilight: The Fall of Singapore* (London: Collins, 1968), and A. J. Swinson, *Defeat in Malaya* (New York: Ballantine, 1970). The best history of the conflict in Burma is Louis Allen's *Burma: The Longest War, 1941–45* (New York: St. Martin's, 1985).

CHAPTER 14: THE TIDE TURNS IN THE PACIFIC

Edwin Palmer Hoyt's *Blue Skies and Blood: The Battle of the Coral Sea* (New York: Eriksson, 1975) is a popular account of this important clash. The best history of the Battle of Midway is Gordon W. Prange's *Miracle at Midway* (New York: Penguin, 1982). Also useful are Mitsuo Fuchida and Masatake Okumiya, *Midway: The Battle That Doomed Japan* (Annapolis: U.S. Naval Institute, 1955), which approaches the struggle from the Japanese perspective, and Richard Hough, *The Battle of Midway* (New York: Macmillan, 1970). Thomas B. Buell focuses on the hero of Midway in *The Quiet Warrior: A Biography of Admiral Raymond A. Spruance* (Boston: Little, Brown, 1974) and on the commander of the U.S. fleet in *Master of Seapower: A Biography of Admiral Ernest J. King* (Boston: Little, Brown, 1980). E. B. Potter has provided the standard biographies of *Nimitz* (Annapolis: U.S. Naval Institute, 1976) and *Bull Halsey* (Annapolis: U.S. Naval Institute, 1985). On the Japanese side, Agawa Hiroyuki, *The Reluctant Admiral: Yamamoto and the Imperial Navy* (Tokyo: Kodansha International, 1979), is also a fine book.

For New Guinea, essential works are Dudley McCarthy, *Southwest Pacific Area: First Year, Kokoda to Wau* (Canberra: Angus, 1959), and Lida Mayo, *Bloody Buna* (Garden City, N.Y.: Doubleday, 1975). The standard volumes on the Guadalcanal campaign are Samuel B. Griffith, *The Battle for Guadalcanal* (Philadelphia: Lippincott, 1963), and Robert Leckie, *Challenge for the Pacific: Guadalcanal, The Turning Point of the War* (Garden City, N.Y.: Doubleday, 1965). In *The Pacific Theater: Island Representations of World War II* (Honolulu: Hawaii University Press, 1989), Geoffrey M. White and Lamont Lindstrom provide a series of articles that reveal the impact of the Pacific war on the inhabitants of the various island archipelagos. Akira Iriye's *Power and Culture: The Japanese-American War, 1941–1945* (Cambridge, Mass.: Harvard University Press, 1981) studies the attitudes of Japanese and American leaders toward their respective enemies, as does John W. Dower, *War without Mercy: Race and Power in the Pacific War* (New York: Pantheon, 1986).

CHAPTER 15: THE TIDE TURNS IN EUROPE

Accounts of the struggle for Stalingrad include Heinz Schröter's grim *Stalingrad* (London: Collins, 1960), V. I. Chuikov, *The Beginning of the Road* (London: Macgibbon & Kee, 1963), and Geoffrey Jukes, *Hitler's Stalingrad Decisions* (Berkeley: University of California Press, 1985). Frederick Ziemke's *Moscow to Stalingrad: Decisions in the East* (Washington: Center of Military History, 1987) focuses in large part on the battle for Stalingrad.

Correlli Barnett provides a sympathetic interpretation of Auchinleck and a highly critical one of Montgomery in *The Desert Generals*. Montgomery's own *Memoirs* (London: Collins, 1958) is anything but self-critical. John Connell's *Auchinleck* (London: Cassell, 1959) is favorable, while Alun Chalfont's *Montgomery of Alamein* (New York: Atheneum, 1976) is extremely negative. Michael Carver criticizes Auchinleck as well as most other British leaders in *Dilemmas of the Desert War: A New Look at the Libyan Campaign, 1940–1942* (Bloomington, Ind.: Indiana University Press, 1986). Ronald Lewin, *Montgomery as Military Commander* (New York: Stein and Day, 1971), is also critical. Lewin's *Rommel as Military Commander* (New York: Ballantine, 1970) and *Life and Death of the Afrika Korps* (London: Batsford, 1977) as well as Kenneth Macksey's *Rommel, Battles and Campaigns* (London: Arms and Armor Press, 1980) are excellent studies of the Desert Fox. Numerous books are available on the Battle of El Alamein, the best of which is James Lucas, *War in the Desert: The Eighth Army at El Alamein* (New York: Beaufort Books, 1983). Others include Michael Carver, *El Alamein* (London: Batsford, 1962), and Fred Majdalany, *The Battle of El Alamein: Fortress in the Sand* (London: Weidenfeld and Nicolson, 1965). Van Creveld's *Supplying War* argues convincingly that Rommel's logistic problems were insurmountable.

CHAPTER 16: PROBLEMS OF A MARRIAGE OF CONVENIENCE

Among the standard works that deal with Anglo-American strategic planning are Maurice Matloff and Edwin M. Snell, *Strategic Planning for Coalition Warfare, 1941–1942* (Washington: Office of the Chief of Military History, 1953), and Herbert Feis, *Churchill, Roosevelt, Stalin: The War They Waged and the Peace They Sought* (Princeton: Princeton University Press, 1967). An excellent recent work on this subject is Robin Edmonds, *The Big Three: Churchill, Roosevelt, and Stalin in Peace and War* (New York: W. W. Norton, 1991). Wilmot's *Struggle for Europe* is highly critical of American strategic conceptions. Two later books, John Grigg, *1943: The Victory That Never Was* (New York: Hill and Wang, 1980), and Walter S. Dunn, *Second Front Now—1943* (University, Ala.: University of Alabama Press, 1980), insist that the Mediterranean strategy was a mistake and that a cross-Channel invasion could have succeeded in 1943.

An excellent general analysis of U.S. participation in the European theater from start to finish is Charles B. MacDonald's *Mighty Endeavor: The American War in Europe* (New York: Morrow, 1986). Kenneth S. Davis, *The Experience of War: The United States in World War II* (Garden City, N.Y.: Doubleday, 1965), is also engrossing.

Biographies of Allied leaders include Nigel Nicolson, *Alex: The Life of Field Marshal Earl Alexander of Tunis* (London: Weidenfeld and Nicolson, 1973), Forrest C. Pogue's three-volume work *George C. Marshall* (New York: Viking, 1964–73), Stephen E. Ambrose, *The Supreme Commander: The War Years of General Dwight D. Eisenhower* (Garden City, N.Y.: Doubleday, 1970) and *Eisenhower: Soldier, General of the Army, President-elect, 1890–1952* (New York: Simon & Schuster, 1983), and Hubert Essame, *Patton: The Commander* (New York: Scribner, 1974). In addition to Montgomery's memoirs, autobiographical works include Dwight D. Eisenhower, *Crusade in Europe* (Garden City, N.Y.: Doubleday, 1948), Field Marshal Alexander, *The Alexander Memoirs* (London: Cassell, 1962) and George S. Patton, *War as I Saw It* (Boston: Houghton Mifflin, 1947). Omar N. Bradley's career is the subject of a work by the general and Clay Blair, *A General's Life: An Autobiography* (New York: Simon & Schuster, 1983).

A brief but useful account is Michael Howard's *Mediterranean Strategy in the Second World War* (New York: Praeger, 1968). The background for the invasion of North Africa is the subject of Arthur Layton Funk, *The Politics of Torch* (Lawrence, Kans.: University Press of Kansas, 1974), and Keith Sainsbury, *The North*

African Landings, 1942 (Newark, Del.: University of Delaware Press, 1976). Charles Messenger, *The Tunisian Campaign* (London: Ian Allan, 1982), deals primarily with the land struggle in Tunisia. Carlo d'Este's excellent *World War II in the Mediterranean, 1942–1945* (Chapel Hill, N.C.: Algonquin Books, 1990) analyzes all the Mediterranean campaigns.

CHAPTER 17: PROBING THE UNDERBELLY

Trumbull Higgins examines the problems involved in the invasions of Sicily and Italy in *Soft Underbelly: The Anglo-American Controversy over the Italian Campaign* (New York: Macmillan, 1968), as does Maurice Matloff, *Strategic Planning for Coalition Warfare, 1943–1944* (Washington: GPO, 1959). Howard M. Smyth and Albert N. Garland, *Sicily and the Surrender of Italy* (Washington: Department of the Army, 1965), Eric Linklater, *The Campaign in Italy* (London: H.M.S.O., 1951), and W. G. F. Jackson, *The Battle for Italy* (New York: Harper & Row, 1967), are all good general accounts.

More specialized and also valuable are Hugh Pond, *Sicily* (London: Kimber, 1962) and *Salerno* (London: Kimber, 1961), Martin Blumenson, *Salerno to Cassino* (Washington: Office of the Chief of Military History, 1969), and W. G. F. Jackson, *The Battle for Rome* (New York: Bonanza Books, 1969). The struggle for Cassino has inspired numerous accounts. The most recent is David Hapgood and David Richardson, *Monte Cassino* (New York: Congdon & Weed, 1984), which is highly critical of Generals Clark and Freyberg. Histories of the Anzio beachhead include Martin Blumenson, *Anzio: The Gamble That Failed* (London: Weidenfeld & Nicholson, 1963), and Carlo d'Este, *Anzio and the Battle for Rome* (New York: Harper-Collins, 1991). Field Marshal Kesselring relates his experiences as German commander in Italy in *A Soldier's Record* (Westport, Conn.: Greenwood Press, 1953). F. W. Deakin, *The Brutal Friendship: Mussolini, Hitler and the Fall of Italian Fascism* (New York: Harper & Row, 1962), is the standard work on the collapse of the Duce's dictatorship.

CHAPTER 18: WAR IN THE ATLANTIC

The official British history, S. W. Roskill, *The War at Sea, 1939–1945,* provides an excellent study of operations in the Atlantic, as does Morison's *Battle of the Atlantic*. Other good overall histories are Dan van der Vat, *The Atlantic Campaign: World War II's Great Struggle at Sea* (New York: Harper & Row, 1988), and Donald MacIntyre, *The Battle for the Atlantic* (London: Batsford, 1961). For the Axis side, Cajus Bekker, *Hitler's Naval War* (London: Doubleday, 1974), Edward P. Von der Porten, *The German Navy in World War II* (New York: Thomas Y. Crowell, 1969), and Marc'Antonio Bragadin, *The Italian Navy in World War II* (Annapolis: U.S. Naval Institute, 1957), are good. Donald MacIntyre, *The Battle for the Mediterranean* (New York: Norton, 1975), is the best book on the naval war in that theater from the Allied side. Herbert A. Werner's *Iron Coffins: A Personal Account of the German U-Boat Battles of World War II* (New York: Holt, Rinehart and Winston, 1969) is a gripping narrative of submarine life. Admiral Karl Dönitz published his *Memoirs: Ten Years and Twenty Days* (London: Weidenfeld and Nicolson, 1959), as did Admiral Erich Raeder, *My Life* (Annapolis: U.S. Naval Institute, 1960), and Admiral Arthur Cunningham, *A Sailor's Odyssey* (London: Hutchinson, 1951). As with so many other aspects of the war, the disclosures regarding Ultra in books such as John Winton, *ULTRA at Sea: How Breaking the Nazi Code Affected Allied Naval Strategy* (New York: Morrow, 1988), have greatly altered our understanding of naval operations.

CHAPTER 19: TARGET GERMANY

Of particular importance in the history of the air war is Webster and Frankland, *The Strategic Air Offensive against Germany.* R. J. Overy, *The Air War, 1939–1945* (New York: Stein and Day, 1980), deals with the conflict in both Europe and

East Asia as well as leadership, organization, training, production, research, and intelligence. Ronald Schaffer offers an extremely critical account of U.S. bombing policy in *Wings of Judgement: American Bombing in World War II* (Oxford: Oxford University Press, 1985). Max Hastings focuses on Britain's part in the great bombing offensive against Germany in *Bomber Command* (New York: Dial Press 1979). Also useful is DeWitt S. Copp, *Forged in Fire: Strategy and Decisions in the Air War over Europe, 1940–1945* (Garden City, N.Y.: Doubleday, 1982). Cajus Bekker, *The Luftwaffe War Diaries* (London: Macdonald, 1966), is a valuable work from the German side, as is Adolf Galland, *The First and the Last: The Rise and Fall of the German Fighter Forces, 1938–1945* (New York: Ballantine, 1957). Earl R. Beck's *Under the Bombs: The German Home Front, 1942–1945* (Lexington, Ky.: University Press of Kentucky, 1986) deals with the German civilian population's efforts to cope with the Allied air offensive.

CHAPTER 20: TOTAL WAR AND THE HOME FRONTS

The best general account of life in Germany during the war is Beck's *Under the Bombs: The German Home Front, 1942–1945*. Charles Whiting's popular work, *The Home Front: Germany* (Chicago: Time-Life Books, 1982), is also interesting. Richard Grunberger examines life in Germany throughout the period of Hitler's rule in *The 12-Year Reich: A Social History of Nazi Germany, 1933–1945* (New York: Holt, Rinehart, Winston, 1971). Milward's *The German Economy at War,* remains the best account of the economic problems and achievements of Germany during the conflict. Marlis Steinert, in the excellent *Hitler's War and the Germans* (Athens, Ohio: Ohio University Press, 1977), relates the attitudes of Germans toward the conflict and the Nazi regime. Leila J. Rupp compares the roles of women in the Third Reich and the United States in *Mobilizing Women for War: German and American Propaganda, 1939–1945* (Princeton: Princeton University Press, 1978). Jay W. Baird explores Goebbels's approach to molding public perceptions in *The Mythical World of Nazi War Propaganda, 1939–1945* (Minneapolis: University of Minnesota Press, 1974), while Michael Balfour compares Nazi and British methods in *Propaganda in War, 1939–1945: Organizations, Policies, and Publics in Britain and Germany* (London: Routledge and Kegan Paul, 1979). The finest study of the German resistance movements is Peter Hoffmann, *The History of the German Resistance, 1933–1945* (Cambridge, Mass.: Harvard University Press, 1977). Erwin Leiser examines film-making in Germany during the war in *Nazi Cinema* (New York: Macmillan, 1974).

For the British war effort, Angus Calder, *The People's War: Britain, 1939–1945* (London: Cape, 1969), is a good beginning. Arthur Marwick's *The Home Front: The British and the Second World War* (London: Thames and Hudson, 1977) presents an interesting photographic and documentary account. Studies of Britain's wartime economic mobilization include W. K. Hancock and M. M. Gowing, *The British War Economy* (London: H.M.S.O., 1949), and Michael M. Postan, *British War Production* (London: H.M.S.O., 1952). Paul Addison analyzes the domestic political background during the conflict in *The Road to 1945: British Politics and the Second World War* (London: Cape, 1975). Other useful works include David Thoms, *War, Industry, and Society: The Midlands, 1939–1945* (London: Routledge, 1989), and Penny Summerfield, *Women Workers in the Second World War* (London: Crown Helm, 1984).

Paul Fussell's *Wartime: Understanding and Behavior in the Second World War* (Oxford: Oxford University Press, 1989) is a shrill and stinging indictment of the Allied conduct of the war. It focuses on the psychological and emotional aspects of the war and is especially critical of the United States. Useful studies of the American home front are Richard Polenberg, *War and Society: The United States, 1941–1945* (Philadelphia: J. B. Lippincott, 1972), John Blum, *V Was for Victory: Politics and American Culture during*

World War II (New York: Harcourt, Brace, Jovanovich, 1976), and Richard R. Lingeman, *Don't You Know There's a War On?* (New York: G. P. Putnam's Sons, 1970). Donald M. Nelson, the director of the War Production Board, has provided his personal account of American economic mobilization in *Arsenal of Democracy: The Story of American War Production* (New York: Harcourt, 1946). Michi Weglyn's *Years of Infamy: The Untold Story of America's Concentration Camps* (New York: Morrow, 1976) deals with the internment of Japanese-Americans during the war. Doris Weatherford examines the various roles played by women on the home front as well as in the military in *American Women and World War II* (New York: Facts on File, 1990). For the role of blacks in the conflict, see Neil Wynn, *The Afro-American and the Second World War* (New York: Paul Elek, 1976). Clayton R. Koppes studies various aspects of the motion picture industry in *Hollywood Goes to War: How Politics, Profits, and Propaganda Shaped World War II Movies* (Berkeley, Calif.: University of California Press, 1987).

Dallin's *German Rule in Russia, 1941–1945,* is still the classic work on life in the Soviet Union during the conflict. Werth's *Russia at War, 1941–1945,* presents a vivid picture of the Soviet home front. A more recent work that provides much useful information and analysis in a brief format is John Barber and Mark Harrison, *The Soviet Home Front, 1941–1945: A Social and Economic History of the USSR in World War II* (London: Longman, 1991). Susan J. Linz, ed., *The Impact of World War II on the Soviet Union* (Totowa, N.J.: Rowman and Allanheld, 1985), links the momentous effects of the conflict on the USSR with the postwar period in a series of informative essays. William Moskoff analyzes the enormous task of supplying the Soviet armed forces and the civilian population with food in *The Bread of Affliction: The Food Supply in the USSR during World War II* (Cambridge: Cambridge University Press, 1991). Robert Conquest presents a scathing account of Soviet policy toward non-Russian nationalities in *The Nation Killers: Soviet Deportation of Nationalities* (London: Macmillan, 1970).

The standard work in English on Japanese life during World War II is Thomas R. H. Havens, *Valley of Darkness: The Japanese People and World War Two* (New York: Norton, 1978). The editors of Time-Life Books have produced an interesting and well-illustrated popular account in *Japan at War* (Chicago: Time-Life Books, 1980). Ienaga's *The Pacific War* provides thoughtful analysis of Japanese civilian attitudes, as do Ben-Ami Shillony, *Politics and Culture in Wartime Japan* (Oxford: Oxford University Press, 1981), and Shunsuke Tsurumi, *An Intellectual History of Wartime Japan, 1931–1945* (London: KPI Limited, 1986). Jerome B. Cohen deals with Japanese wartime production problems in *Japan's Economy in War and Reconstruction* (Minneapolis: University of Minnesota Press, 1949).

CHAPTER 21: RUSSIA MOVES WEST

Clark, *Barbarossa;* Seaton, *Russo-German War;* Werth, *Russia at War;* and Zhukov, *Greatest Battles* all continue the story of the war on the eastern front into 1943–44, and Manstein, *Lost Victories,* is particularly informative on the Battle of Kursk and the Russian offensives that followed. John Erickson's massive book *The Road to Berlin* (Boulder, Colo.: Westview Press, 1983) is especially good for the Russian side during this period. David M. Glantz emphasizes the improvement in Soviet operations during 1943 in *From the Don to the Dnepr: Soviet Offensive Operations, December 1942–August 1943* (London: F. Cass, 1991). Geoffrey Jukes, *Kursk: The Clash of Armor* (London: Ballantine, 1969), is a useful study of that great battle. In addition to Bor-Komorowski's *Secret Army,* Stefan Korbonski's *Fighting Warsaw: The Story of the Polish Underground State, 1939–1945* (New York: Minerva Press, 1956), and Z. K. Zawodny's *Nothing but Honor* (Stanford, Calif.: Hoover Institute Press, 1977), are valuable works on the Warsaw Uprising. For the Katyn Forest massacre, see J. K. Zawodny, *Death in the Forest: The*

Story of the Katyn Forest Massacre (London: Macmillan, 1971).

CHAPTER 22: CROSS-CHANNEL INVASION AT LAST

MacDonald's *Mighty Endeavor* carries his study of the American war effort into the period of the invasion and conquest of Western Europe. Much of Wilmot's *Struggle for Europe* also concentrates on this phase of the conflict, as does Arthur Bryant, ed., *Triumph in the West, 1943–46* (London: Collins, 1959). Russell F. Weigley, *Eisenhower's Lieutenants: The Campaign of France and Germany, 1944–1945* (Bloomington, Ind.: Indiana University Press, 1981), is an outstanding work. Sir Frederick Morgan relates the planning phase of the D-day invasion in *Overture to Overlord* (New York: Doubleday, 1950). A well-known popular account of the landings is Cornelius Ryan, *The Longest Day* (New York: Simon & Schuster, 1959). Books on the Normandy campaign include E. M. G. Belfield and Hubert Essame, *The Battle for Normandy* (London: Batsford, 1965), and Carlo d'Este, *Decision in Normandy* (New York: Harper-Collins, 1991). Martin Blumenson's *Breakout and Pursuit* (Washington: Office of the Chief of Military History, 1961) and *The Duel for France, 1944* (Boston: Houghton Mifflin, 1963) are excellent studies of the breakout and campaign that followed. Studies of individual battles include Alexander McKee, *Caen: Anvil of Victory* (London: Souvenir Press, 1964), and James Lucas and James Barker, *The Battle of Normandy: The Falaise Gap* (New York: Holmes & Meier, 1978).

Alan F. Wilt, *The French Riviera Campaign of August 1944* (Carbondale, Ill.: Southern Illinois University Press, 1981), analyzes the invasion of southern France. Richard Lamb's *Montgomery in Europe, 1943–1945: Success or Failure?* (New York: Franklin Watts, 1984) is a balanced study of the controversial British general. Accounts of Operation Market-Garden include Cornelius Ryan's bestseller *A Bridge Too Far* (London: Simon & Schuster, 1974), General R. E. Urquhart's *Arnhem* (London: Cassell, 1968), and John Frost, *A Drop Too Many* (London: Cassell, 1982). Lewin's *Ultra Goes to War* is essential for the campaign in the west, as is Bennett's *Ultra in the West.* Van Creveld's *Supplying War* is excellent on Allied logistic problems in Western Europe.

CHAPTER 23: THE END OF THE THOUSAND-YEAR REICH

Good accounts of the second Ardennes offensive are John Strawson, *The Battle for the Ardennes* (London: Batsford, 1972), and Peter Elstob, *The Last Offensive: The Full Story of the Battle of the Ardennes* (New York: Macmillan, 1971). Charles B. MacDonald, *The Siegfried Line Campaign* (Washington: Office of the Chief of Military History, 1963), and Hugh M. Cole, *The Lorraine Campaign* (Washington: Department of the Army, 1966), relate the difficult fighting along Germany's western border.

John Toland recounts the campaign from the border to final victory in *The Last 100 Days* (New York: Random House, 1966), as does Charles B. MacDonald in *The Last Offensive* (Washington: Office of the Chief of Military History, 1973). Stephen Ambrose defends Eisenhower's decision to halt Allied forces short of Berlin in *Eisenhower and Berlin, 1945: The Decision to Halt at the Elbe* (New York: Norton, 1967), whereas Montgomery, *Memoirs;* Toland, *The Last 100 Days;* and Cornelius Ryan, *The Last Battle* (New York: Simon & Schuster, 1966), are critical. Ryan's book also describes the Red Army's conquest of the German capital. Another detailed account is General Vasili I. Chuikov, *The Fall of Berlin* (New York: Holt, Rinehart and Winston, 1967). Erickson's *Road to Berlin* is the best general history of the Red Army's offensives from the summer of 1944 to the capture of Berlin. Many accounts of Hitler's last days are available, but the finest of these in many respects is still Hugh R. Trevor-Roper, *The Last Days of Hitler* (New York: Collier Books, 1962). Hans Rothfels's *German Opposition to Hitler* (London: Wolff, 1970) traces the development of the conspiracy against the Nazi leader.

Linklater's *Campaign in Italy* and Jackson's *Battle for Italy* continue their surveys of the struggle in that mountainous land to the bitter end. Deakin's *Brutal Friendship* describes the final days of the Italian dictator.

CHAPTER 24: ISLAND HOPPING IN THE PACIFIC

Volumes 6–8 of Morison's *United States Naval Operations* concentrate on this period. Grace P. Hayes, *The Joint Chiefs of Staff and the War against Japan* (Annapolis: U.S. Naval Institute, 1982), is essential for the strategy of the war in the Pacific. Two excellent works that focus on carrier warfare are Clark G. Reynolds, *The Fast Carriers: The Forging of an Air Navy* (New York: McGraw-Hill, 1968), and James and William Belote, *Titans of the Seas: The Development and Operations of American Carrier Task Forces during World War II* (New York: Harper and Row, 1975). Allan S. Walker, *The Island Campaigns* (Canberra: Australian War Memorial, 1957), is a good general account.

Books on specific operations include David Dexter, *The New Guinea Offensives* (Canberra: Australian War Memorial, 1961), Robert Sherrod, *Tarawa: The Story of a Battle* (New York: Duell, Sloan and Pearce, 1954), John Miller, *Cartwheel: The Reduction of Rabaul* (Washington: Office of the Chief of Military History, 1959), John N. Rentz *Bougainville and the Northern Solomons* (Washington: U.S. Marine Corps, 1948), Philip A. Crowl, *Campaign in the Marianas* (Washington: Office of the Chief of Military History, 1960), and William T. Y'Blood, *Red Sun Setting: The Battle of the Philippine Sea* (Annapolis: U.S. Naval Institute, 1980).

CHAPTER 25: WAR ON THE PERIPHERY

Barbara Tuchman's *Stilwell and the American Experience in China, 1911–1945* (New York: Macmillan, 1970), *The Stilwell Papers* (New York: William Sloane Associates, 1948), edited by Theodore H. White, Albert C. Wedemeyer's *Wedemeyer Reports!* (New York: Henry Holt, 1958), and Charles F. Romanus and Riley Sunderland, *Stilwell's Mission to China* (Washington: Department of the Army, 1953), all relate the tortuous dealings of American leaders with Chiang Kai-shek. Don Moser's *China, Burma, India* (Alexandria, Va.: Time-Life Books, 1978), provides a general account of this theater of operations. G. F. Matthews's *Reconquest of Burma, 1943–1945* (Aldershot, U.K.: Gale, 1966), covers the later period of the Burma campaign. Sir William Slim's *Defeat into Victory* (London: Cassell, 1956) is an illuminating memoir. Studies of specific campaigns include A. F. Campbell, *The Siege: A Story from Kohima* (London: Allen, 1956), G. C. Evans and Anthony Brett-James, *Impahl* (London: Macmillan, 1962), and Charlton Ogburn, *The Marauders* (New York: Harper and Row, 1959). Biographical works on leading figures are Ronald Lewin, *Slim: The Standardbearer* (London: Leo Cooper, 1976), Christopher Sykes, *Orde Wingate* (London: Collins, 1959), Penderel Morn, *Gandhi and Modern India* (New York: Norton, 1968), and John Terraine, *The Life and Times of Lord Mountbatten* (London: Hutchinson, 1968). Francis Clifford Jones, *Japan's New Order in East Asia: Its Rise and Fall* (London: Oxford University Press, 1954), deals with Japanese occupation policies.

CHAPTER 26: THE COLLAPSE OF JAPAN

The standard general histories on the Pacific war devote considerable attention to the final months of the conflict. The Battle of Leyte Gulf has inspired numerous accounts, including Edwin Palmer Hoyt, *The Battle of Leyte Gulf: The Death Knell of the Japanese Fleet* (New York: Weybright & Talley, 1972). Books on specific campaigns include M. Hamlin Cannon, *Leyte: The Return to the Philippines* (Washington: Office of the Chief of Military History, 1954), Robert Ross Smith, *Triumph in the Philippines* (Washington: Department of the Army, 1963), Richard F. Newcomb, *Iwo Jima* (New York: Holt, Rinehart and Winston, 1965), James and William Belote, *Typhoon of Steel: The Battle for Okinawa* (New York: Harper and Row, 1970), and Bemis M. Frank and Henry I. Shaw, Jr., *Victory and Occupation* (Washington: U.S. Marine Corps, 1968), which also covers the Okinawa campaign. The Belote work is especially good. Rikihei Inoguchi, Tadashi Nakajima, and Roger Pineau, *The Divine Wind: Japan's Kamikaze Force in World War II* (Annapolis: U.S. Naval Institute, 1958), is an interesting account of the suicide attacks from the Japanese point of view. Masanori Ito, *The End of the Imperial Japanese Navy* (New York: Norton, 1962), provides an account of the last sortie of Japan's once mighty fleet.

Craven and Cate, in volume 5 of their *Army Air Forces in World War II,* focus on the Superfortress assault on Japan, as do Carl Berger, *B-29: The Superfortress* (New York: Ballantine, 1970), and Wilbur H. Morrison, *Point of No Return: The Story of the 20th Air Force* (New York: New York Times Books, 1979). W. J. Holmes, *Undersea Victory: The Influence of Submarine Operations in the Pacific* (Garden City, N.Y.: Doubleday, 1966), and Clay Blair, Jr., *Silent Victory: The U.S. Submarine War against Japan* (Philadelphia: J. B. Lippincott, 1975), are excellent studies of the impact of the American underwater attacks on Japanese shipping.

Anthony Cave Brown and Charles B. MacDonald have written *The Secret History of the Atomic Bomb* (New York: Dell, 1977). Martin J. Sherwin explores the effect of this weapon on Allied relations in *A World Destroyed: The Atomic Bomb and the Grand Alliance* (New York: Knopf, 1975). The extensive literature on the controversy over the decision to use the bomb includes Herbert Feis, *The Atomic Bomb and the End of World War II* (Princeton: Princeton University Press, 1966), and Gar Alperovitz, *Atomic Diplomacy: Hiroshima and Potsdam* (New York: Vintage Books, 1965). Feis contends that U.S. leaders used the bomb to end the war with as little loss of life as possible. Alperovitz insists that its use was due to the desire to impress the Russians and improve American bargaining power. Keith Eubank's *The Bomb* (Melbourne, Fla.: Anvil, 1991) relates the history of the bomb's development as well as the decision to use it. A number of books have analyzed the debate that led to Japan's surrender. Among the best of these are Robert J. C. Butow, *Japan's Decision to Surrender* (Stanford, Calif.: Stanford University Press, 1954), and Toland's *Rising Sun*.

AFTERMATH

Studies of wartime conferences include Keith Eubank, *Summit at Teheran* (New York: Morrow, 1985), Keith Sainsbury, *The Turning Point: Roosevelt, Stalin, Churchill, and Chiang Kai-shek, 1943* (London: Oxford University Press, 1985), Diane Shaver Clemens, *Yalta* (London: Oxford University Press, 1970), Herbert Feis, *Between War and Peace: The Potsdam Conference* (Princeton: Princeton University Press, 1960), and Alperovitz, *Atomic Diplomacy.* The trial of German war criminals is the subject of Ann and John Tusa, *The Nuremberg Trial* (New York: Atheneum, 1984), while Richard L. Lael's *The Yamashita Precedent: War Crimes and Command Responsibility* (Wilmington, Del.: Scholarly Resources, 1982) deals with the controversial case of General Yamashita.

The literature on the Cold War is vast and varied. Herbert Feis, *From Trust to Terror: The Onset of the Cold War, 1945–1950* (New York: Norton, 1970), views the Soviet Union as primarily responsible. A number of revisionist studies see the United States as the principal culprit in the deterioration of East-West relations. They include Alperovitz, *Atomic Diplomacy,* Joyce and Gabriel Kolko, *The Limits of Power: The World and United States Foreign Policy, 1945–1954* (New York: Harper & Row, 1972), Walter Le Feber, *America, Russia and the Cold War, 1945–1966* (New York: Wiley, 1968), and William A. Williams, *The Tragedy of American Diplomacy* (New York: Dell, 1962). More balanced interpretations, which tend to divide blame between the two superpowers, are Daniel Yergin, *The Shattered Peace: The Origins of the Cold War and the National Security State* (Boston: Houghton-Mifflin, 1977), John L. Gaddis, *The United States and the Origins of the Cold War,*

1941–1947 (New York: Columbia University Press, 1972), and Louis J. Halle, *The Cold War as History* (New York: Harper & Row, 1967).

Among the works on the establishment of the Soviet bloc is William O. McCagg, Jr., *Stalin Embattled, 1943–1948* (Detroit: Wayne State University Press, 1978), which contends that Stalin's policies in Eastern Europe were largely the result of his attempt to crush opponents within the Communist world. Joseph Rothschild argues in *Communist Eastern Europe* (New York: Walker, 1964) that Stalin was determined to maintain Soviet domination and was not merely reacting to pressure from Communist rivals. Ulam's *Stalin* provides a fascinating analysis of the Soviet dictator's postwar policies in Russia, Eastern Europe, and elsewhere.

In *The Reconstruction of Western Europe, 1945–1951* (Berkeley: University of California Press, 1984), Alan S. Milward voices skepticism over the Marshall Plan's effect on European recovery. Other works on Western European economic progress and the movement toward unity include Richard Mayne, *The Recovery of Europe* (Garden City, N.Y.: Doubleday, 1973), and John Gimbel, *The Origins of the Marshall Plan* (Stanford, Calif.: Stanford University Press, 1976). Important books on Germany's crucial role in the division of Europe in the postwar era are John H. Backer, *The Decision to Divide Germany* (Durham, N.C.: Duke University Press, 1978), and W. Phillips Davison, *The Berlin Blockade: A Study in Cold War Politics* (Princeton: Princeton University Press, 1958). Robert E. Osgood's *NATO: The Entangling Alliance* (Chicago: University of Chicago Press, 1962) is a good account of the Western collective security system.

John C. Perry has provided an excellent account of the American occupation of Japan in *Beneath the Eagle's Wings: Americans in Occupied Japan* (New York: Dodd, Mead, 1980). Books on Communist China are numerous. The best biography of Mao is Stuart Schram, *Mao Tse-tung* (New York: Simon & Schuster, 1967). Suzanne Pepper analyzes the Chinese battle for supremacy in *Civil War in China: The Political Struggles, 1945–1948* (Berkeley: University of California Press, 1978). For Korea, David Rees, *Korea: The Limited War* (London: Macmillan, 1964), is a good survey, along with Gregory Henderson, *Korea: The Politics of the Vortex* (Cambridge, Mass.: Harvard University Press, 1968).

Hugh Tinker's *Race, Conflict and the International Order: From Empire to the United Nations* (New York: St. Martin's Press, 1977) and Henri Grimal's *Decolonization of the British, French, Dutch and Belgian Empires, 1919–1963* (Boulder, Colo.: Westview, 1978) are general studies of the waning of imperialism.

Index

Note: Page numbers followed by f indicate figures.